The Complete
21ST CENTURY TRAVEL & HOSPITALITY
Marketing Handbook

Bob Dickinson, CTC
Andy Vladimir, CHE

PEARSON

Prentice
Hall

PEARSON CUSTOM PUBLISHING
75 Arlington Street, Suite 300, Boston, MA 02116
A Pearson Education Company

Dedication

The authors proudly dedicate this book to our wives, children and grandchildren—the source of our energy . . . and serenity!

Contents

Section II Transportation Marketing

Section III Destination Marketing

Section IV Hotel and Resort Marketing

Section V Cruise Line Marketing

Section VI Tour Marketing

Section VII Travel Agent Marketing

Section VIII Luxury Marketing

Section IX Niche Marketing

Acknowledgments

We are deeply grateful to this book's contributors—busy, successful folks who took time to share their thoughts, ideas and visions about the travel and hospitality industries and their own travel-related companies and organizations.

Like us, these seasoned marketers fully understand and appreciate the profoundly symbiotic nature of the travel industry. It is our hope that travel professionals, students of marketing and simply those consumers who love to travel will find this book informative, useful and engaging.

We are thankful to Prentice-Hall for grasping our vision for this book and to our editor, Vernon Anthony, for working diligently to execute it.

Thanks go as well to Janet Simpkins, executive assistant to Bob Dickinson, for her superb administrative and secretarial assistance.

Bob Dickinson
Andy Vladimir

The Big Picture

In the early years of the 21st century, the travel and tourism industry in the United States has been buffeted by terrorism, wars, disease and recession. No sector has remained unscathed. Companies from world-class brands like Disney and American Airlines to mom-and-pop operations such as smaller motels, attractions and travel agencies had their plans and budgets repeatedly foiled by these outside forces. A measure of this disruption lies in the fact that an astounding 378,000 tourism jobs were lost in the United States within only one year of September 11, 2001.

For most of the industry, there is a significant imbalance between supply and demand. Marketers struggle to fill capacity planned and contracted when the economy was booming in the late 1990s, when "irrational exuberance" was the order of the day. The cruise industry is laboring through multiple years of double-digit capacity growth; in many markets, the hotel industry is overbuilt and business travel is dramatically off due to a sluggish economy.

Consolidation and/or ownership changes have created further challenges to virtually every sector of travel and tourism. The Internet has entered the travel distribution picture in a big way—initially as a savior, but to some supply-side marketers as an enormous threat to their brands, potentially robbing them of their distinction: the Internet's focus on the lowest price threatens utterly to commoditize travel products.

At the same time, outbreaks of new virulent, viral epidemics such as SARS and the Norwalk-like virus (NLV) curtailed travel to and from certain major cities and countries. The virtual shutdowns of visitation lasted only several months, but it is likely that the damage to consumer demand for travel to and from those cities and countries could last for years.

The inherent symbiotic quality of our industry exacerbated an already difficult situation. Those who promote travel to certain destinations, such as conventions and visitors' bureaus, now worry about reduced air flights crimping access and consumer demand; cruise lines and tour operators watch in fear as thousands of travel agencies—which provide much-needed new customers—shut down each year. Sagging business travel in particular harms not just the airlines but restaurants, hotels, convention centers, the rental car industry, etc. With few exceptions, as one sector struggles to deal with flagging consumer demand, the others suffer.

To be sure, there are some bright lights on the horizon: The graying of the Baby Boomers and other clear demographic trends bode well for the travel marketer. Information systems will continue to provide new, sophisticated customer relationship management tools, allowing travel suppliers to mine richer and deeper veins of demand. The number of American households with high-speed Internet access will ultimately match the number with television, meaning that practically all Americans will have full, easy, 'round-the-clock access to travel and tourism's increasingly sophisticated virtual retail stores.

In this book, we have challenged some of the industry's best marketers, representing many of the industry's best brands, to give us their views as to marketing challenges and opportunities over the next 10 years or so. We have arranged the chapters by tourism sector so that readers can benefit from a variety of marketing perspectives from multiple well-known players (indeed, they are competitors) within each sector. In some cases, the competitors' operations largely differ from one another. In others, they appear to be more similar than different. In any case, such differences stem from many variables. One, for example, is the business model used by the company. Is it new, in touch with today's consumer? Has it lately been reengineered to be contemporary? Or is it a legacy model that, despite its age, remains profitable, relevant? Each chapter comprises a range of possibilities.

The absolute size or scale of a given company and its financial stability can be a determining factor in the amount and quality of resources that marketers can utilize to establish or strengthen brands and stimulate consumer demand (Amtrak, for example, has scale but is too dependent on the whims of Congress and the annual federal budget.)

Marketing approaches, like business models and scale, vary greatly, of course. Some marketers seem to have tunnel vision, while others have robust bandwidth. Some are more strategically focused while others seem distracted by tactical considerations. Clearly there is both divergence in practice and controversy. Who is right and who is not? Who is realistic? Who has anticipated correctly? Some have forgotten, even disparaged, the basic fundamentals of marketing.

At the end of the day, as always, the marketplace will be the judge. Some sectors and companies will flourish, others will not. It is clear that astute marketing, grounded in fundamentals but attuned to new opportunities, will at least make a difference.

What a time to be a marketer in the travel industry! The challenges are unprecedented. The future is uncertain, but the rewards are still ample. Those marketers who can successfully navigate these troubled waters and enhance their brands, grow demand, grow share in their sector, and provide a solid financial return to their owners, will be well compensated—both in terms of material rewards and the psychic income they receive from the knowledge that they were winners, rare achievers, in an environment otherwise characterized by mundane results.

Section I

Marketing Communications

The codfish lays ten thousand eggs
The homely hen lays one;
But the codfish never cackles
To show what she has done.
And so we praise the homely hen,
The codfish we despise,
Which clearly shows to you and me
It pays to advertise!

This 19th century ditty is often used as a simple way of explaining why advertising is such a powerful sales tool. There's only one problem with it—it isn't true. The famous retailer John Wanamaker is often quoted as saying, "Half the money I spend on advertising is wasted. The trouble is, I don't know which half." David Ogilvy was fond of telling the story of George Hay Brown, a former chief of marketing research at the Ford Motor Company. Brown devised an experiment where he inserted Ford ads in every other issue of *Readers Digest*. At the end of a year, it turned out that the people who had not seen the ads bought more Fords then the ones who had.

The halls of Madison Avenue ad agencies abound with pithy stories like this. Advertising executives like to tell prospective clients that if advertising had just half of the power to persuade that is often ascribed to it, then its creators would be much richer than they in fact are. Why is this? Why can't TV commercials, conceived and directed by some of Hollywood's brightest stars, and costing more to produce per second than most feature films, fail to do their job of selling a hotel room or filling an airline seat?

The correct answer to that question comes down to one thing—the difference between selling a product or service and marketing it. Selling is hard to do—marketing is easy. Selling doesn't work a lot of the time—marketing does. Selling is getting rid of what you have. Marketing is having what people want. Whoever said, "You can't sell a refrigerator to an Eskimo" had it right. Eskimos who live in igloos don't need refrigerators. But in one famous publicity stunt, someone did sell a refrigerator to an Eskimo by convincing him that he needed one—not to keep things cold but rather to keep them warm! If you have something that people want, it is easy to get them to buy it. All you have to do is demonstrate that it does what it's supposed to do at a price that makes it a good value. If they don't want it, you have to try to sell it to them. That's hard. First you have to get them interested in that product that they don't want. Then you have to make all kinds of extravagant claims about its efficacy that may or may not be true. Finally, you have to convince them that at the price you're offering it for, they cannot afford to say no—an unlikely proposition at best. That's why this book is called *The Complete 21st Century Travel & Hospitality Marketing Handbook*. Our contributors want to share this important fact: *Marketing is easy—selling is hard!*

One good question to begin with when you're dealing with marketing is to figure out who are the people you are looking for who will want to buy what you have to sell. This is elementary. Academics sometimes like to think of it the way we think about going fishing. If we want to go fishing, we first must decide what kind of fish are we going after. Do we want yellowtail, grouper, sea bass or sword-fish? The choice of fish will determine our bait, as well as the size boat we will need and the amount of time we'll need to devote to catching something. Next we have to figure out where to find the fish we are going after. There are known fishing spots that we'll want to head for. It would be foolish of us to go to a place where no one had ever caught a fish! All of our contributors in the following four chapters on marketing and advertising think like fisherman. They are concerned with *who* is the target audience their marketing efforts will be directed toward. Are they Baby Boomers or senior citizens? Generation X or Generation Y? Are they couch potatoes who want to sit on the beach sipping Pina Coladas, or are they hikers with their backpacks strapped on and their walking sticks in hand? Would they rather catch fish or ride a glass-bottom boat and look at fish? Will they visit an aquarium, go scuba diving, see a movie about fish, or read *Moby Dick?* These prospects all want different things and if we don't have what they want or need, we're wasting our time trying to communicate with them. They're not interested.

Once we know who they are, we have to know *where* to find them. "Where" has more than one meaning in this case. Are they in Georgia or Arizona? New York or Chicago? In front of their TV sets, listening to their car radios, or surfing the Internet? Watching *60 Minutes, Law and Order* or *The Simpsons.* In some cases we can find them, but we realize that there aren't enough of them to compose a viable market. In other instances we can find them, but there's no efficient way to communicate with them. Selecting the right media and then negotiating the best price is both complicated and time consuming.

Finally there is the creative message. We have a good demographic and psychographic profile of our best prospects. We know where to find them. We've identified the media they read, watch or listen to. We have determined that we have sufficient funds to mount a viable campaign. Our final decision, and possibly the most important one, is what do we *offer* them? What *promise* are we going to make? Good ads offer something or make a promise to solve some kind of a problem that a consumer has. *Advertising is salesmanship,* whether it's in a newspaper, on television, on the Internet, on a billboard, on the side of a bus, or wherever. Why would anyone be interested in an ad from a company that they have no reason to be interested in unless the advertising offers them something they want? Of course, research shows that you can always attract people with pictures of dogs and babies, which is fine if you're selling dog and baby food, but isn't likely to help you sell airline seats and hotel rooms! It isn't enough to get people to see your ads or even love and remember them. If your advertising doesn't help fill rooms and seats, you're wasting your money.

Our contributors to this section all make their livelihoods by hunting down consumers and prospects and learning as much as they can about them for their members and clients. Then they use that information to develop messages that help their clients communicate with those customers and prospects. These are all part of the total marketing mix (product, price, place and promotion), which you'll hear mentioned throughout this book.

1

Meeting Travel Industry Challenges

William S. Norman
President and CEO
Travel Industry Association (TIA)

William S. Norman is president and chief executive officer of the Travel Industry Association (TIA)—a national umbrella organization that represents all segments of the U.S. travel and tourism industry.

Mr. Norman began his career in 1961 as a mathematics teacher in Norfolk, Virginia. In 1962, he was commissioned as a U.S. Navy officer, serving 11 years on active duty and 15 years as a reservist. He holds the rank of captain, (retired).

Between 1973 and 1979, Mr. Norman held a number of increasingly responsible management positions at Cummins Engine Company Inc., a multinational manufacturer of heavy-duty diesel engines and related products.

In 1979, Mr. Norman joined the National Railroad Passenger Corporation (AMTRAK). In 1986, he was named executive vice president—the company's number two position.

Mr. Norman received a bachelor of science degree in chemistry and mathematics from West Virginia Wesleyan College and a master of arts in international relations from the American University in Washington, D.C.

Mr. Norman and his wife, Elizabeth, have two children: Lisa Reneé, an attorney with Bryan Cave, LLP (St. Louis, MO), and William II, media relations manager of the Washington Redskins National Football League team.

The U.S. travel industry is simultaneously one of the shining stars of the 21st century's powerhouse service sector and one that faces very significant challenges. TIA comprises a diverse cross-section of businesses and organizations, such as hotels and lodging companies, airlines, theme parks, attraction, and cruise lines. Also included are rental car companies, ground transportation businesses such as motor coaches and trains, tour operators, restaurants, travel agencies and destination marketing organizations—including all 56 state and territorial tourism offices and many local convention and visitor bureaus.

At the dawn of the century, the U.S. travel industry stood as the third largest retailer in America, second only to automobile dealers and food stores. It was also one of the nation's top employers, with an annual payroll of $174 billion. One in every seven American workers was employed directly or indirectly in travel and tourism. Travel industry businesses generated $584 billion in revenues annually, as well as $100 million in taxes to federal, state and local governments. What's more, the travel industry was producing more growth in good management jobs than the economy as a whole. Additionally, the industry trimmed the U.S. trade deficit. International visitors spent more visiting America than Americans spent traveling to other countries.

The future held much promise for the travel industry as Americans' interest in travel continued to grow for purposes that ranged from attending business meetings and conferences to visiting family and friends, to seeking a respite from a harried lifestyle. There were, and are, reasons to be optimistic about the potential growth in travel to the United States from other countries, thanks to a world that was continually becoming smaller due to the rapid development of new modes of travel and improved standards of living.

But, despite its promise, the travel industry now faces significant challenges as it seeks to transform potential business into actual revenues. The effects of the September 11 terrorist attacks, the war in Iraq and strident international politics showed how vulnerable the industry can be to external events. The rapid rise of the Internet as a travel planning and booking tool has greatly intensified competition in an already highly competitive industry. However, although external events constrain travel desires and intentions, changing demographics and other factors foretell a growing travel market well into the future.

External Events

The effect on the travel industry of terrorists' use of commercial jetliners as weapons of mass destruction had an immediate and painful impact on a broad swath of the travel industry. The industry—which up to that point accounted for six percent of all American workers—suffered 30 percent of post-September 11 job losses. By December 2002, the travel industry had lost 387,000 jobs. A number of travel industry companies—already weakened by a slowing economy—merged with competitors, went out of business or lay severely damaged.

The terrorist attacks also proved the mettle of the industry and American travelers. At the first major industry-wide gathering—TIA's marketing outlook forum—after September 11, travel industry professionals resolved to "march forward with one voice and one purpose to restore consumer confidence in the safety of the U.S. travel product and to restore economic well-being." The conference marked the beginning of an unprecedented industry-wide campaign to "Restore Americans' Freedom to Travel." The campaign was a joint effort across all lines and segments of the industry to speak with one voice to the public. The campaign culminated in a $15 million travel industry message on television featuring President Bush and real-life industry employees.

Americans' attitudes about travel rebounded very quickly. Within a few months, the percentage of those who avoided travel out of concerns for safety had declined to the point where concerns about the declining economy more typically stalled travel. Even in the darkest days following the attacks, more than 80 percent of consumers clung to their freedom to travel. And leisure travel, against all odds and despite an economy weakened by a previous business downturn, grew by almost 2 percent in the next year (2002). Americans' reaction to the national crisis demonstrated that it's not a matter of whether they will travel, but how and where. Auto travel, for example, was up three percent in 2002. Rentals of recreational vehicles (RVs) increased by about 30 percent—on top of near-record RV sales. And the cruise industry reported increased bookings of about four percent, reflecting an acceleration of a trend that had been developing over the previous few years.

In the midst of this turmoil, business travel, critical to the profitability of many organizations, experienced declines affecting airlines, hotel chains and destinations that had traditionally been strong business meeting venues. Overall domestic business travel was down 3 percent in 2001 and by almost 6 percent in 2002. Many people forget that the slowdown in business travel preceded the terrorist attacks and the war in Iraq. The decline began in 1999 (at least in terms of travel volume), although spending by business travelers remained relatively high, even in the face of fewer business trips. As the post-boom economy and stock market cooled, business travel steadily declined from 2000 through 2002 and into 2003.

Another factor in declining business travel was the impact of new technologies. A 2002 TIA report, the *Air Travel Survey*, found that 42 percent of business travelers who fly to meetings had used teleconferencing as a substitute for at least one business trip over a one-year period. Seventeen percent and 15 percent of business travelers used videoconferencing and some form of Web site conferencing over the Internet, respectively. But while two-thirds of these travelers considered technology-based meetings more efficient than travel, only 20 percent rated them equal to or more effective than face-to-face meetings.

International inbound travel to the United States, like business travel, is highly valued for its profitability. TIA research shows that international visitors stay longer and spend more per person than domestic travelers. Conversely, international travelers who visit the United States tend to want to stay as long as possible to take advantage of their transportation investment. International inbound travel had grown by 30 percent from 1990 to 2000 and peaked at almost 51 million in 2000, but it dropped dramatically in 2001 and in 2002 following the terrorist attacks.

The sharp and sustained reductions in international visitors inflicted some of the worst damage on the travel industry among firms that specialized in this area. The silver lining around this desperately dark cloud was an opportunity for the industry to focus national attention on the value and potential of international visitors to the nation's economy. For example, the travel industry was able to impress upon key members of Congress that, while the numbers of international visitors had grown significantly before September 11, 2001, the U.S. market share in this highly competitive marketplace had declined by 30 percent in the previous decade. As a result, in February 2003, Congress appropriated $50 million, via an amendment offered by Senator Ted Stevens (R-Alaska), "in support of an international advertising and promotional campaign, developed in consultation with the private sector, to encourage individuals to travel to the United States . . ."

This partnership with the federal government was a long-awaited opportunity to show that successful public-private partnerships existing in several states were a viable model for a similar, overall partnership between the federal government and the private sector.

Internet

The Internet, used as both a travel-planning tool and to book travel, has changed the industry significantly and will unquestionably continue to have a major impact. It has greatly affected the avenues through which travel products are purchased. Most major travel suppliers sell directly to the public through their own web sites or through online-only vendors. Packaging, long a key marketing element of the travel industry, became a highly developed online phenomenon, spawning new, different and previously unimaginable types of partnerships as late as the mid-1990s.

Statistics tell the story. In 2002, more than half of American adults used the Internet, with 85 percent of those identifying themselves as travelers. Since 1996, the number of travelers who used the Internet had skyrocketed by 256 percent. While the rapid growth in the number of travelers using the Internet slowed by 2002, there were still 96 million people dubbed "Internet Travelers." Of these, 64 million used the Internet to plan trips and 39 million booked travel online. They were rapidly migrating from using the Internet simply to research travel options and compare prices to making their final purchases online.

A related trend has been the rapid move toward booking travel closer to the departure date. Before September 11, only 3 percent of all packaged travel customers booked their trips 30 days or fewer in advance of their trip; however, afterwards, the statistic jumped to 19 percent. This was part of a broader trend away from traditional two-week summer vacations and toward long weekends and combining days off with holiday weekends. It also reflected a move toward tacking a period of leisure travel onto a business trip. Another factor was the increased discounting across-the-board and special promotions such as Web site-only discounts that have encouraged consumers to wait for a good deal on travel—a reversal of historical patterns wherein travelers booked far in advance in order to obtain the lowest rates.

Other Trends

Highway travel, which stood at about 79 percent of all travel in the United States before the terrorist attacks, increased as air travel declined. In addition, Americans expressed a strong desire to "make connections" with family and friends and with icons of the nation. Mount Rushmore National Memorial, for example, set a record for visits in 2002. And it appears that these are longer-term trends, not just short-term reactions to the specific events of the early decade.

One of the most important trends that has developed in recent years and can be expected to accelerate, given the anticipated business climate and the increased globalization of the travel industry, is cooperative marketing and partnerships.

While the large companies whose names frequently appear in television commercials and national periodicals are in virtually everyone's travel industry lexicon, the industry is still overwhelmingly made up of organizations with 50 or fewer employees. Yet, no matter their size, organizations from across the industry want to promote themselves to ever-broader markets. The Internet and other modalities have made it possible for many entities to promote themselves and book business well beyond their previously accepted boundaries. American destinations and states, which have traditionally thought of themselves as strictly regional entities, have been emboldened to market themselves around the world because of research that has shown international travelers—having visited well-trodden gateway cities—are interested in the "authentic" America. Even so, few entities, even the largest players in international markets, have the resources to pursue new markets around the world on their own.

A trend that began in 2000 and that can be expected to grow exponentially throughout the decade is cooperative (co-op) marketing. Co-op marketing programs have demonstrated an ability to serve the interests of the broader travel industry—they have not been limited to either large or small companies and destinations. It is rapidly being recognized that participation in cooperative programs leverages the resources of all who take part in them to help all partners gain a greater return on their finite budgets.

The level of interest in partnerships has been demonstrated across the industry in countless ways. Such interest is growing and is no longer limited to agreements between entities that have obvious coinciding interests. For example, more than 400 industry organizations, many, if not most, of which had never been partners, have embraced *SeeAmerica* cooperative advertising and broader promotional activities.

SeeAmerica is a national brand supported by virtually all segments of the travel industry. It has served as an umbrella under which the industry has promoted itself to consumers internationally and at home, through programs like the "Greetings from America" postage stamp and the associated *SeeAmerica* Sweepstakes promotion with the U.S. Postal Service, along with the *SeeAmerica*'s Byways partnership with the U.S. Department of Transportation. Increasingly, travel industry organizations of all sizes participate in international events, such as major travel shows and seminars, under the *SeeAmerica* banner. Each organization maintains its own distinct identity and branding, but all are identified as part of a unified and exciting U.S. travel product—thanks to the common national brand under which they do business together.

Security

The U.S. government has, understandably and appropriately, worked to increase security at virtually all levels since September 11. This has had a unique impact on the travel industry, a significant portion of which moves people via common carriers such as airlines, motor coach operators, trains and other vehicles. Prime travel destinations such as New York City and Washington, D.C. have already been the targets of terrorists. Many other destinations are considered likely targets. And many travel industry companies that have promoted themselves successfully around the world also carry special security concerns because they are icons for the nation. Even a travel industry that abhors a "Fortress America" image and wants to tap the tremendous potential of growing international travel markets needs workable government initiatives that improve security without discouraging international inbound travel.

The travel industry has, to its credit, strongly endorsed a policy that balances security concerns with economic considerations. The freedom Americans enjoy to travel "where they want, when they want" wouldn't mean much if hindered by enormous security barriers that prevent the exercise of this freedom.

While the travel industry has been generally successful in convincing Congress and the Administration of the need for balanced policies that protect Americans while also preserving their freedoms, the industry will also need to be vigilant about future government proposals.

A Glimpse of the Future

The first decade of the 21st century found the United States and the travel industry in the midst of significant demographic changes. The single largest and most economically important demographic group, the Baby Boomers, accounting for almost half (44 percent) of all travel by U.S. residents, are entering their retirement years. Over the next two decades, the age distribution in the United States will change dramatically. The traditional family market (those aged 25–44) took 44 percent of all domestic trips at the beginning of the decade, while the so-called mature market (those aged 55 and older) took 33 percent. Those shares are expected to reverse over the next 20 years. By 2020, households headed by those aged 55–64 will have increased 74 percent (since 2000), while those headed by adults aged 65 and over will have increased 58 percent. The number of younger households will grow very slowly or even decline in this decade; that is, traditional "family travel" will decline substantially.

However, the graying of the Baby Boomers probably won't mean an expansion of the existing mature market. It is true that Boomers have even more time and money on their hands with which to undertake travel than their elders. But, while only 12 percent of those of retirement age and beyond worked just after the turn of the century, 80 percent of Boomers currently indicate they intend to do so. On the other hand, what they will lack in time for traditional retirement travel, they may make up for by extending business travel with leisure side trips and taking their grandchildren on long-weekend adventures. In addition, the Boomers may vastly expand a relatively new market that combines their apparently insatiable appetite for travel with their unique level of interest in making civic contributions. The market is travel and lodging in pursuit of building stronger communities, a better society, and a "more authentic America" across the country.

As this large group of travelers ages and as medical technology continues to extend life spans and improve the quality of life, another already growing market, travelers with disabilities, could double. A landmark survey TIA conducted for the Society for Accessible Travel and Hospitality made this prediction, providing just a few new measures could be implemented by the travel industry, which would provide: "meet and greet" services at airports; preferred seating on airlines; and lodging in rooms close to amenities with staff specially trained to accommodate guests with disabilities.

In addition, by 2020, Hispanic and African-Americans combined will have grown from 26 percent of the U.S. population to 36 percent. By mid-century, these minority groups will have grown to be about one-half of all Americans. This will greatly affect regional travel, among other segments, since immigration and historic migration patterns have placed very high percentages of these groups in the West and South. Successful marketing to this segment will require an understanding of how minority group preferences differ from those of non-minority travelers and will demand increased cultural sensitivity and appropriate communications.

All of these trends point to a future travel industry that will likely provide increasingly more individualized products to an increasingly diverse population. Then again, the more things change, the more they stay the same: Travel to visit family and friends, long the perennial favorite of Americans, will continue to grow. And as traditional nuclear families decline as a percentage of the traveling public, a broad new class of travel that TIA calls "enrichment tourism," focused on educationally-oriented trips and including historic, cultural and related experiences, will be a staple of the Boomers. One example is a new phenomenon that has been designated "geotourism:" tourism that sustains or enhances the geographical character of the place being visited—its environment, culture, aesthetics, heritage and the well-being of its residents. TIA research has shown that 55 million American travelers (38 percent of all traveling adults in the United States) have a strong interest in this type of travel, which affects their travel behavior and choices.

Finally, making use of changing demographic trends will require a firm understanding of how members of virtually all demographic groups are becoming closely wedded to personal technology and to their changing lifestyles.

In 2002, 69 percent of business and convention travelers and 61 percent of leisure travelers owned cell phones. When combined with the rapidly growing availability of Internet connections while traveling, it is not surprising that the lines between business and leisure travel have begun to blur. Will travel grow because workers can easily attend to both their jobs and their leisure interests while on the road? Or will it grow in that workers will become increasingly desperate to escape, in some sense, ubiquitous technology? Either way, the travel industry stands to benefit if individual organizations can position themselves appropriately.

Conclusions

There has never been a greater need for the various segments within the travel industry to see themselves as part of a greater and more powerful whole—not as a collection of self-interested competitors.

- September 11 was a wake-up call for the entire nation: The end of the Cold War did not mean the end of serious international threats to U.S. security. For the travel industry especially, September 11 demonstrated the country's vulnerability to external events and to world instability. While the travel industry cannot control world events, it has demonstrated that it can influence the government's reaction to them. More importantly, the industry has shown that, on a number of levels, it wields real power to shape its own future when the entities it comprises work in harmony. A key factor in the travel industry's maintaining a strong voice in Washington has been its willingness to accept reasonable and necessary security measures while working with the government to mitigate the measures' negative economic impacts. But if the industry has learned anything from the events that occurred early in the decade, it is that it has power when it speaks with one voice in the halls of government and in the marketplace as well.

- The travel industry was justifiably pleased with the $50 million appropriated by Congress to promote lucrative international inbound travel. If used in ways that prove measurable results and that leverage a national brand bespeaking industry unity, the opportunity exists to transform this one-time appropriation into a longer-term partnership with the federal government.

- The Internet will challenge the travel industry over the long term to become highly competitive and creative in the way it markets and distributes products. Industry organizations, large and small, that invest the time and resources in using the Internet will have enormous advantages in their respective segments.

- Nothing stands still. Markets are constantly changing and growing. As the travel industry is introduced to new domestic and international markets, it will need to develop new and innovative ways to promote its products.

Postscript

Of necessity, much of this essay has focused on rebuilding the travel industry following acts of terrorism, war and economic downturn. But the travel industry should be as proactive as it is reactive. The industry can and should uphold the ideal that travel has the power to bring the world's people together in peace. Only travel brings us face to face with people from different places, with different outlooks. As English literary scholar Samuel Johnson wrote, "The use of traveling is to regulate imagination by reality, and instead of thinking how things may be, to see them as they are." CNN can take us on a world tour every 20 minutes. But it is only when we shake hands with people in the next county or country, or with those visiting from a distant land, that we learn how different things truly are. Despite the wonders of technology, we only truly touch others at distant points on the planet when we travel to their lands and experience firsthand their culture, their prowess and even their dreams.

2

A Look Ahead

Gary C. Sain
Executive Vice-President and Partner
Yesawich, Pepperdine, Brown & Russell

Gary Sain oversees the management of all marketing, advertising and public relations programs for one of America's leading travel marketing firms. His background also includes direct marketing and sales management for leading travel and hospitality companies.

Under Sain's direction, in the early 1990s, Premier Cruise lines, with only two ships, became one of America's most widely recognized cruise lines. His "Big Red Boat" campaign remains a cruise line marketing benchmark for brand recognition.

He has served as chairman for the Association of Travel Marketing Executives and has twice been included in *Travel Agent Magazine*'s "Winner's Circle."

Change, Change and More Change

If you think the travel marketing landscape has undergone a complete overhaul since 2000, hold onto your seat. There are more changes coming. They will happen faster than any of us can conceive.

Those travel marketers who possess vision, courage and financial resources will prosper. Those who fail to adjust to new technologies and new ways of using them will quickly fall prey to changing consumer habits, preferences and booking tools.

In 1993, only 23 percent of Americans possessed computers. In 2000, this increased to 51 percent. That is a very rapid change in a short period of time.

In 1997, only 12 million people used the Internet to book hotels or make air travel arrangements. Six years later, more than 64 million people regularly cruise the Web searching for and booking travel deals, value-packed promotions and special offers. According to Forrester Research, online leisure sales will hit $50 billion in 2007, almost double from what it was in 2003!

The onset of online technology has changed the travel marketing world more rapidly than most travel marketers would ever have guessed. And the changes ahead will be even more dramatic.

Need more proof? Cellular telephones are now being used in ways we could not envision in the late 20th century. Wireless Internet technology is already in place. Televisions now have plasma screens. High definition television (HDTV) capability is being built into the TV sets you will be watching in the 2020s.

If this is where we are in the first decade of the 21st century, imagine what the travel market will be like in the 2020s.

"Noise Level" Means Your Message Has to Be on Target

The onset of rapid technological change has eased many aspects of our lives. But in other ways things are considerably more complicated due to technology.

For travelers in search of a vacation, booking is as easy as a click of the mouse. But that does not mean it is simple. Deciding where to go, how to travel, where to stay, how to travel and what to do has become incredibly complicated. Why? Because the choices available have become so numerous that travelers are overloaded with information.

As new channels of communication emerge and marketers find new ways to present their goods and services, the number of messages bombarding consumers will exponentially increase. Every day, consumers receive more than 3,000 different commercial messages. From the radio commercial you hear when you are dressing for work to the billboards you view enroute to the office, marketers are seeking your attention and your money. Even the foreheads of people are being used to communicate marketing messages!

The number of messages people currently receive is more than they can absorb. But even more messages will be delivered to consumers simply because there are more and better delivery systems with which to deliver them.

Watch television? How many choices do you have on your cable system? And how many choices did you have on television as recently as the early 1990s?

Listen to the radio? AM or FM? How many choices do you have locked in as you punch your way across the dial? How many stations utilize Spanish or language other than English?

Commute on the train? How many messages address you as you glance overhead, browse the daily newspaper or look at your laptop?

The sheer volume of communications is overwhelming. And as the noise level has gone up, consumers have found ways to cut through the clutter.

Television viewers can fast-forward through commercials or imbed programs that skip commercials entirely. Internet browsers can purchase software that obliterates onscreen pop-ups, as well as unwanted email.

Travel Marketers Compete with Everything Else to Do

In addition to watching Tony the Tiger growl "Grrr...eat," or watching an Alka Seltzer tablet "Plop, plop, fizz, fizz," we can now receive elaborate messages about what destination to visit, at which hotel to stay or what adventure or attraction to experience.

Travel marketers now compete in the advertising and marketing mainstream. That is good news for travel marketers, but not all of them can afford to. It also places their advertising dollars in direct competition with pharmaceutical products, fast food and lawn care products. It is not just bookings that travel marketers are seeking. It is the time and attention of a consumer audience whose attention span is already stretched thin.

The travel industry's enthusiastic adoption of the Web as a place to sell its wares has put travel marketers into the middle of a marketing environment that was once the playground of mainstream mass-market products like automobiles, soup and headache powders.

The challenge of driving people to one's Web site has forced travel marketers to market the Web site. The only way to get people to look at one's Web site is to tell people that the site exists and explain why they should visit.

Today's Youngsters Are Tomorrow's Travelers

Travel marketers who have not yet embraced online marketing should take a closer look at tomorrow's customer. A considerable proportion of today's young people already have access to the Internet, either at home or through school computers.

In addition to 65 million homes with Internet access, approximately 54 million youths have access to the Internet at school. The potential for marketing online to the five- to 17-year-olds becomes even more apparent when one considers that, currently, they spend five billion hours online each year.

For travel marketers, the implications are enormous. Marketers will soon be talking to an entire generation that has grown up online. Today's computer geeks are the customers of tomorrow. The marketing changes made on their behalf are already occurring.

Daily newspaper circulations are in decline as young people go to the Web for their news. Magazines are chasing after narrowly defined niches, fragmenting an already fragmented audience.

In broadcasting, the battle for viewers and listeners has become block-by-block guerilla warfare in an attempt to target audiences and efficiently project one's message. Television advertising budgets, already stretched thin as prices have risen, have becoming even more diluted as network viewership has diminished. Viewers cannot only turn to the myriad cable channels available, but technology allows them to preempt advertising messages.

Targeting one's audience on radio is increasingly more complicated. The radio landscape is now about as straightforward as a map of the Baltic—stations offer a bewildering multiplicity of languages and formats. The onset of satellite radio promises even more complicated changes in radio programming and advertising.

What promising media are left? The simple answer: Online media, increasingly the primary choice of an entire generation of knowledgeable computer-savvy youngsters who will be reaching adulthood in the decade of the 2020s.

Personal Computers Will Become Personal Assistants

Imagine a world where your computerized alarm clock wakes you up with a message like: "Good morning, Miss Jones. It's six in the morning. Your Maxwell House coffee is already brewing. NPR will be broadcasting for the next 20 minutes, at which time the television will activate on channel seven. I have confirmed your air taxi to the JFK supersonic jetport, arriving at 8:00 a.m., allowing 45 minutes for you to board your supersonic transporter departing to Seattle at 8:45 a.m."

Indeed, travel marketers in 2020 may find themselves marketing to computers, instead of people. Tomorrow's travelers will likely depend on technology to make their bookings for them. You will simply feed a computer the data it needs to know and it will make choices for you. Better yet, you will not have to keystroke the information into your computer. Simply say it out loud and the computer will do the rest.

For travel marketers, this triumph of technology means a dog-eat-dog competitive environment that will demand creative packaging of travel experience products and services to overcome easily comparable variables like price.

How Will People Receive Messages in 20 Years?

Remember how futuristic projections appeared to you when you were a youngster? Visions of whisking between continents via Space Shuttle-like air transports, exploring undersea in passenger bathyscaphs and even vacationing on Mars all seemed around the corner.

The reality is that travel and transportation in 20 years will not be too unlike they are today. But they will certainly be as challenging, if not more so. Jetting between continents on a swift Concorde was beyond the financial reach of most travelers. Submarines for the rest of us also never got off the ground, so to speak. Mars, in all likelihood, will easily remain unsettled for two more decades.

Because traveling in 2020 will remain relatively similar to traveling in 2004, it requires imagination and insight to envision how marketing to travelers will change by 2020. The onset of the Internet and the Web, and the ability of travelers to explore online, is only the start of a consumer-based travel booking revolution. Lifestyle changes that will affect all of us will have a major impact on how travel is marketed in 20 years. A cursory examination of technological trends we are already experiencing signals what we might expect in our lives over the next two decades.

- *Adoption of HDTV as the standard for home television receivers.*

Sight and sound at home, via television, will demonstrate remarkable improvements and allow travelers to see and explore from their easy chair at home. For curious travelers, HDTV means no more fuzzy imagery, but crystal clear video of almost any place in the world.

- *Commonplace interaction between one's home television and the Internet.*

This is already happening, but will become as routine as turning on your home or office computer. Travelers will be able to watch crystal clear video of their destination or potential lodging—they'll be able to explore and book, all with a television remote.

- *Complex communications tools will become routine.*

Streaming video, Webcasts, Web teleconferences and sharing of video information on an interactive, real-time basis will all become part of our business and home routines. The novelty of transmitting images of people and information on a real-time basis took enormous strides during the Iraqi War in 2003.

By 2023, information will be presented on the next generation of HDTV displays, complemented by the ability of the viewer to pan, zoom and manipulate whatever they are watching.

- *Interconnection will be part of our daily lives.*

PDAs will become personal communications systems. If we want to talk with someone, we will be able to see them as they speak. If we want to learn what the weather is like in Newfoundland, we will be able to punch up a Webcam and see it for ourselves. The computer on one's desk will become a computer on one's wrist by 2025.

What are the implications for travel marketers?

- *The decline of printed materials.*

Travel marketers will be spending the same proportionate amount of money on their marketing program, but where the money goes will be dramatically different. Flyers, brochures, catalogs and printed materials will still exist, but interactive media will be the accepted norm for most people in search of information.

Advertising for newspapers and magazines will undergo massive change. A glance at the downward circulation figures for print media is all one needs to know about the future of advertising in print. The ranks of daily newspapers, already reduced to morning editions, will thin as newsprint and paper costs increase. The same holds true for magazines, which face rising production costs, mailing costs and other pressures that make their continued profitable existence tenuous.

- *Television will morph into online broadcasting*

Once upon a time there were three networks. Period. Viewers now turn to hundreds of choices via cable or satellite dish. UHF stations, once a television oddity defined by fuzzy definition on one's screen, are mainstream and delivery picture quality equal to that of network-affiliated stations. Television, as we currently know it, will likely blur with online media. Your remote will bring up a home page through which you can click to a television channel, movie-on-demand or your home photo library.

Vacation shopping will be run by the customer

No longer will travel marketers control the time and place at which their messages reach the consumer. Rather, in the 2020s, the customer will rule travel shopping. Customers, relying on editorial information that has been customized to their demonstrated wants, needs and preferences, will browse Web sites in shopping for and booking travel.

This implies that publicity and public relations, the usually overlooked, underutilized tool in a marketing plan, will become increasingly important in marketing programs. As advertising becomes more dicey and expensive due to the proliferation of channels of communication, publicity becomes more important because of its ability to cut across those channels and because of its inherent acceptance by audiences seeking news.

Word of mouth will pressure product quality

The onset of chatrooms and blogs (online diaries) has strong marketing implications. Chatrooms and blogs cannot be controlled by advertisers. Whatever people want to say about your product or service can be inserted on the Web and find its way around the world in moments.

The implications?

Customer relationship management (CRM) will become a critical part of marketing plans. Customer relationships will begin at the moment of contact, when a prospective shopper goes to one's Web site. They will end, temporarily, when a customer receives an electronic postcard from your company thanking them for their business. But if a customer is unhappy, hold on tight. They will register their complaint not with you, but to anyone who will listen, via the Web.

Viral (word of mouth) marketing will be king

Keeping customers happy, not ordinarily a marketing function, will become part of the job description of the marketing manager of the future.

Increased pressure on business travel

Why travel when you can talk to people face-to-face or watch a presentation from your television-like computer screen? Technological advances in allowing conferencing to take place over a screen are already causing businesses to think twice before booking trips.

The slide in business travel after the terrorist attacks of 2001 was reinforced by a poor economy, the SARS outbreak and fears about travel during the 2003 Iraqi War. The result has been an adjustment in how people engage in commerce. Businesspeople either adapted to doing business via the Internet or found other ways to do business without taking to the road.

Business travel budgets will continue to be under enormous pressure as attendance at conventions, conferences and meetings adjusts to newfound abilities that allow people to interact via video screen and online technology. Technical advances will likely enhance the ability to engage with clients via long-distance. The same technologies that we will enjoy at home, like real-time long-distance viewing with Webcams and instant messaging, will merge with HDTV, allowing video conferences that almost put you in the room with a client.

Conventions, tradeshows and exhibitions will also change dramatically over the next 20 years. Attendance need not be in person. Interested attendees will be able to visit a virtual tradeshow or virtual general session from their office or home. They will be able to interact with product salespeople on the tradeshow floor, from attending a product demo to placing an order, all via the Internet.

Nothing will replace meeting a client face-to-face. However, with technical advances that can overcome the need to travel, along with the time and cost of having people on the road, business travel will face continued challenges.

What's the future for travel marketers?

Lifestyle trends in the late 1990s and early 2000s point toward increased work weeks and enormous pressures for husbands and wives to work simply to make ends meet. There is increasingly less time for family, less time to vacation and less time to travel.

Everyone is more stressed out today than ever before. Twenty-six percent of Americans need to take something to calm their nerves. Fifteen million Americans include some form of Yoga in their fitness routine.

According to the YPB/Yankelovich National Leisure Travel Monitor, seven in 10 American consumers state life has become too complicated. Four in 10 do not have enough time and six in 10 do not have enough vacation time. One-half of all Baby Boomers are seriously considering slowing down the pace of their lives and 45 percent of American consumers choose the restfulness of being bored over having too much stress.

Since September 11, 2001, there has been a renewed dedication to family. American families are building firewalls to protect their time together. The family market will continue as a top priority for travel marketers in the future.

Americans view travel as a birthright. This has only been enhanced with current world events. As the world becomes safer, travel marketers will be able to capitalize on the aging boomers and their disposable incomes.

Marketing will become the primary driving force to motivate people to change their behavior. Just as lifestyles have changed, travel marketers must recognize the changes and adjust their product and marketing strategy to accommodate a consumer market that has declining leisure time.

Research will be an important marketing tool to identify what the next trend will be or what trends are on the way out. Knowing what customers want and do not want will be critical to formulating product development and marketing programs. Research will also be vital to knowing how to position a product or service. If people are seeking relief from 60-hour work weeks, research will need to identify both the desire and point toward the solution. If people want to travel, but stay close to home, research will have to serve as the barometer that identifies the trend and signal to marketers to market within a certain geographic radius.

Distribution channels will continue to evolve. The Internet will continue to be the driving force and will grow in lookers and bookers. Travel agencies will continue to be under pressure. Travel marketers will need to juggle market share, yield, and customer retention in finding the best channel for product distribution and marketing.

Travel marketers will need to embrace the new value equation. The new value equation is not only price divided by quality, it is also personalization and how much time/energy is expended in the process. Travel marketers who can save their customers time and energy, plus customize their experience, can increase their repeat business and not have to rely solely on price to win them back. This is the value of travel agents who can provide this service.

This is also the next big opportunity for the Internet. According to the YPB/Yankelovich National Travel Monitor, four in 10 Internet users are willing to pay 20 percent more for customized products and services. One size does not fit all. In the future it will be more pronounced. The Internet will allow travel marketers and their customers to tailor each travel experience. No two could be alike. Whether it is a cruise, a safari, a bicycle trip or a spa weekend, each customer will be able to have it their way. And they will gladly pay for these customized, one-to-one travel experiences.

As consumers become more informed, they will become more demanding. Did you know that six in 10 consumers state their IQ is higher than average? This will only increase as the Internet continues to empower consumers. And because of this empowerment, they will demand better service. According to the YPB/Yankelovich National Travel Monitor, six in 10 consumers feel the service people they deal with do not care about them or their needs. Travel marketers in the future will need to spend more quality time on retaining their customers as they do in attracting new ones. Price will always be important; however, value will win customers back. Repeat customers demand more than just price. They want recognition, customization and service. And they want special treatment.

Technical advances, some that we can see and some that none of us have yet discerned, will have enormous influence on traveling. Business travel will remain under pressure. Leisure travel will remain popular, but how people recreate and where they will go to play and vacation will remain influenced by travel marketing.

   None of us know what the future truly holds. As travel marketers, we need to be laying the foundation for future success, even if the immediate future is unclear. The key is having insight into today's consumers—their attitudes and behavior—in order to develop an effective marketing communications strategy. And knowing it can constantly change, based on the world we live in.

3

New Marketing Techniques for an Evolving Marketplace

Ric Cooper, Chairman and CEO
Cooper & Hayes Advertising

Ric Cooper is Chairman and CEO of Cooper & Hayes, one of the country's largest independent advertising and strategic marketing companies. Carnival Cruise Lines is a key client.

Beginning in the early 1990s, Ric was one of the early music and entertainment developers in Branson, Missouri—helping to catapult that tourist destination to national prominence.

He also cofounded American Adventure Productions, a leading producer of outdoor adventure programming such as *Wild Kingdom*, ABC's *Wide World of Sports* and *National Geographic*. Ric's series *The Spirit of Adventure* for ABC and ESPN won seven Emmy awards.

The early years of the 21st century have seen a significant amount of change. Considering that many of these transformations have been in the areas of technology, economics and global politics, the travel industry has especially been impacted.

Of course, one of the key needs of any marketing campaign is the ability to deal with change. We need to understand exactly what changes are occurring and prepare marketing plans that address them. First, however, a key challenge is predicting what these changes will be. As with any type of forecasting, we must begin with an understanding of the marketplace.

Among the challenges that must be understood are the changing demographics of the potential traveler, changing trends in distribution, the impact of outside forces (including the economy and global politics) and the evolving media environment.

Demographic Changes

A key demographic target of the past has been Baby Boomers. This age group, 72 million strong as of 2003, represented about 40 percent of consumers and was a key target for marketers. Moving into the 21st century, we must recognize that this group is aging and that they will eventually be replaced by Generation X and Generation Y. It is critical to understand the wants and needs of these different age segments and adjust our marketing strategies accordingly.

One of the recent challenges with Baby Boomers has been in the area of their free time. At an age when they are highly focused on raising children, performing their jobs, and caring for their aging parents, every minute is at a premium. Fortunately for travel marketers, the boomers are aging and moving toward retirement age. This means that they will have additional free time for leisure activities.

Marketers must recognize that retired Baby Boomers will be different from previous retirees. This age group is most likely going to feel a lot younger than their parents did at retirement age. Current trends seem to indicate that Boomers will live longer. (Some experts predict that by 2050 there will be a million Americans over the age of 100.) Their younger retirement lifestyle will not only impact how to target them, but also will likely impact the type of vacations that they are seeking with a stronger emphasis on "active" vacations than previously seen in this age group.

However, as the Baby Boomers age, Generation X (those born from the mid-60s to the early 80s) will replace them as working America. There is no question that this group is more "extreme"—this can clearly be seen by their choices in music and how they dress. Interestingly enough, the biggest marketing difference, from a travel perspective, between Generation X and the previous generations may be how they plan travel. The fact of the matter is that this is a segment of America that has grown up with the computer. A Nielsen Home Technology Report has indicated that 74 percent of younger adults consider the Internet the "best place" to get information about products and information compared to 69 percent among boomers and 55 percent among older adults. Moving forward, this PC friendly generation is also likely to book more trips online.

From a generation that has given rise to new types of sports such as skateboarding, in-line skating, and snowboarding, it should be no surprise that they are even more likely than their predecessors to seek adventure-type travel opportunities. This group is also more likely to seek out shorter vacations—as opposed to the traditional two-week family vacation.

Generation Y, the offspring of the Boomers, will eventually replace Generation X. This group, also known as Echo Boomers, is even more technologically entrenched than Generation X. They have grown up not only with PCs, but with PDAs and DVDs. As you might expect, this group is highly Internet-savvy. However, marketers can also expect that this group will embrace other technologically spawned forms of communication. In the future, it may be quite possible to send marketing messages directly to consumers' cell phones, which have lately begun merging with their PDAs to form truly portable computers. While it is hard to predict exactly how these technological advances will play out, one factor is known: Generation Y is already acclimated to wielding mobile communication devices (with usage starting in their teen years, if not earlier).

From a psychological perspective, Generation Y has been impacted by global events in a big way. Growing up in the age of September 11, they will fear terrorism; that will likely have a great impact on their values. Disenchanted by certain salable images communicated by the media, they may find it easy to replace their materialism with a desire to give back to the community.

In fact, a Cone/Roper study in 2000 revealed that 91 percent of teens valued companies that supported good causes (and this was prior to September 11). In the future, this group may be considering doing business based not only on the nature of the products manufactured by a certain company, but whether or not the company is a good corporate citizen.

Another interesting fact about Generation Y: 1/3 of this group will be composed of minorities. Accordingly, multicultural marketing will become a much more important issue in the future. However, even among minorities, there is no single homogenous group to be targeted. For example, Hispanics, projected to be the largest minority by 2005, can be segmented into many different subgroups based on their different socio-economic backgrounds.

As America ages, long-held beliefs regarding brand loyalty must also be brought into question. Historically, marketers were told to focus on younger consumers; these consumers would establish brand loyalties that would last into their later years. However, a recent RoperASW study revealed that the long-held belief that older consumers are more brand loyal may be false. This fact may be especially relevant as Baby Boomers move into their senior years.

Changes in Distribution

A key foundation of any marketing program is to influence a customer or potential customer. The key question has always been, "where along the line is purchase decision made?" The travel industry has been somewhat different from other industries due to the presence of the travel agent. Travel agents constitute an intermediary with a unique opportunity to influence the customer's travel purchase decision.

In the past, customers relied on travel agents to pull together information on different travel options. This created quite a service for potential travelers, eliminating, as it did, the need to investigate options on their own through multiple telephone calls and/or extensive research. Now, however, the Internet has given customers previously unheard of access to information. Consumers are now able to do vastly more travel research on their own. In fact, the Travel Industry Association (TIA) reported that 64 million Americans made travel plans online in 2002. This number is only likely to increase in the future. Travel marketers are well aware of this: Nielsen/Netratings has reported that online travel advertising soared 39 percent in 2002 (Nielsen/Netratings—3Q 2002). Once again, all data seems to indicate that this number will only increase.

Of course, a number of travel agents have closed shop due to the latest challenges. The TIA reported that travel agent usage was already trending downward toward the end of the 20th century. The percentage of Americans who used a travel agent for business or pleasure within the previous three years dropped from 32 percent in October 1999 to 26 percent at the end of 2002. However, there are travel agencies that are actually prospering. Customer service still means something and these agents benefit in offering the personal touch in an era when consumers are finding it more and more difficult to receive live assistance. More importantly, the thriving agents are seeing the Internet as an opportunity and not as a threat. These successful agencies are learning to combine the resources of the Internet with their own inside knowledge of the travel industry.

The impact of these new technological research tools has impacted the travel industry in varying ways. Thanks to the ease not only of comparison-shopping, but of easy booking on the Internet, more and more airline business is moving away from travel agents. At the same time, the cruise industry, where the travel agent still plays a key role in helping to explain some of the nuances of the experience, continues to work quite closely and profitably with travel agents. As technology advances and consumers are able to do even more online (and obtain much better online customer service), it is quite possible that many of the functions of the traditional travel agent will be supplanted.

As a result of technology, a new breed of travel agency is emerging. Companies such as Travelocity.com, Expedia and Orbitz (which is owned by a number of airlines) are major players, both in the travel and e-commerce industries. But instant access via the Internet to a myriad of travel opportunities does not mean that the potential traveler now feels comfortable going it alone. These new travel agencies play a definite role in helping consumers wade through the abundant information available on the Internet.

What does the future hold for the travel agent? Travel agents will most likely play a role in the future, but a different role, one heavily impacted by technology. Old-fashioned mom-and-pop companies may become a thing of the past. They will likely be replaced by new technologically driven companies that offer some merger of the traditional online and travel agency experiences.

Economic Influences

The United States has experienced many economic ups and downs throughout its history. While economics clearly impacted the travel industry in the early part of the century, the situation may be quite different ten years from now. One economic factor of continuing importance is value. Of course, a low price alone is not a true customer benefit unless it buys the same or better products and services. It is the responsibility of travel marketers to communicate the true rational and emotional value of any travel program. Price is an important attribute, but mostly because its acceptance makes other customer benefits attainable.

The fact of the matter is that pricing fluctuates in the travel industry more so than in any other industry, with the possible exception of gasoline retailing. The Internet has actually made pricing a much more significant issue than ever before due to the ease with which consumers are able to compare prices. In the past, travel agents would have the opportunity to compare vacation packages based on their merits beyond price. Now, consumers are drawn to online sites that focus primarily on providing the lowest price (priceline.com, cheaptickets.com, etc.) Price versus true value is most likely an issue that will continue to challenge the industry into the future.

It is also now impossible to surf the Internet (even when not seeking travel information) without being barraged by a slew of different travel bargains. These Internet advertisements tend to be very brief and focused on price. Will this still be the case in the future? While economically good times may result in less "bargain" advertising by travel marketers, it may be quite hard to dissuade consumers who have been conditioned for such a long time to seek out online bargains.

Further, tomorrow's consumers are smarter at researching options than in the past. Besides the Web itself, they know to search out prices everywhere from their local paper's travel section to their e-mail inbox. Historically, waiting to the last minute in the travel industry involved high premiums due to limited inventory. More recently, however, consumers are discovering that waiting can actually result in greater bargains as travel companies try to deal with last-minute occupancy issues. Based on anticipated growth estimates in travel capacity, the search for last-minute deals may remain an issue for some time to come.

Global Politics

Since September 11, 2001, threats of potential terror have created challenges for the travel industry. However, it is unknown how long these threats will remain a top-of-mind concern for Americans. Without knowing when or if there will be any future threats, it is hard to make any predictions in this area.

However, while it is unknown whether or not "fear" will continue to play a role in the travel decision process, there is one aspect that will most likely continue to be an issue: increased security procedures. In fact, it is more difficult to travel than ever before. Will this remain a challenge forever? Probably not. Traditional travelers will get used to the changes and new travelers will enter the market never having known any other way. For the immediate future, however, travel marketers need to be prepared to deal with these possible travel barriers.

Evolving Media Environment

Consumers are becoming increasingly harder to reach. Advances in technology and digital delivery systems have resulted in unprecedented programming choices. Unfortunately for marketers, more choices result in greater audience fragmentation.

As of the early 21st century, the average home got reception on more than 80 different television channels. That number is only likely to increase. With a greater number of channels available and viewership split among so many options, the ratings/value of any single channel and, more importantly to marketers, of any single commercial/spot, will be reduced. Five thousand brands are now advertising on national television (with the number reaching close to 25,000 if you factor in local advertisers). This makes it hard for marketers to find an individual voice for the products and services they represent.

It is also important to note that while the Baby Boomers have grown up with television, these new generations will likely embrace several newer forms of media. While statistics have shown that television has remained a viable media vehicle even with the rise of the Internet, we must recognize that television is only one part of the media mix. Moving forward, television alone may no longer be enough. Additionally, considering the predicted increase in the Hispanic population, careful consideration needs to be given to the media habits of the differently growing minority segments. For example, radio has traditionally proven especially effective in marketing to both Hispanics and African-Americans.

Besides the fact that more media exposure is needed to keep up with media fragmentation, there is also the issue of cost. During the past 10 years, the media marketplace has experienced an unfortunate economic trend: media costs are rising much faster than the rate of inflation. TV costs have increased by over 65 percent in the last 10 years, compared to only a 29 percent rise in the U.S. Consumer Price Index (CPI). A review of the history of advertising costs over the past few decades seems to indicate that this is unlikely to change in the future.

One additional challenge is the fact that the media, which serves as a source of delivering marketing communications, has also been a source of increased travel barriers. The news media are always looking for a story and the travel marketplace has always been an easy target. The news media have also most likely increased the fear of terrorism. News media organizations have been known to run stories investigating travel security issues even at times when there are no specific incidents to report.

Answering the Challenges

There are some facets of marketing that are not likely to change. One of the most important decisions for any company will most likely remain how to position its products. You must know your product, the competition's and the needs and wants of the customer base. Positioning should immediately differentiate between your products and those of your competitor. Strong positioning can help to move the market's focus beyond pricing issues. Strong positioning can successfully sell a product regardless of whether the final purchase decision is made in the company of a travel agent or at one's own computer keyboard.

Of course, it is critical both to address the brand image and allow for tactical spending. Short-term needs may call for specific tactical campaigns; however, one must never forget about long-term branding images. Otherwise, price can become a primary consumer decision factor and we will actually find ourselves training consumers to book only when there are deals.

Marketers must simply never lose sight of real customer benefits. Advertising needs to address both the emotional and the rational responses of consumers. There is a great opportunity to romance the leisure aspect of travel products. Leisure travelers anticipate an escape from everyday life; advertising should directly tie into this desire. The stronger the "creative" can be, the greater the chance that the campaign will cut through the increasingly fragmented media environment.

It is also important to find unique ways to reach consumers. Mass media continues to be an excellent way of beginning the process and generating awareness and will most likely remain so in the future. However, it is critical to battle fragmentation through an increasing use of many different types of media, both traditional and nontraditional. The Internet, direct marketing (which will most likely move beyond "snail mail" into new electronic territories), promotions, and event marketing are all tools that will become increasingly important in the future.

Travel marketers also cannot forget the need to monitor how their company is viewed. Public relations will continue to be important; especially considering some of the predictions regarding the views of Generation Y. Moving forward, companies also need to consider the value of co-branding opportunities in which they can combine the attributes of their various offerings to provide greater consumer benefits.

Marketers should also capitalize on the fact that many of the new media offer an unprecedented opportunity to impact consumers in ways not previously thought possible. It is important to turn transactions into relationships. Technology will provide ways not only of creating sales, but of continuing to offer customer service after the fact. Of course, many of these new opportunities also present the prospect of tracking consumer behavior. This data can be used to upgrade product offerings tailored specifically to individual consumer wants and desires.

4

The Travel Landscape

Lou Rena Hammond
Founder and President
Lou Hammond & Associates (LH&A)

Lou Rena Hammond transformed a three-employee, three-client public relations company into an award-winning marketing communications agency with 40 employees, more than 40 clients, and offices in New York, Las Vegas, Miami and Toronto.

Specializing in the premium market, LH&A has for more than 18 years provided expert public relations, public affairs, promotions, product introduction and crisis communications services.

Ms. Hammond developed her specialty in upscale marketing during her 15-year tenure at Pan American World Airways, where she served as director of publicity and public affairs. Lou is cited in *Who's Who in America* and received the Women in Communications' Matrix tribute, along with Hospitality Sales and Marketing Association International's (HSMAI's) Winthrop W. Grice award, the organization's highest honor. A fifth-generation Texan, Lou resides in New York and Charleston.

The Travel Landscape

The shape of the contemporary travel marketplace has changed, perhaps forever. Established revenue streams and long-honored marketing methods are under assault as the industry has faced an unprecedented series of challenges over the last several years. Travel companies are now forced to confront all manner of difficulties, from economic struggles to terrorist attacks, armed conflicts and mystery illnesses. Although more North Americans than ever are predisposed to travel, travel suppliers have discovered that vacationers are also more attuned to national and global developments and thus more willing to postpone or alter their travel plans in light of world events.

In addition, the information technology explosion that began in the late 1990s has created a savvier, more responsive travel consumer. Armed with the power of the Internet, business and leisure travelers are now equipped with the means to compare and contrast competing travel offerings within the blink of an eye, placing increased pressure on suppliers to deliver on the basis of price, product and value. As a result, more than at any time in the travel industry's history, to be successful in today's marketplace, suppliers and operators must build brand identity through nimble and creative promotional initiatives.

Indeed, several segments of the travel business continue to thrive in spite of the extraordinary challenges of the last few years. While savvy marketers have consistently found new ways to present their products, their sustained success is also due to continuing growth in Americans' desire to travel. American consumers have demonstrated time and time again that they will eventually—if not immediately—shrug off all manner of difficulties, from armed conflict to economic hardship, to partake in hard-earned vacation travel.

In fact, several trend studies provide evidence of surprising strength in consumer sentiment regarding travel. American Express Leisure Travel Index polls have found that terrorist attacks and other armed conflicts have historically had little long-term impact on consumer travel. While consumers may avoid certain destinations for a time, few of those who intended to travel will give up on their plans easily, the American Express studies found. Many consumers will instead vacation closer to home, drawn by the competitive, value-added offers that often accompany such disruptions.

This is particularly true for travel's premium market, led by high-end product and service providers. Not only does this segment represent more wide-ranging, frequent travelers, but the upscale category has benefited from a historic shift in consumer buying power, which is now increasingly weighted toward either the premium or mass-market market sectors. Furthermore, premium-market vacationers increasingly view travel as their right, and are quite unwilling to jettison their leisure travel habits in response to outside forces.

In fact, recent research from the Travel Industry Association of America (TIA) confirms that Baby Boomer travelers (age 35 to 54), traditionally a key premium-market audience, have shown a significant increase in their available time to travel. Additionally, Boomers in recent years have also been generally more confident about traveling based on their personal finances.

Thus, while almost all of the major travel market segments—from airlines, hotels and resorts, to cruise lines and international tours—have experienced a challenging environment over the past few years, success remains within reach of marketers who employ techniques suited for today's travel environment. One of the most important of these techniques is public relations.

Successful public relations

The art of public relations is one of influencing public opinion. Successful public relations efforts rely on the clear identification of goals, strategic thinking and impeccable judgment in developing and implementing strategies.

First and foremost, public relations professionals must possess an intimate knowledge of the business, including its customers, employees and shareholders. Only then can the practitioner understand what approaches will prove effective and what specific segment of the audience must be reached. Indeed, once the practitioner has established a complete knowledge of the business, targeting the appropriate audience becomes key. Public relations professionals must continually ask themselves whom they are trying to reach.

The industry's acceptance of public relations as a service that can produce results that affect the bottom line is a relatively new phenomenon. There was a time when public relations professionals were referred to as "publicists" and the profession stood on the fringes of key business priorities.

Today that has changed. Virtually all companies now consider public relations vital to their success or failure and have a greater appreciation of what public relations efforts can achieve.

Updated strategies are required

The ever-widening application of Internet technology to virtually every phase of American life has created a "24/7" mindset among consumers, who are now positioned to expect information on demand.

Additionally, cell phone and Internet technologies have profoundly altered the media's ability to respond to news developments involving travel suppliers.

Increasingly, a disgruntled person armed with a cell phone can create an instant flurry of media activity. Any incident has the potential to spread exponentially beyond the story's initial circle, since Internet-driven research and news is produced almost instantaneously.

These news technologies present new issues for public relations practitioners. Today, when a reporter decides to write about a topic, a quick Internet search provides decades worth of information, instantly providing the journalist with in-depth, long-term research on the subject. As a result, public relations professionals must also utilize the same technologies and move quickly to acquire as much knowledge about specific topics as the reporters they are trying to aid.

In addition, the instantaneous nature of today's news cycle means public relations professionals must be ready to respond to developments within the same advanced time frame—preferably within the hour—or risk seeing the message muffled or even lost in our 24-hour news mindset.

At the same time, the rapid pace of Internet-era communications has also created a crowded marketplace that, while loaded with choices and options, varies widely in terms of promise and product delivery. Because of this, the warm handshake and the face-to-face meeting are more important than ever. No matter how fast and powerful the Internet or e-mail delivery become, the travel business is about relationships, and this makes personal contact of paramount significance, even in the age of technology.

This new media landscape has placed the onus squarely on the shoulders of travel operators, who must immediately respond to news developments and provide the media with accurate information. Today's travel providers also find they must create their own presence in the Internet-driven consumer marketplace by achieving the all-important goal of establishing a clear, motivational brand identity that means something to a contemporary consumer bombarded with choice.

Successful PR professionals employ new tools

As a result, public relations professionals serving today's travel marketers must employ a new range of techniques and tools in creating a marketplace strategy that identifies and establishes the operator's brand while differentiating it from its fast-moving competition.

For example, local-level, grass roots "guerilla" marketing is becoming an effective promotional tool as consumers are increasingly inured to sleek, omnipresent electronic-media advertising and promotion.

For example, Norwegian Cruise Line (NCL) found guerilla marketing techniques particularly effective as the company prepared to launch its newest ship, the 2,224-passenger Norwegian Dawn. NCL needed to publicize the ship's New York-based seven-day cruise series, meaning the company faced the difficult task of gaining attention in the world's media capital during the holiday season, when demands for coverage are at their peak.

As a result, NCL launched a street-level promotional campaign in the weeks leading up to the December christening. A small crew of public relations personnel distributed Norwegian Dawn T-shirts, ski hats and bumper stickers at popular tourist attractions around New York City, all the while videotaping New Yorkers as they "welcomed" the new ship to the Big Apple.

Through a variety of personal contacts, NCL also arranged to have celebrities, including Donald Trump, Regis Philbin, members of the New York Rangers hockey team and even a group of New York City firefighters "welcome" the new ship to New York. The activity met its goal by creating a "buzz" around town and won media coverage for the christening, which included coveted same-day spots on NBC's "Today" show, the entertainment program "Extra!" and the CNBC news program "Power Lunch." The strong media reaction to the ship and the christening ceremony led NCL to change the ship's planned seasonal deployment in New York to an unprecedented, year-round New York-based series.

In another successful campaign that employed innovative strategies, New York's famed Waldorf-Astoria Hotel was able to overcome record-low occupancy and record-high cancellations in the wake of the Sept. 11, 2001 terrorist attack on New York.

In consultation with LH&A, the Waldorf identified new markets created by the World Trade Center collapse, including rescue workers, Federal Emergency Management Agency (FEMA) and Red Cross personnel, displaced residents of Battery Park, and personnel from the Federal Bureau of Investigation (FBI) and other government organizations investigating the attack.

The actions also included leveraging the general manager's position on the executive committee of NYC & Co. (New York City's convention and visitors' bureau) to establish him as a highly visible and knowledgeable spokesperson for New York's hospitality and tourist industries. Finally, LH&A sought to reassure jittery travelers by focusing on the Waldorf's safety and security. Due to its state-of-the-art security measures, the Waldorf has served as an official home-away-from-home for every U.S. president since Herbert Hoover. The Waldorf has also served as the official residence of the U.S. Ambassador to the United Nations.

As a result, the Waldorf-Astoria secured positive coverage for New York City and the hotel in major media outlets including Associated Press, ABC News, "Good Morning America," *The Financial Times*, "The Today Show," CBS News, *The New York Times*, NBC News; BBC News, *The London Times*, the *International*

Herald Tribune, CNN, Crain's *New York Business*, *The Wall Street Journal* and Bloomberg Television.

By the second week in October, the Waldorf-Astoria's occupancy and rates had improved dramatically and most "cancelled" programs and functions had been rebooked.

Building on Brand

Brand building is the essence of successful marketing. Public relations professionals must focus on differentiating their products while ensuring that all materials, events and promotion efforts remain in keeping with the brand's tenets.

Several reports confirm that upscale brands are particularly strong in America's redefined economy, with the hotel segment at the forefront. A number of hospitality companies remain committed to the U.S. market, even when price-cutting is prevalent in the industry.

For example, Mandarin Oriental Hotel Group, a five-star collection of 18 hotels around the world that appeal to discerning high-end travelers, has focused on expansion, moving forward with new properties (including its flagship property in New York City at the AOL/Time Warner Center at Columbus Circle), and other hotels in Washington, D.C., Boston and Tokyo.

One of the most important factors in building image is gaining an understanding of the nature of the brand and the connotations it holds for users. By understanding this, marketers are positioned to utilize the brand's representation of those qualities to appeal to consumer sentiment.

As an example, LH&A faced a formidable challenge generating publicity for the opening of The Spa at The Hotel Hershey in Hershey, Pennsylvania. Despite strong competition from other high-profile spa and resort properties in the region, LH&A successfully generated media interest in this very specialized product by focusing on the established qualities of the Hershey brand. In addition, besides generating a new client base for Hershey, company officials expected the spa to help the resort increase its business in the low and shoulder seasons.

Strategy was built to focus on the core elements of the Hershey brand, not an entirely radical strategy when one considers that the brand is well established in American culture.

Thus, promotional techniques for Hershey included educating the public on chocolate's health benefits and uses in a spa environment; building Hershey's brand identity by alerting the media to novel Hershey spa treatments that utilized chocolate and arranging a "De-Stress Express to Chocolate Paradise" press trip geared to beauty editors. The press trip activities emphasized how a Hershey escape could rejuvenate the senses.

The results of the promotion were overwhelming. Within the first six months, a four-minute segment on NBC's "Today," reaching some six million viewers, had been secured. In addition, enormous media coverage ensued, capturing a national audience of approximately 100 million.

Product segmentation

Recognizing and trading on a brand's specific market segment has emerged as an effective public relations strategy. Focusing on a brand's niches or nuances—such as cruising, golfing, skiing, family travel or honeymooning—and connecting publications with related programs and activities is a proven means of encouraging placements.

LH&A made successful use of the unique characteristics of one company recently in a promotion that featured the upscale Kahala Mandarin Oriental hotel in Honolulu, Hawaii. This classic hotel had undergone an extensive $80 million renovation and needed to attract attention to its re-launch, while downplaying any perception of it as an "old-fashioned" hotel.

The strategy was to capitalize on the hotel's glamorous image as a resort for the stars, while tempering the property's nostalgic image by communicating that the Kahala Mandarin Oriental would uphold the company's high standards in facilities, service and amenities.

By developing press materials focusing on the hotel's combination of "glamour and traditional Hawaii hospitality" and organizing a press trip for journalists to visit, a new perception of the property was achieved. An important element of the campaign was the creation of the term "Kahollywood," which the hotel used to promote the combination of Hawaii hospitality with Hollywood's star power.

As a result of the trip, *Los Angeles Magazine* ran a five-page story entitled "Gone Kahollywood" featuring the property's rich history and celebrity residents, details of the renovation and improvements, food and beverage outlets and recreational and spa facilities. Other placements included prominent stories in such publications as *Bon Appetit, Departures, The New York Post, Southern Accents, Travel + Leisure, USA Today* and the *San Francisco Chronicle*. In all, the promotion attracted a total print circulation of 26 million readers during the first 12 months.

More importantly, the effort signaled to the entertainment industry that the Kahala was back and better than ever. Since the public relations campaign began, numerous celebrities have returned to the property, including Whitney Houston, Sean Penn, Billy Joel, Gary Shandling and John Tesh.

Another form of segmentation is an appeal to value. In virtually every travel category, products that offer value—demonstrable benefits that add to the overall worth of the package—are increasingly important in attracting publicity and promoting business success. "Free" is not a good word when dealing with the premium market, but regardless of market strata, in the present-day environment, people seek added "bang for the buck."

Focusing on what's important

The bottom line is that rapid advances in information technology have prompted changes in the ways in which the public receives information and in which the media delivers it for public consumption. These profound changes have led public relations professionals to respond in kind by creating new tools and methods of their own to provide services to the travel industry's broad scope of companies.

Today's public relations professional must be especially responsive to stay abreast of fast-moving news developments. Practitioners must increasingly focus their efforts on understanding the brand they represent and building strategies around its inherent strengths and characteristics. Additionally, today's challenging economic environment affects the everyday decisions of millions of North American travelers, making it crucially important to link brand to value.

Finally, despite the rapid advance of technology, one thing has not changed— business remains focused on relationships. Perhaps no other industry exemplifies that more than travel, where alliances amongst the various segments—hotels, airlines, tour operators, cruise lines and car-rental companies—are not only prevalent, but also indispensable to the success of all.

The travel industry is a club whose members are fortunate enough to work in an industry where the main goal is providing happiness. The ties that bind members of this group to one another are not only endemic to the business, but also crucial to the success of the club members. Regardless of the latest technology, when editors find themselves hard-pressed for time, they reach out for the sources they trust to provide the information they need accurately and in a timely fashion.

Section II

Transportation Marketing

The travel industry depends on transportation; it is as simple as that. Without the ability to move people from point A to point B, there is no travel industry. The finest hotels, resorts, destinations, cruises and tours in the world will find no takers if folks can't access them.

Since the turn of the century, the transportation system in this country has been reeling like a punch-drunk prize fighter, battered by a contracting stock market, DOT bombs, a sideways economy, SARS, terrorism, Afghanistan and Iraq. The September 11, 2001, World Trade Center attack actually shut down the domestic aviation system—shut it down completely for three days. The ensuing chaos was memorable and unprecedented. Close to 400,000 jobs were lost in the travel industry as a result of that unsettling event. The major airlines bled red ink to such an extent that the federal government bailed them out to the tune of billions of dollars in outright grants and loans. Two major air carriers flew through bankruptcy with massive overhauls of business plans and painful wage restructuring and givebacks. The major hub and spoke carriers were virtually reengineered in less than two years . . . in order to survive. Labor unions gave back billions in wage and work rule concessions to keep companies viable. Literally hundreds of planes are mothballed in places like Phoenix and Las Vegas, reducing capacity by roughly 15 percent in an effort to run the airlines more efficiently by better plane capacity utilization. Thousands of folks opted for early retirement from their management and office jobs where given the choice. The less fortunate were terminated. Similarly, the rental car companies were affected by a fall off in air travel in general and business travel in particular.

The year 2003 witnessed the hub-and-spoke natural carriers struggling to achieve profitability while the point-to-point model, exemplified by Southwest and its latter-day emulators such as Jet Blue and Spirit, enjoyed profitable operations.

But what of the future? Tim Meskill of Boeing suggests that the airframe in 2010 will be evolutionary in nature, not revolutionary. (In the late 1980s, hydrogen-powered supersonic jumbo planes were predicted by the early years of the 21st century. Today, those forecasts seem like pipe dreams.) Delta, Northwest and United are convinced that the hub-and-spoke model is efficient and relevant, today and tomorrow. Point-to-point carriers will have an assured place in the future, thriving on opportunities overlooked by the majors as long as they are able to maintain their "lean and mean" operational style and keep costs low. Global alliances will prosper, creating strong brand associations worldwide while maximizing customer relationship management possibilities. Loyalty programs in both the airline and rental car industry will morph away from pure miles to a metric tied to revenue so that the rewards more properly reflect the customer's contribution.

The national carriers will learn from their smaller, clever competitors and make sure that wage increases are not automatically embedded in annual adjustments but rather are geared to the profit performance of the carrier. Without this fundamental (radical, from the union standpoint) change, the hub-and-spoke majors will quickly return to an uncompetitive cost structure.

Airline marketers need to figure out what features to put on an airplane and which to leave out or charge extra for. First-class seating, meals, beverages: it's all up for grabs with a finicky public careening to the lowest fare while complaining that the product "isn't what it used to be." The cost of efficient airline security, in terms of both dollars and passengers' time, is another issue to be wrestled with. An airline that can streamline and simplify this process has an edge . . . at least temporarily.

And then there's our woefully neglected railroad system, a national tragedy. Anyone who has spent any time in Europe (or Canada for that matter) quickly realizes how far behind the United States is when it comes to rail travel. Amtrak is faced with the daunting perpetual problem of lacking a dedicated source of federal funding. Consequently, it struggles each year to make its case for funding. Against that background of uncertainty and political whim, it's truly remarkable that Amtrak has been able to build passenger volume and add an exciting new product, the Acela Express.

Imagine trying to build that brand and gain volume and passenger acceptance against a background of fiscal quicksand! Notwithstanding that Amtrak has been a beneficiary of airline terrorism threats and security hassles, it has steadily improved its product and made the most of its shoestring marketing budget.

Perhaps Brian Kennedy of Hertz states it best when he says that travel suppliers, to be successful in the future, need to control costs (including distribution costs), create product differentiation, build customer loyalty, utilize technology to achieve their goals and invest in newer, more profitable markets as competitors marginalize existing ones. Pay attention to every shifting customer need, so as not to be outflanked by a competitor!

If the companies represented by the marketers in this chapter perform well, all other segments of travel and tourism will have a much easier time of it.

5

Connecting to the Future: Creating a New Vision of Air Transportation

Timothy D. Meskill
Director, Marketing and Business Strategy
Boeing Commercial Airplanes

Tim is currently director of marketing and business strategy. In this role, he facilitates the development of the commercial airplane group's competitive, market-driving business strategy.

Prior to his current assignment, Tim held the position of marketing director—market analysis. Tim was responsible for providing data, research and forecasts and identifying market opportunities for the commercial airplane group.

Tim earned a master's in business administration with a transportation concentration from Michigan State University and a bachelor of business administration from the University of Notre Dame.

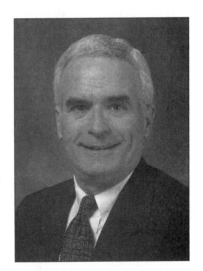

The future of civil aviation began to take shape the day ordinary passengers discovered they could afford to fly. The lure of new horizons and markets drew them to travel the world as never before.

During the last 30 years, airfares have steadily declined, and air travel has just as steadily grown. Over the next 20 years, air travel will increase by 4.9 percent, 2 percent faster than the world economy.

As passengers have become more experienced and sophisticated travelers, they have developed certain demands. They want continued low fares, convenient travel times and comfortable flights. They also want to know that the air transportation system is safe, reliable and secure.

In other words, passengers drive not only the market but also the worldwide system in which air transportation operates. And that system is extremely complex and showing signs of overload.

How can we shape a future system that will meet passenger demand?

Our Vision of the Future

Before you can envision the future, you have to understand the reality of the present. Congestion is a problem we can't ignore, delays are more frequent. The infrastructure that has worked so well for so long can no longer handle the growth in air travel.

How do we fix it? How do we connect people, ideas and technology to create the future we want—a safe, convenient and efficient global air transportation system?

First, we take a look at our concept of what an airplane is and what we think it should do. That concept was formed 100 years ago when the Wright Brothers Flyer flew into history at Kitty Hawk. An airplane was a machine that could move people from one place to another. Through the years, we have embellished that concept: an airplane flies faster and farther than the Wright Brothers ever dreamed, carries more passengers and is much more comfortable.

While we still need a very efficient machine to move people, an airplane is becoming far more than that.

In a world of information, an airplane is becoming an information node, a link to satellites and ground stations, to airline service centers, to the Internet, to Aunt Lou in New York from a wireless phone 30,000 feet up, to a future we are just beginning to imagine.

Information and new airplane technologies are the key to unlocking the new systems that will be the foundation for the air transportation system and passenger experience of this century.

How do we expect to accomplish this revolution in efficiency, comfort and convenience in this brand-new century?

Our approach is fivefold:

- E-enabled airplanes designed to conduct and process information from many sources.
- A new air traffic management system.
- Connexion by Boeings.
- A new airplane.
- A plan for creating an affordable and truly satisfying passenger experience.

E-enabling and Its Exciting Promise

Imagine airplanes with fewer but more intelligent systems capable of connecting and communicating with space and ground systems in a reliable and cost-effective way, of being maintained in a secure and efficient manner, and of managing airspace efficiently enough that more airplanes can use more of it.

In its simplest form, e-enabling creates an integrated network for seamless information flow to a variety of sources. Airplane systems are linked to global air traffic management systems, broadband information and entertainment channels for passengers, and airline service centers. All these systems share a common data core.

In other words, e-enabling makes it possible for an airplane to function as a node in the information flow, and it serves as the basis for our vision of future air traffic management system. We created two special business units to develop our vision further—Air Traffic Management (ATM) and Connexion by Boeing. As information technology improves, e-enabling will become an ever more elegant answer to the challenge of redefining the air transportation infrastructure.

Air Traffic Management— Redesigning Airspace for Growth

Air traffic systems around the world must be dramatically improved to reduce congestion and delays; increase safety, security and convenience; and keep aviation affordable and accessible for everyone.

At the core of ATM's proposed future air traffic management system is the common information network (CIN), which would use secure and encrypted communication links between airplanes, satellites and ground-based users for real-time, integrated information about airplane trajectories, weather and air traffic flow.

Information transmitted through a common information network would give air traffic controllers a far greater degree of situational awareness than they have today. CIN could also be used to detect and monitor anomalies, improve traffic flow and safely increase airspace capacity and efficiency.

Today's controllers must anticipate airplane trajectory because current radar systems cannot predict it. In the future, controllers will be able to view a graphical representation of an airplane's trajectory in real time, enabling them to accurately predict the airplane's future position up to 40 minutes in advance. Potential conflicts will be easier to spot and resolve while giving controllers information and time to avoid congestion and delays.

Using CIN and trajectory-based tracking and planning systems will allow us to redesign airspace. The present complex system of control sectors and segregated flow zones will be replaced with a simple, more open, managed flow configuration.

Under the existing system, controllers reserve large blocks of airspace to ensure safe separation of airplanes on approach and departure because the system cannot provide them with detailed information about flight crew intentions and airplane performance.

Our concept would minimize the airspace needed for safe operation while increasing safety by efficiently managing the flow of information.

The air traffic management system we envision would depend on a ground and satellite system capable of precise positioning in vertical, horizontal and geographic dimensions. It will also enable system-wide connectivity among airplanes, ground-based controllers and authorities, and flight operations personnel.

With its bold approach to a new infrastructure, our proposed air traffic management system will keep air travel even more safe, dependable and convenient.

Connexion by Boeing— Connectivity 30,000 Feet in the Sky

For passengers, crew and operators, connection to broadband services through Connexion by Boeing is invaluable, especially on long flights, and will become even more so as electronic access to the world expands in the coming century.

Leisure passengers can stay in touch with the world through real-time connectivity to the Internet. They can send and receive e-mail, watch streaming video, stay current with the news and listen to the music of their choice.

Business travelers will effectively have a digital office in the sky. They can reach critical customers, work on reports or presentations, adjust travel plans, purchase gifts and conduct research on the Internet.

For airlines, Connexion by Boeing can improve service to their passengers by letting them arrange new connections when a delay occurs and even print a new boarding pass. Flight crews will be able to report maintenance requirements to ground crews, who in turn will have electronic access to airplane records and maintenance manuals. Airplanes in need of repair will spend less time on the ground, and there will be fewer delays due to minor maintenance problems.

Through its dynamic broadband capability, operators can monitor airplane systems, speeding maintenance, reducing delays and retaining the reliability passenger's value.

For air traffic management, Connexion by Boeing will plug the airplane into the new infrastructure efficiently and effectively.

How does Connexion by Boeing work? An antenna mounted on top of the airplane fuselage locks onto a signal relayed from a geosynchronous satellite, which relays transmissions to and from the airplane in flight. The satellite communicates with ground stations, from which the signal is carried securely through a network control center and to the Internet.

As airplanes become more e-enabled, we will be able to reduce the weight, power requirements and complexity of the airplane, creating the potential for many exciting future wireless applications.

For example, on a Boeing 777, we may be able to distribute entertainment to a passenger's seat through a wireless LAN, thus eliminating nearly 2,000 onboard line-replaceable units for the in-flight entertainment center alone. Weight and fuel reduction can, in turn, lead to lower fares.

E-enabling, the proposed air traffic management system being developed by ATM, and Connexion by Boeing will help create and sustain a new and better future infrastructure that will answer passenger needs for convenient, dependable, affordable air travel. And airplanes flying in the redesigned airspace must be just as efficient as the streamlined systems to which they will be connected.

A new airplane for a new world

Our new airplane may look like most airplanes. It doesn't have canards or a blended-wing body, but sometimes revolutions take place quietly.

Aware of the growth in air travel, airlines want an airplane that will take them into the future—profitably. They know that competition for passengers will be keen and that passenger demands are evolving as fast as the speed of information. They also want an airplane capable of taking full advantage of the new infrastructure. Our new airplane will satisfy future airline and passenger needs.

Built with extensive use of composites or new lightweight aluminum alloys, the new airplane will seat 200 to 250 passengers and have highly efficient wings and engines.

Onboard monitoring systems and sensors embedded in the structure will help lower maintenance costs. We expect the new airplane to be 20 percent more fuel-efficient than our 767-300, an airplane known for its efficiency.

E-enabled, the new airplane will be "plugged" into developing air traffic management systems and flight deck technology, making flights even more safe and dependable.

By 2008, when the new, super-efficient airplane will enter service, 42 percent of today's middle-of-the-market, twin-aisle fleet will be at least 20 years old. The new airplane will be an excellent replacement, enabling airlines to fly passengers where they want to go when they want to go.

The new airplane will offer passengers something equally as important as fares they can afford—unprecedented comfort, convenience, and wireless services provided by Connexion by Boeing. Its interior will have wider seats and aisles, innovative lighting, and beautiful aesthetics designed to refresh and relax passengers. For passengers, the new airplane will truly bring back the magic of flight.

Back to the Present and On to the Future

Remember what drives air travel and the systems that support it—passengers and their need to travel where they want to when they want to, conveniently, safely and affordably. The infrastructure that supports air travel is there to support them. It is there to support a flourishing world economy and a world in which everyone has the freedom to travel. We must use vision and conviction to shape travel tomorrow—and today—for the passengers of the world.

6

Changing an Industry to Satisfy a Customer

Lord (Colin) Marshall
of Knightsbridge
Chairman, British Airways, PLC

Lord Marshall has led British Airways for the last 20 years, initially as chief executive officer, then as chairman and CEO, and, since 1996, as nonexecutive chairman.

Lord Marshall came to the United States in 1958 to begin his business career with the Hertz Corporation. In 1964, he was recruited by Avis, Inc. and rose to become president and CEO. Following the takeover of Avis in 1979, he was appointed executive vice president of Norton Simon Inc. and co-chairman of Avis. Lord Marshall returned to the United Kingdom in 1981 as deputy chief executive and board member of Sears Holding, PLC.

He is chairman of Pirelli UK, PLC, a board member of HSBC, and president of The Commonwealth Youth Exchange Council. Lord Marshall is also a former president of the Confederation of British Industry (currently chairman of its international advisory board) and a board member of the New York Stock Exchange. He is a member and past chairman of British American Business Inc.'s and the British-American Council's international advisory board. In October 2000, he became the first non-U.S. business leader to be elected chairman of the board of trustees, The Conference Board, Inc.

He was knighted in 1987 and made a Life Peer in the Queen's Birthday Honors of 1998.

For the travel and tourism industries, the first few years of the 21st century have been traumatic. The effects of terrorism, war and pestilence wreaked havoc as travelers stopped traveling and tourists stopped touring. No sector was more damaged than air transportation, as airlines incurred a collective loss of around $40 billion in three sobering years. Some carriers did not make it and for those left standing, it has been a case of reinventing themselves.

In the absence of further economic assaults on the industry, growth can be expected to resume. For the moment, the annual number of passengers carried on scheduled services—as opposed to charter flights—is something like 1.6 billion. Within the foreseeable future—by, say, 2015–2020—the industry's average annual growth rate should see that number double. In normal times, demand for air travel in existing mature markets is almost insatiable and new markets are opening up. The potential for overseas travel from China, for example, is enormous. Some forecasters believe that before too long there will be more Chinese traveling around the world than any other nationality.

Against the background of the recent past, the nature of airline competition is changing and will continue to change. Steeply dropping demand meant that most airlines had to drive down costs and build up cash reserves to survive. As a consequence, surviving carriers are more cost-efficient.

We have seen the emergence of the no-frills, low-fare airlines and they have had a profound competitive effect. The sector is still evolving, but the new competitors will not go away, nor will their challenges to the now-leaner, traditional, full-service airlines like British Airways. The capability of advanced technology for online booking, fare selection and even self-service check-in is changing the face of the airline industry and will continue to place more choice and control in the hands of the customer. Technology will also come into its own where security, immigration and customs controls are concerned. There can be no let-up on the drive towards fail-safe security and safety precautions; we can only hope that better, more advanced systems will reduce the "hassle factor."

A feature of contemporary air transportation has been the emergence of global alliances. They came about as intercontinental carriers sought to secure market presence and extend market reach across the world in a developing global marketplace. Unlike other industries, such as banking, telecommunications and automotive, airlines have not been given the usual latitude to undertake international mergers and acquisitions.

The situation goes back to the way modern international civil aviation was planned in the Chicago Convention of 1944. It rests on the notion of national sovereignty for airspace and national ownership for airlines. This means that if airline A of X-land bought airline B of Y-land, that carrier would cease to be a Y-land owned entity and could therefore lose its international route rights.

The situation is, however, in the process of changing, following the European Council's and European Parliament's decision to allow the European Union Commission to negotiate airline route rights on an EU basis. The European Union is committed to negotiating an open skies, free-market agreement with the United States and then with other countries. Europe's major intercontinental airlines will then become EU designated and able to effect mergers and takeovers. It is a much-needed process, because Europe has traditionally had a surfeit of hubs. I see, perhaps, just three intercontinental airlines based in Europe in the years ahead. With a single market in air transportation between Europe and the United States, who is to say that we will not have transatlantic airline mergers?

Aircraft development over the past 20 years may not have been spectacular, but it has been truly remarkable. Advances in wing, engine and airframe technology have provided the airlines with fleets that are more economic, more fuel efficient and more environmentally friendly. In the foreseeable future, we are likely to see more of the same kind of development. The latest, greatest aircraft is the Airbus A380, capable of carrying almost 600 passengers. It has, not surprisingly, become known as the "Super Jumbo." As with the Boeing 747 before it, the A380's size and capacity have required airport facilities to be modified.

One of today's ironies is that transatlantic supersonic travel is no longer available, following the retirement from service of Concorde. So far as a successor is concerned, there is nothing yet on the drawing boards. To be viable, a new supersonic transport would need to carry somewhere between 250 and 300 people and be able to operate at supersonic speed over landmasses, a facility that was denied Concorde. This would mean designing out the sonic boom, a feat which is, so far, scientifically impossible. That said, it is hard to imagine that people in this century and beyond will not have the option of supersonic travel.

So far as the business proposition is concerned, not much has changed. There are still two sides to the equation—costs and revenues. Any business that focuses on one at the expense of the other is going to pay heavily.

You just cannot walk away from the fact that somebody can do the job better and cheaper, or that you have a problem and have to do something about it. But at least you can address the situation without undermining the fabric of what you have built up. When business conditions got tough for British Airways in recent years, we did not pull our product apart. We did not reduce costs indiscriminately. We did not stop investing in facilities and training people—we continued making that investment, despite the fact that it would have been very easy not to.

There are different ways to think about how to compete in a mass-market service business such as ours. One is to think that a business is merely performing a function, in our case transporting people from A to B, on time and at the lowest-possible price. That's the commodity mindset—thinking of an airline as the bus service of the skies. Another way to compete is to function on the basis of providing an experience. So far as British Airways is concerned, we want to make the process of flying from A to B as effortless and as comfortable as possible. Anyone can fly airplanes, but few organizations can excel in serving people, because it's a competence that's hard to build. It's also hard for competitors to copy or match.

Today, we operate in a liberalized trading environment and deregulation is the name of the game, as the global economy evolves. The worldwide market is characterized by new freedoms of cross-border investment, pricing, supply, manufacture and access. The new environment generates an intense level of unbridled competition.

A fundamental question has arisen: If governments can no longer fix world markets, nor guarantee national market share, who decides what the standards of quality, service and value are? Who decides who wins or loses?

The answer is obvious: The customer.

It is the essential logic of the new world competitive order in every business sector, but especially in travel and tourism, that customer choice, preference and demand are the exclusive driving forces. This has called for existing thinking to be turned on its head, to bring customers out of the strategic shadows and install them ahead of all other considerations, in every aspect of business activity.

It has meant shifting the center of business gravity, so that the practice most closely concerned, if not obsessed, with what I have come to call "customer science"—marketing—has become pivotal.

Marketing is, above all, a philosophy enshrining a long-term commitment to customer satisfaction and the deployment of a set of intense skills to achieve it.

By definition, therefore, marketing is the key to profitable growth and optimally is part of every business process.

It means that business and its workforces—management, employees and trade unions—must join together in partnership to reduce waste and bureaucracy, to find more productive ways of creating and delivering—that is, of marketing—their products and services.

Management's vital role is to come out of the office and the boardroom to the point of sale or service delivery. If those of us who run companies do not have our customers in sight and earshot all of the time, we shall be passed over.

There is a critical element of British Airways' approach to serving customers: Filling customers' value-driven needs. Every industry has a price of entry—the ante you have to pay to get into the game. In our industry, there are five basic services that everyone has to provide. We must get passengers to where they want to go to; do it safely; go when they want to go; provide some nourishment; and, of course, let them accrue reward points. But our research has shown that, for some time, customers more and more take the basics for granted and want a company to help them, to treat them in a personal, caring way. Fulfilling those desires is at the crux of what I call "orchestrating" our service. By that, I mean arranging all the elements of our service so that, collectively, they generate a particular experience. We try to think about what kind of impression or feeling each interaction between the company and a customer will generate. For example, we ask our cabin crews not to ply passengers with food and drink in one shot, so to speak, then disappear—not for cost reasons, but so that we can create additional personal contacts with customers. That is, according to our research, their just seeing members of our staff, both on the ground and in the air, enhances their satisfaction with our service.

We continually ask customers in focus groups what such an experience should look and feel like and distil their responses into service principles. We have enshrined such principles in at least two of our stated corporate objectives: "To provide overall superior service and good value for money in every market segment in which we compete," and "To excel in anticipating and quickly responding to customer needs and competitor activity."

Our aim remains to create an airline global in scope, but with a homey feel—in deference to that '70s saw, "Think globally, act locally." The global image lets our customers know that we go where they are going and that we are professional. The homey or local aspect of our efforts reassure them that we have orchestrated our services so as to address their individual needs. We want them to know that we carry millions, but also that their individual interactions with us are not mass-produced.

Not all potential customers will recognize the added value of our service. But even in a mass-market business, you do not necessarily want to attract and retain everyone. So far as we are concerned, the key is first to identify and attract those who will value your service and then retain them as customers and win the largest possible share of their lifetime business. Traditionally, around 25 percent of our customers account for 60 percent of all sales. They exhibit a cyclical, repetitive discipline, as new generations become travel consumers, for both leisure and business purposes.

Using database marketing techniques, we have concentrated more of our marketing effort on retaining customers and increasing our share of their business. Consequently, our proportional advertising spend has been smaller than that of our competitors.

The marketing practices of the 21st century may be different and more sophisticated than those of the past, but the essentials have not changed and will not change. Marketing boils down to the timeless proposition of bringing a willing seller together with a willing buyer.

The first task is to study the market extensively and continuously to pinpoint the segments that offer the possibility of generating a higher profit margin—businesswomen, unaccompanied children, for instance—and identify those people among our customers. Then we create extensive lifestyle profiles of each customer, which we use both to increase ticket purchases and to sell other products and services. In addition to tracking how recently and how frequently customers have flown with us for business, leisure, or both, we track their broader purchasing decisions and their value needs. Identifying customers is, however, only half of the battle. Learning from them in order to design and improve services that they will value over time is the other half and it is extremely difficult to perfect.

With packaged goods, you can pull something off the line to test it periodically and adjust it if there is something wrong. A packaged goods business has quite extensive market data available to it. It knows how it is performing by store, even by positioning on shelves in the store. That kind of totally reliable information is just not available in our industry, nor in service businesses generally, because a service business is dealing with people's impressions and feelings. They do not actually buy an object, but an experience.

So many human interactions are involved in producing such an experience that it is often difficult to measure which interaction, or series of interactions, caused a customer to feel satisfied or dissatisfied. At the same time, a customer may have a bad experience because of circumstances ostensibly outside our control—a flight delay caused by bad weather or problems with air traffic control, for instance. As a result, it is often difficult to know if a complaint is the result of an isolated event (an employee having a bad day, for example) or a systematic problem.

The way to overcome such obstacles is by creating an organization that excels in listening to its most valuable customers and by creating data that enables you to measure the kinds of performance that create value for those customers, so you can improve performance and spot and correct any weaknesses. You overcome them by recognizing that the people on the front line are the ones who ultimately create value since they determine the kinds of experiences that the company generates for its customers. We focus intensively on the customer; our marketing, operating philosophy and performance measures reflect that.

In several key places in the company, we have created customer advocates, most notable and importantly in our brand management organization. Instilling a brand culture in a service business is very important, because a service business is all about serving people who have values, ideals and feelings. We need to see the product not simply as a seat, but more comprehensively as an experience being orchestrated across the airline. That orchestration is the brand.

Brand management forces you to recognize that there is a "wear out" factor for consumer products and their branding approach. Delivering consistent, exceptional service is not enough. Service brands, like packaged goods brands, need to be periodically refreshed to reinforce the message that the customer is receiving superior value for the money. Refreshing the service is also a way to make sure you regularly assess how the value you think you are delivering compares with the value customers believe you are delivering.

For consumer products, refreshing the brand may only require different labeling. Refreshing a service brand so that customers will really recognize the change requires something major. It certainly cannot be something superficial, such as changing the menus.

There is another great benefit to be derived from regular brand refreshment: employee motivations. People see that management is genuinely committed to investment—improvement in delivering high quality service. Employees want to be proud of their products and part of a winning team.

Now and for the future, there is much more to a travel industry brand than style, service and value. New factors have come into play.

One of them is environmental concern and it is vital that service providers (airlines, airports, surface transport operators, hotels) and destination areas clearly demonstrate their credentials in sustainable development and care of the environment. Customers will more and more take these factors into account when making their choices. We must remember that tourism's stock in trade is the built and natural environments of the world. Damage them and our core product is seriously devalued.

Another new factor is health risk. Recent scares, such as SARS and DVT, have placed pressure on the travel and tourism industry to ensure that health safeguards for those travelling and visiting overseas are as robust as they possibly can be.

Overall, I am confident about the future of this industry. Foreign travel is, after all, one of the top consumer aspirations. Tourism, like trade, is also a force for peace, prosperity and goodwill across the world.

Price will always be an important consideration, but I am convinced that consumers do not want just a cheap deal. The ongoing responsibility of travel and tourism marketers is to see that the hallmarks of our products and services are integrity and real value for the money.

7

The Future of Commerical Aviation

Frederick W. Reid
Former President and CEO
Delta Airlines

Frederick W. Reid was named president and
chief operating officer of Delta Air Lines in
May 2001. He is responsible for operations,
customer service and marketing across the
company. He oversees flight operations, technical operations, in-flight service, airport customer service, revenue management, route
planning, strategic alliances, global sales and
marketing, brand management, product
development, customer service and all facets
of airline operations.

Delta is the world's second-largest airline in terms of passengers carried and the
leading U.S. airline across the Atlantic.
Together with its worldwide partners, Delta
operates more than 5,000 daily flights to 400 cities in 72 countries.

Reid joined Delta in July 1998 as chief marketing officer, responsible for
Delta's network planning and route development, consumer marketing, and worldwide sales and distribution. During his tenure, he directed the successful acquisition of regional carriers ASA and Comair; rebuilt Delta's revenue management
system; redesigned the network to improve efficiencies and growth opportunities;
re-launched the Delta brand with a new aircraft livery, logo design, and global
advertising campaign; and led negotiations to form SkyTeam, a global alliance
comprising six of the world's leading airlines.

Reid also serves as chairman of the board of Delta Connection, Inc., the airline's subsidiary that operates the world's largest fleet of regional jets.

Before joining Delta, he served as president and chief operating officer of Lufthansa German Airlines, and was the first American national to lead a major non-U.S. airline. Reid played a key role in developing Lufthansa's strategic international alliances, and contributed significantly to the airline's privatization and return to profitability.

Between 1976 and 1991, based in Western Europe, the Middle East and South Asia, Reid held various management positions at Pan American World Airways and American Airlines.

A native of San Francisco, Reid graduated in 1973 from the University of California at Berkeley with a bachelor of arts degree in Asian studies. He is a member of the board of trustees of the Solomon R. Guggenheim Foundation in New York; the Board of Directors for AMB Property Corporation, a leading owner and operator of airport real estate based in San Francisco; and also serves on the advisory board for the Taub Institute for Research on Alzheimer's Disease. Reid, his wife Joyce and their three sons reside in Atlanta, Georgia.

Our industry is at a crossroads. On the one side, we have the prosperous low-cost carriers, growing in even today's humbled revenue environment. On the other side, we have the network carriers who have survived everything from deregulation to recession to the Gulf War, and, for most of us, September 11.

To "survive" is not really the aspiration of the network carrier. To win, to succeed is the goal.

We must evolve as an industry. As always, the strong, the smart and the nimble will evolve and prosper.

There's nothing like an extinction-level-event to accelerate evolution. September 11 was the meteor strike that altered our ecosystem forever—producing a nuclear winter, if you will, as measured by the dramatic and persistent decline in revenue since that day. This is not a change in the weather—this is a change to our climate. Simply put: We have entered a highly compressed evolutionary cycle.

In this evolution, we (the airlines) have a choice about what we keep and what we shed. What we change must be based on survival—what will help us win in the marketplace.

The marketplace is crying out for airlines to meet its needs for fair pricing, global access, reliability, good service and a choice of products. So, in this period of compressed evolution, when the only constant is change and all things seem possible, we ask ourselves the seemingly simple question: What will the network airlines look like that survive and thrive in this new environment?

I think there are three characteristics most successful airlines will share:

First, we must understand that this fight is about "survival of the fittest"—and successful airlines will win mostly on cost and productivity. But to do that, the airline animal must first change its eating habits.

Why cost? Why shouldn't airlines focus on revenue generation? In the heyday of the last decade, network airlines fed—maybe even gorged—off the high yields from frequent business travelers. This food source was produced by a racing economy, coupled with globalization, that produced high demand.

After September 11, business travel slowed; but more importantly, the pricing structure came under intense attack. The disparity between business and leisure fares, as well as the complexity of traditional pricing models, have come under fire.

Personally, I think this debate is misplaced. These are symptoms, not causes, of revenue decline.

The true drivers of change in revenue generation for network airlines—violently accelerated by September 11—can be grouped into four factors:

- Overcapacity

- Recession through many economies

- Rapid growth of low-cost carriers, and

- Unprecedented fare and inventory transparency due to the Internet.

The first two factors—recession and over-capacity—are directly related the meteor strike of September 11, and I believe we will see some correction in these two areas over time.

The last two factors—LCCs and the Internet—are not going away and, in fact, the influence of these factors will grow. The traditional airline revenue model has already been permanently altered.

We must focus on cost reduction and efficiency because there will be less revenue in the future.

We've already seen this in the North America market, in which there was a staggering 22 percent drop in revenues over 15 months.

We've seen revenues drop only twice before in 65 years—even then, by only by 1 or 2 percent. The numbers tell the story of this particular crisis: a 22 percent drop is 10 to 20 times more severe than any precedent. As a result of these factors, revenues have been commoditized.

Between 1995 and last year, U.S. low-cost carrier revenue per available seat mile *grew* 3 percent; U.S. majors unit revenue *fell* 3 percent. The gap between network and low-cost carrier unit revenue narrowed by almost 50 percent.

Revenue is not coming back—at least not as strongly or as soon as we had hoped. Because airlines cannot count on revenue to support the existing cost structure we see today, the battle for survival must move to the cost and efficiency side of the equation.

So where do we spend our money? We buy planes, we hire people to fly the plane, fix the plane, staff the plane, clean the plane; we rent facilities, we buy fuel, and so on. Pretty common pattern here.

A majority of an airline's costs are incurred whether the planes fly or not, so it is vitally important to *control what is controllable* and *maximize asset productivity*.

But what can we truly control?

Roughly 60 percent of the industry's costs are controlled by oligopolies. There is very little cost advantage between competitors when it comes to procuring the necessary infrastructure to run a robust network operation.

Large aircraft and small aircraft are each produced by only two manufacturers. While there can be an occasional and slight advantage in fuel cost due to hedging, the base price is set by the oil-producing cartel—OPEC.

Airports have complete pricing control. As airlines have reduced the number of flights, airports have raised their rates over the smaller denominator—*defying* the law of supply and demand! Airports took no financial hit from September 11. Net income actually rose for airports such as O'Hare in Chicago and JFK in New York. The decrease in airline traffic simply meant higher fees and higher rents.

So, for example, even though Delta reduced departures by *23 percent*, our airport costs ballooned 31 percent. We are paying $160 million more in 2002 than in 2000.

Policy changes such as commission cuts can only go so far. How much lower than zero can you go?

Simply taking on more volume is not a solution—for the airline or, more importantly, for our customers. Load factors have increased from the 60 percent range to the high 70 percent range over 15 years. In our estimation, for a carrier like Delta, once loads begin to creep into the mid-70s, the burden on our system *and* the customer begins to outweigh the marginal revenue that this volume brings.

The benefit from technology is similarly limited. Unless an engine manufacturer finally breaks through the World War II technology of the jet engine and produces a really new power plant, we can pretty much assume this is as good as it gets for the foreseeable future.

Hubs, however, are the powerhouse of a network carrier, and they can be made more efficient.

We can do a better job utilizing our fleets, flying them more per day and, someday, harnessing technology to build better and more flexible flight paths.

We can reduce pilot staffing cost through fleet simplification.

On the customer front, we can leverage technology to increase productivity. By 2005, Delta will have grown from 100 to 800 advanced check-in kiosks in more than 80 cities. We believe that, within two to three years, less than 20 percent of passengers will check-in at the counter. Kiosks, phone banks, delta.com, and curbside will fill this gap.

Our technical operations division employs Six Sigma and LEAN techniques that have resulted in the lowest maintenance cost among our peers, and created capacity for more than $300 million of external work in 2002 alone. This revenue is set to double by 2006. Our engine overhaul productivity is twice that of other airlines our size in America.

So I have covered some matters of savings, some of productivity. But by far the biggest challenge is employee cost.

For carriers like Delta, 60 percent of costs are non-people related, such as fuel, aircraft, landing fees and so on—and this holds true among almost all airlines. So the *huge* difference is employee cost, frankly, between a Delta and Lufthansa on one side, and a RyanAir and JetBlue on the other.

We are stepping up to this issue with vigor. By mid-2004, Delta will have reduced staffing by 21 percent from pre-September 11 levels—although only two-thirds of that reduction is related to reduced capacity; the other third is due to increased productivity.

Our team knows that, in order to survive and thrive, all of us must work harder, producing 7 percent more capacity per head in 2002 alone *and*, for the smaller number of remaining employees, we must embrace some cost reduction to ensure the viability of long-term benefits such as our pension program.

When the dust has settled, we will have reduced unit costs by more than $3 billion between 2001 and 2005, and reduced unit costs by 15 percent.

What's left is a benefits and compensation package that still ranks in the top third of corporate America, but provides a good shot at survival now—and growth, job security and career development in coming years.

This challenge is particularly acute for Delta—with our status as the least-unionized airline of our peer set. We will continue to *partner* with our employees—while some of our peers use a courtroom to abrogate contracts and effect far more drastic wage and benefit cuts than, fortunately, we have even been led to *contemplate*.

But cost cuts and productivity increases alone will not suffice for network airlines to survive. We must also find growth vehicles in an industry that has too many seats for sale today.

That is, the second main competitive advantage of the successful carrier will be the ability to grow via alliances.

The economics of global alliances are attractively simple: What you can't afford to serve or what you're not allowed to serve is a denied market to your customer.

Partnering with another airline and exchanging attractive destinations with each other gives you incremental revenue you otherwise would not have.

Add to this true frequent flyer program integration and you start to see tangible benefits that the customer *values*. Airlines were late to discover alliances. They were out of reach thanks to the steel veil of regulation and dreadfully outdated ownership laws.

Our ecosystem is crowded with irrational revenue limiters, largely driven by "protectionist" policies that ultimately protect no one—neither the consumer, the airline nor the communities the airlines serve. Restricting a European airline from buying control of a U.S. carrier doesn't make any sense.

Why shouldn't Lufthansa or Iberian or Singapore Air be able to make a sound investment and compete on another continent, just like Shell, General Motors, Daimler or hundreds of other companies?

The Germans and Japanese have made a fine go of shaping the U.S. automobile industry in the last 20 years—and the consumer benefited handsomely. Shouldn't airlines be allowed to compete openly in the global marketplace?

Successful airlines must be truly global in today's world, and arcane border-based restrictions upon our industry must be lifted. Alliances are a very large part, to be sure, of the solution, but alliances alone are not the panacea.

The third defining feature of a winning airline will be that it offers the customer a choice of products and services.

Airlines might want to rid themselves of the notion that one product—the hub and spoke network—can be all things to all people. The survivors of this evolution will be those airlines who adapt and segment their products. That means, at least to us:

- Keeping a strong, healthy hub-and-spoke network

- Developing or joining a global alliance that complements our network and offers more reach

- Having *access to*, and preferably *control of*, significant regional jet feed that has become an indispensable part of the U.S. landscape

- And, finally, creating a viable low-fare product that attacks where you need it to attack, and defends where you need it to defend, but above all, pleases customers!

You need all four product elements, in our view, if you hope to have a successful airline system.

Low-cost airlines are large players, but their revenue potential is limited. They will never provide enough point-to-point service to truly replace the network airlines. They can merely create enough value to shrink the network industry somewhat. They will get bigger and stronger, but they won't eliminate hub-and-spokes. Network carriers link more than 115,000 city pairs in North America today. We think that low-cost carriers can serve only 20–30 percent of those city pairs over time. The true hub-and-spokes carriers will still be needed to reach the other 70 percent.

This is an exciting time, no doubt about it. The entire industry is being shaken up and we have yet to see who will make it in today's altered environment. In my opinion, the winning airlines will:

- Align costs to available revenue

- Create new alliances and strengthen existing ones

- Be truly global in approach, push for structural change in the industry, and

- Offer the customer what they want—where they want it, when they want it, with a diverse product mix.

There are two other elements worth mentioning—but they really concern values more than business strategy: Customers must be cherished. We have to provide a clean, comfortable and welcoming environment for them if we hope to win them back from the couch, the road and from other airlines.

And finally, successful airlines must have engaged, committed and educated employees. Our industry's employees (who, when you think about it, work mostly unsupervised), deliver the product to our customers based on what *they believe* about their company and its leaders.

If you have a confused, cynical employee corps, *it won't matter* what your positioning is.

Positive employee relations are a top priority at Delta. In 2002, we invested $2 million in a program called "Our Airline, Our Business" that introduced business fundamentals to more than half of our 60,000 professionals.

I'm convinced that had we not taken the time and money to invest in our people's education, the difficult changes we made last year would have resulted in a decline in employee satisfaction measurements. Last year, as in every year, we measured employee views:

- 74 percent of the respondents said they felt well-informed about Delta Air Lines

- 80 percent knew how to become more strategically informed, and about the same number saw communication from leadership as truthful and credible.

- These results put Delta in the top 15 percent of U.S. companies.

Airlines have to be as engaged with their employees as they should be with their customers. Keeping this trust and engagement lively and intact is probably my greatest single personal challenge as an industry executive.

Our industry is changing rapidly—faster than anyone could have imagined. The path is somewhat uncertain but full of promise for the best teams. I believe that we can adapt to this new reality quickly—besides, we do not have very much choice in this, do we?

8

A Unique Approach to Low-Cost Air Travel

Amy Curtis-McIntyre
Vice President, Marketing
JetBlue Airways

Amy Curtis-McIntyre joined the JetBlue Airways management team in 1998 when the airline was just a concept known as "New Air." In her role as vice-president, marketing, she managed the development of JetBlue's corporate identity and brand platform (as *Travel + Leisure* reported in 1999, she named the airline), web site, advertising, and the in-flight and airport product.

Finding herself truly in a start-up situation, Ms. Curtis-McIntyre even served as a "dummy" for fitting of the brand-new airline's flight attendant uniform design. Jet-Blue started flying in February 2000 and now serves 20 cities around the country with  a fleet of 41 aircraft. Widely acclaimed by consumers, the media and the financial community, JetBlue's list of kudos include a number-one ranking by the readers of *Condé Nast Traveler*, most successful IPO of 2002 and *Advertising Age*'s "Marketer of the Year." Prior to JetBlue, Curtis-McIntyre was vice president of marketing for Virgin Atlantic Airways and director of advertising and promotion for Celebrity Cruises. Amy began her career in travel marketing in the travel and tourism division of Hill & Knowlton Public Relations. She is a lifelong New Yorker, residing in Manhattan with her husband and one son.

The history of JetBlue Airways starts before the words "Jet" or "Blue" were ever uttered. In 1993, future JetBlue CEO David Neeleman sold his first airline, Salt Lake City-based Morris Air, to Southwest Airlines. Neeleman then went on to help launch West Jet, a successful Canadian low-fare carrier, and to develop the e-ticketing system he had implemented at Morris Air into Open Skies, the world's simplest airline reservation system. He sold Open Skies to Hewlett-Packard in 1999.

With three successful aviation businesses under his belt, Neeleman opted to create his fourth—a low-fare, low-cost airline based out of the largest aviation market in the United States: New York City. With $130 million capitalization— the largest capitalization in startup history—Neeleman announced his plans in July of 1999 to create a new kind of airline, the kind of airline passengers would create, and most importantly, the kind of airline that would bring "humanity back to air travel." He rounded up a group of aviation professionals who shared his desire to build a better mousetrap in the domestic coach category and JetBlue was born.

The original business model was very simple: Start with enough money to weather economic storms; buy new, fuel-efficient and environmentally friendly aircraft for low maintenance costs and high consumer appeal; build the industry's strongest management team and fly nonstop to places people really want to go. Add great service, fair pricing and excellent employee care, and you have JetBlue's beginnings. The model hasn't changed much in almost four years and we live by the belief that keeping it simple is the way to go.

We launched JetBlue Airways on February 11, 2000 with the commencement of service between New York City's John F. Kennedy International Airport and Fort Lauderdale, Florida. From that humble beginning, JetBlue has grown to serve 22 cities with a fleet of 45 new Airbus A320 aircraft. It has become the largest domestic carrier serving JFK Airport. Not only is the JetBlue's fleet of planes new, but JetBlue aircraft are customized with comfortable leather seats, each equipped with free satellite TV offering up to 24 channels of free DIRECTV® programming. In June of 2003, JetBlue placed an order for 100 new EMBRAER 190 jet aircraft. The EMBRAER 190 is the manufacturer's newest model in a family of mid-sized aircraft targeting the growing 70- to 110-seat market. JetBlue plans to take delivery of the first seven EMBRAER aircraft in 2005, with the remaining deliveries scheduled to occur through 2011. With the continuous deliveries of Airbus and EMBRAER aircraft, the JetBlue fleet could grow to as many as 290 aircraft by the end of 2011.

Since the airline's launch in 2000, we have distinguished JetBlue as the best coach product in the marketplace by delivering unique and unconventional features. No other airline can claim to have broadcast the Olympic Games and the Super Bowl. Rather than stuffing seatbacks with the same old in-flight magazines, JetBlue provides passengers with a "Crunch Fitness Airplane Yoga" card and an "Every Flight Wisdom" card, designed to bring comfort and peace to passengers. Unlike the first-come, first-served seating methods used on other low-cost airlines, JetBlue provides passengers with pre-assigned seats. Instead of serving up infamous airplane food, JetBlue invites passengers to bring their own meals on board while providing unlimited snack and drink service. And because we are not in the business of giving people the business, fares are fair, very easy to understand and never require a roundtrip purchase.

JetBlue's sales are almost completely consumer direct. When we built our Web site (the Web was just starting to take off as a sales tool in 2000), we constantly had it tested by people who had never been on the Internet before to ensure that it was easy enough for anyone to use. We also offered financial incentives to customers who booked via this inexpensive distribution channel. Today, almost 75 percent of our daily revenue is sold on jetblue.com, and TrueBlue, our one-year-old online rewards program, has almost one million members. For customers choosing to book with a real, live person, 1-800-JETBLUE delivers one of almost 1,000 reservation agents who work from their homes. JetBlue's homework program delivers a very high rate of job satisfaction, as well as cost benefits to both parties. We cannot believe more companies do not do this.

Other JetBlue innovations give our pilots and other crewmembers sophisticated tools to provide the safest possible environment for passengers. JetBlue was the first U.S. airline to introduce "paperless cockpit" flight technology. Our electronic manual program ensures our crews have the most current safety and operations information at all times.

JetBlue was also the first U.S. airline to address post September 11 security concerns by installing bulletproof cockpit doors across its fleet and surveillance cameras in the passenger cabin. We are in constant pursuit of technology that enhances our operation from an efficiency, safety and customer satisfaction perspective.

But it is not just "things" that make JetBlue different. It is an attitude. An attitude that starts with the kind of corporate culture the airline has cultivated. That culture is communicated internally through five simple core values: safety, caring, integrity, fun and passion. We believe that when you take care of your employees (we call them crewmembers), they will take care of your customers, and the business takes care of itself. The airline business is, after all, a service industry—despite the impression most airlines offer these days. A travel experience includes numerous contact points with our crewmembers, from reservations, to check in, to security, to the flight itself—even baggage recovery. We've tried to build great service, coined the "JetBlue Experience" into every contact point we can control, including reservation hold messages, web advice for navigating our airports and a communication for delays policy which requires our crews to update customers every 15 minutes, even if nothing has changed.

It's not a revolutionary concept. Treat people with respect and common courtesy and, more often than not, you will make them feel like they are dealing with someone who cares. We simply acknowledge that traveling can be stressful and that a little kindness and humor can make an enormous difference. We are made up of regular people who understand the difference between passengers and cargo. People who understand that they define the JetBlue brand, and whose individual and collective talents impact the organization every day. The commitment and satisfaction of our crewmembers shows in the job they do, aided by our flexible work hours, initial paid training, free uniforms (custom designed for function and form) and benefits that begin on their start date. JetBlue also provides rewarding compensation packages to crewmembers, including competitive salaries, profit sharing and a discounted crewmember stock purchase plan.

While our people are the flesh and blood of JetBlue, the task of communicating the brand's personality to the outside world falls to public relations and advertising. We believe word of mouth is invaluable and have tried to communicate our unique position in the marketplace as often as possible through third parties. Sometimes with stunts or slightly controversial messaging. Sometimes just with good old-fashioned honesty. We have tried to stretch our marketing dollars by giving the media good reason to report on our activity. The marketing, product development and corporate communications crewmembers are part of the same team and work toward seamlessness in the building *and* selling of JetBlue. As with other aspects of the company, there is an efficiency built into the process that not only often reduces cost, but improves results. JetBlue is remarkably unburdened by bureaucracy.

As of 2003, JetBlue has spent three times more on advertising as a percentage of sales than the major carriers. That said, our budget is still considerably less than the major carriers, so our advertising has had to stand out in a crowd. Major airlines continue to produce "typical airline advertising" that doesn't differentiate one airline from another. JetBlue uses wit and humor to communicate the brand personality as well as our distinct features and benefits. The key to JetBlue's success in advertising has been to capture the voice of the company and the people who make it what it is. Headlines like "Catch us with our fares down" and "Blue for a Better Airline?" have made JetBlue stand out in an often conservative, staid category. Our television campaigns have used humor as well, not just for the sake of humor, but to communicate one of the brand's core characteristics. While we take our operation very seriously, we believe that humor is one of the things that drives our success everyday. All of JetBlue communications are heavily supported with public relations efforts; we believe word of mouth is invaluable and our communications are not limited to traditional media outlets. JetBlue has adopted aggressive guerilla marketing techniques get the word out about the JetBlue experience right at street level. To celebrate the holidays in the JetBlue spirit, marketing crewmembers handed out blue candy canes during the Christmas tree lighting at Rockefeller Center. In 2001, when the airline began service from Washington D.C.'s Dulles International Airport to Fort Lauderdale/Hollywood International Airport, marketing crewmembers invaded the streets of Washington D.C. to distribute oranges to the public. This aggressive marketing provides the public with a lasting impression of the JetBlue experience and personality.

JetBlue also effectively connects with customers through unique sponsorship initiatives—one or two major sponsorships in each core market, in addition to partnerships with charities and events in smaller markets. But JetBlue doesn't partner with just any event or organization. We aim to collaborate with partners who stand for something that connects with JetBlue and its customers from a demographic or psychographic perspective. Golf and tennis tournaments, wine and food programs and family events have provided JetBlue with the opportunity to reach a broad audience of influential decision makers. Additionally, JetBlue has sought out various entertainment, fashion, alternative lifestyle and urban sponsorship opportunities, including L.A. Fashion Week, the Gay and Lesbian Travel Expo Series and the CineVegas International Film Festival. We hope people judge us by the company we keep.

Future marketing plans will be significantly impacted by our expansion. With 245 airplanes planned for delivery, JetBlue receives a new aircraft approximately once a month. This rapid expansion means that the airline will constantly add new markets to the system and increase frequency on its current routes. Rather than most airlines' hub and spoke systems, JetBlue will continue to concentrate on low-cost point-to-point service (though we will happily sell connecting service as well). We will continue to focus on cities that lack low-fare service and are, in our assessment, ripe for stimulation. And, we will continue to focus on taking excellent care of our people, so that they will take care of our customers. Finally, we will continue to work toward our industry-leading low costs and excellent performance, as these are key to our financial success.

Our marketing strategy is challenging but it is not rocket science: Keep building trials by putting the JetBlue message in new places; keep building loyalty with a consistently excellent product and lots of delightful surprises; keep evolving and innovating—challenge everyone on the team to keep making the airline better. And sell it like you own it. Competition is essential to the commercial airline business and all of its customers. That drives us every day to show customers that JetBlue isn't the only way to fly—but it should be.

9

New Age Airlines

Ned Homfeld
Founder and Chairman
Spirit Air

Mr. Homfeld founded Spirit Air in 1969 and served as the company's CEO until April 2000. Beginning in 1982, under Mr. Homfeld's guidance, the company began organizing charter flights to various gaming locations with chartered aircraft. In 1990, the company received its certification as a scheduled airline, operating two 50-passenger Convair 580 turboprop aircraft. In 1992, the company acquired jet aircraft to replace the chartered aircraft, then expanded its operation to offer scheduled service as Spirit Airlines, Inc.

Today, Spirit Airlines is the nation's largest privately held carrier. From 1976 through 1982, the company provided financing, billing and reporting of cargo receivables for eight commuter airlines under the name of Air Clearings; software development and consulting for the initial Part 121 airline certification of Universal Airlines in the areas of aircraft maintenance record keeping, maintenance cost control and crew flight and duty time.

Mr. Homfeld designed and developed the primary portions of the reservations system used by the company from 1982 until 2003. From 1969 through 1976, the company was involved in surface transportation, aircraft charter and airfreight forwarding of critical automotive parts in Detroit. Later it established offices in Cleveland and Los Angeles. Mr. Homfeld attended the University of Michigan from 1967 through 1970, majoring in naval architecture.

The Airline Deregulation Act of 1978 ended government control of airline entry, routes and pricing and forever changed the industry. For the first time, airlines found that they must not only compete, but also control their own efficiency. This act has not only had a tremendous effect on the industry for the past 25 years; it will continue to do so far into the future. The act has also made the airline industry the vibrant, ever-changing engine it is today.

The legacy carriers responded by developing the hub and spoke system. By committing the majority of their aircraft to operate in and out of a minimal number of large cities, a carrier could effectively provide service between large numbers of markets by connecting their flights. While the hub and spoke system is inefficient—it results in high staffing for the periods of arriving and departing "banks" of flights and considerable overstaffing between these banks—it not only expands an airline's reach beyond the hub market, but makes effective competition difficult. A newer, smaller carrier that would compete against a hub carrier with a large number of flights not only has difficulty in obtaining facilities, but in establishing passenger recognition.

In the regulated environment, with the government setting fares, costs incurred by the airlines were simply passed along to consumers. Labor costs could and did spiral to unrealistic levels—there was little need to worry about efficiency since the government insured the airlines' profitability. In the deregulated environment, the legacy carriers (LCs) found other ways to pass along unrealistic costs to consumers. For passengers traveling to and from fortress hubs where there was little competition, carriers could exact higher fares. The growth of computers and sophisticated yield management programs controlled prices to obtain the highest possible fare from each passenger. The most significant method of obtaining higher fares for the LC was by segmenting consumers into those traveling on business and those not traveling on business. The LC then charged business travelers significantly higher fares—and the costs of business travel spiraled upwards. Enjoying a robust economy throughout the 1990s, LCs found most of their profits coming from business travelers. As long as the economy continued to grow, the LCs could expect huge profits and powerful balance sheets.

The Airline Deregulation Act of 1978 also allowed new entries into the airline industry. Early new entrant airlines were often undercapitalized, weakly managed, and initially operated with a weak or flawed business plan. In addition, these new entrants, while no longer facing the barrier of governmental control, still found themselves facing new barriers from the LCs. New entrants found access to many airports difficult, if not impossible, due to the LCs' control of gates, counters and services. Spirit Airlines, certified in 1990, operated without any gates from its founding city, Detroit, for its first seven years.

The LCs also used the strength of their balance sheets to minimize competition from the new, weaker low-cost carriers (LCCs). Faced with impending competition, the LCs could lower prices in competitive markets and, at the same time, increase both flight capacity and flight frequency, driving out the competition before the LCC could establish a foothold. Once the competitive threat was eliminated, the LC raised prices to levels higher than previously charged to recoup the costs of eliminating competition. These actions, clearly predatory in intent, were not in consumers' interest—while consumers enjoyed initially lower fares, they wound up paying considerably higher fares later.

The LCs' fortunes changed beginning with the business economic retreat that began in early 2001. These carriers were hardest hit in the post-September 11 world. They then confronted the SARS scare and the Iraq war in early 2003. The LCs found themselves hemorrhaging—in a few short months, the industry lost more money than it made throughout its history. In many ways, the LCs had spent much of the 25 years since deregulation setting themselves up for difficulty—they had failed to concentrate on efficiency and flexibility; they had relied increasingly on the willingness of the business traveler to pay exorbitant prices for last-minute travel; they betrayed an overall arrogance; and they soon suffered the perception that they had no concern for their customers.

The failure rate of new carriers in the 25 years since deregulation has been astronomical. Still, despite the difficulties of competition, of attracting qualified personnel and of establishing a credible brand, a handful of new entrants has survived the incredible odds and developed into what I call New Age airlines.

In the first quarter of 2003, just four domestic airlines were profitable—each of them New Age entrants. These airlines share common attributes: they have valid business plans, they are efficient, they are well managed, their employees buy-in to their sense of purpose and they treat their customers well and with respect—the same attributes the LCs had forgotten.

As a general rule, LCCs attempted to enter markets by luring customers on the basis of price alone. An LCC was, by definition, efficient. These carriers generally utilized only one aircraft type, which kept their maintenance and training costs at a minimum.

Today these New Age airlines carry about 25 percent of domestic passenger traffic. Many experts predict that, within five years, New Age airlines will carry more than half of domestic traffic.

If these airlines are New Age airlines they must be practicing New Age marketing. What is this New Age marketing? The Merriam-Webster dictionary defines marketing as the process or technique of promoting, selling, and distributing a product or service.

New Age marketing is not new at all; it has been practiced by most established companies at least at one time in their history. The motto for this New Age marketing is *carpe diem*—Latin for "seize the day." Seize the day—what does it mean, how does an airline marketer practice it?

In the 1976 movie "Network," Howard Beale (Peter Finch) shouts from the windows, "I'm mad as hell, and I'm not going to take it anymore!" The movie was a criticism of television journalism, wherein entertainment value and ratings are more important than quality. There has been criticism for a long time that American businesses are no longer concerned with the quality of customer service—that they just don't care about the customer anymore. When, rightly or wrongly— and this is across many businesses—customers perceive arrogance or neglect toward them, more often than not, they radically change their buying habits.

For example, recent poor results among the giants of the fast food industry are attributable to changing customer eating habits—customers looking for more healthy choices. It wasn't long before these companies practiced New Age marketing—addressing their customers' desire for healthier food, seizing the day to look at themselves as their customers see them.

In my own experience, I hit the drive-thru and attempt to place an order at scratchy speaker to an unseen clerk who speaks barely comprehensible English. I order a Coke with no ice. Without fail, at least 60 percent of the time, when I reach the last window, a Coke containing ice is thrust into my hands. The net effect: I'm irritated when I arrive and irritated when I leave. Should I go into the restaurant, I must confront surly, poorly paid counter people in a facility that's anything but pristine—not just "the facilities," but the service, attitude and cleanliness have been, to my mind, inevitably tarnished. Customers who are "mad as hell," along with others, shy away permanently from the establishment, as I am tempted to.

The LCs face the daunting challenge of maintaining customer relations with employees disgruntled by cutbacks and concessions—nearly everyone has heard stories of gruff LC employees. The employees of New Age carriers, on the other hand, have bought into the concept that customer service is paramount. While they have been accustomed to existing in a David and Goliath business, each employee knows that their relationship with customers is the most powerful New Age marketing tool.

Businesses practicing New Age marketing listen to their customers and react. The LCs have heard their business customers' price gouging complaints for some time. While they've heard, they haven't listened and certainly haven't reacted. It's incredible to see the LCs respond to these complaints by increasing the distance between their business class seats; that reaction is akin to a doctor's removal of a patient's appendix when the patient had sought treatment for a sore knee.

At Spirit we've made a habit of listening to our customers and reacting; rapid flexibility is a key ingredient of successful New Age airlines. After September 11, we listened to our customers especially hard. In an attempt to minimize the inconvenience of higher-levels of security, we added magnetometers and screening machines in many of the fourteen airports we serve. We added counter space and check-in positions, and changed some of our gates to allow our passengers to access less congested screening areas. By speeding up the screening process, we were able to provide heightened levels of security without depreciating our customers' travel experience.

We also listened to the LCs' customers. We listened to their business customers' complaints of being gouged by the LCs and responded by adding Spirit Plus, an upgraded coach product featuring two-by-two leather seats, complimentary in-flight snack and beverages, reserved overhead bins, special check-in counters and advance boarding. We added this service at a fair price; the customer response has been so great that we're actually expanding our SpiritPlus section this fall.

Reaching out to small-to-medium sized businesses, Spirit created the Spirit Business Advantage. This program provides discounts in SpiritPlus, our upgraded business class product, allows greater flexibility on name changes and travel changes on our Web site for our SBA members. We recognize business customers not only as a growing part of our customer family, but as partners as well. We learned that, in order to earn their business, we needed to give these customers a product they wanted. SBA addresses this need.

Again, listening to our customers, we've actually increased frequency and added new service at a time when the industry, as a whole, has retrenched. We've listened to our customers, been flexible and reacted—we've marketed to this promising sector—call it New Age marketing.

During most of the time since deregulation, the traveling public has viewed the LCC as a product inferior to the LC. From aircraft appearance to flight reliability, the LCC left the impression that it didn't quite measure up. The carriers who have made the transition from startup LCC to New Age carrier have, for the most part, met or exceeded the product offerings of the LCs. Many of the New Age airlines are operating new aircraft with average fleet ages well below that of the LCs. At Spirit, we've made a dramatic effort to set standards for performance. While not required to report on our performance to the Department of Transportation, nonetheless we carefully compare it to that of the 12 largest airlines. In June, 2003, when we compared ourselves to the 12 largest carriers, Spirit placed first in the following four categories: 1) percentage of on-time flights; 2) fewest flight cancellations, 3) least number of mishandled bags, and 4) fewest customer complaints made to the Department of Transportation.

Price Meets the Value Perception

Like any business successfully practicing New Age marketing, we've developed our product, responded to our customers and honed our flexibility. Coupled with our system-wide rebranding in 2002, our customers have found that the value perception has met price. Our customer support has allowed Spirit to set new profitability levels all at a time when the LCs are losing billions.

As part of marketing Spirit, we've set a standard for the members of our employee family and made a promise to our customers. We recently rolled out a new advertising campaign that highlights our attributes other than our low fares. We've been touting our longevity: "We've been doing this low-cost thing for more than a decade." We've also been touting our efficiency. "Now that's a novel idea. Run an airline efficiently." We also explain to our customers and employees that, by running an efficient airline, we can keep our fares low and our profits high, which benefits all of us. This new campaign not only enforces our promise to our customers, but ensures employee buy-in.

One of the most important attributes of the New Age airline is the utilization of information technology and the Internet. Spirit has embraced technology since our beginning. Our original reservation system, written in-house (I should know, being its author), was unique—it captured various passenger demographics and allowed us to develop a customer database to use for sales. Additionally, it allowed great flexibility in selling various products and allowed frequent customers to receive discounts and other amenities. Although others are given credit for its development, Spirit was offering ticketless travel in 1982, when Spirit was a public charter operator. At the beginning of 2000, our Web site (SpiritAir.com) didn't take reservations. Today more than 50 percent of our reservations are taken on the site and our goal is to be at 70 percent within the next year. As we've developed our Web presence, we were the first airline to offer a Spanish language site; among the first to offer the ability to modify your reservations, and even print round-trip boarding passes on the Web. The Web, as our lowest-cost method of distribution, allows us to pass savings along to our customers and, more importantly, be ever more customer friendly and convenient. Today, in part because of increased use of technology and its low distribution cost, ten years after we first offered flights to Florida, our lowest prices are nearly the same as they were in 1993.

Embracing technology does not mean ignoring what has worked in the past; rather, it means using technology to gain efficiency, to add service convenience. At Spirit, you can make a reservation over the telephone; at any travel agent (who can book on either the customary CRS or on Spirit's Web site for travel agents) or on the Web. Flexibility allows technology to expand reach.

For years, major partnerships existed between the LCs and companies heavily involved in leisure travel. Major tourist attractions, hotel chains, sports teams and cruise lines all sought partnerships with LCs to cross-promote and sell each other's products. Partnerships with LCCs weren't desirable—minimal flight frequency, coupled with less than desirable reliability and the LCCs' inability to provide backup service, made them less-than-interesting partners. As some of the LCCs made the transition to New Age carrier at the same time the LCs were reeling from the effects of economic retreat of early 2001, September 11, SARS and the Iraq war, the destination partners began to reevaluate their partnerships. Thanks to the product quality of the New Age airlines and their potential, partnerships between the New Age carriers and the leisure destination attractions are growing at levels unimaginable just a few years ago. For both sides of these new partnerships, customer service, flexibility and market response will serve to develop and promote new products and offerings. These partnerships will continue to grow and will become an integral part of the offerings of both partners in the future.

Melding these partnerships with the New Age airline's Internet technology creates a powerful Internet marketing tool—at SpiritAir.com, you can not only book Spirit Airlines travel, but hotels, inclusive packages, cruises, and golf packages (with tee times). This product line will continue to expand as long as the customer benefits and both companies see the value in the relationship.

As SpiritAir demonstrates, the major tenets of New Age marketing are simple: be friendly and efficient, continue to improve, treat employees and customers right, take advantage of technology, and choose your partners well.

Be friendly. A New Age marketer's employee group always functions like a family. Outgoing customer service is contagious. As a marketing tool, customer service, in today's environment, allows a company to stand out from the crowd. All of employees must be empowered to make the customer feel like they're a part of a friendly family.

Be Efficient. A New Age marketer must help its company to be efficient. By keeping costs low, a New Age marketer can consistently deliver low fares.

There are no laurels—don't believe your own hype. The practitioner of New Age marketing constantly seeks to improve. You can boast of improvements in customer's satisfaction, but you must continually seek improvement. Listen to customers, be flexible, and be able to change and improve.

You're family. New Age marketing requires that your customers and employees believe in the tenets of the company. Employees must feel like they are a part of the decision-making process and must believe that their voices will always be heard. If employees are treated with respect, they will treat customers with respect.

Treat your partner right. A New Age marketer recognizes that there are many partnerships in business that need to be grown and cultivated. There is, of course, the primary partnership with your customer. New Age marketing also recognizes business travel partnerships, promotional partnerships, leisure destination partnerships and recreational partnerships. New Age marketing constantly seeks to expand the definition of partnership so that the parties grow their businesses and feel the value of that relationship.

New Age marketing motto. *Carpe diem*—seize the day. When you treat customers right, give them a quality product at the right price. Then they will perceive the value of the product. Once a company achieves this value proposition, then that company will be able to seize the day, grow and be successful.

Although new in the airline industry, the concepts of marketing product, performance, customer service, responsiveness, efficiency and flexibility—that is, the fundamentals of New Age marketing—are not new at all. Just look around at the world's most successful businesses—they've been practicing New Age marketing for years.

10

The Hub and Spoke Network System: The Past Is the Present Is the Future

Richard H. Anderson, CEO
Northwest Airlines, Inc.

Richard H. Anderson was named chief executive officer of NWA Inc. and its principal subsidiary, Northwest Airlines, in February 2001.

Prior to his appointment, he was executive vice president and chief operating officer for Northwest, a position he held since December 1998. In that capacity, Anderson was responsible for all operational functions of the company, in addition to facilities, airport affairs and regulatory compliance.

Anderson joined Northwest in November 1990 as vice president and deputy general counsel and later served as executive vice president—technical operations, flight operations, and airport affairs.

Prior to joining Northwest, Anderson was staff vice president and deputy general counsel for Continental Airlines. He began with Continental in 1987 and previously held positions as corporate attorney, assistant general counsel and associate general counsel.

From 1978 to 1987, Anderson, a native of Galveston, Texas, held positions with Harris County, Texas. He was chief counsel to the Harris County Criminal Court judges and served as an assistant district attorney for Harris County.

Anderson holds a law degree from South Texas College of Law and a bachelor of science degree from the University of Houston. He serves on the boards of directors of Northwest Airlines, Medtronic, Inc., Minnesota Life Insurance Company, Mesaba Airlines, the Minneapolis Institute of Arts and the Minneapolis Downtown Council. He is chairman of the Minnesota Business Leadership Network. He is also on the board of trustees of Hamline University in St. Paul, Minnesota, and is a trustee of the Henry Ford Museum and Greenfield Village in Dearborn, Michigan.

Mention the words "hub and spoke" in any conversation and you'll likely have people thinking about wheels. Bicycle wheels, motorcycle wheels, pushcart wheels or maybe the large wooden wheels of a Conestoga wagon, the type that conquered the U.S. prairies in the late 19th century.

And all of those ideas about wheels would be right. To place the words "hub and spoke" in a transportation business context, the notion of collecting passengers and cargo in a central point (a hub) and redistributing the cargo and passengers to other locations, following the path of a wheel's radials or spokes, is a very old idea indeed. It was the concept that helped formulate stagecoach, steamship and riverboat schedules. However, "hub-and-spoke systems" really became a major business model in the transportation world when railroads became the dominant way to move large numbers of people and things around a very large area.

When the Pacific Railroad (the first railroad to be built west of the Mississippi River) was established in 1849 (in response to the demand caused by the California gold rush for rapid and dependable transportation throughout the western United States), it started with a hub in St. Louis, Missouri.[1] In the 20th century, as trucks began to assume a greater role in shipping cargo long distances, the hub-and-spoke model again was employed because of its simple efficiency.

In the airline business, the hub-and-spoke model has been used to some degree since the beginnings of regularly scheduled service (in the case of Northwest Airlines, on September 1, 1926, when the airline started flying mail between its first hub in Minneapolis/St. Paul and Chicago). But it was following the passage of the Airline Deregulation Act in October 1978 that hub-and-spoke airline networks began to grow in substantial quantities.[2]

The act ended the U.S. Civil Aeronautics Board's authority to control routes effective in December 1981 and fares in January 1983 (the board itself ceased to exist in 1984). It also was around the time that deregulation began that low-cost airlines such as Southwest Airlines and the long defunct People's Express made their debuts. Given this environment, there were a host of reasons why inherently efficient hub-and-spoke networks would increase in number in a landscape that now lacked many constraints to growth and profit. One was their ability to allow for increases in load factors. Increased load factors (and the increased revenues attending them) can contribute to greater efficiency, which produces overall cost savings that delights shareholders with higher corporate profits and can be passed on to consumers in the form of lower fares. In a deregulated (and thus much more competitive) marketplace, a hub-and-spoke network system also could prevent passengers from having to change airlines as they change planes.[3] By using a central hub, airlines could, as did the railroads before them, collect many small "loads" and put them together to ship to any number of final destinations.

Still, in the 25 years since the airline industry was deregulated, things have changed dramatically for the airline business as a whole, as well as for the hub-and-spoke system.

"The hub-and-spoke system that the airlines created in response to deregulation is now being exploited by the growing number of discount airlines, which operate on its fringes," said Michael Levine, the noted airlines expert who also is a law professor at Yale University, as well as a former government official and former airline executive. "Yet the established airlines need not abandon the hub-and-spoke system, which has served both airlines and passengers well. They simply need to operate it more efficiently."[4] Levine says that airlines must now do the restructuring that they have postponed for the better part of the last 10 years, and that if they can reduce costs for items such as labor and equipment, airlines will find that the hub-and-spoke system will permit prosperity. "By concentrating their flights at a hub, they can offer more frequent service to more destinations than the discount airlines," says Levine.[5]

And so, our challenges as airlines committed to the efficiency and profitability of our business and to the hub-and-spoke system are to reduce operating costs while making air travel accessible to more people and more communities at ever-decreasing fares. These are not easy challenges, since deregulation alone was intended to drive down costs. One additional problem facing the industry is the fact that there are now only six "legacy" carriers left in the United States (and, as of this writing, two had recently sought bankruptcy protection). Part of this reduction is due to deregulation, which has had similar effects in other high capital cost, capital-intensive, high fixed-cost businesses. Our responsibility now (at least at Northwest Airlines) is to adapt our cost structure as one of the legacy airlines to this difficult and ever-changing economic environment in which we operate. We can do it, and we must do it, because the case for hub-and-spoke system airlines remains clearly viable. One bright spot would be the potential economic benefits of things such as codesharing and loyalty program exchanges afforded by strategic alliances such as the one Northwest has with KLM and the marketing agreement it now has with both Delta Airlines and Continental Airlines.

The hub-and-spoke model is still viable because it remains the predominant way of doing business in the airline industry (the other being point-to-point systems, which tend to operate in dense domestic markets with a total of only 10 flights or so per day). This is true for both traditional as well as so-called low-cost carriers and true for virtually all of the international flag carriers around the world. For instance, British Airways operates a hub at London Heathrow and Japan Airlines operates a hub in Tokyo. One of the best features of the hub-and-spoke system is its ability to allow airlines to provide service to small cities, using small regional jets that accomplish much of what a larger jet can do, but at a fraction of the cost. In Minneapolis/St. Paul, where Northwest Airlines is headquartered, 57 of the 124 nonstop destinations served are small metropolitan statistical areas with fewer than 500,000 residents.[6] In many cases, air service in many a small community is only possible if that community has a solid connection to an established hub.

Hub-and-spoke systems also do a good job of permitting international service. No American metropolitan area, with the exceptions of New York, Los Angeles, and perhaps Chicago, can support international service on a daily basis if passengers were drawn only from the local and regional populations. For a city like Detroit, the hub-and-spoke system is very important because no airline operating in such cities could collect enough local traffic to fill the large airplanes necessary to fly over oceans. Thus, the hub-and-spoke system allows hub communities to receive far better air service than they would if they were not located in an airline hub. Given the increasingly global nature of both regional and national economies, air access to major world business centers is now key to economic development. And the hub-and-spoke system is not just a U.S. phenomenon. Most foreign flag carriers around the world also operate successful hub-and-spoke systems, which can only be of benefit to their national economies. As a matter of fact, several U.S. airlines operate foreign hubs in places like Tokyo and Amsterdam.

The types of service (including international service) available from a hub-and-spoke network benefit both business and leisure travelers. Hubs permit the type of larger-scale service that provides convenience and frequency to business travelers who need to be in any number of places at any number of times. As well, this expanded service increases the availability of seats that qualify for leisure fares, seats and fares that might not be possible for pleasure travelers if the hub did not exist to provide the kind of flight variety business travelers demand.[7]

Hubs also can provide economic benefits to the communities they serve by their very presence. There is a great deal of information that supports the idea that hubs make substantial and positive contributions to employment growth, which is a measure of a region's economic health. In Minneapolis/St. Paul alone, Northwest Airlines employs more than 17,000 people, along with thousands of others at our other domestic hubs in Detroit and Memphis and our international hubs in Amsterdam and Tokyo.

Over the next decade, hub-and-spoke systems *will* become even more relevant and profitable as they move towards a coexistence with the low-cost carriers. Low-cost carriers that operate hub-and-spoke systems and point-to-point carriers have dramatically increased their market share in the United States from about 1 or 2 percent a decade ago to about 25 to 26 percent today.[8] Although it may be in the best long-term interests of legacy carriers to move towards some sort of coexistence with point-to-point carriers, it will not be easy. Legacy carriers are operating in an arena that is still absorbing the changes wrought by deregulation, on top of the ramifications of serious problems posed in the aftermath of the terrorist acts of September 11, 2001, severe acute respiratory syndrome (SARS), a global economic recession and the Middle East wars of 1991 and 2003. Due to the limited range of most point-to-point carriers, they have been able to do business without much concern for these larger issues.

However, many industry experts think that within two to three years, hub-and-spoke system airlines that have been successfully restructured and fitted with viable business plans will reach some sort of equilibrium with low-cost and point-to-point carriers (the two are often one and the same). The legacy carriers that do the best job in reducing their total operating costs will be the ones most likely not only to exist with low-cost and point-to-point carriers, but also survive and see their hub-and-spoke systems grow. From an airline passenger standpoint, the hub-and-spoke model provides the most efficient form of transportation to the most cities around the world.

An additional difficulty now facing all carriers, but especially legacy airlines, is the need to operate (profitably, if possible) in a commodity environment. The Internet has permanently changed the operations of just about every sort of business and airlines are no exception. That's good for consumers—the Internet provides perfect information to consumer for better choices at better prices. Every business must adapt to Internet distribution and the expansion of the Internet to cover all facets of interaction with customers. For leisure travelers, there is an expectation that ever-cheaper fares must always be available at any time from online groups such as Orbitz, Expedia, or Travelocity, and certainly at the web sites of the airlines themselves.

Much has been said and written (especially in the wake of September 11, 2001) about what the legacy airlines must do to reduce costs. The bankruptcy actions of some of these airlines have made this need all too painfully clear. Some of the cost-saving moves undertaken by airlines, including Northwest, include things such as: outsourcing non-core business functions; employing exterior aircraft paint schemes that last longer and are cheaper to apply and maintain; reducing fuel expenses; reducing meal services and onboard entertainment; selling any unneeded assets (such as real estate and idle aircraft); and, of course, cutting labor costs. As is true of most businesses, labor (including items such as fringe benefits) is by far the largest item in an airline's operating budget.

During the year 2003, Northwest Airlines sought nearly $1 billion in labor restructuring cost concessions from our labor unions, as well as from our management staff and officer corps. These changes that took the form of smarter work rules as well as pay cuts. These actions were painful. It may be years before we know if they made enough of a change to propel the airline back into a place where it can both make a profit and provide jobs.

In summary, the hub-and-spoke airline systems are products of deregulation. These systems still offer the most efficient method to collect passengers and transport them efficiently from point A to point B. These systems are operated by both the legacy carriers and newly entering, low-cost carriers in the U.S. and around the world. The hub-and-spoke model will continue to be a predominant model in the worldwide airline industry.

Second, the Internet will continue to be the predominant distribution method for travel in the next decade. We must all adapt and embrace the Internet because that is what our customers demand.

Third, in the coming decade, customer satisfaction will be the most important attribute for our product at Northwest. Customers have a right to expect safe, clean, on-time service built around the most convenient schedules and flight frequency. When we do make a mistake, we must keep our promise to our customers and fix the problem on the spot. Consumer businesses are intensely competitive and we must provide a product that satisfies our customers, whether we run an airline or a cruise line. After all, our customers have perfect information about our products via the Internet and they have choices—it's our responsibility to win our customer's loyalty every day, on every flight.

Notes

[1] Missouri Pacific Historical Society Web site, copyright 2002.

[2] "Transportation Economics: The Deregulation of the Transportation Sector in Airlines" Web site for Economics 145, University of California-Davis.

[3] Ibid.

[4] *"Interview: Professor Michael E. Levine of Yale Law School discusses United Airlines filing for Chapter 11" National Public Radio* Weekend Edition Sunday, December 8, 2002

[5] Ibid.

[6] *Airline Competition Plan for Minneapolis-St. Paul International Airport,* submitted to the Federal Aviation Administration by the Metropolitan Airports Commission, September 29, 2000, p.10.

[7] *"The Impact of Northwest Airlines Minneapolis/St. Paul Hub: A Study for the Hub City task Force of the Greater Minneapolis and St. Paul Chambers of Commerce,"* Daniel M. Kasper (with the assistance of LECG, LLC), p.4, July 2001.

[8] *"Interview notes: Richard Anderson discusses the airline industry," Detroit Free Press,* May 28, 2003.

11

Efficiency and Cost Control: The Keys to Survival

Chris Bowers
United Airlines

Christopher D. Bowers is an airline and travel industry veteran, having spent 30 years at United Airlines prior to his retirement in July 2003.

Bowers joined United in 1973 as a supervisor of airfreight at O'Hare International Airport in Chicago. He has held a variety of marketing and sales positions since then, including district sales manager in Detroit, market manager for the Chicago hub, vice president, market management and vice president and general sales manager.

In 1995, he was named senior vice president, international. During that time, United grew significantly in overseas markets, including new routes to India, and participated in the development of the Star Alliance. In his position, Bowers was responsible for customer service, operations, sales and profitability in cities served by United in Europe, the Pacific and Latin America.

In 1998, he became senior vice president, North America, with responsibility for operations, customer service, sales and profitability in all North American markets.

From 2002 to his retirement, he was a senior vice president with responsibility for marketing, sales and reservations, and was an architect of United's strategic realignment in which it transformed itself into a more competitive, customer-focused carrier.

Bowers holds a bachelor's degree in business administration from Monmouth College, Monmouth, Illinois. He served in the U.S. Army from July 1969 to May 1972, attaining the rank of Captain.

Bowers has been a guest lecturer at Northwestern University's Transportation Management Program, served as national chairman of the Travel Industry Association of America, was a member of the executive committees of the Chicago Convention and Visitors Bureau and the Chicago Chamber of Commerce, and is a trustee of the Field Museum of Chicago.

People want to travel; to explore; to visit friends and family; to travel on business or just to escape. Their needs are simple: A good value at a fair price. That should be easy to provide; in fact, it will be necessary for survival.

Air transportation will become more accessible worldwide as the economies of highly populated countries strengthen, expand and more of their citizens are able to travel. The "shrinking of the world" via television has an impact on generating interest and curiosity. Seeing images of cities or other specific destinations emboldens people and makes them more comfortable once at the destination because of familiarity—they've seen the place before.

Our business will adapt and flourish in the new world economy. The primary reason is our ability to meet customer demand by shifting capacity. I offer a couple of assumptions that buttress my longer-term beliefs:

1. Prices will remain mostly inelastic.

2. Load factors, on average, must rise to 80 percent.

3. Low-cost competitors will force continued cost controls on network and international carriers.

4. Consolidation will take place both domestically and internationally.

5. Traffic will grow worldwide at 2.5 to 3 percent annually.

Our nomadic ways will increase discretionary travel, while business travel will reflect worldwide economic conditions. Price and value will be the key components to carrier selection—we can either be a commodity or differentiate ourselves with various services. The easy approach is to adopt to the commodity model, where everything moves on price, there are no product differences. Costs are kept in check, service expectations are minimized and complexity reduced. However, would there be any customer loyalty?

The global scope of our business, I believe, points us in a different direction. With flights ranging from 30 minutes to 16 hours and crossing 12 time zones, we need a broader range of products to address our future customers' demands.

An airline is really in the hospitality business. We differentiate ourselves by the services we provide: seat 32B between Chicago and Des Moines is just a seat, but seat 1A from Chicago to Hong Kong is a self-contained suite. It's an easy chair, recliner and bed. It has an entertainment system, and an attentive staff serve its occupant great quantities of food and beverages. I suggest you enjoy this now—because the economics don't work, the space is expensive and our customers are less and less willing to pay for that space and service. Business class, with lay-flat seats, will migrate forward, replacing first class. Amenities will abound to maintain the panache of riding up front. This will, however, be limited to international flights.

International economy will advance with improved entertainment systems such as distributed video for movies and games. Many are already in place; however, the passengers will pay for the services they use. This will keep fares down, but allow for investment in more onboard entertainment products to keep pace with technology. Domestic onboard services and amenities will more closely reflect the fares the passengers are paying. First class will offer more space and meals, but not all aircraft will be configured with a first-class cabin. Short-haul and leisure routes will see all-coach aircraft with fares to match. Food service in coach will be available onboard for purchase, allowing the customer to decide if and what they want to eat. Quantity, quality and variety of menu items will improve dramatically.

Air transportation is labor and capital intensive, with very low margins even in the best of times. Therefore, the industry must make greater use of technology to attract, sell, service and retain its customers.

The Internet will account for 40 percent of sales within 10 years, up from 11percent today. All the more so, customers will buy only if they believe they are getting the best rates. The complexity of the fare structure undermines customer confidence in online sales. As capacity and demand come closer, the fare structure must be simplified. The gap between the highest, unrestricted and lowest, most restricted fares will narrow. The fares that only exist today online will migrate to agencies and airline reservation offices. The method for specific date, destination-type low fares will move to direct customer marketing tools. Rather than publish for all to see, staff will put more effort into customer relationship management to improve customer satisfaction and improve revenues. There will be fewer fares; the fares with clearly stated and understood rules, and that provide value, will prevail.

The increased use of online booking is reducing the need for carrier-specific reservation operations. While there will always be the ability to speak to a reservation agent, that need will diminish as online services mature, allowing for cancellations and credit, simple itinerary changes and, of course, simpler fare structures. Already, online automated products exist that notify customers of schedule changes, flight irregularities, rebooking actions and real-time flight data. Voice recognition technology will further speed customer information and response times—there will be no more busy signals or sitting on hold. Of course, all of this is dependent on the customer having confidence in the information provided and not calling reservations for the human touch to verify what they have already done online. Airline reservations will confine themselves to sales, complex itineraries, international bookings, special requests, e.g., those relating to medical conditions and disabilities, and servicing the carrier's highest-revenue customers. Those customers will qualify for a special status based on their annual revenue (spend). They will be invited to use a special phone number and will enjoy preferential treatment. Of course, such preferential treatment exists today, but it will be more important in the future as carriers identify a more select group of customers for such treatment, while allowing price to meet the needs of the majority of their customers.

Reservations specialty desks will handle group and meeting business; they will have the ability to negotiate price and services for those customers. All other service-related reservation activities will be outsourced. Outsourcing is not only more cost effective, but allows for demand peaks and valleys—you can buy more help when needed. There will be fewer airline call centers, but they will more often handle multiple carriers, most likely those associated through alliances, and will operate 24/7 with multiple language capability.

Travel agencies will still be a significant source of revenue for us. Today, they sell 74 percent of our revenue. Although that number will decline over time, their presence and influence is a major factor in our sales and marketing efforts. They are an integral part of distribution, providing more "shelf space" and assisting in top-of-mind awareness with our customers. Agencies, tour operators and consolidators are most effective as market makers. This ability to sell to specific customer segments cannot be replicated by the carriers at the same cost. It is quite possible, therefore, that they will buy scheduled airline seat inventory to bundle with hotels for re-marketing and pricing, spreading their risk but also enjoying greater revenue rewards. They do this today with charters, on which they own all the seats; on scheduled service, they would only purchase a portion of the inventory with the carrier selling the rest.

Airport services are in the midst of significant change—but many more changes will be wrought. Customers want to spend less time on the ground at the airport, less time in lines, and less time (in fact, no time), dealing with confusing fare rules when they make changes. Customers will tolerate security as long as it is efficient, consistent across all airports and effective. To improve the ground experience, airlines will increase their efforts to make the customers "travel ready" when they arrive at the airport. By "travel ready" we mean just that—travelers with no reason for ticket or itinerary changes, customers who have utilized the Internet, a remote kiosk, voice recognition unit or call center to make any necessary changes prior to arriving at the airport. They will be able to utilize electronic check-in on their own PC and printer before leaving for the airport or, once there, the units available in the terminal designed to check-in customers with or without their baggage.

At the boarding gate there is less hassle and fewer last minute changes, except for seat assignment adjustments. Boarding pass readers, almost universally deployed by the larger carriers, further speed the process of boarding, eliminating errors once passengers are onboard. The point of the aforementioned enhancements on the ground is that customers traveling without checked bags will make their first contact with an airline employee aboard the aircraft.

Perhaps the most difficult issue facing the industry is maintaining competitive unit costs. Network carrier infrastructures have developed over many years. While there is dramatic change taking place, those costs must be contained going forward. When the carriers return to profitability, they must find new innovative ways to share a portion of those profits with the labor groups. Embedding regular wage increases only causes the differential between full-service and low-cost carriers to grow to a point where the full service group is again uncompetitive. We're in the service business, thus labor needs to be aligned with customer performance goals and given incentives to exceed corporate profit targets. Sustained profitability is a necessity for survival and growth.

The future for new aircraft—faster, bigger, more onboard room—is not good. The customer is not ready for the fare increases necessary to bring a faster, larger aircraft into solution. Therefore, for the next 10 years, new products will look a lot like today's—they'll have different designators such as A380 and 7E7, but from a customer's standpoint, not much will have changed on the exterior or in speed. The sizzle will come, as previously discussed, from the continued development of entertainment systems and online capability while in the air. The real savings for the carriers will be in improved unit costs; more efficient engines, less maintenance, ease of conversion of interiors—this, in turn, will help control fare increases.

If load factors must be in the low 80s for sustained profitability, there must be rationalization of capacity. Economic cycles result in the purchase of aircraft in good times, inefficiencies and price wars in bad. Mature industries consolidate to gain cost and capacity efficiencies, and, while in our business alliances can address market coverage for the customer, they fall short in the other areas. For instance, there is little incentive to drop routes because, at present, domestic alliances don't allow for revenue sharing between the carriers.

Today, the U.S. government is concerned about service to small communities, about the commitment to the Civil Reserve Air Fleet, about competition and prices. I believe market forces, both domestic and international, will put more pressure on our government to approve mergers, acquisitions and the lifting of the cap on foreign investment and stock voting rights in U.S. airlines. This will allow the forces in the market to size the industry properly. Inefficiencies will not be tolerated nor compensated for by the customer. Will there be fewer flights in some markets? Yes. Will profitability improve? Yes. Will this spawn new competition? Yes.

The large U.S. carriers operate multiple hubs that have proven to provide more choices, in terms of frequency and destinations, to the customer. As the market fragments, more flights will operate on a direct (nonstop) basis between markets, but hubs will remain the principal core-scheduling tool for the airlines. Most hubs are located in large, multimillion-resident population centers, geographically situated to serve either east-west or north-south markets (in some cases both). And while the infrastructures that have been built are too costly to abandon, they do need to be more efficient. Additional runways and terminal facilities are needed to handle peak demand and weather. Local communities, well-versed on the economic value of a hub, will push politicians to keep up with the needs. For the carriers, hub schedules will be adjusted to increase utilization of both aircraft and gates; technology deployment in customer service will reduce manpower dependencies and speed customer processing. However, given capital constraints, there won't be evolutionary changes in how bags and cargo are loaded. This will continue to be a factor limiting quick turns and manpower efficiencies. Finally, due to increased point-to-point competition and a small local market base, some hubs may not survive.

Loyalty programs are the cornerstones of large airline marketing efforts. We've seen the value of advertising diminish as customers have already settled on a destination and are more interested in price. Most of our marketing efforts, therefore, will be directed at the individual customers. We already have a wealth of data on each, such as trip purpose, destination, price paid, how many traveled, who bought what meal on board, luggage checked (golf bags or not), and frequency of trips. We'll use customer relationship management to offer special price programs by destination, remind customers of past trips, alert them to special events, see why their patterns have changed and use them as a real-time focus group tool. Advertising will serve two principal roles: 1) highlight price promotions, and 2) develop the brand image to distinguish us from the competition. Corporate sponsorships will be fewer but more aligned to the likes/desires of our key customers. Again, this intelligence will come from one-on-one market communications. Direct marketing will also play a larger role in alliances—since our customer base basically expands to all those flying on an alliance partner, segmenting their needs and then addressing product enhancements consistent throughout the alliance partners will require a broader/international expertise. Finally, pure loyalty programs will move from a mile-for-mile award to a mile for dollar spent. Perks will be more reflective, therefore, of true customer revenue value. It is also quite possible that there will be membership fees for the loyalty programs to help enhance value-for-dollar perceptions.

While aircraft design and technology may not change much in the next 10 years, the preflight and in-flight experience will. The ground will be less about personal customer contact and more about speed, efficiency and simplicity from booking through check-in to boarding. In-flight, there will be more seats, more entertainment choices the customer will pay to use, higher quality and quantity of meals for sale and, most importantly, a continued primary emphasis on safety and punctuality.

The air transportation business is a dynamic, exciting, highly competitive, visible, global, vital, challenging, and glamorous industry in which to work. Our future will be marked by significant changes in all areas of the business. There will be a renewed emphasis on customer service, making it easy, enjoyable and a good value. Consolidation will bring down excess capacity but allow for more point-to-point schedules, resulting in improved aircraft efficiencies, frequency of service for the customer and less pressure on prices. Evolving use of technology while reducing personal interfaces will speed processing time for customer activities such as reservations, check-in and boarding. Product innovations both on the ground and in the air, such as all-business class A320s/737s for market specific routes will continue to spur interest and keep us from becoming a commodity. Finally, our future will see a dramatic increase in discretionary travel worldwide as we nomads venture to enjoy new experiences.

I like the fact that everyone, no matter what age, has a story to tell about travel. We are fortunate to get to play a part in most families' lives and, regardless of the reason, we look forward to sharing that time with them. Although manned flight is 100 years old, the vast majority of the world's population has never been on an airplane—I think we have our work cut out for us in the next 100 years.

(Note: The opinions expressed in this contribution are those of Christopher D. Bowers and do not necessarily represent those of United Airlines, Inc.)

12

The Car Rental Industry: Driving to Success on Unfamiliar Roads

Brian J. Kennedy
Executive VP, Marketing & Sales
The Hertz Corporation

Brian J. Kennedy is executive vice president, marketing and sales, for the Hertz Corporation, based at Hertz Worldwide Headquarters, Park Ridge, New Jersey. Mr. Kennedy, who joined Hertz in 1983, is responsible for worldwide marketing, including marketing planning, marketing information systems, market research, marketing programs, automation marketing, airline and hotel marketing, pricing and travel industry sales.

Prior to joining Hertz, Kennedy spent 17 years with Trans World Airlines in a variety of senior marketing/sales roles, culminating in the position of corporate officer, vice president, advertising and sales. A native of New York City, where Kennedy currently resides, he graduated from Georgetown University's School of Foreign Service in 1963. Subsequently, he graduated at the top of his class from the Defense Language Institute in Monterey, California, and served for two years in Sapporo, Japan, working on civilian intelligence assignments with Japanese officials.

Predicting the future of the travel industry, including the car rental sector, is risky as we look ahead this decade. U.S. and worldwide travel revenue declined at the beginning of the decade, following years of steady growth, and many travel businesses struggled to survive. Three well-known U.S. car rental brands, in addition to several airlines, went bankrupt. Yet a few financially healthy, forward-looking companies are pushing forward, working to influence trends shaping the travel industry.

Car rental companies—and others in the travel industry—hoping to thrive in the future must successfully manage several related trends, which include:

- Achieving unit cost preeminence;

- Differentiation versus commoditization—companies that are not lowest cost/lowest price providers must provide reasonable value at competitive prices and find/retain customers willing to pay more for basic service plus;

- Targeting and rewarding customer loyalty based on revenue/profit potential;

- Refining the use and cost of all distribution channels;

- Utilizing technology effectively to drive the evolution of the other trends;

- Wisely acquiring and deploying capital to develop new markets while existing, profitable markets are attacked by competitors.

While you'd have to be very lucky to accurately predict travel trends for the next several years, it is important to understand the macro-forces shaping the travel industry and emerging travel patterns. Only at that point can we analyze the trends and the strategies companies could deploy to succeed in these uncertain times.

The Rise and Fall of the Travel Revenues: Trend or Aberration?

The travel industry was certainly among the great success stories of the world economy during the 1990s. Worldwide industry revenues increased from $277 billion in 1991 to $476 billion in 2000, representing an annual growth rate of 5.6 percent, according to the World Tourism Organization. The annual growth rate during the same period in the U.S. rental car industry exceeded 7 percent. This period was marked by robust growth in the leisure travel segment, combined with steady business travel growth during the period, with a spike in the latter segment during 1998 though the first half of 2000.

Due to a combination of a slower global economy (which initially became evident in the U.S. business travel segment during late third quarter 2000), and the temporary, catastrophic impact of the September 11, 2001 terrorist attacks, overall travel revenue decreased by almost 6 percent in 2001 (7 percent in U.S. car rental). Worldwide revenues decreased, again, by less than 1 percent in 2002, and 2003 was another year of relative stagnation, driven by decreased business travel in particular.

Several years will have passed before overall revenue is expected to exceed the record achieved in 2000—and, unfortunately, costs have continued to grow throughout the period. No one is currently forecasting a return to high single-digit, annual growth rates in the foreseeable future. And no one is able to predict the stability of the international geopolitical environment, as it might affect travel, or the long-term prospects for the global economy, both of which will be significant drivers of travel behavior in the immediate future.

Trends—Near Term

Travel industry revenues declined in 2001–2002 and slow growth is projected for the middle of the decade. Businesses in the United States show no sign of relaxing corporate travel restrictions, and it may be at least the end of 2005 before business travel gets back to the record levels achieved in 2000. Leisure travel, by comparison, was robust throughout the recession of 2001–2003, but in itself cannot buoy the entire industry. This segment may be equally sensitive to concerns about travel safety and international political unrest.

To the extent tourists and business people travel, they are becoming more cost conscious—their behavior is driven to a great degree by price/rate transparency available to individual consumers via the Internet. Internet travel bookings, which were insignificant in the mid-1990s, have become a major source of business in the United States, and there is rapid growth in online distribution in Europe as well. These trends should continue. Unsurprisingly, and somewhat as a result of the impact of the Internet and growing price sensitivity, we have seen the launch of low-cost, low-fare airlines—copying the Southwest Airlines model—such as Jet Blue in the United States and Ryanair in Europe, a trend that shows no signs of abating. The entire airline industry will continue to be affected and repositioned as a result.

Demand and pricing will continue to be the major factors affecting the financial results of major travel suppliers—from travel agents to hotels, car rental companies and airlines. However, other factors, many within the control of individual companies across the industry, will be important for years to come.

Trends—Long Term

It is always difficult to predict the future, particularly when there is so much volatility in the current period. Nevertheless, a few long-term trends may take hold. These may include:

- Less competition in the airline and car rental industries due to contraction;

- The proliferation of lower cost business models in the airline industry—there will be rapid growth in this segment, but customers will expect safety, reliability and a decent service attitude;

- Low-cost/high-service segmentation in the airline and car rental segments;

- Further cost-consciousness among many leisure travelers;

- Service-oriented business and high-end leisure travelers will pay for extra services;

- Great emphasis on cost management by all travel providers, greater use of Internet to reduce costs; greater emphasis on data mining to capture customer data/trends;

- More premium on customer loyalty, and rewards for revenue/profit generation by customer segment (e.g. high paying business/leisure travelers get more frequent flyer miles).

Keys to Success in Car Rental

Control Costs; Find and Hold Loyal, Paying Customers; Leverage Technology; Spend Wisely.

The twin overriding themes for the car rental industry will be cost management and sales growth—there are companies addressing these issues today, while others struggle to survive. There have been low-cost, low-price car rental companies for years, but cost-conscious, price-savvy customers, educated by Internet travel portals, are generating, some believe, a race to the bottom on the pricing of many travel products and services, including rental cars. This development, along with slower demand, has made it even more difficult for companies to remain profitable, hence the need to manage costs carefully.

Yet, we know that many, if not most, customers are willing pay for better service and extras as long as the underlying product or service is priced at reasonably competitive levels. But travel demand is not likely to expand as it did in the 1990s. Will it still be possible to compete on price and provide premium service and a wide range of options? Where will companies find a stable, growing customer base to support a goal of long-term viability and profitability? Technology holds the key to some answers, but not all of them.

These competing forces, as well as crucial decisions about capital allocation—as companies compete in new markets and fight to protect existing markets—will shape the future of the car rental sector. Many companies that lacked solid balance sheets at the beginning of the decade ended up in bankruptcy when demand decreased. In the future, financial strength will be essential for car rental companies that need capital to compete and grow. Executives and others in marketing roles will have to be as conscious of these factors as anyone in operational, accounting or executive roles.

Unit Cost Preeminence

Whether a car rental company competes for low-price customers, or primarily for less price-sensitive business, rising costs and intense price competition make unit cost control mandatory, not optional. Regardless of a company's market strategy, it will not succeed if costs are out of line with its competitors in target markets. Accurate capacity (fleet) planning, while not a focus of this paper, will be a key to success, because fleet costs are the major cost in this industry.

For those company employees involved in marketing, a greater understanding of costs, as well as products and services, will be even more critical in the future. Will new business generate an acceptable profit at the price demanded by the customer? Is existing business profitable, or are rising costs and soft pricing cutting deeply into profit margins? Can a new business segment be developed profitably and how will it affect peak cost/demand periods? Can new business generate off-peak revenue to help offset peak costs? How effective is the marketing strategy to generate necessary price increases, assuming continued cost pressures? Can prices be set accurately to reflect the cost drivers in each segment (e.g., short rentals on peak days v. longer-duration off-peak rentals)?

Undoubtedly, the quest for achieving optimal unit cost efficiency must be a company-wide effort. A successful company will have expected and planned for an operating environment in which costs will continue to increase, and downward pressure on pricing will be maintained. To the extent that such a mindset creates cost discipline, the company will be positioned to take advantage of business opportunities, and achieve greater profitability when price increases are possible, and at least maintain viability when prices are depressed.

There is a possibility that the travel industry "shakeout" that started in the first half of the decade will result in fewer competitors and less capacity in the car rental and airline industry. This trend cuts two ways. Less supply may mean higher prices, or the potential for higher prices, despite downward pricing pressures evident in today's market. However, the reduction of airline seats may create further downward pressure on car rental demand, which could have a depressive effect on prices, and force the surviving companies to fight for market share, both on and off-airport. Whatever scenario plays out, achieving unit cost efficiency will be critical to survival and improved profitability.

Commoditization Versus Differentiation

Will the car rental business become a commodity business or not? Some people argue that, already, there is nothing to compete on except price. These people conclude that there is no difference between car rental companies, the vehicles they rent, or car rental experiences. In this world, price=value, value=price, and little else matters.

There are still many customers who value something more than the lowest price, and that's not likely to change. However, those companies that operate with a philosophy that value equals something more than the lowest price will remain under great pressure to provide better service and options while maintaining competitive prices. Customers will only pay so much more for good service, even if the lower-cost competitors provide, at best, mediocre service.

Beyond careful cost management, the challenge is to locate and lock-in the "price plus" customer. What do these customers want or need, beyond a reasonably competitive price? How much more will customers pay for good or superior service and convenience compared with average or below-average service at a low price? What additional services and options will customers pay for? How inexpensively can a car rental company provide better-than-average service? How can you keep those customers coming back time and again? For the lower-cost providers, isn't the challenge to provide a consistent, baseline level of service that avoids turning off customers accustomed to some of the better-known, high-value providers?

Building and Rewarding Loyalty

The convergence of technology and marketing is enabling businesses to learn more about customer preferences and help companies determine who their best customers are. In the future, we can expect greater segmentation of customer groups, focused targeting of individual customer groups and more emphasis on building loyalty and rewarding customers for it. However, this trend evolves at a time when personal and data privacy are potent political and social issues, and travel companies will be forced to accommodate new laws, regulations and judicial rulings in this area.

In the car rental context, that will mean knowing which customers generate the most profitable revenue, ensuring their needs are met every time, and enticing them to rent frequently. Companies will use data creatively to find these customers while strictly complying with new privacy rules. With respect to the rental process, companies will identify and nurture customers who demand a transparent pick up/drop off process and who want certain vehicle types, options and special services.

Customer loyalty will be rewarded, helping to make the decision to rent with a particular company a non-decision. Most importantly, it will be critical to know the costs of building, maintaining and rewarding loyalty, as well as the cost of delivering higher levels of service and options. Finally, companies will have to decide whether they can simultaneously serve both the high-service and low-price customers, as well as customers in between.

Nevertheless, the company serving the price-plus customer will be challenged to moderate unit costs while providing levels of service that generate long-term customer loyalty. Customers will only pay so much more for even the highest level of service. Furthermore, the company competing in the "high-service" segments will be continually challenged to communicate that customers get tangible value for the premium they pay.

Distribution Channel Efficiency

Travel agents, tour operators, call centers, proprietary Internet booking sites, GDS, Internet travel portals and other distribution channels are a fact of life in today's travel business. While there has been phenomenal growth of online bookings during the late 1990s and during the current decade, the other distribution channels remain vital for travel providers like car rental companies.

Undoubtedly, Internet booking potential has not peaked. But it is hard to see the Internet completely overwhelming other channels, even in the very long term. Many people still want some human interaction—it's more than a little ironic that many Internet travel portals are investing heavily in call centers—at different points in the travel booking process. That's especially the case for more complex travel decisions involving multiple travel services, and for solutions to problems that arise during a vacation or business trip.

This creates a dilemma for travel service providers, such as airlines, hotels and car rental companies, operating in this highly fragmented environment. No one will want to eliminate lucrative sources of business, but what is the optimal business strategy for building relationships, compensating and committing resources to individual distribution channels? How will travel service providers work with new cut-rate Internet travel providers and avoid having the portal control price and profit margins? How will the company continue to work successfully with agents and tour operators as the importance of the Internet continues to grow? How will the cost of each distribution channel be rationalized and reasonably reflect the contribution to revenue growth and profitability? As important as Internet-based distribution channels have become, are the cost-saving benefits greater than overall participation costs, when the low rates offered over these channels are taken into account? Will customers become more comfortable making complex travel plans without assistance from travel professionals?

Technology: Untapped Potential—But at What Cost and for What Benefit?

Technology is a theme that weaves throughout all of the other trends car rental companies must address. Technology is a valuable tool to drive unit cost efficiency and improved service (e.g., flight arrival tracking systems, expedited rental returns), and it is the basis for product and service options (e.g., onboard navigation systems, satellite radio) and reservations. Many of the important technological advances—data mining, rate engines, yield management, customer relationship management—are entirely transparent to the customer, but will become critical to the success of the company.

Undoubtedly, technology will provide answers to future operational, marketing and service issues businesses face. The key question is whether the benefits are worth the cost, and these decisions will have to be made jointly by operational, systems, marketing and financial management. We've all learned that technology is not a panacea, but even when companies are limiting technology investments, some technological tools will be invaluable. Assuming the technology can deliver as promised, the question remains whether the costs and benefits justify the investment.

Capital Investment: The Key to Growth

It will continue to be impossible for travel businesses, including car rental companies, to stand still and hope to survive, let alone succeed, in the future. It is clear today that the companies best positioned to thrive in a volatile business environment will have been financially strong beforehand. Major investments in the future, such as the development of new markets, require significant capital. And while the price of money has been inexpensive in the first part of this decade, it can be difficult to acquire working capital for a variety of reasons, including the risk aversion of lending institutions.

Assuming capital markets remain tight or the cost of money increases, car rental companies will need strong balance sheets, along with sound reasons for investing in new markets, to acquire additional working capital. Those companies that are unable to finance growth or market expansion, because of underlying financial weakness, may see their financial difficulties escalate rapidly as healthier companies invest and move ahead.

Conclusion

Changes in travel trends, uncertainty about the future, as well as emergent changes in the travel marketplace will require car rental companies to be efficient, have a clear plan to capture and hold profitable business, and make wise capital investment decisions to expand and hold onto markets. The industry shakeout that has occurred during the first half of the decade will create opportunities for some companies, but the underlying volatility in the global economic and political environment makes long-term planning difficult.

The successful company will have relatively lower unit costs, per market segment, and a strong focus on their customer base(s), as well as a rational capacity planning process. These are keys to success, also, for the entire car rental industry. For leaders in each company, a clear head, strong stomach and an iron will be critical skills for making and implementing the tough business decisions that can result in growth and profitability during uncertain times.

13

All Aboard: Marketing Train Travel

Barbara J. Richardson
Vice President of Marketing & Sales
National Railroad
Passenger Corporation (Amtrak)

As vice president for marketing and sales for the National Railroad Passenger Corporation (Amtrak), Barbara Richardson is responsible for passenger ticket revenue generation, overseeing marketing and branding, pricing, revenue management, call center operations, e-commerce, customer and travel industry relations and corporate communications.

Possessing more than 15 years of travel experience, Ms. Richardson serves on the executive committee of the Travel Industry Association (TIA) of America, the Board of the Travel Business Roundtable, the allied committee of the American Society of Travel Agents, and the Women's Transportation Seminar.

Before joining Amtrak in 1994, Ms. Richardson served as director of the office of public affairs for the Federal Railroad Administration. Other positions she has held include director of communications for the New Jersey Department of Transportation and director of public information for the Triborough Bridge and Tunnel Authority in New York City. She holds a bachelor's degree from the University of Nebraska.

The introduction of Amtrak's Acela Express, America's first high-speed train service, signaled the start of a new millennium in travel. With the launch of the first train in December 2000 between Washington, D.C. and New York, Americans no longer had to fly to Europe to experience fast, modern and comfortable train travel. But far from a replication of a European model, Acela Express was tailor-made for American travelers—the service reflects Amtrak's extensive research on their design and amenity preferences.

Acela Express' popularity increased as more trains were added to the schedule. It was not long before Acela Express dominated the air/rail market in the northeast corridor. Prior to the launch of the service, air travel enjoyed a 64 percent share of the New York-to-D.C. market with rail at 36 percent. In just two and a half years, the air share decreased to 47 percent and the rail share increased to 53 percent, powered by the success of Acela Express.

The demand for the service is not an aberration. Instead, there are a number of factors, including those that are instructive to marketing train travel in the future. First, there are the trains, which are futuristic, but also appeal to Americans' love of trains. Acela Express is a good quality product and service that distinguishes itself from the norm of previous U.S. train travel offerings, which had become unreliable and age-worn as a result of years of under investment.

The attraction to the trains also reflects a change in the mindset of travelers today. The glamour days of air travel have been replaced with air's "hassle factor"—security lines, onboard meals of pretzels and peanuts and non-existent legroom. As for those who seek more control of their lives by driving, they are finding themselves locked behind a wheel for hours in traffic as thick as molasses. Travelers are yearning for an alternative that does more than get them from point A to point B, one in which they have a certain latitude to make the experience whatever they choose.

Also relevant are the changes that have occurred in travel since the terrorists' attacks of September 11, 2001. A higher value is being placed on spending time with family and friends. Economic uncertainty is also a consideration as Americans travel shorter distances, stay closer to home and search for travel bargains and values. They are demanding, for less money, the same or more of a travel experience.

The same travelers are also demanding more as consumers. Products once reserved for the wealthy are becoming commonplace—cell phones, designer clothes and luxury cars. Individuals not only strive to own large luxury items, but also routinely treat themselves to daily lattés or weekly massages. Luxury and status symbols are within reach of more and more Americans because they are affordable. Consumers want to feel special and to treat themselves to the best, but at a reasonable price.

The current consumer demands are tailor made for rail service, which is able to offer a civilized transportation alternative in an environment that provides luxurious freedom to do whatever travelers choose with their time. Business travelers may choose to set up a mobile office with a cell phone and laptop or work with colleagues at conference tables. Or they may want to recharge their own batteries by sneaking in a nap. Leisure travelers may choose to read a book, see America's scenery, dine while watching the sunset or simply spend time with family and friends.

In short, selling travel is all about personalizing travel. As Amtrak emphasizes in its brand positioning statement: "With Amtrak, you're an individual, not a seat number. We won't just take you somewhere; we'll take you somewhere you've never been."

Amtrak Services

Founded in 1971, Amtrak provides intercity passenger rail service to more than 500 communities in 46 states across a 22,000-mile route system. Almost 34 percent of Amtrak's customers are traveling on business on the short distance rail corridors, such as Acela Express or on successful commuter trains such as the Surfliner and Capitols in Southern and Central California; the remaining are leisure travelers on the corridors, but primarily on the long distance overnight trains.

From the beginning, gaining awareness has not been a problem for Amtrak. When the nation's freight railroads wanted out of the money-losing passenger business, the federal government consolidated the passenger rail services under a private corporation incorporated in the District of Columbia, the National Railroad Passenger Corporation (Amtrak). Unfortunately, missing from the charter was the identification of a dedicated source of federal investment, which the federal highway and aviation systems currently enjoy. Consequently, Amtrak struggles each year to make a case for federal funding to supplement its passenger ticket revenues (which exceed more than $1 billion annually). Contrast that plight with the situation of any other passenger railroad in the world—none operate without some form of ongoing government support.

The funding situation presents a significant marketing challenge. Over time, Amtrak has been forced to defer investment in new equipment, stations and other passenger facilities. The exception, of course, is Acela Express and the services supported by the states. The other result of the annual funding debate is that it creates an uncertainty about Amtrak's future. This was especially true in the summer of 2002, when passengers were not sure if the railroad would operate through its high-demand season.

Marketing intercity rail service in the United States is not a traditional commercial challenge—one must consider the impact that the transportation policy debate has on consumer decisions.

It is important to note that despite some of the uncertainty, Americans continue to want to take trains. In an Amtrak survey, 49 percent of those questioned said that they would consider Amtrak for their travel choice and 9.5 percent of those have moved from consideration to usage. Amtrak's future success will depend on its ability to literally move people from thinking about a train to stepping on board, as well as to retain its loyal base of train travelers, who together take 24 million train trips a year.

The foundation for future marketing programs will depend on six basic principles:

Demonstrate product stability, reliability and availability: Marketing starts with the product. Before making a commitment, customers must have a comfort level that Amtrak will not only be in service, but will deliver dependable quality service. To recover from years of underinvestment, efforts are underway to stabilize the railroad through management efficiencies and, more importantly, the implementation of a long-term capital program designed to repair track, equipment and other passenger facilities. Rebuilding the railroad will build credibility with passengers, who, over time, will experience improved equipment interiors, better on-time performance and an enhanced dining experience (among just some of the improvements). Additionally, the gradual improvements could help build support for further investments in intercity passenger rail service, as federal leaders see the possibilities.

As resources become available, marketing should assume a product development role, providing guidance based on consumer preferences for equipment enhancements, amenities, food service, ticketing, pricing, stations and all aspects of the train travel experience. Lessons from the past plus research identifying emerging consumer demands and trends will provide a foundation for decisions.

Proof of changes will position Amtrak away from the struggling railroad image, and consequently entice first time and younger consumers to try the service. All communications and marketing tools will need to emphasize changes that are underway to build confidence. In particular, marketing programs that invite writers and travel agents to experience improvements firsthand will be more effective in telling the story of change than paid advertising.

Rebuild long distance service: Given today's consumer desires, a tremendous opportunity exists for Amtrak to offer transportation that makes travelers feel special and gives them the luxury to use time in whatever way they choose. An overnight train trip fits the bill for those who want to spend time with family and friends or those who want to take trips at home in the United States. Unlike plane or car travel, the train trip is an experience in itself—passengers travel through America's most scenic sites.

In 2002, more than 3.5 million trips were taken on Amtrak's long distance trains. The top reason for choosing Amtrak, according to long distance travelers, was to gain "a unique train experience." Other reasons included the travelers' dislike of flying or driving.

To capture even more of this market, Amtrak will need to reassess its offerings in the context of the changing consumer demands and the lack of investment over the years. Similar to Amtrak's Acela Express, Surfliner and Portland-to-Seattle Cascade services, new offerings should represent the culmination of concentrated efforts focused on one long distance train at a time, starting with research to determine what travelers want from the experience and what today's train travelers view as shortcomings of existing service on that route. In the past, long distance train travelers have said that they want to see reliable, timely service, improved food and beverage service. They have also cited equipment problems or limitations, such as faulty heating and ventilation, or worn materials.

Marketing should take the lead in such a review, providing research that will serve as the compass and help to shape what customers want. However, such an effort will involve all touch points of customer service, and a 360-degree effort from within the railroad, calling upon expertise from onboard services, mechanical forces, food and beverage service, train dispatching, station staff and every area that indirectly or directly impacts the passenger experience. By focusing on one service at a time, the changes will be done faster, and will be more evident to potential customers.

Position rail service as an experience: Rail travel's inherent advantage is that it offers more than basic transportation. It is an experience within itself—the vacation begins when the traveler steps on the train. Every communications and marketing tool provides an opportunity to position the product. From photographs in a sales brochure to video on an Internet site, the focus must be directed to optimally position rail service to provide a glimpse of the experience to newcomers and ignite the memories of those who have previously traveled on trains.

For short distance trains, the focus could be on café car amenities, freedom to move, laptop plugs and tables for productive meetings and casual conversation. The experience on long distance would be conveyed with images of sleeping car quarters, diners enjoying meals at tables outfitted in linen, passengers viewing America's scenic beauty from the seat of a lounge car or families enjoying time together. All of which would be intended to convey that train travel is far more than traveling from point A to B; it's actually a luxury in today's fast-paced world.

Simplify the purchase: Train travel is a straightforward, relaxing way to go that allows travelers to individualize their experience. Likewise, purchasing a ticket should reflect the simple, unique requirements of individual travelers. This is true for both pricing and ticket distribution.

In a value-conscious environment, pricing needs to be simple and understandable. Today's price savvy travelers comparison shop through the Internet, newspaper advertising, travel agents and by consulting friends and family. Overcomplicated fare structures are losing out to those that provide easy-to-understand guides, mapping out high-demand and low-demand periods with respective prices. Value airlines are among the best at displaying their fare structures on Web sites and advertising. Amtrak will gradually return to a publishable fare structure to provide travelers with an open book on when they can expect to pay the most and least for train tickets.

Equally important is to offer distribution that matches customer purchase preferences. Again, distribution needs to be simple, straightforward and accessible. But a distribution strategy must also recognize that one size does not fit all. The role of travel agents provides an illustration. Over time, short distance and business travelers have come to prefer purchasing tickets directly from Amtrak via its www.amtrak.com Web site or by calling Amtrak's call center. Knowing train schedules, some have gone to stations and purchased tickets from machines. Businesses have also petitioned Amtrak to offer direct access to the railroad's reservation system, allowing businesses to save commission fees. Amtrak is working to meet this direct sales demand. Web site sales account for nearly 25 percent of Amtrak's ticket purchases (though mostly for short distance travelers). And new technology is emerging that would provide access for businesses to book tickets from their offices.

However, as the advances continue, there remains a strong demand for one-on-one customer service among long distance travelers. Personalized attention is best provided by call center agents or travel agents, who are able to describe overnight sleeping accommodations, meal service, baggage handling and in general, can set realistic expectations for the overnight journey. This is especially important for first-time train travelers.

While some travel providers have eliminated travel agent commissions, Amtrak mirrors its commission policy to customer preferences. Because of the important role that they play for long distance travelers, agents continue to receive commissions for booking travel on those trains. But commissions no longer exist for short distance tickets as customers have turned to other avenues and are demanding even more direct means.

Observing traveler preferences, remaining flexible and being responsive are critical to offering competitive fares and distribution methods. It is difficult to predict what will come next, but the ticketless world that has become common among airlines may find its way into the world of future North American train travel.

Rely on supporters and partners: Through its years of struggling for funding, Amtrak has gained strong local support across the country. While starting out as advocates for increased national rail funding, many of the individuals or groups have taken on marketing and promotion roles that supplement corporate efforts. An example is found in the state of Texas. In 1996, because of a shortage of funds, Amtrak sought to eliminate some of its long distance trains, including the Texas Eagle, which travels from Chicago south through Texas and west to California. Rallying to the defense of the train were Texas' mayors, city council members, and Amtrak employees, whose efforts ultimately saved the train. The advocates evolved into a grassroots marketing group that supports rail service, but also markets and promotes the train currently operating in their communities. On the West Coast is a very successful example of regional marketing. Throughout the country, Amtrak operates services that are funded by the states. States such as California, Oregon and Washington, besides covering the operations cost, fund marketing programs. With Amtrak marketing staff providing the management (similar to an in-house advertising agency), the states and Amtrak cooperatively develop and implement regional programs that have led to successful ridership and revenue growth. In fact, Amtrak's West Coast trains are the fastest growing in the nation, experiencing record ridership and revenue increases. The West Coast marketing programs serves as a model for the future, as more and more states turn to train service to fulfill basic transportation needs.

These are just two examples of the nontraditional marketing partnerships that provide lessons not found in the private sector on how to use every available marketing ally to extend corporate-level efforts.

Save advertising for last: Advertising should be treated as the icing on the cake. It may be the easiest avenue, but it is the most expensive and may not always have the greatest credibility. The most effective, long-lasting and cost-efficient way to build a brand is by providing an experience or product that speaks for itself, delivering service that exceeds expectations and stimulates others to speak on your behalf, whether they are grassroots supporters or your own employees. Harley-Davidson motorcycles is an example of such a brand.

While success for Amtrak may follow a similar route, it is important for Amtrak to take advantage of the public exposure (or scrutiny) it receives. Such media coverage may not always be positive, but at least it provides an avenue by which to reach a large audience with commercial messages. At Amtrak, external and internal communications are integrated into the marketing and sales work, which also includes market research, promotion, pricing, field sales, revenue management, charter services, call center operations, Web site and customer relations.

In building marketing programs, each of these areas is put into play, depending upon the target market and planned outcome. A truly integrated approach takes advantage of the most efficient methods and saves the most expensive method, advertising, as the topper—a way to punctuate the plan.

All six principles are important to a successful rail marketing program. Ultimately, the success of attracting future rail travelers will depend on understanding consumer trends and desires before they become commonplace; candidly assessing the product and service in context with passenger expectations; and recognizing and highlighting the attributes that distinguish train travel from other travel options. Whether it's the train cars themselves, the scenic vistas or America's nostalgic love of trains, there are many aspects of train travel that make it a distinctive experience in its own right. Keeping a watch on the changing consumer environment without losing sight of the train's unique qualities will help fulfill the six marketing principles and help achieve the larger objective of convincing future train riders to come aboard.

Section III

Destination Marketing

In this section you will find sound "how to" marketing techniques from marketers of some of the most popular travel destinations in the world.

Any discussion of marketing travel destinations needs to start with an understanding of why people travel. Unless we can assess a destination in terms of how it satisfies our basic need to "get away from it all," there's no way of targeting our market. According to various research studies, there are five reasons in general why people travel:

1. **Recreation:** Whether you like to go skiing, swimming, dancing, camping, roller coasting or golfing, you fall into this category. You want to get out there and play.

2. **Culture:** You want to get out and learn things. Cultural travelers want to see Broadway shows, operas, museums, ruins of ancient civilizations, and they want to learn new languages.

3. **Business:** Business travelers often combine their travel with recreation and culture. Sometimes they bring their families—especially to meetings held in resorts and on cruise ships.

4 **Visiting Friends and Relatives (VFR):** A lot of people travel to visit friends and relatives, and their numbers appear to be growing in recent years. Unfortunately, these people not only visit friends and relatives, but they tend to sleep in their homes and eat at their dining tables. That means they don't contribute much to the local economy—not unless they're all there for a massive family reunion!

5. **Health.** This is a popular category. Some people go to spas. Others to soak in hot springs. Like VFRs, they're not out shopping and running up high bills at the local clubs.

There are different segments of the market. When you read the following chapters, keep in mind that each contributor targets a certain segment, making a carefully planned appeal.

Destinations are like brands—they have personalities. Think about it. "Snap, Crackle, and Pop"—that's personality. "The Fun Ships"—you can count on having fun aboard a Carnival ship. Walt Disney World—think Mickey Mouse and exciting rides with names like "Tower of Terror," and faux Japanese, German, Mexican and French food served in exotic-looking settings. Yellowstone Park— Old Faithful, bears, bison, moose, flowers, hiking trails and waterfalls. Branson, Missouri—country music. Las Vegas—gambling. Now, for contrast, here are some perfectly good destinations with no, or hardly any, personality: South Dakota, Minnesota, Belize, Uruguay and Slovenia. If these places want to attract visitors, they need to develop a brand image for themselves, so that if someone says to you, "Let's go to Slovenia," you'll say, "They have the most wonderful food. I can hardly wait to try sauerkraut and sour turnip soup and walnut Slovene bread."

You might not care for those particular recipes, but indeed, many destinations, like California's Napa Valley, have given their brand a unique identity associated with good wine and food. If you want lobster, go to Maine and for steak, Kansas City.

Let's go back and take another look at that list of why people travel. Take business travelers. Many want to take their families with them when they go on vacation. A destination that wants that kind of business must first have a special product available. First, they need transportation. If convention delegates can't get there conveniently and cheaply, they won't go. Next, the destination needs meeting areas, space to accommodate the convention. That calls for hotels with plenty of bedrooms, meeting rooms, ballrooms, and display space. Larger destinations require convention halls, maybe more than one. How about the children and the rest of the family? What are Mom or Dad, and Billy and Grace going to do while the one spouse is in meetings? Hopefully there are hotels that have a good children's program so the kids can be safely and happily parked somewhere for a few hours. Or maybe there's a sightseeing tour everyone can take. Horseback riding, tennis, swimming and ice-skating are good family activities too.

How does it all come together for a destination? Clearly there is a symbiotic relationship going on here. To develop an attractive destination requires the coordinated efforts of many groups. What is the role of each of them?

Arguably, it is government's responsibility to provide the basic infrastructure needed to develop a viable program. Government needs to take the lead. Air treaties need to be negotiated. It is government's job to provide attractive, comfortable, user-friendly airport and seaport facilities, as well as highways and accessible bus transportation. To encourage airlines to fly to a new destination, other incentives may need to be offered such as opening tourist offices abroad and doing cooperative advertising. Private investors are needed to add hotels, car rentals, taxis, shopping and restaurants. In some countries, governments must do more things than others. In international locations, construction of a resort becomes very complicated. Duty fees need to be negotiated to bring in materials, furniture and fixtures. Labor is often a controversial issue. Destinations want to provide jobs for the local population. But that is not always practical. Large chains such as Marriott have their own architectural and construction teams. In some countries, developers need to negotiate labor contracts. This often involves changing laws concerning the use of imported labor. When Club Med wanted to open in Bermuda, the issue of their multi-cultural staff was raised. Club Med's ambience, an essential part of their branding, requires "genteel organizers" who come from all over the world. Bermudan law, at the time, required that almost everyone involved be Bermudan. Bermuda needed to amend the law to accommodate the needs of Club Med.

There are other special issues with all-inclusive resorts. As a practical matter, all-inclusives need some control so only paying guests can enjoy their lavish buffets and other amenities. But local laws in some countries don't allow for private beaches or hotels that are closed to the local populace. Casinos are another issue. Developing nations worry about the social consequences of allowing gaming. All of these resort development issues can be enormously complicated, yet they must be resolved before anyone can move ahead.

Then there is the role of private enterprise. Developers need financing to build hotels and vacation condominiums. That money generally comes from private sources. Retail space has to be built so small businesses can sell souvenirs and T-shirts and open restaurants. Tourist attractions must be added. These include everything from distilleries and vineyards to alligator wrestling. Where adventure travel is popular, access such as whitewater river rafting must be offered. Hiking and horseback trails have to be built and maintained. The list goes on.

Successful destinations are ones where everyone's role has been clearly defined and where all parties agree that tourism development and promotion are top priorities. Good destinations do not develop by themselves. Not only is growth planned, but everyone knows when to stop growing as well. Overdevelopment can spoil 100 years of planned growth. Like other products, destinations have life cycles. Look at the histories of Miami Beach and Atlantic City. Both were born in the 1920s, crashed in the1960s, and were reborn in the 1990s.

Similarly, tourism promotion of a destination has to be coordinated among many disparate and potentially competing entities at or near the destination. In this section, you have sound "how-to" marketing techniques from marketers of some of the most successful travel destinations in the world.

All too often, as these entities look to the future, they coalesce remarkably on issues surrounding how to keep the destination popular and successful. These destinations never stray too far from Marketing 101!

14

The Story of a Public/Private Tourism Marketing Partnership

John Ellis "Jeb" Bush
Governor of Florida

Jeb Bush was born in Midland, Texas. After first arriving in Florida, he helped start a real estate development company that today is one of the largest, full-service commercial real estate companies in South Florida. In 1987–88, he served as Florida's Secretary of Commerce and promoted Florida's business climate worldwide.

Following an unsuccessful bid for governor in 1994, Governor Bush founded the Foundation for Florida's Future, a not-for-profit organization designed to influence public policy at the grassroots level. As chairman of the foundation, he co-founded the state's first charter school—Liberty City Charter School—with the Urban League of Greater Miami.

He was elected Florida's 43rd governor in 1998 and re-elected in 2002, becoming the first Republican to be re-elected governor in the state's history. Since taking office, his top priority has been creating a world-class educational system through high standards and increased accountability. To achieve this goal, he helped secure a record four-year increase of $2.9 billion (26 percent increase) in statewide K-12 funding. He believes passionately that all children should learn a year's worth of knowledge in a year's worth of time.

Governor Bush also boosted the state's reserve funds while reducing the state's tax burden to its lowest level in a decade. He has focused the state's resources on protecting Florida's natural environment with an historic $2-billion commitment to saving Florida's Everglades. He has also increased health insurance coverage for needy children and provided unprecedented levels of funding and services to the elderly and the developmentally disabled.

By taking advantage of online technology such as the state's Web portal, www.myflorida.com, and thanks to outreach programs like his monthly "Open Office Hours" around Florida, Governor Bush continues to be the most accessible governor in the state's history, providing all Floridians with greater opportunities to directly participate in and communicate with their government and elected officials.

Those of us who are lucky enough to live in Florida appreciate the unique diversity of the state's attractions. From the Florida Keys to the Everglades; from the historic beauty of St. Augustine to the wonderful world of Disney in Orlando; from the unspoiled beaches along Highway 98 to the vibrant international culture of Miami, Florida has something for everyone. Fortunately for the rest of the world, we're willing to share.

Every year we welcome more than 70 million tourists from around the world, making Florida the number one tourist destination in America (if not the world). With that kind of volume, it's no surprise that tourism is the state's number one industry. More than 860,000 Florida residents work in the industry, and almost as many are indirectly affected by it as well. Today, Florida tourism is a $50 billion industry, providing $3 billion in sales tax revenue to the state's treasury each year. This revenue supports critical services including education, health, law enforcement, public infrastructure, and environmental protection. Tourism accounts for about 20 percent of our total state economy. In Florida, tourism is a serious business and we manage it like one.

It wasn't always that way. Prior to 1996, Florida managed and marketed tourism like most other states. Armed with an insufficient annual budget (under $18 million in 1995), the state's division of tourism was responsible for developing and executing the state's tourism marketing initiatives, including advertising; promotions; public, media, and travel trade relations; hospitality programs; and research programs.

The division, later dubbed the Destination Board, was part of the Florida Department of Commerce, and was run as a government office. Leaders in the tourism industry had limited access and little influence. Instead, the board was staffed by government employees and funded by a yearly appropriation from the Florida Legislature. The board competed for funding with other state programs and operated under cumbersome, bureaucratic rules and policies that hindered its effectiveness.

Aside from modest trade show and promotional opportunities, the board had no programs to encourage private sector financial investment into the state's tourism marketing efforts. This lack of resources limited the state's ability to launch and sustain an effective tourism marketing initiative. Florida's tourism businesses, as well as local convention and visitors bureaus and tourist development councils, concentrated their efforts on promoting individual destinations, rather than actively participating in statewide promotional efforts.

By the late 1980s, other domestic and international destinations began to seriously challenge Florida in the competition for tourists. The success of their well-financed marketing initiatives made it clear that our statewide tourism marketing program needed greater funding.

Florida's marketing effort also needed a long-term unifying vision that strongly established the state as the tourist destination of choice. Historically, Florida's marketing direction changed with the political tides. Any announcement of a new commerce secretary or division head was usually followed by a new tourism marketing campaign and slogan. Not exactly the best way to establish brand recognition for Florida tourism in the marketplace.

As competition for tourist dollars increased, something had to give. It turned out to be state government's grip on Florida's tourism marketing. In a move that was both revolutionary and evolutionary, in 1991 the state began to transition the responsibility for tourism marketing from the government to the private sector. The result was the creation of The Florida Tourism Advisory Council, an industry-driven organization under the direct control of leaders in the state's tourism industry who worked with the state to promote tourism.

The first step in this revolution was to establish funding. Independent funding was critical to the success of this transition. A dedicated public revenue source would free the new organization from the yearly scramble for general revenue dollars that had plagued its predecessor, while ensuring that tourism remained a top priority in any budget year. It was important that primarily tourists, instead of residents, provide the revenue since all money generated would be earmarked to support that sector.

Florida ultimately opted to fund the tourism marketing initiative through a surcharge on car rentals. Since 1991, all car rental transactions and the first 30 days of new car leases are subject to a $2.00 per day surcharge. Of the revenue collected from this surcharge, 15.75 percent goes to the Tourism Promotional Trust Fund. These funds are dedicated to promoting tourism in Florida, replacing the annual allocation bestowed by the legislature. The rest of the revenue generated by the surcharge is primarily used for transportation infrastructure, since the state's roads are significantly impacted by the influx of tourists each year.

The next step in the revolution of Florida's tourism industry gave a greater voice to the industry's advisors. From 1992 to 1996, the industry's Florida Tourism Advisory Council continued to evolve as the driving force behind the state's tourism sector. In 1996, the Council emerged with considerably more power and prestige as the Florida Commission on Tourism. The commission recruited 28 advisors from every geographic region in the state to represent all segments of the tourism industry. The governor also joined the commission representing the public sector's interests, as did a member of the Florida House of Representatives and a member of the Florida Senate.

Although Florida's private tourism industry assumed more responsibility for directing the state's tourism marketing efforts, the commission still encountered the government model for the day-to-day execution of these strategies. It was soon apparent to everyone involved that the model was woefully inadequate. The multiple layers of management, protracted approval processes, and massive paperwork requirements, so integral to the function of a state agency, were at odds with the lean, fast-moving organization the commission needed to be. It was critical that we remove all bureaucratic barriers to the organization's ability to effectively support Florida's tourism industry. For instance, it is common practice in the "real world" to accept meals offered during business meetings, to make on-the-spot marketing decisions, and to enter into cooperative relationships that make sense from a purely marketing perspective. But the government model actively suppressed these practices.

The bureaucracy of the government model also prevented rapid reaction to unexpected or urgent situations. In the wake of one hurricane, the division of tourism requested additional advertising money to inform concerned vacationers that Florida was fully open for business. By the time all the proper approvals were finally secured, hurricane season was over and the state had suffered lost tourism revenue.

In 1996, the state's tourism industry led the charge for change. In response, the Florida Legislature abolished the Florida Department of Commerce and its various divisions. All economic development activity formerly conducted by commerce is now the responsibility of several private/public organizations. In the case of tourism, the Florida Tourism Industry Marketing Corporation (FTIMC), a 501(c)6 organization, assumed responsibility for development of the state's tourism industry.

Reporting to the Florida Commission on Tourism, the FTIMC adopted the operating culture of a private business rather than a government agency. The new staff quickly streamlined policies and procedures. Rules covering employee travel were reduced from 30 pages to one by empowering staff to be responsible, prudent, and reasonable within the confines of their budgets. Other policies were simplified, and obstacles to performance and organizational responsiveness were either eliminated or improved dramatically.

In keeping with world-class marketing practices, FTIMC quickly created a consumer-friendly name for the organization, "VISIT FLORIDA," as well as a unified brand identity for the state as tourist destination. The "FLA USA" brand is now used in advertising, promotional activities, consumer publications, and everything else connected with marketing Florida tourism around the world and is readily recognizable in the marketplace.

With stronger checks and balances between input from the government and private sector, VISIT FLORIDA is far less vulnerable to political pressure. The president and CEO of VISIT FLORIDA is appointed by the Florida Commission on Tourism. The VISIT FLORIDA Corporation has full discretion over all other hiring decisions. This ensures the most qualified candidate, regardless of any political expediencies of the moment, fills each position.

A hallmark of a successful private business is the ability to identify and secure new sources of revenue. In addition to the funding it derives from the rental car surcharge, VISIT FLORIDA built additional financial support from the state's tourism industry through three revenue mechanisms.

The first of these mechanisms is investor association. Businesses and government agencies may affiliate with VISIT FLORIDA as "partners." Partners pay a modest annual fee, determined by their industry sector category and gross revenues. In return, these organizations receive a wealth of special marketing opportunities, either at low cost or no cost to them. This program provides far greater marketplace visibility for tourism businesses, especially smaller organizations, than they would be able to obtain on their own.

Strategic alliances provide a second stream of income. Freed from cumbersome mandatory government bidding practices, VISIT FLORIDA negotiates alliances with a select group of industry leaders. For each alliance, the private sector partner provides a combination of cash and in-kind services, while VISIT FLORIDA offers a featured marketing position and special marketing advantages. Today, strategic alliance partners include the Florida Hotel & Motel Association, Delta Airlines, Dollar Rent-A-Car, and American Express.

A third private sector funding mechanism is advantage marketing through VISIT FLORIDA. Both partner and non-partner businesses can participate, with partners having first right of refusal, in a multitude of marketing programs including trade and consumer show participation, brochure distribution at the official Florida Welcome Centers, media missions to key origin markets, cooperative advertising opportunities, and research study participation. These opportunities are priced attractively through the economies of scale, and provide the added value of co-branding with the state's official tourism marketing corporation.

The VISIT FLORIDA program has been an unqualified success. The number of visitors to Florida has risen steadily since the creation of the organization in 1996, with the notable exception of 2001, a year impacted by the September 11 tragedy and a soft economy. Visitor spending has also grown, from $37.9 billion in 1996 to $51.1 billion in 2002. This growth increased state tax revenues derived from tourist spending during the same period from $2.3 billion to $3.1 billion.

VISIT FLORIDA's success extends well beyond those indicators, which likely would have risen to a limited degree under the old model. The legislation that created VISIT FLORIDA mandated a dollar-for-dollar match of private-to-public funding by July 1, 2001, five years after the Corporation began operations. VISIT FLORIDA met that mandate in less than half that time. In 1996, VISIT FLORIDA had 407 industry partners, by early 2003 that number exceeded 3,300. These partnerships contribute more than $2.5 million to the corporation's marketing efforts.

VISIT FLORIDA has garnered countless industry awards for outstanding and creative marketing. Perhaps the highest accolade came in 2002, when the Tourism Industry Association of America (TIA) proposed the creation of a tourism marketing organization for the entire United States based on the VISIT FLORIDA model.

Nothing is more indicative of an individual or an organization's character than response in the wake of a crisis. The events of September 11, 2001, provided just such an occasion for VISIT FLORIDA and the State of Florida, as the tourism industry worldwide received a shock of seismic proportions. Empty airliners sat silently on the tarmac while millions of vacationers stayed home and Florida faced an unprecedented economic crisis.

Within two weeks of the attacks, VISIT FLORIDA had crafted the most audacious tourism recovery campaign in the nation's history. As governor, I repledged the support of state government in the form of $20 million in supplemental advertising funds—provided VISIT FLORIDA could stretch that funding cooperatively with private sector partners. Nearly 90 industry partners, from every sector of the industry and geographic region of the state, put up a total of more than $25 million to more than match the $20 million dollar state funding. Additionally, various state government agencies, such as the Florida Lottery, Department of Citrus, and Department of Agriculture and Consumer Services, partnered with VISIT FLORIDA to provide exciting and highly visible promotions. When all was said and done, the massive campaign pumped more than $76 million into the marketplace. As a result, while most other U.S. destinations were still struggling a year later, Florida's visitor numbers were actually exceeding those of the previous year. Florida ended 2002 with the largest visitor estimate in state history—over 75 million.

The success of VISIT FLORIDA extends beyond our state. It has crossed our borders to become a model for a growing number of states and nations. Several states have already begun to experiment with a privatized tourism board, always using VISIT FLORIDA as their foundation. My personal philosophy has always favored an approach in which government and the private sector work together to achieve better outcomes than either could achieve separately. VISIT FLORIDA is an outstanding example of this philosophy in action; a new way of thinking that *works*.

15

Hawaii . . . the Islands of Aloha: An Integrated Marketing Model

Tony S. Vericella, President and CEO

Visitors & Convention Bureau

Tony S. Vericella became president and chief executive officer of the Hawaii Visitors and Convention Bureau in October 1997.

At the time of his selection by the HVCB board of directors, Mr. Vericella was vice president and general manager, Hawaii and Asia/Pacific, for Budget Rent-a-Car Systems, Inc.

Prior to joining Budget Rent-a-Car in 1992, Mr. Vericella was vice president and general manager of American Express Travel Related Services Co., Inc., from 1985 to 1992.

Mr. Vericella came to Hawaii in 1983 as a vice president of sales and market planning with Hawaiian Airlines.

A native of Pennsylvania, he graduated from Purdue University with a bachelor's degree in biology and chemistry in 1975. He earned a master of business administration degree at UCLA in 1980.

Mr. Vericella began his career in the visitor industry in customer service positions with Western Airlines in 1976. He later joined Continental Airlines, where he held senior analyst positions in long-range planning and marketing before becoming director of domestic passenger pricing. He has been an active member of several Hawaii business, education and community organizations, and is currently a sustaining board member of Travel Industry Association of America (TIA), board member for Pacific Asian Travel Association (PATA); Assets School Board of Trustees; St. Louis School Board, Aloha United Way (co-chair, tourism committee), U.S. Department of Commerce, U.S.-Japan Tourism Export Expansion Initiative Committee member, and a member, board of directors, Hawaii Wellness Tourism Association.

Mr. Vericella and his wife Dana have "triplets" (2 boys and a girl).

Over a hundred years ago, a group of enterprising business and community leaders began sharing Hawaii with the world. It was a time, 1903, that marked the entry of the islands into what we refer to today as destination marketing—the global tourism industry.

What magical foresight did they possess that inspired them to believe that people would traverse the waters of the Pacific for relaxation and respite? Whatever their vision, it was a vision that set the stage for tourism in the islands today. A $10 billion-plus industry, tourism to the islands is the leading economic engine in the state. Surpassing all other industries in contributions to the economic health and welfare of our community, it showcases the lost Hawaiian culture and is a catalyst for diversification of other emerging knowledge-based industries around the state.

The surveys of those who have traveled here indicate the highest visitor satisfaction rate of any global destination—consistently in the 98th percentile. Hawaii is a place that also consistently leads U.S. and Japanese polls that attempt to determine the most satisfying vacation experience; the most desired destination for the Japanese; the number one honeymoon destination in the world; the number one favorite city (Honolulu); the number one island in the world (Maui). In addition, Hawaii received an award of excellence for superior service to the meetings and incentive travel industry. The people of Hawaii and all those who've worked together over the years to nurture, shepherd and evolve the Hawaii brand can be justly proud.

Hawaii's pristine natural environment, the diversity of each of Hawaii's islands, and the multicultural mix and welcoming spirit of the resident population inspired President John F. Kennedy to say, during a brief stopover to the islands in 1963, "Hawaii is what the rest of the world would like to be."

Growth of Tourism

In the early days, it could almost be said that Hawaii sold itself. Through the 1960s and 1970s, the allure of the destination was unrivaled and the envy of would-be competitors. The growth of visitor numbers from all parts of the world was short of remarkable, not seen in any other U.S. destination, and comparable to the most glamorous cities around the globe. As the economic face of the world changed, many other countries and locales entered the tourism marketplace. After all, tourism is an industry that's "clean," has the ability to generate revenue from many diverse sectors, is able to support the culture and heritage of a place, and utilizes all that a destination has to offer (i.e., cuisine, crafts, arts, environment, etc.). Tourism is pursued by cities, states and nations of the world.

- The World Tourism Organization (WTO) projects that, by the year 2020, 1.6 billion people will travel to another country, and spend nearly $2 trillion in U.S. dollars.

- In 2002, WTO reported 715 million international tourist arrivals (22 million more than 2001 and almost 19 million more than 2000).

- In 2003, in North America directly and indirectly, the World Travel & Tourism Council (WTTC) projects:

  - 21,801,000 million jobs, representing 11.8 percent of total employment

  - $1,330 billion of gross domestic product (equivalent to 10.8 percent of total GDP)

  - $228 billion of exports, services and merchandise (or 13.5 percent of total exports)

  - $232 billion of capital investment (or 10.6 percent of total investment)

And over the next 10 years, the WTTC only expects the North America travel and tourism industry to achieve more annualized real growth:

- +4.1 percent in total travel and tourism demand to $3,016 billion

- +2.4 percent in employment to 27,571,000 jobs in the travel and tourism economy overall

- +6.7 percent in visitor exports, rising to $269 billion

Although Hawaii is constantly studied by competitors and although we welcome and share our knowledge with emerging destinations (regarding our research methodologies, infrastructure, planning, marketing and promotion), we continue to learn from other destinations. The road Hawaii has and continues to travel has not been as easy as others might suspect. Since the mid-1990s, the opportunities and challenges have become increasingly interconnected and dynamic. We've faced global, regional and national challenges, some unleashed by nature and others instigated by man. In this global, instantaneously connected world, there have been and will continue to be impacts created by geopolitical, economic and social changes, natural disasters or discoveries, and new emerging or reborn destination choices.

Throughout it all, we have seen Hawaii through the eyes of its repeat visitors. Indeed, our high repeat visitor count tells us that Hawaii continues to excel at delivering its essence and experiences to its guests and consistently satisfies their needs and interests. We try to keep Hawaii as a welcoming, rejuvenating place that's "everyone's home," and do so in a warm, sharing spirit of "Aloha." Our residents are really our heart and soul. They explain Hawaii's enviable repeat visitor ratio—nearly 62 percent of Hawaii's annual visitors are repeaters. We have the highest repeat percentage of any global destination.

Be Who You Are

The key for any organization or destination is to truthfully know and thoroughly understand itself—its core essence, its strengths and opportunities, its areas of improvement and challenges to its sustainability. At the same time, it is critical that an organization deliver on its brand. "Brand promise" is what resonates with consumers; it is what generates the all-important repeat business that is crucial to an organization's success and growth.

Hawaii knows who and what it is. We have fostered a resurgence at our core—the Hawaiian culture. This will keep Hawaii true to itself and broaden and evolve Hawaii as a brand. Communicating this essence, involving and connecting our residents and sharing the real experiences of the Islands with our guests are key to continually generating desire, intention and actual visits to Hawaii. Delivering to our "guests" what they expect and desire is critical to building repeaters and referrals and creating ambassadors for Hawaii. The destination has been delivering on its promises. We provide genuine, welcoming people and interactive, rejuvenating experiences that naturally bring residents and guests together—in fact, that's what today's consumers expect. Further, they know when those experiences aren't being delivered. Events and festivals from the grassroots community level to those of world-class broadcast quality are not only providing more "reasons" to come at specific times but also are the source of higher levels of satisfaction.

With all of the positives of the islands, it has never been enough for Hawaii simply to assume "We're unique, so they'll come," or that the marketing of the destination can or should be generally the same year after year. What worked in the past won't necessarily continue to be effective in the future. We cannot assume or take anything for granted in a world that is increasingly interconnected and "smaller," and where the quantity and pace of change is staggering and constant.

As more destinations enter the marketplace and aggressively target more active, higher-spending consumers, the need has intensified for Hawaii, and all other destinations, to continually reposition its brand to appeal to the diversity of interests among consumers, while being true to itself, and to reinvent our marketing approach to increase effectiveness and improve efficiency.

Know your customers better than yourself

As information has continually doubled in ever-shorter periods of time, consumers have fragmented into smaller groups, driven by a unique combination of interests; and thus, the "customer of one" is a reality. Consumers are being increasingly and constantly bombarded with messages and images. As a result, consumers are more brand savvy and the landscape of targeting messages to people is overloaded and drastically altered. Multiplying choices and combining them with advancing technology allows consumers to be in total control of what, when, and how they receive information. The power of knowledge has shifted and is clearly in the hands of the consumer.

Consumers can do whatever they want, whenever they want and from wherever they want. They are more knowledgeable, more in control, and their expectations are escalating. Consumer fragmentation has permanently altered traditional media, as we've known it. There's been large-scale convergence of media, news and entertainment.

This array of choices, with the plethora of communication vehicles and methods, and the emergence of devices to selectively pick or block communications, presents ongoing challenges and opportunities in the marketplace.

There are going to be more broadcast media channels, not fewer; more and shorter commercial messages in between program segments, not fewer; more messages embedded into TV/cable shows, not fewer. And, there will be easier, more convenient, and effective devices that will allow consumers to select what they desire (thus eliminating/blocking out what they don't want to see or hear).

The marketplace demands that you *know your customer better than yourself* (your destination/product). Not only your customers' demographic/psychographic profile, but their combination of interests and expectations. You must also know when and how they are most receptive to your messages and who and how they're influenced. You must continually invest more energy, time and resources into knowing, understanding and listening to your customers than knowing your brand. Your customers will demand that you integrate your brand with their needs, desires, and interests and that you honestly and truthfully communicate and deliver what you promise.

A destination must know who it is and what it offers. You must know who your customers are and what your customers want. And to break through all of the clutter and be more effective, you must be able to make a personal connection with your targeted customers. You must be able to showcase your brand essence with real, relevant and authentic experiences. Your customers must not only be able to visualize themselves being there but also be satisfied by the overall experience. The relationship you are strengthening, establishing or wanting to establish must be "visual," intellectual (interactive, learning) and emotional.

Lifelong Relationships with Your Customers

Once you've identified your targeted customers, you're continually trying to move them along a cycle from awareness to desire, to intention to visit, to travel and then to becoming a repeat visitor.

Knowing your customer enables you to deliver a memorable, experiential relationship, and, through your marketing, touch your consumer in the stage of life and through the lifestyle interests in which they're living today. Here's how we've assessed the typical life stages and lifestyles of visitors to Hawaii:

- Life stage—Young Adults; Honeymoon/Wedding, Couples, Families, Mature Adults

- Lifestyle—Nature/Culture/History; Romance, Cruise; Wellness; Golf; Sports

The *relationship* you develop must continually evolve and grow stronger while remaining transparent. Thoroughly understanding the consumer is critically important and is the foundation for successful, effective and efficient marketing. Knowing the needs and interests of the consumers allows you to craft messages that are *relevant*. Identifying their media habits and how they are influenced determines the communication channels and methods through which your messages are best delivered and when the consumer is most *receptive* to them. This "dialogue" with the consumers should drive *response*.

In an effort to leverage resources, increase effectiveness and improve efficiency, try these "four Ps" of marketing":

- **Personalize** your messages

- **Profile** to find more of the target customers

- **Partner** with like-minded companies

- **Promote** to drive desired response

Hawaii is a "sensual" destination—sight, sound, smell, touch, taste and feel need to be utilized in the marketing efforts undertaken. A balance of physical (bringing your brand to the customer), virtual (Web-based promotion) and other communication channels should be used to "surround" the customer. This multi-front attack is delivered, based on customer research, in appropriately timed "waves" of marketing to our targeted audiences.

Integrated marketing—Align and unite

How are you organized? What are your people focused on? Are your systems and databases interconnected and seamless? Are the messages you deliver internally and externally in sync for all stakeholders? Does each marketing program build upon and add value to the other?

Integrated marketing enables us to organize, focus and interconnect our people, systems, strategies, markets, tactical programs, messages, etc. Everything is aligned around Hawaii's brand and its four major customer groups: consumers; media; travel planners; sellers, suppliers and partners (traditional or not). A single-minded purpose of more effectively and efficiently delivering value to the consumer unites all stakeholders and thrives upon more inclusiveness. Adding value, leveraging resources and building lifelong relationships increases momentum and creates opportunities.

The quantity, pace and constant atmosphere of change, coupled with the rapid expansion of knowledge, continually changes the dynamics of reaching targeted consumers. Progressive, leading-edge organizations, over the last two decades, have had to increase their levels of connectivity, both internally and externally, from cooperation, to coordination, to collaboration, to synergy and now, in the last five years, to integration.

Integration requires continual energy and attention by everyone within and connected to the organization. Whether vertical or horizontal, it should permeate your organization. When it becomes a natural part of your thought process and actions, you're just about ready for the next level—co-evolution. That's where partners proactively plan how they will evolve together. While it might seem that some partners have nothing in common, partners always have targeted customers to reach.

It's all about choices and value

All of us receive a relentless bombardment of marketing messages and are given a myriad of choices as to how, when and where to respond. We also face an increasing number of distribution channels through which to make a purchase. Of course, everyone along the way is promising to deliver added value.

Through it all, we know that consumers are smarter; that they have the knowledge, power and control. Whether travel is intended for leisure, corporate meetings or both, consumers are increasingly focused on destinations they believe will offer them "authentic" experiences that satisfy their needs and interests and provide "real" value. In a recent Yankelovich study, nearly two-thirds of the respondents said that they prefer to spend money on experiences that will enrich their lives; another 77 percent said that doing enjoyable things and going to interesting places means more to them than material goods. And nearly 60 percent said they want to spend more time exploring their "spiritual" side.

At the same time, the Travel Industry Association of America (TIA) reports that nearly 93 million Americans included at least one cultural, arts, heritage or historic activity or event while traveling in 2001.

We know, too, that people, ourselves included, don't believe they have as much time as they had in the past. We're double-booked, over-stimulated, and 24/7-connected. You constantly hear that people are looking for ways to simplify their lives; and that they yearn for a pace of life that they control and into which they can place meaningful and emotionally rewarding experiences and relationships.

Hawaii is fortunate in that the essence of our islands comprises peace, harmony and the welcoming spirit of our people. Hawaii's unsurpassed natural beauty, near-perfect climate, diversity of terrain and experiences, and multicultural population combine to deliver a rejuvenating quality to travel there.

We must continue to remain flexible and on the leading edge of the changing attitudes and behaviors of travelers. At the same time, we must be sure that we continue to provide our guests with what they want within the context of who we are. There will always be somewhere new and different to go to. Broadening the diversity and aloha of Hawaii and each of its unique islands will keep the Hawaii brand fresh and relevant for our guests coming here, whether for the first time or on their 50th repeat visit.

As we've seen in the past, what will keep Hawaii in the forefront of the world's destinations is forward-looking knowledge, continuous evolution, creativity, desire and action to forge new alliances with our integrated marketing partners, and the sharing spirit of our people and communities.

For nearly 100 years, it has been this combination that has assured Hawaii's visitor of high satisfaction . . . and it is what will enable the Islands to thrive and prosper into the future.

'A 'Ohe Hana Nui Ke Alu 'Ia
"No task is too large when we work together."

16

Convention and Visitors Bureaus

John A. Marks, President and CEO
San Francisco Convention
& Visitors Bureau

John A. Marks has served as President and CEO of the San Francisco Convention & Visitors Bureau since 1987.

Marks was the 2003 national chairman of the Travel Industry Association of America (TIA); is co-chair of the U.S./Japan Tourism Export Expansion Initiative; was a founding member of the California Travel and Tourism Commission (CTTC, 1998–2003), and is past president of the California Travel Industry Association (CALTIA, 1999–2000).

He served as chairman of the International Association of Convention & Visitor Bureaus (IACVB) during 1988–89, and was vice-chairman of the American Society of Association Executives (ASAE) in 1996–97.

Keeper of the Future

Convention and visitors bureaus (CVBs) have been in existence, in one form or another, since 1896, but the last decade has seen an exponential shift in how bureaus will move forward into the future. Challenges of product distribution and technology, funding, accountability, product development and leadership are swirling around cities as never before. Despite these challenges, however, the primary reason cities created destination marketing organizations hasn't changed in more than 100 years: "Bring in the business."

Elected public officials, along with local business and community leaders, have learned that convention, leisure and business travel are not only powerful economic engines, but also job providers and lifestyle enhancers for local residents. To that end, it has become clear that the long-term financial health of many communities lies in the travel and tourism industry. The CVB, working most typically as a public-private partnership with the host city, performs the sales and marketing function on behalf of the destination. Although a CVB structure may differ somewhat from city to city, the function doesn't change appreciably. In most cases, the bureau operates as a 501(c)(6) business organization with private sector funding coming from members.

Additional funding in almost all cases comes from the city through a portion of the local transient occupancy tax (hotel or room tax). The bureau is typically the one community organization solely responsible for the future health of the travel and tourism industry—therefore it's the "Keeper of the Future."

One of the greatest challenges facing bureaus today is the pressure to fill hotel rooms *tonight!* The robust times of the mid-1990s, followed by an industry record-breaking year in 2000, have shifted to a more difficult period from a performance perspective. The downturn is the result of a declining economy, dot-com meltdown and global disquiet. Although pressure will continue to mount to fill hotel rooms to support related hospitality industry services in the near term, sales and marketing decisions must look beyond the next few days or months. If left to their own devices, many hotel executives would give away the future to fill rooms tonight—a direct result of immediate performance expectations from investors and Wall Street.

While that strategy may work in the short term, it cannot possibly prevail over the long haul. For a city to be successful into the future, the bureau must develop and maintain long-term relationships with domestic and international tour operators, travel agents, and other transportation partners, along with association and corporate meeting planners. These individuals are not only the influencers and decision makers for a community's long-term business, but also their providers.

The bureau, in its role as the "Keeper of the Future," must always remain focused on value and long-term returns.

Funding . . . Create an Entrepreneurial Spirit

Any bureau executive worth his or her salt will tell you they never have enough money to adequately market their destination. They will quickly point to a handful of other cities that have what are perceived to be enormous budgets. One fact is undeniable: You need money to market. However, approaching this subject in a traditional manner simply will not work in an increasingly competitive environment. Going forward, the lazy or unimaginative will continue to wait for members' dues checks to arrive, and pray that their municipality continues to fund them at the same, or (with a little luck), at an even higher, level through the room tax or city's general fund. Their days are numbered.

Creating an entrepreneurial spirit within the bureau is critical to the future success of destination marketing organizations. Partnerships and alliances provide the necessary resources to successfully market the destination. It will also become the accepted practice, and those who don't engage in this endeavor will be left behind. As financial resources become tighter, new and innovative ways of selling the city will become essential. Traditional "endemic" partners such as hotels, airlines, car rentals and attractions, will be enhanced by "non-endemic" partners including, but not limited to, financial services, consumer goods and technology.

These endemic and non-endemic partnerships are "leveraged" through the use of cooperative partnerships. Business entities, either public or private, that share like goals come together to stretch their collective message and financial resources through marketing, advertising and sales initiatives. As a result, the frequency and reach of the message is expanded for all involved. The key to success is through the process of identifying compatible brands that seek a similar audience. The cost of the message, through any distribution channel, must be shared by all. In many cases, as the result of multiple partnerships, the bureau is able to return three or four dollars for every one-dollar invested. Now you can begin to see why this makes sense. The San Francisco Convention & Visitors Bureau has partnered with such diverse companies as Visa, See's Candies, Colavita Olive Oil, Buick and the San Francisco Giants—and this doesn't even take into account our traditional hotel, airline, car rental and attraction partners that have been regulars with us for years.

Get with it: create an entrepreneurial spirit, look at advertisers already in the media you wish to be positioned in, seek them out as new cooperative partners, and watch your sales and marketing program grow by leaps and bounds.

Product Distribution and Technology

The CVB has traditionally acted as an intermediary between the consumer, professional travel trade, meeting planner and the various resources of the host community. While that premise hasn't changed, the dynamic nature of technology has created a new platform for community information and ultimate booking solutions for all concerned. Although printed materials about a destination certainly still exist, they are quickly being usurped by information that resides in an electronic environment.

It is a fact that travel remains the number one requested segment on the fast moving Internet. As a result, convention and visitor bureaus have little choice but to enhance their technology offerings or face the risk of becoming dis-intermediated in the sales and marketing process. If a bureau is to adequately represent its destination in the future, it will be an absolute necessity to be on the leading edge of technology.

Destinations, like their lodging and transportation partners, must be in a position to deliver information and services to the customer when and how they want it, 365/24/7. "One size doesn't fit all" has never been more relevant. General city information vehicles, encompassing hotel rates and amenities, meeting room specifications, transportation options and local attractions, along with their hours and pricing, will not only be informative, but bookable. Bureaus will need to establish and grow alliances with technology companies that will facilitate these bookings via the Internet. Many forward-thinking organizations are already doing this today, but it will become pervasive in the coming years.

A by-product of this technology revolution is the ability to track customers in a very direct and accessible way. Through technology, the CVB has the ability to talk to the customer about areas of particular interest to them. For example, if a customer has come to your Web site seeking information on fine dining or wine tasting, it's probably safe to assume that he or she has an interest in this area, and in fact may be what is referred to today as a "foodie." If that indeed is the case, the individual's name is collected in a niche bucket—he/she will be sent future information regarding similar offerings. In other words, the CVB can help attract business to the community by marketing directly to the consumer utilizing those areas of predetermined interest.

To develop this further, consumers will be able to opt-in to become part of a "community loyalty program," as currently exists with airlines, hotels, car rentals and cruise lines. We recently developed a program along this line in San Francisco called "Riley," a virtual tour guide to the city. To date, more than 40,000 people have opted-in to receive regular information from "Riley" about what's going on in San Francisco, thus providing compelling reasons, coupled with specific offers, to entice a return visit, soon! Exciting, interactive information is provided, including the appropriate links to facilitate booking the trip. We're just beginning to realize how significant this type of loyalty program can be for a city, and look forward to its continued growth and development in our city and elsewhere.

The area of convention housing is one that will continue to cause great consternation for CVBs, their members and convention planners. Typically, major conventions reserve large room blocks at hotels years prior to the actual meeting. On the surface this is good. The planner is guaranteed that sufficient rooms are under contract for the future convention, and the hotel can plan on filling a prescribed number of rooms over a given time period. Unfortunately, that's where the good ends. Because of the pervasiveness of product distribution via the Internet, hotels will often provide unsold rooms, not contracted for the convention, to online booking services at very reduced rates. This practice is commonly referred to as "dumping." In fact, these rates are often lower than the published rate guaranteed to the convention group prior to their meeting. The result is that the convention delegate may well have the ability to "go around the room block" and reserve a lower-priced room, at the same hotel or another, through a third-party booking service.

A few problems occur when this happens—a number of the contracted rooms between the meeting planner and hotel go unfilled, and there is no record of the attendee's use of a hotel room in the city, a fact that's often important in securing future space at the local convention center. Additionally, hotels have moved towards "attrition penalties" when contracted rooms go unfilled. The theory is simple. The meeting planner contracted for "x" number of rooms, but only "y" number was utilized. The hotel took these rooms out of the sales inventory for the convention, therefore the planner must pay the hotel just as though they had been used. Of course, the meeting planner replies that if the hotel hadn't made lower priced rooms available over the same dates this wouldn't have happened. I'm sure you get the picture—two unhappy campers, the meeting planner and the hotel executive. I guess the only winners, at least for the moment, are the convention attendee who paid less for the room, and the online broker that made the sale!

To counteract this trend, hotels and planners may have to build "incentives" for attendees to stay within the room block at the contracted rate.

Technology can work for you or against you, and in this case the convention and visitors bureau ends up in the middle, between the member hotel and convention planner. This problem will be solved in the coming years, but it will take the concerted effort of all parties. CVBs will have to readdress how the value of a convention to a city is measured. Is it by number of hotel room nights filled, total attendees or a new metric that has yet to be created? It will happen. Convention customers and hotel executives, with the help of the local CVB, will find a way to live in harmony, and yes, the Internet will ultimately be their friend!

Strategic Role in Product Development

In order for a destination to be successful into the next decade and beyond, it will take the leadership of many, including the local convention and visitors bureau. Product development is what will differentiate one destination from another. It will be essential to understand what community ingredients will be required to lure current visitors back, and encourage new ones to visit. In short, communities and their bureaus will need to better understand the customer, determine what they want, and, within reason, find a way to develop and deliver it. This could be as large and costly as building or expanding a convention center, or as simple and basic as packaging information that already exists about local history and museums. Both efforts have the potential to enhance the visitor experience, although they differ greatly from an investment perspective.

In the coming decade, CVBs will, by necessity, take a more prominent role in product development decisions within their community. With proper leadership, they'll actually help drive these initiatives. It will be important to look to the future with each step, and not attempt to simply cure current deficiencies, today.

In most communities, the bureau remains the responsible entity for strategically positioning the destination from a tourism perspective; therefore it's only fitting that the organization have a significant hand in shaping the future. With the trend towards "sameness" from city to city, it will become increasingly difficult, yet essential, to avoid becoming yet another "generic destination" where one's retail, restaurant and visitor experience replicates others, without distinction of location. It will, however, fall to the bureau and others to create unique points of difference and values that make the destination attractive to the visitor. If this process is to be effective, it will be necessary to become the "voice of the visitor" on all levels—what they desire, like or dislike about the destination.

Beyond product development, bureaus will need to insure that quality of life issues are addressed within the community, particularly given that the visitor has little voice and no vote, yet holds one powerful trump card: the ability to refuse to return to the destination.

As tourism positions itself to become the largest industry on Earth, the leading provider of jobs and economic growth in many communities, the industry, through the CVB as its spokesperson, will need to be prepared for the media scrutiny that will follow. History chronicles industries such as mining, forestry, fishing, and even technology as they glimmered, then shriveled, under the media spotlight. For significant and valid reasons, the most likely focus will be on whether or not we, in the travel and tourism industry, are "environmentally responsible." The debate will no doubt focus on land use, congestion and traffic, infrastructure requirements and the cost of public services.

Accountability, Education and Integrity

As the value and visibility of travel and tourism increases from town to town, all affected stakeholder groups will demand an increased emphasis on performance evaluation. Research vehicles will need to be developed to accurately measure the economic impact, and job creation, of the industry in a given community. Additionally, the effectiveness of the convention and visitor bureau will be measured against a clear return on investment (ROI) metric. This will come as the result of cities contracting with bureaus to provide promotional services utilizing public funds.

This paradigm shift will cause the organization to be more aggressive and results-oriented. Other stakeholders, including bureau members, cooperative partners and customers, will share similar performance expectations. Measurement, by its very nature, will take place in both good and bad times. It will be essential to maintain the highest degree of honesty and integrity, with all information that is presented. The news media and others will demand accurate, reliable, timely and comprehensive information.

Benchmarking will become of even greater importance as a measurement tool against "competitive set" cities in such broad areas as funding, membership, and organizational "best practices." Additionally, gauging the productivity of convention and tourism sales departments, and their individual sales managers, will provide insightful information to all stakeholders. Although significant disparities may exist between competitive destinations, the basic assumption of measurable ROI per sales manager is sound from one convention and visitors bureau to another.

Should complete accountability not be achieved, it is entirely possible that the bureau's funding sources may seek other alternatives to execute the community's sales and marketing function.

The escalating lack of trust in many public and private institutions, including a few bad decisions made by other convention and visitors bureaus along the way, will affect how we do business for a long time. The actions of bureau sales and marketing staff will need to be above reproach. In fact, if you have to question the appropriateness of an action, then it is probably inappropriate.

To further gain the support of the local community, the bureau will need to do a much better job of telling its story of how important the industry is to the economy of the city, and the essential role that the CVB plays in delivering the business. To accomplish this, a strong communication strategy will be required; however, these actions should prove helpful in securing long-term funding for the organization from the host city. The theory is simple. If local elected and appointed leaders understand the value of travel and tourism to the community, they're far more likely to continue to support the bureau's sales and marketing efforts.

Bottom line: Keep everyone informed of the industry's value. Report your results regularly and accurately. Educate the local community and politicians. Do all of this with a high degree of integrity and you are bound to succeed.

A Final Thought or Two

Most convention and visitors bureaus are structured as independent not-for-profit organizations. However, a few remain as divisions of the local chamber of commerce or a department of local government. In almost all cases, regardless of current structure, the key to success in the coming decade will be to act with an entrepreneurial spirit and a for-profit mentality. We're not in the business of charity. What bureaus do is relevant, essential to the economic well-being of the community, and affects the lives of countless people and their products.

In the future, fewer people will support the bureau because it's the right thing to do for the community, but rather will ask the question "What's in it for me?" That being said, bureaus will be compelled to adapt to the changing environment or run the risk of being something one only reads about in history books.

Yes, there will be profound changes in the distribution of the travel product, and yes, the local CVB will play an active role in the technology that makes all of that possible; and yes, accountability, integrity and community education will be essential to success. But at the end of the day, nothing will have changed. It's still "Bring in the business!"

17

New York City and Company

Cristyne L. Nicholas
President and CEO
NYC & Company

Cristyne L. Nicholas was appointed president and CEO of NYC & Company, formerly the New York Convention and Visitors Bureau (NYCVB), in October 1999.

NYC & Company's principal mission is to enhance New York City's economy through tourism development by promoting the city as the destination of choice for business and leisure travel. NYC & Company is a private nonprofit corporation with a current membership of more than 1,400 businesses and cultural organizations.

As a leader of one of New York's key industries, Ms. Nicholas has spearheaded numerous initiatives that have placed her at

the forefront of the efforts to revitalize New York City's $25 billion tourism industry following the events of September 11, 2001.

These initiatives include: creating the city's first-ever consumer television advertising campaign; crafting New York's first city-wide travel packages; relaunching NYC's official tourism Web site, www.nycvisit.com, and producing major citywide winter and summer marketing promotions. Ms. Nicholas has formulated innovative partnerships with major national corporate leaders, such as Delta Air Lines, American Express, Coca-Cola and the NFL to assist in marketing New York City. Understanding the importance of the convention sector to tourism, Ms. Nicholas has implemented aggressive programs to increase the number of meetings and conventions coming to New York, and has consistently advocated the need to expand the Jacob K. Javits Convention Center.

Prior to joining NYC & Company, Ms. Nicholas served in the administration of New York City Mayor Rudolph W. Giuliani as director of communications. In that capacity, she was charged with globally promoting New York's renaissance.

A Brooklyn native, Ms. Nicholas attended New York-area public schools and graduated from Rutgers University in 1987 with a bachelor of arts degree in political science and a minor in French. She began her career as a volunteer for Senator Bill Bradley and later served as New Jersey campaign spokesperson and press secretary for President George H.W. Bush. In addition to her career in public service, Ms. Nicholas has competed in the New York and Boston marathons and coached in the City Sports for Kids program.

Ms. Nicholas also heads the NYC & Company Foundation, a charitable and educational organization that promotes New York City by encouraging tourism through its arts and cultural organizations. She has recently been appointed to the International Association of Convention and Visitors Bureaus (IACVB) board of directors and to the arts, education and tourism advisory council of the Lower Manhattan Development Corporation. She has been named one of the 25 most influential people in the meetings industry by *Meeting News* and one of the most powerful women in travel for two consecutive years by *Travel Agent Magazine*. She has served as an adjunct professor at Baruch College and sits on the boards of the Yale Women's Campaign School, Big Apple Greeter, the Broadway Association, the New York University Tisch School for the Arts, the New York Society of Association Executives, and NYC2012, New York City's Olympic Committee.

She resides in Manhattan with her husband, golf writer Nick Nicholas, and their basset hound, Gabriella.

In the beginning of the 21st century, visitor destinations need to compete for travelers' dollars with greater intensity than ever before. As the travel industry continues to recover from September 11, increasing travel options, more competitive pricing and changing demographics are making the cost of complacency unacceptable. Constant innovation, diversification, infrastructure development and improvement of existing attractions are essential to the successful branding of a city as a premier tourism destination. Staying on top requires an increasingly market-oriented approach from convention and visitors bureaus.

New York City begins this competition for visitors from an enviable position. We are the world's second home. Recently, approximately 36 million people a year have come to our city to enjoy some of its 18,000 restaurants, countless retail stores, 39 Broadway theaters, 150 museums and six professional sports teams spread throughout the five boroughs of Manhattan, Brooklyn, the Bronx, Queens and Staten Island. With something for everyone, America's largest and most diverse city is a "no-compromises" destination for visitors of all ages from around the world.

But the quality of one's product is only half of the marketing equation; the other half is how to communicate its strengths and address its weaknesses. To succeed, destination cities, like any multi-billion-dollar product, need to successfully brand and market themselves to their customers.

For example, the transformation of New York City from what was considered the crime and grime capital of the country to what is today the safest large city in America has been key to the city's rising fortunes over the past ten years. Innovative policing strategies that focused on reducing quality of life crimes, which intimidated visitors and residents alike, allowed the city to cut crime dramatically beginning in the early 1990s.

But making the city safe wasn't enough. It was necessary to communicate. Only by repeating the safety message at every opportunity to the worldwide media over a period of years were we able to begin to change what had become a misperception: the now false idea that New York is dangerous.

From a tourism marketing perspective, it didn't matter whether or not the city was safe—what mattered was whether people around the world believed the city to be safe. Simple product development does nothing without the ability to communicate about it effectively.

That said, the best marketing and communications program is equally ineffective without a quality product to back it up. In the case of crime, each time visitors would return home from a trip to New York City, they would reinforce the message to their friends and family that the streets were indeed cleaner and safer. These visitors were the most credible emissaries of our message—if we were marketing something that wasn't true, eyewitness accounts would have quickly reversed all our hard work.

In the same way, following the events of September 11, our tourism marketing efforts focused on the fact that New York City was still open for business and was in fact stronger than ever. Thousands of visitors answered our call to visit and, by experiencing what was actually happening in New York at that time, they helped send a message through word of mouth and through the national and international media about the resilience our city. As a result, visitors began returning and many businesses that were struggling survived their most difficult winter season intact. Happily, we remain the nation's number one destination for international visitors.

Looking to the future, we at NYC & Company—the innovative public-private partnership established to promote the city's $25 billion tourism industry at low cost to taxpayers—are building on our new product strengths while continuing the effort to re-brand our city as the most diverse and inviting destination in the world.

Today, we are a city that has successfully embraced the 2004 Republican Convention and secured the U.S. candidate city status for the 2012 Olympic Games. Both these accomplishments will lead to continuing infrastructure improvements as well as tremendous opportunities to show off New York to worldwide television audiences.

Another major initiative is that of moving forward with the long-overdue expansion of the Jacob K. Javits Convention Center. Currently, New York City is automatically excluded from hosting the 65 largest conventions in the nation. Between 1999 and 2000, the Javits Center turned away 43 conventions that wanted to come to our city. We're literally losing billions of dollars annually because we can't accommodate the nation's largest conventions. The proposed Javits Center expansion will bring the exhibition hall space to a very competitive 1.6 million square feet, placing New York City among the top five convention cities in the United States.

The larger point is that even America's biggest city cannot afford to ignore any segment of the tourist or business travel industry. Nothing less than constant product development and improvement will keep you on top.

Diversity of Product— Travelers Want It All

A recent nationwide study by Mediamark Research Inc. showed that modern middle-class Americans enjoy watching professional wrestling and attending Rembrandt exhibitions. Hockey fans increasingly attend live theater and open-air concerts; football fans listen to jazz; rural Americans read *Forbes* and watch CNBC while readers of the *New Yorker* like to unwind with a beer while shooting a game of pool.

True to their generation's sense of independence, middle-aged Americans no longer feel constrained by traditional societal divisions. They want it all: instant access to both "high" and "low" entertainment and recreation while on a vacation. This is an insight Las Vegas has ridden to great profit in recent years with the proliferation of art galleries and satellite branches of established high-end restaurants that began in New York.

In turn, we have realized that offering the widest array of attractions will make New York City an even more desirable vacation destination for a wider array of visitors. For example, visitors to Times Square can visit a World Wildlife Federation (WFF) themed restaurant, eat at Virgil's Bar-B-Que or catch a basketball game on a wall-size screen at ESPN zone. They can then walk a block to catch the latest revival of "Gypsy," "La Boheme" or Eugene O'Neill's "Long Day's Journey Into Night."

The Importance of the Private Sector

Like major corporations, major destination cities must constantly focus on keeping their brand image up to date. For CVBs, this means using limited municipal dollars in more innovative ways, partnering with the private sector to promote their city and directing investment toward the development of new areas and assets. It also means anticipating the desires of tomorrow's visitors by studying today's demographic trends.

In times of consecutive years of billion-dollar governmental deficits, CVBs across America are being asked to do more with less. There is no use complaining about this condition. Instead we just have to meet the challenge. Increases in tourism benefit both local businesses and governments with more jobs, greater profits and more tax revenues. Thus it makes sense that public-private partnerships would begin to shoulder the promotional burden once believed to be the sole responsibility of the taxpayer.

At NYC & Company, we look out our office windows to the spectacle of Times Square for inspiration in this area. The well-documented resurgence of the crossroads of the world was built squarely upon increased partnerships between the city and visionary corporations such as Disney, which could look at what was one of the city's greatest challenges and see opportunity.

NYC & Company has an extended base of private sector partners ranging from small businesses to multinational corporations, each paying annual membership dues in exchange for inclusion in various promotions and outreach. Additionally, we have formed strategic alliances with well-known corporate brands such as American Express, Delta Air Lines and Coca-Cola, which provide additional resources and assistance with promoting New York City around the country and the world while they seek simultaneously to expand their own market presence and visibility.

Marketing to a Changing Audience

CVBs can also learn a valuable lesson from big business in the way we use demographic data. One of the most significant long-term trends facing the travel and tourism industry is the graying of America. Furthermore, our aging population is matched by population shifts throughout Europe and Asia, New York's two most significant sources of international travelers.

At NYC & Company, one of the ways we are adjusting to this shift is by emphasizing New York City's unparalleled cultural offerings—from internationally known museums to neighborhood art galleries, from an elegant dinner at a four-star restaurant to the unforgettable experience of live theater on a Broadway stage.

We have been bolstering our assets in this category with new events such as September's CultureFest, which brings together almost 100 of the city's best-known artistic and cultural offerings from all five boroughs in one central location, and June's Broadway Under the Stars, a free celebration of the stage and screen that kicks off the city's summer outdoor concert season.

New York is famous for its 24-hour energy. We're working to educate more travelers about the fact that our city is also home to some of the world's most relaxing day spas, romantic carriage rides, landmark historic sites, dozens of beautiful parks and 578 miles of coastline. New York is a memorable and exotic trip for anyone and for everyone.

The Importance of Value

While we're proud of New York City's reputation as a place where you can buy the best of everything, we cannot afford to ignore the growing value-consciousness of today's traveler. That's why we've organized annual events where New York's best restaurants offer *prix-fixe* meals from their famous menus during Restaurant Week in January and June, as well as Paint the Town—a promotion of savings packages with participating hotels, theaters, restaurants and museums throughout the traditionally slow winter months.

Attracting Repeat Visitors

When more than a hundred million people have visited your city in the last three years alone, it is important to give them a reason to come back. That's why we're working to promote the many exciting attractions in the neighborhoods outside of well-traveled midtown Manhattan. Much of New York's cultural riches lie in diverse neighborhoods scattered throughout the five boroughs that make up our city.

Brooklyn is home to some of our city's cutting-edge artistic neighborhoods as well as classic communities like Brooklyn Heights and hundreds of churches. The revival of Coney Island is in full swing with the third sold-out season of the minor-league Brooklyn Cyclones (named after the famous roller coaster still open for business a few hundred yards down the boardwalk). New interest in this historic borough has been encouraged by the opening of the first new hotel built in downtown Brooklyn in 50 years, the Marriott at the Brooklyn Bridge, the success of which supports the idea that if you build it, they will come.

The surprise is not the increased commercial and visitor interest in boroughs like Brooklyn and Queens, but that these assets were not developed long ago. When you consider the fact that more people live in our least populous borough, Staten Island, than live in St. Louis, you begin to understand the depth of our city. Exploring the many community jewels off the beaten path gives longtime lovers of New York another reason to visit New York again "for the first time."

Improving the Visitor Product

In the same way that the opening of the new downtown Brooklyn Marriott has encouraged more people to visit that area of our city, we are aware that constantly improving our infrastructure promises to bring increasing numbers of visitors to our city in the coming years. The selection of New York as the official U.S. candidate city for the 2012 Olympic Games promises to set off a spate of infrastructure improvements such as improved access to our waterfront, new public transportation options and state-of-the-art sporting facilities that can attract major events before, during and after the Olympics.

The overall picture is of a dynamic growing city that has only begun to tap the real depths inherent in its communities. The diversity of experiences available to travelers in this single destination means that we are well-positioned to take advantage of the demographic trends that will transform the tourism industry while increasingly leveraging its already impressive benefits to local businesses and government alike.

New York City's best days are still ahead of us. A glance at the plans already in place to improve our ability to accommodate more visitors here on business and pleasure gives us reason to feel confident as we look to the future. The restless spirit of reinvention and constant improvement that built New York from a group of villages into the capital of the global village will continue as we head into the 21st century.

18

Branson, Missouri

Steven L. Presley, President
Presley Communications, LLC

In 1967, 10-year-old Steve Presley began his career as a performer in Branson's original music theater on Highway 76. As the Branson area grew into a national destination attracting more than seven million visitors annually, Steve became a respected community leader and representative for all that the town has to offer.

Numerous organizations in the Branson area have looked to Steve for his expertise in tourism marketing. Dedicated to the tourism industry, he has served as president of the Ozark Marketing Council, producing several successful marketing programs to increase the number of visitors to Branson. As president, he led the development of a multimillion-dollar marketing partnership between Branson and General Motors. In addition, Steve chaired the marketing council responsible for a substantial First USA and Branson Visa promotional campaign.

He is past chairman of the marketing advisory council for the Branson/Lakes Area Chamber of Commerce, and currently heads up the advertising council for the Branson/Lakes Area Convention and Visitors Bureau.

Throughout the explosive growth of Branson, Steve's constant anchor has been his love of performing on stage nightly with his family. Today, as co-producer of Presleys' Country Jubilee, he still performs over 200 shows a year. Off stage, he is president of Presley Communications, LLC, and vice president of Presleys', Inc., which coordinates the marketing, program for Presleys' Country Jubilee.

Steve married his wife, Raeanne, in 1976. They have three children: Nick, John and Sarah.

What will Branson, Missouri look like in the next 10 years? That is a very challenging question our community continues to ask. The biggest obstacle as a public entity is that we have very little control of product development. This is still very much a private sector decision on new attractions and new entertainers that perform in the theaters. What we are able to do is provide up-to-date, accurate research data to new or existing companies that are considering investing in Branson as a vacation destination. We feel that this information is critical to our community in answering the question that any mature tourism destination faces: "What do you have that's new?"

One answer to that question is a new theme park called Celebration City that opened in 2003. This park was developed by Silver Dollar City as an evening attraction to complement their daytime park. The target for this park is young families and young adults—it features a giant wooden roller coaster as its main amusement ride. It also presents the Midwest's largest laser light show on a giant water curtain.

Another project that's in development is in the city's control. The city recently purchased over 20 acres of the property adjacent to Lake Taneycomo in downtown Branson. This, in addition to the 50 plus acres already controlled, will provide space for a sizeable project. The development will most likely be a public/private partnership. Preliminary designs call for a boardwalk along the lake with a themed plan of shopping and entertainment. It may also include a city-owned convention center. One current challenge in the development of convention business is adequate air service. The Springfield/Branson Regional Airport is located approximately one hour away from downtown Branson. The distance is less of a deterrent than the small size of the airport. Fortunately, a new terminal is in the design stages, but it will not be built for another five years. Thanks to that limitation, the short-term target for convention business is the drive market located within a 500-mile radius.

In developing our future marketing plans, we must understand whom we are competing against for travel dollars. For the past two years our main competitors have been Las Vegas, Nevada; Orlando, Florida; Gatlinburg, Tennessee; and Myrtle Beach, South Carolina. These destinations continue to compete with Branson. Another, much stronger, competitor is the cruise ship industry. With cruise ships now departing out of ports in the Midwest such as Houston and New

Orleans, it is much closer and inexpensive than in the past for our regional customers to embark on a cruise instead of visiting us. Both Branson and the cruise industry are working to position their product to a younger audience.

One disadvantage for Branson is that we have never been a destination that is sold by travel agents. This is where we will strategically use the Internet to our advantage. As Generations X and Y start to travel with their young families, they are much more inclined to use the Internet for their travel needs. Whether they are seeking information for their vacation or booking reservations, the Web plays a much bigger role for them. Fortunately for Branson, we can use this to our advantage. It is considerably less expensive to be visible on the Internet with proper placement on search engines than it is to buy television or print advertising. With our limited budget, we will continue to purchase television advertising, but will support that with a strong Internet campaign.

An example of one campaign is the use of innovative URL names to stay current and look fresh to the customer. The site we have chosen to use for our marketing partner campaign is www.Branson2003.com. We have also secured sites for future use, i.e. Branson2004, Branson2005. We feel this projects an up-to-date image to use in our ads. Of course, we will retain all past sites in future years and route them to the current year's site.

As Branson moves forward into the 21st century, we are taking a hard look at the perception of the brand of our community. In competing for the leisure traveler, we are working to shake the image that Branson is the place your grandparents go on vacation. In all of our paid media, we are very careful to keep a youthful look that includes a mix of families and young adults, but we still intersperse our ads and presentations with youthful-looking 50-year-old adults. We do not want to alienate this mature audience, because spring and fall are great times for these empty nesters to visit. In recent years, this approach would seem to be working—we have seen the average age of our visitors drop from the late 50s to the early 50s. We have also seen a significant percentage increase of families in our overall visitor mix.

We are also in a wonderful position to target the new generations of families that will be traveling over the next couple of decades. With the growth of eco-tourism, Branson can offer a variety of experiences to the vacationing family. Most of Branson's attractions and shows are located along the ten-mile strip of Highway 76, but the beautiful scenery of the Ozarks surrounds us. This allows for us to continue to develop the area surrounding Branson and still offer miles and miles of the great outdoors for hiking, biking and kayaking. We feel it is a strong competitive message.

19

Las Vegas: To Brand the New Destination

Manuel J. Cortez
President and CEO
Las Vegas Convention
and Visitors Authority

Manuel J. "Manny" Cortez has been a Las Vegas resident since 1944. He began his service on the Las Vegas Convention and Visitors Authority (LVCVA) board of directors in 1983 and was chairman from 1985 through 1990. On July 2, 1991, he became president of the LVCVA, the largest convention and visitors organization in the United States. That year, Southern Nevada tracked visitor volume at just over 21 million. Visitor volume has grown significantly since that time, reaching 35.1 million leisure travelers and convention delegates in 2002.

Travel Agent magazine named Mr. Cortez the United States Person of the Year for 1999, calling him "one of the most astute marketers in the tourism industry." During his tenure as president of the LVCVA, the organization was consistently honored at the World Travel Awards. In 2000, the LVCVA received numerous WTA honors, including the World's Leading Convention & Tourist Bureau and the World's Leading Conference and Convention Center.

Mr. Cortez and the LVCVA have also been honored with awards from *Facilities Magazine*, the Government Finance Officers Association, *Meetings & Conventions* magazine, *Successful Meetings*, *Incentive Magazine* and the American Society of Travel Agents, among others.

Elected in 1976 to the Clark County Commission, Mr. Cortez went on to serve four terms, during which time he was chairman of the county commission as well as chairman of the Clark County Sanitation District and the Clark County Liquor and Gaming Licensing Board. He was also on the governing boards of the University Medical Center and the Las Vegas Valley Water District and on the Fiscal Affairs Board of the Las Vegas Metropolitan Police Department. Prior to taking office as a county commissioner, Mr. Cortez served as administrator of the state taxicab authority, by appointment of the governor. His background also includes employment with the Clark County District Attorney and the Clark County Public Defender.

Mr. Cortez was a participant in the White House Conference on Travel and Tourism in 1995. In addition to other tourism industry affiliations, he currently serves on the board of directors for the Travel Industry Association of America. He is also active on several community boards and associations.

Las Vegas was built on odds. Through the years, it has been delighted to defy them.

The city is a cacophony of color, of swirling sights and sounds. It is a place where stunning resort hotels—each its own destination—rise dramatically from the desert floor. Las Vegas is a study in human imagination.

It is a place with 18 of the 20 largest hotels in the United States and 127,000 hotel rooms, more than any city in the world. It is a place where you walk down the street and marvel at striking replicas of an Egyptian pyramid, the Sphinx, Venice and the Eiffel Tower, improbable neighbors to an erupting volcano and dancing waters. It is a place where time appears suspended but, at the same time, rushes forward.

In retrospect, there was a seminal event that helped to shape the destiny of the "Entertainment Capital of the World"—the Nevada State Legislature legalized gambling in 1931.

After the war, and through the 1950s, Las Vegas became engrained in the public consciousness as a neon-lit jewel in the desert. The Rat Pack held court and reigned supreme here, and the names of countless other show business luminaries brightened hotel marquees along the ever-growing Strip and downtown. Neon lights punctuated desert nights.

Neither clocks, nor time, nor sleep mattered much. People played craps on a floating green felt table in a sun-soaked hotel swimming pool, rubbed shoulders with celebrities, and slept in. It was all here, and all within reach.

During these times, Las Vegas pretty much fed off its own reputation, and the public's need to escape. There wasn't much in the way of a sophisticated marketing effort—nor in the way of any comprehensive marketing effort, for that matter. Las Vegas was "marketed," if that's the right word, through news coverage of people and events that took place here. The public fascination with anything Las Vegas goes back a long way: a Las Vegas dateline on a news item, or photo, was solid gold to members of the media. Then, as now, America's appetite for anything Las Vegas is insatiable.

Many of the classic images of Las Vegas—Sinatra and the boys in smoky showrooms, Elvis and Liberace on stage swapping musical instruments, the frenetic casinos, the cheesecake pictures—were both captured and staged by a group of creative public relations executives and photographers at hotel properties, along with those who worked at the Las Vegas News Bureau, then part of the chamber of commerce, and now part of the Las Vegas Convention and Visitors Authority (LVCVA).

More than anything, these photos, distributed via wire services and printed in newspapers and magazines around the world, defined Las Vegas for subsequent generations of visitors. If a picture's worth a thousand words, then the thousands of pictures that the bureau fed to a hungry public spoke volumes about the nature of this resort town. Which is to say: This is a place unlike any other, anywhere.

Mixing Business with Pleasure

The 1950s brought unprecedented prosperity to America, and Las Vegas continued to benefit from both a strong economy and a lingering post-war need to celebrate. Even so, leisure travel is nothing if not cyclical, and that affected Las Vegas to a fairly large degree. Hotel operators found that, while business was strong on weekends, weekdays sometimes presented a challenge.

Out of this scenario came a decision by the 1955 Nevada State Legislature to form the Clark County Fair and Recreation Board, the precursor to the LVCVA. It would be funded by a newly instituted five percent tax on hotel and motel rooms; with this money, the LVCVA would promote Las Vegas on an ongoing, comprehensive basis. Room tax dollars would also be used to build and operate the Las Vegas Convention Center. The thinking was: If Las Vegas would spend real money promoting itself, and if it could attract convention business, it would be much stronger overall as a destination.

A convention industry was born. And so, too, was the LVCVA. Today the LVCVA is recognized as one of the premier tourism and convention marketing organizations in the world. The LVCVA's primary mission is to fill hotel and motel rooms in Clark County, which encompasses a sizable chunk of Southern Nevada. Under the direction of its 13-member board of directors, including seven elected officials and six resort industry executives, the LVCVA fulfills its mission by marketing Las Vegas around the globe. The organization also owns and operates the Las Vegas Convention Center (now 3.2 million square feet) and Cashman Center, a multiuse convention and entertainment facility.

Building a Winning Team

The LVCVA's marketing division has about 100 members—of a total of about 500 LVCVA employees—and an annual budget of nearly $85 million; about $60 million of that is spent on advertising. The LVCVA still receives a large part of its budget through the countywide room tax, which now stands at nine percent, retaining slightly less than half of this money (the remainder used by local government for infrastructure needs). The rest of the LVCVA's budget is derived principally from facility rental revenue.

Since a large part of our budget comes from room tax dollars generated by visitors, as our resort industry and room inventory have grown, so has our ability to market the destination. It's been a wonderful domino effect. More rooms have meant more dollars to market Las Vegas, and, consequently, we have been able to fill more rooms. This financial structure has enabled us to do something most other destinations could not: we have doubled our room inventory in the 10 years ending in 2003, and at the same time have maintained our occupancy levels. (Average citywide occupancy levels stood at 84 percent in 2003, about 24 points above the national average. Many hotel properties in Las Vegas—exceeding 3,000 rooms—commonly have annual occupancy levels that surpass 90 percent.)

Today the LVCVA's marketing division continues to look for new ways to respond not only to changing market conditions, but to changes within the local marketplace. (In this case, encompassing Clark County in Southern Nevada, all of which is the LVCVA's area of responsibility. This includes the Las Vegas metropolitan area, as well as Laughlin, a resort town on the Colorado River about 90 miles south of Las Vegas; Primm, on the California-Nevada state line, about 40 miles south of Las Vegas; and the resort town of Mesquite, about 80 miles north of the city.)

The division is composed of the following departments:

- Marketing services

- Convention/corporate incentive sales

- Domestic/wholesalers, international tourism

- Special events

- Consumer/trade advertising

- Public relations

- Research

- Internet

All entities work closely together, as well as with representatives of the resort community, to reinforce the Las Vegas brand.

Ultimately, everything is based on research. Virtually every advertising and marketing campaign that the LVCVA has done in the past 30 years is born out of extensive research. From its relatively modest roots in the early 1970s, the LVCVA research department now budgets about $1 million each year to test the waters of the marketplace and get input from, and give visitor data to, the Las Vegas resort community (especially metrics on consumers' attitudes and behaviors). This includes primary and secondary research, visitor profile studies, intercept studies, data collection and dissemination, ongoing tracking studies, phone surveys to measure consumer awareness, and surveys of attendees at special events (many of which the LVCVA sponsors).

It is all done in close concert with the LVCVA's longtime advertising agency, Las Vegas-based R&R Partners, as well as with entities such as the Nevada Gaming Control Board, McCarran International Airport, the Nevada Department of Transportation, the Las Vegas Chamber of Commerce, and the Nevada Development Authority. The relationship between the LVCVA and R&R Partners spans more than two decades, and is arguably one of the most successful such marriages in destination marketing.

Fast Forward in a Very Fast City

Las Vegas' resort industry has changed in ways that are unprecedented in the history of the leisure and business travel industry. In 2002, Las Vegas hosted 35 million visitors, who collectively pumped nearly $32 billion into the local economy. Las Vegas' visitor volume has increased by 12 million people a year in just the past decade.

The number and scope of new properties that have opened here in just the past 15 years is mind-boggling, as is the money invested by the resort industry.

Las Vegas' "newest" modern era began at the end of the 1980s, with the opening of the 4,000-room Excalibur and the 3,000-room Mirage (it's worth noting that one of the original and successful "theme" hotels, Caesars Palace, was built more than 20 years before that). Since it had been more than a decade since a major resort hotel had opened on the Las Vegas Strip, these properties began to fundamentally redefine Las Vegas—and spawned a flurry of construction not seen anywhere else.

Just four years later, in 1993, in the space of just months, the megaresorts Luxor, Treasure Island (now called "T.I.") and MGM Grand opened. Between them they have nearly 11,000 hotel rooms, more than in many American cities, and they again took Las Vegas to another level.

The nature of these properties, and the fact they opened in such a short period of time, led many to believe that Las Vegas was suddenly trying to transform itself into a "family" destination. But that was never really the intention of the resort industry in Southern Nevada.

Says LVCVA Executive Vice President Rossi Ralenkotter: "We are the destination marketers, and we have never actively pursued the family market. We don't discourage it per se, but we have always been primarily an adult destination. The megaresorts that opened in the late 1980s and 1990s were really 'entertainment centers.' They had something for everyone, but, remember, they were still hotel-casinos that catered to adults."

In the late 1990s and into 2000, more megaresorts came on line: the Bellagio, Mandalay Bay, the Venetian, Paris and the Aladdin. These represented some 15,000 rooms and several billion dollars in capital investment. These properties, too, redefined the concept of resort hotel.

Selling the Dream

As Las Vegas evolved, the way it marketed itself did, too, and that has prompted a sea change in the evolving public perception of the destination.

Las Vegas was changing, all the while becoming more of a multidimensional resort destination, because the competition had changed. Until the late 1970s, Nevada had a monopoly on legalized casino gaming in the United States. The competitive landscape now is a vastly different place. Indian reservation casinos, riverboat casinos, other land-based casinos . . . some 35 states now have some form of casino gaming. Forty-eight states have some form of gaming, including lotteries and horse tracks.

It used to be that, if you wanted to legally gamble in a casino in the United States, you had to come to Nevada. That changed forever, of course, in the late

1970s, when Atlantic City built its first casinos. Industry observers were saying at the time: "Las Vegas could be in trouble. A quarter of the United States population lives on the East Coast, just a few hours' drive from Atlantic City. Why would anyone get on a plane and fly across the country to gamble in a casino, when Atlantic City is right in their back yard?" (Perhaps there had never been a time before when state leaders' prescience in forming the precursor to the LVCVA in the mid-1950s was more in evidence. Nevada's monopoly on legalized gaming was gone forever; it wouldn't be long before the competitive floodgates opened fully. Having an organization whose singular responsibility was to proactively and aggressively brand and market the entire destination suddenly became vital.)

Las Vegas had begun its first comprehensive market research in the early 1970s, and also had started television advertising for the first time. Research formally identified key feeder markets, chief among them Southern California (then and now). Market research essentially laid the foundation for all advertising and marketing programs that were to come. Resort industry leaders recognized that it was vital that Las Vegas be able to respond quickly and effectively to whatever challenges arose. The advent of casino gaming in Atlantic City was certainly one, and perhaps the biggest challenge Las Vegas had ever faced. The LVCVA responded with a multimedia national marketing campaign, "Nobody Does It Better," in the early 1980s.

Las Vegas had met Atlantic City's challenge, but then there appeared another form of competition: a national recession that refused to go away. Consumers were watching their discretionary travel dollars carefully, and wanted reassurance that they were receiving value for their money. The LVCVA unveiled another national advertising campaign, calling Las Vegas "The Resort Bargain of the World."

The remarkable thing about Las Vegas, in any event, is its resiliency: its ability not only to survive, but thrive, given so many changes and challenges on the competitive landscape.

The way we market Las Vegas today, the messages we're sending out, are much different than just a few years ago. But then, Las Vegas is so different nowadays. It used to be that Las Vegas was seen as a destination with one or two primary facets: gaming and entertainment. Now we're a world-class destination for dining, shopping, golf, special events, health spas, etc. Inherent in all of our advertising and marketing messages is that, while Las Vegas is an adult destination, it has something for everyone.

We don't have to tell the public that there are casinos here. What we tell them these days is that you have to come to Las Vegas for the Las Vegas experience. It simply cannot be replicated anywhere else.

Meeting the Challenges

The tragic events of September 11, 2001, of course, presented by far the biggest challenge in history to the nation's travel industry. Immediately after the tragedy, Las Vegas pulled all of its advertising. A number of intense strategy sessions, concurrent with exhaustive research and focus groups, led a few weeks later to a series of television spots showing images of visitors in Las Vegas and featuring the previously unreleased Frank Sinatra song, "It's Time For You." The spots, which had undergone extensive focus group testing, were aired in drive-in and short-haul airline markets. They worked because they managed to strike the right tone during a very difficult time. Also during this period, the LVCVA significantly stepped up its Internet marketing efforts.

During extraordinary times, Las Vegas' resiliency was again in evidence. Though recovery was slow, it was steady; it became apparent once again that one of Las Vegas' strengths was its "newness" as a destination—that is to say, all of the new resort hotels and other amenities and attractions made Las Vegas a very desirable place to visit once people began traveling again.

Las Vegas' recovery was also aided greatly by the fact that, once it was again appropriate to be out in the marketplace, Las Vegas was the first major destination in the United States to be up and running with an entirely new marketing and advertising campaign. What would normally have taken months took a matter of a few short weeks. The message was that it was OK to get away, to escape for a few days—and Las Vegas was the perfect place in which to do that.

All the while, Las Vegas' target audiences were expanding. There was a time when nearly half of all visitors to the "Entertainment Capital" came from Southern California. Not surprisingly, most advertising and marketing efforts—TV, radio, print, outdoor—were focused there. While it's true that California is still by far Las Vegas' largest feeder market, accounting for almost a third of the 35 million visitors last year, the resort now has become a truly international destination. More than 3 million visitors last year came from other countries. Las Vegas still views the international marketplace as having great growth potential in the future.

Our sales teams are grouped under separate "tourism" and "meetings" umbrellas, corresponding to the two distinctly different audiences we are trying to reach. The message to prospective leisure travelers, and the means by which that message is delivered, are not the same as the message and delivery method used to address those responsible for planning corporate meetings, trade shows and conventions.

The LVCVA has official representatives in Chicago, Washington, D.C., and Laughlin, as well as in the United Kingdom, Germany, France, Australia, Korea and Japan. Industry leaders include trade shows, client appreciation events, educational seminars, media/industry familiarization trips, and many others. The tourism team actively markets the destination to prominent industry associations, travel agents, tour operators and wholesalers, among others, throughout the world.

On the meetings side, marketing efforts reinforce Las Vegas as the world's premier destination for corporate meetings, conventions and trade shows. "We Work As Hard As We Play" is the tag line for Las Vegas' campaign to attract conventions to its nine million square feet of meeting space. (The LVCVA sells space in the Las Vegas Convention Center, and also works with the resort industry to fill meeting space citywide. In 2003, the LVCVA sent out 3,000 business leads to other convention facilities and resort hotels citywide.) Corporate meeting planners, associations and other groups are regularly courted by the LVCVA's offices in Las Vegas, Washington, D.C. and Chicago.

The campaign is based primarily on trade print advertising, direct mail pieces and industry and client events. It underscores the fact that, while Las Vegas means business when it comes to the meetings themselves—more than five million convention delegates came to the destination in 2002, pumping more than $6 billion into the local economy—it also offers more nighttime entertainment and lodging options than any other destination. (Another way to look at it: Las Vegas has a world-class airport, more hotel rooms, more meeting space and more professional support staff than any other major convention city. It also has Danny Gans and Wayne Newton.)

We've got a great product to sell on the leisure and business travel sides, but that doesn't mean we can afford to be cavalier. Las Vegas is competing with everyone and everything: every major convention city—and these competitors are ambitiously expanding their facilities—along with domestic and international destinations, Indian reservation casinos, cruise lines, theme parks, you name it.

20

How Disney Targets the Family Vacation Market

Randy A. Garfield, President
Walt Disney Travel Company

Randy A. Garfield, CTC, is president of the Walt Disney Travel Company, and executive vice president of sales and travel operations for Walt Disney Parks and Resorts. Garfield heads up one of the country's largest travel wholesalers, marketing a variety of packages for travel to Disney resorts in Florida and California. He leads the worldwide sales efforts for the Walt Disney World Resort, Disneyland Resort, Disney Vacation Club and Disney Cruise Line.

He is also responsible for the development of theme park and resort packaged products, manages the central reservations operation, and provides leadership to Walt Disney World Sports and Recreation.

Walt Disney revolutionized the concept of the American family vacation when he opened the world's first theme park in 1955. At the time, Walt's "Saturdays with the girls" consisted of taking his daughters to various amusement locations from fairs to carnivals that were great fun for his kids, but not experiences he could enjoy with them.

Much has changed in the travel industry since Walt's pioneering contribution almost 50 years ago. Likewise, the American family has also changed.

In 1955, the nuclear American family consisted of a married couple with 2.2 kids. By 2000, the "average" family had changed dramatically, and now reflects a vast series of diverse possibilities.

With those demographic changes have come dramatic shifts in the way Americans vacation. Today, travelers are more diverse—in their composition, in their age and in their ethnicity. To be successful in reaching these guests, the tourism industry will have to cast aside the "one-size-fits-all" approach that's been popular in the past and transition to a strategy of segmentation that's as diverse as the markets the industry is eager to target.

The "family segment" offers a great deal of opportunity provided a destination leverages the right communication message featuring the right product with the right offer to the appropriate market.

Those trends have been further compounded by the economic and psychological challenges of the early part of this new century. The tragic events of September 11 and the acts of terrorism across the world have resulted in a craving for increased interaction with friends and family.

Today, the "traditional family"—married with children—represents only 24 percent of all U.S. households according to Census 2000 data. And while 73 percent of those family types took at least one vacation together in 2000, they do not represent the bulk of American family travelers. Of all adults who took one vacation with a family member in 2000, fewer than one-third (30 percent) fit the married-with-children mold.

What's emerging is a family travel market that includes a growing number of nontraditional family types: grandparent travel, multigenerational travel, single parent travel and friends-and-family travel. To properly target these segments, travel suppliers will not only have to change their traditional "one-size-fits-all" advertising messages, but their pricing, packaging and accommodation offerings will have to change as well.

Grandparent Travel

The significance of the Baby Boomers—comprising the more than 77 million Americans born between 1946 and 1964—has been well documented for decades. With the dawning of a new century comes a new life stage for this generation, which enters the "mature" years healthier, more active, better educated, more affluent and better traveled than any other age group before it. In 2001, this segment generated the highest travel volume in the United States, registering more than 248 million trips, according to Travel Industry Association of America (TIA).

Naturally, as this sizeable market transitions, there will be a significant rise in grandparent-hood. By 2010, more than 80 million Americans—about one-third of all adults—will be grandparents, according to AARP.

Like grandparents throughout history, Boomers tend to dote on their grandchildren. In the past decade, annual spending on grandchildren has increased 56 percent—from an average of $320 in 1992 to $500 in 2002. But rather than use that money to buy "things" for their grandchildren, Boomers are increasingly looking to invest those funds in *experiences* they can enjoy with them.

Baby Boomers were the first generation to travel extensively. Having enjoyed the enriching benefits of travel firsthand, they are eager to introduce their grandchildren to the social and educational advantages of visiting abroad, with the fringe benefit that travel with grandchildren will provide meaningful memories.

According to a study by the TIA, grandparent travel represented 20 percent of all trips taken with children in 2000, up significantly from just 13 percent in 1999. Twenty-one percent of grandparents take their grandkids on at least one leisure trip (without their parents) each year.

Since, in most cases, grandparents have more than one grandchild, and because the average Baby Boomer is likely to have as much as 30 years of grandparenting ahead of them, there is also the prospect of high repeat business.

According to Helena Koenig, grandchildren and grandparents are natural-born travel companions.

"These two generations enjoy the most fabulous relationship there is. There are no expectations. And, their acceptance of one another makes them incredibly compatible, which makes for a fantastic vacation," says Koenig.

A grandparent herself, Koenig knows firsthand that grandparents have traveled a great deal, and have an appreciation of other cultures they're eager to share with their grandchildren. With that pairing in mind, Koenig launched her organization, Grandtravel, in 1986, by offering four escorted trips annually. Today, her organization escorts more than 40 tour groups per year to more than 27 world destinations, including native American sites in the southwest United States; the Alaskan wilderness; estates and castles in England, Scotland and Ireland; and wildlife preserves in Kenya.

And while the concept is clear, the implementation is not easy. Koenig attributes her success to keeping the tour groups small and organized, and to sending along a teacher with every group (so that the kids have someone to help them appreciate the culture from their level).

"Grandparents know that meeting new people and seeing new places in the company of someone who loves you is the best way for grandchildren to learn about the world and to gather the skills they will need to keep it wonderful."

Multigenerational Travel

Not just Boomers have caught the travel bug. A renewed dedication to spending quality time with the family is also resulting in an increase in multigenerational or intergenerational travel. Grandparents, parents, kids, in-laws, aunts, uncles and cousins are variously vacationing together. Vacations are becoming a great "excuse" for people to come together, as families move away from their hometowns and become dispersed across the United States.

A Meredith Travel Marketing study revealed that about four in 10 family members (38 percent) who have traveled with three generations on the same trip in 2001 say they will take more vacations with the family over the next five years, up from 30 percent who expressed that intent in 1999.

Multigenerational travel is also expected to get a boost from the shift in the ethnic make-up of the country. Strong family ties and a desire to please their children are common motivators in the African-American and Hispanic segments, two markets experiencing growth in both numbers and buying power. In fact, a pleasure travel poll of 1299 Americans conducted by the marketing firm Yesawich Pepperdine & Brown showed that 60 percent of blacks and 51 percent of other nonwhites (including Hispanics) plan to take at least one family vacation with children in the next 12 months, compared with 25 percent of whites.

For her 8th birthday, Amber Johnson enjoyed a celebration with "All-American" flare—a trip to the nation's capital. Escorting her to the historical treasures and museums in Washington, DC were her mother and grandmother.

"I had the opportunity to extend a business trip, and arranged for my daughter and mother-in-law to join me for a long weekend," said Vicki Johnson. "Watching my daughter soak in the historical and political significance of Washington DC was amazing. Knowing she'll always remember seeing it for the first time with her mom and her nana made it priceless."

"It might have been her birthday, but there's no doubt in my mind that I experienced the greater gift," said Betty Jane Johnson, Amber's "nana" and a former teacher who says she qualifies as a "mature adult." "Our children and grandchildren provide us some of the most enriching life lessons, and traveling with my daughter-in-law and my granddaughter delivered more than I could have ever anticipated. I can't wait until we do it again."

Single Parent Travel

Single parent travel is another emerging family travel segment. According to the U.S. Census Bureau, the number of single parent households increased 20 percent in the past decade, from 7.7 million in 1990 to almost 9.4 million in 2000. In addition, this segment is being augmented as busy parents are vacationing with the kids (but minus their spouse), and by doting aunts and uncles eager to travel with nieces and nephews. The percentage of all trips taken with children that consisted of just one adult chaperone jumped from 30 percent to 38 percent between 1990 and 1999, according to TIA.

While it may be true that on average single parents have less money than two-parent families, the industry cannot ignore this segment. Single parents are particularly distressed by the traditional industry concept of double adult occupancy package pricing. Quality Time Travel is a New York-based travel agency that targets this niche by offering a list of vacation destinations and resorts that offer single occupancy rates and top-notch children's programs. In addition, several resorts, like the Eastover Resort in Lenox, Massachusetts, have recently begun to feature dedicated weekends that offer single parents the opportunity to mingle with one another.

Julie Heizer is vice president of tourism for the Washington D.C. Convention and Tourism Corporation. In addition to heading up the marketing efforts for the nation's capital, she also represents a growing travel niche—nontraditional family travel. Heizer, who spends eight to 10 weeks a year on the road, has a travel arrangement with three of her nieces that she hopes will introduce them to a "lifetime of travel."

Walt Disney World was the destination of choice for Heizer's initial excursion with the girls minus their parents; a place the girls—14, 11 and 9 at the time—had never visited. The trip was two years in the making, during which Heizer made them allocate half of any money they received as a gift for the Disney vacation fund. And while the $200 they saved didn't cover the cost of the trip, it did allow them to tip the skycap $4 for handling their bags, to pay for the afternoon snack they were anxious to purchase, and to reinforce the concept that "Saving for something you really want is worth the effort," said Heizer.

"What an incredible experience it was for them," she said. "It introduced some of the nuances of travel—the fact that people have to make a concerted effort to save for vacations, tip for service provided, etc."

Heizer now plans to take the concept one step further. For each niece's 16th birthday, Heizer's gift will be a trip to any U.S. destination they select. The deal gets sweeter when her nieces turn 18—that's when Heizer has promised a trip anywhere in the world.

Friends & Family Travel

Not to be left out, Generation X—consisting of Americans born between 1965 and 1977—is establishing an emerging travel niche of its own. Call it the "Friends" factor (after the popular TV show). An increasing number of such younger Americans are traveling together and not just with friends, but with families.

Gen-Xers were the first generation to be dramatically shaped by divorce. Between 1970 and 1990, the number of children living only with their mothers doubled from 11 percent to 22 percent. For this reason, Gen-Xers have an expanded definition of family that encompasses new lifestyles such as cohabitation, same-sex partnerships, and communities of close friends.

With a feeling she's neglected the great places her home state has to offer, Nikki Botwinik is undertaking a maneuver that will offer tremendous value to her group of friends and family. Botwinik, a Gen Xer who entered the ranks of fulltime motherhood in 2002, is coordinating a monthly outing to some of the Sunshine State's old-time attractions and off-the-beaten path alternatives.

On the fourth Saturday of each month, Botwinik and as many as 40 members of her Central Florida-based circle of family and friends spend the afternoon at locations such as Ybor City and Edison's Home in Ft. Myers or experiencing an airboat ride for the first time. The group is predominately Gen Xers—some with children, others without—eager to experience areas of Florida they've heard about, but have never gone out of their way to visit. Right now, people coordinate their own means of travel to the month's designated location, but with the research and communication legwork being done for them, Botwinik thinks the assembly will eventually grow to a size that will dictate dedicated transportation.

The Right Product

Regardless of the composition of the traveling party, to successfully sell to the family market, suppliers have to be prepared to navigate through all of the diverse needs, generational expectations and the unique makeup of families of all shapes and sizes. The key to successfully meeting the diverse requirements of a family's wish list is to deliver a vacation that matches *all* of these expectations. Historically, when planning a vacation with young children, parents typically put the needs of the kids first. But it doesn't have to be that way. More adults are finding ways to cater to the needs of all the members in the traveling party.

Cruise vacations are all-inclusive and all-encompassing. From rock climbing to ballroom dancing (with menu items from lobster to fish sticks), today's products offer even more for people of all ages—especially families. Not to mention all the exotic destinations that a cruise ship can safely take families to without missing out on all the comforts of home.

Since Disney Cruise Line's entry into the cruise business in 1998, major cruise lines have become increasingly focused on catering to families with children. Lines that had traditionally targeted older passengers have allotted considerably more space to children and expanded children's programming aboard their ships. Some lines have even factored the increased number of youngsters on board in the *design* of new ships. Included in this appeal to families with children is further segmenting of offerings by pumping up the entertainment and gathering areas available for both younger teens (12–14 years old) and older teens (15–17 years old), as well as providing more options for families with toddlers (beyond traditional babysitting services).

Hotel chains also are adjusting their products and services with families in mind—from more all-suite accommodations to in-room video games to special meals and complimentary milk and cookies. But success in the new century will require more than just incorporating a kid's menu at food and beverage locations.

In an attempt to draw more family travelers, many hotels and resorts across the United States and Canada now offer activities for every member of the family. While the kids are playing or participating in structured enrichment activities, older members of the party can golf or enjoy spa facilities. Later, parents or grandparents can enjoy a relaxing, romantic dinner without interruption, or reconvene with the kids to have some fun together.

The Montecito-Sequoia Lodge in Los Altos, California, caters to families with children of all ages. Its High Sierra Vacation Camp features age-appropriate activities for groups from Guppies (6–23 months with parent), to Bears (13–18 year olds), and all ages in between. "Family Time" is held each night before dinner in the sports arena, including horseshoes and table tennis, with counselors on hand to help with the children. Babysitting for children under age three can be arranged and there's a special play area for the infant to two-year-old set.

The Mohonk Mountain House in New Paltz, New York, offers a similar range of family activities and also features a house doctor available daily during the busy summer season and on most weekends.

There are also a number of nontraditional travel industry players that are setting an example as to proper catering to family travelers.

According to the American Camping Association, family camps have increased 500 percent over the past 15 years. More than 450, run by organizations like the YMCA, Camp Fire Girls and churches and synagogues, now offer four- to seven-day camps that the entire family can attend.

A number of colleges and universities, like Cornell, are making it easy for families to go to college with the kids. Summer programs let family members choose their own courses for a week of study. Adults can sample ornithology, bronze casting, physics, landscaping, cooking and more. Kids ages 3 to 8 enjoy a mix of games and science activities; kids ages 9 to 12 can pick from comedy, adventure or animal behavior; and teens can delve into logic, science, law or writing.

Not to be outdone, rural destinations have realized their success is a family affair. Farm vacations are becoming a popular travel niche for families, as farmers in Michigan, Ohio, Vermont, Indiana, Utah, and Kansas offer travelers the opportunity to milk a goat, feed a cow, and stay in an authentic farmhouse.

The Right Message

For many, a trip allows a family to reconnect and accentuate what's really important in their lives—an emotion that takes on added significance in the post September 11 environment. And the special memories that travel creates are viewed as the most valuable keepsake of time spent together. Just a few years ago, nearly all of the television advertising for Walt Disney World theme parks was devoted to new attractions and special events. The objective was to let people know about the newest, biggest flume ride, the most spectacular parade, the hottest motion picture tie-ins. The rewards that were promised were "excitement" and "thrills" and "escape."

And that would have been just fine—except for the fact that almost every competing theme park in America could promise similar rewards.

A tactical adjustment was made to leverage the emotional connection Disney enjoys with travelers worldwide and deliver a message that was more subtle, but a lot more powerful.

Travel marketers have to avoid getting caught up in the product facts and figures, the hardware instead of the emotional software. The way to sell vacation travel is not with *facts*, like the speed of your roller coaster or the size of your atrium, but with plenty of *feeling*.

The communication objective of the marketing tools should be to help the consumer picture themselves splashing in warm, turquoise-green water off the shore of an uncharted island, or meeting and making new friends in the relaxed, friendly setting, or discovering romance.

Ironically enough, the ultimate goal is to hook them with a once-in-a-lifetime experience that we hope will result in a mindset that has them returning five, 10, or 25 more times throughout the stages of their lives.

Customer Is King

Technology will play a major role in allowing companies to efficiently and effectively target these unique segments and deliver even greater customization. The advance of the Internet, enhanced cell phone technology and wireless applications have created a new type of consumer, and reinvented the way travel is marketed and purchased.

Today travelers can research and plan their own vacation, sample pricing across a number of channels, decide where and how to book, and ultimately, call all the shots.

Understanding why and how consumers make their choices and then perfecting the means of capturing and evaluating those preferences will be the sales and marketing brass ring for the industry over the next 10 years.

Customer relationship management (CRM), is becoming a way of life for organizations and a means by which to put their customers in the center of all their processes. CRM leverages technology to understand the unique preferences of customers so that a business can differentiate them from one another, provide special offers for loyal clients and those that have the strongest affinity for their products, and establish and maintain a lifelong relationship.

Establishing this enhanced relationship will allow companies to customize a guest's vacation or make suggestions on how to vary their vacation experiences from year to year. Armed with this information, travel providers can mine the data to identify marketing opportunities to present the right deal at the right time, communicated effectively, and without invading a customer's privacy. This ultimately will influence the frequency of guest visits, and result in higher yields, more effective and efficient marketing campaigns, and shorter intervals between vacations.

CRM will not be limited to marketing tactics and booking processes. Ideally, companies will also integrate CRM with the actual vacation experience itself—by maintaining the relationship between visits. Properly leveraged, CRM will effectively link the marketing and operating computer systems to enable significant employee interaction in order to deliver vacations tailored exclusively for each guest.

Some companies have already taken this strategy to heart. The Rey Juan Carlos I hotel in Barcelona offers a choice of nine different pillow types with various fillings and degrees of firmness. But that pales in comparison to the Pan Pacific in San Francisco, which actually makes pillows according to guests' preferences—pillows that can be made, even fluffed, to the guest's specification.

Ideally, CRM will help enable long-term relationships that will continue even after a traveler returns from vacation. Successful companies will add a personal touch by sending a welcome email, or sending them a note to wish them a happy birthday or recognize an anniversary.

Summary

Families come in all shapes and sizes and so do family vacations. Today's family travelers are more numerous and varied than ever before. They come from all over this country and the world, they speak a variety of languages, they have their own customs, they enjoy diverse foods, they have different physical abilities, they represent varying age groups, they have nontraditional families, and much more.

The challenge is daunting, but successful travel organizations who target their product, their marketing strategies and their customization will reap substantial rewards—not only for business for the next five to ten years, but for the generations of business that will follow.

21

The Theme Park Perspective

Fred Lounsberry
Senior Vice President
Universal Parks & Resorts

Fred J. Lounsberry is senior vice president for Universal Parks & Resorts. He is responsible for the oversight, development and coordination of sales activities for Universal Studios' theme parks worldwide, including Universal Studios Japan, and Universal Mediterranea in Spain. He also is responsible for Universal Parks and Resorts Vacations, Universal's in-house wholesale tour operation, which packages and markets Universal Orlando and Universal Studios Hollywood vacations. Further, Lounsberry is responsible for leading the development of the marketing and sales plans for Universal Studios Shanghai, scheduled to open in early 2007 in Shanghai, China.

Lounsberry, most recently executive vice president of sales and marketing for Universal Orlando, has been with Universal since 1987. One of the original members of the Universal Studios Florida startup team, he was instrumental in both the launch of Universal Studios Florida in 1990, and in the successful expansion of Universal Orlando over the last several years into a full destination resort.

A veteran of more than 25 years in the entertainment and tourism industry, Lounsberry was director of sales and marketing for Expo '86 in Vancouver, British Columbia, Canada, prior to joining Universal.

181

Lounsberry served in 2001–2002 as chairman of Visit Florida, the public-private partnership responsible for promoting tourism on behalf of the State of Florida. During his term, Mr. Lounsberry worked directly with Florida's governor and legislature to successfully secure a $20 million appropriation for additional advertising to assist Florida's tourism recovery, post-September 11.

Mr. Lounsberry served as 2002 national chairman of the Travel Industry of America (TIA), and remains a member of the TIA executive committee.

He holds a baccalaureate degree from the University of Iowa, and resides in Orlando with his wife Michelle and their three children.

Being in the travel industry at the outset of the 21st century was like witnessing Columbus' proving the world to be round, Fulton's invention of the steam engine, Henry Ford's Model T and the Wright brothers' launching the era of air travel. As with these other great watersheds, nothing again would ever be the same. The change was forever. It became part of our very fabric.

Unfortunately, and sadly, the tragic events of September 11, 2001, in America launched a new decade for the tourism industry. It made a profound change and tore at the very fabric of the tourism industry. At this writing, the long-term effects of September 11, as well as those of the 2003 war in Iraq, and the continued hot spots of unrest in the world, are yet to be clearly defined for the industry. What we do know is that travel and tourism were profoundly impacted by these events. The uncertainty generated by these events has created a new definition for "normal." This industry is determining how to adapt as we enter the 21st century.

What I do know is that our business, the theme park/resort segment of tourism, was profoundly changing even before the geopolitical events of the early 21st century had their impact.

Distribution and Vacation Planning

The Internet has changed the way consumers plan and purchase travel. We knew that this was coming when significant Internet travel purchases and travel information came about in the mid-1990s. Early apprehensions about security issues in making purchases on the Internet are long gone. Internet travel sales continue and are expected to grow exponentially. The ability for consumers to conduct extensive vacation and travel planning and research via the internet and compare products, features, etc. will continue to make all in the travel industry rethink our sales and marketing channels and pricing and product strategies.

Consumers have now been trained to find the "best" deals and offers for travel on the Internet. While this may send minor shock waves through some of the traditional travel industry channels, this is a reality of today's consumer thinking and behavior. As we enter the 21st century, it is mandatory for all businesses in the travel industry to remodel pricing, product, and distribution channel strategies which address and respond to this consumer mindset, while also still supporting other, more traditional travel industry distribution channels.

The Internet will continue to provide other benefits for the travel industry. The Internet provides a unique opportunity for efficient testing and experimentation of new products, added value and pricing. This allows the travel industry to react quickly to the consumer trends, and events that will impact travel in the 21st century.

The Internet also will continue to provide the travel industry the most cost-effective distribution system for sales transactions, fulfillment, information distribution and communication. This will help offset the increased value offerings that will continue to be required for competitive reasons through the Internet channel by the travel industry.

My final point on distribution addresses a question that is asked repeatedly—What is the future of travel agents? Travel agents and agencies are still, and, I believe, and will remain, an important segment of the travel industry. True, the Internet and new technologies are, and will continue to, impact this channel. However, travel agents and agencies provide a valuable function for the travel industry—*personal service*. Consumers will pay for service. The technologies of the 21st century will challenge the travel agency segment to be creative and continually evolve themselves in the services and products that they provide.

The Theme Park Perspective

As with many of the changes of the late 20th century and the dawn of the 21st century, much has been driven by technology. Technology is, and will always be, at the core of the entertainment business, including theme park resorts.

Entertainment has always been about creatively arousing senses, emotions and ideas. Laugh! Cry! Scream! Reflect! Technology helps us do it better. And, better it must be. The consumer of the 21st century expects and, yes, demands it at all levels.

Consumers want services that not only are better, but faster, more realistic, more personalized, more intense, more convenient, more diverse, more creative and a true value. They (we) want it all. That's what's expected day to day in everything, including food and household products, to TV and movies, the Internet and games.

Just imagine what's expected when it comes to a vacation destination representing a substantial investment of family discretionary income. Imagine it. Anticipate it. Create it. Deliver it. Theme park resort vacation destinations like Universal Orlando must continue to do it. This is particularly true in Orlando, the "Super Bowl" of theme park vacations.

Totally Immersive, More Realistic, More Intense

By way of examples, I'll focus on a few of our many landmark rides at our two Universal Orlando theme parks.

At our "Ride the Movies"–based Orlando theme park, Universal Studios, as early as 1991 we introduced what is still today an industry landmark: "Back to the Future: The Ride." It is a true one-of-a-kind marriage of creativity and technology. It was minute-for-minute the most expensive film of the time. It puts you in the middle of a favorite motion picture story as has never been done before. A blend of Imax film and cutting-edge motion-based simulation technology, it remains after a decade one of the most popular rides at the park. It "raised the bar" for the entire theme park industry. We continue to do so.

Based on the success of our original Universal Studios theme park, which opened in 1990, we opened Islands of Adventure in 1999 along with our City-Walk entertainment complex, and launched our on-site hotels as we transitioned to a full vacation destination theme park resort. Two rides at the second park further exemplify our response to consumers' desire for the earlier mentioned characteristics demanded for the then approaching 21st century. That remains true to this day and as we look ahead further into our new century.

At Islands of Adventure we introduced the first roller coasters in the Orlando market. Roller coasters have been around since the late 1900s and have virtually defined "thrill rides" for over a century, from their beginnings at New York's famous Coney Island. Not exactly a new concept. What to do?

Universal created The Incredible Hulk Coaster inspired by Marvel's super popular character, The Hulk. Universal's designers created state-of-the-art roller coaster technology, married it with a dramatic theme, a well-known story and hugely popular comic book character to tell a story and create a true "thrill" experience that emotionally engulfs guests. It was voted "the world's best steel coaster" by the Discovery Channel in May of 2002.

At the same time, we introduced a whole new ride category at Islands of Adventure. A true industry "threshold attraction." It didn't go unnoticed: "(The Amazing Adventures of Spider-Man) . . . undoubtedly the greatest virtual reality ride."—*U.S. News & World Report*, May 10, 1999; "The Amazing Adventures of Spider-Man…is a technical marvel."—*The Washington Times*, May 8, 1999.

"The Amazing Adventures of Spider-Man," based on another Marvel comic, is the first attraction in theme park history to combine rapidly moving, highly mobile ride vehicles hurtling through acres of vivid scene sets and extraordinary, specially filmed 3-D action with pyrotechnic special effects.

It's an experience unlike any other ever created. Traditional 3-D films require viewers to remain in one location. The challenge of Spider-Man was to get guests directly involved in the action as they view three-dimensional films and move at high speeds past various movie screens and props—at unusual angles and varying distances.

Called a "moving point of convergence," the new technology was developed along with pioneering motion-picture techniques by a handpicked team to achieve astounding results. The effect relies on 25 large-format movie projectors and dozens of smaller projectors. Guests see 3-D wherever they look.

What makes the images remarkable is the pioneering effort to project heretofore flat, two-dimensional comic book characters who have no dimensional form into three-dimensional characters via CGI (computer graphic imaging). The results are staggering. People are unable to discern the boundaries between fantasy and reality. But success in the 21st century will yet require more than inspiration and technology. Broad family appeal will also be key.

More Personalized, More Convenient, More Diverse

Not everyone yearns for the in-your-face excitement of the Hulk or the Amazing Adventures of Spider-Man. Our theme parks do, and must continue to, offer diverse, broad family appeal. The counterpoint and broad appeal of the rides I've already described is perhaps best exemplified at Seuss Landing at our Islands of Adventure theme park.

Seuss Landing is a place of fantastical whimsy and colorful delight for young and old alike, where fish fly and cats wear hats. Where green eggs and ham are always on the menu and blue hair is not a bit unusual.

The most colorful of five themed islands at Universal Orlando's Islands of Adventure theme park, Seuss Landing, is a dream world for fans of the late

Theodor Geisel's work (as the brilliant children's author, Dr. Seuss). For everyone else, it's simply a dream world.

The island's centerpiece is the Caro-Seuss-El, an interactive merry-go-round that gives life to the animal characters created by Dr. Seuss. Guests hop aboard a cowfish and can ring its bell to some "wonky" music—an original soundtrack that plays throughout the island.

The splashy One Fish Two Fish Red Fish Blue Fish ride is an exercise in following directions, where the reward and the punishment are the same—the opportunity to get wet. A rhyming song tells the flying fish captains when to take their fish up and when to take it down. But look out . . . there are fish below that are ready to squirt at any moment.

A three-story red-and-white striped stovepipe hat marks the entrance to one of Seuss Landing's most popular attractions—The Cat in the Hat, where traveling couches await to whisk guests through one of the world's best-loved children's books. The journey begins with two long-faced children at the start of a rainy day, hopelessly bored and utterly depressed until their strange visitor, along with Thing One and Thing Two, drop by to make a mess.

Even the food in Seuss Landing is fanciful. Whether it's a Green Eggs and Hamwich or some Moose Juice a guest is looking for, there are plenty of whimsical choices for the discerning Seuss fan.

The rides and attractions I've mentioned point to some of the characteristics demanded for success in the 21st century. No matter how exciting, entertaining and awe-inspiring they all might be as they immerse you in their themes and stories, they are but the "hardware" of our business.

The heart and soul of the business, its "software," its spirit, is very human, at the core of exceptional world-class guest service.

Universal invests heavily in its guest service mandate. Employee recruiting and training is intensely guest service driven. Guest service incentive programs for Universal Orlando team members routinely fuel the emphasis on guest service.

This guest service "spirit" of the Universal Orlando Resort plays out in many ways beyond the core of personal, friendly, helpful services by our team members. For example:

On-site resort guests at our three hotels can use their room key for direct express access (a 10–15 minute maximum wait) for all major rides and attractions at our two theme parks. This on-site resort benefit is unprecedented in the theme park resort category and provides the "ultimate benefit" for theme park visitors.

Universal express ride access. The Express access feature for rides and attractions, available to all on-site hotel resort guests, is also available to park guests on a limited basis, subject to capacity limitations.

On-site resort guests enjoy a growing list of special vacation benefits and privileges—in-park purchases delivered to the room, free water taxi or shuttle bus to both theme parks and CityWalk, "first available" seating at select Universal Orlando Resort restaurants, and use of hotel key card to charge food and merchandise at Universal Orlando locations where credit cards are accepted.

For guests with disabilities: Disabled parking permit parking; wheelchair or electric convenience vehicles for rental. All shopping, dining and restroom facilities, as well as outdoor stage shows, are wheelchair accessible; amplified handsets for hearing disabilities are provided at all phone locations and telecommunication devices for the deaf (TDD) are available at guest services and throughout each park; amplified audio for assistive listening at many of the theme park queues with assistive listening headsets are available for loan at guest services; captioning on request is provided in queues with television monitors; sign language interpreting services are available with advanced notice; service animals are welcome in all restaurant and merchandise locations, as well as attraction queues and on some select rides. A Universal Orlando *Rider's Guide for Ride Safety and Guests with Disabilities* is available at Guest Services.

Staying Ahead of the Curve

The technology curve will continue to increase and the industry's speed will accelerate thanks to two kinds of competition: 1) The competition for the destination driven leisure dollar from locales across the world—it will continue based on economic appeal; likewise, 2) the competition for the consumer's time and discretionary income will intensify, driven largely by technology. (Will virtual reality be the family parlor game of the future, transporting the family anywhere in a virtual world?)

Along with the characteristics and values already mentioned, anticipating and identifying new themes, new "classics," as well as new trends, and quickly responding to them through new or transformed product, will be the basis of holding a competitive edge in this new millennium.

We at Universal continue to ride the curve with all-new attractions regularly. The latest in our attraction lineup for 2003 includes Jimmy Neutron Nicktoon Blast and Shrek—the new classic "greatest fairytale never told."

Jimmy Neutron's Nicktoon Blast rockets into action this April and brings Nickelodeon's famous boy genius to life—along with the largest collection of Nickelodeon characters ever assembled for a theme park attraction. Jimmy Neutron is the first CGI (computer graphic imaging) character developed by

Nickelodeon for television, film, Internet—and, now, theme park—use. Using sophisticated computer graphics, state-of-the-art ride technology and programmable motion-based seats, guests experiencing the attraction will spin, crash and career during an action-packed trip through the universe.

The "Shrek" saga continues at Universal Orlando with the 2003 opening of "Shrek 4-D" (opening simultaneously at our sister parks in Hollywood and Osaka, Japan).

The all-new multi-sensory "Shrek 4-D™" attraction, a multimedia continuation of the "Shrek®" fairy tale, will be the first major attraction to be introduced simultaneously at Universal theme parks in Hollywood, Orlando and Japan.

The comic talents of Mike Myers, Eddie Murphy, Cameron Diaz and John Lithgow will return to give voice to the swamp-dwelling ogre, Shrek; his faithful chatterbox companion, Donkey; his bride, Princess Fiona; and the vengeful ghost of Lord Farquaad in an all-new animated saga that will pick up the story where the Oscar-winning feature film "Shrek" left off.

With 12 minutes of all-new 3-D animation, "Shrek 4-D" will bridge the narrative between "Shrek," "the greatest fairytale never told," and the upcoming sequel from DreamWorks Pictures. The "Shrek" saga continues with spectacular visuals and multiple special effects yet to be seen, heard and felt in a "4-D" attraction.

"Shrek 4-D" will mark the first animation to be created for a theme park by the animation wizards at PDI/DreamWorks, the creators of "Shrek," as well as the earlier computer animated hit "Antz." The addition of three-dimensional depth to the animation and the creation of in-theater effects by attraction designers at Universal Creative will be parts of the new OgreVision multisensory experience.

Expansion continued in 2004 with "Revenge of the Mummy" at Universal Studios. Based on the phenomenally popular "Mummy" films that have grossed nearly $1 billion worldwide, and heralding a new era in thrill rides, Universal Studios ride designers have unveiled plans for "Revenge of the Mummy"—the first attraction in history to feature an unprecedented fusion of threshold technology, high-speed roller coaster engineering and space-age robotics to propel guests through authenticated ancient Egyptian catacombs and "live" pyrotechnic effects.

Ten years in research and development, the indoor thrill ride debuted simultaneously in 2004 at both Universal Studios Hollywood and Universal Orlando, integrating design concepts by visionary Stephen Sommers, who reinvigorated the classic Universal monster film "The Mummy" in 1999's worldwide smash, and its even more popular sequel in 2001, both of which he wrote and directed.

Indeed, the design and construction of the ride marks an unparalleled collaboration between a director and producers from the worlds of moviemaking and theme park design. Sommer's longtime creative partner, Bob Ducsay, also applied extensive creative input into the ride.

Unique methodology in themes and technical elements for the ride have been conceived by the combined team resulting in a unique "High Velocity Show Immersion System" that completely engulfs the riders' senses in the eerie, haunted world of "Revenge of the Mummy."

The ride possesses the most advanced animatronics ever engineered, elaborately staged "dark ride scenes" and a revolutionary new ride track employing new linear induction motors to create a series of visual, visceral and motion-based effects that continually surprise guests while drawing them into Sommers' immersive storylines—storylines that have thrilled hundreds of millions of moviegoers worldwide.

This new ride continues Universal Studios' successful tradition of creating attractions from its own library of hit films, including "E.T.," "Back To The Future," and "Backdraft," all of which have become popular attractions at its theme parks.

The ability to harness the newest technologies, adapt, anticipate trends, remain "current" and new with popular appeal to diverse and rapidly changing consumer tastes has always been the characteristic of our entertainment "hit" and entertainment industry business success. And so it will be, we feel, through the 21st century.

22

Marketing the Thrill of Skiing, the Serenity of the Mountains, the Luxury of Travel

Adam A. Aron
Chairman of the Board and CEO
Vail Resorts, Inc.

Adam M. Aron is chairman of the board and chief executive officer of Vail Resorts. Vail Resorts manages Vail, Beaver Creek, Breckenridge, Keystone, and Heavenly, all of which rank among the best ski resorts in North America. Vail also manages the Grand Teton Lodge Company in Jackson Hole, Wyoming. And it runs RockResorts, with its ten luxury resort hotels throughout the United States. Vail Resorts manages many other hospitality, dining, retail and real estate businesses. Vail Resorts has 15,000 employees and $700 million in annual revenue. Mr. Aron previously served as President and CEO of Norwegian Cruise Line; senior vice president, marketing, for United Airlines; and senior vice-president, marketing, for Hyatt Hotels.

Stand atop a majestic mountain, some 12,000 feet above sea level. Feel refreshed by the brisk cold upon your cheeks, all the while basking in a hot and brilliant sun. As you gaze out across snowcapped peaks for as far as an eye can see, you can't escape admiring fields of lush six-story-high evergreen trees under a bright blue sky. Survey a landscape that looks nothing short of a winter wonderland. Then, breathe deeply the cleanest air that will ever reach your lungs.

When you've had your fill of Mother Nature, flip your hips gently. Your skis will prove the power and force of gravity. They will do all the work, and you will move down the mountainside. Slowly at first, then your speed will increase. Within seconds, you will be moving at the fastest pace a human can without motorized assistance. Adrenaline will pump throughout your body. No matter what your ability level, you will push yourself to your limit—and with all the motion, you will experience an odd blend of excitement, freedom, fear, grace and pride. When you come to rest, the athleticism of your run will fuse your body and your mind. Physically and mentally, you will feel just great.

And then it is time for dinner. Not just any dinner, of course. You may savor some of the finest dining that can be found anywhere, in a throwback setting of historic, charming and authentic small mountain towns.

What a day, what a day, what a day. And tomorrow, you'll do it all again. This is the essence and the joy of a modern U.S. ski vacation.

In 2003, approximately 10 million Americans spent 58 million days on the slopes of more than 500 ski resorts across the United States. Those adherents have turned skiing into a big multibillion-dollar business and an important niche in the U.S. travel industry.

The Market

About 10 percent of the U.S. population consider themselves to be, or to have been, snowsports enthusiasts. Of these, about three-fifths have actively skied or snowboarded in the past few years. And some 10 million do so in any given winter.

By a three-to-two margin, more men are skiers than are women. But, despite the physical demands of skiing, it is apparently ageless. Children start skiing at about age 4, and seniors in their 70s are often found to be avid skiers. The average age of the typical skier/boarder is about 40 years old.

About 7 percent of the nation's skiing and snowboarding aficionados are children. About three of 10 are unmarried single adults. Almost two-thirds of skiers and boarders are married. Of these, half have children living with them at home, a fourth are empty-nesters with children who are fully grown, and a fourth are married but, as of yet, childless.

It goes without saying that college students and 20-something singles do ski in great numbers. But with so many skiers representing families with young or grown children, it should be no surprise that skiing is also often seen as an ideal family vacation experience. After all, adults and children alike enjoy the fun of the sport. And avid skiing parents, carrying their own memories of youth, seem to get a special thrill from teaching their own children to ski. While teenage boys vacationing on a beach, for example, may want their parents as far away as possible, by contrast those same teenage boys seem to love skiing with (and usually outperforming) their skiing parents. (Indeed, the old joke: "What are the three most dangerous words in skiing?" Answer: "Follow me, Dad!"). Not to be outdone, increasingly grandparents are buying mountain real estate, creating a focal point for multigenerational family vacations.

About 85 percent of the U.S. skiing public does so on traditional alpine skis, with the remainder choosing a snowboard as their winter sports equipment of choice. Recently legitimized as an Olympic sport, snowboarding is especially popular among younger skiers. And, as a result, in the decade of the 1990s, snowboarding has grown at a rate of about 20 percent per year.

While snowboarding has been growing at a galloping clip, the world of skiing itself—even including all of those new snowboarders—has seen growth that has been much more modest. Over three decades, total skier days have grown at a compounded rate of less than 1 percent per annum.

Many think the reason for this tepid growth in skiing has been a declining number of adolescents in America in the 1970s and 1980s—the infamous Generation X is about 20 percent smaller than its predecessor Baby Boom generation. On the other hand, there is hope that the U.S. ski industry will soon enjoy growth in industry-wide demand. The population of the children of Gen-Xers—dubbed by demographers the Echo Boom generation—is not only larger than Gen-X, it is now larger than the Baby Boom group. A growing Echo Boom generation is taking to snowsports with a fervor. Accordingly, year-over-year growth in sold lift tickets was some 11 percent in the year 2001. And despite the slowdown in travel caused by September 11, the Iraqi War and a weak national economy, 2003 was the best year ever for the U.S. ski industry—annual growth between 2000 and 2003 was about 20 times the annual growth rate between 1975 and 1995.

Skiers come from all over the nation, and ski all over the nation. Most skiers, of course, stay close to home—choosing to ski for a day or a weekend within a few hours' drive of their primary residence. But, interestingly, fully 25 percent of all skier visits are multi-day vacations to destinations more than 500 miles away from home. The recipients of more than 85 percent of this out-of-state wanderlust are ski resorts offering the famous "blue skies and champagne powder" of the Rocky Mountain West.

The Mecca of U.S. skiing is, of course, the Rocky Mountain West. About 30 percent of all U.S. lift tickets are sold along the Continental Divide. Colorado's 20 or so ski resorts host fully one in five U.S. skiers. The Utah ski market is one-third the size of that of Colorado. And the various Rocky Mountain states of Wyoming, Idaho, Montana and New Mexico split the remainder. Given that these six states represent less than 5 percent of the U.S. population, the Rockies' prominence in skiing cannot be denied. Indeed, Colorado, which accounts for 20 percent of all U.S. skiing, has less than 2 percent of the U.S. population.

About 20 percent of U.S. skiing takes place in the Pacific Northwest and West Coast, with half of these skiers doing so around the crystal blue waters of Lake Tahoe, and the balance at a variety of resorts in California, Oregon and Washington.

About 25 percent of all U.S. lift tickets are sold in the Northeast. While New York, Pennsylvania and Massachusetts each have ski resorts with regional appeal for day and weekend skiers, most Northeast skiing takes place in Vermont, New Hampshire and Maine. Another 25 percent of lift tickets are sold in the Southeast (10 percent) and Midwest (15 percent), almost entirely at smaller regional ski hills that cater to nearby population centers and to beginner skiers.

While skiing cuts across the geographic landscape of the United States, its demographic breadth is less egalitarian. Skiing is not inexpensive, and as a sport and vacation experience skews to the more affluent. Indeed, a whopping 20 percent of skiers have a household income exceeding $200,000 or more per year. Fully half of skiers come from households with annual incomes above $100,000. And some 90 percent of skiers have annual incomes above the national median.

The Competitive Landscape

Ski resorts, like skiers themselves, come in all sizes, shapes and price points. With more than 500 ski resorts and ski hills in the United States, the average U.S. ski resort hosts about 115,000 skier days annually. But this distorts the magnetic appeal of key larger resorts. Vail, Colorado, is America's most visited ski resort with some 1.6 million annual winter visitor days, followed closely by Breckenridge, Colorado with 1.4 million. In Colorado, Keystone, Aspen/Snowmass, Steamboat Springs and Copper Mountain each traditionally host one million-plus skier days in any given year. And Winter Park and Beaver Creek are not far behind. So, too, Mammoth and Heavenly in California, and Killington in Vermont get close to or exceed one million annual visitor days. Indeed, fully 20 percent of all U.S. skiing takes place at the top 10 most-visited (of the approximately 500) U.S. ski resorts.

With so many resorts, skiing is still a highly fragmented industry. The industry was long dominated by strong but under-capitalized (if nonetheless visionary) pioneers. As but one example, a middle-aged Alex Cushing brought the 1960 Winter Olympic Games to Squaw Valley, California. In the same year, General Dwight Eisenhower ended his glorious career, and a dashing John F. Kennedy defeated Richard Nixon for the U.S. Presidency. It was neither Eisenhower nor Kennedy nor Nixon who became *TIME Magazine*'s 1960 Man of the Year, but Alex Cushing. Incredibly, 43 years later, Cushing still runs Squaw Valley day-to-day, with the same verve and passion he did more than four decades earlier.

Since 1996, six companies, owning only about 35 resorts, have consolidated control of more than one-third of all U.S. skiing. The largest of these in the United States is Vail Resorts, with more than a 40 percent share of the Colorado market. It also owns the most visited ski resort at Lake Tahoe. Indeed, among other resort ventures, Vail Resorts owns and operates the first, second, fifth and 10th most visited U.S. ski resorts. The American Skiing Company is to New England what Vail Resorts is to Colorado. Powder Corporation owns the most visited ski resort in each of Utah and Oregon, namely Park City and Mount Bachelor. Booth Creek Ski Holdings owns or manages a handful of smaller ski resorts, including Telluride. Canadian-headquartered Intrawest Corporation, in addition to controlling the two largest ski resorts in Eastern and Western Canada (Mt. Tremblanc and Whistler), also controls the most visited ski resort in California, and of all places, West Virginia and New Jersey. Boyne USA Resorts features second-tier but well-known ski resorts from Michigan to Montana to Washington.

When contrasted with the rest of the industry, these larger companies have effectively used their market power to attract and invest capital to enhance their resorts, create a competitive lead in marketing programs and technology, and achieve purchasing synergies. Despite the obvious advantage that economies of scale may give the larger firms, the independent resorts—often owned as trophy assets by very wealthy entrepreneurs—have nonetheless, in most cases, held up well.

Competitive Advantage: Who Wins and Who Loses

For sure, economies of scale are a real competitive advantage. So, too is the quality of managerial decision making and marketing aggressiveness, which, to be sure, vary by resort.

But other almost obvious factors are of huge import. Any of the following ten factors can help a ski resort generate oversized profits:

1. Proximity by modern road to a large nearby population.

2. Availability of sizable and convenient nonstop jet aircraft capacity to and from major U.S. and/or foreign cities.

3. A large, tall ski mountain—the more the ski terrain in acreage, and the greater the vertical drop from summit to base, the larger the number of probable skiers.

4. A big nearby bed base—the more rooms that are available nearby in hotels and condos, the more active skiers in the day.

5. A charming activity-filled nearby ski town or base village, that provides added vacation appeal.

6. Continued investment in state-of-the-art high-speed lift equipment, snow-making systems, and various resort amenities and facilities.

7. Natural snowfall, elevation and corresponding ski season length—you can't ski at a resort that is closed or one that has little actual snow.

8. A cooperative political climate in the surrounding communities, that allows innovation and positive change.

9. An available workforce, with affordable housing, high quality medical care, and good schools for the children of resort employees nearby.

10. Generally, it takes the same amount of brainpower to run a small resort as a big one. Usually, the larger resorts have higher margins and the capacity to produce bigger returns.

Skiing and the Five Ps

Product. To a skiing visitor, nothing is more important than the quality of the overall vacation experience and, more specifically, the quality of the ski experience that each resort may offer. Product quality and product innovation are king in attracting more skiers—not to mention those willing to pay skiing's increasing prices. Innovations in the product come in many different ways.

Some resorts in recent years, namely Vail, Breckenridge, Beaver Creek, Park City and Telluride, have added more ski terrain and ski lifts. Others have built almost wholly new base villages, including Mammoth, Squaw Valley, Heavenly and Keystone. Whistler, Beaver Creek, and Jackson Hole have added new luxurious world-class resort hotels. Some resorts, like Aspen, have focused on the quality of their retail stores throughout town, given the popularity of shopping as part of a ski vacation experience. Almost all major resorts have added special features and terrain parks aimed at snowboarders. And many have increased the amount of "grooming"—a technique that flattens and smoothes the snow surface, making skiing easier on the hips, ankles and especially knees of aging Baby Boomers.

Many ski resorts in recent years have improved their offerings for non-skiing spouses with new destination spas; for children, with a variety of youth-oriented facilities; and for international guests, with increased signage and collateral materials in Spanish, Portuguese, French and German.

People. While much of the experience results from physical facilities and amenities, good old-fashioned personal service is immensely important in creating guest satisfaction and repeat patronage.

Generally, ski resorts with winning employee attitudes are winning resorts. Does the lift operator smile and ask how the day is going? Is the cafeteria cashier pleasant and engaged or an uninterested I-could-care-less automaton? Is the ski instructor a helpful and friendly goodwill ambassador or a demanding taskmaster-martinet? Does the ski patroller handle medical emergencies with competence and sensitivity?

Skiers, like all other vacationers, know the difference between great service, good service and bad service. They reward, with their continued visitation and spending, the resorts that excel and punish those resorts that do not.

Price. Given that a single round of golf can cost anywhere between $100 and $250 at the nation's leading golf properties, an adult lift ticket priced anywhere between $40 and $75 at the nation's leading ski resorts almost seems like a bargain.

But add in ski equipment, ski lessons, pricey on-mountain food, shopping, dining and expensive ski lodging, and the total cost of a ski trip can be daunting. The cost of skiing a nearby mountain for a single day can merely be that of a deeply discounted local operator's lift ticket and a tankful of gas. By contrast, a family of four could easily spend from $4,000 to as much as $20,000 for a week-long ski holiday several states away.

As a result, especially in a weak national economy, and when all sectors of the travel industry seem to be offering one low-priced package deal after another, the importance to ski resorts of cleverly packaging their low prices and special deals cannot be overstated.

One recent trend is the advent of low-priced season passes. All around the country, resorts have been dropping the price of season passes by as much as two-thirds or more. But the price cut is not as disadvantageous to the issuing resort as it may at first appear. Higher-priced passes were traditionally only bought by avid skiers who might ski 40 or 50 days per season. The new, lower-priced passes are actively being purchased by skiers with only five to 10 ski days per season. As such, the average lift ticket price per day skied has actually risen with the new cheap passes. It's counterintuitive, but true.

Some resorts are also creatively packaging many different components into a single one-stop shopping purchase. Skiers increasingly are offered air, hotel, and car reservations along with lift tickets and ski school reservations—all with a single phone call or online purchase. This not only enhances the buyer's convenience, but also allows a resort to bundle certain discretionary discounts in a manner that neither cannibalizes nor showcases individually good deals that might otherwise dilute previously confirmed prices.

Promotion. Smart resort operators create a unique and distinctive personality or image for their resorts. Skiers not only pick ski mountains that match or challenge their ability, but resorts that match their idealized sense of where they should be vacationing based on a psychographic segmentation.

For example, Vail is billed (and is almost always reviewed) as the best and biggest U.S. ski mountain, a place where "real skiers" will simply find "there's no comparison." Aspen is a Hollywood redoubt, a place to see and be seen. Steamboat Springs and Jackson Hole are promoted as down and dirty Old West cowboy towns. Heavenly has its heavenly views of the magnificently blue waters of Lake Tahoe. Mt. Tremblanc in French-speaking Quebec touts its *joie de vivre*. Deer Valley, Utah features its world-class cuisine, while Park City, Utah is still milking the fame it garnered as host to the 2002 Winter Olympic Games. Mammoth hypes the size of its aptly named mammoth-sized ski mountain in California. Big Sky, Montana highlights the wide-open, uncrowded spaces within Montana.

Each resort fosters its image in everything from media advertising to collateral, trail maps to direct mail, web sites to outbound emails.

In recent years, airline frequent flyer-type loyalty programs have become part of the ski marketing universe. While developing close relationships with repeat customers is a much-pursued goal, classic loyalty programs per se are not as immensely powerful as in other parts of the travel industry—given the inherent lack of frequency of vacation purchase (often only once per year). Therefore, other vehicles are used to drive loyalty, including the creation of on-mountain high-end club buildings, and one-on-one interpersonal relationships with ski instructors and real estate sales personnel.

Place of Sale. Distribution issues for ski marketers mirror other sectors of the travel industry, but have some unique differences.

To be sure, like other travel companies, ski company marketing and sales departments chase group travelers, and market both online and through travel wholesalers and packagers.

One surprising difference, though, is the relatively small role played by travel agents in booking ski trips. Many agents, of course, promote skiing. But most do not. There are many reasons why. One is that almost all travel agents like, if not love, to travel and familiarize themselves accordingly, so as to properly advise their clients. But many agents simply are not skiers, so they are unsure of the subtle differences that separate one major U.S. ski resort from another. Second, since the lodging in many ski towns consists of small, unbranded lodges and condominium complexes, it is harder for agents to recommend lodging without the familiar understanding of major lodging brands. Just about every travel agent can readily and easily explain the difference between Best Western, Hilton, and Four Seasons hotels—but most ski resort lodging is unbranded. Third, there are many ski resorts, and the marketing budget for each is usually small. Rightly or wrongly, only the largest ski resorts think they have the resources to court the tens of thousands of U.S. travel agencies. And fourth, skiers become loyal to particular ski resort towns and mountains very quickly, tending to return year-after-year-after-year, over and over again, to their favorite ski resorts. In such an event, their product knowledge is high and their tendency to seek out professional travel advice decreases. Instead, they book directly.

Just look at the travel industry trade press to see what little coverage is given to skiing versus, say, cruising or major lodging chains. Again, this is the direct result of both smaller ski resort trade press advertising budgets, and the propensity of skiers to book their ski vacations directly, without an intermediary.

The Internet

Never in the history of mankind has a new communications medium grabbed the attention of the country or the world as quickly as has the Internet. As such, it deserves its own special mention.

The Internet is a boon to ski marketers. Thanks to the World Wide Web, literally reams of up-to-the-minute information, including stock and live photography, can be communicated to current and potential customers at negligible cost. It is common for ski resort Web sites to have live photo-cams showing current ski conditions, and active Doppler radar weather updates to showcase near-term weather (skiing is the only sector of the travel industry where a big storm in the next few days is considered a good thing that will actually drive increased, not decreased, near-term visitation).

The Internet conveys both long-term image and short-term "deals." It communicates written and photographic information. At any hour of the day, it details dynamic inventory availability. And travelers use it. Over 80 percent of ski vacationers say they study the Internet for hours on end to help them plan their ski holiday. And they say that more than half of all their information about prospective ski trips comes from their online investigations.

Trends in Ski Resort Marketing

Three trends stand out as paramount in recent years in ski resort marketing.

First, many resorts now sell more than lift tickets. In the old days, ski resorts were "uphill transportation companies." They primarily sold lift tickets and little else. These days resort operators are also in lodging, dining and retail businesses. Indeed, non-lift ticket revenue may be as much as two to three times lift ticket revenue for many major ski resorts.

Second, resort marketing staffers are now working a full 12-month year, because they are transforming their resorts from winter-only resorts to year-round resorts. Most winter-peaking ski resorts are open from November to April. Some are open in October, a few stay open until May, and a handful are actually open well into the summer months. But, increasingly, almost all ski resorts are determining that theirs can become a 12-month year. After all, the mountain communities are generally charming tourist destinations, the hotels are already built, and summer is just a glorious time of the year at most resorts.

What used to be only "ski marketing" is now ski marketing in the winter *and* golf marketing in the summer—along with the marketing of hiking, biking, fly-fishing, white water rafting, kayaking, horseback riding, hot air ballooning, not to mention cultural events such as concerts, theater and festivals.

Third, ski resorts are not only broadening the diversity of their winter offerings, and creating new summer offerings, they are also actually constructing wholly new ski towns and villages. The creation and sale of mountain real estate has become an increasing focus for most operators and marketers.

In short, in yesteryear, a ski marketer figured out how to sell a lift ticket—and that was it. Now, in the winter, he or she also sells a hotel room, a high-end dinner, and the rental of ski equipment, not to mention a ski lesson. In the summer, there is the promotion of a golf course, a full-blown major-city symphony in residence, a Shakespearean play, and a film festival. And all year long, there is also the sale of everything from a cute, cozy and cramped ski condo to a 7,000 square-foot palatial vacation home.

What Will Keep You Up at Night

What are the major obstacles for ski marketers?

Well, for one thing, a little snow would be nice. Oodles of early-season and well-communicated snowfall makes a ski marketer's job much easier, and the absence of that snow makes for a much tougher challenge.

Similarly, in recent years, ski marketers have had to cope with declining demand for travel both because of a weak national economy and the fallout from September 11 and the Iraqi War. In the simplest terms, and for reasons that are far more important than just the success of resort marketing efforts, peace and prosperity would be good for the world, for our country and for the travel industry.

And, regardless of the state of the world, many ski resorts are small businesses that need to market regionally or nationally, but whose marketing budgets are insufficient to do that with ease. In that case, marketers need to think more boldly and creatively, to target better, and to maximize the use of less expensive communications techniques including the Internet, outbound email, and public relations. Guerilla, not gorilla, marketing often becomes the order of the day.

It's All Downhill from Here

Given that only 10 percent of the U.S. population considers itself to be skiers, skiing will always be only a niche within the broader U.S. travel industry, not a dominant force. On the other hand, some of the country's most prominent and accomplished individuals are fanatically devoted skiers, and their billions of dollars spent on ski vacations each year says it all.

Thanks to the getting-bigger-every-day Echo Boom generation, demand for ski vacations should only increase in the years to come. Those resorts that commit themselves to providing an excellent and differentiated vacation experience, combined with an aggressive and imaginative marketing and sales program, in winter and in summer, are almost certain to thrive.

Section IV

Hotel and Resort Marketing

Hotel and resort marketing has, like the industry itself, undergone huge changes in recent years. To begin with, hoteliers now have a much better understanding of the 4 "Ps" of marketing.

They understand that the first "P," the product, is in fact a marketing decision. There is no new technology that affects the way people sleep. They lie down and close their eyes. This hasn't changed in thousands of years. The hardware, of course, is different.

What has changed is the number of choices people have when they choose a hotel, which is still basically nothing more than an eating and lodging establishment. There are now airport hotels, road warrior hotels, business hotels, convention hotels, resorts, suites and conference centers. When Marriott thinks about building a new hotel, it has 11 different brands to choose from. These include Marriott Hotels and Resorts, Renaissance Hotels, Courtyards by Marriott, Fairfield Inns, Towne Place Suites, Ramada International Hotels and Resorts, and Ritz Carlton Hotels and Resorts. Which one they choose is to a large extent, we would suppose, a marketing decision. Where are the customers and what kind of hotel do they want? Can we exceed their expectations? This is a key question. Professor Ted Levitt of Harvard reminds us that when we go into a hardware store we don't buy a quarter-inch drill—we buy the expectation of a quarter-inch hole.

The second "P," price, used to be set by the accountant. Now it's determined by the marketing director, who is more sensitive to what people are willing to pay. This person understands all of the different segments the hotel has an opportunity to pursue. Many hotels use revenue management computer programs to set prices. These programs seek to optimize the revenue a hotel receives in any given period by adjusting the rates that are offered to different market segments, based on the projected supply of rooms and the demand for them. These numbers change constantly as reservations come in, and forecasts are adjusted accordingly.

The third "P" is place, which refers to distribution points. This is one crucial issue hotels must deal with. Traditionally, only 20 percent of hotel business has come from travel agents. Most of it comes over the phone, in the mail and through reservation systems. But the Internet is rapidly taking over. Hotels need to be online with their own Web sites. They also need to understand how to work with companies like Expedia and Travelocity to maintain and grow their market share. And they need to decide if the brick and mortar travel agencies might possibly represent a significant opportunity for business they may have missed.

The fourth "P" is promotion, which includes personal selling, advertising, public relations, sales promotion and direct marketing. Here there are revolutionary changes in advertising media. Cable TV has made it possible for hotels with small advertising budgets to use this tremendously powerful media to reach target audiences at a reasonable cost. Specialized channels like the Travel Channel and the Wedding Channel are good examples. The Internet too is not only a wonderfully effective opportunity, but it is, as previously mentioned, a necessity in today's marketplace. But effective Web sites are interactive and have many pages. These are not easy to design and they can be expensive. Moreover, you can build the best site in the industry, but if no one looks at it, you're trying to save souls in an empty church. That's where the real expense comes in!

Public relations offer new opportunities as well. Savvy hotel owners have learned how to attract movie and TV production companies to use their properties for filming and to house entire casts and crew when they go on site.

To summarize, here are the main issues in hotel marketing as we see them:

Overcapacity: In up markets we build a lot of hotels to satisfy current and future demand. We built them and they (the customers) haven't come for a whole lot of different reasons. What do we do now?

Commodization of product: A room is a room is a room. Or is it? Hotels can offer their clientele grand ballrooms, meeting rooms, salons, saloons, solariums, business centers, nurseries, playrooms, bedrooms, sitting rooms, boudoirs, dormitories, parlors, restaurants, dining rooms, cafes, cafeterias, wine cellars, lobbies and more. What kind of rooms, amenities, and service a hotel offers is what makes one different from another. Today's independent travelers want different kinds of hotels to choose from, and they want to know what the differences are. Only hotels that can separate themselves from the crowd in a meaningful way are going to make it.

Brand Image: The first thing you do to separate yourself from the crowd is to create a brand image. A clear one. One that creates expectations associated with that brand. You make promises. Then you deliver on those promises, or even better, over-deliver. That's what a successful brand does.

Future Business: People are traveling less. Business travel has been curtailed. Everybody is after the affluent, retired Baby Boomers, but are there enough of them to go around? These are serious questions that need to be addressed. Every hotel needs to decide whether it wants to go after business travelers, leisure travelers, niche travelers (golfers, persons with disabilities, etc.), or what mix.

23

The Hotel Industry: Looking to the Future

Robert Dirks
Senior Vice President
Brand Management & Marketing
Hilton Hotels Corporation

Robert E. Dirks assumed his current position as senior vice president, brand management and marketing, in January 2001. He is responsible for the overall management of the Hilton branded hotels which includes strategic brand positioning, marketing programs, brand communications, both external and internal, hotel support in maximizing revenues, training, customer relationship management, development of brand expansion, customer satisfaction, and implementation and oversight of brand standards. Prior to assuming the above position, Dirks was senior vice president, sales and marketing, for Hilton Hotels Corporation, a position he held since 1994.

During the time period of 1997 through 2000, Dirks was a key driving force in the consummation of the sales and marketing alliance with Hilton International, Hilton's sister company located in London; as well as the integration of the Promus acquisition, which occurred in December 1999. The Promus acquisition brought the Embassy Suites®, Hampton Inn®, Hampton Inn & Suites®, DoubleTree® and Homewood Suites by Hilton® brands under the Hilton umbrella . . . and these brands became part of Hilton Hotels Corporation.

During his 31-year career with Hilton, Dirks has led the company in introducing many of the company's leading marketing programs. These have included Hilton Honors Worldwide (Hilton's frequency guest program), BounceBack Weekend and Easy Escapes, Hilton's Travel Lifestyle Center Rooms, Hilton's Sleep Tight Rooms, 30-Second Zip-In/Check In, as well as involvement in the positioning of Hilton's new brand—Hilton Garden Inn.

He began his career in 1972 at the Hilton New York as a sales trainee. He then served as convention service manager, conference center manager, sales manager, and then assistant director of sales at the hotel. From there he moved to the Capital Hilton in Washington, D.C, as director of sales, and from there to the Fontainebleau Hilton, also as director of sales. He was later appointed as the company's first director of marketing before transferring to The Waldorf-Astoria in 1982, in that same capacity.

In 1984, Dirks assumed the position of regional director, sales and marketing, for Hilton's southern region comprising eleven states, with an office in Atlanta. In 1988, Dirks was appointed vice president, marketing programs and moved to the corporate headquarters in Beverly Hills, California. From 1992–1994, Dirks was vice president, marketing, before being appointed senior vice president, sales and marketing, Hilton Hotels Corporation.

A native of Bloomington, Illinois, Dirks earned his bachelor's degree in hotel administration from Michigan State University. After serving in the Army for two years, he returned to MSU to obtain a master of business administration degree in marketing. He is currently on the board of the Travel Industry Association of America and the National Business Travel Association. He is immediate past chairman of the Institute of Business Travel. Dirks, his wife, Kathy, and their two children, Lauren and John, live in Westlake Village, California.

Someone anonymous and astute once made the observation that "The future isn't what it used to be." That's the *one* forecast unanimously accepted today by the entire travel industry. The future of travel is *not* what it used to be. It looks better; it looks worse. It's more personal; it's more technical. It's back to basics; it's driven by innovation. It's about success; it's about survival.

At Hilton, we believe the future of the hotel industry is all of these things. But, most importantly, the future of the hotel industry is what we CREATE. In a marketplace increasingly characterized by uncertainty, those who think boldly and act decisively will hold the competitive advantage. At Hilton, CREATE is a very specific call to action. It's an acronym for the forces that shape our own future: Customer relationships and relevance, experiences, accommodations, technology and extraordinary service (CREATE).

In the next pages, we will share with you our perspective on these forces and our ideas for making them work to our advantage.

Customer Relationships

There is a good reason why customer relationships lead our call to action for the next decade: they're the most important factor that will influence brand leadership. We can expect to see significant marketplace changes over the next ten years, with the distance between leaders and the rest of the pack becoming more and more pronounced. Today's challenges will continue—from maintaining product quality, to managing difficult owner relationships to retaining the best employees. But the greatest future threat, by far, will be the loss of brand and hotel identity as new electronic buying channels try to capture customer loyalty, and thus reduce hotel companies to commodity suppliers.

To fight that threat, *tomorrow's leading hotels must differentiate themselves through a passionate focus on knowing their customers individually, knowing the travel experiences those individual customers want and building greater trust with them by delivering consistently at all touch points*. As a result, their customers will choose to do business with them directly because they get higher value from the relationship. The rest of the pack will be forced to take business the leaders find less attractive.

Advances in technology provide travelers with more choices for shopping and buying than at any other time in history. Personal computers and digital assistants—on corporate desktops and in homes, along with the explosion in Internet usage, emerging wireless connectivity and new merchant channels, make it easier for savvy travelers to electronically compare various travel options and price points. While advances will continue to enrich the future with new options, one thing will remain constant—buyers will ultimately select the option that delivers the highest value to them personally.

In the future, successful hotel companies will recognize and harness the value of technology in order to own the customer relationship. That means building a closer bond with guests by relating to their individual needs for each travel occasion and then matching experiences to those needs in ways they cannot find elsewhere.

Even today, the typical leisure customer does not want to buy a rate plan or a travel package. Increasingly, he wants to build his own travel package. He wants to drag and drop his own preferred rate plans as he creates his own price-value relationship. Similarly, today's business customer wants to be remembered. The moment his frequent traveler number or name has been introduced, he wants to be acknowledged. What room does he like? What rate does he pay? What does his purchasing behavior tell us he will later need on his trip? Future success depends on finding ways to manage the customer by allowing the customer to manage the travel company.

Over the near term, hotel companies will recognize their most valued customers, provide them with incentives, collect information about their preferences and empower their employees to consistently deliver individualized service at each stay. Brand loyalty will be earned and preserved based on guests' trust.

Over the intermediate term, winning companies will further strengthen guest relationships by recognizing and providing individualized products based on an expanded guest knowledge base. Instead of separately marketing leisure or business products, these companies will use their overall knowledge of high-valued customers to recommend appropriate business or leisure experiences driven by the needs of the particular stay.

For example, when a valued business traveler, who usually stays in city-center luxury hotels, shops for a vacation experience, the hotel company might recommend resort properties at various locations around the world based on the traveler's past preferences, as well as the size and ages of his family. For a family reunion in the mountains, though, the company might recommend a mid-priced hotel with special amenities and a recreation program for children.

In the longer term, truly successful hotel companies will know their customers so well that they could become a "personal concierge," recommending unique services beyond the hotel. For example, by knowing the traveler's unique profile and building electronic alliances with other service providers, the company could even recommend a sitter for a stay-at-home pet or a bonded housekeeping service for spring cleaning at home during an extended vacation—all within the online reservation process.

Technology will play a major role in making these stronger future relationships possible. As prices of data storage decline, the capacity for larger guest databases will become economically attractive. As access to consistent public networks becomes more widespread and affordable, buyers and suppliers will come together in new ways, without the need for intermediaries who impede the flow of information between them. As graphical interfaces make underlying complexities transparent to end consumers, we will realize previously unheard of possibilities for "anytime, anywhere" customer transactions. The years ahead will be exciting times for the leaders who have the foresight to use advancing technology for building innovative bonds with their best customers, instead of blindly implementing new technology for technology's sake.

Overall, the companies who win in the next decade will master the power of technology to provide unique customer knowledge, targeted service and an infrastructure for delivering it at all touch points. They will forge stronger guest bonds than their competitors, enter alliances that add to the overall guest experience without restricting customer knowledge and enable employees to do what they do best—deliver high-quality service to meet ever growing guest expectations.

As a result, they will also enjoy market premiums based on the overall value of the guest experience. The losers, on the other hand, will be companies that allow others to capture the customer information advantage and become relegated to competing in the general marketplace based on rate alone.

Relevance

Technology gives us the ability to forge relationships with millions of customers, but it's understanding what is relevant to those customers that makes bonds last. Relationships are by definition emotional. While anyone in the hotel industry understands that rate and location are key stay determinants, rate and location alone do not—and cannot—build client relationships. Relevance builds client relationships.

At Hilton, we work hard to understand our guests' wants and needs. We also work hard at predicting how those wants and needs might shift over time.

Changing demographics are and will continue to affect the relevancy of hotel products and promotions. The two most significant demographic shifts today are increasing diversity and the aging of our population. People today are living longer lives, having fewer children and spending more time alone—whether they are single, divorced or widowed.

The "average" American family is becoming a meaningless descriptor. Families now come in all shapes and sizes and their shapes shift as members move from one family unit to another. There are increasing numbers of single-parent households, "blended" households and multigenerational households. There is also a trend toward identifying friends as family or "family of choice."

These demographic shifts have wide-ranging implications for hotel companies. The aging Baby Boomers, who grew up traveling America's highways and byways, are at or near their peak for discretionary income. This spending power, coupled with the belief held by many of this generation that "traveling is our inalienable right," should bolster leisure travel for the foreseeable future.

Of course, hotel companies will have to adjust to the needs of an older traveler, including equipping rooms appropriately, changing food service and offering relevant packages.

On the other end of the age spectrum, children are wielding unprecedented buying power as well. They're increasingly influencing the wheres, whens, whos and whats of their family vacations as busy, guilty parents seek to create family memories.

Equally as significant to demographic shifts are changes in American values. We were a stressed-out culture before September 11. Now we're stressed out and scared. It's unlikely that we will see a return to the relative security of America before the World Trade Center tragedy. As uncertainty increases in our society, confidence decreases. We are taking fewer risks—with our money, with our careers, our families and our personal safety.

This has obvious implications for the hotel industry. We will need to reassure our customers that it is safe to travel. Leading brands have a psychological advantage in uncertain times. Customers know what to expect and feel safe in choosing familiar brands. At Hilton, we always feel a responsibility to meet guest expectations, but, in these times, we doubly do. Hotel companies are taking security measures very, very seriously and we can expect increased attention on safety in the years ahead.

Interestingly, there is a countertrend that is encouraging Americans to travel even as their safety concerns increase. Our country has been experiencing a move back toward "family values" over the past several years. The events of September 11 did not create this return to family, but they did push it along. At its heart, this trend is a return to connectedness. It's about a desire to be close to the people we love. We might expect this of Baby Boomers as they age, but it's also true of Generation X and especially true of Generation Y, which is the most conventional and conformist generation since WWI. For the hotel industry, this has implications ranging from multigenerational leisure packages to family reunions. Winning hotels will need to keep in mind that "connectedness," an emotional need, is as relevant to leisure customers as being "connected" to technology is to business travelers.

A continuing trend that is equally relevant to both business and leisure travelers is lack of time. Americans work more hours than citizens of all other industrialized nations. We describe ourselves as chronically time-crunched. One of the ironies is that we're so busy that we "don't have time for vacations." One could argue that "time" is what hotels actually sell—time to connect, time to refresh, time to enjoy, time to be more productive.

Acknowledging our time scarcity, Americans have been saying for the past decade that we want to "simplify" our lives. This continues to sound good to most of us. But it also continues to be more of a goal than a reality. So far, as a society, we haven't simplified our days or our dreams. We have high expectations of what we can and should achieve—and we have equally high expectations of what others should do for us. That includes what hotels should do for us in terms of service.

Multi-tasking is the norm in our culture. So it should come as no surprise that rather than simplify our travel experiences, we increasingly multitask within them. It used to be that leisure travelers went on vacation and vacationed. Today, a high percentage go on vacation and *work*. A recent study shows that 40 percent of travelers do not leave work behind them—they stay in touch with the office via technology. Conversely, we're seeing more business travelers extending their trips for leisure. The delineation between work and play will continue to blur, not simply because of our driven natures, but also because technology makes the blur possible.

To build strong customer relationships, hotel companies must remain relevant to their customers' lives. They must respond to shifts in demographics and values with products and programs that make sense, that deliver emotional as well as tangible benefits. Relevance is second only to customer relationships in our call to CREATE our brand future because it provides the context for all of our other efforts.

Experiences

Richard Branson of Virgin Airlines has always said that he doesn't sell air transportation, he sells entertainment. Starbucks says it doesn't sell coffee; it sells an experience. So does Hilton. So does the hotel industry.

We are not in the business of selling beds, conference rooms, ballrooms or meals. We are in the business of selling an experience, an experience relevant to the specific wants and needs of the individual guest. Hilton has a proprietary name for our customer relationship management program: "Customer Really Matters." Note that customer is singular, meaning we focus on every customer, one customer at a time.

No two customers have the same hotel experience. We don't want them to. From booking one of our rooms to checking out of one of our hotels, we want them to have an experience that is uniquely and wonderfully their own.

That means that everything we do—from booking to check-in; housekeeping to room service; greeting to problem-solving—is connected and important to creating a satisfying guest experience. Hotel employees at all levels and in all departments need to understand that they are personally a part of the "total guest experience."

In the future, we believe "connectedness" will not only be a relevant consumer trend and technology trend, but also an organizational trend. Every hotel employee has one overriding responsibility: To provide guests a special and satisfying experience. Successful hotels of the future will understand and embrace this.

Positive experiences build customer relationships. Customer relationships build business. It's that simple.

Accommodations

An undeniably important part of the guest experience is quality accommodations. A century ago, hotels attracted customers with such simple promises as "comfortable beds" and "quiet rooms." While such basics are still important, no longer are they the defining traits of a hotel or a hotel chain.

The hotel room of today, and that of the future, is a fusion of functionality and style set against a backdrop of technology. It is more than a place to sleep; it is, in many ways, much of what defines the travel experience, whether that be business or leisure.

A great hotel is not always one that has the grandest lobby or the most elegant furniture. Seasoned travelers will tell you that a great hotel is one that makes you feel at home. It's an environment where you can be relaxed but do not have to want for anything. It's a place that offers that perfect combination of comfort, quality and safety.

Today, one of the most fundamental challenges for hotel brands is to deliver *consistently* high-quality accommodations. This challenge will only intensify tomorrow. Hilton family brands have approached this challenge by setting high brand standards for accommodations—and constantly moving them higher.

The basics, like a comfortable bed, a large, well-lit room and a sparkling clean bathroom, will never go out of style or cease to be important. For more than 100 years, great hotels have been defined by such basic elements. But, as we begin to explore the opportunities that the 21st century offers, we see the value and necessity of combining these basics with the technology that is shaping other aspects of our lives.

To stay ahead of the curve, the Hilton brand family painstakingly researches and tests concept rooms that will shape our standard rooms of the future.

Room 267 at the Hilton Garden Inn near Los Angeles International Airport is officially our "Room of the Future." It is an experiment in balance between "homey" and high tech; luxury and affordability; practicality and pizzazz; familiarity and novelty; American tradition and international innovation.

Even the bed is different. It uses air baffles supported by wood slats instead of springs to mold to the body. And it can be adjusted, like a hospital bed, to a variety of positions. The standard lounge chair has been replaced by a leather massage chair. The standard TV-in-the-armoire has given way to a 14-inch flat panel display that not only entertains you, but also enables you to see who is at your door via videophone.

The bathroom has a separate shower with multiple showerheads. The Jacuzzi is equipped with a TV and the toilet comes complete with heated seat. There also is a bidet and a towel warmer.

Security "extras" include motion-sensor lights, a safe with digital keypad and an electronic "do not disturb" sign. It goes without saying that there is high-speed Internet service and a cordless phone.

This union of basics, luxuries and technology provides guests with a greater sense of comfort and control than ever before possible. Yet we know that this "Room of the Future" will be outdated within two years. The next version is already under development. It, too, will strive for balance with practicalities such as a self-cleaning bathroom and with luxuries such a climate control system that emits the soothing sound and fresh smell of rainfall.

Physically, a hotel is many things. It is ballrooms and boardrooms, dining rooms and lobbies. But, for most customers, what matters most are the comforts and amenities found in the private room or suite. The comfortable bed advertised a century ago is still important, but hotel accommodations of the future will be sculpted from a broader blend of technology, comfort, need and convenience.

Technology

Technology is woven into every aspect of our commitment to CREATE our own future, from customer relationships to accommodations. But it is so important, so strong a factor, that it also must stand alone.

Consider how technology has impacted the hotel industry—beginning with reservations. The invention of the telephone in the early 1900s provided a means for guests to book reservations directly with the hotel owner. Not much changed until the 1960s, when the advent of the computerized reservations system and 1-800 numbers gave guests the ability to book reservations for multiple stays across the country. The 1980s brought the global distribution systems (GDS), and the 1990s brought websites. Both gave guests the ability to "book direct" without ever contacting the hotel owner or operator. The year 2000 ushered in the "third party channel." This new distribution channel presents yet another change in how guests "purchase" their hotel room. But, as we discussed earlier, it is the first change that truly presents a danger to push the industry into complete commoditization. Moving forward, how/if the hotel industry gains control over this rapidly growing channel will determine just who actually "owns the relationship" with the consumer—the hotel or the channel by which they book their accommodations.

Every component of the travel industry, from sales and marketing to inventory control and purchasing, has been impacted by the Internet. In the hotel industry, most companies started their e-business initiatives by attempting to move their traditional strategies for managing the customer online. But it didn't take long for them to realize that that was not going to be enough. Fewer than seven years after their Web sites were launched, most companies found themselves in the position of trying to "take back the Internet." The new frontier had become a battleground, not the windfall opportunity that it appeared to be in 1995. Why?

More than anything else, the Internet provides content. It brings the customer face to face with information about products and services in a way in which no other medium can compete. Any marketing strategy that was based upon keeping information away from the customer was now transparent. For example, wholesale rates, which for years had been shrouded in indiscernible margins and mark-ups, were now transparent. Retail rates could no longer be justified if the customer had seamless access to both retail and wholesale prices at the same time. The Internet provided that content and completely changed the way customers could shop for values and bargains.

The Internet has also completely changed the way Americans work and communicate, creating the second major technology impact on the hotel industry. Before hotels became consumed with the challenge of Internet booking, we were challenged with wiring hotels for Internet connectivity. That need has spurred the introduction of a new networking technology known as Wi-Fi (short for "wireless fidelity"), which is quickly becoming a *necessary* offering for major (and even minor) hotel operators.

A high-speed wireless Internet connection, Wi-Fi has been gaining popularity where large groups of people gather. Information industry analysts at the Yankee Group project there will be 5.37 million users of public Wi-Fi networks in North America by 2007, up from only 30,000 this year.

Once relegated to homes and offices, Wi-Fi is clearly making its way into the mainstream. Schools and hospitals, even Starbucks and McDonalds, are offering wireless Internet connections. According to the Yankee Group, 40 percent of workers spend less than half their time in the primary work space. For people who travel on business and want frequent and convenient access to a broadband connection, Wi-Fi offers greater mobility and productivity than a conventional dial-up solution.

According to the research firm IDC, the worldwide number of Wi-Fi locations will increase to 118,000 by 2005, up from just over 19,000 at the end of 2002. More relevant to the hotels courting the business traveler, the percentage of Wi-Fi-enabled corporate laptops will grow from 20 percent in late 2001 to more than 90 percent by the end of 2007.

The race to continually implement new technology solutions has led many hotel owners to think of technology both as a blessing and as a curse. For example, in the early 1980s, innovative properties started introducing high-speed Internet access. This quickly became a point of differentiation to the business traveler.

But as technological advancements are conceptualized and implemented at astonishing speeds (think gigahertz), hotel companies can "catch up" with competitive technological offerings much faster than in the prior decade. Claims of "new" different, unique or special technology can barely be made before a competitor offers the same service. The evolution is so fast that, soon, not offering Wi-Fi may be equivalent to not offering a normal phone line.

Technology also is racing ahead in in-room entertainment, challenging hotels to keep up with both consumer expectations and business opportunities. This is the third major area of technology impact.

The hotel industry is no different than any other in that it wants to service the customer to the best of its ability while, at the same time, increasing its margins and profitability. In-room entertainment offers that opportunity.

From a broader perspective, the consumer electronics industry has grown by leaps and bounds in the past 10 years, predominantly from the influence of globalization and the pressure of international competitors. This has allowed for a fairly consolidated industry to come up with a vast and diverse array of products. From video recorders to compact discs, from Walkmans to PlayStations, people have a plethora of choices by which they can acquire media content.

Today, the bigger trend is the convergence of all of these devices; the idea is to make a whole range of devices more useful by linking them in a networked home-entertainment system. And while the notion that the television and the personal computer will increasingly resemble each other is not new, their convergence can't be effectively assimilated until broadband speeds catch up with the expanding "width" of content.

Once relegated to movies, in-room entertainment has expanded its own breadth and depth to include video games and online shopping services. Tomorrow's successful hotel companies will look for ways to offer more multimedia capabilities as the technology and consumer demand drive the market for these services.

Extraordinary Service

The final factor contributing to our vision for the future is arguably a more important contributor to creating customer experiences, and therefore, relationships, than either technology or accommodations. That factor is service—extraordinary service.

After location and rate, quality of service is the most often-cited criterion when selecting a hotel. In today's sophisticated hospitality world, "added value" to guests can no longer be obtained by simply outfitting a property with fancy amenities, five-star restaurants and luxurious frills. For hotels to attract their share of today's finicky travelers, they must provide a level of service that goes well beyond the "one-size-fits-all" formula of the past.

For years, the traditional hotel service-training program referred to guests in general terms as "they or them." Today, it's more about "him or her" or Mr. Douglas or Ms. Pearson. The point is, each guest is viewed as an individual person with specific interests, wants, needs and desires.

In one of our recent proprietary studies, frequent travelers described the "ideal hotel" as one that acts as a responsive and caring "personal assistant" catering to a guest's specific and individual needs. More and more, today's savvy travelers are viewing customized service at hotels as a requirement, rather than an option. This is even more apparent when you read some of the actual guest responses expressed during the Hilton study:

" . . . my needs are more important than the hotel's bureaucracy. I want a hotel that fits what I want versus what their daily regimen requires."

" My hotel experience has to be more personalized . . . I want to feel as if they're taking care of me as an individual."

"I want to feel as if [a hotel] cared enough to understand my personal needs. Most hotels are in a reactive mode [rather] than ahead of it."

In light of this new breed of "I/Me" guests, hotels today, regardless of their size or pricing structure, are searching for ways to provide their customers with consistent five-star service. Robert Nozar, editor-at-large for *Hotel & Motel Management* magazine, explains it this way:

"Whatever rate a hotel charges for its guestrooms, the customer knows that there are less expensive accommodations somewhere else. That means it becomes even more important for the hotel to do everything it can to help a guest perceive that he or she has found value in a lodging."

To maintain our own edge in this endeavor, Hilton combined our proud tradition of top-quality service with a zeal for innovation. The result: Our client relations management program, a potent mixture of training, communications, employee recognition and consistent operational execution. This intricate network of initiatives allows Hilton to capture key personal insights about each guest, enabling the hotels to provide specific amenities and services customized to their stay, right down to their own favorite pillow.

With the infrastructure of CRM now in place, the new millennium will experience a level of guest service never before seen. Imagine one day walking into a hotel room that is precisely outfitted to suit your specific needs and interests—from your own personal in-room "hello" to a pre-programmed selection of your all-time favorite television shows. Accommodations, technology and service will all merge to create an experience for you that is uniquely relevant to your own wants and needs. This tomorrow is really only steps away. For eight decades, Hilton has been synonymous with the word "hospitality." We have maintained and strengthened our brand equity through focus, innovation and passion. We will continue to CREATE a future for our brand, our industry—and most importantly, for our customers—that exceeds all expectations. At the end of the coming decade, Hilton will still be synonymous with "hospitality" because we will continue to set the standards that define it. We will build customer relationships through a relentless focus on what is relevant to our guests, creating special and satisfying experiences through unparalleled accommodations, technology and extraordinary service.

24

Competing in an Increasingly Hostile Environment

Bruce Wolff
Senior Vice President
Distribution Sales & Strategy
Marriott Hotel Corporation

Bruce Wolff is senior vice president of distribution sales and strategy for Marriott Lodging with responsibility for e-commerce sales and marketing and worldwide reservations sales.

Before joining Marriott in 1984, he was vice president, sales, marketing and customer service for New York Air; and president of Hickory Travel Services. Prior to this, he spent 13 years with TWA, where he led reservations sales and airline training.

A graduate of Lehigh University, he is a board member of Pegasus Systems, Inc., TravelWeb, LLC and the Travel Industry Association of America (elected 2004 national chair). He serves on the board of DRADA and Good Shepherd Ministries.

U.S. hotel occupancy in 2002 was 59 percent, the lowest in 31 years. With low occupancy come low rates. The U.S. decline in revenue per available room (REV PAR) in 2002 was 14 percent for upper-upscale and 12 percent for upscale hotels. There are reasons to be even more concerned about the future. Supply continues to grow faster than demand. Uncertainties such as SARS and terrorism must be calculated into any long-term planning. At the same time, the air transportation system is in disarray. Financial difficulties experienced by airlines make it challenging to project long-term low airfares. The hassle of air travel adds a new and significant "cost" to travelers who do not want to stand in long lines to remove their belt and shoes in order to get to a business meeting. Finally, the Internet is increasing price transparency in the lodging industry and has spawned a new generation of intermediaries who are adding significant costs.

In the face of this perfect storm, many would ask why Marriott would continue to grow its portfolio of 13 brands by about 25,000 rooms per year. A strong corporate culture that focuses on meeting the needs of our associates, customers, owners, and shareholders gives us the confidence to compete in an increasingly hostile environment. How can a strong array of brands, supported by a quality management team, navigate through a changing environment? The answer lies in three basics tenets: do not abandon one's core values; take advantages of emerging trends; and seek ways to change the economic environment where possible. While the next decade will certainly show dramatic changes in many aspects of our business, from how people buy to the products they demand, to the very uses for lodging products, a few things will not change. We must stay focused on attracting and retaining quality talents at all levels. Seventy-five years ago, Marriott was founded by J. W. Williard Marriott, Sr., who said, "Take care of your employees and they will take care of the customers." The more complexity we add to our business, the more this basic tenet helps differentiate those companies that see their associates as a principal asset from those companies that view their employees as expenses or liabilities. While many companies were cutting their workforce, Marriott knew it could never weather this storm on the backs of its associates. Marriott made sure that its associates did not bear an undue share of the difficult times. Key training programs and our systematic associate feedback initiatives helped ensure that our workforce is well positioned to capitalize on new market opportunities.

Customer's needs were also paramount during the past few challenging years. Short term-savings at the customer's expense can lead to serious brand erosion and long-term disasters. Relationship selling through a global network of integrated sales offices, capable of selling our 13 brands and over 2,600 properties, will continue to be a mainstay of our future plans.

While our industry is changing dramatically, a wise manager looks to benefit from inevitable trends. Marriott is well positioned to benefit from consolidation, globalization, demographic shifts, the Internet, and enhancements in marketing techniques (customer relationship marketing).

Consolidation

Many believe the lodging industry is dominated by a handful of major players. In fact, we are a fragmented business. Marriott's U.S. market share is less than 9 percent of total U.S. hotel rooms. Over the past two decades, there has been a movement toward consolidation. Economies of scale, efficiencies in sales and distribution channels, as well as customer preferences for predictable, reliable, quality lodging have fostered steady consolidation. This trend will continue for the foreseeable future. Without an array of products in desirable locations to meet an individual's or corporation's spectrum of needs, independent properties and small chains will have an increasingly difficult time remaining relevant.

Globalization

Global travelers are demanding global brands. There is little interest in someone investing their valuable leisure time or business travel budget exploring unproven, risky lodging decisions. There is enormous opportunity here for global brands, such as Marriott, to increase penetration and have an even greater impact on the global marketplace. For example, in Europe and the Middle East, branded hotels represent less than 20 percent of the market supply. The Asia Pacific region provides even greater opportunities.

Internet

The Internet is a two-edged sword for the hotel industry. It provides impressive opportunities for low-cost distribution, high-quality information transfer with consumers, as well as a mechanism to enhance our customer relationship with people who choose to do business online. Marriott.com has capitalized on this trend and will continue to support the organization's growth and cost objectives.

In 2002, more than $1 billion in Marriott room nights were sold on Marriott.com. In 2003, sales will increase 50 percent. The Internet now delivers more than 10 percent of our business. This could more than double in the next five years. Three-quarters of all our online business comes via Marriott.com. On a fully allocated basis, the Internet is our lowest-cost distribution channel. With more than 100 million page-views served each month, the value of Marriott.com far exceeds the tally of its online transactions. More than just a sales channel, Marriott's Internet sites empower customers with the ability to do business with the company when, where and how they want. The approximately five million customers who visit Marriott.com each month appreciate the quality of information and the ease of doing business. Marriott.com enables the company to establish personal relationships with customers by providing desired services and important information. Today, the scope of the service offering on Marriott.com is primarily pre-travel planning and booking in a traditional business-to-customer (B2C) construct. Tomorrow, the Internet will permeate the key business-to-business (B2B) markets as well, with customized online booking tools for corporate accounts, travel managers, and convention and meeting planners.

While the Internet has favored us, there are two significant concerns that could adversely impact hotel profitability. The Internet has enhanced price transparency and spawned powerful new intermediaries.

An Example of Changing the Economic Environment

In the Internet space, oligopolies are forming in virtually every segment. Priceline and Hotwire dominate the opaque market place; Sabre is a major player in on-line corporate sales, retail sales, and packaging. They plan to increase their merchant presence. Of particular concern is the rise of the merchant model, which threatens to have impact on long-term hotel profitability. Interactivecorp (owner of Hotels.com and Expedia.com) controls more than 75 percent of merchant sales.

A little background: The standard method of sales, by third parties, was agency or commission-based sales, where the intermediary would sell products offered by the lodging company at prices defined by the lodging company for a commission. Commissions ranged from 3–15 percent, based on a variety of factors. Merchant model, however, relies on a merchant negotiating a fixed (low) price for a block of rooms. The merchant accepts no inventory risk but marks up the rooms (generally 25–40 percent) and distributes them via the Internet. Growth in this space has been phenomenal. During a three-year period of declining hotel occupancy, merchant hotel sales have increased at a compound annual growth rate of more than 150 percent to sales in excess of $2 billion. Interactive's market cap of $19 billion exceeds the market cap of Marriott or Hilton or Starwood. The growth is exacerbated by the strong negotiating power the merchant had during periods of low occupancy. There are three primary difficulties with the merchant model:

1. **Pricing Integrity**. Because of the bulk nature of the room purchase, properties find their product for sale at prices lower than available through their own channels.

2. **Inventory Integrity**. Because of the imbalance of negotiating power, merchants are able to require properties to agree to fixed room blocks throughout the year. A fixed room block means that during peak periods a property could find itself unable to meet customer needs even though the merchant still has an allocation available for sale.

3. **Cost of the Channel**. Markups of 25–40 percent are taking significant money from the transaction without benefiting the consumer. In addition, dealing with merchants at the property level could be expensive because of lack of automation.

To create a supplier-friendly competitive alternative to the existing oligopoly, Hilton, Hyatt, Starwood, Marriott, Six Continents and Pegasus, a leading technology company, created a venture called Travelweb. All hotel chains and independents were encouraged to participate on terms comparable to the founding members. The first operating year of Travelweb has proven to be very successful. Approximately 10,000 hotels have signed up. They are enjoying sales at an annual rate in excess of $100 million dollars, at competitive prices.

Will the Internet Commoditize the Hotel Industry?

There is a growing belief that the Internet will commoditize the hotel industry so that, within a given tier (upscale, mid-tier, economy, etc.), consumers will become indifferent to the brand selected and will buy solely on price. We believe that the Internet will enhance pricing transparency to better facilitate customers who make value decisions. This prospect should be encouraging to superior brands. The Internet is a great provider of information. Information is the ally of brands with superior products, locations, service reputations, and amenities, etc. There are three reasons we believe that our brands will not be commoditized in the Internet environment.

1. Unlike true commodities, our basic product is highly differentiated in ways that are important to the consumer. Leisure travelers do not want to

squander their hard-earned leisure time at a location that does not provide them with the value they deserve. Business travelers do not want to risk the productivity of their trip on unreliable or unproven products.

2. We do choose not to be commoditized. This is an important aspect. At Marriott, as at other important brand companies, a significant amount of time is spent ensuring that we create brand value and differentiation. We make enormous efforts on product development, program development (such as Marriott Rewards), and support systems to ensure consistent reliable delivery of our products and services. Throughout our almost 3,000 hotels, they are developed to ensure that we remain differentiated in the consumer's mind. For those who question the impact of this approach, consider Purdue Chicken. Many in the past would have considered chickens to be a commodity, yet Purdue Chicken has been able to consistently command premium prices for its product. If this can be done with chicken parts, it clearly can be done by a company that manages an array of brands designed to meet business, leisure, and extended-stay travelers' needs.

3. Of greatest importance, consumers do not see our product as a commodity. On an average business day, Marriott receives over three reservations per second from customers and travel agents around the world. The impact of these millions of reservations, month in and month out, consistently results in revenue per available room premiums for our brands compared to those of our competitors. Informed customers and travel agents are reaffirming, every minute of the day, that they see value in the Marriott brand. Their preference is reaffirmed in tracking studies of business travelers, leisure travelers, corporate travel managers, and meeting planners. The very way people make reservations demonstrates their affirmation of brand preferences. In Marriott's case, the bulk of our customers, both online and offline, choose to book directly with us vs. an intermediary. Among guests who choose travel agents, a disproportionate share of their business is booked in Marriott rooms. Marriott currently commands about 20 percent market share in the major Global Distribution Systems (GDS). It should be remembered that the travel agents who make these bookings have complete transparency about rates for all competitors.

There is one channel designed for people who think of hotels as a commodity product. Priceline offers consumers a proposition whereby the consumer makes a binding commitment to purchase a hotel room within a given star category, if Priceline can find a hotel at the price the customer has bid. Some consumers are attracted to the prospect of lower rates in exchange for foregoing brand choices.

This year Priceline expects to sell about 5.6 million hotel rooms to such brand agnostic customers, less than 1/2 of 1 percent of the total rooms sold in North America. While Priceline is an excellent service for those who choose to buy that way, they do help demonstrate that the overwhelming majority of consumers are willing to pay a premium for their ability to select a brand. Successful future relies on maintaining core values, capitalizing on and responding to major structural changes and where possible, influencing the course of the marketplace.

Conclusion

Few industries are transforming themselves as fast as the travel industry. Hotels face new forms of competition and new intermediaries. Soon, the Internet will become to travel what the ATM is to banking. Through it all, successful companies, like Marriott, will remain true to their core values of a "spirit to serve" and will strive to satisfy and delight their guests at every opportunity.

25

Getting Close to Our Customers

Bob Gilbert, CTC
Vice President,
Worldwide Marketing and Sales
Best Western International

Bob Gilbert is vice president, worldwide marketing and sales, Best Western International, the world's largest hotel chain. He has more than 30 years' experience in the travel and hospitality industry. He is an opinion maker. He started his career in London as a travel agent in 1965. Bob is well known for his innovative and aggressive business solutions in competitive environments, both domestically and internationally.

Earlier in his career, Gilbert held senior executive positions with Walt Disney Attractions–Disneyland, SuperClubs, Choice Hotels International, Creative Tourism, Crest Hotels International, Utell International, and Charisma Records (where he worked with Phil Collins and Genesis).

Among his accomplishments, Gilbert was a lead in the hotel industry's first-ever strategic hotel alliance (between Crest Hotels and Quality Inns International in 1981); a member of the senior management team that gave birth to hotel brand segmentation (Choice Hotels 1983); Choice Hotel's "suitcase" advertising creative; he created and implemented the "world's largest sales blitz" (33, 000 worldwide sales calls in seven days—(Choice Hotels 1992); on executive team that introduced the hotel industry's first-ever real time Web booking engine (Choice

Hotels, 1995); created Disneyland's "Kids Fly Free" initiative with Southwest Airlines (Disneyland, 1998); developed first ever online educational program, Travel Agent University, with *Travel Agent* magazine—at www.tau.com (SuperClubs 1999); and repositioned Best Western under the brand position of World's Largest Hotel Chain (2001).

A frequent travel industry speaker, Bob serves as a board director with Travel Industry Association of America (TIA), and is active with NTA and ASTA. He has been recognized for numerous travel industry achievements, including a *Brand Week* feature article (July 2003), 1997/98 "Attractions Person of the Year" by *Travel Agent Magazine*, 1996/97 "Hotel Person of the Year" by *Travel Agent Magazine* and also listed in "The 25 Most Influential Executives in the Tour & Travel Industry" by *Tour & Travel News*. Bob has played leadership industry roles including chairman of AH&MA's international marketing committee; chairman of Pow Wow Europe; executive board director, TIA; board director, TIA; board director, Viator Networks; advisory board SpaView.com. He has worked on executive committees with ASTA, AAA, USTOA, ETOA, HSMAI, CTO, CHA and ICTA and is on the board of the Junior Diabetes Research Foundation.

He speaks French, German, Italian and Spanish. Educated in London, he holds the MinstM diploma (Institute of Marketing diploma, 1983) and ICTA's CTC (Certified Travel Counselor) accreditation, which he gained in 1998. He lives with his wife and two sons in Scottsdale, Arizona.

The world is changing fast. Of course, the world has always been changing fast. Only the *speed* of change is faster.

We are in sales and marketing; there must be speed. There must be change. There must be a sense of urgency. There must be a continual quest for creativity and innovation. As we read all the latest hot news on customer relationship management (CRM), we see more and more the infamous "E" (for "electronic") being placed in front of CRM. ECRM entails all the aspects of interaction a company has with its customer. If managed well, it can also predict behavior. Giving the customers what they need when they want it. CRM is all about the customer-or at least it should be. It's about creating and perpetuating that special "one-on-one" dialogue. Sound familiar?

It's a one-to-one marketplace and has been since the first two cave dwellers struck a deal on a flint knife. Down at its most basic, bedrock level, selling involves two people, one with something the other wants or needs or desires. Throughout the history of organized commerce, sales has been a one-to-one science. When we've forgotten that most basic tenet or when we've let it get lost in trendy theories, numbers drop. We become so enamored of the process that we lose sight of the objective: To sell more of whatever it is we are selling.

I believe this is a contemporary problem, a product of our love affair with technology and all things new. Of course, somewhere along the line, someone may have sold us on the need for all things new.

In truth, it's only been in the last generation or two that the personal touch, the personal relationship, has been displaced. For countless generations before, it was the only way to sell.

Master salesmen were, traditionally, the ones who built the relationships with those to whom they were selling. In the opening scenes of the popular musical, *The Music Man*, we're told "You've gotta know the territory." That's simply another way of saying you've got to know the people. You've got to know what they want, what they need and how you can be the one to supply those wants and needs.

That was easier to do in simpler times. The door-to-door or traveling salesman was practically an institution. Indeed, he generated an entire cottage joke industry devoted to his extracurricular activities.

Some master salesmen became legends by following that creed and their creations are still with us: J.C. Penney. Sears. And, of course, one of the real legends of the sales art . . .

It was 1906, on a cold day, when a young Nova Scotian huddled over his workbench between the furnace and the coal bin in his sister's home as he struggled to create "the best products of their kind in the world." Selling from door to door, with his suitcase full of custom-made brushes, Alfred C. Fuller created the Fuller Brush Company and the selling icon, the Fuller Brush Man. Fuller had three basic rules:

- Make it work.
- Make it last.
- Guarantee it no matter what.

He sold his brushes door-to-door, one personal relationship at a time. Today, his old fiber suitcase is a 12-acre plant that produces more than 2,000 items. That's the power of relationship selling.

The world that gave birth to the likes of Alfred Fuller has changed almost beyond description. We live in complicated times now. We move people, goods, ideas and information—vast amounts of information—at speeds that exceed sound and thought. We get the news in real time, as it happens, live in our living rooms, in full color. We carry miniature wireless devices and sound systems wherever we go. We are bombarded every second of every day by sophisticated messages, designed to exact specific responses—buy this, buy that, vote for John, vote for Jack, don't do this, do support that.

And things aren't getting any simpler. The world is changing, as I already pointed out. It's also getting more complex.

Every day, there are more and more people, all trying to be heard, all trying to make sense of what they hear and read and each expressing differing points of view on an endless array of subjects.

At the heart of this cacophony of sound and sight is the very simple human desire to say something to someone else and be understood. Or rather, to say anything and be heard.

The ability to communicate, which includes listening as a basic principle, is an elemental part of the human experience. It makes possible everything that distinguishes man from the rest of creation.

The ability of one person to relate to another through an exchange of ideas is the beginning of civilization. The ability to record those ideas is the basis of all experience and knowledge. The ability of an individual or a group to communicate with others is the beginning of all mankind's achievements, from the first cavemen hunting down a creature many times their size to the exploration of space.

If you would succeed in selling and if you would understand the success of others, nothing is more important than an understanding of the process by which we exchange ideas, by which we inform, by which we influence, by which we explain, by which we learn.

Personal relationships are basic to the everyday existence of every modern individual and every organization.

The complexity of a society can be measured by the amount of information, opinion and speculative knowledge necessary to keep it operating with reasonable consistency. We do live in complicated days.

The amount of information required to keep our society functioning is mind numbing. Machines process information at speeds we can't comprehend, using communications systems that are unlike any in the history of our species. We've had to create new words to even describe the process to ourselves. Nanosecond. Internet. Interface. Under it all is the nagging sense that our humanity is being threatened.

Bill Joy, co-founder and chief scientist of Sun Microsystems, one of the leading manufacturers of web site servers, confirmed that feeling a couple of years ago in newspaper interviews.

He predicted that technology is very close to causing "something like extinction" for mankind, probably by the year 2030. Others of his ilk agree. Hugo de Garis, an Australian computer genius who works for the Japanese in communications research, says machines will match human memory and thinking speed by 2020.

These are, indeed, unusual and unsettling days. And it goes far beyond the technology. The technology is designed and created by a group of people over there. It is used by another group of people over here. Each group has different skills and different agendas. It is unusual if they ever meet. And they very poorly understand the separate languages they speak.

The resulting messages conflict. Everyone seems to have something to say. Driven by that incredible technology, the competition for your listening time and understanding is vicious. Messages overlap. Some are blotted out completely. Not all are heard. Fewer are understood. Many go by so quickly they never register at all.

For the average individual, the result is a sort of numbing self-defense. We develop selective filters . . . or we shut down.

Some are overwhelmed by the rush of information. Like Bambi in the headlights, they simply don't understand what is happening around then. They go from day to day blaming their problems on the most convenient scapegoat—the press, the government, others. They let information control them without understanding why.

Some people simply don't care. They let information control them and they understand what is happening. They've shut down and they just don't care.

Some people do care. They work hard at coping with the vast flow of information. They develop their own filters. They are critical consumers, informed about what is happening around them.

We who sell or market try to reach all these people. We've created special television channels and direct marketing opportunities. We've whipped up an alphabet soup of theories and programs. We use CRM, ECRM, VCR, TV, CD-ROMs and more.

And lost in the middle of all the chaos of communicating, selling, advertising and marketing is the rock on which we built the whole Tower of Babel: the one-to-one marketplace. At Best Western International, we are working to bring the selling experience full circle, back to our most basic roots.

The hotel business is, after all, a very personal business. I invite you to spend the night under my roof. This is especially true of an organization that is made up of hundreds of individually owned businesses, many of them family owned and into second and third generations. Because of this, there is the pride of ownership. I want you to like my hotel and appreciate what I've done with it.

In the pleasant northern Arizona community of Williams is the Best Western Williams Inn, owned by Eva Vandiever, a veteran hotelier and Best Western owner. Eva understands about pride and personal relationships. "I have been in this industry a long time, and have seen a lot of changes in what our guests' expectations are. I have a personal desire to exceed those expectations and work diligently to achieve this goal. My personal philosophy is to exceed guest expectations with my accommodations and then deliver the best possible friendly service to enhance the guest's experience, one guest at a time."

Eva believes her personal philosophy is also the philosophy that must drive Best Western. A regular guest at the Inn of Williams agreed. "The staff is always friendly and helpful. The location is wonderful and the thing that makes the Inn really so special are the 'touches of Eva' so obvious in the design and furnishings. She works so hard for perfection and it shows."

"The importance of a quality property is what we should all strive for. It only takes one bad experience to turn a Best Western regular guest into a guest for the competition. I want my property to be the best I can make it, and in turn, I expect other Best Western members to do the same. Their guests tonight could be mine tomorrow night . . . It's a matter of pride, I believe," says Eva.

Eva Vandiever is just one member of an organization of fiercely independent hoteliers who understand that the one-to-one marketplace is where their bread and butter is.

One-to-one marketing means truly understanding the real needs of your customer. This, in turn, translates to more research on customer needs and desires. What makes them tick? Do they tick differently than last year? Without understanding the "tick," how can we meet their needs and beat their expectations?

Best Western International, not long ago, undertook a major research project to understand the needs of global clients. Interestingly, the results were pretty similar all over the world. The immediate result was the creation of a program called "Best Requests." Best Requests ensures that every Best Western property has the same consistent amenities and standards worldwide. The program retains the nonhomogeneous nature of our entrepreneurial hotels, while downsizing risk or apprehension on service levels. That is why you will find in-room tea- and coffee-making facilities, laptop data ports, free local calls, kids staying for free, hot or cold breakfast, irons and ironing boards, hairdryers, etc. The list goes on. Add to that that Best Western is the world's largest hotel chain and you have a strong, compelling marketing message. We are saying to consumers that we listened when they told us what they wanted and we now have it ready for them. That's important, for we see a future in which the world is dominated by a handful of great world brands. We also see companies learning from each other and developing what we call "Best Practices."

We also see that, because of the speed of disseminating this information, coupled with the speed of its adoption and adaptation, we all end up looking the same to the consumer. Breaking through the clutter and the sameness is critical. This demands creativity and it demands focus. The consumer looks at hotel chains (especially mid-scale chains) and has a difficult time differentiating between them.

Best Western's strategy is simple, clear and compelling. We must and will increase our global brand awareness. We will do this with our World's Largest campaign, and a series of tactically inserted memorable and fun promotions that capture the targeted audience's imagination.

Examples of this will be the creation of a golf event that pits amateurs from across North America against two world-class golf professionals; John Daley and Lee Trevino. The winners get $100,000. Runners-up receive $50,000. As they say, "That's a compelling value proposition." This is the first time in golfing history an event like this has taken place. We are marketing this as Best Western's "People Vs. the Pros." And it's only open to those who join our loyalty program, Gold Crown Club International. This not only drives acquisition but also pride of membership.

Building and keeping loyalty has to be the cornerstone of any business. It's an important part of life in the one-to-one marketplace. Loyalty, for the most part, will always be fleeting. There must be a continual drive to increase acquisition and usage. The future successes will be built on the ability to keep customers as loyal as possible. This will involve "Loyalty Handcuffs," making it very difficult for a loyal guest to even consider "jumping ship." Loyalty programs will need to become very creative and go beyond the obvious double, triple or even quadruple miles promotions, moving into the entertainment business and conjuring up sizzling offers on a monthly basis. And—a critical point—we must communicate all of this in a one-to-one personalized framework.

So where are we headed in this rush of change?

I believe that data mining specialists will be worth their weight in gold as we research hidden behavior that will hopefully predict future travel booking patterns. Data mining will also assist in identifying common interest groups that can be communicated with a simple call to action or offer. True data mining software of the future will actually discover previously unknown relationships and make our jobs as marketers a little easier.

Anti-junk mail programs will become very popular. Pop-up messages will disappear. Opt-in programs will become as redundant as the fax machine, as more memory resident programs are developed, allowing consumers to hit a button on their desktops and read all the offers that are created and selected "just for me."

Do you understand what all this really means, what all this technology allows us to do? It gives us the ability to get as close as possible to the customer, to reestablish that special one-on-one relationship of earlier generations of door-to-door selling. That's our Holy Grail, after all.

Disintermediation will be the future battlefield, but make sure you are on the winning side of the disintermediation battle. Do you want to relinquish control of your message or even your pricing to a third party that cares nothing about you or your brand? Rhetorical question, of course, but many will suffer the long- term consequences for a short-term gain.

Traditional companies, which thrived for many years on providing connectivity links to broadly based audiences, will be challenged to survive.

Many companies undervalue the superglue of the travel industry—the much maligned travel agent. Some say travel agents will totally disappear due to the current rise of online travel companies such as Expedia, Travelocity and Orbitz. Travel is not a commodity, although a point-to-point airline ticket, the purchase of which has been made so simple by the Internet, is. It is interesting to note that those airlines—Jet Blue and Southwest Airlines, as obvious examples—that will be profitable tomorrow are those that break through the clutter and focus on the customer today, and have fun doing it.

Travel agents who can create value for their clients will be around forever. There is a big difference between an order taker and a "consigliore" who can offer real hands-on expertise on travel. A true travel agent/professional provides counsel for business trips, Caribbean cruises or honeymoons. Their success will be in getting as close to their customer as possible. The savvy travel supplier will work hard to carve out special relationships with those agents who know how to effectively sell products and services. This relationship is similar to a car dealer's relationship with his automobile manufacturer.

Many times we either make this marketing stuff very scientific or too mystical. The reality is that marketing's job is really very simple. Here's my definition (stolen and abridged from several sources): "The sole purpose of marketing is to get more people to buy more of our product, more often, for more money. That is the only reason to spend a single nickel, euro, yen or peso."

If your marketing efforts are not delivering consumers to the cash register to buy your product—don't undertake them. Do something different. And do so quickly, because you can bet your competition is doing just that—and watching you in their rearview mirrors.

"We don't make any money until we sell the stuff, and we can't sell the stuff until we've gotten people to know that we have it and to create a demand for it. And that's what marketing does. "

At the end of the day, a clear and concise strategy with thoughtful and simple execution of the plan will win. And of course, when all is said and done, we hope we will have more customers than the competition.

But always remember this: In the rapidly changing, highly complex world that is our marketplace, hope is not a strategy.

26

Harrah's Entertainment and the Future of Casino Marketing

Gary Loveman
President and CEO
Harrah's Entertainment, Inc.

Gary Loveman is president and CEO of Harrah's Entertainment, Inc., a Fortune 500 Company publicly traded on the New York Stock Exchange. Harrah's is a leading casino entertainment company with 43,000 employees and $4.1 billion in revenues in 2002. Prior to his appointment, Loveman oversaw brand operations, marketing, information technology, and day-to-day operations at Harrah's 26 properties during his four-and-a-half years' tenure as CEO.

Loveman serves on Harrah's board of directors, and is an outside director of Coach, Inc. (NYSE:COH), a leading marketer of modern classic American accessories.

Before joining Harrah's in May 1998, Loveman was associate professor of business administration at the Harvard University Graduate School of Business Administration, where he taught service management in the M.B.A. and executive programs. Loveman was awarded a Ph.D. in economics from the Massachusetts Institute of Technology, where he was an Alfred Sloan Doctoral Dissertation Fellow; he earned a bachelor or arts in economics from Wesleyan University.

Harrah's Entertainment's Growth Challenge

Founded in 1937 by William F. Harrah, Harrah's Entertainment, Inc., is the premier U.S. gaming brand, operating 26 casinos in 13 states. In the 1990s, Harrah's expanded from its operations in Nevada and New Jersey into the new gaming jurisdictions of Illinois, Mississippi, Louisiana, Missouri, Indiana and elsewhere. Although the company enjoyed considerable growth from the opening of these new markets, subsequent entrants into each market narrowed margins and reduced earnings growth. With revenue stalled and the company's stock price in decline, Harrah's Chairman and CEO Phil Satre sought ways to leverage Harrah's brand recognition and geographic diversification to stimulate same-store sales. Satre believed the right technology could serve as the foundation for the growth of cross-market revenues, i.e., sales generated by customers outside their home markets. So he approved a significant investment in development of a national database to track customer play, determine player value and suggest marketing interventions.

Harrah's Turnaround

To counter stagnant performances at existing properties, many casino operators—particularly in Las Vegas—adopted a strategy of building billion-dollar properties complete with "must-see" attractions. Visitors were impressed with the fountains dancing at the Bellagio, the canals flowing through The Venetian, the pseudo-volcano erupting at The Mirage and the pirate ships battling at Treasure Island. This "build it and they will come" strategy was designed to draw new customers to casinos and generate incremental revenues from the properties' gaming, food and beverage, retail and entertainment venues.

Harrah's chose a very different approach, adopting a gaming-centric focus in which greatly improved marketing effectiveness and enhanced service delivery would build enduring customer loyalty. In 1998, Satre hired Harvard Business School professor Gary Loveman, who had been a marketing consultant to the company, as Harrah's new chief operating officer. This gamble countered the prevailing wisdom that gaming industry leaders could come only from inside the casino business. Gaming was perceived as a complicated business, shrouded in mystery with intricate strategies that no outsider could understand. Satre, a lawyer, knew otherwise and was determined to hire a marketing powerhouse who could turn around the company and create solid, sustainable growth.

When Loveman arrived, he faced the challenge of creating and executing a turnaround strategy targeted at generating growth in a highly regulated business with limited new development opportunities. The proliferation of gaming in new jurisdictions had slowed to a trickle, with growth centered mostly on difficult-to-obtain Native American casino management contracts. Loveman quickly realized he could not easily change the merchandise that was for sale, as other retail businesses could. He was constrained by the existing and inconsistent quality of the assets and the static nature of his "products." It was apparent, though, that he could influence the way gaming customers made decisions about where to make their gambling visits. He could do this by improving the mediocre customer service that characterized all but the "high-roller" segment of the industry, and by developing decision-science marketing capabilities to enhance the customized value delivered to each of the millions of Harrah's customers. Loveman set out to transform Harrah's from an organization focused on the operating performances of individual properties into one guided by decision-science-based marketing strategies developed at the corporate level. Building on a platform established by Satre, he wanted to change the culture—ubiquitous throughout the industry—from one based on properties as individual fiefdoms that frequently discouraged *their* customers from patronizing other company casinos, to a branded enterprise approach in which customers were encouraged to frequent as many Harrah's casinos as possible. Finally, he mandated personnel changes to elevate the level of intellectual capital and talent in the organization, especially in the marketing area. Casino operational experience was no longer the most valued attribute in the hiring of new professionals.

Harrah's Growth Strategy

With an effective organizational structure in place and clarity about customer "ownership"—players belonged to the company, not to the individual properties—Loveman devised an organic-growth strategy aimed at boosting same-store sales. He launched extensive surveys of members of the company's nationwide player-loyalty program, Total Rewards. He discovered that those customers were spending only 36 percent of their annual gaming budgets at Harrah's properties. The opportunity to capture a share of the 64 percent of those budgets spent at competitors' casinos afforded enormous revenue and earnings potential—if Harrah's could increase customer loyalty. Loveman knew Harrah's didn't need customers to gamble more; they merely needed to consolidate their existing spend at Harrah's. The company estimated a mere 100 basis point increase—from 36 percent to 37 percent—in customer spend at Harrah's would boost the stock price $1.10 a share.[1]

Loveman's same-store growth strategy focused on three key initiatives: Create brand identity and stimulate trial, envelop customers with great customer service to drive loyalty, and use proprietary decision-science capabilities to optimize customer profitability. The overriding goal of the strategy was to make customer relationship management (CRM) a core competency at Harrah's. A customer-centric approach to marketing and operations, CRM is technology-intensive, automates key business decisions and processes, and is anticipatory—not reactive—in nature. CRM success requires delivery of consistent, high-quality customer service across all touch points.

Consumers become loyal to brands because they develop trust based on the value propositions and their individual experiences with the brands. Before Harrah's launched its branding campaign, casino companies were rarely able to gain lasting traction or affinity for their brands. There was little brand differentiation in the industry aside from Caesars, which had properties only in Las Vegas, Lake Tahoe and Atlantic City. Based on customer research, Harrah's decided to focus its brand messaging on a gaming-centric platform that re-created players' descriptions of the "exuberantly alive" anticipation and excitement they experienced as the principal emotions of gambling. Cognizant of its nationwide property distribution, Harrah's also needed to bolster customer preference and trust in a brand that offered consistently exciting entertainment experiences. But it first had to address service-delivery issues to ensure Harrah's customers actually had experiences aligned with the brand's positioning.

Many consumer businesses cite customer loyalty as the key to their successes. But few measure customer loyalty, and fewer still actually implement customer-loyalty initiatives. Loveman realized Harrah's needed to employ the concepts of the service-profit chain[2], which holds that only very satisfied customers become loyal customers. Great service delivery, a key factor in building customer loyalty, required well-trained, satisfied and loyal employees. Harrah's launched an extensive training program called FOCUS to prepare its employees to provide truly great service. And it implemented a plan that paid quarterly bonuses to non-management employees based on improvements in customer-satisfaction scores. Individual employees earned up to $200 per quarter based upon service improvements. The improvements were measured by customer surveys sent to Total Rewards cardholders after their visits to company properties.

The development and implementation of decision-science capabilities were the final components of the strategy. The first capability Harrah's developed predicted customer worth—the theoretical amount the company could expect to win over time based on the customer's pattern of casino play, demographics and other detailed transactional information. Thus armed, Harrah's was able to model the predicted behavior of certain customer segments. Although each customer was measured to compare actual versus predicted behavior, the application focused on "avid, experienced players" (AEPs) whose average gaming spend was from $100 to $399 per visit. The potential upside was the difference between observed and predicted behavior. Opportunity segments showed the greatest upside and received heavier reinvestment in the form of complimentary rooms, food and beverage, show tickets, cash and other rewards. Segments at their predicted full potential were targeted for reduced reinvestment. After properly segmenting customers, Harrah's sent them appropriately customized marketing inducements.

For example, a Las Vegas visitor staying at a competitor's property might enter a Harrah's casino, sign up for a Total Rewards card and play slot machines for an hour. Based on the customer's tracked play, the traditional marketing application would call for Harrah's to send an offer, such as a free buffet ticket, based solely on that hour's gambling. By contrast, the competitor's property would offer the customer complimentary rooms, food and beverages only after he or she had played many more hours there. The customer would have remained loyal to the host property and would not be likely to visit Harrah's again. Under Harrah's new CRM strategy, however, that customer—identified by the company's decision-science tools as a member of an opportunity segment—would receive an offer for complimentary rooms after a mere hour's play. That would be a powerful incentive for the customer to revisit Harrah's. Using processes modeled after epidemiological research methods, Harrah's splits customers into test and control groups. This methodology allows marketers to test optimum reinvestment figures for AEP customers and track the most popular offers. The goal is to produce growth in opportunity segments through appropriate increases in reinvestment, while maintaining the current levels of visitation from the full-potential segments despite reduced reinvestment.

Harrah's also introduced a hotel yield-management decision that optimizes high customer demand against the scarce supply of hotel rooms to maximize total profit per room. The system forecasts demand at a detailed customer segment level for a year into the future, based on current bookings, historical demand patterns and competitive market conditions. After the forecast is validated, the optimal hurdle rate for a particular date is calculated, and customer segments are priced and offered room availability. When a known Total Rewards customer phones Harrah's call centers or logs on to the website www.harrahs.com to make a hotel booking, the system recognizes the customer and offers the appropriate yielded access and rates. The most valuable customers typically have such a high gaming value that they are offered complimentary rooms. This system is the only revenue-optimization tool in the industry that takes two revenue streams—casino and hotel—into account. The yield-management system is an excellent example of how Harrah's adapted a proven capability from other industries such as airlines or hotels and brought it to an operational CRM level using the company's technology and marketing systems.

Results of Growth Strategy

After implementing its same-store strategy, Harrah's has recorded 18 consecutive quarters of same-store sales growth despite a challenging economy and the impacts of the terrorist attacks on America. The database of customers enrolled in the company's Total Rewards player-card program grew from 13.8 million members in 1998 to more than 26 million in 2002. Harrah's introduced a tiered Total Rewards loyalty-card program in 2000 in which customers are able to achieve higher levels of rewards based on their annual spend at the company's properties. As a result, customer consolidation of gaming spend rose significantly, with 40 percent of those who achieved higher-tier status increasing their play by a factor of more than three. This was a direct result of the better services and products offered to the higher-tiered cardholders. Customers truly appreciated the aspirational aspects of the loyalty program, and showed it by increasing their loyalty to the brand. The most telling measure of the success of this strategy has been the growth in Harrah's share of customer gaming budgets. In 2002, Harrah's captured a 43 percent share of its cardholders' annual casino spend, up from 36 percent in 1998.

Harrah's has also progressed in its quest for brand recognition. With consistent award-winning advertising, operations and service delivery across its properties nationwide, Harrah's has become the preferred brand in the gaming industry. When surveyed in 2000, gamblers gave Harrah's the highest unaided awareness of any casino brand. Another measure of brand loyalty and power is growth is cross-market revenues. Tracked revenues from Harrah's customers outside their home properties are called cross-market revenues. In 2002, revenues from Total Rewards cardholders at Harrah's properties outside their home markets exceeded $1 billion, up from $323 million in 1999.

The strength of the Harrah's brand has led to strategic marketing alliances with such entities as Coca-Cola, Sony Entertainment, Macy's, Maxim and Foyt Racing, which sought to reach customers with similar interests and attractive demographic profiles. These relationships have allowed Harrah's to create unique affiliations with other strong brands that resonate with customers, enabling the company to gain competitive advantages over other casino operators. For example, NASCAR is one of the fastest-growing sports in the United States and boasts extremely loyal fans. Through its sponsorship of driver Larry Foyt in the Winston Cup Series, Harrah's has been able to host "fan fests" at Harrah's Las Vegas with popular NASCAR drivers. The company also was the largest purchaser of tickets for the Winston Cup race at the Las Vegas Motor Speedway, enabling it to reward loyal customers with complimentary access to an exciting racing event. Its partnership with Macy's offers another example of how Harrah's benefits from strategic alliances. Harrah's customers were able to earn entries to win a December shopping excursion at Macy's flagship Herald Square store in New York City. The five winners were treated to private $10,000 shopping sprees before the store opened during the heaviest shopping period of the year. Harrah's will continue to use mutually beneficial events and promotions with existing and new partners to further solidify its brand leadership.

As a company offering 24-hour, 365-day-a-year entertainment to millions of customers nationwide, Harrah's has placed an emphasis on delivering great customer service. Thousands of customers conduct millions of transactions daily with valet, hotel, food and beverage, cashier, slot, table-game and Total Rewards employees. Thanks to its rigorous training programs, the company has seen significant improvement in customer satisfaction. As a result, Harrah's paid more than $14 million in customer-service bonuses to non-management employees in 2002.

Harrah's created metrics to determine the validity of the service-profit chain theory[2]. Guests were surveyed to gauge the effect of a change in service experience on their gaming behavior. Customers who gave the same ratings each year increased their gaming spend 10 percent. Those who lowered their ratings by one point increased their gaming spend only 4 percent, while customers who raised their ratings by one point boosted their gaming spend 20 percent. Guests who reduced their ratings two points or more cut their gaming spend at Harrah's 10 percent, while those who increased their rating by two points or more spent 24 percent more in the company's casinos. This evidence clearly demonstrates the efficacy of the service-profit chain and the service-excellence initiatives executed by Harrah's.

Harrah's proprietary decision-science capabilities have fueled the expansion of its customer database, the consolidation of customer spend and the growth of cross-market revenues. The capabilities allow Harrah's to maintain a consolidated view of its customers and to treat them according to their predicted lifetime value to the brand. In 2002, the Total Rewards tiered loyalty-card program saw 161 percent growth in gaming spend from players who were promoted to higher-tier status. In addition, Harrah's recorded higher same-store sales growth rates than the competition in markets across the United States, achieving a distinct competitive advantage through the intellectual capital and technological capabilities employed across the enterprise.

The customized hotel-yield management system has proven highly profitable to Harrah's, generating $120 million of incremental revenues in its first year of operation. The system helped boost revenue per available room an additional 13 percent in its second year despite a downturn in the lodging industry nationwide.

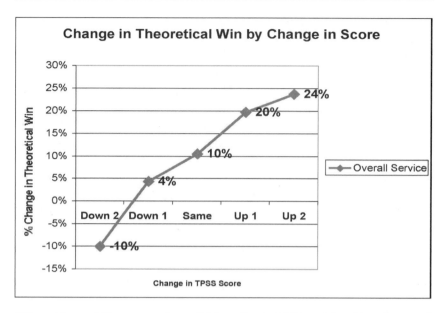

When this capability was made available online in 2002, web bookings increased 384 percent, as customers benefited by being able to get the best available yielded rates. For each online booking, Harrah's saved $3 on the estimated cost of processing a traditional phone reservation.

The Future of Marketing at Harrah's

As the gaming industry's leading practitioner of operational CRM, Harrah's knows it must continue to evolve its successful growth strategy. With strong, sustainable revenue growth in its AEP and high-end VIP business, Harrah's has begun to focus more on the retail-customer segment, comprised of players who have a daily gaming spend of less than $100. While such customers tend to have a lower value per visit than AEP or VIP customers, they comprise the majority of casino players and may visit Harrah's properties with greater frequency. Business from the retail segment was flat in 2002 because such customers were not often included in marketing activities. But in 2003, Harrah's turned its attention to enhancing the Total Rewards program for the retail segment to offer such customers a better value proposition.

Total Rewards was, by design, extremely popular with the AEP and VIP segments, but offered little of value to retail customers. Because the Total Rewards complimentary matrices were based on a six-trip average spend rather than cumulative spend, retail customers rarely earned rewards through the program. Customers who visited frequently had to negotiate with Total Rewards representatives to receive complimentary rewards. The representatives would manually review database records of customers' play and reward players accordingly.

Harrah's knew enhancements offered in the next phase of Total Rewards would have to encompass the retail segment by allowing those customers to have greater control over their rewards and enable them to "bank" rewards credits and spend them as they wished. Under the enhanced program, introduced June 17, 2003, reward credits have a currency value and each property offers an aspirational menu from which customers can select rewards. The transparency of the rewards menu and the value of the credits provide incentives to all customer segments and dispenses with the need to negotiate complimentaries. The new version of Total Rewards is expected to generate revenue growth from the retail segment.

Harrah's next phase of CRM development will allow the marketing of direct mail and email offers that specify a particular slot product and a particular value for its use. The practice will be very similar to the way retailers and grocers offer coupons and in-store promotions. Those businesses typically don't give customers direct cash incentives, as the gaming industry does, but offer specific discounts valid only on specific products during specific time periods. Harrah's plan is to mail coupons called "Reel Rewards" that can be inserted directly into slot machines. For example, a customer may receive an offer in the mail to play The Price Is Right slot machines at Harrah's. The Reel Rewards coupon may tell them the value is $40 if they visit on Friday or Saturday, $60 on any other day. The coupon would work on the specified game and would credit the player with the appropriate amount depending on the day of the week. The customer may have received the coupon because he or she has shown a preference for The Price Is Right slots or for similar game show-themed slots or to stimulate trial on a game they haven't played before. Test and control groups will be used to assess the effectiveness of different incentives.

New Gaming Distribution

Whenever gaming has been legalized in new jurisdictions, it has experienced rapid growth. Detroit's three commercial casinos, for example, hit the billion-dollar revenue mark within three years of opening, in spite of competition from an existing casino in nearby Windsor, Ontario. Its widespread popularity notwithstanding[3], commercial casino entertainment is available in only 11 states. The next wave of gaming innovation will address this supply-demand imbalance and lead to gaming expansion through both traditional and nontraditional channels. Casino operators will emulate other industries that have succeeded in filling customer demand for access to highly popular products and services through innovative distribution outlets. It wasn't long ago that a cup of coffee was sold only at restaurants or diners, or served at home. Today, fresh coffee can be bought at grocery stores, malls, hotel lobbies, gas stations, airports, bus terminals, book terminals, Starbucks and more. Similarly, new distribution systems for gaming products and services may include the Internet, interactive television, cellular telephones and events simulcast over radio and/or TV. New gaming products will be different from traditional table games and slot machines and have to be developed for delivery over such nontraditional channels. For example, one of the most popular games on the Internet today is Solitaire. No existing casino offers wagering on Solitaire because of the personnel and time required to oversee and complete a game. Yet it is possible to design a secure Solitaire game that allows consumers to play over a variety of channels and to wager on the outcome. The differences between such convenience games and live-action casino games must be analyzed to create viable new products.

The pace of gaming's expansion will depend in part on the realization by political leaders that for the vast majority of adults, casinos merely offer another form of entertainment, similar to movies and professional sports. Those adults demand convenient access to gaming entertainment, much as they do to movies and sports. A future major wave of growth in gaming will come in the form of readily accessible new distribution channels for the single most popular form of entertainment in America. Harrah's has built the capabilities to drive this evolution in gaming distribution, and will be the leader in providing great gaming experiences through emerging distribution channels.

Notes

[1] This was calculated by applying the appropriate margin to a 1 percent gain in revenues from Total Rewards cardholders, capitalizing the benefit at the then-current multiple to the stock price, and dividing that by the total number of shares outstanding.

[2] "Putting the Service Profit Chain to Work", *Harvard Business Review,* Heskett, Jones, Loveman, Sasser, and Schlesinger

[3] Seventy-nine percent of Americans believe casino entertainment is acceptable for themselves or others, according to a 2002 poll by Peter D. Hart Research Associates, Inc. and The Luntz Research Companies.

27

How to Compete in the "Get-Real" Decade: Rethinking Travel and Tourism in the 2000s

John T. A. Vanderslice
President and CEO
Club Med America

John T.A. Vanderslice joined Club Med on July 10, 2000 as president and CEO. His responsibilities include all sales, marketing, finance, operations and human resources for both the North and South America business units.

Mr. Vanderslice brings 20 years of brand development experience in the consumer products industry to this new corporate position, which was created to facilitate the worldwide decentralization of Club Méditerranée, the parent company. Currently, North America represents the second-largest market for Club Med after France.

Prior to joining Club Med, Mr. Vanderslice was with the Triarc Company from 1994-2000. He served as senior vice president, concept development at Triarc Restaurant Group (Ft. Lauderdale, FL), a subsidiary of Triarc Company, NY. At Triarc, he focused on strategic repositioning and brand development for Arby's®, T.J. Cinnamons®, and Pasta Connection®.

Mr. Vanderslice began his career in 1983 at Kraft General Foods in White Plains, NY. Over the next 12 years, he gained a wealth of experience in product repositioning and brand development in senior brand management and category management positions for a host of products including Post® Cereals, Kool-Aid®, Country Time® and Crystal Light®.

Born in February 17, 1961, Mr. Vanderslice holds a bachelor of science degree in marketing from Boston College School of Management. He lives in Boynton Beach, Florida with his wife and two children. His hobbies include entertainment, skiing, golf, and tennis.

Twenty. That's the number of people who set a world record by squeezing into a VW Beetle back in the "bug's" heyday. Today, that record is history. Twenty-seven Penn State students managed to fit themselves into the new updated Beetle—the one that appeared on the scene in 1999, introducing a new generation to "BeetleMania." At least one student helped to write a new page in the *Guinness*  *Book of World Records* by lying atop the car's redesigned, wider dashboard. After all, the new beetle has been updated.

But a bug is still a bug. It is the same—completely recognizable as the world's all-time best selling car. It has all the charm of the old bug. It creates the same "buzz." Like the old Beetle, it speaks to us of simpler, more relaxed times.

And yet today's Beetle is different. Compared with the old bug, its body is more substantial, offering greater protection and security to drivers who navigate an anxious era. Its colors are more vibrant. And its interior is a bit roomier, as the new record-holders showed.

In short, as consumers' ideas about value evolved, so did the product. For those in the travel industry, this is an important story. It reminds us to take a glance over our shoulders, to rethink the trends and icons that have taken hold in previous decades. Which were fads? Which had enduring appeal? How can we update yesterday's more successful business models to address today's concerns and tomorrow's trends?

Just as Beetle consumers have changed over time, so have definitions of value. So the most critical question may be, how can we understand and respond to changing perceptions of value? Some have compared this to changing the tire on a moving vehicle—a difficult challenge even with a bug! It requires holding firmly to the sacred qualities that differentiate your product while, at the same time, adding features that are relevant, new, and surprising.

"In the Air on Land and Sea"— In the 1940s

Images of tanks racing across the Iraqi desert reminded Americans that war is about many things—but, of course, it is about travel. In the United States, World War II brought rationing of all the "musts" associated with travel. Gasoline, tires, and leisure time were hoisted high on the list of scarce commodities. But the war years sparked interest in the world beyond America's hometowns. As they bussed and trained across the country, on their way to basic training or overseas postings, soldiers caught glimpses of places they promised themselves they would revisit with their families. Despite the trauma of war, many GIs returned from abroad with tales and memories that excited the imagination.

Wartime also inspired new visions for the nation's travel infrastructure. Frustrated by the difficulty of moving tanks and heavy equipment across the country, along poorly paved one- and two-lane roads, Dwight D. Eisenhower and other military planners envisioned a more efficient interstate highway system. The network of highways that sprang from this impulse did not come into being for another decade, but the value Americans placed on car trips and U.S.-based travel was well established in the1940s.

"On the Road"—In the 1950s

The book that most powerfully emblemized the 1950s—Jack Kerouac's *On the Road*—also reflected the passion for travel, as well as the pursuit of the American dream, that followed World War II. This was a period of economic growth. The interstate system built during these years spawned a new icon of American life— the motel. The separate tourist cottages of the 1930s and 1940s gave way to rooms assembled under a single roof and lit with neon to attract weary travelers. The rooms themselves were nothing special, but the owners used stucco, adobe, stone, brick, or other materials on the motels' facades to reflect regional styles.

Some of the rooms were inhabited by lone travelers, but others held mom, dad, and the kids. The decade that gave us "Ozzie and Harriet," "Leave It to Beaver" and "Father Knows Best" emphasized family togetherness and witnessed the growing popularity of family vacations. Though the terms "quality time" and "family-friendly" would have confused the Nelsons and the Cleavers, these concepts, as well as efficiency and affordability, were vital to consumers' evolving notions of value.

"Like a Rolling Stone"—In the 1960s

In the realm of the economy, the boom years of the 1950s gave way to turbulence in the 1960s. Turmoil characterized the decade's political and cultural scenes as well. "Flower power" was the watchword of the day, and the focus shifted from the idealized nuclear family—from the family home and the family car—to the restless experimentation and wandering of teens and young adults. A search for new sensations and new experiences characterized the decade, as the very idea of taking a "trip" took on a whole new meaning.

Travel across America continued—but now parents were less visible. The television show *Route 66* debuted in 1960, featuring two young guys who take off in a shiny new Corvette to discover America. By the time another pair of travelers took off across America, in the 1969 road movie *Easy Rider*, much of the youthful idealism of the early 1960s had dissolved, and the view was far bleaker. But the urge to travel and discover, while taking an inward journey as well, remained an enduring theme.

To be sure, not all of the trips taken in the 1960s were psychedelic. America's romance with the road continued. But now, small local motels gave way to brand names. Founded in the 1950s by a man who had trouble finding a place for his family to stay on road trips, Holiday Inns expanded in the 1960s, offering not only a night's lodgings, but predictability and respectability. Other chains grew at the same time, dotting the nation's highways with familiar logos as well as familiar lodgings. These chains responded to consumers' changing priorities and expectations. Now, in addition to efficiency and affordability, travelers prized comfort and improved services. Beyond bed and bath, they now wanted color televisions and swimming pools.

"Goodbye Yellow Brick Road"— In the 1970s

The zigzagging trend lines of the 1960s settled into the relatively flat economy of the 1970s. As the Baby Boomers moved into their twenties, the disco scene dominated popular culture. Some think of the 1970s as the decade fashion would rather forget: it featured women in loud dresses or flared pants and super-high cork platform shoes; men wearing wide collars and ties, Starsky and Hutch sunglasses and patterned polyester shirts tucked into too-tight pants.

As the 1970s moved along, Americans said goodbye to the idealism and revolutionary fervor of the 1960s, urging each other to "mellow out." The passionate hues of the 1960s softened into pastels. Exotic islands frequented by the decade's "beautiful people"—often in lavish movies—created an interest in tropical travel. Florida and Hawaii became favorite destinations. As in the late1960s, young people with means made trips to Europe, often traveling farther than their parents had ever ventured. But most Americans looked for mellow destinations closer to home.

At the same time, American hotel chains began expanding in size and reach. Marriott—a company whose "roots" can be traced back to a root beer stand— opened its first international hotel in Acapulco in 1969, its first European hotel in Amsterdam in 1975 and, by decade's end, operated nearly 100 hotels. Marriott was not alone. Americans seeking the comforts of home while traveling abroad now could choose among several brands.

In the 1970s, consumers' perceptions of value became more sophisticated. For many, the comforts of home were no longer enough. They began to seek accommodations that were more luxurious and better appointed than their usual surroundings—a set on which they could play out their own dreams and fantasies. Moving well beyond the basics, they were drawn to full-service hotels.

"Working 9 to 5"—In the 1980s

The workplace was the site of the 1980s most popular movies—such as *Wall Street* and *9 to 5*—and the focus of many Americans' lives. It was a time of economic growth and upward mobility. On the roads, VW bugs became an endangered species, replaced by upscale BMWs. In the realm of travel, European destinations were *de rigueur*.

While money occupied a central place in the culture of this era, some vacationers wanted to dispense with it altogether. Club Med had had pioneered the all-inclusive concept since its founding in 1950, and its appeal grew immensely in the 1980s. Boomers with growing families joined the single travelers who had always flocked to Club Med villages, eager for a "no-hassle," fun-filled experience that would take them away from the pressures of their everyday nine-to-five lives.

In the 1980s, consumers placed new importance on leisure travel as a break from—and reward for—hard work and long hours. More companies held meetings in desirable locations, often at plush resorts. Frequent flyer programs and incentive travel changed the shape of the travel industry.

Exploring "The Matrix"—In the 1990s

In the 1990s, the Internet revolution not only grew the economy, it changed Americans' ideas about exciting settings. In the arts, movies like *The Matrix* envisioned alternative environments—places bounded only by the limits of the imagination. Cyberspace became a favorite destination, and surfing the Web became an engrossing activity. Virtual adventures ruled.

In the real world, money earned in the bull market went for bigger cars (sport utility vehicles—SUVs—began to dominate the roads) as well as more exotic travel. As the Internet made the global village a reality, destinations that once seemed distant and inaccessible now beckoned. Americans enjoyed adventure travel, especially to Asia. For those with families or more limited budgets, Carnival cruises and similar packages offered a chance to explore exotic ports while remaining "anchored" in an American experience.

The heady optimism of the 1990s did not last, however. The bull market faltered as the Internet economy imploded. Millions of Americans saw their savings diminish and, as scandals were exposed, faith in the nation's corporate leaders plummeted. Many believe that the door on the decade, and on the old century, slammed shut on September 11, 2001, when terrorist attacks shocked the nation. During much of the decade, it was possible to imagine that good times and economic growth would continue nonstop. After September 11, America entered the "get-real" decade.

The 2000's—The "Get-Real" Decade

How will consumers define value in the new century? Of course, the history of its first decade has yet to be written. Its watchword may well turn out to be "Let's roll," the words spoken by one of the heroes of September 11 who resisted the hijackers in the skies over Pennsylvania. Additional themes and trends are sure to emerge in coming years.

But this much is clear: In the 2000s, harsh economic and political realities are shaping not only national priorities but those of everyday life. As priorities shift, so do values. On the day the World Trade Towers fell, people across America and around the world reached for their phones to connect first with family and then with friends and relatives in places near and far. Many Americans heard from old friends with whom they had been out of touch for years. These times saw a maturation of Americans, after the more self-indulgent times of the 1980s and 1990s. The "Get-Real" decade is characterized by more genuine, basic values and a more sober view of America's place in the world.

In the 2000s, human contact has emerged as the strongest value. This may reflect not only the difficulties of terrorism and wartime, but also the aging of the Baby Boom generation. As the theme song from the classic film *Casablanca* goes, "The fundamental things apply/As time goes by."

For travelers, the fundamental things include spending time with loved ones, relaxing together, sharing adventures and reconnecting emotionally. For some, it may mean returning to their roots through heritage travel. The sense that life is fragile has inspired, in many people, the impulse to "seize the day." Those who might have put off a vacation, telling the kids "maybe next year," may be more likely to take the time—and spend the money necessary—now.

Seeking a Managed Paradise

But not just any vacation will do. The Get-Real Decade has also changed travelers' values and their ideas about how they want to spend that vacation time. Safety has become an important consideration in every facet of life. Vacationers still want a week in paradise, but now it has to be a managed paradise. Anxious about spending time away from home, many travelers want experiences that bring them in contact with other people and places, while assuring their security and round-the-clock access to family, friends and colleagues via telephone and/or the Internet.

As our review of past decades noted, the appeal of travel has always involved not only an away-from-home adventure, but some kind of inward movement as well. That is certainly true today for many types of travelers. Some may be less concerned about destinations than about destinies—in other words, life's deeper mysteries and questions. Their journeys may take on a spiritual dimension.

In addition to spending time with loved ones, vacationers are seeking out experiences that engage their minds and bodies, test their limits, and put them in touch with powerful feelings. They may be feeling what author Graham Greene once called "a nostalgia for something lost"—perhaps the simplicity or innocence or romantic love of earlier days.

The Quest for Authenticity

In short, today's travelers want authenticity—a sense that their time away from home connects them with experiences that are meaningful and memorable. The challenge for the travel industry is to provide affordable vacations that also offer authentic, in-depth, unique experiences.

For different travelers or different families, this quest can take different forms. For some, it may mean adventure trips—journeys that take them up mountains, down little-explored rivers, across deserts. Rigorous walking tours and bicycle trips now attract tourists of every age.

For others, authenticity may mean ecotourism—a trip that includes an exciting nature component while contributing to environmental conservation. Ecotourism can range from small, highly focused study tours to large numbers of resort tourists who make day trips to nature reserves during their holidays.

For still others, authenticity may demand adventures of the mind. They may seek out educational tourism—holidays that emphasize learning through travel. Many people are willing to invest in high quality, exhilarating, enjoyable learning experiences for themselves and their families. As they make travel decisions, many people are moved by the same desire for aesthetic and intellectual stimulation that has fostered the spread of book clubs. At Club Med, we have found great interest in themed vacations, whether they focus on fiction, photography, art, or cinema.

Authenticity Redefined

To be sure, the desire for unusual "behind-the-scenes" experiences is not new. But the intensity of the quest seems stronger today, and strategies for reaching this goal tend to be more insightful and intentional.

Authenticity means thinking of oneself more as a traveler than as a tourist. It may mean traveling in the off season, getting off the bus tour, or visiting smaller galleries and cafés rather than those highlighted in all of the guidebooks. More and more, it also means seeking out experiences with other people that are genuine and thoughtful.

In past decades, travel professionals could satisfy tourists' desire for authenticity by setting up an itinerary to remote places, engaging a knowledgeable guide, and waiting for the inevitable "snafus" to occur. Tourists were often intrigued by the locals who would offer to tow their jeeps out of deep ruts on rain-soaked back roads. A few hours (and snapshots) later, the travelers would be on their way, happy to have caught a glimpse of how people in other places live and eager to share their experiences with friends.

Today's travelers still appreciate the kindness of strangers, but they are more apt to appreciate the complexities of other cultures and places, as well as their own natures, as more self-constrained observers. They realize that "authentic tourism" is often a contradiction in terms—that tourists change the nature of an experience or the realities of an "untouched" destination simply by being there. Rather than demanding an "insider's view" of life in another place, they may be seeking honest, sincere contact with people from another place or culture. Of course, there are many exceptions—but, generally speaking, there is greater awareness that travelers have a personal responsibility to respect the people and places they visit and to leave those destinations as unchanged as possible.

And that is why, as one ecotourism expert wrote in 2002, "Authentic experiences are just as available at popular tourism destinations like Costa Rica and Thailand, as they are in remote Mongolia or the Bolivian highlands. It all depends on how we conduct our business and integrate our tour operations—from trained guides to informed guests. If authenticity is genuineness, as I believe it is, then the level of cultural or economic development, or the degree to which people live according to their traditions, should not be factors in how we judge the value and meaning of our cross-cultural encounters."*

Travel as a Fundamental Freedom

There is no doubt about it—the events and uncertainties of the early 2000s have had a significant impact on travel and tourism. Many people stayed away from airports, choosing to vacation closer to home. But industry observers have said that the public will not be denied leisure travel, and that they view it as one of their fundamental freedoms. Travelers want the flexibility to cancel or reschedule vacations if necessary, but they continue to put a high value on enjoyable getaways with friends and family. This fact will provide a basis for growth in coming years.

At the same time, travelers are harder to please, and travel professionals are going to have to work harder and smarter to earn their business. The cookie-cutter approach won't work. Vacationers want experiences and activities that reflect their particular preferences and needs. This is a crucial point: While they value authenticity, vacationers will not compromise on comfort. They may want to experience the jungle, but while they are there, most want not only mosquito netting, but also air conditioning and white-glove treatment. They place a high premium on feeling good. Given difficult economic conditions and worries about homeland security and world events, Americans want no hassles when they are on vacation. And they want good deals. As a result, the All-Inclusive concept is more important than ever.

---

* *Presentation by Kurt Kutay at a conference on "Ecotourism and Conservation in the Americas," Stanford University, May 2–5, 2002.*

Updating the All-Inclusive Concept

All-inclusive was a great concept half a century ago, when Club Med invented it. And it is the right concept today. Back in 1950, the idea was to create, in the somber atmosphere of post-war Europe, a colorful, intense, diverse universe. Club Med's founders understood that in a world filled with worry and uncertainty, there are three keys to a fulfilling vacation adventure: 1) no hassles; 2) a relaxed setting that fosters easy exchange and friendship; and 3) activities that are exhilarating, yet easy to join in. The brand that emerged had incredible appeal, and Club Med expanded from the Mediterranean to Africa, Asia, Australia, and the American continent.

Today's context has striking parallels with the era when Club Med came into being. Now, as then, life can be fraught with anxiety. The economy is uncertain, job security is shaky, the world is on edge, and travel can be truly nerve-racking. The imperative in our industry is to take the stress out of vacationing.

Given the pressures of day-to-day life, vacationers want not only to gain new experiences—but also to lose themselves in engrossing activities. They crave not only beauty and sunshine—but also a lightness of being. That is Club Med's unique contribution to the history of tourism. The All-Inclusive concept that Club Med pioneered half a century ago has become the fastest growing segment in the tourism sector. In fact, the term All-inclusive is now used to mark an offering as cheap . . . less than first-rate.

And that is why the time has come to update all-inclusive. In 2003 Club Med launched *Total All-Inclusive*—with the goal of maximizing freedom and flexibility. Total All-Inclusive means an open bar and all-day snacking at many villages. And of course, we include activities and instruction in the widest possible array of sports. But the Total All-Inclusive concept is not simply a marketing approach. It goes well beyond drinks and snacks. From the start, All-Inclusive has been a philosophical framework. Yes, it meant freedom from hassles—no hidden costs, and no surprises. But it also meant a commitment to living more fully, to a wider array of experiences and social contacts, to more involvement and inspiration.

Before the advent of Club Med, the way to sell vacations was to promise something "exclusive"—a holiday that required a serious wardrobe, called for lots of attitude, and surrounded you with lots of people doing their best to be elegant. Club Med changed all that. Our founders changed the way people around the world relax and play by making vacationing "inclusive"— in every sense. It wasn't just a matter of price. All-inclusive meant more than a package deal. It spoke to an entire ethos—part of the spirit of liberation and democratization that followed World War II. That spirit is just as important today.

Re-engineering Club Med for the Get-Real Decade

Today, we are in the process of reengineering Club Med for the Get-Real Decade. We are rethinking everything we do: every activity, every amenity. In coming years, as we reinvent the concept of all-inclusive, we will be looking for ways to meet—and surpass—vacationers' expectations. Research is critical to this process. In particular, we will continue to ask a lot of questions that allow us to evaluate the needs of vacationers in North America. As consumers' ideas about value change, so will our product.

Once again, the key concept is value. In any industry, there are usually three factors that consumers trade off when they make purchasing decisions. In the car industry, the three factors are price, performance, and quality. There was a time when Mercedes Benz owned the luxury car market. Then Lexus came out, lowered the price, offered great performance, and raised quality. They changed the paradigm.

That is what Club Med has done in the travel industry. In our world, consumers trade off location, activities, and value. We have focused on all three. To stay in the game, you have to make a case for your product in all three areas. But to win, you have to pick one that you will be committed to in good times or bad. And for us, it is value.

Total All-Inclusive is a total value strategy. We think it is the right strategy at the right time. Look at the trends. Consumer confidence is down. Disposable income is still up. Of course, decision-making is not just about the pocketbook. Vacationers want a lot of things. They want multigenerational travel. They want environments that are both exotic and secure. But most of all, they demand value.

We are meeting that need—and all of our marketing and PR efforts are geared to that message. For example, to support our Total All-Inclusive offering, we mounted a new Total Escape campaign. Based on significant research, this campaign included TV spots, print ads in major newspapers and trade publications, radio ads, and a significant Internet presence.

To succeed in the Get-Real Decade, you have to step back and look at the trends—not only industry trends, but also demographic, social, cultural, and economic developments. Big-picture thinking can help you succeed, but only if you also sweat the details. Small changes at the right time can make an enormous difference. Just one example: At Club Med, we are rethinking the way we offer spa services. We think vacationers will enjoy a massage more without the usual claustrophobic, table-in-a-cubicle experience. So we're thinking out of the box—literally—offering massages in the open air. By offering privacy in natural settings, we are translating a big-picture trend (the desire for authenticity) into specific services that consumers value.

The bottom line: At Club Med, we believe that the experiences we offer need to change with the times, but still take into account enduring values. Like VW Beetles, the services and products we provide must be the same . . . but, over time, different. They must offer the authenticity, flexibility, freedom, and comfort that vacationers demand in the Get-Real Decade. In the decades to come, this strategy will sustain Club Med's position of leadership in the travel industry.

28

It's Not Simply the Product—It's the Entire Experience

The Hon. A. David Dodwell, JP, MP
The Reefs, Southampton, Bermuda

An hotelier and politician, David Dodwell was born in Bermuda. He began his career in the hotel industry between 1967 and 1971, when he worked summers at a number of well-known resort hotels in Bermuda. In 1972, he was appointed manager of The Reefs—then a 43-room resort overlooking its own beach in Southampton, Bermuda. Over the years, and beginning in 1981, he has acquired a majority interest in the hotel.

During this time, The Reefs has been expanded and upgraded to 67 rooms, suites and cottages, and enjoys occupancies among the highest on the island. This year, The Reefs was listed in *Travel + Leisure*'s "500 Greatest Hotels in the World"—#1 for the Caribbean / Bermuda / Bahamas, and also #1 in "World's Best Service" and "World's Best Hotel Values" categories for the same region. In August 2002, The Reefs was awarded "the best resort in the entire Caribbean, Bahamas and Bermuda region" in the *Travel + Leisure*'s World's Best Awards; and ranked #23 in the world and #11 in the region in "Small Resorts of the World."

In 1989, Dodwell purchased the Nisbet Plantation Beach Club, a 38-room beach resort on the island of Nevis in the West Indies. Recently, Dodwell has begun, with a small group, a new entity, the Island Resort Collection, that focuses on the development, ownership and management of small, distinctive hotels and resorts worldwide in extraordinary destinations.

In 1992, he was named Bermuda Hotelier of the Year. He is currently the regional vice president for Bermuda of the Caribbean Hotel Association.

Dodwell has a long record of community and public service. He was elected to Bermuda's Parliament as a member of the United Bermuda Party for Southampton West in 1993 and was appointed Bermuda's minister of tourism from August 29, 1995 through November 1998. In the general election of November 1998 and July 2003, he retained his seat. The United Bermuda Party is the loyal opposition; he currently serves as the shadow minister of tourism and development.

He attended Cornell University in Ithaca, New York, graduating with a bachelor of science degree in hotel administration.

Excellence in service is a journey, not a destination! And what a journey it has been for me with my two boutique resort hotels—The Reefs in Bermuda and Nisbet Plantation in Nevis, West Indies.

The importance of the "experience" is absolutely what we in the travel industry are facing today. And there is no silver bullet or magic formula for a resort hotel, small or large. In reality, it is a "work in progress"—with no end in sight . . . it is ongoing, and always will be. So, buckle up and get ready for the ride—we have no choice!

And it's even tougher these days, with everyone else striving to perfect the experience—in tourism or whatever! Tom Peters, noted speaker and author, said "Customer service is the battleground of this decade." I agree completely—except for his timeline. It will probably be forever—not just a decade.

The customer wants more and more, is receiving it, and wants it not just from hotels. Thus, expectations run high and we now have the "on demand" customer who wants everything personalized and customized. So, in the boutique resort business, it is whoever delivers the experience that you and I want—when, where, and how we want it—who wins and wins and wins!

I feel privileged to be able to tell you what we do at The Reefs and Nisbet Plantation. We are not perfect by any means. However, we have been fortunate in winning awards, primarily customer selected, in significant travel publications over the past few years. I am proud of my colleagues and associates at both resorts.

So, this chapter is about a philosophy. It is not ours alone—it belongs to everyone. We did not write the rules about service—the customer did, and will continue to do so. Long may it continue!

I know *the product* is very important, but is that really what I want to write about? I'm not so sure I do. At least not exclusively. Are there lessons to be learned from The Reefs' and Nisbet Plantation's success and our shortcomings? I suspect there are, and I would like to share them with you.

But I'm not really going to focus solely on the product as we think about it! No, I am going to talk about The Reefs' and Nisbet Plantation's "brand." That's right . . . the "brand"!

You see, I firmly believe that, in order to be successful in today's ultra competitive environment, you have to be thinking about *the total* resort experience—not just the product and its service. Our brand is more than the product we offer our guests.

In fact, our brand is "The totality of the thoughts, feelings, associations, and expectations that our guest experiences when exposed to our company name, trademark, products, or design or symbol representing them. Our brand is our reputation and, therefore, its promise of quality."

The Reefs and Nisbet Plantation make a promise before customers arrive, and we must absolutely deliver on it. When you look at it from this standpoint, our brand is so much more than the resorts we hold or the people we employ. It's a slightly different way of thinking about a resort, but one that has helped us to be successful.

When you look at it this way, you can see that every point of contact with a customer, or anyone who can influence the decision to stay with us, represents an opportunity to build our brand and strengthen our reputation—our promise of quality and service.

At The Reefs and Nisbet Plantation, we like to look at our brand-building as a circle of continuous improvement at three distinct points of contact.

1. Before the customer arrives

2. While the customer is at the hotel

3. After the customer leaves

Before the Customer Arrives

Like many resort hotels, we do spend a considerable amount of money marketing to customers, enticing them to choose us over a multitude of alternatives—both hotels and destinations.

Several years ago, we decided to make a major shift in the way we market. Prior to that we were like most resorts—advertising in different magazines and participating in various programs, hoping they were reaching the right audience and that our message would have an influence. But never being able to track return on investment (ROI). In addition, we had what most would call "brochureware" Web sites. They were nice, but did little for our overall marketing effort.

In 1998, we decided to embrace the principles of integrated one-to-one marketing (as in one-to-one guest service) and, with the help of Madigan Pratt & Associates, a consulting firm, turned our entire marketing efforts upside down.

We decided to talk to prospects individually and not en masse—you know, just like you and I want to be addressed. Here are just a few of the things we did:

a. We revamped our Web sites—to add much more content and to provide reasons for Web visitors to come back time and again. We added more packages that we update and change regularly. We also began adding more information on Bermuda and Nevis, since we needed to expand the visitors' experience beyond just what we have at the resorts.

b. We added a sweepstakes wherein we give away four free vacation stays a year. In order to register for our sweepstakes, customers and prospects have to give us their name, address and email address. We mobilized the entire team at the resorts in an effort to encourage our guests to sign up for the sweepstakes.

c. We built a database of customers, prospects and travel agents.

d. We launched a monthly e-mail newsletter known as the Island Vacation Update. The newsletter is highly personalized and we can send out different messages to customers past and present, prospects and travel agents. We talk to them one-on-one—as they want to be addressed. The newsletter drives traffic back to the Web, where they will learn more about the resorts, our awards and packages.

But driving traffic and selling packages are not the main, nor even the most important, purposes of the newsletter. We are using it to begin building relationships with readers. When you are trying to build a brand, you need to establish trust and the first step toward that end is to establish and then deepen a relationship.

e. We do still encourage readers to contact us by phone, but now primarily by e-mail. This was one of the most difficult things we have done because it required a new set of thinking and skills to handle questions promptly and efficiently. The importance of this was brought to light by a survey recently conducted by Purdue University's Center for Customer-Driven Quality. That study showed that:

- 92 percent of U.S. consumers decided how they like a company by their experience at the call center. And we view our e-mail correspondence as call center activity.

- 63 percent of consumers will stop using a company's products or services based on a negative call center experience.

- 95 percent of consumers will use a company again when a call center exceeds their expectations.

- And finally, 100 percent of consumers between the ages of 18 and 25 will move to a company's competitor once they have a negative call center experience. Anyone trying to attract the honeymoon market like we are should heed this.

What's interesting here is that we don't strive to meet customer expectations, we strive to exceed them in everything we do.

We track every click-through to every link in our newsletter. We know who clicked on every single package and can address targeted direct mail, for example, to people who have looked at our wedding package.

We cut way back in our advertising and now spend a small amount in *Bride's Magazine* and a few newspapers. In every case, we try to drive traffic to the web site and encourage them to sign up for the sweepstakes.

As you can see, we really are doing quite a bit of marketing designed to get people to consider visiting The Reefs and Nisbet Plantation. To every extent possible, we are personalizing all of our communications and tracking their effectiveness.

In essence, we are trying to capture the hotels' experience and communicate it to people before they even arrive at our doorsteps. We believe we begin our service before they arrive!

Before I tell you what we do when the customer is at the resorts, I would like to leave you with this thought. If you would like to market as we do, hire a professional! There are far many more things that need to be done than you can ever imagine. Integrated one-to-one marketing is a science and there are far too many ways you can hurt your brand if you do not get things right.

While the Customer Is at the Hotel

So . . . the time has come to deliver on the promise; to deliver on the trust that we have hopefully built up prior to the customer's arrival at The Reefs and Nisbet Plantation. Are we ready? We must be—there is no choice, because the customer is!

Millions of words have been, and will continue to be, written on the delivery of product at an hotel. Remember, product consists of three attributes—

physical plant and facilities, service and activities. In our case, all three have been critical to our success. From the moment of their arrival to the time of their departure, we try to meet and anticipate our guests' needs through the facilities that they live in and use, through our one-to-one service approach and through, if they choose to participate, the things we offer them to do.

I could list the obvious—and go on forever—about beaches, accommodations, restaurants, pool, the services and activities we provide, etc. I won't, because I believe you know what is required to truly please a guest in a resort hotel. But what I will say is that investment is critical—both in physical plant and people—to our success. Commitment to ensuring the best facilities we can offer at the high quality level we set—four-star in our case—is expected if you want to be in the resort business. What is even more important than ever before is investment in our people, staff, associates, etc. Without them we, and our guests, are lost.

We try to recruit the best we can find, and then train, motivate and incentivize them to simply wow our guests! I like to say that we are tough on our standards and tender on our people. Simply put, they count, we need them, they need us.

One of the major advantages small resorts have had over larger ones has been their ability to provide more highly personalized service. It's certainly an opportunity that both The Reefs and Nisbet Plantation have enjoyed. But that is changing also, as larger resorts have initiated many specific guest programs. The bar is constantly being raised and we must continually stretch our efforts to remain competitive. Remember, all we are selling in this business is a memory.

While our guests are with us at The Reefs and Nisbet Plantation, our culture of enhancing the experience is Number 1. If it works, we all win!

After the Customer Leaves

What is the most effective form of marketing for resort hotels, large and small? In my experience, it is positive word-of-mouth.

Some hoteliers may think it's easier to let past guests recommend their resorts whenever that guest happens to think about it. Easier, yes! A good idea, no!

At The Reefs and Nisbet Plantation, we have always taken a more proactive view toward generating positive word-of-mouth. Let's face it, it doesn't take long for that "vacation glow" to wear off. That just means you have to work harder to keep your name in front of past customers and continue to remind them of what a nice time they had.

Without that reminder, how can you expect them to have you fresh in their mind when the topic at home or a cocktail party turns to vacations?

That's why, many years ago, The Reefs launched "Smart Casual," a newsletter specifically targeted to past guests. It was the first newsletter of any resort in Bermuda and one of the first by any resort in the Caribbean. Mailed three times a year, "Smart Casual" has since become an immensely popular communication among our guests.

Nisbet Plantation continues the tradition with its own publication "Nisbet News Waves." Past guests see stories and pictures, information on improvements, promotions and the staff—all news from "their" hotel!

So we send out paper newsletters and highly personal e-mail newsletters to keep The Reefs' and Nisbet Plantation's name top-of-mind among the most highly desirable individuals out there—past customers, interested prospects and travel agents. Timely messages are delivered to their mailboxes—outside their homes or inside their computers.

So there you have it, some thoughts on survival in today's competitive world. If there is one thing you should take away from this chapter, it's that the secret is *not* simply the product—it's the entire experience. Yes, the entire experience! It's every touch point before, during and after a guest's visit to your resorts—your island. It's the way you build a brand. It's the way to survive. The only way!

Remember, excellence in service is a journey, not a destination!

29

Selling the All-Inclusive Resort Concept

Gordon "Butch" Stewart
Founder and Chairman, Sandals

Gordon "Butch" Stewart, the "Cupid of the Caribbean," is the founder of a billion-dollar Jamaican-based empire that includes 16 resorts, Air Jamaica, Appliance Traders Ltd., and *The Observer* newspaper. Stewart was born in Kingston, Jamaica in 1941. In 1968, Stewart formed his first enterprise, Appliance Trading Company. In 1980, he purchased an old hotel and founded Sandal's Montego Bay, the first all-inclusive resort of its kind in the Caribbean. Stewart now owns 18 resorts in Jamaica, St. Lucia, the Bahamas, Antigua, the Turks Islands and the Caicos Islands under the brand names Sandals, Beaches, and Royal Plantation Golf Resort.

Air Jamaica, which he acquired in 1994, carries almost 50 percent of all passengers onto the island.

Stewart's philanthropic efforts have been widely recognized. Sandals actively supports more than 150 projects in host communities. This support ranges from building schools and paying teachers to providing hospital linens and bringing healthcare to the doorsteps of those who cannot afford it.

We keep our product simple, and the reward for such simplicity is having some of the highest hotel occupancies in the Caribbean. Simple, of course, does not mean inferior. Sandals is an upscale all-inclusive resort company, and that upscale image is something we strive for in every facet of our operation.

In nearly three decades of business experience, I have learned one lesson better than any other: your success is ultimately based on the quality of the product that you sell. Without an exceptional product, your brand is weak from the start, and no amount of marketing or advertising will make it strong. As much as things change in the travel industry, that will not.

Like any company, we have faced stiff challenges in the opening years of the 21st century. Challenges posed not only by our competitors, but by the shifting forces affecting a very complicated industry: the world economy, the health of the airlines, concerns about terrorism, and the impending mass retirement of the Baby Boomers—are all factors we must manage every day.

For the uninitiated, a brief explanation of the all-inclusive concept. In this system, the guest pays one price that covers everything: drinks, room, activities, meals, etc. The concept works well on many counts. After paying for their vacation up front, the guests feel more relaxed, enabling them to enjoy themselves. Also, the concept permits our employees to concentrate on serving the customer rather than collecting money.

In the all-inclusive market, where we are the most upscale hotelier, proliferation is our greatest future challenge. Some may practice the all-inclusive concept, but don't deliver a quality experience to their guests. Because of this, the term "all-inclusive" does not always convey a positive image. At Sandals, we must chip away daily at the misconception that "all-inclusive" is a lower-end product, when we are, and will never be, nothing of the kind.

Countering this perception requires unceasing improvement. Sandals Resorts International began operations in 1981, and the product has been forever evolving since that time. King-size four-poster Mahogany beds, satellite TV, hairdryers, and marble baths, among many other features, are all standard at the resorts. Our improvements didn't stop there. We continue to serve more discriminating consumers who will, among other things, want a bedroom as nice or nicer than their bedroom at home. And when you aim at an upscale, aspirational market, as we do, that bedroom must be very nice indeed.

Currently we have 21 properties spread throughout the Caribbean. More than half of these hotels are in Jamaica, and we have others in Antigua, St. Lucia, Turks & Caicos, and the Bahamas. Two of our properties, located in Cuba, are not marketed in the United States.

A decade from now, I predict Sandals will boast a portfolio close to double its current inventory. However, I do not envision us leaving the Caribbean in the foreseeable future. The reason we have been so successful is that we have always concentrated in the Caribbean. Others have struggled because they tried to be all things to all people—or perhaps in all places for all people. If you lose your focus, you lose your way. And there is definitely enough room to develop in the Caribbean. We have hotels in only six destinations. There are more islands to be explored and, with the many cultures and countries in the region, there will be no shortage of exciting, attractive places for our resorts.

How we grow over the next decade or so will probably be different than in the past. Sandals has a proven track record in developing and marketing the whole all-inclusive experience, from the television ad to the resort, and this makes us attractive for management deals.

With only about one property opening per year, we have grown somewhat slowly. This is, in part, because we carefully select our ownership partners. That discretion will remain constant in coming years. To us, having quality partners is more important than growth. A partner must be willing not only to secure a good property and financing, but also be committed to keeping the resort at our brand's standards.

Your brand must be consistent for travel agents and wholesalers to be comfortable selling it. It is a changing market, and you have to keep your sellers focused. You do that by maintaining the clarity of your product and keeping your message simple.

We like our brands, and why not? Sandals, with 12 properties, is exclusively for couples and is especially popular among honeymooners. Beaches, with six hotels, is intended for families as well as singles and couples. We have since created a third brand, which are boutique-type upscale hotels, of which we currently have two—Royal Plantation Spa & Golf Resort in Ocho Rios and Dragon Bay in Port Antonio.

To maintain our freshness in the minds of consumers, Sandals has always concentrated on improving and upgrading our hotels and our amenities. Not a year goes by in which the company stands still with its product. Look at our history. We were the first all-inclusive hotelier to put hair dryers in every room. Then we added a la carte dining, giving customers a true restaurant experience—not the buffet and trough of other all-inclusives. We had waiters and menus and daily specials and, by the way, there was never a check. We recently introduced our world-class Signature Spas in many of our hotels. We're ahead of the curve by any standard, and we will continue to be so. Through constant improvement and renovation, we will maintain our appeal and quality.

Our growth in the next decade will likely continue with the same proportion of brand-types in the portfolio. Sandals, the brand, will maintain its greater proportion but, of course, as the company develops, Beaches and the boutique hotels could also increase in number.

The three brands complement each other nicely, but we also add other travel elements. There are things you have to think about, such as entering the cruise market. Certainly the cruise industry is of interest to us, and we have discussed the idea, but the cost of entry into the market has been, so far, prohibitive. You must be smart about what will work and what will not, for gambling with your brand is a dangerous pursuit. Sometimes the best idea is to sit tight. Of all the dangers that we face in our part of the world, one of the chief challenges is airline lift. People go where it's easy to go. If you don't have planes flying to your destinations, filling rooms can be difficult. Wherever there is a predominance of leisure business, the airlines find it less interesting to fly. But as the industry changes, I think you'll see airlines further involve themselves in destinations that are leisure dominated. The American business traveler is tired of being fleeced, and airlines, forced to adapt, will try different revenue mixes.

We have an advantage in some markets because of our relationship with Air Jamaica, but as we develop in other areas of the Caribbean, we must be more clever.

For example, in the late 1990s, when we opened Beaches Turks & Caicos Resort & Spa, one of the region's best family resorts, there simply wasn't enough airlift. To reach the critical mass necessary to make the hotel work, we basically had to enter the airline business ourselves. We used to operate as many as five charters weekly out of key gateway cities, but now we fly only one. Why? The resort, and the destination as a whole, took off, largely because of the flag we planted there. Now the Turks & Caicos is served by US Airways, Delta, Air Canada, and British Airways.

In business, you sometimes must deal with trends that occur on a massive scale. In the next decade, we will encounter such a trends. We are moving into the vaunted period when the American Baby Boom generation retires. They are truly a segment that is important to everybody with anything to sell.

We have been targeting that older market for a long time and you see it in our marketing even now. A lot of our guests are customers who have stayed with us before. But, as their tastes become more refined with age and increased wealth and their needs change, we need to become more and more upscale to retain them. Of course, we must market this differently, and our collateral and advertising will reflect the continued pursuit of that segment.

Although we may want to appeal to this more mature audience, the younger clientele will remain a huge part of our business. The Sandals brand, for couples only, tends to skew younger. As demographics change, and those Baby Boomers want to take vacations, family-oriented Beaches and the boutique line, which we only dabble in now, will increase in size to better serve the needs of that clientele.

At Sandals, we do not overly concern ourselves with the luxury market. Our goal is not necessarily to grab that top 1 percent of the luxury market, but to position ourselves to attract the aspirational consumer. And that aspirational mass market is willing to pay a bit more for something they perceive to be worth it. As an obvious example, consider coffee: at a fast food restaurant, a cup of coffee may cost less than a dollar, but a cup of gourmet coffee sells for $3. The coffee may be better, yes, but the customer also pays that price because he or she is attracted to other values inherent in the brand. At Sandals, our marketing and advertising has that customer in mind: we target the person who wants to drive the Jaguar, not necessarily the person who drives it. To appeal to such a customer, you have to adhere to high standards. You have to show off your beaches, your hotel, your employees, your commitment to service and even the environment. You have to show off, period, and what you show must deserve that cachet of class. Again, it goes back to the product.

The best source of information will always be your customer. When you communicate with guests, you might be shocked to hear what they have to say. They often know the hotel better than you do. I spend lots of time at the properties talking with customers. We sometimes hear tales about what a man from Milwaukee said while sitting in the Jacuzzi. It sounds funny, but that is the most solid research you can do. When you stop communicating with your audience, when you stop learning what they like and dislike about your operation, then you quickly lose touch. In fact, that it exactly how our Beaches brand was born. So many of our customers came to me and said "Butch, we love Sandals, we honeymooned with you, we've returned again and again, but now we have kids. We want the same vacation experience for the entire family. Build a place for us." So we did, and now we have four Beaches Resorts for families.

Bottom line is that the worldwide consumer is becoming more discriminating, and that is obviously not something exclusive to the U.S. market. Because of the abundant information available in magazines and on the Internet, today's customer is much more aware of what constitutes a good product than yesterday's customer. If that is true, then tomorrow's customer will be even more particular.

As consumer tastes become more articulated, marketing must become more focused. The challenge is, how do you find these customers to bring them to your property? There must be an appeal to niches. People don't want to sit on the beach—well, some do—but many have other interests. For us, the markets are fun: honeymoon, scuba diving, golf, and spas, among others. In the future, people are going to travel more frequently with such interests firmly top of mind.

Perhaps our most prominent niche is honeymoons and weddings. We even developed a concept for it called the WeddingMoonTM. Many couples come to our resorts to get married because they can't bear the expense, grief, or drama of a wedding at home. In 2002, we hosted more than 10,000 weddings. This is obviously a very attractive demographic. Young couples that are ready, willing, and able to spend—all very good things—and we want to help them make their dreams come true.

The honeymoon and wedding market is becoming more and more competitive. We can't take anything for granted. To stay on top of a niche market, you must innovate and improve your product. Not long ago we suggested that, with so many honeymooners staying at our properties, we, too, should give them a wedding present. Our first partnership in this regard was with Royal Doulton, a British china manufacturer. More recently, we have paired with Waterford Wedgewood to give our customers a choice of crystal or china from the world-renowned providers of the finest place settings and glassware. In late 2002, we formed a relationship with WeddingChannel.com, the top online source for wedding planning information and one featuring the largest online registry. This was an industry first wherein honeymooners were able to register their Sandals Honeymoon on-line.

Another niche we've entered is the spa arena. Spas are upscale, and spa service, being expensive, cannot be given away as part of the all-inclusive concept. But it also cannot be done hesitantly, because customers are knowledgeable about spas and will reject any half-hearted attempt. So you give the customer a quality product and you charge for it. Even though spa costs are not covered within the all-inclusive price, customers still go to the spa. Thus, we have award-winning spas in many of our hotels and plan to add more to the lineup.

Groups account for only a small percentage of our business. Although we have handled groups of up to 5,000 people before, it is not a sizable part of our operation, and intentionally so. We are, and will continue to be, cautious in how we handle the group market. First and foremost, the size of our hotels prohibits activity on such a scale; but we also do not want to confuse other customers about our brand. If our guest had wanted to stay at a resort that could host a big meeting, they would have gone to Florida.

While advertising is undoubtedly a significant part of our marketing strategy, it is limited in its abilities. Our all-inclusive product is not simple to sell. A customer needs to understand why the price is what it is, and that is not easy to communicate in a 30-second commercial or a print advertisement. We need a third party to do some of the selling for us, and that takes us to distribution.

The distribution system in the travel industry is, as always, shifting. There are wholesalers who want to cut out agents by going straight to the consumer; there are agent consortia acting as their own wholesalers; and then there are suppliers that seek to sell to the customer direct. It is a maze, and the maze changes daily.

At Sandals, we will continue to respect all parts of the distribution system, because relying upon a range of heterogeneous booking sources is the healthiest place to be. If one source is not performing, another can pick up the slack. To have a single entity bringing in all of your business is not a good situation—unless, of course, that entity is you.

Some suppliers may believe they can avoid the fee paid to the wholesaler or dodge the commission paid to the travel agent, but you cannot become so concerned with the different modes of distribution—whether wholesaler, agent or consumer—that you lose sight of reality. You still have inventory that needs to be sold. Who will sell it? In the end, the formula is simple: there is a cost of doing business, and if that cost is sustainable—that is, you don't pay too much for it—the origin is irrelevant. It is only worthwhile to cut someone out of the deal if you can sell your product for, say, the same $100 you did before. If you bypass third party commissions and sell for $80, you're net revenue remains the same, *and* you're devaluing your product. If you fall into that pit, you may never get out—it's already a pit from which many hotel companies are trying to extricate themselves. The distribution road map going forward will be constantly changing. We want to have a successful Web site, and we want to sell direct, but only to the extent necessary to sustain the room inventory that we have. There is no point robbing Peter to pay Paul. Rather, let Peter and Paul gain mutually from a win-win relationship. As a source of distribution, the Internet has proven to be as dangerous as it is beneficial. In the United States, business-focused hotels, for example, have so much inventory devoted to Internet sources that maintaining a desired price point has become a problem. The Internet is perceived as a foolproof way to reduce distribution costs, but the big question that the travel industry must answer is this: What happens when it's no longer cheaper to book online?

The travel agent has always and will remain a crucial distribution source for our company in the future. Because our average sale is more than $3,000, customers usually don't try to book us through the Internet. Customers feel more comfortable talking to someone face-to-face when they're considering spending several thousands of dollars. That's only human nature. And, by definition, human nature isn't changing anytime soon.

Leisure hoteliers need agents. At Sandals, we have always said that we have a longstanding love affair with agents. It's that relationship that has made us what we are today, and it works both ways. We will continue to reward the agent, perhaps increasingly so in the future, if that agent focuses on our product. But there is more to the partnership than simply paying overrides. Agents must have the tools and knowledge to sell the hotels. This is achieved through educational programs such as our Certified Sandals Specialist (CSS), Sandals Nights, Ultra Conventions, in-store agency collateral, and referral programs, among other methods.

The relationship shouldn't end with the sale. It is important for our mutual customer to return to the agent and thank them for a great vacation. The agent then knows our product is reliable and will book us in the future. Both Sandals and the agent benefit from this arrangement. Of course, it is incumbent upon Sandals to deliver that incredible experience to the customer. After more than two decades of doing exactly that, I'm confident our resorts will continue to exceed customers' expectations again and again.

Section V

Cruise Line Marketing

The cruise industry has been the fastest-growing segment of the North America travel industry for the last 30 years. Amazingly, over 70 brands that were marketed in the United States at one time or another, over the last 30 years have gone out of business. Consolidation has certainly been the rule in recent years. Three companies, representing 10 brands, controlled 90 percent of the market in 2003.

Ten years ago, lines were easily differentiated: As the price of the cruise increased, fewer consumers could afford the time and the money for the cruise. Luxury cruises, for example, were typically two-week cruise duration or longer, with exotic, worldwide itineraries. Premium cruises were typically 10–14 days in length, featuring Alaska, Europe and Transcanal itineraries. The mass-market and bottom feeders were generally in the three to seven days range, dominated by Caribbean, Bermuda and Mexican Riviera itineraries.

As competition for the cruise vacation market intensified, cruise lines took advantage of scale economies to build larger ships with more "bells and whistles." The new ships began to blur the distribution between mass-market and premium lines. The premium lines countered by building larger and larger ships themselves, making it far more challenging for premium lines to offer the type of intimate service on which they had built their reputations. Moreover, as premium lines added capacity, they found themselves marketing to broader (mass-market) segments of the population. Today, these brands are vying for the family market, ethnic markets, younger ages, etc.—a far cry from their narrow "country-club-at-sea" heritages. As a result, these brands can't always fulfill the implied expectations that folks on board will be "just like me."

In effect, the premium lines were moving down market in terms of price, product and customer demographics to keep pace with expanding capacity. (After all, there is a reason why large hotels are found in Las Vegas and Orlando, but not in Palm Springs or Palm Beach!)

The expanding mass-market lines' fleets forced those lines to venture into Alaska, the Panama Canal and European cruise itineraries to get out of their own way—further blurring the premium/mass-market historical distinction. Upgraded accommodations (including suites and balcony cabins), high-end supper clubs, elaborate children's facilities, a vast array of nightclubs and lounges—literally something for everyone—were features newly offered by mass-market lines, creating a significant lure for the traditional premium customer. Along the way of course, the bottom feeder lines like Regency, Premier and Commodore went out of business—despite the price advantage derived from operating older, fully-depreciated ships—because the new, larger ships' economies of scale allowed the mass market lines to close the price gap. Consumers, faced with price parity, opted for the feature-laden new ships. This drove the bottom feeders into bankruptcy.

The luxury segment has also had its challenges, primarily as a result of a too-rapid expansion in capacity. Prices of these typically small (two to six ship) fleets of small (110—700 passenger) luxury ships have been rolled back significantly (up to 50 percent or more) from price levels at the turn of the century, wiping out profits and putting significant pressure on costs. The luxury segment is clearly at the highest risk of extinction. It will take many years for the overall cruising industry to grow sufficiently to get the luxury segment back in line.

Contracted and planned new ship construction over the next ten years will only heighten the competition for the cruise vacationer, with every brand feeling it has a shot at acquiring every customer! Further blurring of the brands and segments is thus inevitable.

At this point, it should be noted that the graying of the Baby-Boomer generation is certainly viewed by many of the cruise lines (as well as other travel segments) as a fortuitous circumstance that will help marketers absorb new capacity in an expanding vacation market. Is this optimism warranted or merely wishful thinking? Will rising medical costs, longer life expectancies, and shrinking retirement plans conspire to blunt this anticipated growing propensity to travel? Is it possible that by 2015 it will be common to work full-time to 72 or 75 years of age? If so, wouldn't that lifestyle change crimp the expectations of more, not less, leisure time to invest in vacations?

We believe the best marketing strategy for the cruise industry is to focus less on cruise market share and more on market expansion by attractive non-cruisers who are vacationing on land. At every level, cruise marketers should look to generate trial of first-time cruisers. In any given year, cruising captures only three percent of the hotel, resort and cruise market of leisure trips consisting of three-night stays or longer. Further, only 15 percent of the American public had ever cruised by 2003. Curiously, most premium and luxury brands don't even track first-time cruisers but rather focus on first-time-to-brand cruisers. Perhaps a luxury line should think about converting consumers from land competitors like

Four Seasons and Relais & Chateaux to its brand directly. It's clearly a much larger lake to fish in than just focusing on the other lines in the luxury segment.

Lastly, what our cruise contributors say, or don't say, about the changing distribution channel landscape is instructive. Do some lines believe it is business as usual? Do they run the risk of being late to the party? Or worse yet, are they in danger of losing control of their brand to third parties such as the large, Internet players? Cruising firms form an oligopoly, irrespective of who owns what. Brands within Carnival Corporation or within Royal Caribbean International fight fiercely with one another, as well as with the brands not in their family of cruise brands. Those brand managers that are not looking far enough ahead—to the customer, to the product, and to its distribution—will lose the race!

30

Carnival Cruise Lines' Winning Formula

Vicki L. Freed, CTC
Senior Vice President
Sales & Marketing
Carnival Cruise Lines

Vicki Freed is senior vice president of sales and marketing for Carnival Cruise Lines, the world's largest cruise operator, and former chairman of Cruise Lines International Association (CLIA), the marketing and travel agent training arm of the North American cruise industry. She is one of the highest ranking and most recognizable female executives in the travel industry.

Freed began her career with Carnival in 1978 as Southern California regional sales manager, earning the company's "Rookie of the Year" award for outstanding effort. In 1982, she was promoted to sales director for Southern California, responsible for the territory spanning Los Angeles north to San Luis Obispo.

After being named Carnival's "Salesperson of the Year" in 1984 and again in 1987, Freed was promoted to director of sales, western region, in May 1989. In this position, she directed 19 sales representatives in 10 states throughout the western portion of the country.

In June 1993, Freed was appointed to her current position of senior vice president of sales and marketing. Based at the company's headquarters in Miami, she has overall responsibility for all sales and marketing activities of the largest cruise line in the world. Under Freed's direction, Carnival's sales department has won numerous accolades, including being named one of "America's Best" by *Sales & Marketing Management Magazine.*

Freed recently completed a two-year term as chairman of CLIA. In her role as chairman, Freed oversaw CLIA's various programs designed to build consumer interest in cruising and help travel agents expand their cruise sales.

Over the years, Freed has also been recognized for her role as a leading cruise industry marketer. In August 2000, Freed was appointed by Florida Governor Jeb Bush to the Florida Commission on Tourism, a private/public partnership that is responsible for promoting Florida tourism.

She has also been nominated by the Association of Travel Marketing Executives (ATME) to serve on that organization's board of directors, and has been named one of the "100 Most Powerful Women in Travel" by *Travel Agent Magazine.*

Freed attended San Diego State University, earning a bachelor's degree in business with an emphasis in marketing from the University of Colorado. She also holds a Certified Travel Counselor (CTC) designation.

Freed also serves on the board of directors for the South Florida chapter of the Make-A-Wish Foundation, an organization dedicated to enriching the lives of children with life-threatening illnesses. She was recently invited to become a founding member of the Institute of Shipboard Education's board of directors and is a trustee of the United Way of Miami-Dade County.

Freed resides in Weston, Florida, with her husband and three children.

A winning cruise marketing formula in the 21st century is no different than in the last century, and we suspect no different than it will be in future times—it's all about enticing prospects to try your brand and then delivering a product that at the very least meets—and hopefully exceeds—expectations.

The challenging part of this formula is that the marketing components—particularly product—must always remain fresh and relevant in order to expand the cruise industry's currently lackluster three percent share of the vacation marketplace. Marketers must diligently push the envelope in not only the product arena, but in the arena of the other classic "4 Ps" (price, place/distribution and promotion), as well.

Market Opportunity

In the early 1970s, the entire cruise industry sailed roughly 500,000 people per year, and only one percent of the American public had ever been on a cruise.

Cruise line marketers saw lots of opportunity for "new blood" with this great vacation alternative. The proof of the opportunity for success in this industry is with the incredible, early turnaround and continued growth of the Carnival brand. Carnival started with one old ship—a converted transatlantic ocean liner—back in 1972. By 1975, Carnival was carrying 50,000 cruisers per year on this single vessel. Carnival quickly developed its "Fun Ship®" brand positioning, continued investing in the product and the marketing, and, by 1984, became "The Most Popular Cruise Line in the World!®", sailing a record 300,000 guests. In 2003, Carnival carried 2,800,000 guests—a full third of the industry's approximate 8,500,000 North American patronage!

Additional opportunity abounds: consider that the most popular land-based resort areas in North America, Orlando and Las Vegas, generate about 70 million visitors per year and, since only about 15 percent of the North American market had ever cruised as of 2003, the industry certainly *still* has a huge opportunity for expansion. Due to capacity limitations, however, the cruise industry can only improve upon its penetration of the North American market by one or two percent per year. No wonder the cruise lines are building fabulous floating resorts as quickly as possible to move the needle in the direction of gaining the vacation market penetration our fine product deserves.

While during certain heavy capacity growth years, and/or economically/geopolitically sensitive years, the industry finds itself in a temporarily demand-challenged state, the cruise industry has consistently been able to generate higher levels of overall consumer satisfaction with a product that beats all other vacations (at Carnival, overall guest satisfaction runs about 98 percent vs. land-locked hotels/resorts at 71 percent) and provides an experience guests long to repeat. Cruising simply offers the better vacation choice . . . we just need to increase trial among first-timers! The cruise lines know that once first-timers experience cruising, they will come back again and again.

It is critically important that the lines focus their marketing efforts on developing their first-timer base. Carnival has been the clear leader in this arena, and is credited with almost single-handedly creating first-time demand for the industry. The percentage of first-time Carnival cruisers is roughly 50 percent, which heavily skews the rest of the industry's overall 33 percent first-time cruiser ratio to a "net net" of 40 percent first-timers.

While first-timer trial is key to the continued successful growth of cruising, the repeat cruiser is also of great importance. Today, roughly 60 percent of industry-wide cruise passengers are repeaters. And although Carnival leads in developing first-timers, the product improvements and terrific customer satisfaction with Carnival's brand value are evident in the growth/loyalty of repeat guests. Of the 50 percent of our guests who are repeat cruisers, 65 percent of those are *repeaters to the brand.*

Overall, this data speaks volumes about the cruise experience in general versus land-based vacations, and also speaks to the huge strides we have made specifically in enhancing the "Today's Carnival" experience.

Product—Theoretical Brand Formulae for Success

It is postulated that there are two sure-fire formulae for success when it comes to brand positioning:

- Acceptable Product w/Superior Value (*e.g., Toyota and Wal-Mart*)

- Superior Product w/Acceptable Value (*e.g., Mercedes-Benz and Nordstrom*)

Up until about 10 years ago, Carnival fell into the first category. We built a reputation early on, in the late 1970s and early 1980s, of being a "bottom feeder" . . . offering an acceptable product at the lowest price (superior value). Today, we remain loyal to our original brand promise of "Fun and Value" (it's what people want in a vacation experience). However, over the last ten years, we have enhanced that core brand promise with "Quality & Choice" . . . and we have done so with consistent strides in product upgrades and terrific service, yielding a superior product with acceptable value. Some may consider our latest goal to be unthinkable: Offering a superior product with superior value.

The Blurring Distinction of Cruise Experiences

While yesterday the product within the "cruise pyramid" had distinct categories (starting from the smaller top-of-the-pyramid to the broad bottom: luxury, specialty, premium, contemporary and budget—"bottom-feeders"), today there is a fascinating blurring of distinction among the contemporary, premium, and luxury product categories from a qualitative standpoint . . . and the bottom-feeders are gone! By 2010, we anticipate a continued blurring of the product as the cruise lines provide better experiences at more favorable consumer pricing. Given the tremendous increase in quality in the contemporary and premium lines, the luxury and specialty ends of the market are at risk of shrinking.

Carnival is now a premium product at contemporary pricing. Economies of scale realized with the growth in our brand, coupled with strategically-focused product-improvement initiatives, gave us the opportunity to offer the consumer a better experience on Today's Carnival than on many traditionally-known "premium" lines with older ships. The companies that operated these ships failed to make a serious investment in improving human resources through training.

"Today's Carnival" is staking a new claim . . . it represents new and unique brand positioning with a premium product that still offers superior value. So, we've used our consistent management and "category killer" economies of scale to maintain the superior value proposition and provide far more than just an acceptable product; we have enhanced the quality component beyond "acceptable" . . . to that of the premium lines!

Today's Carnival: Carnival Cruise Lines has made inordinate strides over its 30-year history. In the1990s, Carnival introduced "Today's Carnival," which lets travel agents and consumers know that this is not "your father's Oldsmobile." In addition to the ongoing upgrades in hardware and the commitment to a new-building program that blows away the competition, Carnival continues to enhance/improve our menus, wine lists, itineraries, hospitality/training and service investments . . . and to include more of what's most important to today's consumer. Carnival repeaters are coming back to the brand in droves. However, as the graph shows, it takes years to change long-held perceptions.

What is Carnival's formula for success? Clearly, one secret of our success is that we understand we're in the larger, "making vacation memories" business, not just the cruise business. And, we're also the only supplier in the cruise industry that is fun and *owns* fun (we're riding the boot heels of the two most successful North American vacation destinations, Orlando and Las Vegas). Another huge piece of our success is a dedicated, consistent management team. Add to that significant financial resources and economies of scale as the largest company in the cruise industry. These strengths allowed us to look at the product of "Old Carnival" and identify where our shortcomings were. In 1993, we developed a vision statement and acted upon it! Carnival's vision statement is to "*Provide quality cruise vacations that exceed the expectations of our guests.*" This credo remains a core focus throughout our company, and is the platform from which our marketing strategy emanates. As the result of this vision, Carnival dedicates a sizable annual budget to ongoing personnel training at all levels, and continues to invest in food, service and entertainment upgrades.

Carnival Cruise Lines' "Homeport Strategy" is simple yet brilliant—we know that travelers prefer to spend three hours or fewer to get to their vacation destination. We've set the trend in growing cruise home ports from just a few in the domestic United States to almost 20 North American ports of embarkation. Talk about choice! We're making it easier and easier for prospects and past guests alike to enjoy our product.

While the "Fun Ships" positioning was created early on in the history of Carnival Cruise Lines, "fun" has transitioned through the years. In the very early days, it meant "young, party ship," and, today, it's a quality of fun that is personified by our colorful promotional and collateral materials, by the advertising . . . and themed throughout our marketing program. The clear message to the prospect is that nobody offers more vacation value, choice, and fun than Carnival. Carnival's unique ownership of "fun" in the cruise industry (via entertainment architecture and product delivery) is yet another element of our success.

At Carnival, we work with our ad agency to always refresh the "fun" brand so that it breaks through the clutter. And, speaking of fun, according to the Yankelovich National Leisure Travel Monitor (among other sources), having fun is a top-rated choice among leisure travelers!

Pricing

Our largest competitor is really the land-based vacations sector, which leaves on average about 30–40 percent of its inventory unutilized; by contracts, the cruise industry works on a model approaching 100 percent occupancy (Carnival leads in stateroom utilization at 99.9 percent). We are driven to fill every berth given our desire to grow the market and our "constraint" of limited capacity.

This model has given way to the cruise lines' development of very sophisticated revenue management techniques in recent years, which provide the tools for us to make smart decisions regarding the tightrope we walk between maximizing revenue and ensuring that each and every sailing is full.

It is our belief at Carnival that this model has allowed the cruise industry to be incredibly resilient in the face of the "Perfect Storm" of the September 11 attacks, NLV, SARS. Not to mention the other intermittent economic, geopolitical, or security challenges we're continually faced with.

Bottom line, the aggressive pricing of today, coupled with our product improvements, make cruising a "no brainer" consumer vacation opportunity. The operational efficiencies of the industry, particularly with the latest product offerings, allow the industry to thrive in profitability even in the most challenging economic times.

The Distribution Channel (Place)

While vacations, on the whole, are primarily purchased direct by the consumer from a supplier (calling hotels and resorts to book), the vast majority of *cruise* vacations have always been booked through the valued travel agent distribution system. As that system has gone through consolidation and a reduction in the number of retail "outlets" available (essentially since the airlines' commission caps/cuts began in 1995), and as other communication/distribution systems have created value propositions to the consumer, a still significant but smaller percentage of business is being booked through agents.

The consumer used to rely virtually exclusively on "traditional" (retail, mom-and-pop) travel agents to provide information on the relatively complex and unknown (to most) cruise vacation product. Even this model morphed—it was standard practice through the early 1990s to visit a retail location. Now, most people call agents (most of whom have 800-numbers in addition to local access). The new reality of the 21st century is that the world is much smaller. The Internet has provided prospects and past cruisers alike with the opportunity to learn about the vast cruise vacation offerings right in the privacy of their own homes . . . at any time of the day or night. Various booking sources include suppliers' Web sites, travel agents' web sites, and the "new" Internet travel agents' Web sites such as Travelocity, Expedia, and Orbitz.

At Carnival, we believe that, given the rapid growth/success of Internet travel agencies, there could be a huge opportunity for someone to "own" cruise on the web—to create a "Cruise Orbitz," if you will—at a lower cost to suppliers. In addition, the cruise lines must find a way to regain "price parity" no matter the channel used by the consumer . . . nor the productivity of the agency. Pricing, which makes smaller agencies uncompetitive with larger ones, makes no sense. The traditional travel agencies have already suffered at the hands of the airlines (many died). The cruise lines should create an equally competitive pricing environment for all agencies so that they're *all* motivated to sell cruises.

Choice—It's all About the Customer

Gone are the days where the consumer is not responded to by the cruise supplier, who used to graciously bow out of the selling process and allow the travel agent to drive all the business. The new reality is that the consumer of today is savvy and demanding . . . and no good businessperson would or should ignore the consumer who raises his hand and asks for help in understanding the product supplied. The cruise lines today are responsive to consumers' needs and wants for information. They all have Web sites and push out brochures on request. And most recognize the fact that the consumer has a choice in how they wish to book their travel. We are supportive of that choice—we just want the business, whether it be through our valued travel agent partners, through an Internet travel agency or directly through a supplier. The choice is ultimately the consumer's.

The responsiveness by cruise lines today to consumers' inquiries is also evident in the development, in the late 1990s and the early 2000s, of outbound telemarketing and other direct initiatives (Carnival is a leader is this arena. We expect others to follow, if for no other reason than they, too, wish to be responsive to consumers' needs/wants). Particularly in light of the very challenging economic and political conditions affecting the travel industry today, it's more important than ever to proactively go after qualified leads and reach out to those leads quickly and professionally, in order to close the sale.

The distribution channel conflict that exists today is interesting and certainly worth some press. Some retailers believe that they are "owed" business by the suppliers without working for it by "owning" their business through passionate and enthusiastic sales skills. They believe the supplier should pay for their marketing, give them preferential pricing and pay them high commissions. The reality is that cruise lines have always been uniquely loyal to the travel agent distribution system and have always paid fairly for this terrific relationship; they continue today to hold that same loyalty. This will not change in the future. Sellers of cruises who are out there proactively selling and getting the business will enthusiastically and wholeheartedly receive the cruise lines' support . . . in a big way. However, the folks that are waiting for the bus to drop off 40 people at a shot with their credit card in hand, without working for it . . . those agents will be off the map, based on their own lack of initiative.

Promotion

As the cruise product continues to evolve, as the Baby Boomer market ages, and as children of cruisers become "entrenched" in the unbeatable value of a cruise vacation, the demographic appeal of cruising will continue to widen.

At Carnival, our core media demo is where the bulk of our business falls—that is, among those adults who are 25–54 years of age. But, as with other cruises and vacations, Carnival appeals to a wide range of folks with varying ages and interests.

So how can we continue to capture these folks and convert them to cruising? What works today? As always, there are many forces at work to ultimately garner response and create bookings for the cruise product. Traditional channels include brand and tactical broadcast advertising (national network and cable TV, spot TV, radio), brand and tactical print advertising (consumer magazine, newspaper) and direct response (direct mail). The new reality is that the immediacy of the Internet and e-mail are a powerful force in creating interest in, and garnering response for, the cruise product. In addition, particularly with interactive TV models just a few short years away from development (we're very excited about some of the models in place in the United Kingdom), putting infomercials in the media mix facilitates direct response initiatives and helps cruise marketers drill down to prospects who are interested in cruising.

Passion: The Fifth "P"

Passion for making the product better and better (service, hardware, etc.) is no longer optional. Today's consumer is savvy and wants nothing but the best.

Carnival recognizes that there's no "free lunch" or "silver bullet" here—the passion and enthusiasm (and financial resources) to deliver to the customer an even better experience than what they think they're going to get is the order of the day. Basics go a long way. A smile. A friendly greeting. Attentive, pampering service. Given the rapid growth of the cruise industry, Carnival and the other cruise lines must commit to ongoing training of shipboard staff to ensure that exceptional product delivery remains consistent. There are so many great products out there today, so many wonderful vacation alternatives. As in every other aspect of life, things are more and more competitive and we need to proactively and positively differentiate ourselves with the fifth "P" in everything we do.

31

Building Our Brands

Jack L. Williams
President, Chief Operating Officer
Royal Caribbean International
and Celebrity Cruises

Jack Williams, president and CEO of Royal Caribbean International and Celebrity Cruises since 2001, has been instrumental in reorganizing the lines' revenue management, marine operations and environmental policies, and in redefining the corporate culture.

Prior to joining Royal Caribbean International as the line's president in January 1997, Williams was an executive with American Airlines. He began his career in San Diego in 1972 as an operations agent, and subsequently served as supervisor of budgets and cost control; he was manager-budgets and cost control at Chicago O'Hare Airport; and was general manager-Denver, where he opened American's operation at that airport in 1981. He later was named managing director-passenger sales for the western division, then general sales manager in 1987, and ultimately, vice president and general sales manager in 1990.

Williams has maintained a longtime commitment to a number of professional and charitable organizations. Since 1994, Williams has been on the board of directors of the Andre Agassi Foundation, which has raised more than $8 million in support of charitable causes in the Las Vegas area. He also is the featured auctioneer at several annual fundraisers, including the American Airlines Celebrity Ski event for Cystic Fibrosis, the American Airlines Celebrity Golf event for the Komen Foundation and the Michael Bolton Foundation for women and children at risk. Through his association with charities, he has helped raise more than $6 million annually. In 1999, Williams was elected to the national board of directors for the Cystic Fibrosis Foundation and to the board of directors of SunTrust Bank / Miami.

Williams has won many awards for his charity work, including the 1994 "Breath of Life Award," the highest honor bestowed on an individual by the Cystic Fibrosis Foundation. He also received the 1995 "Breath of Life Award" from the San Francisco chapter of Cystic Fibrosis and, in November 1996, shared the stage with Bob Hope in Los Angeles, where he received the "Joel McCrea Merit of Achievement Award" from the American Cinema Awards for his humanitarian efforts.

Williams is a graduate of San Diego State University, where he earned a degree in communications and was an associate professor for two years.

"Mindset": Creating Powerful Marketing Platforms

The great mistake of many corporations is to chase a demographic without creating a mindset about your brand.

In the eyes of some cruise lines, consumers are a faceless audience. These potential customers fit general demographic targets composed of age, gender and socio-economic level—essentially, a snapshot of American travelers.

If these potential customers ever take vacations, goes the traditional thinking, they are candidates to take a cruise.

But research into present and future cruise guests reveals much more about the audience than traditional thinking has allowed. The research goes beyond demographics, venturing into psychographics. These are preferences based on behavior and attitudes. Psychographics can yield a treasure trove of insights and hot buttons likely to steer a consumer toward a cruise. Psychographics, in a sense, can serve as the gold standard in target mindset marketing.

Getting inside a prospective customer's head to design and build a product that meets their desires or expectations, then creating a mindset, a brand promise, and marketing the product in an alluring way, is the goal of a successful marketing platform. More than just statistics in a database, these insights have guided much of the brand development and marketing initiatives by Royal Caribbean Cruises Ltd. over the past several years.

The results have been striking. We have proven that, by taking a more thoughtful and thorough look at what guests want, as well as who they are, our marketing and sales teams can better develop the brands and fill the ships' berths—now and in the future.

Who Cruises?

The cruise industry remains a ripe market for today's traveler. In 2002, the cruise industry had 8.7 million guests worldwide, up 15.5 percent from 2001, according to the trade group Cruise Lines International Association (CLIA). Even in times of deep economic stagnation and concerns about security, the North American cruise market outperformed expectations, with 7.4 million guests in 2002, up from 6.9 million in 2001.

Consumers are cruising. But research reveals that an overwhelming majority of Americans (88 percent) have not yet cruised. Why? The issue is that most prospective cruise guests simply don't realize how much there is to do on a cruise vacation, onboard the ship or during onshore excursions. That's why our marketing and sales teams at Royal Caribbean International (RCI) and Celebrity Cruises have studied the vacationer's mindset to learn what travelers want from their vacations.

We have two brands under Royal Caribbean Cruises Ltd. RCI positions itself as an active, energetic brand. Celebrity Cruises offers itself as a premium brand, serving a more upscale audience. What these brands already have done bodes well for our approach to marketing them in the future. We have differentiated our two brands based on what research revealed of prospective guests' present and future desires. We have defined a unique positioning statement to set our brands apart. We have marketed aggressively across traditional and nontraditional advertising media. And we have tested and retested the results.

By being keenly aware of changing consumer demographics *and* psychographics, our company will evolve our products as well as our marketing efforts to meet those desires and create a positioning statement to speak to different consumer groups.

In essence, think Nike. The athletic apparel company doesn't sell tennis shoes or running shoes or hiking shoes. The company sells a *mindset* of exercise, health, and adventure. That positioning speaks across all demographics—from kids wanting an edge on an inner-city basketball court to seniors looking for comfortable walking shoes. Once marketing has established the mindset, you can pretty much target any demographic you want.

For several years, RCI has worked to know the minds of our guests. Like other cruise lines, we face a variety of challenges related to marketing to our potential audience. One challenge was simply that among most potential cruise guests, the various cruise brands are poorly differentiated. Cruise lines are viewed as a homogeneous category of similar ships offering similar amenities and visiting similar destinations. While the thoughtful cruise guest will discern the differences, most cruise guests aren't inquisitive enough to spend the time discovering the subtle or even striking differences between cruise lines. To stand out, RCI needed to market our products differently.

Mindset and consumer segment marketing at RCI became central to our product marketing efforts. Marketers can always chase demographics, but mindset tells tales about future desires—insights that are instrumental in guiding a product's placement and positioning, today and tomorrow.

The Challenge

The challenges for today's cruise lines are twofold. First, you must break out of the mold of traditional cruise-line positioning. Product differentiation has become essential to setting apart any cruise line from the pack. For RCI, it has meant creating a brand promise—that is, what guests can expect when traveling with us. A cruise with RCI is an excursion into adventure and recreational activities not found on other cruise lines or land-based vacations, reflecting an explorer mindset. A vacation with our sister brand, Celebrity Cruises, brings an unparalleled cruise experience with a touch of luxury on an upscale ship, so our campaign focuses on the guest experience and how guests are treated onboard. Other cruise lines have instituted programs catering to the preferences of guests, such as open-seating dining rooms and a smoking-prohibited environment.

The second challenge is to find new audiences. It is not enough to market to the static pie of existing cruise guests. To grow the market, cruise lines must target *prospective* cruise guests—not just those who have cruised previously.

Throughout our 34-year history, research has told us much about our guests: Where they want to travel to, how they want to get there, and what they want to do and experience along the way. The concept of "options" has been a common denominator.

Our marketing and sales teams looked at the company's brands and wondered where our products and options fit among the competition. We looked at the competition's onboard programs and amenities, shore activities, and the way sales and marketing initiatives positioned those offerings to the consumer. At RCI, we call the process SEAS (Strategy, Execution, and Approach for Success). The process helps us approach and define any strategic problem, opportunity or issue, and it assists executives to better understand the competition and the entire playing field.

Our company turned to consumer research firms Simmons Market Research Bureau and Yankelovich Inc. to gain an understanding of the competitive landscape and consumer mindsets. The goal was to discover how to market RCI so that we could effectively differentiate our brands amid consumer impressions of this poorly understood and homogeneous vacation category.

The result was the development and creation of a brand positioning with a working strategy line, "The freedom to experience the unexpected."

The most tangible and obvious evidence of our company's research (and options) is the array of amenities on RCI's Voyager-class ships. Some 40 percent larger than our next-largest Radiance class, the five Voyager-class ships feature first-ever attractions, such as a horizontal atrium—a shopping and entertainment promenade almost the length of two football fields—a rock-climbing wall, ice-skating rink, scientific research laboratories, and sports decks for basketball, inline skating, and miniature golf.

This speaks a great deal to today's cruise guests as well as to tomorrow's. Many guests want more than to just retreat to the pool and spa. Research has shown that as Baby Boomers age, they are seeking more active-lifestyle vacations. If the cruise industry is going to grow, those options available on our ships have to appeal to many more slices of the audience pie. Think of it as an almost bi-polar audience: One half wants the traditional relaxing vacation; the other, a more energetic, adventurous getaway.

As with many industries, marketing is essential to the cruise trade in getting word of the brand out to consumers. Cruise prospects are more likely than past guests to cite television and radio advertising as key informational resources when deciding to take a cruise (54 percent versus 20 percent, according to the CLIA). Research continues to reveal that consumers who have not cruised are misinformed about what cruising has to offer. They want action, engaging shipboard activities, entertainment, and experiences they cannot find on another vacation. But they perceive cruising as not providing those amenities. Making the situation even more challenging is that our competition's advertising continues to focus on the old perceptions—shipboard scenes of smiling couples dining in tuxedos and dancing.

Defining the Brand Expectation

Through additional research, executives from RCI and Arnold Worldwide, our Boston-based advertising agency, refined the brand positioning. The strategy essentially was to increase first-time cruisers by advertising the exciting, off-ship activities. In this way, RCI would break the mold, break out of the pack, and sail away from traditional cruise marketing.

Research revealed a sea change in the cruise line's target audience. We discovered potential cruisers were the millions of Baby Boomers who increasingly view themselves as adventurers instead of vacationers, and who seek active vacations in exotic destinations. The list of prospects exceeds 30 million Americans—a group distinct from what other cruise lines target in their marketing initiatives. This was important for us, as it revealed the future role that segment marketing would continue to play in our product and message development.

In 2000, RCI unveiled new print and television advertising campaigns supported by the consumer insights gained from research. The new advertising brought the new brand positioning to life. Shipboard shots gave way to images of snorkelers, jet-skiers, parasailers, rock climbers and joggers on the uppermost deck. Print ads showed scenes of a Yucatan cave and other shore destinations. Our campaign was entitled "Explore the world" with the television tagline "Get out there."

This new creative strategy met the challenge in cruise marketing to attract a wider range of people, from babies to seniors. To get those people, we needed to deliver a compelling message—one that isn't delivered solely from the deck of a cruise ship. Among the key strategies was the mission to educate consumers as to what amenities and offerings were available onboard—and on shore—and thereby entice more people to cruise.

All of this active-lifestyle positioning could not come at the expense of our past guests. Research revealed that while many Baby Boomers enjoy active vacations, a large population still enjoys the more relaxing elements of cruising. While we aimed to bring new guests into the fold, it was important to serve the future needs of our best, most loyal guests and keep them interested in booking another vacation.

Finally, between the print and television advertising, collateral and travel-agent materials, online marketing and the company Web site, all marketing was presented in a consistent and integrated message across all media. This helped increase the campaign's reach and effectiveness, boost awareness of a centralized brand message, and ensure our company did not have splinter messages and campaigns separated by medium.

The balance between offline (print, television, and radio) and interactive, online marketing could shift dramatically in the coming years. The travel industry is preparing for this change. Just as online booking sites such as Expedia.com are becoming recognizable brands and destinations for travelers to study their options and purchase travel, the Internet is becoming a key tool for the cruise industry, too. Prospective guests increasingly are visiting cruise-line Web sites to explore ships, itineraries, and schedules, and to learn what options exist.

To wit, RCI has used television to steer traffic to our Web site. Once at the Web site, prospects learn about individual ships and more about the brand, viewing shipboard shots, views of and from staterooms, and other onboard and shore activities. In fact, traffic to www.royalcaribbean.com doubled once television was used to increase awareness of our Web site. The Internet will become a growing and important element in any cruise marketing initiative.

Sister Brand's Success

Though positioned as a premium line since its inception in 1989, Celebrity Cruises' marketing now seeks to present the brand as one appealing to experienced travelers who appreciate the best in this vacation category. The "Faces" campaign, begun in late 2002, and the follow-up, "Treated Famously," were the result of a redefined target—a better understanding of who the audience is and exactly why its members select (or should select) Celebrity.

Not unlike the work done with RCI, research into Celebrity's guest psychographics revealed insights that have helped steer the brand to better serve its audience. Prospects and guests are savvy vacationers, slightly older than the mass-market cruise audience (between 35 and 60). These educated individuals appreciate culture, are optimistic and unpretentious, and have a high degree of social interaction.

Focusing on this target audience changed Celebrity Cruises' marketing approach. Today, Celebrity's key brand assets are rejuvenation (relaxation), connections (meeting new people or traveling with friends), and enrichment (learning something while onboard). Those brand pillars have become the linchpins of our marketing efforts as we look to communicate those product offerings that aim to serve the prospects' expectations.

This brand transformation initiative has introduced some 75 elements designed to enhance the consumer experience. A few examples include cold towels available when returning from a tour, and complimentary sorbet offered poolside on sea days. More than just meeting expectations, constant improvement to the product will be critical to creating a memorable cruise and furthering brand differentiation.

Celebrity's advertising campaign speaks to how consumers can expect to be welcomed and treated while onboard. More than an expectation of service, it touches an important internal identifier: A perceived feeling of deserving the finer amenities a cruise vacation offers.

Finally, addressing how guests are treated onboard, as well as how they are treated once they return home, is a natural extension of the brand promise.

Loyalty marketing programs seek to create brand-loyal customers through outreach marketing initiatives. Instituted by the marketing and total guest satisfaction departments, these efforts extend our company's outreach efforts to create a more loyal, committed guest. They receive marketing materials, like direct mail, brochures, and special offers, to encourage them to book a future cruise.

Celebrity Cruises, like RCI, has seen the future of travel marketing, and the future is this: Further targeting of the cruise market and cooperative marketing initiatives. The latter brings awareness, affinity, and a greater likelihood of a customer attaching goodwill from one brand onto our cruise brand and vice versa. For example, a Celebrity sweepstakes campaign with a financial services company targeted three million similar customers and prospects. Similar initiatives with groups, organizations, and associations will deliver greater marketing value to Celebrity, while also targeting a highly differentiated and segmented audience. Synergistic marketing drives down marketing and media costs and makes a wider audience available for prospecting.

The success of these efforts, of course, depends upon shipboard employees becoming ambassadors of the brand. Employees help personify the brand and the message, creating an additional touch point for the company to interact with and influence the experience of the guest. Therefore, not only is it critical that guests get the right marketing message, it is also critical that employees understand and personify it. At RCI and Celebrity Cruises, employees are educated in the GOLD Anchor Service and Savvy Service standards, respectively, to ensure that the right message is presented.

The result has been unparalleled recognition for both brands. RCI's advertising has been judged by travel agents as the best in the cruise industry, and five Celebrity ships were ranked in the top 10 of Best Large Ships in a 2002 poll of readers of *Condé Nast Traveler*. In fact, our two brands combined for 16 of the top 26 large ships!

The Future of Cruise Marketing

Glance at the variety of television ads for cruising and it becomes apparent that many of the same attributes that were marketed yesterday are being pitched today. Remove the cruise line's name from the ads and they're too often the same. Astute marketers have realized, however, that the cruise industry cannot grow solely by "stealing share" from rivals. Brand differentiation will prove essential to carving out a separate, distinct identity for tomorrow's successful cruise brand. Companies then will build upon those identifiers to lure a distinct type of vacationer.

As Royal Caribbean Cruises Ltd. continues to grow its fleet to 28 ships and more than 60,000 berths by the middle of 2004, further brand differentiation and segmentation will be employed to fill the staterooms.

Moreover, to be perceived as an enticing vacation option and attract the consumer's time and disposable income, cruise lines will need to see themselves not only competing against each other but also against land-based destinations. Cruise lines must watch consumer trends and become category-builders by enticing vacationers who otherwise might not choose to cruise to consider doing so instead of visiting theme parks and other land tours and destinations.

If consumers are evolving, the travel industry must evolve, too. This will determine the future success of travel providers. By studying consumer values, demographics and psychographics, by keeping product evolution in line with changing needs and values, by tying together online positioning and a robust Web site to educate potential customers and by always serving the consumer's desire for value and choice, the cruises will become even more prominent among the choices for vacation travel.

32

Building Loyalty Through CRM

Peter G. Ratcliffe
Chief Executive Officer
P&O Princess Cruises PLC
and Executive Director
Carnival Corporation

Peter Ratcliffe began his career in the cruise industry in 1973 when he joined one of the most recognized maritime companies in the world, the Peninsular and Oriental Steam Navigation Company (P&O). After rising through the ranks of the venerable British-based company, he was named president of Princess Cruises in 1993. Following a de-merger from P&O in 2000 to form a separate cruise division called P&O Princess Cruises PLC, and a subsequent merger of that company with Carnival Corporation in 2003, Ratcliffe oversees seven cruise brands as chief executive of P&O Princess Cruises, and is an executive director with the Miami-based Carnival Corporation, the largest cruise group in the world.

P&O Princess Cruises brands under Ratcliffe's responsibility include Princess Cruises, one of the best-known cruise companies in North America; P&O Cruises, the UK's largest cruise operator; Aida, one of the best-known brands in the fast-growing German cruise industry; Swan Hellenic, a distinctive operator of British "discovery" cruises; Ocean Village, a cruise brand in the UK emphasizing informal and contemporary holidays; Arosa, a destination-oriented product catering exclusively to German-speaking customers; and the successful P&O Cruises Australia, offering contemporary seagoing holidays for Australians.

Ratcliffe was appointed head of P&O's cruise division in February 2000, and chief executive officer of P&O Princess Cruises PLC at its inception in October 2000. The company, the world's third-largest cruise operator at the time, merged with Carnival Corporation in April 2003.

Ratcliffe joined Princess Cruises in 1986 as chief financial officer and subsequently was appointed senior vice president of customer services, then chief operating officer in 1989. Prior to Princess, his earlier career was spent with P&O Containers Limited in London and Sydney, where he ultimately became group financial controller. Prior to joining P&O, he worked for the London accounting firm of Coopers and Lybrand, after graduating from Cambridge University in 1969 with a baccalaureate degree in economics and mathematics. He served as the chairman of the International Council of Cruise Lines (ICCL) in 1997 and 1998.

Ratcliffe was born in Manchester, England, in 1948, and now resides in a suburb of Los Angeles with his wife, Alison.

Strategic Context

Over the past two decades, the cruise industry has grown dramatically—at a rate four times greater than demand for vacations in general. Forty percent of this demand comes from "first timers" who are trying a cruise vacation for the first time. Through our marketing and travel agent partners, we have convinced them to try a cruise vacation versus other vacation alternatives. The other 60 percent of the demand comes from "repeat cruisers" who have previously cruised. Growing both of these demand streams is critical to the success of the cruise industry going forward as we continue to aggressively grow our capacity.

As an industry, we must first generate a healthy stream of first timers. Then our products must exceed their expectations so that we retain them as frequent cruise customers. These repeat cruisers will, in turn, refer their friends and begin the virtuous cycle again. Customer retention and word of mouth marketing are the most cost-effective ways for the cruise industry to grow its business.

Fortunately, cruising dramatically outperforms alternative vacations in terms of customer satisfaction. A recent study showed satisfaction rates with cruising in the 90th percentile, in contrast with land-based alternatives, with satisfaction rates in the 60th percentile. This disparity in performance testifies to the outstanding value proposition of a cruise vacation.

It also creates a competitive challenge. If all of cruising delivers such outstanding customer satisfaction rates, how can we differentiate our particular cruise line? We at Princess continually strive to distinguish our product by way of its modern fleet, affordable balconies, flexible dining and entertainment options and a wide selection of routes and destinations (perhaps the industry's widest).

In addition, we recognize that it is often the intangibles that make an experience memorable. These are the personal touches that say "We know you and we appreciate you—so why cruise with anyone else?" We believe our customer relationship management (CRM) strategy is critical to our industry and to our product growth over the next decade.

CRM

What is CRM? Customer relationship management is the marketing buzzword we use for creating and fostering a unique, personal relationship between Princess and our passengers. It's not a new idea—our crew has been making these personal connections with our passengers for decades when they learn their passengers' tastes and preferences and then surprise and delight them. We've received many letters over the years from passengers thanking specific crew members for making them feel special by remembering their favorite drink or food and preparing it for them in advance, etc.

Our business challenge was to determine how we might foster and maintain that personal relationship in every interaction a passenger has with our company. We wanted to create a small company feel even while growing dramatically.

First, we set out to review all the ways a prospective customer interacted with Princess. We found that an average Princes passenger can have literally dozens of interactions with Princess Cruises. There are many "moments of truth" when we make an impression on our customers.

1. They may see our ads or receive direct mail/e-mail

2. They may call us or their travel agent for our brochure

3. They may research specific cruises on our Web site

4. They may make a booking

5. They may call with questions about their upcoming vacation

6. They will receive our pre-cruise preparation materials

7. They may pre-reserve their shore excursions

8. They spend on average nine days on vacation with us

9. They may write a letter offering feedback on their experience

Our challenge is to take a comprehensive view of all of these interactions and create a dialogue with our passengers as to what their hopes and expectations are for their vacation and use that information to deliver an exceptional, personalized Princess experience.

Technology enables us to do this on a large scale. We are unlike other industries in that we spend considerable amounts of time with our customers and are responsible for their entire vacation experience. While they're aboard, we provide all of their hotel, dining, entertainment and transportation services! Consequently, we have the ability to capture a tremendous amount of information about our passengers' wants and needs from their varied communications by phone, mail, Web, and in person onboard. In turn, this information can be organized and used by many different departments internally like customer service, passenger relations, marketing, and fleet operations.

Principles of CRM at Princess Cruises

Because CRM efforts involve people from many departments, we believed that it was important to agree on a set of common, basic principles to guide our activities. While many of these are simple and common sense, they are operationally more complicated than one might think. We believe that this constant attention to, and refinement of, our basic processes will be a competitive requirement over the next decade.

Principle #1: Ask for information only once—then remember it

We used to ask passengers to complete their basic contact information for us each time they cruised. Even if they had cruised with us five times before, they were asked to fill out the same information. This had the unintentional, undesired effect of communicating to our loyal passengers that we did not know them or recognize their history with Princess. It also resulted in additional administrative hassle for them during their vacation preparation. At a time when they should be excitedly anticipating and planning their vacation, we were giving them duplicative work.

We now store this passenger information in a central repository and give them pre-filled-out applications. They can confirm or revise their basic information and invest their time in changing only those items that may change over time, like emergency contact information or dietary restrictions. We encourage them to validate and confirm this information via our Web site, www.princess.com. This reduces our paperwork costs and risk of errors. Most importantly, this process reinforces the message that Princess remembers them and desires to make their vacation as easy and enjoyable as possible.

Going forward, we will be constantly looking for ways we can "remember" information passengers share with us in order to personalize and improve their vacation experience.

Principle #2: Contact them in ways they want us to

Market research studies indicate an increasing trend in consumer frustration with intrusive advertising by corporations. We all read articles each week condemning generic e-mail "spamming," highlighting privacy concerns, etc. The business challenge is to create and maintain a meaningful relationship and dialogue with our customers between cruises while respecting their preferences.

We know that our passengers are successful, busy individuals. Therefore, we have recently begun to record their communication preferences and reflect them in our marketing communications. We more actively track how they wish to communicate with us whether by e-mail, mail or phone. We ask them how they would like to be addressed, then store and use their preferred name in our marketing materials. Lastly, we closely monitor our response times to passenger inquiries so that we will promptly respond when a passenger proactively contacts us.

Principle #3: Tailor our communications to their individual interests

With the explosive growth of e-mail use, the world wide web, cable channels, etc. we increasingly recognize that consumers are bombarded with information each day on a wealth of topics. This information overload can compromise our effectiveness at maintaining a positive dialogue with our repeat customers.

In order to nurture our relationship with them, we believe that our communications must be relevant and timely. Therefore, we are increasingly working to understand our passengers' individual interests and support them. In direct marketing, we analyze where each passenger has cruised with us and where he or she would like to travel next. We then send them relevant offers at the appropriate time given their vacation planning cycle. In fleet operations, we analyze what activities on the ship interest each passenger and then tailor our promotions to their interests.

Once again, this type of targeted marketing creates a win/win situation. Our passengers learn what activities we offer are most attractive and relevant to them; simultaneously, we improve our acquisition cost efficiencies.

Principle #4: Communicate that we value their loyalty

We recognize that consumers have many vacation choices and that we must give them great reasons to 1) return to cruising and 2) return to Princess every time. We recognize that it is much more cost-effective to retain our customers than to find new ones each year. Therefore, we can afford to invest in offering additional recognition and reward to loyal customers. The lifetime value of a loyal cruise passenger is quite substantial!

In designing our loyalty program, our intention is to deliver such an exceptional experience to passengers that they don't want to vacation anywhere else. We also provide them with a real incentive to return to us. To this end, we recently updated our Captain's Circle loyalty program to better recognize and reward a passenger's cruise history with Princess. After completing their first Princess cruise, a passenger is given free membership and "gold status" in the Princess Captain's Circle. After completion of five cruises, a passenger attains "platinum" status.

We have created program elements that provide recognition of their patronage like priority embarkation and special event invitations, among others. We additionally offer meaningful rewards for loyalty to Princess in the form of special deals on cruise prices and onboard benefits like free Internet access.

We have increased our emphasis on service and communication with our past passengers. We have created a new, unique functionary onboard, the Circle Host, who is responsible for looking after the past passengers' needs while on vacation. Between vacations, we communicate via a quarterly magazine and a special section of our Web site exclusively dedicated to news relevant to Princess Captain's Circle members.

We anticipate that the battle for past passenger loyalty will accelerate over the next decade. The cruise industry will need to continue to deliver a vacation experience and a value that outperforms all other vacation options. To do this, we will have to maintain the highest product standards while offering real value and incentives to return. On average, an experienced cruiser cruises only once every three to five years. If we could halve that, we could double our demand!

Principle #5: Listen closely to their feedback

The best way for us to stay on top of consumer trends is to listen very closely to our passengers' and employees' feedback. At Princess, we constantly measure our performance with onboard evaluations and record call or correspondence history in order to track trends. This information has been integral to our product and service development process. Armed with consumer insights, Princess has led the industry with its product innovations

For example, we were increasingly hearing complaints from some passengers that they wanted greater flexibility when dining. For some portion of our passengers, they wanted discretion as to where, when and with whom they would dine while cruising. They found the traditional dining option of two seatings at fixed times to be too restrictive, given all the other things they wanted to do while on the cruise—go to the shows, visit the bars, play the casinos, etc. They wanted the option to dine as if at any fine restaurant at home.

Consumer trend research also indicated that the Baby Boomer generation valued choice. It suggested that consumers like to know their options and choose what suits them best. This was the genesis of Princess' "Personal Choice Dining." Princess is the only cruise line to offer its passengers a choice between traditional fixed seating and restaurant-style anytime-dining. In addition, we offer a number of alternative dining venues like the Sterling Steakhouse and the Bayou Café.

Similarly, consumer trends indicated that there was increased interest in "edutainment." Passengers were interested in learning while relaxing on vacation. In response, Princess has taken shipboard programs to a whole new level with our ScholarShip @ Sea program, which offers full schedules of enrichment and entertainment programs for our passengers. It is yet another way we can customize a Princess cruise to respond to our passengers' diverse needs.

Critical Ingredients: People and Technology

People. In order to design, execute and evolve this CRM strategy, we need two critical ingredients: people and technology. First, we ensure that Princess'

employees share a common mission and service ethos. Then we give them the tools to be able to perform their jobs at a superior level. Over the next several years, we believe that we will need to continue to invest in both people and technology to maintain our leadership position in service excellence in the cruise industry.

The foundation of Princess' service culture is a program known as "Courtesy and Respect Unfailing In Service Excellence" (CRUISE). The program, started in 1996, was originally launched on the ships with a cornerstone statement:

At one point everyday, one of our customers will come into contact with me, the Princess employee. At that moment, I will be Princess Cruises. Our entire reputation as a company will be in my hands and I will make an impression. The impression will either be good or it will be bad and I will have spoken to our customers more loudly than all our community involvement, all our advertising and all our public relations put together. I will always remember that I am a Princess person . . .

"I am responsible, and I can MAKE THE DIFFERENCE."

The CRUISE program features training and competitions that emphasize teamwork and educate our employees on Princess' service expectations. It empowers our crew to strive to deliver an exceptional vacation experience for each passenger. When problems arise, employees take ownership of determining a solution.

Within the past few years, we have also implemented a form of the CRUISE program onshore in our offices. Our credo includes the phrase:

Even if you're not serving our passengers directly, you are serving somebody who is.

By offering classes, appreciation programs and special events, the CRUISE program maintains our company's focus on service and its critical role in attracting and retaining our passengers.

Technology. Technology is an essential component to improving our CRM over the next several years. We have made and will continue to make significant investment in tools that help us better understand and serve our customers.

Consumer trends support this direction. An increasing number of consumers (even in the older age brackets) are using e-mail as well as the Web for information and research. Unlike other travel business, we see only a small percentage of consumers actually making cruise bookings via the Web today. But we expect that to increase as well over time. In the interim, we certainly can expect to see an increase in use of the web to request brochures, inquire about their bookings, etc.

We will continue to create a central repository for all of our customer information so that we may have a single place with a 360-degree view of our customers. This repository will gather information regardless of how it was collected (by phone, mail or via the Web).

We will give technology tools to our employees to enable them to more efficiently respond to our passengers' needs and document and track their interactions. This will help us to reduce our costs over the long term so that we can continue to offer a great price and value proposition to our cruise customers.

Conclusion

The future success of the cruise industry in general, and of Princess in particular, relies on our ability to continue to deliver an exceptional cruise experience for both new and experienced passengers. We must inspire them to cruise again and again, as well as share their experience with their friends and family. This customer retention and word-of-mouth marketing are essential to generating sufficient demand to fill our ships for many years to come.

In order to deliver this high quality experience, we believe we will need to invest further in CRM over the next decade. We must challenge ourselves not to lose the personal touch as we grow larger in size. Inspiring true loyalty requires building a unique, personal relationship with our customers. In every interaction they have with our company, they must feel that we know them and so can serve them better.

This requires a clear vision that outlines how we expect to treat our passengers in each interaction. We must evolve our CRM principles to adapt to changing consumer tastes and preferences so that we are timely and relevant in our communications and product offerings. Using the techniques of personalization and customization, we can also improve our efficiencies with targeted marketing.

We recognize that our future depends on the further support and development of our employees and our tools. We must maintain and improve the service culture of our company and enhance their capabilities by providing improved information and technology for their decision-making. With this approach, we can make a difference.

33

Adapting the Cruise Product to an Evolving Travel Market

A. Kirk Lanterman
Chairman and CEO
Holland America Line Inc.
and
Chairman, Windstar Cruises

Alton Kirk Lanterman is chairman of the board and CEO of Holland America Line and Windstar Cruises, a subsidiary of Holland America Line. Lanterman has been a member of the board of directors of Carnival Corporation, the parent company of Holland America Line Inc. since 1989.

Lanterman began his career in the travel industry in 1970 as vice-president of finance for a company then known as Westours Inc. In 1972, he was promoted to executive vice president of Westours Inc. the position he held when Westours was purchased by Holland America Line one year later in 1973.

In 1979, Lanterman was promoted to president of Westours Inc. Four years later, in 1983, Holland America Line consolidated its total operations in Seattle, Washington and it was at that time that Lanterman was named president of the combined cruise and tour company. Lanterman remained president of Holland America Line until 1997. Carnival Corporation purchased Holland America Line-Westours Inc. in 1989, at which time

Lanterman assumed the duties of CEO. In 1997, Lanterman was named chairman and chief executive officer of Holland America Line.

Lanterman has served two terms as chairman of the Cruise Lines International Association (CLIA) and served two terms as president of the Alaska Visitors Association. He is a lifetime trustee, and past vice-chairman and treasurer, for the Institute of Certified Travel Agents (ICTA) and also served as vice-chairman of the International Council of Cruise Lines. Presently, he is the chairman of the North West Cruise Association and a member of the board of the Academy of Travel and Tourism. He was twice voted Travel Executive of the Year and was chosen the Outstanding Travel Supplier of the year by ASTA.

In 2002, Lanterman received the Sioux Award from the University of North Dakota, the highest award given by the university to any individual for outstanding achievement in their professional arena.

In 2003, Lanterman was honored by Her Royal Majesty, Queen Beatrix of the Netherlands, by being made an Officer of the Order of Orange-Nassau, the Netherlands' highest civilian honor, in recognition of his outstanding achievements in his field of work and for his service to the people of the Netherlands and its Royal Family. This order of knighthood is bestowed on individuals who have contributed exceptional value to the Dutch society through their dedicated labor and exceptional achievements in their profession and because of their benevolent community service.

Lanterman was born in Bismarck, North Dakota and graduated from Bismarck High School. He served for two years in the Korean War. He attended both the University of North Dakota and the University of Washington, where he graduated with a degree in accounting (he is a CPA). Lanterman is married, has four grown daughters and nine grandchildren, all residing in the Seattle area.

Perhaps the single most significant trend in the 21st century travel market is the maturing of the American population. The Baby Boom Generation—those Americans born between 1946 and 1964—are turning 50 at the rate of one every seven seconds.

According to the 2002 Randall Travel Marketing Report, the number-one U.S. population trend—more important than increasing affluence, rising educational levels, household variety, cultural diversity or the growing influence of women—is the increase in the mature adult demographic group.

The latest 2002 U.S. Census found that adults 50-plus represent 79 million people, or 28 percent of the total U.S. population and 37 percent of the population over 18 years old. Demographic trends associated with the aging of the Baby Boomer population, plus gains in longevity, are expected to grow the 50-plus market to more than 106 million by 2015 when they will account for 45 percent—

nearly half—of the adult population. This market has more than $1.6 trillion in spending power and a net worth that's nearly twice the U.S. average.

That comprises a market force that presents both new opportunities and challenges for companies that sell travel products. The opportunities lie in an increasingly affluent and discriminating customer set. The challenges lie in providing a level of quality and depth of experience that can fulfill the expectations of a diverse and demanding market segment.

Demographically, these consumers seek products, services and activities that complement their desire to live life to the fullest.

Here are some more facts about the 50-plus market:

- Larger than the African-American and Hispanic market segments combined.

- Most affluent of any age segment.

- Acquires 41 percent of all new cars.

- Purchases 25 percent of all toys.

- Controls a household net worth of $19 trillion.

- Owns more than 75 percent of the nation's financial wealth.

- Owns 70 percent of all money market accounts and certificates of deposit.

- Has a per capita income 26 percent higher than the national average.

- Spends more than $1 trillion annually on goods and services.

- Spends more per capita on travel and leisure than any other age group.

- Travels more frequently than any other age group and stays longer.

There is no question that this market segment will become the single most important segment for Holland America Line and others in the cruise industry. By virtue of our product, we may be uniquely positioned to capitalize on the market. However, like others, must continue to watch trends and innovate to fulfill market demands.

As we continue to define and redefine the premium cruise experience that is Holland America's, we have the perfect opportunity to meet the expectations of this important market segment. We will continue to be mindful of two other important markets for our company: past guest mariner society members, which makes up 40 percent of our business; and mature adults.

However, the population of mature adults is expected to grow 14 percent over the next five years, while our capacity will grow at 33 percent through 2006.

This illustrates a most critical point: While our current core customer franchise is growing, our capacity is growing even faster.

For this reason, our marketing effort has expanded to address certain segments of the Baby Boomer market.

As mentioned earlier, these key boomer segments are over the age of 45—affluent and mature in their careers, they seek new experiences. They want spacious verandahs and suites. They want choices in dining. They want the freedom to be as active or relaxed as they choose while on vacation.

Boomers and Money

According to a 2002 Yankelovich study, the Baby Boom generation's expectations, life skills and values were created and shaped by the postwar expansion of their formative years. They have confidence that progress and prosperity, which created a generational sense of expectation and entitlement, will never stop.

As they move through their peak earning years, Boomers remain focused on accumulating experiences and possessions that fulfill a need to remain in control and acquire rewards to which they feel entitled. As they grow older, they are not willing to sacrifice these goals to ensure a secure retirement. That is not to say Boomers are not saving for retirement, only that they will not trade a fulfilling today for a secure tomorrow.

Boomers have always been strong purchasers and that is expected to continue as they mature, according to Yankelovich. But their purchasing decisions tend to be based on the emotional benefits they bring—self-fulfillment and confirmation of their intelligence. Boomers do not accumulate possessions as tangible signs of success, preferring to view material goods mainly as facilitators of worthy experiences. Yankelovich found that:

- Only 19 percent of Boomers think that the only really meaningful measure of success is money.

- Only 21 percent think that money can buy happiness.

- When given the choice between two weeks' salary or two weeks' vacation time, 63 percent of Boomers would take the extra time.

- Sixty-six percent say they prefer to spend money on experiences that enrich their life like travel, vacations, cultural activities or fine dining.

- Most Boomers (82 percent) feel there should be less emphasis on money in our society.

- When it comes to symbols of success and accomplishment, the emphasis is on intangibles over tangibles.

Boomers and Fitness

On average, Baby Boomers define old age as beginning at 67, a full decade older than the oldest Boomers today. In considering that future, 50 percent name "staying active" as a major challenge facing most people over age 55 today. According to Yankelovich, 86 percent of Boomers are conscious of the need to take measures to ensure that their health will be good when they get older. In general, boomers view themselves as approaching aging in fairly good health.

Boomers seem fully aware that overall good health is the key to enjoying their anticipated longevity. The majority (63 percent) are concerned about taking care of themselves, a proportion that has been increasing as more Boomers move into their middle years. The majority of Boomers who exercise at least two to three days a week do so for the health benefits, while only 10 percent do so for appearance reasons.

Given their emotional investment in staying active and their propensity to accumulate health information (62 percent actively seek out information on health), Boomers are likely to explore a variety of resources, including fitness programs and sports activity, to maintain their youthfulness on a physical level. Yankelovich found that Boomers' favorite form of exercise is walking (55 percent), followed by doing outside work (43 percent) and using exercise equipment (37 percent).

Having been enthusiastic participants in a variety of fitness fads, it's likely that Boomers will continue to experiment with different exercise forms, from pilates and spinning to water aerobics and tai chi. The group aspect of many health club programs—in terms of providing mutual support and social opportunities—is attractive for Boomers who enjoy sharing their experiences with others.

At Holland America, we also are seeing that, more and more, demographics are defining what cruise lines are all about. Our guests today are more active in terms of health, fitness, and leading an active lifestyle.

The premium cruise target audience is fast growing, composed of affluent experienced travelers, with a five-year growth rate of nearly 40 percent.

The Baby Boomer market is looking for travel experiences that are beyond the ordinary. They are experienced travelers, who don't want to squander precious vacation time with routine travel options. Certainly, with our premium cruise offerings, five-star cruising with Holland America provides Oceans Apart adventures on all seven seas.

More and more of our guests are focused on individual experiences and on enrichment. So the newest cruise ships are offering new dining experiences, Internet cafés, larger and more customized spa facilities, and e-mail ports in all staterooms and much, much more. It's not hard to see that as the Baby Boomer market grows older, cruise lines and others are carefully tracking behavior and buying habits to cater products to this market. If we don't, we won't exist in the future.

What's exciting about this is that great things are in store for the cruise line industry and especially for our guests. Look at the innovations today compared to the industry just 10, 15 or 20 years ago. We have extensive spas, world-class restaurants of all food specialties, cigar bars, video rooms, slides, rock-climbing walls, ice-skating rinks, coffee houses within the confines of the ship's promenade deck, a variety of shows and entertainment, innovative shore excursions such as Holland America's Soldier for a Day—in which a guest can literally relive a bygone era for the afternoon—and private island experiences such as our Half Moon Cay, which allow for very personalized experiences and give us flexibility to adapt quickly to the market.

Inveterate Travelers

It's no surprise that the over-50 segment likes to travel. They represent 80 percent of all luxury travel purchased in the United States, making up 65 percent of all cruise passengers and typically spending 74 percent more on vacations than the 18-to-49-year-old population segment.

People in this demographic category travel more than three times each year—more than any other age group. Nearly half, 46 percent, travel by car, 42 percent travel for relaxation and a third travel for adventure.

A travel survey of 50-plus consumers revealed that experiencing new cultures and meeting the local people were most important to these active travelers. They want an experience, not just a tour. Here's what the survey found out about these lively travelers.

- 43 percent want to experience and learn about new cultures firsthand, especially through meeting and interacting with the locals.

- One in five wants expert tour guides who can share their culture.

- 15 percent said they want plenty of time to fully explore each travel site.

- One in 10 wants worry-free experiences.

- Meeting and socializing with fellow travelers was another high priority for respondents.

These same travelers wanted more free time, and when it came to pet peeves, airline travel, including delays and overcrowding, was the biggest headache.

Multigenerational Travel

Another trend among this demographic group is their propensity to travel with their families, a phenomenon known as "multigenerational travel." According to the Travel Industry Association, more than 5 million U.S. families consisting of three generations travel each year, accounting for 14 percent of all U.S. travelers.

More than 60 million Americans—31 percent of the population—are grandparents, and that figure is expected to grow to 80 million by 2010. It is interesting to note that these days the average age of a first-time grandparent is 47.

Grandparents spend a median of $489 per year on their grandchildren, about $30 billion annually. Lower-income grandparents spend $239; the middle-income bracket spends $637; and those with higher incomes, $840. Grandparents with only one grandchild spend about $500.

From the travel perspective, it is noteworthy that one in five trips with children in 2000 consisted of travelers who were grandparents and their grandchildren.

Adventure Travel

According to Purdue University travel expert Alastair Morrison, the Baby Boomers are responsible for the most recent explosion in the travel industry—adventure vacations.

Morrison, a professor of tourism management, notes that when the 50-plus crowd goes on vacation, it doesn't want to be passive, it wants to do something. Boomers also want a high-quality experience and have the discretionary income to support their demands. Adventurers may choose to visit a rainforest, go birding or hike to Incan ruins.

When viewing the above trends in travel, it's not hard to let your imagination go when it comes to the cruise industry. A cruise ship allows for a very comfortable and secure vacation environment. But that doesn't mean the experience has to be seen as dull. On-board activities that cater to the emerging market tailor each cruise product to the appropriate Baby Boomer. You find kids programs with adult activities so all can enjoy the experience. And shore excursions allow for the utmost in flexibility to tailor an experience to the specific likes and dislike of our guests.

There was a day when the simple motor coach city tour was what you found offered from a cruise ship. Don't get me wrong; they are still popular. But now, we have dog sledding on a glacier, rock climbing in Alaska, diving in the Caribbean, spy museum tours in Moscow, wine tasting in France, and more.

Holland America Evolving

Although the cruise line business has changed in many ways, Holland America Line has experienced a steady evolution, through what we might call "130 years of attention to detail."

We find that small, careful, well-focused changes work best. And our guide for such careful but significant change is the customer—our guests.

Responding to our guests has led us to some major innovations common throughout the cruise line industry today. For example, after listening to suggestions from guests, we established what we call the "Lido" dining area—a café that provides a casual dining alternative.

Our brand promise is to deliver service, comfort and an exceptional premium cruise experience each and every time to our clients and those of our travel agents and distributors. Our HALmarks include:

Unequaled Value: We offer an extraordinary value for the dollar. Our ships are designed to provide guests with space and comfort. We provide the most extensive menus at sea, award-winning entertainment and our "tipping not required" promise—we're the only cruise line in the industry that can make that statement.

Superior Products: Our ships are designed to carry fewer passengers, meaning more space per guest than any other premium cruise line, including staterooms that are, on average, 25 percent larger than those on ships of similar class. And Verandah staterooms on many of our ships provide a whole new level of cruise experience.

Innovative Deployment: We offer a wide choice of exotic ports on seven continents, and more time to enjoy these ports than any other cruise line. Our corporate staff is constantly searching the world to find new and exciting ports for a travel client's next cruise adventure. We sail on more than 440 cruises a year to more than 280 ports of call and utilize 15 North American home ports.

Oceans Apart Service: Our guests enjoy the best crew/passenger ratio in cruising today, with gracious attentive service from every member of our crew.

And to prove we continue to deliver on that brand promise, we've been honored once again, with a number of distinguished awards, including being rated the highest-rated premium cruise line in the world in *Travel + Leisure* magazine's "World's Best" awards.

With the recent introduction of our Vista ships, we have been able to further improve and innovate our premium product offerings through more verandah staterooms, expanded dining options, increased activity choices, spas, children's programs and facilities and other elements that provide guests with more of what they are looking for: a cruise experience that's something special and more.

Holland America Line's fleet will continue to grow for the foreseeable future with our Vista-class series. By 2006, Holland America will increase its capacity by 24 percent—and its fleet to a total of 15 ships—with the introduction of three additional 85,000-ton, 1,848-passenger Vista class ships (the largest ever built for Holland America Line). After that we are going to begin to focus our efforts on conceptualizing the next series of vessels beyond the Vista class, which will be designed specifically for longer, worldwide cruise itineraries. These will also adapt to the growing and experienced travelers in the Baby Boomer market segment.

We Know the Audience; The Trends Will Develop

In the cruise industry, the major future trends will be driven by an aging Baby Boomer population with greater leisure time, higher disposable income, more travel experience and more access to information about travel products and suppliers. These consumers will seek convenient, value-oriented vacation options that are increasingly international in scope. Cruise vacation products will continue to be segmented to meet the diverse needs of these customers ranging from low-priced, close-to-home cruises to more expensive, highly personalized exotic cruises. And Holland America Lines' premium product will serve those customers who demand a level of quality, service and choice that is above the industry norm, yet still within their economic reach and personal definition of value.

34

Cunard's Queen Mary 2: A Case Study

Deborah L. Natansohn
Sales and Marketing
Senior Vice President
Cunard Line Ltd.

Deborah Natansohn, senior vice president of sales and marketing, joined Cunard Line in November 2000 and was charged with spearheading the re-branding of the line. A well-known industry veteran, previously she was president of Orient Lines. When appointed, she was the only female president of a premium cruise line.

Natansohn began her career in the travel field as an editor with *Travel Trade* magazine. Her background includes holding positions as director of marketing for Travelers International and director of marketing for the tour company Arthur Frommer International. She also served as vice president of marketing for Ocean Cruise Lines and Pearl Cruises.

More than any other sector of the travel industry, the cruise industry succeeded in reinventing itself during the last decade of the twentieth century. The 1990s saw unprecedented growth, corporate consolidation, and, most importantly, new developments in product both onboard and ashore. There were a greater number of vessels to choose from, economies of scale kept prices low, and new, exciting vacation features were offered—all of which benefited the consumer tremendously. For the cruise lines themselves, especially those on the upper end of the market, these developments presented new marketing challenges.

Between 1990 and 2004, more than 125 new ships entered the worldwide cruise market, with each new class of ship seeking to outdo the last. The building boom was fueled by three factors: attractive loan guarantees and building subsidies by European shipyards; the need for the now publicly-held cruise companies to reinvest profits on behalf of their shareholders to ensure future growth; and the maturing of a key target market, the Baby Boomer generation.

Led by the large, mass-market cruise brands—cannily re-christened the "contemporary" segment—the building boom replaced older tonnage with megaliners featuring soaring atriums, balconied staterooms, elegant showrooms, themed bars, multiple dining venues, spacious spas, greater sports facilities and even such unique features as rock climbing walls, moving walkways and ice-skating rinks. With better technology and larger facilities, onboard entertainment was upgraded to more closely resemble lavish Las Vegas productions than cabaret acts. Dining also improved, with menus offering greater choice and reflecting current culinary trends.

The contemporary brands had raised the bar in defining the cruise vacation experience. They had compressed the differences between themselves and the next highest segment of the cruise industry, the "premium" sector. The premium lines, who were also building bigger ships to improve the economies of scale of their businesses, had to similarly upgrade their products to justify their price differentials, thus putting pressure on the upper tier, the "luxury" sector.

Into the fray came Cunard Line with the announcement that it would build the biggest, tallest, widest, grandest and most expensive ocean liner ever: the Queen Mary 2. At a cost of nearly $800 million, the 2,600-passenger ship would have to deliver a reasonable rate of return to its investors by being priced at the luxury end of the market. With all the superlatives attached to it, Queen Mary 2 had generated very high expectations from the consumer, the travel trade and the media alike. In fact, it became the most anticipated cruise ship ever built.

A Bit of Brand History

Cunard Line, one of the most venerable brand names in the cruise industry, had operated transatlantic crossings since 1849, and world cruises for nearly a century. Among its many historic liners were the Aquitania, Mauretania, and Lusitania, and the legendary Queen Mary, Queen Elizabeth and Queen Elizabeth 2 (QE2). The line, with its British registry, had played a key role in many historic events as well. Its ships carried all of the horses to Crimea for the Charge of the Light Brigade, rescued the survivors of the Titanic, brought countless immigrants from Europe to a new life in America, served as troop carriers in both world wars (Winston Churchill credited the Queen Mary and the Queen Elizabeth with shortening World War II by a year), and served Britain in 1982 during the Falklands War. Cunard's advertising slogans, such as "The Only Way to Cross" and "Getting There is Half the Fun" entered the common lexicon on both sides of the Atlantic. The line's illustrated posters became collectibles. For a good part of the 20th century, it was the carrier of choice for movie stars, industrialists, political leaders and the world's elite.

But, by the 1990s, Cunard had lost much of its luster. Only the QE2 reflected the line's former glories: she had iconic status, a loyal following and was still viewed by many as an aspirational product. She was the last ship purpose-built for Cunard. The line had acquired a hodgepodge of other vessels since QE2's launch in 1969—at one point even marketing riverboats in its mix— but its owners failed to invest in new tonnage as other lines expanded. The result was a blurred image in the marketplace, and uncertainty among many retailers as to how or why to sell the brand. Cunard's business primarily came from its past passenger base.

The Carnival Corporation came to the rescue in 1998, acquiring Cunard and determined to restore the line to its previous stature. Within months of the acquisition, they invested a considerable amount in refurbishing QE2 and announced that they would build the first true ocean liner in more than 35 years, the Queen Mary 2. At 150,000 tons, it would be the largest ship ever built. Later, they announced a subsequent new-build for Cunard, the Queen Victoria.

Cunard's new executive team was charged with revitalizing the brand and expanding market demand for their new vessels. Having the largest new ship in the world, the historical context of previous Cunarders and the backing of the Carnival Corporation certainly gave them a head start: there was significant press generated about the Queen Mary 2 project from the moment it was announced.

But the novelty of size and innovative maritime technology would eventually wear off. For the ship and the overall brand to be successful in the long term, Cunard's onboard product would have to be reengineered to suit the needs and desires of the 21st century traveler. Like Burberry and Jaguar—two other established British brands that reinvented themselves for a new generation—the Cunard brand name still had resonance in the marketplace but was perceived as old fashioned. Now it set out to regain its role as a trendsetter.

The Target Market

With an average price point of over $300 per day, Cunard set its sights on the powerful, affluent Baby Boomer generation. That's not a surprise—so did virtually every other marketer of upscale goods and services. Boomers (those born between 1946 and 1964) represented the largest segment of the population snake, and controlled the lion's share of the nation's spending power. Wealthier, better educated, and better traveled than any previous generation, they had had an enormous influence on every decade through which they passed. When they were children in the 1950s, there was a rush to build schools and the nation saw a great migration to the suburbs. Their rebellious youth sparked the cultural and political upheavals of the 1960s. During their early earning years, they became the self-indulgent "me" generation, driving consumerism to new heights, and when they settled down in the 1980s, the housing market soared. Their peak earning years spurred the bull run of the stock market in the 1990s, as they sought to secure their financial future.

Everyone wanted a share of the Boomer wallet, but for a luxury travel brand like Cunard, their demographics couldn't be better. By the end of the century, 10,000 Boomers a day were turning 50 in the United States alone. Their nest was almost empty. The mortgage was manageable, if not fully paid. They were still working, but had more discretionary income to spend on themselves. They were set to come into $2 trillion of inherited wealth in the next decade. And, unlike their parents' generation, which may have saved for years for their one grand tour of Europe, the Baby Boomers were comfortable with international travel and saw taking vacations as almost a divine right. (The tragic events of September 11 and subsequent Iraqi conflict dampened the enthusiasm among the affluent for travel abroad, but most travel companies saw this as a temporary aberration.)

Demographics were one thing, psychographics another. Fifty wasn't what it used to be. Indeed, most Boomers saw themselves as 15 years younger. They were physically active, health-conscious, and almost obsessed with looking, feeling and acting young—what else could explain the meteoric rise of the spa industry, exercise gyms, skin treatments, health food markets and plastic surgery? They also saw themselves as stressed and time-starved, never having enough hours in the day to accomplish what they sought out to do. In fact, in Cunard's target market of boomers with $150,000 or more household income, time was viewed as a more precious commodity than money.

Affluent Boomers had other behavioral attributes that had to be taken into account. They were choice-oriented, and expected excellent service, if not instant gratification. This attitude can be best summed up by a call button installed on the phones of the trendy "W" hotel in New York: instead of the usual "concierge" label, hotel guests could summon service by pushing the "whatever, whenever" button.

Boomers also viewed themselves as independent thinkers, and were referential rather than deferential when evaluating a product. Instead of deferring to the pronouncements of the media, corporate brochures, guidebooks or even the travel agent in their vacation selection process, they sought the references and advice of people whom they knew and trusted. Failing that, they preferred to consult the anonymous chat rooms of the Internet than blindly take the word of someone in authority. Positive word of mouth would thus be a critical determinant in the long-term success of QM2; the product had to have "wow" factors and deliver promised service levels from the moment of its launch.

Boomers were not oblivious to advertising—indeed, they appreciated clever imagemakers like Nike and Absolut—but they were cynical about the message. Competitively aware, they were also value-conscious. That didn't mean that they wouldn't pay a fair price—as long as they valued the return they got in product, service or status. And their expectations were high. Asked what they assumed would be offered by Cunard's Queen Mary 2, the largest ocean liner ever built, a group of target customers came up with this list:

- A variety of food and fine dining experiences

- The best spa and gym at sea

- Better entertainment

- Elegant service

- "Best of Europe" shopping

- State-of-the-art hardware

- Large cabins

- A children's center

- Activities that were both varied and interactive

The last item was interesting because it underlined the Boomers' proclivity for active participation, even in areas other than sports and fitness. To quote one focus group attendee, "I don't necessarily want to attend a lecture on "Great Painters of the 20th Century." If I had the time, I'd rather learn how to paint."

Creating the Product

Cunard already was well on its way to surpassing its customers' expectations. Their hardware *was* state of the art: staterooms ranged in size from the industry standard to lavish penthouses and duplex apartments, the ship had such unique features as the only planetarium at sea and the largest ballroom at sea, and it had greater speed, power and stability than any other ship afloat except the QE2 itself. Cunard's famous White Star Service was a brand hallmark of which the line could be justly proud.

The real challenge for the Cunard team was in convincing the time-pressed Baby Boomers to spend six days crossing the Atlantic—a journey that they could make in six hours by air. Cunard would have to make it time well spent—by offering dining, entertainment, spa and learning options that would fulfill the vacation yearnings of their potential customers. A transatlantic crossing already had a degree of built-in romantic appeal, its image fostered by such Hollywood movies as *An Affair to Remember* and *Titanic*. Sailing across the mighty Atlantic was, in fact, an awe-inspiring experience, from the changing seascapes to the drama of entering or leaving New York harbor. But to lure the required number of customers, Queen Mary 2 had to become an attraction in itself. If time was a more valued currency than money, what better indulgence was there than to give yourself six days of peace, pampering, fine dining and the chance to pursue hobbies and interests that escaped you at home?

The first step Cunard took in its quest for an unparalleled onboard product was signing an exclusive agreement with Canyon Ranch, the preeminent name in health resorts, to operate the spa, fitness and beauty club. Spa management aboard other cruise ships was generally dominated by a single operator, so there was little differentiation in spa services between the many cruise brands. Canyon Ranch would bring its unique healthy living treatments and services, for which it had received so many accolades, to the sea for the first time aboard QM2. For those familiar with spas, there was no better marquis name to put on the Queen.

Another incomparable institution—Oxford University—was enlisted to design and manage the ship's enrichment program, a college at sea that would offer entertaining lectures, classes and, yes, interactive learning programs. QM2 had more space dedicated to learning than any other ship: 20,000 square feet divided into seven classrooms and a planetarium, which doubled as an auditorium. Dubbed ConneXions, the program was designed to explore the cultural links between Britain and America as the QM2 crossed between them. From literature to garden design, film studies to language courses, wine appreciation to acting classes, Cunard guests would have the unique opportunity to learn from Oxford scholars and other notable experts. There would be lectures on great artists *and* you could learn how to paint.

For its entertainment program, Cunard wanted to create the atmosphere of a city at sea, where guests could walk down the ship's "avenues" and see different amusements in every venue. Musical production shows were commissioned for the Royal Court Theatre; a jazz club would present a variety of featured acts; would-be singers could join the karaoke fun in the pub; Big Band music would lure dancers to the largest ballroom at sea; classical strings would play in the peaceful Winter Garden; and disc jockeys would spin tunes in the ship's nightclub.

Because QM2 would be traveling between the two greatest theatrical cities in the world, New York and London, the line wanted to present legitimate theater as well. The Royal Academy of Dramatic Arts (RADA), the greatest acting school in England, if not in the world, agreed to put a repertory company of recent graduates on board. The list of alumni of RADA read like a who's who of British theater: it included everyone from John Gielgud to Anthony Hopkins to Glenda Jackson to Ralph Fiennes. The marketing angle was that you could see the stars of tomorrow today on the QM2: something that would appeal not only to the cultural interests of QM2's target audience, but to their desire to be ahead of the curve.

As with entertainment, the ship offered a panoply of sporting activities. There were five swimming pools, including one just for kids, a basketball court, paddle tennis, deck games, simulators where golfers could play the greatest courses in the world, and more. Cunard wanted their guests spoiled for choice.

Dining Options Fit for a Queen

Some of the most significant changes in the cruise industry's on-board product during the 1990s came in the area of food service. Traditionally, cruise guests were assigned a specific table in the dining room, which was open at designated times for each meal, and they were served by the same waiter/busboy team, who got to know customer preferences, thereby creating a personal touch. Passengers could also enjoy more casual breakfast and lunch buffets in the "Lido" area, usually located near the pool. There were differences in the quality of food for each line, of course, depending on their price point, but the overall structure of the dining experience crossed all brands.

This began to change around 1990, as lines sought to differentiate themselves further through the dining experience. Celebrity Cruises introduced the notion of menus designed by a celebrity chef (Michel Roux) and some lines, particularly the smaller luxury brands, followed that model. Crystal Cruises introduced alternative Italian and Asian restaurants separate from the main dining room, and others soon followed suit by offering at least one alternative-dining venue. Interestingly, however, it was an upstart Asian brand, Star Cruises, and not one of the U.S.-based majors, that completely revolutionized the concept of onboard dining.

Star, based in Malaysia, had studied the U.S. cruise industry for some time before creating its own line for the untapped Asian market. Although they adopted many standard aspects of leisure cruise operations, they felt that more restrictive elements of operations, like telling passengers where and when they could dine, would not play well in their arena. (Fixed dining would also empty out their casino, a major source of revenue, during certain periods.) Instead, they mirrored a large land resort, creating numerous restaurants on board and charging supplements for some of them. When Star purchased Norwegian Cruise Lines in 2000, the "Freestyle" dining concept, with multiple dining venues and no assigned seating, was brought to the US and Europe. Although operationally there were some teething problems, the concept was embraced by the marketplace, and other lines quickly sought ways to offer as many dining options as their hardware would allow.

For the QM2, Cunard decided to offer the best elements of the industry's various dining models while also improving upon them, giving their passengers exceptional quality, variety and choice. In the tradition of the great ocean liners, Cunard created a grand, three-story dining salon called the Britannia Restaurant, where diners would always have a reserved seat and the gracious, knowing service of their usual waiter. For their highest-paying customers, there were the exclusive Princess Grill and Queens Grill, another Cunard tradition. The most acclaimed chef in New York, Daniel Boulud, was brought in as a culinary consultant to help design the menus of all three restaurants. Another celebrity chef, rising star Todd English, would have his own restaurant on board, offering a casually stylish atmosphere and serving innovative Mediterranean cuisine. There were six other dining venues as well: Kings Court, which served breakfast and lunch buffets, would at night be transformed into four separate restaurants offering various types of cuisine. One of the restaurants, Chef's Galley, would be an interactive experience wherein diners would learn how to cook the meal they were about to eat. There would also be traditional English fare in the pub; burgers and such at the Boardwalk Café; and, of course, 24-hour room service. With the "whatever, whenever" Boomers in mind, Cunard managed to offer the comfort of reserved seating, the quality of name chefs, and the flexibility of dining alternatives all on one ship.

The Role of Co-branding

In every area of customer service described so far, Cunard had paired itself with a famous entity known for delivering excellence in their field: Canyon Ranch, RADA, Oxford—even chefs Daniel Boulud and Todd English—each could be considered to be his own brand. The intent was to communicate instantly to the consumer the level of quality they could expect, especially to those who might not be familiar with the attributes of the Cunard brand itself. (Research showed that cruise brands in general—with the exception of Carnival—did not have clearly defined images in the minds of the consumer.) Cunard pursued this strategy in other areas of the on-board product as well. Chanel would open its first boutique at sea aboard QM2. Veuve Cliquot would sponsor the champagne bar. Waterford and Wedgwood would design the crystal and china. Microsoft would provide X-Boxes. Simmons would create a privately labeled mattress, which would be covered by Frette linens.

In addition to providing consumers with a picture of quality through its association with other respected companies, Cunard's widespread co-branding had other benefits, as well. Its partner brands targeted the same upscale audience, so there were joint marketing and cross-marketing opportunities of which both sides could take advantage. New, on-board retail opportunities were created. But, most importantly, affluent customers could envision themselves experiencing a wide variety of upscale and fashionable activities at a single destination: the QM2. Cunard, in fact, took a fashion approach towards its advertising. Targeted towards women, who were usually the prime movers in selecting a couple's or family's annual vacation, the ads were anticipatory and aspirational in tone and broadly featured Cunard's co-branding partners in the copy.

Early Signs of Success

Although (at the time of this book's printing) it is too early to determine if Cunard's strategy worked in the long term (the ship was launched in early 2004), early indications have been positive. Within a few weeks of opening reservations, Cunard had $50 million in revenue booked; this was significant because it occurred 18 months before the ship's first voyage, in an environment where the market tended to book at the last minute for most other travel products. The Athens Olympic Committee chartered QM2 to be the flagship of the 2004 Olympic Games, another vote of confidence in the ship's stature. But the best indicator of all was that more than 60 percent of passengers booked were new to the Cunard brand. The company had succeeded in expanding its market.

Cunard had done what any good marketer, in any century, should do. They had studied the market, analyzed their place in it, listened to the needs and wants of their prospects, and changed their product to fulfill those needs and wants. If they could deliver successfully on their marketing promise, the Baby Boomers would keep their ships full for the next 30 years.

35

Luxury Cruising, Revisited

Mark S. Conroy
President and CEO
Radisson Seven Seas Cruises

As president and chief executive officer of Radisson Seven Seas, Mark Conroy is responsible for the overall management of the line's six luxury cruise ships—as well as for forecasting revenue, profit goals and company growth. The line's sixth vessel—the second all-suite, all-balcony ship of the modern cruise era and sister ship to the first—was christened in March 2003.

Previously, Conroy was president and CEO of Diamond Cruise, which merged with Seven Seas Cruise Line on January 1, 1995.

Beyond the instrumental role he played in bringing about the merger of Diamond Cruise and Seven Seas Cruise Line, he oversees all operations, marketing and sales for the luxury line as well as key strategic issues relating to Radisson Seven Seas' growth and its distinctly varied, ultra-deluxe product.

Mr. Conroy's three decades of experience in managing and operating cruise ships encompasses some of cruising's most prominent names. He has served as president of both Renaissance Cruises and Commodore Cruise Line and as vice president of sales, Royal Viking Line.

Over the years, his expertise has been sought by major industry interests, casting him into the role of inside consultant to both ship owners and corporations seeking to enter the cruise industry or to expand capacity. His behind-the-scenes consulting work has led to everything from the creation of new luxury lines to the development of niche products in specialty cruise markets.

Mr. Conroy, respected as one of the industry's most knowledgeable executives, often serves on travel industry panels. He is currently chairman of the Cruise Lines International Association (CLIA) executive committee, having served on various other committees in the past.

Mr. Conroy's cruise industry career began in 1974 in the mailroom of Norwegian Cruise Line, while studying at the University of Miami. Conroy graduated summa cum laude in 1976 with a bachelor's degree in business, and currently lives with his family in Ft. Lauderdale.

"It's deja vu all over again."

This timelessly apt comment of that master of the English language, Yogi Berra, might well have been said of luxury cruising. Here's why:

Cruising began in the era of the great ocean liners that sailed from the Old World to the New World and Asia. What is it you remember about those vessels? What do the *Queens Mary* and *Elizabeth*, the *Normandie*, *Titanic*, and *Lusitania*, and *Imperator* have in common?

It might have been their speed or graceful lines or, to some, their tragic demise, but most likely what you recall is the lavish interiors, grand ballrooms, sumptuous dining rooms, wide promenades, grand staircases and marble-appointed suites. These were the features that each of the lines used to differentiate themselves. However, their primary focus was tourist- and emigrant-class accommodations. The luxury class revenue was no more than the icing on the cake.

Fast forward to the year 2003—some 50 to 90 years later—and it is still the case. Not that I am comparing today's contemporary and premium ship accommodations with steerage of yesteryear. Far from it. In fact, the many distinguishing, often innovative features of large modern vessels would overwhelm even the luxury guests of yore.

That said, luxury cruising has also evolved. Today's luxury is rooted in the last vestiges of the grand ocean crossings aboard the likes of the *Queen Elizabeth*, taken up and transformed by such names as Swedish American Line, Norwegian America Line and Royal Viking Line, now part of the history of cruising.

Today, Crystal Cruises, Seabourn Cruise Line, Silversea Cruises, Radisson Seven Seas Cruises & Windstar Cruises primarily serve the North American luxury cruise market and Hapag Lloyd's *Europa* caters to the German market. These cruise lines have a capacity of approximately 8,000 beds, or less than 4 percent of total cruise industry capacity. And, due to the greater length and lower occupancies of our cruises, this accounts for only about 3 percent of the total number of guests who cruise.

Many have commented that the fast growth of the overall industry has made luxury cruising insignificant from a "big picture" perspective. Indeed, such observations seem to question our ability to survive in such a huge market. Ironically, it's the very growth of the industry—in particular, the size of the ships—that will continue to spur the development of the luxury market.

I can remember bristling at the pronouncement of an unnamed industry leader who suggested that cruising was the beneficiary of the "trickle up theory," namely, that many guests begin their cruise life with one of the contemporary or premium cruise lines and, as their experience grows, they inevitably search out more exotic and more luxurious cruise experiences. At the time, my reaction was: Why would anyone who can afford the best select a three-star property on their first trip to Europe? Similarly, I didn't think they'd choose that approach to cruising.

But time and the marketplace have proven him right. The power of the large cruise marketers—evident in their continued growth and product improvements—has expanded the market for cruising dramatically. In winning over millions of first-time cruisers each year, they have enlarged the market to some 43 million experienced cruisers in the U.S. in 2003, 23 million of whom have cruised in the last five years.

Since 80 percent to 85 percent of the guests of the luxury lines have sailed before, this has created a much larger pool of experienced customers to whom we can sell. Because these cruisers are already convinced of the value of cruising, all the luxury operators need do is bring the exceptional value of their own products to life convincingly.

Underlying these changing marketplace factors are significant social changes that include:

- The aging of the Boomer population and its devotion to "personal growth"

- Increased longevity and, along with it, enhanced quality of life of those who live longer

- Travel has not only become more experiential, but also more clearly oriented towards "life-enrichment" (meeting the Boomers' demand for personal growth)

- As personal lifestyle expectations have risen steadily, so, too, have the expectations guests bring to travel (for example, that it's an entitlement rather than reward)

- The increase in the number of wealthy households created by business success, stock market gains and inheritance

As the last few years prove only too well, nothing that remains static can stay viable. Nowhere is this more obvious than in travel—and yet the threads of consistency are equally profound. A relationship with a loyal customer base is critical to ongoing success.

So what must a luxury cruise offer?

- An environment that meets the affluent traveler's desire for a cruise experience that is both intimate and social, and, most of all, non-confining in its generous allotments of personal space

- No inside cabin anywhere aboard, thereby assuring every guest of a spacious ocean view, regardless of purchase price

- All-suite and or all-balcony accommodations—providing every guest on the ship with either a separate sitting area or private balcony to serve as their own eagle's perch on the world

- Many of the same amenities that our affluent guests enjoy in their own homes including walk-in closets, richly textured fabrics and spacious marble-appointed bathrooms with full bathtubs

At the same time, the hallmark of luxury is found in such elements as:

- A commitment to providing a highly personalized experience for each and every guest

- A steady monitoring of guest feedback to assure that trend setting concepts are incorporated into each vessel's design

- A distinctive, destination-intensive style of cruising that fulfills the experiential urges of travelers today

- A wide variety of cuisines from multiple outlets with the flexibility of open seating and the option of dining when, and with whom, you like

- Professional service staff who strive to delight and surprise guests each day, in spite of the fact that gratuities are not expected

- A blend of hardware and software, ships' facilities and programming, including such hands-on, participatory "personal growth" options as exclusive cooking workshops, computer classes and language programs

What do these guests look like and where do they live?

- Target households, about 3 million in the United States

- 45 years plus, living longer and better than their parents did

- High income $200,000, or high net worth (more than $3 million) or great savers
- Empty nesters with lots of disposable income
- The "Millionaire Next Door," not the super rich, tend to be retired or working rich, enjoying the fruits of their labors
- Self-made and/or inheritance from their parents (the "great generation")
- Experienced travelers
- Educated and married or widowed
- In major urban and suburban areas

Why should they cruise on luxury ships?

- Desire to travel with people like themselves (successful)
- Recommended by family or friends
- Recommendation of a travel agent
- Security and comfort
- Destinations and life experiences
- No compromise to their lifestyle
- Exclusive, one of an elite few versus one of many
- Choice versus regimentation
- Price value equation, the best they can get for the money

What are they looking for in a travel counselor?

- Professional, like their CPA
- Knowledgeable and well-traveled, up to date
- Diligent and responsive
- Trustworthy
- Successful, an expert, an insider
- Technically savvy

Why offer a luxury cruise?

- High guest satisfaction—which leads to repeat business

- Profitable sale, higher commission
- Ease of booking
- Pride in the effort
- Higher profile

How do you find potential luxury cruisers?

- Experienced cruisers
- Have traveled to Europe
- Have taken a deluxe tour or stay in upscale hotels or deluxe resorts
- Fly first or business class for business and/or leisure travel
- Private, yacht, country or social clubs
- Charity supporters
- Live in gated communities and luxury condos
- Special interest groups, museum councils, alumni clubs, professional associations
- Through the Internet
- Recommendation of family or friend

Tools to use?

- Guest knowledge—data trust
- Direct mail, e-mail, the Internet
- Phone
- Social and charitable functions
- Network of friends and associates
- Referrals
- Guide books, topic experts
- Marketing alliances
- Newspaper, advice or social column
- Radio

To summarize:

- There is a growing market for luxury cruises, that actually reaches back to the days of the classic ocean liners

- The new fleet of luxury ships has evolved from an early promise of elegance and grace to offer far more than was possible at the outset of the cruise era

- There is a wide variety of products to offer affluent travelers that fit their varied lifestyles

- There are tools to find them and introduce them to the varied opportunities

- When you do there are ample profits to reward you for your efforts

So what are you waiting for?

Section VI

Tour Marketing

The tour operator industry is far more fragmented than the cruise industry, but far less so than the hotel and resort industry. There are hundreds of tour companies in the United States of varying sizes. Not one, however, has as much as five percent of the national market.

The dynamic packaging capability of online travel agencies presents a serious risk to those tour operators who have not focused on a narrow specialized product offering that can give the operator a perception of branding, unique expertise and superior product delivery. Without this differentiation, the operator will likely try and survive on price alone—and, in all likelihood, will fall prey to dynamic packaging automation, which virtually assures the consumer the lowest price.

Consumers are willing to pay more if the operator has a known brand or known brands associated with expertise in a destination and/or high quality. Overall, the ability of an operator to do something special, to provide customization of the tour components to meet the customer's needs, will continue both to drive a price premium for this superior service and insulate those operators from the low-price, run-of-the-mill tour products that will increasingly be the domain of online agencies.

Unlike the cruise lines of today, most tour operators traditionally have had 20–40 percent of their business come directly from the consumer. Their channel conflict is not with the traditional travel agency channel (which has historically been price neutral from a consumer standpoint). Rather, as stated above, the threat is from the online agencies that act as tour operators by offering customized, dynamic packaging available 24/7 to the consumer. A robust, easy-to-navigate Web site, backed with rich product information and graphics and offering the lowest possible pricing will, in time, make this model the dominant channel, save for the branded or niche operators described above. AA Vacations derives strength from the American Airlines brand. It's equivalent to sporting the Good Housekeeping seal of approval to many consumers: the implication is that if American puts its name and reputation behind a product, it must be good.

GoGo Tours has the unique advantage of a strong retail agency chain (Liberty) pushing its products. Yet, as it looks to the future, it sees the need to replicate the online agency operator model as well as retain its traditional travel agency distribution model. Moreover, they are planning to be a business-to-business solution for other online agencies—offering them their tour content in a manner transparent to the consumer.

GoGo is well-resourced to invest in this technology. Many small operators, on the other hand, simply don't have those resources. Some operators have followed the Far and Wide model where smaller, niche operators are rolled up under one brand and supported by scalable home office solutions. Others, like Classic Hawaii, have been purchased by deep-pocket entities (Expedia, in Classic's case).

As with the cruise lines, the tour operator industry is focusing on the Boomer generation as a likely avenue to grow sales. Yet almost all the marketers in this section see the need to know the customer, manage the relationship, customize the product and supply "something extra." However it is verbalized, the operators are moving to de-commoditize their products. They plan to thrive on a model that creates high customer value for an acceptably higher price. It's a very reasonable strategy, but scale is an issue. Online agencies, as they grow, can simply purchase their tour operator competitors. Larger operators will buy smaller ones. After all, with few exceptions, this is a low-margin, low-capital cost business!

In years to come, we should expect that suppliers will enhance their own abilities to package their products and offer them directly to the consumer through their own branded Internet sites with dynamic packaging capability. As the Internet provides ready consumer access to their brands, we anticipate that more suppliers will disintermediate by being their own tour operator where possible, pocketing the operator margin. The nonspecific, price-driven operators will be at most risk when this happens–their ability to provide unique customer value will be minimized and marginalized by their competitors, both online and offline.

36

Changing Customers Require Product Change

Robert E. Whitley, CTC, President
United States Tour Operators Association
(USTOA)

Robert E. Whitley, president, United States Tour Operators Association (USTOA) has served the group since 1978, when he was selected by the board of directors to head the national nonprofit organization. His association with USTOA is the latest in a distinguished career that spans more than 30 years in tourism, including both private sector and government positions.

Before joining USTOA, Whitley held positions as director of the Florida Department of Tourism, director of the Pennsylvania Department of Tourism and director of the Virginia Beach Convention and Tourist Bureau. During his tenure at USTOA, the organization has grown to become one of the leading associations of its kind in the travel industry.

Mr. Whitley is the recipient of numerous marketing awards for travel promotion, and has served on the boards of directors of many travel industry associations. For the past seven years, he has been recognized by a leading trade magazine as one of the travel industry's 25 most influential executives, and was named in 1996, 1997 and 1999 as "Person of the Year for Travel Industry Associations" by *Travel Agent Magazine*. As an expert spokesperson for the travel industry, Mr. Whitley has appeared on television and radio stations throughout the United States.

A Word about USTOA

Founded in 1972, the United States Tour Operators Association is a professional organization representing the tour operator industry. Among USTOA's goals are consumer protection and education, maintaining high standards of professionalism within the tour operator industry, and facilitating travel on a national and international level. USTOA numbers among its active members some of the leading tour operators in the industry, who must subscribe to the organization's strict code of ethics, stringent membership requirements, and participate in the USTOA's $1 million consumer protection plan. Combined, the active tour operator members of USTOA annually move more than ten million Americans, both domestically and internationally, accounting for over $8 billion in sales.

The 21st century started with enough challenges to the tour operator industry to fill 100 years. However, this has proven to be the most resilient of industries, and quality tour operators have proven they can respond to challenges and succeed.

The 1990s were a high point for the tour operator industry. Americans were traveling as never before and 2000 was the best year in history for the tour operator segment. But things began to change in 2001—even before September 11—because of a slowing economy and international events. The September 11 tragedy, coupled with the Iraq War, accelerated those changes. Nothing was the same, it seemed, afterwards.

In the aftermath of the events of September 11, the industry proved itself by ensuring that travelers on vacation packages and tours around the world were safe and well cared for. Following those events, and the Iraq War, the industry moved fast to assure the public that they were in good hands with a tour operator.

Tour operators proved that they could adapt effectively. However, it became apparent that adaptation was not to be an occasional posture—it is now institutional. We must respond continuously in order to function in a world where change has become a constant.

This is where we find ourselves as we look ahead. It is no longer necessary to convince consumers that travel is pleasurable—they are aware that it is an important part of a modern lifestyle. We do have to demonstrate to them that travel is safe and secure—and that our products have adapted to their ever new and changing lifestyles.

Evolution of the Market

In the late 1990s, with the stock market at a peak, and technology driving the economy, a trend that had been affecting other travel segments finally reached the tour operator industry. That trend was consolidation. A number of investor-driven firms purchased smaller companies to form a new business model: larger, consolidated corporations offering more diversified products.

While it appeared that the traditional, family-owned business might give way to these investor-owned—and, in some cases—public companies, that did not happen. The future will tell if family-owned businesses or the larger corporate models will dominate—or if they can thrive together side-by-side. However, we will continue to see the smaller, independently-owned companies succeeding on their own well into the next decade. The difference is that even the smallest tour operators will need to be not only strong marketers, but flexible enough to adapt their products quickly to market trends.

Diversification of destinations is another trend we will be seeing as we continue into the future. Since the mid-1980s, because of changing geopolitical conditions, tour operators have had to diversify the destinations they offer in order to profit. Single-destination tour operators learned that specializing in one destination made them too vulnerable to changing world conditions. As we have seen time and again, natural disasters, conflicts and diseases can affect business suddenly and dramatically. Events such as England's outbreak of hoof-and-mouth disease, the SARS epidemic in China and Hong Kong, terrorism in the Middle East and other countries, and armed conflicts in countries such as Iraq, are deterrents to travel. Tour operators who depend on a single region are vulnerable to a host of situations that can virtually impact their business overnight. By offering multi-region products, a tour operator is better able to insulate operations from sudden negative events, selling into regions perceived as safer and more secure.

Not Your Father's Package or Tour

The tour operator industry today is unrecognizable to anyone who remembers the way it was just 30 or 40 years ago–the days of the well-known Hollywood movie, *If It's Tuesday, This Must Be Belgium*. The film was about the adventures of a group of Americans on a whirlwind tour of Europe. While the multi-destination escorted tour is still popular among first-time travelers, there has been a noticeable shift toward more independent travel and escorted products covering less territory with more depth. In a nutshell, packaged travel products have changed dramatically.

Today, tour operators have diversified their product more than ever to meet the needs and expectations of a more active, well-traveled population; and entire new population segments—like younger travelers and families—are increasingly seeking the convenience of packaged travel.

People on every budget have come to seek "experiential" travel. They don't want to simply check "sights" off a list. They want to experience a place in depth—whether in the form of "soft" adventure or by interacting with locals or participating in cultural events. For escorted tours, that can involve more free time or staying in one location for a longer period.

Monitoring Consumer Patterns

Six distinct consumer patterns have emerged in the beginning of the 21st century. Consumers are better informed than ever, the U.S. traveler is far more sophisticated, an increasing number of travelers are discount-driven, late bookings continue to be a growing trend, all types of travelers want value for the dollar, and the pace of modern-day life has made the pursuit of leisure even more important.

Thanks to the Internet, the American traveler is much better informed today than ever. In fact, it's hard to overestimate the importance of that wealth of information. Travelers now know much more than they ever have, before they even contact a travel agent or tour operator. They will research their trip on the Internet, and then consult a travel agent for final recommendations and booking.

Travelers today are far more sophisticated and experienced, and more likely to have traveled to more places. They are also savvy about bottom line issues like pricing, and they have become accustomed to discounting—a practice pioneered by the cruise lines. The consumer of the 21st century shops until that person is satisfied that they have found the best price, before they even make a booking.

The search for discounts has also become a contributing factor to the rise in late bookings, a pattern that is no longer a trend, but has fast become entrenched as the norm. We expect this pattern to continue.

The late booking pattern is also driven by two other factors. The first is the consumer's belief, conditioned by the airlines, that discounts become more available as departure dates approach. The second factor can be attributed to busy lifestyles of many travelers who don't know until close to the last minute whether or not they can actually get away.

A poll of USTOA members and *Travel Holiday* magazine readers conducted in the fall of 2002 indicated that 70 percent of USTOA respondents reported that passengers were booking their vacations 30 days prior to departure. And 30 percent of USTOA members said passengers booked only 14 days ahead. Passengers who previously booked as much as a year in advance were down to 30 days advance booking, while those who used to book up to six weeks in advance were booking two weeks prior to departure.

When it comes to luxury travelers, rather than discounted travel, they want value for the dollar. Whether on a golf vacation in Scotland or on a once-in-a-lifetime expedition to Antarctica, getting their money's worth means more than lavish furnishings and superior service. They want to return home with the feeling that they have actually learned something or done something memorable.

And, while it seems that many are working 24/7/365, in fact, market segments like seniors have more leisure time than ever. Events like those of September 11, 2001 have made many previous workaholics treasure their leisure activities more than ever.

Demographically Speaking

As is the case with cruise passengers, the profile of the tour and vacation package customer has changed markedly; for escorted tours, the average age has dropped from the 60s to the 50s.

Even those who seem to fit into traditional demographic patterns are not the same. A senior citizen today is a different kind of traveler from his or her counterpart a generation ago. Today's senior traveler is likely to be more active, seeking more from a tour than simply seeing the major sights and covering a lot of ground. In fact, it is sometimes difficult to differentiate by age alone what trip is appropriate for which traveler.

Family travel is another trend that will continue to strengthen. With the growth of two-parent wage earner households, the need to spend quality time with the kids becomes ever more critical. Travel fills the need for quality time, and with less free time for planning, parents will continue to turn to the vacation package or tour to solve the problem of having to make complicated arrangements.

In response, tour operators will continue to create more family-specific packages and tours. Already-existing incentives such as discounts for three in a room, or for a family group traveling together, will entice a growing number of American families to select tours and vacation packages.

Niche markets that didn't exist a decade ago are also gaining momentum. They include gay travel and women-only travel. And Baby Boomers, always eager to pioneer trends, are sure to create their own patterns. In fact, according to an article in *The New York Times*: "The major influence of the next two decades will be the aging of the Baby Boomers, the approximately 79 million people born in the United States from 1945 to 1965. This generation has about 27 million more people than the one that preceded it, and about 10 million more than the one that followed."

As those Boomers become seniors, they will have an even greater impact. The Travel Industry Association of America (TIA), a trade group, estimates that the Boomers account for $130 billion in travel spending and take one-third of all trips (which the association defines as journeys of 50 miles or more, or at least one night away). Within that group, older working couples account for 80 percent of luxury travel.

The Distribution Evolution

The distribution channel for tour operators' products has undergone tremendous evolution, and will continue to do so. While the Internet has not produced some of the dramatic changes envisioned by many observers in the early 1990s, its impact is undeniable. Some experts say the online travel market is expected to grow to more than $60 billion in 2006.

About 64 million Americans used the Internet for travel planning in 2002. And wired travelers planned a greater proportion of their trips online—42 percent said they did most or all of their planning on the Web in 2002—up from 29 percent in 2001. Online bookings also rose, with 39 million people saying they bought travel (mostly airfare or hotel rooms) on the Net, up 25 percent over 2001, according to TIA.

To date, consumers have tended to buy simple elements, such as an airline ticket or hotel arrangements, online, relying on travel agents for more complex itineraries. In time, however, consumers will overcome the fear of buying more complex products over the Internet.

That said, we in the industry feel that there will always be a need for travel agents. While the Internet enables consumers to be more knowledgeable, they still need professional advice because they are, in fact, overloaded with information. In addition, agents have proven themselves the most efficient distribution system for the tour operator product.

From 2000 to 2002, the industry saw rapid growth of online travel agencies. According to *Travel Weekly's* ranking of the Top 50 Travel Agencies of 2002, several of the top agencies were online companies—including Expedia, Orbitz and Travelocity. However, that report also shows that almost all 'traditional' agencies are realizing rapidly growing bookings online. While online agencies will continue to thrive, "traditional" agencies will be competing for those electronic bookings.

Travel agents—whose income has been driven downward by the cutting and elimination of airline commissions—will continue to play a crucial role in the 21st century, but they will never resume the role of "order takers," as they were prior to the 1990s. Only those who provide real service and stay a step ahead of their information-loaded (and overloaded) customers will survive.

Those agents who do make it may no longer be found in brick-and-mortar offices, preferring home-based operations where transactions can be done electronically. But they will retain the expertise necessary to help clients choose the right tour operator and the right vacation package or tour.

The Internet will also result in even more direct marketing to consumers. In the 21st century, the ability to target consumers directly with precision will mean that the revolution in one-to-one marketing will continue and accelerate. In fact, we foresee direct marketing playing a significant role in targeting the right product to the right consumer.

Product Evolution

All these changes—in demographics, in consumer values and in distribution—have and will continue to trigger product evolution. In response, the tour and vacation product will be increasingly active and not passive—with travelers becoming engaged participants rather than watching the world go by.

The escorted tour product will provide more active and in-depth experiences. Some tour operators refer to this as "sightdoing vs. sightseeing." Tours and packages will include features such as meetings with influential artists, "behind-the-scenes" visits to art galleries and museums, and meetings with local people who live in a destination. A growing number of tours and packages will focus on special interests, including "soft" adventures like day hikes and whitewater trips; culturally enriching experiences like wine tasting; or sports activities, such as golfing and golf tours.

At the same time, tours will incorporate more leisure time for travelers to pursue their own dreams and goals. Consequently, we will see a balance of experiences that travelers would find hard to do on their own, combined with time for individual pursuits, so that each traveler can follow his or her own interests.

The tour operators who succeed will be those who meet the new challenges of the Internet; of value-conscious consumers; and of travelers driven by a passion to pursue their own interests. These successful operators will deliver high value for the dollar. And the tour and vacation package product will continue to evolve to meet ever-changing demands.

The next decades will see the changes that began in 2001 continue to play out. Even during the boom years of the 1990s and 2000, signs of change were apparent. New products were being introduced and the distribution system was beginning its electronic revolution.

In the end, it is the customer who will determine the future. Tour operators must continually adapt to a public that wants to "do" rather than "see," to "experience" rather than "visit," and to "participate" rather than "watch."

37

The Changing Face of Packaged Travel

W. James Host, Chairman
Host Communications, Inc.

W. James Host is chairman of Host Communications, Inc. (HOST), a subsidiary of Bull Run Corporation (NASDAQ: Bull).

Host opened Jim Host & Associates, later to become Host Communications, Inc., in 1972. Today, the company is nationally known for the administration of affinity, lifestyle, sports marketing and association management.

Active in civic and charitable activities, Host has chaired many campaigns and has been associated with more than 40 organizations and boards, including the White House Conference on Travel and Tourism, The Tourism Works for America Council, the Academy of Travel and Tourism national advisory board, the Freedoms Foundation, the National Basketball Hall of Fame executive committee, and the American Football Coaches Association Foundation board.

Host has also been inducted into the Travel Industry of America Association's Hall of Leaders and the National Tourism Foundation Hall of Fame.

There was a time when a successful tour package consisted mainly of sightseeing—a glance at a famous monument or two through a bus window, the obligatory walking tour of a well-known hot spot and the mailing of a few "Wish you were here" postcards. It was, more than anything else, a chance to get away from work and stress, an opportunity to discover America or a distant land. And it was enough.

No longer.

Today's savvy and independent traveler is on the constant lookout for new, customized experiences. The "been there, done that" attitude prevalent among modern tuned-in customers has altered the landscape of the packaged travel industry. They've already seen it on TV. They've read about it on the Internet. Today's traveler is smart, experienced and hungry to explore those new, hands-on frontiers that they've heard so much about.

"People don't want to come to Banff Springs and look at a mountain," says Marilyn Bell of Fairmont Hotels Banff Springs, Banff, Alberta. "They want to climb a mountain."

Barbara Bowman, director of sales for the Grand Junction Visitor and Convention Bureau in Grand Junction, Colorado, agrees, commenting that travelers are no longer saying, "I want to go there." They are asking, "Where can I go to do that?"

One commonality between today's tourist and those of the past is that they are both looking for a stress-free experience. The difference between them in this regard is that today's traveler doesn't expect to have one. In fact, with global and economic threats always looming, there is a heightened sense of cynicism when it comes to travel. People no longer feel completely safe away from home, and for some it can be even more stressful to take a vacation than to abstain from one.

According to a National Tour Association Strategic Travel Action Resource (STAR) report entitled "The Psychology of Travel—The New Normal," there has emerged a new kind of "normal" traveler. People have settled into an awareness that the relatively stress-free experience of travel will not return to what it once was. Global unease will continue to be a factor in their decisions over where to go and what to do. According to NTA's STAR, "gaining trust is more important than ever and keeping the new stresses of travel to a minimum and helping consumers obtain their goal of relaxation can all positively affect a consumer's behavior and loyalty toward your company."

To achieve this, travel professionals must create the kind of environment that travel participants respond to, including giving travelers a tangible sense of control over their experience, as well as working behind the scenes to make sure there is less reason to worry over stressful factors.

According to Mikie Wall, CTP, director of sales and trade development for the North Carolina Travel & Tourism Division, keeping up with change will be the name of today's travel industry game.

"Tour operators are listening to new ideas," she said. "They understand that you can't do the same old thing. Because of that, we will have a better, stronger market."

Some areas of the packaged travel industry are proving to be pivotal in this regard.

Family Travel

In an age of economic downturns and unpredictable change, time in which families can be together as a unit is growing increasingly rare. Because of this, family vacations are becoming very precious commodities—times when they can reconnect and experience together, re-forging their familial bonds in the process.

"We see family travel as a long-term cultural focus," said Steve Born, director of marketing for NTA tour operator member Globus/Cosmos. "Demographics have shifted to family units that put a higher premium on being able to travel together. The time is so precious that if they can put it together and spend time with the grandparents and the kids all together, then it's a very attractive activity for them."

Globus/Cosmos' research indicates that there's nothing quite like the experience of traveling together; it is considered the perfect quality time.

"The idea of discovering a new place together, of physically being in the same place to explore, is very important in terms of quality family time," said Born. "Whether they're a part of a family that's separated or whether they're still together, there's a real premium on the time that the family spends together. If they can schedule it around a vacation, then it's sort of that ultimate quality time."

One example is today's popular, entertainment-packed ocean cruise, where the whole family can be a part of the same experience, even while doing different activities. The kids have the liberty to explore and play, while parents can relax, enjoying the knowledge that they are in a safe, enclosed environment.

According to Born, children play the largest role in deciding where to go during a family vacation. And with grandparents who are generally younger and more active than they used to be, multigenerational travel packages are leaning more toward soft adventure and interactive educational itineraries.

"In planning the trip, (parents) want to interact and experience a bit more with the kids, as opposed to just traveling together. Then, once they're at the location, they all run in separate directions," said Born. "They want to experience things together."

According to Born, this attitude extends to the grandparents, who also are more interested in getting out and keeping up with the kids. "That has had a real significant impact on how these packages are put together," said Born. "They can get out and really be grandparents, whereas, at home, they would be much more likely to get saddled into playing the 'babysitter' role. On vacation, they can enjoy discovering with the kids."

Born noted that many families are choosing the shorter, regional getaways, versus the longer and "big production"-style vacations of the past. "They may have concerns about traveling far from home," he said, and this has changed their focus as to what they can experience locally.

On the technology end of family travel, the rise of the Internet has enabled grandparents and grandchildren to connect much more than they used to, inspiring many more multigenerational travel packages.

Addressing how the family market values its time, Globus/Cosmos has created a special product called *On The Road*, specifically designed for families.

"It's the great American driving vacation," said Born. "We offer a selection of twelve itineraries that are already selected and pre-packaged, and we provide roundtrip airfare, pre-selected hotels, rental car options, recommended sightseeing and on-call service. Travelers also receive a "TripKit" that includes detailed maps, driving instructions, local history and suggestions of what to do and see along the way, enabling the days to be free with no details to handle. With one call to Cosmos, families can book the vacation that is already built for them."

According to Born, many Boomers don't have time to piece all of their own vacations together, and by building it for them, Globus/Cosmos removes many of the various stress factors for their customers.

"I think that the future of family travel is taking experiences and creating customized packages specifically according to what the family is looking for," said Born. "The thing is, I don't think we can just label something 'family,' because there are many factors to take into consideration. It's a product that needs to be built from the ground up."

One of the main factors to take into account in the coming years is the aging Baby Boomer segment. Boomers, as they move into their retirement years, feel that they have earned the right to have some fun and they have built up the savings to do it. This group can be targeted for very successful multigenerational tour products.

Greg Schmid is director of the strategic planning group at the Institute for the Future, a forecasting firm in Menlo Park, California. Schmid believes that anything travel or leisure-related will be in high demand among this group. This belief is based, in part, on the idea that Boomers don't see their final decades as any time to start pulling back on luxury. They want to age well, stay active and continue to broaden their experiences.

Targeting this well-traveled, mature group means successful re-branding of product, and creating new and different experiences.

"The rule of thumb always has been that once people reach 55 or so, they're out of their heavy consumer phase," said Schmid. "But the (leading-edge) Baby Boomers are going to continue to be an economic force. Marketers ignore them at their own risk."

Also important to take into account is a younger, trailing-edge Boomer segment. These Boomers are less secure because of safety concerns. They have grown up in an age of violence, and this will impact their travel choices in the years to come.

Experiential Tours

According to NTA's Market Assessment Plans, which explore growing trends in the industry, one of the biggest growing trends is that of experience-based travel. Travelers want to touch, to taste, to interact with the environment. They want to be a part of it, not just to see it.

Clients who are looking for these kinds of adventures tend to be well educated, according to the report. They are often financially secure and goal-oriented. Knowledge, personal enrichment, unique experiences and socialization with like-minded people motivate them. Their desire is to remain intellectually active, to create memories and learn about people, places and cultures. It's not enough for them to look at everything from "behind glass." Whether the itinerary includes a special visit to a hidden-away, authentic Mexican town, taking a scuba certification program during a cruise vacation in the Bahamas, or stopping for wine-tasting while on a bike ride down a mountain, experiential travel is catching on.

Being able to physically interact can guarantee that their trip will be stimulating, and that they will carry home with unique and cherished memories.

Ron Drake, president of Royal Palm Tours, Fort Myers, Florida, specializes in cutting-edge, experience-based travel packages. Drake pointed out that there's a certain economic stability inherent in packaging to the more hardcore experience-seekers, as well as to those who actively pursue volunteerism within their vacation structure. There is a level of passion involved in this special interest group that often supersedes feelings of caution.

"There is a definite loyalty factor built into whatever the experience is, and since much of experience-based travel is special access, they don't want to miss it by canceling and waiting until another date." said Drake. "If it's just escape or entertainment, they can always cancel and do it later. It's harder to do that when it comes to experience-based travel."

For example, Drake created a horticulture-based travel package experience. Inspired by the best-selling publication, *The Orchid Thief: A True Story of Beauty and Obsession* by Susan Orlean, Drake used the popular nonfiction work to build a fascinating horticultural journey for one of his most loyal special interest markets. The five-day *Orchid Thief* tour featured actual characters and sights from the book, woven into a mosaic of floral and historic experiences created specifically for those who have a passion for plants.

"The tour has so many layers of experience," said Drake. "The kinds of folks who travel on this kind of program very much want to learn about the heritage, and participate in hands-on activities and restoration projects. It gives them a sense of ownership and the chances are very good that they'll come back in the ensuing years."

According to Suzanne Slavitter, CTP, vice president of Lakewood, CA-based Sports Empire, Inc., one of the main advantages of a special interest tour is that participants are often so devoted to the theme of the tour that business is guaranteed through stable economic times as well as turbulent ones. For the travel planner, their devotion and loyalty result in an invaluable commodity: predictable, year-round business.

"Our car racing packages have done unbelievably well through some difficult times," said Slavitter. "Most of my clients just don't care about the potential obstacles to traveling. They're not first-time travelers, and nothing's going to stop them from attending the event."

"I see the popularity of experience-based travel holding into the future, almost regardless of the economy or terrorism threats," agreed Drake.

Technology and the "Human Element"

In this age of ever-increasing access to information and services, Web-based bookings/travel sites are quickly adding to marketplace competition. Sites such as Expedia and Travelocity are all aiming to establish dynamic packaging online, and the future of the industry will shift greatly as the technology and software platforms make packaging online easier and more understandable.

According to a recent report from PhoCusWright Inc. ("Online Travel Overview: Market Size and Forecasts, 2002–2005"), online travel booking will continue to experience a steady increase into the future as people become more familiar with technology and new products are offered. The ever-increasing ability of travelers to easily customize their own itineraries is going to become one of the future strengths of Internet planning and booking.

According to NTA's "*The Psychology of Travel—The 'New Normal*,'" "As our world becomes more and more reliant upon technology, a company that can offer the benefits of this technology, while keeping their human element, will be ahead of the curve."

One way for tour operators to keep the "human element" that will differentiate them from the online services is by creating more customized tours now, directed to the individual packaged traveler.

Gerald DiPietro, founder and president of Hyannis, Massachusetts-based Tourco, a receptive operator, specializes in these kinds of packages, and sees them growing only more popular and necessary over time.

"There's no question that it's the product of preference for the future, especially if it's packaged correctly," said DiPietro, who noted that most Europeans who come here are looking for an FIT product (FIT tourists generally consist of families, couples, single travelers, or very small groups; F.I.T. originally stood for Foreign Independent Traveler, but has since come to refer to any independent traveler). "The demographics of the domestic marketplace are pointing toward more FIT-type products in the future."

According to DiPietro, that's where tour operators come into the picture. "To be successful in the future, operators are going to have to understand that the FIT market is going to be more and more of a product preference," he said. "Creating individual itineraries that are exciting and have value to them, and creating experiences that people want, will be crucial to this success."

Flexibility and Customization

Also according to NTA's "The Psychology of Travel—The 'New Normal'" STAR, today's "live for today" spontaneity "creates the need for flexible booking options and for tour suppliers and operators to work together to create more customized product available on shorter notice." NTA tour supplier member the Cendant Corporation is on the vanguard of addressing this need.

"In every way we recognize that tourists are requiring more customization," said Robert Chafey, senior director of tour marketing for Cendant. According to Chafey, there are two main steps in staying ahead of the curve in this regard.

"Step one is identifying where the need lies, and really listening to our customers," said Chafey. "Step two is developing solutions, including the technology that will get us there. That applies to both group and FIT operations."

Cendant—whose mantra is "customer-focused solutions"—is proactive when it comes to both of these steps. By taking their customers through an interview process and asking in-depth questions about their needs, pre-planned customization can be developed. And by developing and using dedicated technology, including a special group tracking system, Cendant can help its customers figure out what kind of business trends they've been experiencing, as well as what opportunities remain to be explored. In this regard, they become a partner and a consultant for their customers, creating new customizing opportunities before their customers even ask for it.

"There are many opportunities to do cooperative marketing and to provide additional support for programs they're trying to run to their clients," said Chafey. "We create good customizing resources that make it easy to do business with us."

Likewise, DiPietro's company has created a diverse menu of itinerary options that customers can use to create a unique travel package.

"We give our clients the opportunity to put together their FIT tours as they wish," said DiPietro. Tourco works in a region, and within that area they have enough areas contracted, with daily blocks of rooms, for a consumer to basically connect the dots. "It's a concept that works," said DiPietro, with the key component being a comprehensive product line.

Thanks to today's more intelligent and demanding traveler, modern customized tours truly run the gamut of combinations. From traditional history-based travel packages that also pull in elements of architecture or the arts, to the successful merging of an ocean cruise vacation with an extended on-land hiking adventure, anything goes in today's packaged travel industry.

"I think that things are going to become more and more customized," said Chafey. "The end user is going to demand it even more than they do right now, and the technology is going to give us the capabilities to more easily deliver it. The key is that we have to stay ahead of it to be a part of it. That's certainly our commitment."

Control

In an industry that is, to a great degree, subject to the winds of change, the traveler's need for perceived control over his or her experience has become a major factor in customer satisfaction. According to NTA's "The Psychology of Travel—The 'New Normal'" STAR study, heightened focuses on security (especially related to air travel) and stresses connected to various perceived threats have caused customers to feel out of control, vulnerable and helpless.

Giving these individuals a renewed sense of control over their travel experiences will play an important role in ensuring successful travel packages. The professionalism of the travel planner or tour operator, and their ability to alleviate as many of the stressful components of the travel process as possible, will be vital to customer enjoyment of the experience—and to repeat business.

According to the STAR, "by offering first quality service and providing travelers with a range of options, a feeling of control can be regained." And by eliminating as many stress-causing factors as possible in a package, other unavoidable stressors, such as airport security, can seem less daunting for the customer.

One thing's for sure—there's no going back. And for industry professionals who stay attuned to these important trends in the coming years, and who do the work that it takes to adapt to constant change, many unexpected and exciting opportunities await.

Research and editing assistance for this article provided by Paul Ramey, copywriter for the National Tour Association.

38

Sending People on Vacation in the Future: Trends and Developments in the Marketing of Leisure Travel

Daniel E. Westbrook, President
American Airlines Vacations

Daniel Westbrook, CTC, has been involved for many years in the leisure travel industry. He started his career as a commercial trial attorney and joined American Airlines in 1986 as an attorney in the legal department. He served also as senior attorney and assistant corporate secretary. In August of 1991, Mr. Westbrook became managing director of American's international market development group, which was responsible for American's leisure sales programs and international sales. In August 1996, he was named president of American Airlines Vacations.

American Airlines Vacations is the industry's largest airline-owned tour operator. AAV offers individually customized vacations at locations around the world, including Florida, Hawaii, the Caribbean, Las Vegas, Mexico, Europe, Canada and all the major U.S. cities. These packages are available through the Internet at aavacations.com or by calling a local travel agent or AAV's toll free number, 1-800-321-2121.

Introduction

An invitation to write about the future of travel marketing is a mixed blessing, to be sure. On the one hand, it forces one to take time—time which most persons generally do not set aside—to reflect upon emerging trends in travel, evolving markets and likely developments. In an industry where most people have become accustomed to crisis management, the time set aside for thinking about the future is precious indeed. On the other hand, committing long-term predictions to paper in as dynamic an industry as travel leaves one open to scorn and ridicule—the pace of change outstrips even the most farsighted prognosticator. Most technologists still cherish this wonderful quote attributed to Bill Gates: "640K ought to be enough for anybody."

In light of that quote, I approach this subject with abundant humility, if not trepidation. Still, there are certain trends that become sufficiently evident that some discussion of them, and of their long-term implications for a travel marketer, can be productively undertaken. Having thus admitted the folly of predicting what is ahead of us, I intend nonetheless to offer, in the first section of this note, three developments that I believe we can anticipate. First, continued technological advancement will drive greater demand for leisure travel. Second, traditional retail and wholesale channels for travel distribution will merge over the course of the coming years. Third and finally, even as the distribution channels merge, the consumers of leisure travel will become increasingly polarized along a number of disparate continua. The latter section of this note will then, again humbly, identify some of the implications that I foresee as a result of these trends, both for travel distributors and for the ultimate suppliers of travel services.

Three Emerging Trends

The Global Community: In 1869, the final spike was driven on the first transcontinental railway, an accomplishment that historian Stephen Ambrose characterized as the greatest of the American 19th century. It was an enormous industrial leap forward and its effect on the American West cannot be overstated. No longer was the West accessible only to frontiersmen and pioneers. It became, both literally and figuratively, a gold mine; the land of opportunity open to all who could scrape together the rail fare. In short, the techno-industrial advancement created a new market.

There are other, more recent examples of a connection between technology and what I refer to as an "expanding community." The invention and refinement of the automobile made possible the weekend visit to neighboring cities and, ultimately, led to huge metropolitan communities such as Southern California, Greater New York, Dallas-Fort Worth and Seattle-Tacoma. Air travel, particularly jets, brought continents together. In each case, the community in which we live has grown dramatically as our ability to "get to" more places expanded. To paraphrase an old maxim of political philosophy, where technology enables people to go, they will go.[1]

Nothing in today's technological world is as pervasive or as "impactful" as the Internet, wholly apart from considerations of online commerce. Everyone from children to grandparents is surfing the Net. Increasingly, the allure of the Net is the sense of community. Whether tracking down old, long-lost friends or making new ones, people are chatting and messaging others, connecting with a new and much larger "community." That community, in the online world, has lost all reference to geographic borders or regions.

It has been fashionable in some circles to worry that improved communications and, in particular, the Internet's capacity for video and for messaging, will make travel unnecessary. It seems to me likely that the inevitable consequence of increased Internet usage is increased travel. As people make friends or read about new and different places, they will want to see those friends and places. Just like the transcontinental railroad, then, the continued development and acceptance of the Internet will expand the scope of the community and will ultimately stimulate leisure travel demand. In short, where people can travel in cyberspace, they will ultimately travel in fact.

Channel Merger: A second development that appears likely to continue, both in travel and in other industries, is a blending together of the traditional retail and wholesale travel distribution markets. Examples abound, even on a single drive through any commercial area. Make your way to Sam's Club or Costco, wholesale-like distribution centers selling directly to "members." If you shop long enough, you will no doubt get hungry and you can either go to the McDonald's location in the store, or head across the street to the combined Taco Bell/Pizza Hut/Kentucky Fried Chicken. The same sort of considerations that drive these distribution anomalies have, if anything, even more forceful effect among those involved in travel distribution.

At one point, the retail side of the leisure travel trade was pretty clearly defined. The leisure-oriented travel agents had attractive offices in strip shopping centers or in trendy areas with lots of "foot traffic." The typical customer interaction took place either within those offices or on the telephone and the customers relied heavily upon the cumulative knowledge and experience gathered by the travel agent over the course of many years in the industry. Particularly in situations involving more complex travel experiences—cruises, trekking expeditions, multidestination tours—the customer was, and should have been, extremely reluctant to investigate, select and book the vacation components without that critical advice.

The emergence of the large online travel sites has clearly changed much of that "transactional dynamic." For better or worse, the "e-tailers" have entered the retail channel in a significant way, providing virtually unlimited amounts of information and broad booking capabilities. While few would yet conclude that the e-tailers are a solution for all travel planning needs, that certainly is their goal and their enormous technological resources suggest that they will continue making progress toward that goal. Clearly, the large online travel sites are and will likely continue to be very formidable competitors in the retail channels. The traditional travel agent must adapt to a fundamentally different competitive environment than was foreseen just a few years ago.

The phenomenon that was not so immediately apparent was the evolution of those same travel sites into the wholesale channel. Not satisfied with the revenue streams generated by commissions and transactions fees, and very likely with an eye toward enhancing Wall Street's view of their relative value, the e-tailers aggressively pursued "merchant models" that would boost their margins and allow them to report dramatically higher revenue figures. The merchant model that they adopted is essentially the same as the more advanced traditional model that tour operators have used for years. The distributor receives net rates from various travel suppliers, from airlines to hotels and car rental companies, among others, and marks the various components up discreetly. The online shopper then can assemble his or her own package of components in a "real-time" shopping environment. By shifting to this business model, the e-tailers became the new competitive challenge in the wholesale channel, as well.

Predictably, existing competitors at both levels of the distribution chain have responded to the competitive development of these emerging online players. The more progressive, traditional tour wholesalers have adopted, or already were using, technology that automated the same dynamic packaging capability, offering component-based tours. They also have become much more aggressive about selling directly to the traveling public and doing so both online and through their existing inbound call centers. This merger of the distribution channels will accelerate as the technology grows even more flexible and more "intelligent" in terms of enabling customers. As in other industries throughout the years, computers and databases will do more and more of the role of the traditional travel agent. Ultimately, there will be no meaningful distinction between a retail agent and a wholesaler of travel services—there will simply be travel planning and booking services, both large and small, specialized and general, online and offline.

Polarized Purchasers: The third of my theories relates not to the distributors, but to the customers. In many respects, it is a natural consequence of the first two anticipated developments. As the world "community" expands and the demand for leisure travel grows, the merger of the traditional distribution channels will polarize customers at opposite ends of a number of identifiable spectrums. Again, some historical reference points serve to demonstrate the likely development.

As this book goes to print, the global economy is still struggling to right itself. Unemployment is higher than it has been for decades and likely to grow worse yet. Consumers' fears of terrorism or diseases of various forms have combined with an unsettled geopolitical environment, and all of that economic uncertainty, to depress travel dramatically. A general survey of current automobile advertising, though, would be very instructive. Ads for low-priced cars are abundant and are replete with rebates, discounts, special no-interest financing and other promotional offers. And yet, the higher-priced cars, such as SUVs, seem to be selling best. The example used earlier reinforces the observation; while the wholesale shopping clubs may be full on Saturday mornings, the luxury, high-service, high-touch retail stores in the fashionable areas are also full and doing quite well.

At one level, the United States is facing increasing challenges with the allocation of wealth among the "haves and have nots," an issue that has plagued societies throughout history and occasionally has led to violent sorts of adjustments. For our purposes, however, it is sufficient to note that consumers will basically come in two forms in the coming years. One subset of travelers will want price. They will want little else. Whether they plan to go to Las Vegas or on an African safari, the overriding consideration once they have made their initial decision about destination and activity will be the price at which they can fulfill those plans. Another, in some respects more interesting, subset of travelers will be at the other end of the "price continuum." They will be much less sensitive to price and much more willing to pay premiums for service and for quality. They will be less likely to book obscure products online, though they may well book online if attractive brands with the right sorts of quality assurances are available. The confidence that comes with qualified advice received from an experienced travel agent is more likely to be valued, and to be paid for, by this subset of travelers.

As a supplier or a distributor of travel services, however, it is important to note that the price continuum is just one of several relevant spectrums. Purchasers will also become more polarized in terms of the nature of the experience they seek. At one end of the spectrum, the short, weekend escape to a city hotel or to a casino with little else in the way of pre-travel arrangements will appeal to a population working much harder than they would like and needing just a break of some kind. At the other extreme, travelers will want pre-travel arrangements for a biking trip, theatre tickets, multiple destinations and special handling of particular needs. So the continuum is basically one of complexity and of specialization. Another relevant variable may be the geographic range of interest; some adventurous souls will finally head off for that Himalayan trekking expedition or to scuba dive in the Seychelles. Others will decide to stay closer to home, taking perhaps a three-day cruise from a U.S.-based home port or visiting an attraction, even an area of primarily historical interest, close to home.

The important observation is that there will be a complex matrix of variables relating to group travelers. Each group will have a different set of interests and resources and each will drive different planning and sales dynamics. My expectation, however, is that people will increasingly insist upon having what they want when they want it, rather than settling for what is available at any given time. Again, the other trends that I have suggested reinforce this tendency. As the community grows larger and people want to experience a world about which they know much more and that feels much closer to them, as their ability to book travel to that world in whatever form they choose increases, their tendency to book travel only in the form that appeals to them will be greater.

Implications of Three Trends for the Travel Marketer

If I was at all diffident about making predictions, then it is outright fear that I feel when it comes to suggesting to anyone how best to market travel in the coming years. My first reaction when invited to contribute to a book on that topic was to call to mind Mark Twain's old quote, "I was gratified to be able to answer promptly, and I did. I said I didn't know." Still, if my three trends ultimately prove to be even reasonably accurate, then there are certain implications for anyone charged with responsibility for marketing travel. Rather than offer advice, then, let me suggest to you what I intend to do and encourage each of you to form your own judgments. Also, since I seem to be doing things in threes, I will identify three marketing strategies that seem to me likely to be successful.

Know the Customer: Gertrude Stein once admonished that "Everybody gets so much information all day long that they lose their common sense." In deference to her warning, my first principle for marketing travel in the coming years is little more than common sense: know the customer. If my observations above are correct, every customer, or potential customer, will tap into and become a part of some larger community. That community will be defined not necessarily by geographic boundaries, but by interests, experiences, price elasticity and resources and capabilities. Each of us must understand the complex matrix of polarized customers and understand, as well, to which subsets our particular products may appeal. Alternatively, we must understand how we can *make* our products appeal to as many of those customers as possible.

Certainly, the concept of knowing the customer is no flash of insight. Segmenting the customers, however, will become more important. As well, the technology that drives the three trends we have discussed will also dramatically enhance the ability to gather information about customers and to respond to customers' interests and desires directly on a one-to-one basis. This lesson incorporates not just marketing and "messages," but actual product design and planning. For example, if one's customers are more likely to be in the more price-sensitive, less complex purchasing subset, product should be simple, easily delivered and absolutely low-cost. More to the point, thoughtful marketers should anticipate creating alternative brands—indeed, many companies already have created them—to address the various market segments.

In the midst of this somewhat self-evident suggestion, I want to offer one less popular observation. Use technology without relying upon it. Understand what you or your company can do with technological tools, but never lose sight of the fact that your customers, ultimately, are people. Albert Einstein once said, "Not everything that can be counted counts, and not everything that counts can be counted." Whether I am eventually proven to be right or wrong about polarization, expanding communities and distribution practices, we all know that travel is ultimately an intensely personal experience. Whatever our theories, every travel product or service must first appeal to a prospective customer on some visceral level. Even before questions of price or of quality or reliability are resolved, a customer must want to go someplace and/or to experience something.

Tap into your own humanity and that of the people with whom you work. Never rely so completely on data and statistics that you lose sight of that basic fact. Each of us is essentially a focus group of one. What do *you* like to do? With whom? What about your family and friends? If you cannot imagine someone wanting to take the vacation you offer, chances are that no one will. On the other hand, if you cannot imagine someone passing on the opportunity that your product or service provides, you are a long way toward marketing that product or service successfully.

Know Your Partners: This policy may be slightly less obvious, but is equally reducible to a common sense denominator. The travel industry is and almost certainly will remain a hopelessly—or I should say, hopefully—intertwined industry with little vertical integration. It relies for both marketing and delivery of travel experiences on the collaboration of multiple parties. We tend to throw around the word "partnership" a bit too glibly, perhaps, but there is indeed a sense of partnership that pervades the industry and is, in fact, necessary for the customer to be satisfied. Yet, simply put, not all partners are created equal.

As the distribution channels merge, for example, there will almost certainly be distributors who amass a tremendous amount of potential leverage; in whose hands, in other words, is amassed a significant amount of market power. As a marketer of travel products, those distributors can be very helpful and can be very good marketing partners. Still, prudence dictates that no one should become too reliant upon any single partner or class of partners. According to another Mark Twain witticism, "Put your eggs in one basket, and then watch that basket carefully." For all his folksy wisdom, I must disagree with Twain on this.

Suppliers of travel products should develop a "stable" of distribution partners based upon several criteria. First, are the partner's long-term economic interests aligned with yours and likely to remain so? The answer to that question is likely dependent upon the extent to which the distributor is, in one way or another, "invested" in your product, destination or market segment. Second, does this particular partner offer a means to distribute a travel product at a favorable cost-of-sale and with otherwise low distribution costs? Third, do these distributors, as a whole, enable you, the travel marketer, to reach all of the relevant areas of that matrix of purchasers we described? Is there a dive operator, a soft-adventure operator, an upscale, full-service agency? Finally, and perhaps most important of all, will this marketing partner actually help to create demand for a travel product, or will it simply process transactions and capitalize on demand that you yourself must work to create?

From the distributor's point of view, the lessons should be obvious. Be a good partner. Invest in the long-term success of your suppliers and of the destinations you sell. Work hard to lower the distribution costs of your partners and to enhance their ability to manage inventory and yield. A distributor must prove every day that it is interested in contributing to the success of its suppliers. Develop tools to create demand and do so in a myriad of submarkets. The technological tools available today offer almost unlimited flexibility to brand product dynamically and to appeal to niche markets. Understand the submarkets where your suppliers' products are likely to have the greatest appeal and tap into those markets. Also prepare to help the supplier target new markets and to reach those markets in creative ways, particularly during those times of the year when demand for the suppliers' products typically weakens. The days of looking to suppliers to find what they can do for you in exchange for selling their product are gone. The challenge now is to maximize your value to the suppliers, so that they will see you as the most effective and efficient distribution tool for their products.

You're in the Dream Business, Stupid! At American Airlines Vacations, we seldom talk about room nights or seat miles or rental car days. We certainly track all the business metrics necessary to manage the business, but we work hard to recall that we are in the business of sending people on vacation. Unlike today's business traveler, when our customers return home, they have a memory that we hope they will cherish for years to come. They have experienced a honeymoon in a romantic beachside villa, have enjoyed a family escape to a theme park that they can discuss when the grandkids come along, or perhaps have finally gotten to play the Old Course at St. Andrews. Each of us carries with us memories of special times and special places, usually with special people in our lives. No one involved in the leisure side of the travel business should ever lose sight of the value of what we do.

On the door of the conference room in our office is a quote from Theodore Roosevelt: "Far and away the best prize that life offers is the chance to work hard at work worth doing." Even as we struggle with a host of circumstances that challenge us, from wars to diseases to generally poor economic conditions, we celebrate that all the trouble, at least, is worth doing.

Go ye, therefore, and send some people on vacation.

Note

[1] Machiavelli, "What the Prince permits, the Prince commands."

39

Survival of the Fittest

Ron Letterman, Chairman
Classic Custom Vacations

Ron Letterman is chairman of Classic Custom Vacations (CCV), an Expedia company. In his position, Letterman focuses his attention on building and maintaining relationships with preferred travel agents and suppliers and implementing new products. Letterman had been president of CCV since 1992, and previously served as vice chairman, president and CEO of Global Vacation Group, Classic's former parent company.

Prior to joining CCV, Letterman was president of retail travel for Carlson Travel Network, where he was responsible for more than 1,000 travel agency locations in Carlson's wholesale tour operation.

During his 20-year residence in Hawaii, he was president and co-owner of Cove Enterprises, which operates the Paradise Cove Luau, the Charo show, and Cove Expo and Design, a convention exposition company. Letterman previously held the positions of vice president and general manager for inbound travel USA for American Express which, under his leadership, created the largest inbound operation in Hawaii's history. Earlier in his career, Letterman worked as a travel writer, travel escort, travel agent and agency manager.

Because of the rapidly changing political, economic and technological world in which we live, many no longer feel that the lessons of the past can help us navigate the future. One has simply to look at what has happened in recent times to communication giants like WorldCom, energy companies like Enron, media giants like AOL Time Warner, the dot.com start- ups and the once proud airline industry, to recognize that when you forget the ethics and fundamentals of good business practice, the business will ultimately fail.

There is a path that I have tried to follow in business and, for that matter, in my personal life, that has kept me on track, happy, reasonably successful and in this crazy world, sane. That path is based on a life and business commitment, to stay true to my values, to try to always do what I say I am going to do, to behave and perform in a way that brings pride to me, my family, my associates, my customers and my employees. My business bias, which has evolved over 40 years, was based on continuing to do what I and my company do best—to maintain the culture of our organization, a belief that honest confrontation is not a bad thing if it comes from the right place, and that strategic alliances are often a more successful business strategy than vertical integration.

That is why, in the case of Classic, we stayed true to our travel agency distribution model while the airlines did not. They found that their yield decreased far more rapidly than the expense of travel agency commissions. They lost a partner that could sell their high yield product and bias the business towards them. They lost their brand and became a commodity because their pricing strategy could not be communicated to consumers in a way that established the value of what they were buying. The prices had little integrity and the game became who can find the cheapest fare versus which was the best airline with the best service. Now when you bought a ticket, you felt uneasy and somewhat taken advantage of, because the person next to you was smarter and got a better price for the same or better seat.

Hundreds of millions of dollars have been spent marketing this insecurity and the downward yield cycle was accelerated. We cannot blame the middleman who responded to this pricing strategy; you have to blame the airlines that created it.

Many of us who went to business school and who worked for public companies were told that the only objective of business is to increase profits and shareholder value. I have come to believe that if that is your company's only objective, over the long haul, you will increase neither profits nor shareholder value.

The business world has spent more time wooing the investor and less time serving the customer. Venture capital companies that have invested in many businesses were looking to take them public and for an exit strategy with high returns in a short period of time. Hype and financial engineering were often more valued than good operating savvy and a clear vision to build a sustainable brand that would last a lifetime.

What does all this lead me to believe? It leads me to believe that consumer values have not changed all that much; business values have.

My belief is that while we respond to the new business challenges before us and continue to invest in the future, you still must feed and nurture your core business.

The culture of your organization, the relationships and trust you have built with your customers, vendors and employees, must be respected and maintained. The basics are still there.

- Do what you say you are going to do.

- Charge what you say you are going to charge.

- Respond when you say you are going to respond.

- Always deliver what the customer paid for and more.

Once you have that in place and have built a dedicated team of employees sharing those values and participating in a common vision, then and only then can you respond to the challenges of the future.

Classic built its reputation on the quality of its services, the flexibility of its vacation packages and a commitment to serving the high-end market with the best hotels in the destinations we served. We built strong relationships with the most professional travel agencies in the industry. We supported those relationships with a dedicated group of district sales managers and a reservations staff recognized and rewarded for its superior service and aggressive sales efforts. Such efforts were supported by technology that allowed them to create a completely flexible, customized itinerary that could be confirmed in writing within minutes. We were a strong, sales-oriented organization and our marketing department was primarily there to serve the needs of our travel agency partners with collateral and co-op marketing support. We built our brand via word of mouth, one agent at a time, one agency at a time.

Agency needs have changed and they are now behaving differently to stay alive. Currently 98 percent of all agencies have Internet access, 95 percent charge fees and 60 percent have their own Web site, according to *Travel Weekly*. Forty percent of travel agencies' vacation package bookings are made online via GDS and Internet access.

Agencies want more technology to improve their productivity and empower them with information to serve their customers better. Wholesalers have to have the financial and human resources to develop this technology. This is the big difference versus the past and companies without these resources will have a very difficult time competing. Travel agencies' continuing role is to protect consumers from making poor choices while proactively selling the travel products and companies they believe in. Too often they try to protect the consumer from spending more to get a better vacation experience. Consumers have to be more vigilant, so that they are secure that they are working with ethical, professional travel agencies and that their agents are recommending companies with robust balance sheets and a history of providing superior service and products.

It's also more difficult for companies that have made large investments of capital in technology, ship production or hotel construction, to rely solely on the travel agencies as their sole distribution source. There are fewer small independent agencies and consolidation is accelerating causing the distribution cost through the agency channel to increase. Fewer and fewer agencies control a larger and larger share of agency business.

Having a strong consumer brand and direct channel is no longer an option for tour operators and cruise lines, if they are to continue to grow.

As we grow and enter a world with ever-increasing dependence on technology, you have to bring new skills to the organization, not only up from the bottom but down from the top. It's hard to be the strategic leader of your organization without strong technology skills. So it's also important to recognize your limitations and know when to bring in new skills to your organization. We have done that at Classic by bringing in a new president with the technology skills to help navigate our future. I see my new role as chairman as the keeper of our core values and to maintain the trust and relationships with the agency community and with our vendor partners that we have so painstakingly built over the years. In a nutshell, we must make sure that we do not discard what got us here as we embrace the future. Marketing is product and trust is earned. These fundamentals never change.

Having said that, where does this leave the travel agency community in the future? It is my firm belief that for some in that community, their future will be brighter than ever. Survival of the fittest will cull those who have gotten into this business for familiarization trips, or because they thought this would be a fun avocation. It will cull those whose skills were limited to delivering easy transaction products at the lowest price they could find. It will enrich those who embrace the future, who have developed professional and business skills and who have developed a sales culture in their organization, through recognition programs, training, empowerment and financial rewards tied to successful selling.

Historically, 50 percent of the traveling community has never purchased their vacations through a travel agency. This will not change, but a large percentage of the remaining travelers, especially on the high end, will want and need the services of a professional travel agent empowered by technology and able to deliver highly personalized services. More and more consumers are willing to pay for this service. High tech, high touch will be the theme of most successful companies if the future.

So what do I think our industry will look like in the future? Internet travel companies will continue to grow. It is estimated that this $24 billion industry will grow to at least $75 billion by 2006. It's important to remember, however, that we are talking about $75 billion out of a $3 *trillion* industry. On the low end are Internet companies focusing almost totally on price. These companies include Priceline, Cheap Tickets.Com and perhaps Hotel.Com. Addressing the mid-market are Expedia, Orbitz and Travelocity, which are focusing on building a brand that represents reliability, value and convenience delivered by the best Web sites, using the best technology. Currently there are no major Internet travel companies focusing on delivering vacation packages that would satisfy the discriminating traveler interested in staying at the world's best properties or resorts while enjoying a special sightseeing, dining or shopping experience. That is the space we think Classic can occupy in the future.

I believe the Internet companies mentioned above will continue to grow exponentially, with perhaps one or two falling out or merging. The newer and smaller entrants to the Internet travel world will have an increasingly difficult time keeping up with the financial and technology advantages of the existing industry leaders and there will be significantly more fallout among this group.

Hotel and cruise lines will continue to invest in their own sites and connectivity. On the hotel side, the industry is very fragmented. The 50 top hotel brands represent only15 percent of hotel inventory. Internet travel companies in this environment will always be important to the hotel industry. Just as credit card companies vie for share of wallet, hotels will continue to compete for share of site. On the cruise side, the industry is much more consolidated. In this environment, a strategic partnership will be forged with selected Internet travel companies that have a greater focus on growing the market.

More than ever, the hotels will have to invest heavily in developing their brand position. Clearly Internet travel companies like Priceline.com commoditize all hotels, promoting only the best price available on a given day amongst their designated two-, three-, four- or five-star hotels. Sites like Expedia and ultimately Classic are looking for long-term marketing and merchandising relationships with the best brands and properties in their price range, while delivering customers at acceptable yields and guaranteeing a fare that will not be undercut by the hotel or cruise line.

Travel agencies will use the Internet more and more frequently as an alternative to their GDS systems and will increasingly develop more and more sophisticated Web sites. These sites will be supported by travel agents, both at home and in the headquarters office, who have very strong selling skills focusing on a limited number of vendors. The Web sites will break down the geographical boundaries that limit travel agencies today. The ones that will thrive in this environment will have the best Web sites, and navigators who can direct hot inquiries to agents who are trained to call back instantly at anytime and close the sale. These agencies will not have to know everything about every destination or vendor; they will only have to be trained experts in the products and destinations they choose to sell.

I expect there also to be significant fallout among travel wholesalers (package and tour operators). The credit card companies consider all tour operators and even cruise lines high risk because they collect money first and deliver their product months later. That leaves the credit card companies highly exposed during that period of time. The liquidation of Renaissance Cruises and Kingdom Tours cost the credit card companies millions of dollars. Those companies that do not have very strong balance sheets will be sorely pressed to keep their credit card merchant agreements. Without these agreements, it is almost impossible to survive as a tour operator. Also, as I have said previously, tour and package operators are under increasing pressure from larger and stronger agency groups to increase their commissions and marketing support. They are under increasing pressure from the hotels and airlines who want to reduce the wholesalers' margins, especially on their best consumer offerings. So, unless you have a strong consumer brand position, supported by significant financial and technology resources, you are very vulnerable.

The consumer, as has been noted many times before, is more demanding, more knowledgeable and less trusting than ever. If the travel agent gains the consumers' trust by knowing them better than any travel wholesaler or cruise line can, and by always offering superior service and superior products, they will survive and thrive. The travel wholesaler has not only to deliver a vacation whose price is better than a consumer can normally obtain for themselves; they also have to earn both the agents' and consumers' trust by always delivering what was paid for and more and by delivering the total vacation experience from the time the consumer leaves home until the time they return.

The vacations offered in the future will be more personal, more flexible, and satisfy consumers' need to feel special, while enjoying an experience they feel was designed especially for them. This is more important than ever, now that the world that Americans feel they can safely visit is getting smaller and smaller. We are challenged to deliver safe, frequently visited destinations in uniquely different ways.

Survival of the fittest will be especially true in tomorrow's world of travel. All of us will have to be more fit than ever.

40

Travel Packaging in the Coming Decade

Steve Perillo
President and Owner
Perillo Tours

Steve Perillo is the president and owner of Perillo Tours, America's largest travel wholesaler to Italy. He was a lifelong apprentice to the legendary Mario Perillo, "Mr. Italy," and represents the third generation in the family business.

Mr. Perillo has expanded the company slowly and methodically through years of tremendous change in the travel business. Aside from their renowned Italy tours, Perillo also offers one of the finest Hawaii vacation programs on the market. Spain is the company's most recent product.

Perillo Tours is further distingushed as a bona fide "brand name" after 25 years of national broadcast advertising. Always pitched by a family member, the ads come with the important proviso, "See Your Travel Agent."

Steve has developed one of the most extensive tour operator Internet booking sites. The ability to book live land inventory with live air reservations in five steps is one of the site's more notable features. Travel agents can also build customized Perillo brochures for printing and e-mailing to clients.

Mr. Perillo, a graduate of Boston University, is also a widely recognized composer of concert music.

Introduction

There's a good chance people wanted to visit the moon when they first realized it wasn't just a hole in the celestial canopy. And what a great business opportunity it would be! But why did it happen precisely in 1969 and not 1372 nor 2080? Because the technology was ready in 1969—and, the way NASA insiders tell it, just barely.

Well, moon tourism is no longer contemplated for the next decade. But the premise that travel entrepreneurs must wait for technological innovations in the broader society still applies. From the flying machine to the Internet, the travel industry is very much intertwined with advances in technology.

From Juan Trippe to Arthur Tauck, Sr., to Sir Freddie Laker, the great innovators have used technology for the same goals—to make travel cheaper, easier and more fulfilling for each individual traveler. So what innovations should we look for in the next ten years in travel packaging? First, we need to agree on our terms.

Definitions

To date, travel packages have been sold to the public directly by the "wholesale packager," or through an intermediary known as a "retail travel agent." Retail travel agents have traditionally received a 10 percent commission on each package sold. The wholesaler offers this commission because the travel agent does the job of pre-selling the product, while the wholesaler needs simply take the order. However, in the aftermath of the airlines' recent travel agent commission cuts from 10 percent to 0 percent, and the availability of wholesaler products directly on the Internet, travel agents have found themselves in a weakened position. This issue will be explored later.

Now, let's establish what a "travel package" is, and what it is not. It's not "independent travel," wherein consumers buy all aspects of their trip separately; nor is it "VFR Travel," an acronym for "visiting friends or relatives." These two styles of travel account for the vast majority of American vacations each year. Unfortunately, they are not of much interest to the travel packager, because there is little profit margin in arranging them. There is, however, a great interest in converting these travelers to package deals. We'll see how technology is gearing up to do just that.

For the purposes of this article, cruises, which are very much "all-inclusive packages," will not be considered. Cruises have a sufficiently varied history and evolution from air/land vacations that it is best to entrust that story to cruise specialists elsewhere in this book.

Currently, air/land travel packages come in four flavors. Because these terms have had overlapping connotations throughout the years, we'll establish the following definitions for this article:

1. Independent package—Usually just air, airport transfers and hotels.

2. Escorted tour—A guided trip, usually by motorcoach, covering several cities or countries, including sightseeing and some or all meals.

3. All-inclusive beach vacation—Packaged air, hotel, drinks, meals and activities.

4. FIT—An old acronym for "foreign international travel," which has come to describe a trip customized in varying degrees of detail by a travel expert, usually for a small group of family or friends.

A Brief History of Travel Packaging

The customized FIT was the most common type of travel arrangement all through history until the 1950s. This is when affordable jet travel replaced steamship travel. While the jet aircraft also enhanced the FIT experience, it brought us the first prepackaged escorted tours. However, these tours were limited by law to so-called "affinity groups," which consisted of established clubs, company trips, family reunions, etc. Nineteen-fifty is also significant for the birth of the first all-inclusive beach vacation—Club Méditerranée.

The next major change came in the early 1970s, when the U.S. Civil Aeronautics Board abandoned the above mentioned affinity group law and now allowed "inclusive tour charters," wherein an operator could charter an aircraft and offer an inclusive tour to go along with it. This was like striking gold for those lucky enough to be positioned to exploit it. Because the charter seats were so cheap, a tour operator could throw in a two-week tour with sightseeing and meals for the same price as a regularly scheduled airline seat! This was the birth of modern mass tourism. In the consumer's mind, any perceived regimentation of a group vacation was more than offset by the amazing travel value—especially to Europe.

The fully escorted tour has continued to thrive in the present day. However, by the 1990s, it was no longer feasible to charter an entire plane because of the surge of competitors into the field, the need to offer flight connections from smaller U.S. cities, and the growth of low-cost "bulk rate fares" now offered by the airlines to their larger customers. Airline charters do, however, still find a place in beach packages to the Caribbean, Mexico and Las Vegas during the winter months. In fact, all-inclusive beach vacations continue to flourish using the same model as the original Club Med.

Bare bones independent packages and fully escorted tours have always been uneasy bedfellows. Wholesalers and travel agents would tout the superiority of each style of travel—one promising freedom from regimentation and an initial low cost, while the other highlighted the security of fully escorted travel and knowing all costs up-front.

From a profit margin point of view, there is no doubt that escorted tours and all-inclusive beach vacations are preferable for the wholesale operator and travel agent. They are able to add small markups to the many activities of a vacation—from sightseeing admissions to meal costs. The independent packager can only markup the air and hotels. Still, some travel packagers offer both independent and escorted trips in order to broaden their appeal.

All the while, the FIT trip never really died. But it has remained painstaking work and the time/profit ratio has never made it a particularly lucrative business. But we will soon see how the next ten years of increasingly intelligent computer systems might revive the FIT as real money-making option for travel packagers.

Demographics

Tour operators and travel packagers view America's population trends as the brightest factor in their future. The fabled Baby Boomers (born between 1945 and 1964) are expected to be the largest and wealthiest generation of retirees in history. When you consider that seniors have traditionally preferred packages and tours, one can understand the jubilant prognosis for the industry.

At the same time, Baby Boomers are the most sophisticated market the travel industry has encountered. While the World War II and Korean War generations were certainly discerning customers, Boomers have traveled all their lives and can quickly assess the merits of a travel offer. Given their lifelong travel experience, simple air/hotel packages should continue to sell very well.

But what about the highly profitable escorted tours? Many wonder if the Boomers are too sophisticated for all-inclusive escorted tours. Indeed, will Boomers be willing to "line up for the bus" as their parents did? The answer is "yes," with certain modifications.

With age, people become more vulnerable to the stresses of travel. After all, the word travel comes from "travail," which can often describe even the best-planned trips. So, if you ask a 30-year-old man if he'd enjoy traveling around Europe with a busload of strangers, he'll usually say, "No way, I can get around on my own!" Ask the same fellow 30 years later, when the feet are less willing to run after trains, and the eyes are weary of deciphering foreign road maps and, indeed, by the age of 60, that bus is starting to sound as necessary as it is comforting!

Still, the escorted tour formula must address the specific preferences of the Baby Boomers versus their parents. These preferences include smaller group sizes, more independent time, opportunities to mix with local people, more in-depth sightseeing, and unique experiences such as regional cooking and exploration of the back roads away from the main tourist thoroughfares.

The Baby Boom, now more properly called the "Senior Boom," is certainly a welcome trend for travel packagers of every kind.

Trends

Shorter Vacations: While European workers get four to six weeks off a year, Americans average two to three weeks. But with low-cost airfares, Americans are cleverly combining a few paid vacation days with weekends to get half a dozen mini-vacations each year.

An independent package, including air, hotel and activity vouchers, is perfect for these short vacations. There is tremendous opportunity for creative packaging and unique destinations in the years ahead. And, when you add the power of the Internet to handle everything from advertising to printing airline boarding passes, it's easy to get excited by the possibilities.

The long weekend concept is even being applied to London, Paris, Rome and beyond, particularly in the off-season (from November through March). While these packages have just a tiny profit margin, a smart travel packager will recommend air and hotel upgrades, additional nights and excursions, as well as travel insurance—all to enhance the bottom line.

Spur-of-the-Moment Trips: Deciding on Tuesday to go to Las Vegas on Friday has a universal appeal, not only for consumers, but for airlines and hotels. But there was no practical way to make it work. Until, that is, a standard communication device used by the airlines, hotels, tour companies, travel agents and consumers was invented. Again, the Internet is radically changing the face of travel.

Last-minute travel sites grew up right alongside the Web. It's a concept perfectly in tune with the technology—joining suppliers eager to sell last-minute unused inventory with consumers looking for exciting weekend plans. The operators who stand between these suppliers and consumers can only grow stronger as the technology improves and more participants sign on to the concept.

Special Interest Travel: Standard sightseeing and beach vacations are giving way to trips geared specifically to families, art lovers, nature enthusiasts, adult learning and much more. This trend is a result of the growing travel sophistication of the U.S. population.

After one has seen the Eiffel Tower, the Colosseum and the Grand Canyon, there is a need to dig deeper into these familiar destinations. Cooking classes in Dijon and villa rentals in Tuscany, once activities for the *cognoscenti*, are now growing niche industries. "Family friendly" vacations also surface as a new trend from time to time. However, this concept fails when adults realize their vacation will be disturbed not only by their own children but by dozens of others! Of course, Disney packages, theme parks and some beach resorts are obvious exceptions.

While shopping and sightseeing are still cited as principal interests in travel, packagers are increasingly adding unique activities to differentiate their offerings in the marketplace and to address the new consumer interest in deeper learning experiences.

New Destinations: Asia is often cited as the "new Europe" of the 21st century. China, Japan, Malaysia and Indonesia are surely as rich in history, sights and activities as Europe. However, their development has been limited by the enormous travel time from America's populated East Coast and because most Americans remain of European descent. Still, these destinations are perfect for escorted tours; even sophisticated travelers are reluctant to take on Asia independently.

Meanwhile, the hugely populated West Coast is comfortably close to Asia and many residents are of Asian descent. The time for major tourism initiatives to Asia is at hand.

Information Technology

There is no doubt that our immediate future holds something relatively new in tourism—information—massive amounts of information, before, during and after traveling.

It was only as recently as 1975 when travelers bought their European vacation from a black-and-white flyer. Once-in-a-lifetime trips were purchased with information limited to an itinerary, sightseeing highlights and hotel names.

With the Internet, today's traveler has a chance to see their aircraft's seating chart, check out a 360-degree view of their hotel room, enjoy videos of the important sights, read restaurant menus and review a detailed biography of their tour guide. While all of this is still cutting edge for the average travel packager, it will be standard "brochureware" by 2010.

As usual, the information explosion is a two-edged sword. Consumers who have ready access to your informational site have equal access to your competitor's. For that matter, they have direct access to your supplier's site as well. An educated consumer should not be a threat to travel companies with good products at fair prices. However, it does disturb the traditional sales hierarchy of supplier, packager, travel agent and consumer.

Who will sell travel packages?

Consumers can buy travel from three entities:

1. Travel agent

2. Travel packager/wholesaler

3. Direct from suppliers, i.e. airline, hotel, cruise line, railroad, etc.

This has always been the case and will probably continue to be the case for years to come. Note that the Internet does not sell travel as such; it is merely a way to communicate with the above travel entities.

Before the Internet, consumers could make phone calls or visit these entities in person. So it's clear why travel agents once had an advantage. Wholesalers and suppliers in distant cities could not service consumers in the way a travel agency on "Main Street" could. Suppliers understood this and readily gave travel agents a commission for their sales. The consumer paid the same rate, whether they booked with an agent or directly with the wholesalers and suppliers. In fact, travel agents often knew how to get lower rates.

But the Internet leveled the playing field by making supplier and wholesaler information available on consumer computer screens. Airlines were the first to seize this opportunity by putting their rates and schedules on the Internet. Intelligent routing and pricing software that was once accessible only to agents was simplified and made available to consumers. The airlines' success on the Web emboldened them to cut the travel agent commission—first from 10 percent to 5 percent, then to 0 percent. Agents were furious until they realized they had to sell air as part of their services or go out of business. In fact, many have gone out of business due to the loss of air commissions. Others are charging their clients a fee for booking air tickets. Either way, the Internet has not been good to travel agents—and it even gets worse.

The old airline reservation systems, Sabre and Worldspan, also had hotel and car rental inventory in their systems. So why not create self-service travel agencies by simplifying these systems for consumer use? That's exactly what occurred in the form of Travelocity and Expedia. With ever-increasing sophistication and ease of use, these travel sites have quickly become the largest "travel agencies" in the country. Although no one claims they are better than an experienced professional travel agent, they have further eroded the agents' customer base.

While the airlines and their reservation systems have eliminated pay to travel agents, hotel owners have yet to follow suit. While they, too, have vigorously embraced the Internet, they continue to pay agents an 8–10 percent commission. A consumer cannot be expected to visit the Web sites of each independent hotel in a distant city and book a room on that basis alone. The recommendation of a travel agent is still highly valued by consumers and hotel managers alike. Large worldwide hotel chains can, however, command many visitors to their Web sites and book thousands of rooms directly from the public. Of course, so do Travelocity, Expedia and electronic agencies.

Tour operators and travel packagers were the last to join the Internet fray. Fully escorted tours, with a set departure and return date and no options at all, were relatively easy to offer online. But travel packages with many options were just too complex for a novice consumer to assemble coherently on a Web site. That is changing rapidly. With artificial intelligence programs, elements such as air, transfers, hotels, rail tickets and car rentals can be assembled in a practical sequence. The experienced eye of a human tour packager is only required to quickly verify the practicality of the itinerary choices. This is an amazing development, as it brings us full circle to customized FIT vacations, which was once the labor-intensive job of the most experienced travel professionals.

What will become of storefront travel agents? There are two possibilities, which are already visible: 1) They will be bought up and consolidated into mega-agencies that have the clout to buy air seats and hotel rooms at wholesale prices, along with the money to advertise and compete on the Internet; and 2) They will become very knowledgeable specialists in cruises, vacation packages or a particular destination. A small specialist still stands a chance because real expertise will always be a rare and valuable commodity.

Therefore, of the 25,000 agencies at this time, perhaps 5,000 or fewer will remain in the next 10 years.

Conclusion

Of course, predicting the future is impossible. The future unfolds randomly and doesn't follow the patterns of the past. Even if we might confidently say that travel will get cheaper, easier and faster, unimaginable outside forces could change everything we ever knew about travel. Political unrest could ground the travel business for years. Global warming could flood cities and seriously alter the weather at our most revered destinations. Vast progress in computing power could make "virtual travel" far superior to the real thing—turning the travel business completely over to programmers.

Thankfully there are two things we *can* be somewhat certain of:

1. Humans have basic needs that will never change: Food, water, love, sex, warmth, camaraderie, a feeling of worth, and a curiosity about what's over the next hill.

2. Even if you can't predict the future, it's better to be ready for a few possible scenarios then just wait to see what happens!

Whether we use the most advanced 3D computers, or personally fine tune a trip on our client's front porch, somehow, travel packagers must cater to the basic human desires. Good food, a caring face at the airport, a comfortable hotel room, good friends, fascinating discoveries and yes, the prospect of re-igniting old romance or the excitement of finding a new one. The client doesn't care how you pull it off, but if a travel packager doesn't fulfill at least a good portion of the above, they will be quickly out of business. The sad truth is most travel packagers *do* go out of business.

Preparing for several possible future scenarios is prudent. Travel packagers should be prepared to work with and support travel agents, but also be ready for the demise of agents by promoting their brand to the general public. Packagers should have a strong Internet booking site, but also an excellent telephone staff for those who will always prefer human contact. Travel packagers should have a specialization, but also a hand in other destinations and styles of travel in case their specialty becomes unmarketable in the future.

Finally, the future is never as radically different as we predict, and hard work will always and forever be the number one ingredient to success.

41

The Future of Vacation Package Distribution and Marketing

Michelle Kassner, President
GOGO Worldwide Vacations

Michelle Kassner earned her bachelor's degree from Hamilton College in 1979 and began her career in the finance department of Sotheby's. Michelle then turned to her lifelong interest in gardening, working as a garden designer for a New York City landscaping firm.

In 1988, the family business—GOGO Worldwide Vacations—turned her attention to the landscape of leisure travel. Co-founded by her father, Fred Kassner, in 1952, GOGO Worldwide Vacations had grown into the largest privately owned tour operator in the country. Michelle learned the business from the ground up, and served as director of European marketing and senior vice president of marketing.

As president of the company, Michelle has maintained the firm's prestigious reputation and become a leader in the travel industry. She has served on the board of directors for the United States Tour Operators Association (USTOA), sits on several industry advisory panels, and is active on the board of the Travelers Conservation Fund (TCF).

Michelle lives in New York City with her husband and their young daughter.

Background

At $1.9 billion in sales, GOGO Worldwide Vacations is the leading wholesaler of vacation packages. Based on more than 52 years of experience, dependability and financial stability, GOGO satisfies over one million customers each year. Widely recognized as the pioneer of the wholesale mass-market packaged vacation, GOGO has evolved into a company known best for its extensive vacation product and its unmatched marketing ability.

As the preeminent distributor of leisure travel packages in the United States, GOGO offers the broadest selection of vacation packages, destinations and accommodations worldwide. The GOGO product line features over 200 destinations on five continents, encompassing more than 4,000 hotels and 50,000 allotted rooms nightly, in addition to airlines, ground operators, sightseeing and rental car companies.

GOGO is now celebrating its 52nd anniversary. Its combined retail, wholesale, outsource business, and electronic distribution network makes it one of the most successful marketing and distribution companies in the industry.

Introduction

In this chapter, we will cover the critical issues in marketing and distribution—the areas driving today's travel commerce—relevant to traditional and online vacation package companies alike. To help you navigate the future of vacation package sales and marketing over the next decade, we will explore four areas undergoing radical change in the vacation package arena:

1. How traveler demographics/psychographics and researching/purchasing behavior are changing the vacation package landscape;

2. Which product lines may evolve as a result of changing customer needs;

3. How the evolution of dynamic packaging—and direct distribution via Web sites—may be a key differentiator, providing a future competitive advantage to some major wholesalers;

4. How the distribution channels are rapidly changing, affecting how all packages are bought and sold.

The Changing Vacation Traveler

Today's vacation package travelers are better educated, earn more money and have traveled more than their predecessors, making them more sophisticated, demanding, even cynical, than previous customers. According to Forrester Research's April 2002 travel survey, 65 percent of package travelers regularly go online—meaning they have the ability to search out travel deals and bargains at will. More than half view themselves as avid leisure travelers, according to Forrester. That is not surprising, since they are better traveled than previous generations. But traveling isn't just about taking a trip: It's about finding enriching experiences. Vacations are shorter, so the demand to get as much value as possible is more critical than ever before.

While most—46 percent—vacation package travelers are married, 21 percent are still single, and the rest are separated or divorced. Family travel—regardless of the parent's marital status—is emerging as an important trend in vacation package travel, as is travel by singles. Destination trends have come and gone in the past 20 years, but the old mass-market standbys—the Caribbean, Florida, Las Vegas, Mexico, and California—still sell and will continue to sell. New hotspots, such as Punta Cana and Cuba, continue to emerge.

Not only do destinations emerge. So do new transportation trends. Concerns about personal safety, an uncertain political and economic climate, and a desire for more family travel, are increasing the demand for drive market vacations in U.S. markets. In the United States, 86 percent of travelers used their car for their entire trip in 2002, versus 81 percent in 2001.

One thing is certain. Vacation package marketers must know what is relevant to their customers. Whether mass marketers or niche players, vacation operators and travel agencies must constantly test the waters by developing new products. Then they must know who their most valued customers are through customer relationship management (CRM) technologies. Managing customers—talking to them, servicing them, delivering a memorable experience that will help maximize profits—is essential if tour operators are to succeed in travel's next period.

Stay current with the marketplace— Conduct ongoing customer research programs

We already know our customers. Why do this?

- To determine current attitudes and perceptions toward wholesale travel companies and their products, and contrast/trend them over time;

- Position the company to respond to needs before the competition does;

- Develop insights from which to develop or modify programs and services;

- Include questions that will draw out information regarding e-commerce, problems, questions, plans, future spending.

These seem like obvious good business practices. But it is amazing that many travel marketers do not effectively follow these precepts. Data mining is key— knowing the preferences of your customers and how you can effectively communicate your value proposition to these key customers. Marketers must make it possible to give customers what they really want, and get them to spend what their products are really worth.

Beyond discounting— How can you market value?

There is one marked difference in the makeup of today's vacation traveler, one that will likely continue into the next decade. Since the popularization of the Internet and the events of September 11, 2001, travelers have been conditioned to seek out vacation bargains. Beginning in 2001 and continuing to the present, travelers have been researching perceived "bargain sites" for the best package price. Wholesalers have been working with their suppliers to deliver the bargains that their customers want—but at a price.

According to Forrester Research, 73 percent of all U.S. leisure travelers will research their 2004 travel plans on the Internet—by 2007, that will exceed 83 percent. This critical mass of travelers, with unfettered access to a mushrooming volume of travel and destination information available on the Net, stymies industry managers combatting better-informed customers, and the devil that Forrester calls "Internet deflation." Face it: on the Web, there's no such thing as invisible pricing. Thus, it's increasingly easy for travelers to find ways to pay less to travel.

And, as the younger generation, used to doing everything from downloading music to researching term papers online, grows into the target market for packagers, they will gravitate even more towards the Internet—and to seeking out travel "deals."

All of this increases pressure placed on operating and profit margins. It's likely that we'll see a wholesale shakeout in the marketplace during the next three to five years. Attractive net rates will be granted to a precious few—those that can produce the customers, and have longstanding relationships with suppliers, will continue to receive favored rates. Those who don't provide value to suppliers—primarily though volume, margin, and reach—will simply disappear.

Consider innovation & new products

One way to counter the trend of package selection purely based on price is to lead the market whenever possible by innovating and offering new and better choices for customers.

By developing and implementing new travel services and products to meet the changing travel demand nationwide, wholesalers will ensure providing additional value as intermediaries. These may include:

Last-Minute Weekend Packages

A significant behavioral trend, which began in 2001, is the major shift in planning/buying curves. They are much shorter now. Americans are booking later and planning more weekend getaways.

American Express found in its annual summer travel survey that Americans are embracing short, weekend getaways. Sixty-three percent of survey respondents say they are planning a weekend getaway this year, and the average number of weekend trips will be four, up from three in 2001.

- Last-minute travel products are in high demand by online travel portals. Travelocity's acquisition of Site 59 speaks volumes.

- They are excellent for brick and mortar travel agents to offer in their stores.

- Weekend getaway products make an excellent introductory product for new distribution partners.

Providing value—How do tour operators provide value to customers and suppliers?

How then, do some intermediaries provide value to suppliers, as well as the changing package buyer? Where does value lie? Is it a balance of what consumers will pay to get the value? Is it just price, or something more than that? How do wholesalers add more value—or access—to a package, so that a product is sold on more than just price? And what is the state of the package industry—with its current leaders and newer entrants—in 2005 and beyond?

In the past, good product, a good customer base and basic marketing would ensure a wholesaler's survival both nationally and regionally. Going forward, however, packagers need to develop the most sophisticated technology to connect the buyer to the seller. As an aggregator of product, this connectivity is key. In the past, wholesale distribution relied solely on the retail travel agency channel. The future indicates that Web site distribution—perhaps as a direct "merchant model"—may take precedence.

In order for intermediaries to provide value, they must develop and market the best priced/valued package. They must offer the discerning customer one-stop shopping, and offer inventory on a real-time basis. In fact, the very essence of wholesaler survival in the years to come will be superior customer service.

Suppliers have always been competitors to wholesalers. However, a strong packager can offer all of the major brands.

Tackling the five distribution issues that keep you up at night

The priority for most vacation package companies is to reduce the high costs of distribution which, over the years, have escalated due to the various fees paid to third parties. Since e-distribution entails the lowest cost per unit sales, companies need to increase the proportion of their reservations booked online. However, most companies have not yet embraced the concept in a structured way—they don't have yield management integrated into their online systems.

1. The times, they are a changing . . .

With the appearance of new "merchant model" players on the block, such as Expedia and Travelocity, vacation package distribution will never be the same. They have had a profound effect on the entire vacation package business. For the first time, these aggregators of net supplier rates can dynamically package product, enabling the traveler to bypass retailers and wholesalers to buy directly online at a perceived price advantage.

Another distribution change is that, although suppliers have always been wholesalers' competitors, they can market online more intelligently than in the past. They can now control their pricing and yields in ways they never could before.

Third, hotels.com and Travelweb are great conduits for suppliers to move distressed merchandise, and therefore the consumer sees those distributors as offering enormous added value.

For these reasons, and many others, consumers are moving towards the Internet channel rather than to travel agents. As wholesalers who have traditionally distributed our product exclusively through travel agents, and the GDSs that connect to them, we must take a long hard look at alternative distribution, including the "merchant model."

GOGO will conduct at least 70 percent of its transactions electronically over the next four to five years, and then increase it from there. Today, electronic sales account for only 20 percent of our total volume. To that end, GOGO is investing more than 20 million dollars in new technology to further electronic distribution. And, GOGO will invest significantly in marketing and training programs that will shift agents off the phone and onto the Web.

Wholesalers' customers are travel agents. Going forward, will the customers continue to be travel agents? At this point, GOGO's intention is not to change its model as a traditional wholesaler distributing exclusively through travel agents. Looking forward to the next three to five years, that model may indeed be altered radically; the traveler may become the direct customer. That depends in large part on the retail travel agent's ability to survive. As travel agencies continue to shrink, going directly to the travelers may be a possibility.

Travel Agent survival is paramount if the wholesale model is to continue: If travel agents learn how to be proactive marketers and seven-day-a-week retailers, they will most likely survive. Agencies must then take an aggressive marketing position by targeting their client base through media placements, direct mail, and email marketing. They no longer have the luxury of sitting in their "store" and waiting for the customer to come in. They must provide value and expertise.

2. Make certain to have the right distribution relationships in place . . . and should you look for new and more productive ones?

Wholesalers need to partner with the big retailers and travel suppliers who have brand and web presence. Going forward, GOGO intends to expand its reach by partnering and developing product with airlines, hotels, large Internet portals, and with national retailers.

Travel suppliers, such as airlines, hotels and car rental companies, are finding that they are attracting lookers, but not necessarily bookers, on their sites. They are realizing that keeping bookers is difficult if they don't offer complete packages in conjunction with their own products.

There is a great opportunity to bring these suppliers into a wholesaler's network by offering them custom product priced for resale on their sites. The major groups of these suppliers are:

- Hotels

- Airlines

- Car rental companies

- Specialty suppliers (ski resorts, etc.)

- Large online retail agencies and consortia, including Carlson, American Express, GIANTS, etc.

Demand for Vacation Product

Major travel retailers with extensive distribution are finally realizing that having airfares are not enough. They need vacations. They need high margins for vacation package elements that bring high margins online.

Lifestyle, activity & other niche sites

There is significant potential for partnerships with a variety of "content-needy" commercial Web sites. Delivery of custom content to commercial sites represents a new market and new group of products for wholesalers.

These partnerships will be able to obtain a specific subset of wholesale content to be integrated with the niche Web site in a co-branded or private label arrangement.

Through these proposed partnerships, lifestyle sites will gain quality bookable content to enhance their Web site offerings, while building and retaining targeted traffic.

Further, they are designed to stimulate vacation commerce by augmenting existing site content with more descriptive information about purchasing vacation packages.

Branded, e-commerce sites

Significant e-commerce players could provide huge new distribution opportunities for wholesalers. The retail market (regardless of channels) is in a period of rapid technological advancement, where information technology strategies and capabilities drive the business. Travel is a familiar product for most of these "e-tailers," though many in this group do not now offer travel.

Companies that do NOT now offer travel but that have:

- Strong consumer brand recognition

- Significant marketing budgets

- Very high e-commerce revenues . . .

. . . can, as distribution partners, add very large increases in sales. The advantage for these companies is that, with wholesalers' technology, customer support and product, they can move into the travel space with relative ease and economy. The challenge is to move them into a new and unfamiliar space. To do this, they need to see the potential numbers.

3. How is distribution consolidation likely to impact business?

Currently, GOGO books the majority of its business through an aggregation of many small mom-and-pop agencies. Distribution through traditional travel agents is fine for now, but if the numbers significantly diminish, GOGO is prepared to shift its emphasis to channels, which produce the greatest return, at the most attractive margins. Over the next five years, the industry will experience even more shakeouts (ARC figures). However, it is difficult to get a true feel, since many agencies are rolling into others.

4. How can you reduce the cost of distribution?

It is essential that wholesalers migrate to the Web. Even though there is an initial cost associated with training and conditioning agents to book directly through a web site, doing so will quickly pay for itself. Dynamic packaging for agents is key—delivering real time packages within seconds—and necessary to ensure a wholesaler's survival. In addition to providing excellent customer service and ease of booking for agents, dynamic packaging through a wholesaler's Web site reduces the third-party costs associated with GDS fees, which are currently between seven to eight dollars on top of distribution costs.

5. Should you focus on maximizing direct reservations via your own Web site, or look for strategic alliances to drive leverage and efficiency in online reservations?

In addition to building a compelling site for agents to access directly, wholesalers should distribute product through as many e-commerce sources as possible. But, for large wholesalers, such as GOGO, the focus should be on maximizing direct reservations on our own Web site.

Visions of Tomorrow

The online landscape

We've already seen how today's climate for travel product suppliers is characterized by weak pricing and a stalled travel industry recovery, coupled with weak airline traffic and low hotel occupancy rates, versus a year ago. However, interactive travel sector companies are experiencing a unique dynamic—they still have the ability to grow. Given the counter-cyclical nature of online travel agencies, this climate has helped increase the supply of inventory.

The current climate

Online vacation package sales are still a small portion of total U.S. travel; packages are $8.5 billion out of $215.7 billion consumer (leisure plus business) travel revenues (airline tickets, lodging-sleeping accommodations, cruise sleeping accommodations, rental car base fees, vacation packages, Amtrak tickets).[1]

- $594 million in packages will be bought online, out of $20.4 billion leisure travel online this year (United States only).

- 1 in 10 each of Web bookers and lookers took a vacation package in past 12 months.

- Among bookers and lookers who are considering taking a vacation package, 44 percent of bookers and 19 percent of lookers plan to book one online within the next 12 months.

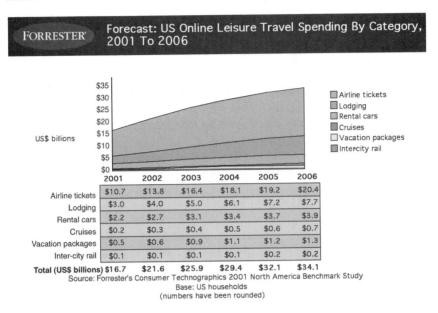

FORRESTER	Forecast: US Online Leisure Travel Spending By Category, 2001 To 2006					
	2001	**2002**	**2003**	**2004**	**2005**	**2006**
Airline tickets	$10.7	$13.8	$16.4	$18.1	$19.2	$20.4
Lodging	$3.0	$4.0	$5.0	$6.1	$7.2	$7.7
Rental cars	$2.2	$2.7	$3.1	$3.4	$3.7	$3.9
Cruises	$0.2	$0.3	$0.4	$0.5	$0.6	$0.7
Vacation packages	$0.5	$0.6	$0.9	$1.1	$1.2	$1.3
Inter-city rail	$0.1	$0.1	$0.1	$0.1	$0.2	$0.2
Total (US$ billions)	**$16.7**	**$21.6**	**$25.9**	**$29.4**	**$32.1**	**$34.1**

Source: Forrester's Consumer Technographics 2001 North America Benchmark Study
Base: US households
(numbers have been rounded)

Even those not buying online are still researching trips; although cruise and tour sales booked online will only account for $1.8 billion in 2007, Jupiter analysts expect investments in online marketing initiatives for those products will boost off-line bookings.[2]

Discount Buyers Aren't Who You Think They Are

A recent Forrester Research analysis shows that online discount buyers are actually the most attractive target markets. Forrester has found that they are wealthier than all other leisure travelers, take nearly twice as many leisure trips per year, and fly twice as often as others. This means that product designed for vacation package buyer must have price appeal as well as destination and travel appeal. And, this is where wholesalers can implement their years of experience in combining attractive consumer pricing with attractive margins, and may triumph over some of the newer online merchant-model entrants.

Online vacation package buyers are an attractive target

Forrester's Technographics 2000 Travel Online Study of more than 9,500 online households allows us to identify what distinguishes vacation-package bookers—online consumers who have purchased a package online in the past 12 months—from all online bookers.

They spend more on leisure travel

Vacation-package bookers spend an average of $3,554 on the 3.4 leisure trips they take each year. Their annual leisure travel spending is 40 percent higher than that of average online bookers. On a per trip basis, they spend 42 percent more than the average booker.

Package bookers are more self-sufficient than all bookers: 33 percent of package bookers do not like dealing with travel agents, compared with 25 percent of all bookers.

Twenty-three percent of online travelers have researched vacation packages on the Web—more than airline tickets, 21.3 percent, or lodging, 18.8 percent.

Forrester suggests that, rather than targeting the larger audience of travel lookers—consumers who have researched travel on the Web but have not purchased it online—savvy vacation-package marketers will target just package lookers for three important reasons:

- They are wealthier (spend 23 percent more a year on leisure travel)
- They're more interested in the product
- They're more comfortable with technology and shopping online.

Setting the stage for growth

GOGO is moving into the future with a keen sense of both history and changes. Our philosophy is to provide our valued customers with a complete travel experience, our partners and suppliers with new ways of marketing their products, and our employees with great career opportunities and long-term growth. Our strategy is to match our strengths with the right affiliates and partners to reach our future goals.

Building Systems for Tomorrow— New Technology Will Trump Legacy Systems

The travel industry was the birthplace of real-time, online travel distribution. Originating in the late 1960s through the 1970s, systems like American Airlines' SABRE and GOGO's SARS were on the forefront of cutting-edge technology. Powered by highly stable mainframes, they pioneered the way travel was sold and distributed. Due to continuous investments and the nature of the mainframe as a monolith, these powerful systems *still* fuel the operation of today's firms. Experts estimate some 70 percent of the world's data still resides on these "legacy systems." [3]

Not so surprisingly, in our Web world of the 21st century, a vast majority of travel bookings are transacted through these decades-old systems. Retrofitted or "extended" with handsome and functional Web "frontends" or interfaces, the data, rules and transactions ultimately occur on the legacy "backend." This is true for all the GDS and the systems that fuel leading edge e-commerce firms such Travelocity and Expedia (for air), as well as traditional dominant distributors like the Mark Travel Corporation and Liberty Travel/GOGO Worldwide Vacations.

Why should this matter? Simply put, these decades-old systems work. They are very reliable and they are very stable. One thing they are *not* is flexible and adaptable—which puts business relying on them at a disadvantage in today's rapid-fire environment. Additionally, their processing power is falling behind the innovations of today's technology. Compare a cluster of a dozen PCs to a mainframe—the cluster can often perform billions of fare searches more effectively than a multimillion dollar mainframe legacy system. One example of this particular technology application is Orbitz. The case of Orbitz reveals how a new entrant can usurp incumbent market leaders (Expedia and Travelocity) by leveraging superior, non-legacy technology. In simple terms, firms that utilize new technologies can also identify and attain a competitive advantage in travel distribution.

Wholesalers need to develop and implement dynamic packaging

Legacy technology works for today's needs—but the future of travel distribution has a new set of requirements. Dynamic packaging capabilities allow wholesalers to pull live inventory—real time—to create unique packages online. Companies like GOGO are a part of that future and will rely on this new technology for the following reasons:

1. Capture greater market share

2. Generate greater revenue at more attractive margins

3. Build on strong supplier relationships

Before e-commerce as we know it today, look-to-book ratios were on the order of one transaction for every eight searches. At that time, it made sense to deliver real-time, "down to the penny" live pricing and availability. Today, in our Web world, look-to-book ratios are on the order of approximately 49 to one[4]. This dramatic change therefore requires a reprioritization in delivery of rates and inventory, given the tradeoff between pinpoint pricing precision (due to pricing complexities) and speed and flexibility. Moreover, low conversion rates need not mandate this pinpoint precision any longer. Hence, the industry recognizes that today's applications need to emphasize rapid response time in searches, and revisions need to occur to traditional faring and searching architectures. Future systems therefore require a greater degree of *sophisticated* caching and other techniques leading to indicative pricing, so that online travel delivery is optimized for maximum speed and flexibility. As consumers drill down further into the booking process, the system can switch to real-time dynamic packaging. Most of today's legacy systems can't successfully enable these techniques.

Dynamic packaging, however, must be the norm for wholesalers' distribution through travel agents. Technology investments to speed up time for search results will be paramount in moving forward to educate and shift agent booking behavior.

Redefining the way travel is marketed and distributed, for tomorrow

While GOGO's current e-business offerings are among the best in the industry today, GOGO's mission with respect to its next-generation system is to *redefine the way travel is marketed and distributed, for tomorrow*. To do so, current technologies and applications, while functionally sound, are not able to deliver at the levels we require. While there are countless key features and objectives for this new system, there are several of note:

New "Backend" —

- *Utilization of a Web Services Model.* Web services are a best-of-both-worlds model. They enable information technology to centralize information and processing but distribute services remotely. Here we envision that, via a services model, we can provide distribution partners with booking and pricing interfaces (via services) that plug into their various pages. Essentially, each partner will then be able freely to integrate travel distribution solutions among strategically placed points on its site and have 100 percent control over them. Integration of a Web service can take as little as several minutes. For these and other reasons, Web services will be a core component of GOGO's future technology platform.

- *Scalability via Caching.* As sophisticated caching is an important part of travel distribution—particularly for wholesalers who also operate as merchants—in the future, it will enable independence from legacy systems, greater flexibility, better response time and ultimately far more scalability— letting millions of users view rates and inventory.

- *Ability to Direct Connect to Supplier Backend Systems.* Already in talks with airlines and already in development with a major worldwide hotel chain, GOGO believes direct connections to the computer systems of major supplier partners and distributors will be an important part of its new system. While GDS connections will also be utilized, they will not be solely relied upon. The new system architecture will effectively manage and account for multiple direct connections to suppliers' backend systems to enable efficient information exchange in large volumes.

Multichannel, Integral Customer Relationship Management (CRM)—

- A CRM solution for a multichannel distribution needs to be holistic in its approach. Relational profiles on all users, irrespective of channel, need to be accounted for and seamlessly integrated into the multi-channel distribution systems. In other words, distribution partners' customers, buying online, need to be seamlessly integrated into call center profiles. Moreover, they need to be integrated into external CRM systems, as well, such as each partner's internal systems.

Collaborative Filtering and Other Personalization—

- In our complex world, travel users often require recommendations and advice on travel choices. In the absence of an agent, we anticipate online customers will greatly benefit from both explicit and implicit personalization. When one visits amazon.com, personalization engines fire off those "we recommend" or "other customers who bought X also bought Y." If set up correctly, with the appropriate know-how embedded into the logic and rules that manage said recommendations, GOGO feels this will be a powerful online travel distribution tool. Lastly, GOGO's new platform, being a Web-based one, will seek to embed these engines and their statistical intelligence gathering throughout the enterprise's sales interfaces. The concept is that users will effectively benefit from the knowledge captured and incorporated into the personalization engine from thousands of professional travel agents making purchases on behalf of their customers, as well as from online consumers (via Libertytravel.com and other affiliate Web sites) throughout LIB/GO's vast distribution network.

CRM in multi-channel distribution

Many consumers will mostly research online, and will continue to book offline. Forrester Research calls this group "sideliners." Forrester's recent report indicates that, after researching, at least 35 percent of this group will contact some offline source (50/50 split between supplier or travel agency) to continue to investigate vacation prices.[5] LIB/GO has witnessed these phenomena where the Web has complemented offline, retail/store business. According to internal data, Liberty's *offline* retail stores and web call centers close approximately 10–15 times as many Web leads than Liberty online (its Web-based booking engine) closes.

Along these same lines, we have witnessed pure-play online retailers expanding into offline travel distribution and therefore identifying similar trends. Important examples include eTrade's move into traditional brick-and-mortar retail stores and Expedia's acquisition of traditional travel wholesalers so they can "slowly grow roots in the offline travel world."[6] Understanding this, Liberty Travel's re-launched Web site has deliberately exploited bricks-and-clicks strategies. The result has been a 350–400 percent increase in closure of offline business originating from the web. This is just the beginning of the continued optimization LIBGO expects to exploit in its online strategy. The table on the following page, of close ratios by channel, alludes to the potential synergies that can continue to be exploited by LIBGO and its potential partners.

Therefore, multichannel distribution is a key facet of online distribution, due to the complexities of travel offerings and the need for users to close online inquiries with offline sources. This being said, a key technology strategy to enable offline/online customer management is the deployment of a true multi-channel CRM system. These types of tools would effectively (1) create a seamless user experience across various media that consumers may access and (2) create a rich source of mineable data that identifies optimal marketing opportunities on the aggregate and individual level. Clearly, the effective management of customer relationships across channels is a key success factor for an online travel distribution strategy.

Web Site Only	Email	Phone/Web Call Center	Retail Store (Phone, Walk-In)
1–3% Close	4–7% Close	10–15% Close	30–+40% Close

Powering online travel

As the originator of the merchant model, GOGO's operations, scale economies and know-how produce best-of-breed products and solutions for our partners. The first "powered by" relationship was our supply of Caribbean product to American Airlines Vacations in 1982, a relationship that continues today. Today, GOGO powers five private-label enterprises and continues to provide content to Travelocity Vacations and other online retailers. An essential component of GOGO's growth strategy is to not only to supply product to its traditional agency partners but also to the new agency entrants: online travel agencies.

While the largest of the players attempt their own forays into the merchant model, the vast majority of distributors look to focus on their core competency and outsource this product development, merchandising and even e-distribution activities.

As the online world expands and more affinity opportunities grow, GOGO expects to capture a significant portion of this market and be the preeminent "powered by" solution in the industry.

Distribution Objectives

The goal is to strategically showcase travel product to appropriate audience members through a broad distribution of media. It's no secret that major players are carrying out this vision today, as seen with USA Network's acquisition of Expedia. The firm's stated interest is to develop a travel channel that provides "a toll-free line

[to] buy vacation packages."[7] We believe this is a truly viable opportunity in the future and GOGO is preparing for it in its technology development, today.

Vacation packages for the Web vs. retail agency

While airline tickets have exploded online, other categories of travel, such as packages and cruises, have not migrated online as quickly. Vacation package penetration has been slower than airline and hotel and will represent about five percent of the total online market by the end of 2004.

More complex travel

Travel packages have seen slower acceptance because they are:

- More complex, requiring more planning
- Packages cost more
- Vacation packages have very little online brand identification
- Travelers often need more advice, reassurance on their planning
- Current booking engines are more cumbersome and awkward in dealing with complex trip planning.

Travel buyers need reassurance that they have made the correct choice; after all, it's their vacation. In the offline world, this has been traditionally achieved through either the travel consultant or friends and family; there is no online equivalent to date.

What this means to wholesalers

It is even more important to offer online packages based on recognizable and trusted travel suppliers that the majority of consumers feel comfortable booking, allowing the Internet consumer to self-validate vacation choices and purchase vacations online rather than opting to book offline through a travel agent or call center.

This means that:

- We need to be selective about what packages are marketed online

- By managing the price and complexity factors of offerings, we increase the likelihood of online booking to completion.

Conclusions

Knowing your customer, giving superior and consistent customer service, developing appealing products, and remaining on the cutting edge of new distribution and marketing technology are all essential to maintain leadership in the increasingly cluttered landscape of leisure travel marketers.

There are several key things that all wholesalers must do if they are to profit in the years to come:

- Stay current with the marketplace by conducting ongoing customer research;

- Develop new product to meet the needs of the changing profiles of travelers;

- Make certain you have the right distribution relationships in place;

- Find ways to reduce the cost of distribution;

- Don't just develop packages based on price—provide unique value propositions;

- Invest heavily in building technology systems that will lead you into the future;

- Develop and implement dynamic packaging capabilities;

- Make sure you have the ability to direct connect to supplier backend systems;

- Invest in multi-channel, integral CRM systems; and

- Maintain and grow your relationships with suppliers to ensure better access to the most sought-after inventory

Those wholesalers who invest wisely in technology today—to enable better customer management and provide better access to competitively-priced, real-time inventory—will not only survive the changes in the leisure travel landscape, but will continue to thrive in the decades to come.

Notes

[1] Forrester Research

[2] Jupiter Research

[3] Information week, "Legacy Systems: Reinvest Or Restructure?" Garvey, Martin

[4] Per an unnamed senior technologist at a major GDS.

[5] Ibid.

[6] *New York Times,* 3/18/2002, "E-Commerce Report" Bob Tedeschi

[7] *New York Times,* 3/18/2002, "E-Commerce Report" Bob Tedeschi

Section VII

Travel Agent Marketing

Every sector of travel and tourism is grappling with changes in the distribution possibilities for its products and services. The last few years of the 20th century saw the airlines slowly and methodically disintermediate those traditional brick and mortar travel agencies that could not move market share, by first capping, then reducing, and then finally eliminating, the airline commission structure. (Make no mistake, however. Those agencies that provide significant volume and/or shift share continue to be well-compensated by the airlines in terms of back-end override commissions and other perks, such as free tickets, based on productivity.)

As a result of this disintermediation, roughly one-third of the ARC appointed agencies went out of business in the eight years since the process started in 1995. This trend will continue for years to come. The first casualties, of course, were the typically small, mom-and-pop agencies started by folks who love to travel and got into the business for the perks (familiarization trips, free tickets, reduced rate fares for hotels, cars, cruises, etc.). These agencies were slow to introduce fee-based pricing and did little to stimulate new business. Essentially they were order takers.

This group has its apologists, however. The American Society of Travel Agents (ASTA) argues that traditional travel agencies can survive and thrive if they morph in this changing environment into new enterprises that enhance their value to the consumer.

Travel marketing organizations (TMOs) like Vacation.com, suggest that they can provide critical technology, purchasing power and scale to assist the small, independent agency to grow and prosper. Their promise is to take financial resources from preferred suppliers and nominal annual dues from hundreds or thousands of agencies and create Web sites, accounting packages, marketing programs and volume purchasing plans of unusual benefit to a small agency.

But can the member agents collectively move market share? Especially when "preferred suppliers" frequently number in the hundreds? As suppliers themselves get larger, through either natural growth and/or acquisition, will they agree that the TMO does in fact provide a reasonable return for the incremental acquisition cost the TMO demands from the supplier? As suppliers look to constantly reevaluate and trim their cost structures, distribution costs, historically one of the highest costs a travel supplier incurs, will be under constant scrutiny and challenge.

On the other end of the agency continuum is the 800-pound gorilla, American Express. Clearly it has the scale and resources to keep pace with changing consumer needs. But they, too, have competitors, including burgeoning online, robust travel sites like Expedia, Orbitz and Travelocity. Not to mention the growing trend in the cruise and tour industries of direct distribution to the customer. American Express' avowed strategy of staying close to its (mainly affluent) customers and providing superior service is a recipe for success, but not without competition. As online agency sites grow and add more services, it's just a matter of time before they'll offer 24/7 concierge-level service to make a run for their share of the affluent customer market. Perhaps American Express will look to explore ways that their credit card can provide enhanced features for their retail agency customers?

The online agencies are now, and will continue to be, catalysts for change for many years to come. Initially focused on the travel commodities of airline seats, rental cars, and hotel rooms, these Internet sites are being continually enhanced to showcase cruises and tours through terrific product information, advantageous pricing, dynamic packaging, chatrooms, cruise and destinations reviews, side-by-side product comparisons, etc. The fact that all these consumer friendly features are available 24/7 at no cost or hassle to the consumer provides an enormous benefit to the customer. It's no wonder that online agencies are the fastest-growing segment of travel distribution. One of our prognosticators in this chapter suggests online sales will be responsible for about 50 percent of all cruise and tour sales by 2015! Heady stuff, indeed.

Unfortunately, from a supplier standpoint, online agencies' business is typically at lower yields and with higher acquisition costs than either the traditional agency or direct channels.

Initially used to move close-in, distressed inventory, especially during the so-called millennium trough (the first several months of the year 2000 showed an unexpected and pronounced dip in consumer demand across virtually all segments of travel and tourism), suppliers were amazed at how quickly and efficiently these sites could communicate travel bargains and drive sales. Like drug addicts on heroin, suppliers kept coming back to these online sites with lowball pricing to stimulate demand after September 11, 2001, Afghanistan, the Norwalk-like virus, Iraq, SARS and other influences that disrupted demand.

While their technological benefits are undisputed, make no mistake about it: online agencies have benefited enormously by preferential pricing provided by suppliers. Will this continue? Can, should or would suppliers establish price neutrality across all the distribution channels? Or have online agencies created an unstoppable momentum? Will their continued growth, stimulated by low preferential pricing, risk the commoditization of experiential products like cruises and package tours, with the consequent substantial loss of brand value for those suppliers?

And, finally, the last few years of the 20th century saw the initial forays of the cruise lines into direct distribution. Previously, this was considered agent bypass, a huge no-no for the cruise lines. Lead bravely by Carnival in 1996, direct initiatives have grown to an estimated 10 percent of industry sales by 2002. While Carnival faced the channel conflict issue head on, other lines didn't "come out of the closet" on this issue until years later. From Carnival's viewpoint, the strategy was not about disintermediation but rather, opening up a channel to the consumer that had been exploited for many years by the cruise industry's direct competition—land-based resorts and hotels. The enormous increases in capacity the industry had contracted for in the 1998–2002 period, coupled with the significant retrenchment of traditional agencies, made the direct channel strategy even more compelling. The 70–80 percent direct distribution of hotel rooms is the result of presenting well-known commodity products. A textural, experimental product like cruising lends itself to value interpreters such as traditional and home-based agencies, as well as online agencies supported by knowledgeable call-center employees. How far will this direct channel extend by 2015? One pundit in this section suggests 40 percent or so . . . we suspect that 20–30 percent is a reasonable range, depending on the individual cruise line's degree of commitment to the channel and ability to manage and grow an effective in-house sales force.

Finally, what's fascinating about this section are the widely divergent points of view. No wonder marketing is such an interesting subject! Cut through to the fundamentals, however, and you can draw prudent conclusions on what's likely to occur, versus what is more likely to be wishful thinking!

42

Travel Agents as Travel Influencers

William A. Maloney, CTC
Executive Vice President and CEO
The American Society
of Travel Agents (ASTA)

William A. Maloney, CTC, a 30-year veteran of the travel industry, was named ASTA's executive vice-president and CEO in March 1999.

Prior to joining ASTA, Maloney was the vice president, travel industry sales for the Hertz Corporation in Park Ridge, New Jersey, where he built and led the U.S. travel industry sales force. He was responsible for the company's sales and marketing activities with travel agents, tour wholesalers, airlines, hotels, and cruise lines.

He also served as senior vice president, sales and marketing, for Allnet Communication Services of Birmingham, Michigan, where he was responsible for sales, marketing and customer service activities for the $400 million corporation.

He served as executive vice president and chief operating officer for Woodside Management Systems, Inc., of Boston, Massachusetts, from 1980 to 1985, where he converted the company from a nonprofit to a for-profit stock company and grew the company-owned franchise location from startup to $40 million. Maloney has also worked as vice president sales for Hughes AirWest of San Francisco, California, and worked for American Airlines. He was a 1st lieutenant in the U.S. Army.

Maloney has served on the board of the Travel Industry Association of America (TIA), the Institute of Certified Travel Agents (ICTA), the National Academy Foundation and the Association of Travel Marketing Executives.

He holds a BBA degree in finance from St. Bonventure University in Olean, New York, and is certified by ICTA as a certified travel counselor (CTC).

The mission of ASTA is to enhance the professionalism and profitability of members worldwide through effective representation in industry and government affairs, education and training, and by identifying and meeting the needs of the traveling public. The society is the world's largest and most influential travel trade association, with more than 20,000 members in 140 countries.

In the past, travel agents were paid by the airlines for issuing tickets. Travel agents had access to all the lowest fares at their fingertips and clients automatically went to their local travel agencies because the idea of doing it themselves was unimaginable. But now the landscape has changed dramatically. Airlines have eliminated commissions, car rentals have tinkered with their commission fee structures as well and today's traveler has a panoply of choices as to how he will make his travel arrangements. Still, there are plenty of consumers and suppliers who appreciate and value the role travel agents play, and they will be the ones to provide agents with their income. In turn, travel agents will have to prove their value in new and different ways.

While many agents have increased the fees they charge their clients to make up for lost revenue, others are looking at new and creative ways of doing business. Today, it's not stretching the truth to say that the biggest mistake many small business owners make in terms of marketing is not marketing. Either owners feel they do not have the resources for marketing or they do not realize its importance. With forces such as the Internet and online booking services, the traditional travel agency must market itself aggressively and consistently in order to survive in this ever-evolving business.

Decades of Change

As all travel professionals who have been in the business for a while know, since the advent of deregulation in 1978 until the fall of 2001, the market had been characterized not only by a huge expansion in the number of retail travel outlets, but by a rapid increase in the demand for travel. Regardless of whether deregulation was a good idea, the fact is, it is here and, by all accounts, here to stay. While deregulation certainly has brought with it its share of problems, it also meant the onset of dramatically lower airfares, which have afforded most Americans the ability to vacation virtually anywhere in the world.

Prior to deregulation, the average American thought of vacation as time at the beach or mountains or a once-in-a-lifetime trip to Europe. Now, thanks to the combination of airline expansion, a marked decrease in real-dollar pricing and the mass marketing of destinations (Europe and the Caribbean, for example), people think nothing of going to China for a week!

Over time, but most dramatically within the past 15 years, travel agents have lost their monopoly on information. With the advent of Internet travel sites, agents no longer were the only people who could access travel and flight information via their computers, nor were they the only outlets for travel documents. Today, for example, people can print their boarding passes from their home computers before leaving for the airport. The appropriate role of the travel agent, accordingly, has shifted from order-taker to travel retailer.

Just as the role of the travel agent has changed, so have the faces of American travelers. Today, they are just as likely to be older adults as they are to be young families and singles. Perhaps one of the most marked changes in the demographics of the American traveler is the increase in active older Americans. Mature adults today are not what they used to be. They're on the move and visiting more diverse locations.

It's no surprise, then, that today's older adults are the world's best travelers. They are more active and in better health than their predecessors, with considerably more disposable income and time on their hands than previous generations had. A 2001 survey conducted by AARP's *My Generation* found that its readers had taken almost 4.8 million international trips in the previous three years and had spent $5.6 billion on domestic vacations in the previous 12 months.

Today, there are more Americans who are 65 years old and older than there are Canadians of any age. Many of these Americans grew up as children of World War II—the offspring of the Depression generation. Combined, these powerful societal influences have led to an entire generation that, ultimately on behalf of their children, have managed to pass on substantial wealth. In fact, according to the Alliance for Aging Research, Americans 50 years and older control more than $7 trillion or 70 percent of the nation's total wealth. Many of their children—Baby Boomers, born between 1946 and 1964, who make up nearly a third of the total U.S. population—will one day inherit that wealth.

Unlike their parents, Boomers as a group never have denied themselves anything. For them, travel has been an entitlement, not a luxury. So, as empty nesters in their retirement years, they have it all—time, money and the inclination to travel.

The Business of Selling Travel

Suppliers who sell their wares only through travel agents are few and far between these days, as are those who only sell direct to consumers. More common are suppliers who use a variety of distribution methods to get their products before the public eye. To truly understand the nature of the business, one first must have a clear understanding of what a distributor is—that is, someone who takes a product or service and brings it to market either through wholesale or retail channels.

In the travel industry, there has always been a great deal of overlap in these two arenas. An airline, for example, sells its flights directly to consumers to eliminate distribution costs, but it also will sell its seats through wholesalers and retail travel outlets. Destinations tend to rely on a combination of tour operators and direct sales to reach consumers, while hotels tend to sell direct to the public. Increasingly, however, the Internet is accounting for a large portion of all direct sales. Cruise lines, meanwhile, historically have relied principally on retail travel outlets to reach consumers even though they, too, like the hotels, are increasingly selling direct via the Internet.

Retail travel sales today center on the market selection of either commercial or leisure travel or a mix thereof. A growing number of business agencies will sell their travel management services to corporations for a fee. Leisure retailers, meanwhile, predominantly sell pre-packaged vacations and FIT travel.

Current trends are such that simple travel transactions are rapidly heading toward self-booking on the Internet. Consumers now must decide which site will get their business. The question faced by many retailers is whether they should keep trying to be all things to all people and supplement their phone and walk-in business with an online presence, or become a specific market facilitator, specializing, say, in mature adult travel, Mediterranean cruises or sports travel.

No one can deny that the face of the travel industry is becoming more and more technology driven. In fact, consumers spent more than $13 billion buying travel online in 2001, and the figure is only expected to grow.

But that hardly forecasts doom for travel agents. The new travel marketplace merely requires new strategies. Technology is like a steamroller: travel agents who aren't on the steamroller are destined to become part of the road.

It stands to reason that if the public is turning to their computers, travel agents must turn to theirs, using the technology to their own maximum advantage. They must create their own Web sites, discover what Internet sites give them the best information (with which to better serve their clients), and they must send e-newsletters and personally tailored e-mail messages to their clients, matching their client's profiles.

Selling What to Whom

When it comes to marketing, retail travel agencies have two choices in their approach. Will they aim for a targeted market or will they opt for a broadly based, mass-market appeal?

The latter is by far the more difficult arena in which to succeed, because travel agencies are up against competitors that also have access to the lowest prices, the latest technology, 24/7 sales and service teams and the ability to allow customers to tailor their trips. Adding to the odds against succeeding in the mass-market world is the fact that suppliers who target a broad segment of the market don't need travel agents to the extent that their niche-market competitors do. They have products that sell themselves. Suppliers offering Spring Break or Super Bowl packages, for example, don't need a complex system to reach the market. Consumers know about the events, anticipate them on an annual basis, and book accordingly.

Suppliers who offer themed cruises or unique tours, on the other hand, rely on travel agents to spread the word about their products, be it through open-house events, special-offer e-mails or direct solicitations. The more narrow a supplier's focus, the more that supplier needs the distribution services such as travel agents provide. Suppliers also need travel agents if they offer particularly high-priced products or extremely unusual tours or services. These suppliers especially need travel agents to help them reach the right client. Travel agents know that the key to customer retention is matching the client to the right product and that benefits the supplier quite as much as the agent.

For these reasons, most agencies today are better off engaging in a targeted market approach, whereby they achieve a successful balance of suppliers who want them, on the one hand, and customers who need them, on the other.

As for customers today, the typical traveler who relies on the expertise of a travel agent is one that has a history of buying from providers—someone accustomed to using tax preparers, grocery delivery services and other amenities—and is willing to pay an additional premium for customer service. This traveler has a unique profile and, just as importantly, is not afraid to express his likes and dislikes.

Travel Agent: Facilitator or Influencer?

The greatest returns in the travel business go to those businesspeople who are influencers and not facilitators. Suppliers and customers alike will pay a premium for sellers who know their product, have the skill to make the match between product and person, and who will stand behind their recommendations. Thanks to the Internet, consumers these days have a wealth of data at their fingertips, be it on hiking trails in Oregon, the best place in Maui from which to watch the sunset, the top ten places in Madrid to eat paella or the best spas in Eastern Europe.

What consumers are looking for, though, is reliable, credible information. For example, are the spa services touted on a Web site really what the site claims they are? What restaurant in Madrid serves the best paella? This is where the travel agent's firsthand knowledge of a destination, as well as the agent's global connections, pay off. Agents must not only qualify a client or supplier, but must quantify them, too.

Travel agents must start with the basics—what are the clients' time constraints, if any? Are they flexible about when they travel and even where? What's their budget like? And, above all, ask prospective customers about previous trips they've taken, what they've liked about them and what they've disliked, and what they want to get from their upcoming vacation. Some people might be looking to unwind and get away from it all, while others might be looking to jump into a host of activities. The answers to these questions give the agent a framework from which to work.

It's crucial, especially in these times, that professional travel agents always charge for their services—be it trip planning and providing advice or canceling and rebooking tickets.

Travel agents should make it a habit to always provide their clients not only with a travel recommendation but a reason why that particular destination, location or vacation is the right one for their client.

And, don't forget, people are always looking for a little something extra—something to make them feel special and to justify their having paid a little more for a product or service. So, when you help someone plan that dream vacation or that quick business trip, throw in a little something for free, even if it's just some extra advice or a brochure on tipping overseas. Thanks to human nature, they'll feel that they got a better deal and you'll have a repeat customer.

Travel agents need to qualify suppliers with the same degree of care as they do their clients. Find out about suppliers' target markets; learn what differentiates their products from their competitors; and get a commitment from them that you and your clients can be happy with.

Getting to Know You

It wasn't all that long ago when it was enough to keep a Rolodex file on customers with only the minimum amount of vital information—name, address, phone number and maybe one or two personal items of interest. But with the advent of Global Distribution Systems (GDS) in the 1980s, travel agents had access to GDS-based Star files and profiles, which in turn gave them easy access to all types of customer information.

Today, running a business for profit means having an eye to the future. One of the best ways a travel agency owner can track his or her progress is not only through financial gains, but by the increased worth of the business as a growing concern. Especially during slow periods for travel, agents must go to their arsenal to stimulate business. One of the strongest weapons in that arsenal is a computerized database and knowing how to use it.

More than a simple list of clients, this business weapon is a meaningful database of clients' travel consumption histories, including their airline and hotel preferences, frequent flyer membership numbers, past destinations and any mention of places they would like to go, birthdays, and anything else of possible relevance. More and more, suppliers today are telling their sales forces that they shouldn't even think of entering into a co-op marketing agreement with an agency unless it has a database. Moreover, several leading consortia are conducting more marketing campaigns involving the use of their members' databases.

Databases are the key to improving an agency's profit performance, an important tool for survival and a passport to increased personal wealth. It is vital that agency owners and managers use this technology to develop, cherish and grow their unique and most precious asset—customer information—because when it comes time to make the sale, it all boils down to what kind of car does the client drive. Is it sporty and sleek and seats only two? Is it comfortable and spacious, with room for two car seats, several beach chairs and a load of groceries on top of it all?

A solid marketing strategy depends on first picking the group to which you will market your products, and from there, focus, focus, focus. In order to be successful, a travel agency owner must recognize that they cannot be all things to all people. In fact, they would be hard-pressed to be all things to any individual. Rather, every travel agent should be able to tell a client or supplier what separates his agency from the herd, be it in two minutes or on the back of a postcard. This "elevator speech" or "two-minute drill" needs to make a claim the agency can backup and one that clients can understand. A succinct mission statement will prove a useful tool, not only in attracting new clients but in reinforcing existing relationships. Agents must focus on what sets their agency apart and repeat it frequently.

It's important that travel agencies maintain strong relationships with their community, their clients and their supplier-partners. Solid relationships are based on having a deep understanding of the other party. One way for agents to get to know their clients is via a short survey that will provide the agent with a demographic snapshot of their clients' travel personality. From this, agencies can target clients' travel needs with vacation-offer coupons and individually tailored inducements. Even small gestures go a long way. Consider sending customers new luggage tags when they move, with their new address printed on one side and the agency information on the other. And, think about sending those tags to people who have recently joined the community—they're a quick and inexpensive means to alert them to your agency's existence and the services you provide.

Anything a travel agency can do to add value to the transaction is a plus. Today's travel agency must offer full-service planning—it's more important than ever that travel agents not simply provide documents, but that they carefully craft vacations. Agency owners and their employees must go the extra mile in learning about their clients' preferences, their habits and their desires. They must sell the total trip from airport pick-up to trip insurance to car rental to hotel. And then they need to fill in the gaps with such things as side excursions to museum openings, dinner reservations and theater tickets. Agencies should consider being more than trip planners—they're vacation experience planners, partnering, if necessary, with a pet-sitting service or a company that provides limo transfers to and from the airport, so that they have had a hand in their client's vacation experience from stem to stern.

In today's world, travel agents must exceed a client's expectations. They do that by making a commitment to quality control, growing revenue and listening to their customers' feedback. No longer can travel agencies aim to provide customer service alone—they must offer total customer service—because, in return, they want total customer satisfaction. A totally satisfied customer, as the saying goes, is a totally loyal customer.

It's a new business landscape out there. The old rules don't apply. Agents who are flexible enough to make the right choices about the resources they use, the services they provide, the products they promote and the clients they serve will be the agents who thrive as the industry continues to change. Travel agents' ability to transform themselves from document dispensers to dream makers will ensure their viability.

American economist Lester Thurow once said, "A competitive world has two possibilities for you. You can lose. Or, if you want to win, you can change." Changing to meet challenges is the key to success in the travel industry.

43

The Future—
It Ain't What
It Used to Be!

Joel M. Abels
Editor and Publisher
Travel Trade Publications, Inc.

Joel M. Abels is owner, editor and publisher of Travel Trade Publications, Inc. (TTP), which will celebrate its 75th anniversary in 2004. With his wife Lenore, he has edited and published TTP for more than 40 years.

Abels is a decorated U.S. Army infantry veteran and a cum laude graduate of the Wharton School of the University of Pennsylvania.

Together with his high school sweetheart, his wife Lenore, he has edited and published travel trade publications for over 40 years. He is best known for his hard-hitting weekly editorials on behalf of travel agents, covering subjects ranging from travel agent presence on the Internet to travel agency bypass and commissions, to the urgent travel industry need for a major consumer public relations campaign, as well as forceful lobbying and legislative action in Washington, D.C. They have earned him the publishing industry's Neal Award, "The Pulitzer Prize of the Business Press," as well as entry into the "Travel Industry Hall of Fame."

In addition to publishing Travel Trade's weekly newspaper and monthly Cruise Trade and Tour Trade magazine editions, Abels conducts three major travel industry conferences annually for travel agents and industry executives, in addition to the Annual Travel Trade Summit Conference for industry leaders.

A 45-year resident of Woods of Larchmont, New Rochelle, New York, Abels has been active in national political and local community affairs, and currently serves as an elder of the Larchmont Avenue Presbyterian Church.

With thanks to world-renowned wordsmith Yogi Berra for his insight in developing the title for this chapter, I would like to state from the onset that attempting to forecast the future role of the travel agent industry 10 years down the line, and the fate of today's travel agents, is about as possible as picking the right number in the next multimillion dollar lottery.

Be assured that, if I were given an analysis of U.S. and world economic factors over the next decade, foresight into the scientific and technological inventions that will emerge during this period, had the ability to foretell the final chapter of the global battle against terrorism and its impact on tourism, and could control the advertising, public relations and lobbying programs conducted by travel industry principals and travel agents alike, it would be a relatively simple task to accurately forecast the fate of the travel agent industry a decade from now.

Having none of the above-mentioned working credentials available in any manner, shape or form, I'd like to develop with you, our readers, an overview of where the travel agent industry is right now, and down which series of crooked paths it might be headed during the years ahead.

Many years ago, while an undergraduate at the Wharton School of the University of Pennsylvania, I developed an economic thesis which, in the opinion of my economics professor, Dr. J. Weldon Hoot, who later became director of the Wharton School's graduate division, represented a significant departure in economic thinking. My concept then, as it remains today, is that there is no such thing as the proverbial "long run" in economic terms, only a series of short runs.

In commonsense English, anyone attempting to predict an economic cycle longer than 12–18 months out is a tea leaf reader, and is neither an economist nor a realistic observer of industry trends.

The fact is that the world of travel, as well as the entire economic world, is changing at a constantly accelerating pace, and none of us can even dare to imagine what the next technological advances might be and how they might or will affect our tomorrow.

For example, who would have dared predict, just eight years ago, that then very profitable and very travel agent–friendly Delta Air Lines would decide to "cap" travel agent commissions, and make no bones about letting the travel agent industry know that travel agents were unnecessary to Delta's future? (They even announced it during Delta's famed "Travel Agent Appreciation Week.")

Yet here we are today, eight years after the fact. Once profitable Delta lost billions of dollars in 2002 and 2003. Comparable losses have been racked up by each of Delta's lemming-like competitors, who also first capped, then cut and eliminated, travel agent commissions.

Although airline losses have all been attributed primarily to the aftermath of the September 11 catastrophe, it remains a fact that the cruise and the tour segments of the travel industry have remained relatively profitable throughout this period. I think that is due in large part to their ongoing close working sales/ marketing relationship with the travel agent industry.

But, what about travel agents, what is their real role today and where are they heading during the next five to ten years? It's an open secret that the number of brick-and-mortar travel agencies has been sliced roughly in half during just the past three years—down from 33,000 travel agencies to some 17,000 at the time this chapter is being written. I predict that there will be only 3,000 to 5,000 brick and mortars three to five years from now.

Consumer travel writers/broadcasters, who would prefer that their readers/ listeners/viewers rely on their words of questionable wisdom, rather than the advice of travel agents, have been stating for years, louder and louder, that the days of the travel agent industry are all but over.

Nevertheless, I think that five to ten years from now, although the number of so-called brick and mortars may sink to well below the 5,000 mark, most of the growing number of cruises, tours and resort vacations will continue to be sold by the travel agent distribution system.

The big difference between travel agency sales five to ten years from now and those today is in the ways travel will be sold, the means by which it will be sold, and the types of travel agencies and of travel sellers of the future.

I believe that it is important to think and plan and dream completely "outside the box" when forecasting travel selling in the future. Anything and everything that we are doing today, and that we think will be the way of the future, will probably be in the travel sales/marketing ashcan in just five years. Skyrocketing changes in technology will continue to alter everything we think and do. After all, as I stated earlier, there is no such thing as a long run, and even the proverbial 12–18 month short runs are being shortened.

Travel Trade, which was the industry's first trade publication, established in 1929, has been published continuously throughout this period by the Lewis/Abels families. We will be publishing our 75th anniversary edition in 2004. Looking back at our 50th anniversary edition, which included a brilliant 50-year look ahead by the world's then-leading futurologist, Dr. Herman Kahn, chairman of the renowned Hudson Institute, I discovered that all of his major predictions proved incorrect within less than a decade after publication.

Why were Dr. Kahn's predictions wrong? Because they were all based on the two most popular concepts of the day—that (1) the speed of travel (as evidenced by the birth of the Concorde, now about to be deceased) would continue to accelerate. And that (2) consumers would have an increasing amount of leisure time during which to spend longer and more leisurely vacations. Well, we all know how that baby went out with the bath water.

The travel industry, like every other element of world society and world industry, is today being shaped by the fast-growing age of technology, which has swept over everything in today's society and economic development. The lightning-like changes in computer technology, and in every other form of technology, have made it all but impossible for anyone but the so-called "techies" to keep up with it all. And, yet, travel agents must keep up with technology and must utilize it to market and sell travel.

As far as I am concerned, any travel agent in business today who doesn't have a Web site with which to market and sell travel, and who doesn't use all of the newest technological advances to maintain his/her back-office record keeping, as well as sales, will be out of the travel agent industry by the end of 2004 at the latest.

It goes almost without saying that travel agents who want to be able to continue and to expand their profitable presence in the travel industry of tomorrow are going to specialize in cruises and tours and resort vacations and groups, of all sizes and sorts. Of course, there will always be some agents who will keep doing business the old-fashioned, unprofitable way. But they are the agents who are in business for the perks and the kicks, not to make a meaningful living.

Contrary to the opinion of many travel agents, travel agent doomsayers and suppliers foolish enough to believe, or even hope, that travel agents will soon become equivalent to cigar-store Indians—I believe that the best days of the travel agent industry lie ahead, not behind, us.

Because I feel so strongly that the best days of both the total travel industry and of the travel industry's travel agent sales distribution system lie ahead, I am convinced that a decade from now will see at least a quintupling or more of today's vacation travel market.

I don't have an equally robust prediction for the corporate travel market, since so many businesses have learned how to curtail and cutback on their business travel expenses. Also, most larger corporations will undoubtedly make far greater use of advanced videoconferencing techniques to further reduce convention and meeting, as well as air travel, expenses.

So, while business travel will undoubtedly continue to grow as the world of business expands throughout every corner of the globe, I think that technological advances throughout every element of the business community, coupled with expense considerations, will limit travel growth in this area.

However, I am confident that the vacation travel market in the year 2014 will be exploding in terms of U.S. vacation/pleasure travel, with Americans spending far more time and money vacationing on the seas, in every part of the United States, worldwide, and, yes, even in outer space. I don't doubt for an instant that ten years down the line Americans, and others will be taking rocket rides to space stations on the moon—maybe even to Mars.

What about so-called ordinary vacation travel—cruises and tours all over the world? I would be astounded if cruise and tour and resort vacation travel by Americans failed to at least quintuple over the decade, with more and more cruise ships being built, tour programs packaged and resort hotels being built to accommodate the American public's growing and insatiable demand for greater travel opportunities.

Surprisingly, perhaps, I see tourism growing more slowly within the 48 contiguous states than elsewhere in the world. This is because the United States has no viable promotion authority capable of promoting itself, either to our own citizens or to the citizens of the rest of the world. The Travel Industry Association of America (TIA) is, in my opinion, a moribund, stuffed-shirt organization controlled by hotel chains and other industry segments concerned primarily with the business travel/meetings/conventions markets, and is totally out of tune and out of step with the vibrant leisure travel industry.

And, with the overwhelming majority of state travel directors unaware of the value of packaged tours or how to promote them, and equally unaware of the value of the travel agent sales distribution system, there appears little likelihood that this situation will change significantly during the coming years.

But, how about that fast-growing leisure travel market and the role that U.S. travel agents might, could, should and surely will play in this huge travel growth arena?

The reason I am so confident that the travel agent sales distribution system throughout the United States will grow and thrive far into the foreseeable future is my firm belief that travel agents "do it" better than do-it-yourself travelers and cheaper than cruise lines and tour operators and resort hotels and, yes, even airlines, can do it for themselves.

As long as travel agents can market and sell both more effectively and at lower expense for travel principals (suppliers) than the travel principals themselves can market and sell directly to the public, there will always be a travel agent industry.

Nevertheless, this does not mean that travel agents can sit still and expect to be the beneficiaries of the tremendous increases in vacation travel products and services that will be pouring onto the market in coming years. Travel agents must continue to work harder and smarter, in an increasingly broad number of ways, if they hope to thrive, not merely survive, in the dynamically changing world of travel that lies ahead.

The next question that travel agents, principals, writers and observers continue to ask is whether there will still be a need for travel agents a couple of years down the line. They also wonder how many travel agents will be needed in the new workplace world of technology, and if cruise lines, tour operators and others, many of which have already begun to operate internal direct sales organizations, will remain dependent on travel agent sales in the foreseeable future.

The airline industry, led by Delta, proved me wrong seven years ago when I declared that the carriers would always sell their seats via travel agents, as long as travel agents could sell airline tickets cheaper and more effectively than the airlines could do it themselves. Now, let me go out on a very long limb and declare that I believe the carriers will eventually learn their lesson. Yes, I believe the airlines will come back to the travel agent industry and will develop some new means of compensating travel agents for the sale of airline tickets.

No, I'm not dreaming. I am trying to be practical and I am confident that the U.S. airline industry has learned that by cutting out travel agents, they have commoditized their product, resulting in bargain basement pricing over the Internet, thereby leaving nobody out there selling the true potential value of air transportation and of servicing the traveling public.

In my admittedly limited view of airline marketing, I see the airline industry as having destroyed its system of travel agent sellers in favor of inanimate Internet marketing, which reduces fares to their lowest levels.

The travel agent commission savings of 10 to 20 percent, which the airlines achieved, has been more than offset by airfare reductions of 40 percent and higher. It doesn't make sense to continue this airline/travel agent adversarial relationship and I'm betting that significant changes will be made. The airline industry needs someone out there marketing and selling their seats. Travelocity, Expedia, Orbitz and the like don't market air travel—they just sell seats at the lowest price possible.

As recently as two weeks ago, American Airlines—the carrier that travel agents, in a poll conducted by *Travel Trade* just a few years ago, voted "The airline agents dislike least"—told the Department of Transportation that travel agents were important to American. According to the testimony of American's spokesman at the DOT hearing, "It is important to take a moment to discuss the role of travel agents in airline distribution, particularly for a large network carrier like American. It is difficult to overstate how important travel agents are to American."

Yes, I do believe that the major air carriers will decide in coming years that it is better to remunerate travel agents for their sales/marketing efforts rather than to leave air seats up for low price grabs over the Internet.

The biggest question of all for travel agents, as well as for cruise lines and tour operators who are so dependent on agents for their sales and marketing, is whether enough travel agents will survive the current crunch to sell today's and tomorrow's rapidly increasing supply of berths, seats and beds.

The steep decline in brick-and-mortar travel agency locations from the 33,000 of three years ago to the 17,000 and still declining number that we have today, scares many cruise lines and tour operators. They are justifiably concerned that there may not be enough travel agents left to sell their products. I feel certain that the number of brick-and-mortar travel agency locations will continue to decline and will eventually bottom out to no more than 3,000.

Interestingly, in a survey conducted by *Travel Trade* just three years ago, when the industry stood at 33,000 brick-and-mortar locations, 89 percent of our agent responders declared that they still expected to be in the travel agency business three years from then—83 percent expected to still be in the business five years from then. Well, half of them are gone already, so it is obviously pretty difficult to predict one's own business demise.

As an aside, while 60.3 percent of these same agents stated that they had a Web site, on average they could trace only three percent of their sales to their Web site.

Of course, tremendous change has been occurring at a constantly increased tempo during the same past three years. There has been extraordinary growth in outside sales, in independent contractors, and in people working from their homes, either independently or through large host agencies.

In my opinion, this is where tomorrow's travel market lies for travel agents and for the rest of the travel industry, which so heavily depends on the travel agent sales distribution system. One important factor that I do not think will ever change, is the need for personal service and advice and information when buying a vacation package—be it a cruise or a tour or a stay at a resort property.

The public wants service. That is one big reason why the number of outside independent home-based agents is now estimated to be at the 200,000 level. And it is growing and will be well over the half million mark or higher before this decade is over.

Here is where today's vacation business is evolving and where it will continue to evolve at an increasing pace. To the surprise of the brick-and-mortar segment of the industry, it is already a fact that at least one-third of all cruise sales are being made today by home-based agents. That number is growing fast and will grow faster as these same agents start booking more tours, hotel rooms and even airline seats.

I assume that cruise lines and tour operators will still grow their direct business via their in-house sales teams, and that the travel agent market share might drop to two-thirds or perhaps less of total cruise/tour sales. However, the growth in overall berths and beds will be so huge that agents will still have double and triple the cruises and tours to sell tomorrow than are on the market today.

And, what do you think might happen to the co-ops and consortia and franchised travel agency groups that are so vital to the health and welfare of agents and suppliers both? Well, having supported their growth so vigorously in the pages of *Travel Trade* and at our nearly 100 trade shows over the past quarter century, I am not about to predict that they are going to disappear. But, they will surely change.

If I had to guesstimate as to their future, I would expect that parts of today's co-op movement will survive a decade from now by becoming giant host agencies, each with a vast network of home-based, independent agents; and so will many brick-and-mortars. And, if the likes of Expedia, Travelocity and Orbitz are still around, you can bet that the giant co-op-style host agencies will be driving them crazy, due to their ability to provide personalized travel agent services, above and beyond the Internet screen. While the Internet will be used extensively as a sales and marketing tool by every knowledgeable travel agent sales professional, the key to the travel agent industry's future will always be based on the agents' ability to provide personalized service and knowledge.

Whether or not ASTA, the travel agent industry's premier trade association, will survive the coming decade is surely another highly debatable subject. However, since I'm in the process of making predictions, I wouldn't want to overlook ASTA. So here goes! As I see it, ASTA cannot possibly survive in its present form and will go out of business within five years at most, unless it sheds its lawyers and its lawsuits and becomes strictly a lobbying and a public relations organization on behalf of both its active and its allied members.

Furthermore, if ASTA does survive the decade, it will almost surely have a paid, permanent president running the organization and its elected officers will be advisory only. Elected officials will not be running the show. The society is one of the last remaining major trade organizations to be run by elected officials—the change to a permanent paid CEO is inevitable.

By now, I have probably shaken up, disturbed and uprooted so many of the industry's "sacred cows" that you are asking yourself whether there will still be a trade press a decade from now and, if so, what shape it will take—or will everything take place over the Internet?

Well, while I wish that I knew, I don't have the answer to that one. At least not now. However, next year, when *Travel Trade*, the industry's first trade publication, celebrates our 75th anniversary, we will attempt to provide a realistic forecast of *Travel Trade*'s own future 10 long years from now.

Meanwhile, keep selling and marketing travel harder and smarter and faster than you ever have before!

44

The Travel Agency Landscape

Robert L. Darbelnet
President and CEO
American Automobile Association (AAA)

Robert L. Darbelnet is president and CEO of AAA, a not-for-profit federation of 79 motor clubs that serves almost 46 million members in the United States and Canada.

Darbelnet became AAA president and CEO on January 1, 1995, after serving 11 years as CEO of the Canadian Automobile Association (CAA)-Quebec and more than two decades after beginning his AAA career as an emergency roadside service driver for the Quebec Automobile Club.

Darbelnet is a member of the National Petroleum Council, chair of ITS America, and a board member of the Ontario Corp.

On the international front, Darbelnet serves as president of Alliance Internationale de Tourisme (AIT) and is deputy president of tourism for the Fédération Internationale de l'Automobile (FIA). As AIT president, he chairs the AIT management committee. He currently chairs the AIT/FIA world board, and is an elected member of the FIA Senate. He also serves on the executive board of the Federación Interamericana de Touring y Automóvil-Clubes (FITAC).

Darbelnet is a graduate of Sainte-Foy College in Quebec and earned a bachelor's degree in law from Laval University, Quebec.

Overview

The travel industry is undergoing tremendous structural change, driven by the application of technology and the growth of online distribution. The way travel is researched, bought and sold is changing, and a struggle for share of market between suppliers and travel agents and the evolving role of other intermediaries continues. Travel agencies must sell the value of their services and their expertise to support long-term relationships with customers and remain profitable.

The Current Travel Agency Landscape

This section discusses the ongoing channel shift taking place in the industry, the efforts by suppliers to take advantage of new technologies and changing consumer needs.

Channel shift

Forecasted rapid growth in Internet usage, continued improvements in the online travel shopping experience, and an increased willingness to book travel online are helping the rapid migration of travel bookings from offline to online channels.

    Overall, 64 million travelers used the Internet to make travel plans (researching and/or buying travel online) in 2002, and of these, 41 percent actually made travel reservations online, up 25 percent over 2001. Among those who bought travel online, 77 percent purchased airline tickets on the Internet, 57 percent made hotel reservations and 37 percent made rental car reservations[1]. PhoCusWright Research estimates that, by 2004, up to 17 percent of all air, 14 percent of all car rental and 12 percent of hotel bookings will be made online.[2] More complex products such as vacation packages and tours are less likely to be sold through direct channels.

Supplier direct efforts

Fueled by the need to cut costs, suppliers—predominantly airlines—are capitalizing on the increased use of the Internet as a direct conduit to consumers. The Internet provides consumers with more control over the selection of carrier, equipment and seat assignment, and a perception that better prices are available online.

Supplier online initiatives are taking two main forms:

- Proprietary Web sites: Suppliers' proprietary Web sites are their lowest cost distribution channel, given that most distribution fees, including travel agent commissions, are eliminated on travel booked through these supplier sites.

- Supplier Backed Portals: Travel portals developed by groups of suppliers are the industry's response to online travel agencies. Sites with discounted fares from participating suppliers provide additional competition to travel agents. The direct distribution of travel is having significant repercussions for travel agencies who are facing reduced commissions and revenue from other sources.

- Commission Cuts: The fragmented nature of the industry has prevented travel agencies from effectively blocking commission cuts, which have essentially cut their take to zero in the past few years. Smaller travel agencies remain the most vulnerable in the industry, losing share to both online entrants and other larger offline agencies, according to PhoCusWright.

- GDS Pressure: Global Distribution Service (GDS) providers receive a booking fee per transaction from the suppliers, which have been highly dependent on these intermediaries. The GDSs, in turn, have been paying the larger travel agencies incentives and rebates in order to attract their business. With the arrival of the Internet, and the rise of direct distribution, the pricing power of GDSs has been threatened. And, as the adverse impact on GDSs increases, this will, in turn, likely impact the incentives these companies pay to travel agencies, and may even entirely change the current compensation structure.

Vertical integration

The travel agency industry remains highly fragmented, with no single intermediary having the scale to control or influence industry actions. Large, well-capitalized players have now entered the market, aggressively growing by acquisitions and capitalizing on structural changes occurring in the travel distribution arena: the same companies that supply product or serve as intermediaries for agencies are now effectively competing directly with them for customers. Travel agents have expressed concerns that such vertical integration may lead to possible information biases on intermediary systems and may also negatively impact access to travel products for key markets.

Aging U.S. population

One of the major demographic trends affecting the travel industry is the aging of the U.S. population.

By 2020, American adults 55 years and older will account for 29 percent of the population (96 million), up from 21 percent (or 58.8 million).[3] In the same period, younger age groups will see less rapid growth.

This has implications for the amount and types of travel that will be popular in the years to come. For example, those 55 and over are more likely to take longer vacations, book cruises and play golf and less likely to visit theme parks or the beach. They are also more likely than those under 55 to have used a travel agent in the recent past.

Distribution

Research conducted by AAA in 2002 found that points of booking for travel products are now relatively evenly distributed between direct sources, online sources (agencies and supplier direct) and traditional travel agencies. However, the number of leisure travelers who say they have used a travel agent in the past 12 months continues to decline and, for the purpose of planning a leisure trip, the Internet is increasingly dominant.[4]

Consumers also report a decrease in the degree of confidence placed in the recommendations of a friend or family member (84 percent report being confi-

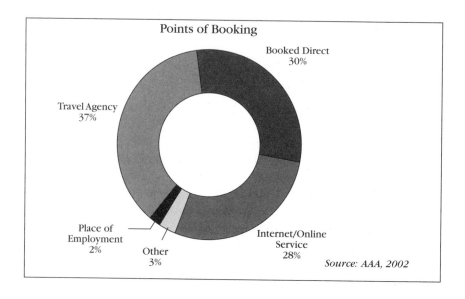

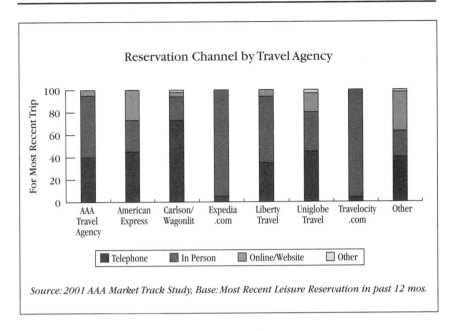

Source: 2001 AAA Market Track Study, Base: Most Recent Leisure Reservation in past 12 mos.

dent in 2002, down from 88 percent in 2001). Other sources for travel destination information with a high degree of confidence include travel guidebooks (55 percent of leisure travelers), travel agents (50 percent) and travel Web sites (46 percent). Advertising continues to be the least credible information source, with only 28 percent of leisure travelers reporting a high level of confidence, according to YP&B. In addition, research has shown that access through multiple channels is important, even for those agencies that provide service primarily through one medium. For example, even though the most recent reservation made at Expedia.com was through the Web site 95 percent of the time, just over 3 percent used the agency's call center.[5] The mix of corporate and leisure travel sold by the agency affects the channels used and multiple channels are important for brick-and-mortar agencies such as AAA, Liberty Travel and Uniglobe.

Drivers of Satisfaction for Travel Agency Usage: Research conducted by AAA focused on the reasons why travelers did not use a travel agency to book their most recent leisure trip.

Key reasons why travelers did not use a travel agency

- Trip was simple and did not require any travel agents
- I can get a better deal myself without using a travel agent

- I don't want to pay for travel agency services

- I wanted to deal directly with the travel provider such as an airline, tour or cruise line.

- I wanted to make my reservations directly through a travel provider.

Source: AAA/CAA Leisure Traveler Profile, November 2001, AAA Market Research

Satisfaction research confirms that the performance of the travel agent is the most important factor driving overall satisfaction with travel agency services (more than 90 percent of the variation in overall satisfaction with travel agency services can be attributed to the performance of the travel agent). Ease of service (4 percent) and trip experience (4 percent) also contribute to overall satisfaction.[6]

The research established the importance of individual attributes that must be addressed in order to maintain traveler satisfaction with the in-person agency experience. These are presented in rank order and pertain directly to the performance of the travel agent. However, relatively small differences in importance were found between the different attributes listed, emphasizing that all of these are critical for overall satisfaction with travel agency services.

Key attributes for maintaining satisfaction with travel agency services

- Providing objective information

- Making planning pleasant

- Ability to explain travel arrangements to you

- Making correct travel arrangements for the first time

- Understanding your needs/tailoring a package

- Interest in serving you

- Going out of the way to help

- Specific recommendations to improve trip

- Knowledge of all types of travel

- Courteous and professional manner

- Thoroughly check options for best price

- Service without distractions/interruptions

- Ability to utilize the travel booking system

- Providing different travel arrangement options for you to choose from

- Knowledge of services

- Courtesy follow-up after you booked your trip

- Ability to make recommendations based on their own travel experiences and feedback from other travelers

- Knowledge about requirements when traveling to a foreign country (passports, visas, immunizations, etc.)

- Help if plans change

Source: Travel Agency Services Satisfaction Study—Phase II, AAA Market Research, April 2002

The accessibility of the travel agent in case of problems during the trip is also a driver of satisfaction for those users who gave a satisfaction rating (members who are either concerned about potential problems during the trip or members who actually experienced such problems). This issue will likely become increasingly important, particularly at times of heightened security perils during travel; providing advice on security to clients is an effective way to add value to travel agent services.

Moving Ahead: Facing the Challenges

Moving forward, success in the travel agency industry will be about demonstrating the value that agents bring to travelers. This section focuses on travel agent training and development, supplier relationships and internal (organizational) efficiencies.

Agent training and development

The travel agent is the most important component of customer satisfaction with a travel agency and is the key point of delivering service, demonstrating value, and building trust in this channel. As such, agents are increasingly called upon to become travel consultants, counselors or specialists, not mere ticket agents.

The training, development and continued positioning of travel agents as experts and customer advocates will remain a key challenge for the industry. Providing opportunities for incentives, offering attractive compensation and offering training opportunities rank among the top most successful retention practices for travel agencies.

Recruitment

Sales ability, customer service skills and a positive attitude are key components of a good travel agent. In addition, the agent must be able to support the organization's values, with a commitment to provide service as opposed to least-cost options.

Employee referrals and word-of-mouth recommendations provide the most successful pools of travel agent candidates, according to research conducted by AAA. Highly experienced agents are also becoming available as the number of agencies continues to shrink due to market pressures.

Development

Particularly at a time when an increasing amount of travel research is being done by consumers, and the economics of the industry necessitates the charging of service fees, agents have to demonstrate specialized knowledge and excellent customer service skills. Agents are also expected to drive sales of preferred supplier products and to understand the balance-sheet impact of the product mix they sell. Training includes traditional instructor-led activities, on the job coaching, familiarization (fam) trips and, increasingly, self-guided learning through online tools.

Ongoing agent training is becoming even more important, not just on how to work with customers, but how to prospect for them and how to interface with the technology tools, which are constantly changing.

Rewards and Recognition

Effective reward and recognition programs, in conjunction with training, keep the agent labor pool stable. In addition to keeping costs under control, a stable employee pool is critical to building and enhancing customer trust in the agency.

Most successful compensation practices are those designed to reinforce desired behaviors and practices. Often, these link the pay of agents to performance, either in the form of a base salary plus incentives or pure commission, on an annualized basis (to reduce seasonality).

Successful recognition practices include a combination of monetary (gift cards, for example) and non-monetary incentives (plaques, awards dinners, or trips, for example). These usually work best when designed to meet specific agency goals, such as retention or driving sales towards profitable products.

Most agencies also weigh the incentives towards sales of preferred supplier or more profitable products. All other things being equal, preferred partner business that provides overrides (or incentives) and sales of higher commission products such as cruises and tours will likely be more profitable for the agency. While a commission based on all transactions booked during a period of time is the most easily available measure of an agent's productivity in almost every information system, the inherent and problematic assumption is that each dollar earned by the agent is equally profitable to the agency, regardless of service or product sold. For example, while individual sales of air tickets are loss leaders for the agency, such sales may lead to cross-selling opportunities with clients.

Successful agencies tend to reward agents for sales of higher profit margin products and services, focusing on broader agency goals, rather than simple gross sales.

Supplier relationships

Access to product, a key component of a successful travel agency, can be gained through a variety of methods, some of which are discussed below. These include preferred supplier agreements, merchant models for volume purchases, and participation in consortia to build leverage.

Preferred Supplier Agreements

Preferred supplier agreements give agencies the opportunity to acquire products geared to the agency's customer base, often with access to exclusive, branded benefits. The level of access and exclusivity offered by such agreements is often directly dependent on the amount of volume the agency is able to drive to each supplier. In 2002, 65 percent of U.S. travel agencies' revenue was derived from sales of preferred supplier products.[7]

Demonstrable scale—the ability to shift market share of a preferred supplier—remains a key point of leverage in negotiating preferred supplier agreements.

Consortia

To maintain or build leverage with preferred suppliers, agencies continue to affiliate into agency consortia: 59 percent of agencies reported in 2002 that they had such an affiliation, up from 54 percent in 1997.[8]

Moving away from pure revenue volume generation to commission leverage strategies, typical tactics employed by consortia today include strengthening relationships with preferred suppliers, enhancing communications between members, assisting with technology developments and exploring new business models.

Merchant Inventory

This model bypasses the GDS altogether and the agency contracts directly with the supplier for volume purchases and guaranteed availability of air tickets, rooms, or cruise berths (albeit without incentives or commissions). The agency then marks up the price for resale to its customers. The highest risk to this model is from suppliers themselves, who might then undercut such agency offers.

Merchant inventory has the potential for offering stable revenues to agencies, particularly in lodging and other product sectors with decentralized distribution. The ability to manage such inventory acquisition effectively will become an increasingly essential skill.

Vertical Integration

The benefits of vertical integration are highlighted by aggressive consolidation by some in the travel industry, and the resulting leverage they have built up in terms of access to distribution channels, access to products in niche markets and leverage with suppliers.

Vertical consolidation and strategic alliances will be driven by continued fragmentation in the industry, a need for scale, access to technology, exclusive products and customers.

Internal efficiencies

In addition to recruiting and managing the right agents and finding and partnering with the right industry players, managing internal assets is a key component of the agency's maintaining its financial well-being.

Product Mix

In the face of a zero-commission environment from airlines, travel agents need to refocus their efforts on products with the greatest potential for profit and growth. However, in the longer term, as the use of the Internet increases and technology improves, direct distribution of more complex products such as cruises and vacation packages will also increase. This will continue to negatively impact travel agencies who are not positioned to migrate with their customers to the Internet or indeed, to other new media.

Agents need to focus their efforts not only on selling the more complex products—such as cruises and vacations—but also understanding the loss-leader impact of commodity products such as airline tickets and promoting the value of the services they provide.

Recovery products: In research conducted by the AAA, 40 percent of respondents indicated that they would travel somewhat or a lot less in 2003, in the event of a war. This highlights the need for agencies to develop and promote travel products that address safety and security concerns.[9]

A growing number of travel agents are providing auxiliary products such as travel insurance and alerts in case of schedule changes. Particularly in times of uncertainty, recovery-based products help to allay fears that consumers may have in committing to travel.

Partner Programs: Customer loyalty can be enhanced by providing partner programs. Networks of retailers and suppliers are joining together to offer customers rewards and incentives that can be used across their various product lines and locations. AAA's Show Your Card and Save® program is one such program, with members gaining discounts through a wide array of partners.

Such programs offer customers more opportunities to leverage their participation, while allowing agencies to get more complete trend data and access to new prospects.

Multichannel Access

Research has shown that there is a need for multiple channels of access, even among those who have booked leisure travel online.[10] As expected, the principal point of purchasing airline tickets and booking car rental for online leisure travelers is on the supplier's Web site; for lodging, it is over the phone. However, 16 percent purchased air tickets by calling the airline's call center, and 26 percent did so for car rentals. PhoCusWright found that half of all online travelers who have researched travel online bought that travel product offline.

This emphasizes the need to allow customers to contact the agency when and how they wish to do so: either through the traditional storefront, a Web site, or a call center.

Technology

After cost savings, managing customer interaction is the major reason travel companies are leveraging the Web and related integration technologies. However, most travel companies are faced with divided operations supporting their online and offline customers. This continues to be an area with disputed ROI implications. Learning and retrieving preferences at the point of sale will continue to become a key tool for building loyalty and overcoming price sensitivity. This is particularly relevant on the Web, where it is much easier to simply switch to another travel Web site.

Technology tools have been able to cost effectively administer basic upselling tactics—such as querying a customer who is buying an airline ticket as to whether they may also need a hotel or rental car—and more complex tasks such as dynamically changing offerings to meet shifts in demand.

To counter the effect of lower fares being available directly to consumers from supplier and discounter Web sites, a host of new tools are being made available to agents and corporate booking managers. These tools seek to facilitate easy access to Web fares and reestablish agents as the lowest fare source.

Building on the need for multichannel access for customers, travel agencies need to integrate data collected through call centers, Web sites and agency operations to offer enhanced customer service, personalization and loyalty features.

Service Fees

Ninety-eight percent of travel agencies responding to a survey indicated that they charge fees as part of efforts to bridge the gap left by commission cuts from airlines and other suppliers.[11] Service fees, according to PhoCusWright, position the travel agent as a provider of professional services, an advocate of the buyer, rather than the supplier.

Building on the expertise developed by agents, service fees can be used to educate travel agents' customers of their usefulness. This includes highlighting value-added services on everything from room upgrades and seats on sold-out flights to handholding and trouble-shooting when a trip goes awry.

Brand

Consolidation, vertical integration and supplier direct efforts are increasingly impacting the travel agency business. In addition, unexpected players, beyond travel, are entering the online arena. The ease with which such organizations are able to affiliate with others that provide complementary services is rapidly eroding traditional agents' competitive advantage. In addition, intense price cutting on the Web is driving first-time travel buyers to online booking. However, PhoCusWright notes that brands, not just prices, will affect purchase loyalty over time. Those who buy a great deal of travel eventually become partial to a brand or set of brands and use branded sites.

In addition to conveying a specific image—trust, value, commitment to service, etc.—branded agencies can compete more effectively for employees, supplier relationships and incentives. Organizations such as AAA will continue to emphasize their value and capability for broad-based membership services by cross-promoting travel agency, travel content, automotive and financial services.

Notes

[1] Travel Industry Association of America, 2002 at www.tia.org. Used with permission.

[2] PhoCusWright Research at www.phocuswright.com. Used with permission.

[3] Travel Industry Association of America, 2002 at www.tia.org. Used with permission.

[4] 2003 National Leisure Travel Monitor, Yesawich, Pepperdine, Brown & Russell (YPB&R)/Yankelovich Partners. Base: those who have taken a leisure trip more than 75 miles from home requiring overnight accommodations in the last 12 months. Used with permission.

[5] Market Track Study, 2002 AAA.

[6] Market Track Study, 2002 AAA.

[7] Travel Weekly, 2002 at www.twcrossroads.com. Used with permission.

[8] Travel Weekly, 2002 at www.twcrossroads.com. Used with permission.

[9] Travel Intentions Study, 2002, AAA.

[10] Forrester Research, 2002 at www.Forrester.com. Used with permission.

[11] Travel Weekly, 2002 at www.twcrossroads.com. Used with permission.

45

The Travel Agent of the 21st Century Lives in Your Ear

Richard Barton
Founder and Former CEO
Expedia

Richard Barton is the founder and former CEO of Expedia, Inc., the leading online seller of travel in the world. Mr. Barton led the spinout of Expedia from Microsoft in 1999, selling a portion of the company to the public in an IPO. In 2003, Expedia was purchased by Barry Diller's InterActiveCorp (NASDAQ: IACI).

Mr. Barton retired from Expedia, Inc. in 2003, though he still advises the leadership of the company from his seat on the InterActiveCorp board of directors. He is also a director of Netflix, Inc. (NASDAQ: NFLX). Currently, he is living in Italy with his wife and three children.

To date, the increasing ubiquity of the personal computer, coupled with near-costless connectivity through the Internet, has enabled a rather sudden lurch forward in the way travel is planned and purchased by leisure and business travelers alike, driven by services like Expedia. This strong shift in behavior from offline travel planning to online will continue for decades, until, in my opinion, it is complete. There are broad implications for the marketing of travel assuming I am correct, but I am not going to dwell on these, as they are fairly well debated by now. Rather, I'd like us to try to think about how currently emerging technologies may significantly change and improve the travel experience itself in the decades to come. I believe a combination of wireless broadband, GPS or geo-location technology, and the relentless progression of Moore's Law, will enable a whole new kind of 21st century travel agent—not one that is human, but one that comprises super-smart, adaptive software that travelers carry with them, perhaps in their ears or directly in their brains, and which utilizes the wireless broadband network to constantly produce advice on how to make a trip better and, indeed, is available to answer any question that a traveler might have about a trip.

In 2001, my wife, Sarah, was pregnant with twins and she was instructed to remain horizontal all the time, be it in bed or on a couch. Sarah is a very active woman and did not take this news well. After catching her ten times sitting up at our computer sending e-mail and surfing the Web, I decided to attempt to "un-wire" the house by installing a wireless broadband "wi-fi" network, and getting her a laptop with a wi-fi card. This would enable her to lie on the couch with her wi-fi connected laptop on her laptop and do e-mail. After some tinkering, I got the network working and Sarah stayed on the couch, at least when I was around. What I couldn't predict, however, was how having wi-fi in the house would change our everyday lives. We now have two laptops in the house. These roam with us wherever we happen to be plopped down, in the kitchen, in the TV room, on the front porch, even in bed, though that's not a popular spot. We've found that the Internet has embedded itself much more deeply into our lives as an advisor, information resource, and communication device than ever before. I remember when personal computers first came out when I was in junior high school, and my mother asked me why they were useful. I told her that she could store her recipe file in there. She gave me a confused look and asked me why on earth she would ever want to do that. She was right, of course, until now. Sarah and I have found that we actually use our wi-fi laptop to get recipes off the Internet on demand. Did you forget how long to cook the turkey for Thanksgiving? How about making that gravy? Tired of Mom's old recipe? How would Martha Stewart do it? It's now all there, instantly, waiting for us to simply ask.

We've even incorporated the laptop into our meals. We had some friends and their kids over recently for Hanukkah candle lighting. Our friend, Dan, wanted to be able to tell the Hanukkah story to the kids and find the correct Hebrew prayers, but we didn't have any of the books at our house. So, we picked up the laptop, and, in about 20 seconds, with a little help from Google, we had everything we wanted, and Dan was standing up and reading the Hebrew prayer, holding the laptop like a prayer book.

Why am I telling you all of this, and why is it relevant to the travel agent of the 21st century? Well, I believe that in such stories lies what is to come for travelers. Assume for a moment that this wi-fi network that I have in my house is literally *everywhere*. Wherever I am, the network is available, too. Okay, now assume that I have a really powerful and really tiny PC with built-in wi-fi so that I am on the Internet all the time. Perhaps this PC is actually so tiny that it lives in my ear—literally. This is not so farfetched. I live in Florence, Italy right now, and I'm told that the penetration of mobile phones in Italy is 102 percent. Yes, greater than 100 percent (like those cruise ship occupancies), because there are many people that have multiple mobile phones. Leave it to the Italians to make the mobile phone a fashion accessory. I walk down the street in Florence and it's a little spooky because it looks like everyone is walking around talking to themselves. What they are really doing is talking on their mobile phones using hands-free devices. Some of them are "wireless" headsets, which means all that is visible is a little nub nestled in the user's ear that connects wirelessly to the base mobile phone that is in the user's pocket or purse. Well, it is not at all unreasonable that, in a few years, the computing power of a 2003-era PC will be built into just that little nub. It's also pretty easy to imagine that voice recognition and natural language processing software will have reached the point in this decade such that you can speak to your computer and ask it questions, much the way the folks on TV's "Star Trek" have done for years. So, if you can speak to your computer, and your computer can be the size of a small earpiece, and it is always connected via a broadband wireless network to the Internet, then you will be carrying around your "software" travel agent in your ear. Let's call her Speedi.

Not only will she be in your ear, ready to answer any question you might have, but Speedi will always know exactly where you are. This is due to a magical new technology called GPS (global positioning system), a satellite system for captains of planes and boats that tells them their exact latitude and longitude (it was originally developed for the military). Many of you have already come in contact with GPS systems embedded in some newer cars as "trip computers," allowing you to never really get too lost. You can see your "car" on the screen of the trip computer with a roadmap overlay, and, voila, you now know exactly where you are. How this works doesn't really matter; what matters is how this GPS technology might change our lives as it expands beyond being embedded in vehicles. Why not carry a GPS system around with you all the time? You'll never get lost. Why not embed a GPS chip in your child's wristwatch (or, more reliably, his Gameboy) and then you'll always know where he is? Why not put one in every mobile phone? How might that be useful?

Well, obviously, one great use for this technology will be to access our synthetic travel agent, Speedi, who you, a traveler, are now carrying around in a tiny, connected, voice-enabled computer in your ear. Now that Speedi knows exactly where you are, she can better advise you on where to go and what to do, in real time, based on exactly where you are at this moment. Let's close our eyes together and try to dream up a couple of potential future traveler scenarios for how Speedi might work for you.

Pretend for a moment that you, your husband, and your three kids are doing the Disneyworld vacation some time in the future. Speedi will serve as the family's tour guide and park advisor for the day, amongst other things. She will enable you and your family to never completely lose each other: *"Will is with Daddy in Tomorrowland on Space Mountain."* She will also be able to advise everyone on how long the waits are at various attractions: *"The wait for "Pirates of the Caribbean" is now 45 minutes . . . However, the Jungle Cruise is right around the corner and only has a 10-minute wait . . . Shall I guide you there?"* She'll be able to help everyone meet for lunch, by giving them turn-by-turn directions on how to get to the best spot: *"There's an air-conditioned restaurant where you can sit down at a table next to the Country Bear Jamboree . . . Shall I guide you there and let the others know? Well?"* Speedi will even be able to warn you about the weather: *"A thunderstorm is headed our way . . . Perhaps we should head out of the park early today to avoid getting everyone wet . . ."*) She also knows exactly where you parked the car this morning in the infinite parking lot, so that you don't have to wander around for an hour searching for it.

Speedi can also help you out on the business trip you are taking the following week to New York City. She knows where you are and what time it is, so, of course, she can remind you that it's time to head for that meeting midtown: *"Your meeting with Mr. Anderson is in 30 minutes . . .The weather outside is nice, so it might be a nice walk . . . Shall I guide you there and we can walk through Times Square and Rockefeller Center along the way?"* When it's time for lunch, you can ask Speedi if there is a great New York deli within walking distance: *"Yes, the Stage Deli is three blocks away and is known for the best corned beef sandwich in the world. Shall I guide you there?"* Following your afternoon sales meeting, Speedi knows that you have no evening plans and also knows that you're not flying back to Seattle until tomorrow: *"Would you like me to buy you a ticket to the Broadway show, 'The Producers'? There is a last-minute seat in the orchestra available for half price."* You had planned on getting some work done in your hotel room, but you've always wanted to see *The Producers*, so you say, *"What the heck, let's go see The Producers. Book it."* After seeing the show, Speedi might even wake you up early the next morning, because she notices that traffic out to JFK airport is particularly bad this morning, and she knows that the security lines are running slowly at the airport as well.

Speedi is an all-around helpful travel cybergal, who is simply part of the trip. She has access to all information that is available on the Internet (or what the Internet becomes) in real-time, and is at your service. Scenarios like Disneyworld and the New York City business trip ones above, abound. It might be fun to dream up a few for yourself or with your friends, coworkers, or classmates. How might Speedi be useful in Las Vegas for that bachelorette party you are planning? How about on the Mediterranean cruise you've been dreaming about? Would she be useful on the obligatory post-graduation backpack trip around Europe?

You may be skeptical as you read these scenarios and develop your own, noting all the hurdles to delivering a service like Speedi. How is Speedi going to know about the lines at Disneyworld or at JFK security? How is she going to buy a show ticket from Ticketmaster? How is she going to know about the Stage Deli? How is she actually going to understand what I'm saying and then speak back to me in a way I understand? Won't it be weird to have a computer in my ear?

Sure there are hurdles, but I've learned that when it comes to advancements in computer and telecommunications technologies, we tend to *under*estimate how rapidly advancements will take place. The World Wide Web did not even exist until 1994, and by 2002 the majority of travelers in the United States used it to help them plan their trips. In 1994, when the Expedia team first started building what was then known cleverly as "Microsoft Travel," personal computers could not do what the mainframes at Sabre could do. However, we had no doubt that advancements in PC hardware and software would enable us eventually to rewrite the complex searching and pricing algorithms from mainframes onto PCs, and we were highly confident that it could be done for a fraction of the price of a mainframe. We didn't have to invent the new chips and software that enabled this, we simply had to build our modern system and let Moore's Law catch up to us.

My intuition is that Moore's Law, GPS technology, and wi-fi wireless broadband, will drive an *acceleration* of the way technology will change and reshape the travel industry, making the immense changes we've seen in the way people plan and purchase travel seem *minor*. The changes we will see in the decades to come will completely remake how we actually conduct travel, not just how we plan it. Strap on your seatbelt low and tight around your waist . . .

46

A Perspective on the Evolving Online Travel Marketplace

Sam Gilliland
President and CEO
Travelocity

Sam Gilliland is executive vice president of Sabre Holdings, and president and chief executive officer of Travelocity, the most popular travel service on the Web.

Prior to being named CEO of Travelocity, Gilliland served on the board of directors at Travelocity and was executive vice president and chief marketing officer (CMO) of Sabre Holdings. As CMO, he was responsible for corporate strategy and for driving enterprise-wide alignment with the Sabre Holdings business strategy. That responsibility included authorizing and managing product investments.

Gilliland also has served as group president of the company's airline solutions business and senior vice president and general manager of product marketing, where he managed the company's global product and service portfolio for the travel industry. Gilliland spent more than three years as senior vice president and general manager of Sabre Business Travel Solutions, a business-to-business e-commerce unit. He also has held various leadership roles in sales and product development since joining Sabre in 1988.

Prior to his career at Sabre Holdings, Gilliland worked for Lockheed Missiles and Space in Austin, Texas, developing hardware and software for land and air-based defense systems.

Gilliland holds a master's degree in business administration from the University of Texas at Dallas and a bachelor's degree in electrical engineering from the University of Kansas.

Beyond the Internet Bubble—
The Electronic Marketplace

While a great deal of technology and business model innovation emerged from the go-go days of the Internet in the late 1990s and early into the new millennium, it was clear that much of that innovation came without the benefit of viable business models. By late 2000, the "irrational exuberance" of the late 1990s met head on with the sobering reality that businesses without viable business models simply cannot survive.

That reality led to the elimination of nearly 100,000 jobs created by the Internet revolution just several years prior.

But it also led those of us who survived the Internet implosion to balance our views of the world. The focus upon market share and revenue growth that fueled the Internet boom turned to one that certainly maintained those ambitions, but with a clear mandate toward profitability and sustainable business models.

And fortunately, online travel was and is a business model that works. Why is travel different from other online businesses? Quite simply, because it relies upon a foundation of e-commerce that had been created by the airlines and other travel suppliers almost 30 years ago. The airlines, through the systems they developed for travel agents, invested in the systems . . . the automation . . . to sell their products electronically. And while some wish to criticize the collective foresight of the airlines on a number of strategic issues, they clearly envisioned a more efficient marketplace of thousands of travel agents selling their products, whether through large travel brands, such as American Express, or through smaller mom-and-pop travel agencies on Main Street, USA.

Thus, riding upon technology originally developed by the airlines and then dramatically enhanced by spun-off technology companies, such as Sabre Holdings (NYSE: TSG) or Cendant (NYSE: CD), online travel agencies were able to quickly enhance travel agency technology to make it "friendly" enough for consumer use.

Consumers were hungry for that technology and information. During the Internet's short life, the online travel marketplace has grown from $400 million in 1996 to over $35 billion in 2002. Online travel agencies quickly grew to rival in size the largest traditional travel agencies in the world. Three online travel companies, none of which has been in operation for more than seven years, now rank among the top 10 largest travel agencies in the United States.

Incredible Innovation

During those seven years, incredible innovation occurred in online travel. The competition initially focused upon airline pricing and ticketing. Early adopters and then more mainstream consumers were immediately empowered by the ability to see all of the lowest fares and flight options for themselves. No longer were they dependent upon a call center agent on the other end of a phone to interpret and articulate their options. The consumer could now "see through" to the agent's desktop, shopping and buying a ticket from one of 400 airlines from a single online site.

In short order, car rentals, hotels, vacation packages, and cruises were added to the online travel mix. In a few short years, online sites evolved into "one-stop" shops for travel. Consumers no longer needed to either call or shop online with individual travel suppliers as they were now all in one place.

Online travel agencies quickly evolved into electronic marketplaces, linking suppliers (air, car, hotel, cruise, etc.) with buyers, offering great value to both sides of the supply-demand chain. They had become online retailers, creating additional value through the unique ability to market through these systems. Unlike traditional discount stores, where proprietors rarely know who is shopping in their stores until the point-of-purchase, online Web sites could tailor their offerings to the individual shopping experience . . . in real-time.

An example of this type of customer-specific shopping experience is the FareWatcher feature on Travelocity. FareWatcher monitors the prices on routes of interest to the individual shopper, providing e-mail alerts when great deals are available between, for example, Dallas and San Francisco. In addition, through the visual experience available online, cruise lines can display deck plans and photographs of the cabins on their ships. Not only that, consumers who had shopped for cruises during the past six months, as an example, might receive promotional e-mails when great cruise deals came available.

One-to-One Marketing?

No longer was online marketing about mass marketing. Thanks to the Internet, it was about marketing to the individual, or groups of individuals. While "one-to-one" was the marketing buzz phrase of the 1990s, it's not clear that anyone has ever truly achieved that nirvana—that ability to create a very specific, unique product tailored to the needs and tastes of an individual buyer. This one-to-one capability, even with the expansive set of tools available to Internet marketers, hasn't been fully realized. Some question whether it ever needs to be.

At Travelocity, we have implemented what we call "one-to-some" marketing. Sociologists have long known that people like to consider themselves a part of a group or community of people with similar backgrounds, tastes, and preferences. Amazon.com, the online retailer most known for reselling books and CDs, recognized this fact early on, offering book recommendations to the individual shopper that reflect the shopping preferences of a larger group of shoppers. It's an incredibly simple concept when you think about it. When I search for a book about Lyndon Johnson's presidency, Amazon lets me know that "Customers who bought this book also bought . . ." It's been an incredibly powerful concept with consumers who, regardless of their desire for individuality, really like to know that they are part of a larger community.

Travelocity has embraced this "one-to-some" concept. We may get to "one-to-one" some day, as we continue to invest in understanding the individual preferences of our customers. But rather than just focus upon individual preferences, we look for groups of people with similar demographics. And we find that our promotional campaigns, whether on our Web site, in our e-mails to members, or in our print advertisements, are much more effective when recognizing that larger set of tastes. If, for example, I'm an "educated working woman," I have a different set of travel preferences or destination preferences than an "affluent couple with children."

But it need not stop there; compelling e-mail campaigns can take advantage of individual-specific information. The most obvious is "cross selling" a hotel to a customer who has purchased an airline ticket to San Francisco, but has not purchased a hotel. In addition, when promoting a cruise out of Ft. Lauderdale, Florida, to customers who have either shopped or booked a cruise in the past, we might also choose to promote it to those within driving distance (based upon ZIP codes), of Ft. Lauderdale.

Are You Relevant?

These illustrations demonstrate the power of knowing your customers. Using that power allows us to deliver *relevant* offers . . . offers that matter to our customers. However, relevance and good marketing are not just about promotions, they are about delivering information of relevance in very uncertain times.

As the travel industry has struggled in the early years of this century with terrorism, war, a down economy and a lethal virus, Travelocity has provided comprehensive information to our customers. Examples have included posting "monitors" at the 25 largest airports around the country during the Thanksgiving holiday of 2002, as the Transportation Security Administration (TSA)—its people and systems—was first tested by throngs of travelers seeking to spend time with their families. Those monitors provided up-to-date information not only to our Web site, but also to 24-hour news organizations. We take a similar approach each day, as our "Eye-on-the-Sky" provides up-to-the-minute air traffic delay information on major 24-hour news channels and on our Web site.

This type of information provides assurance to customers that they *know* before they buy and that they *know* before and during travel.

Challenge or Opportunity?

But challenging world events and their impacts on the economy also lead us to seek out new products for our customers, based upon their changing attitudes or uncertainty about travel. The good news is that a large portion of our population will always have a need to travel. And Americans have increasingly viewed travel, particularly leisure travel, as an expression of their freedom. So the key to success in this environment—an environment I believe will prevail for many years—is again having a deep understanding of your customers and delivering relevant products.

That understanding led us to develop and enhance a category of products we call "Last-Minute Deals." This offering recognizes two new aspects of the current travel environment. First, travel suppliers (airlines and hotel companies in particular) have excess inventory left unsold very close to the day of departure. Second, consumers are now more likely to book closer to the date of departure given the uncertainty of the world around them. They still want and need to travel, but certainty in their minds is less about securing a reservation well in advance, and more about the comfort of knowing the environment around them is safe as they travel.

The Evolving Electronic Marketplace

"Last Minute Deals" are a good example of the requirement of online travel sites—and any retailing environment for that matter—to continue to evolve not only based upon consumer needs, but also supplier needs. The perfect electronic marketplace strikes that delicate balance between those two constituencies. A marketplace favoring consumers to the exclusion of suppliers alienates one side of the equation, just as a marketplace representing just the interest of suppliers quickly becomes irrelevant to consumers very quickly.

And while one would expect common sense to remind us every day that we must evolve with the times, it takes a concerted effort to understand how buyer and seller attitudes change, and how an electronic marketplace can best adapt to those changes.

47

The "Online" Phenomenon

Brad Gerstner
Co-CEO and President
National Leisure Group (NLG)

As co-CEO and president of National Leisure Group, Inc. (NLG), Brad Gerstner is responsible for the strategy and operations of one of the fastest-growing companies in the travel distribution industry. He joined NLG from General Catalyst, a Boston private equity firm that along with Softbank Capital Partners purchased NLG in May 2000. Over the three years since he joined NLG, Brad has helped position NLG as one of the leading sellers of trips, vacations, and cruises in the country.

Prior to joining General Catalyst, Mr. Gerstner served an appointment as deputy secretary of state for Indiana. In this capacity, he ran the department of state—a division of state government responsible for securities regulation, elections, and incorporations. Prior to this assignment, he practiced law at the firm Ice, Miller, Donadio & Ryan, where he worked in the mergers and acquisitions practice specialty of the firm.

Mr. Gerstner received his undergraduate degree from Wabash College and Oxford University. His subsequent academic degrees include a JD from the Indiana University School of Law and an MBA from Harvard Business School.

One could not talk about travel over the last couple of years without talking about the Internet. And for good reason. In a few short years, millions of people have shifted from using their local travel agent to purchasing their travel online. And if millions are buying, then tens of millions—or nearly 70 percent of all travel buyers—are shopping online.

But the real story is not about who is selling "online" versus who is selling "offline." Because, after all, even at the major online travel brands, more than 60 percent of the cruises they sell are over the phone—not over the computer. The real story is that the Internet awoke many very sophisticated investors to the fact that travel is one of the largest industries in the world and that travel distribution is a business with huge opportunity for change and improvement.

Wal-Mart, Staples, Kinkos and Home Depot all have something in common. They all had entrepreneurs and investors who realized that the distribution channels for general merchandise, office products, printing services and home improvement products, respectively, were highly fragmented and relatively inefficient—and that a better solution for buyers and sellers could exist. Capital investment attracted talented people who put together business plans that helped to revolutionize these massive industries. In fewer than 20 years, the once robust networks of local retailers who worked with regional wholesalers to ply the wares of powerful suppliers became virtually extinct—replaced by powerful intermediaries that have become the principal hubs of exchange for these goods and services.

So what does this mean for the future of travel marketing and distribution? What follows are my top five predictions of how the forces that reshaped these other industries are currently at work to reshape the world of travel. As all prognosticators know, predicting the future is a losing science (unless, of course, you get paid to be wrong, like my stock broker and our local weatherman), but making educated guesses based on other industry transformations may help us better understand how to shape and react to this changing environment.

Prediction #1—The Big Get Bigger

Conventional wisdom would have us believe that the "online" travel providers (a.k.a. Expedia, Orbitz, and Travelocity) only wanted to sell travel to the 10–20 percent of customers who today are willing to book their travel completely online (or those who will, over time, be willing to book online) and that they will leave the other customers for offline travel agents. Wrong. These companies want to be the Wal-Mart equivalent in the world of travel services, and the early indications are that they (or others like them) may just succeed.

But why will they succeed when others before them (AMEX, Liberty, Carlson) failed to build dominant national travel brands? The secret is in the business model.

Before Wal-Mart, few retailers had innovated enough to turn the low margin business of general merchandise retailing into a scaleable endeavor. In other words, a local retailer earned enough to get by—and maybe even enough to expand to a few stores—but not enough to build a national network of stores and to run the huge advertising campaigns needed to attract millions of customers. But Wal-Mart changed all that by investing in the "big box" store format and technology-enabled distribution mechanisms that dramatically changed the business. The big box led customers to spend more dollars per customer and satellite- enabled distribution centers radically reduced the cost of stocking the shelves. The result—Wal-Mart's operating margins became (and remain) the envy of the retailing world—allowing them to invest even more in expansion and technology to further reduce the cost of doing business.

A very similar phenomenon is playing itself out in travel. Except think of the Internet travel site as the "big box"—and booking engines as the highly mechanized distribution centers. Because the Web site is a 24-hour superstore, consumers are spending more per customer (not necessarily per visit) and often doing most of the work themselves. When they buy online—they eliminate much of the direct sales cost–which for many travel agents accounts for nearly 30 percent of their total cost. And even when the consumer picks up the phone—because they have pre-qualified themselves on the Web—they convert at nearly three times the industry average, accounting for another massive cost savings. Combine these savings with the increased margin that these retailers get by selling a more extensive line of products and services, and this new breed of travel agents is nearly three times as profitable per transaction as the best traditional agencies—and they often provide as many or more services to the customer.

So while Liberty Travel was able to do a little better than most traditional agencies (by doing their own packaging, having more access to capital, etc.) they never transformed the business model. They were marginally more profitable per transaction–not radically. And with a radically better business model, the online agencies can reinvest hundreds of millions of dollars on an annual basis back into growing their brands, growing the portfolio of services they offer, and building even more cost- saving technologies.

Michael Porter, the well-known professor of strategy at Harvard Business School, refers to this state as sustained competitive advantage. Arguably, pre-Internet, no agent had such advantage. But when someone alters the competitive landscape—as happened in each of the industries mentioned above–a tipping point is often reached where those firms that have the advantage quickly crowd out those firms characterized by the "Old World" economics.

And crowd out they will. As the graphs on the next page illustrate, my bet is that the major online brands will go from selling virtually no hotels, cruises, or vacation packages in 2000 to 25 percent, 33 percent, and nearly 50 percent in those respective markets by the year 2010! That is not their percentage of the "online" market, but rather their percentage of the total market—an amazing transformation by any measure.

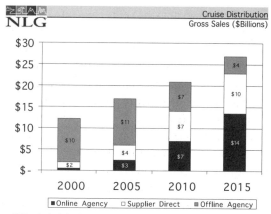

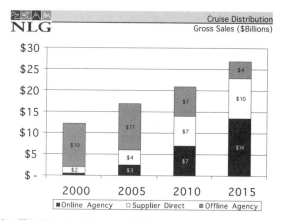

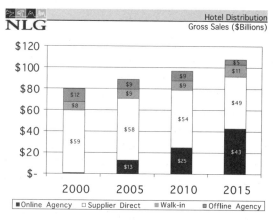

Is this forecast overly aggressive? Consider that in 2002, when the total consumption of travel remained flat, as compared to 2001, and nearly 5,000 retail travel agents went out of business, the leading online brands grew at over 50 percent. Moreover, consumers' unaided awareness for these brands, often considered a leading growth indicator for consumer marketing companies, reached above 60 percent—numbers beginning to approach the levels of awareness previously only achieved by the travel suppliers (Carnival, American Airlines, etc...).

And several forces seem to suggest that the pace of consolidation will continue to accelerate. First, consumers' fast adoption of broadband Internet access—giving them an "always on" characteristic similar to television—will lead to dramatically higher usage of the Internet, including online agencies. Second, online agencies looking for growth and experience, will continue to use their cash and stock to buy many of the traditional offline travel assets, from hotel consolidators to vacation wholesalers to large retail agencies. Third, struggling suppliers will continue to cut distribution compensation, making it ever more difficult for the marginal traditional agency to stay in business.

While it is still too early to predict the exact names and sizes of the firms that will emerge as the Wal-Marts of travel (particularly given the extensive merger and acquisition activity), there is little doubt that five years from now the competitive landscape will look much more like the other distribution industries that we have referenced, than the highly fragmented industry that travel still is today. Is this a good thing? Many people have mixed emotions because they are nostalgic for the good old days–but whether it's a good thing or not, it seems to be an evolutionary fact.

Prediction #2—The Channels Converge: Online, Phone, Retail

In the late 1990s, Expedia still described itself as an "Internet travel provider." Today it defines itself as the world's "fourth largest travel agency." While the move sounds subtle, it underscores a very important point. In the early days of the Internet, people often confused the online channel for the business model. However, the successful online brands quickly realized that customers don't live in channel silos. People often like the convenience of shopping online, but may want to buy over a phone or in a store. So while the Internet stimulated the unprecedented growth of a few powerful travel brands—those brands now recognize that the Internet is one (albeit the dominant and preferred) among several channels where they will interact with their customers.

This is not to understate the power of the Internet. Even in the first inning of its development, which has been characterized by rudimentary shopping engines and content, it has transformed the way that consumers shop for travel. Unlike the challenges associated with physical goods distribution, travel (and other information services like personal financial management) has proven to be a great fit for online commerce, precisely because it requires an accurate and efficient exchange of real-time information.

The next generation (which will last three to five years, versus the three to five months that early pundits predicted) will be about optimizing these basic functions and building seamless integration with the phone and retail outlets that will undoubtedly become part of the equation. The phone, untethered in its wireless form, has become nearly as pervasive and powerful as the Internet—and it's becoming increasingly difficult to tell where one ends and the other begins. And physical locations, once the antithesis of online commerce, will have a role to play, albeit one very different than their current role now, in attracting and retaining loyal customers.

No matter what the channel, each will be glued together by technology that understands and facilitates highly tailored personal interactions with a specific customer. It will be back to the future—with big brands attempting to replicate the best feature of the travel agencies that they have put out of business. Personalization—as it has come to be known—is not the abstract promise of over-engineered customer relationship management (CRM) software, but the very real possibility that, by analyzing customer data, brands can tailor marketing, promotions, product, and services to the specific need state of an individual.

This is already leading brands to rethink the business they are in—rather than thinking of themselves as ticket providers, they are broadly defining their business as "the whole trip." From the time the customer begins thinking about the trip, to the time they return home—and everything they do along the way–the new breed of travel agents will attempt to facilitate. Think of it as a massive shopping cart, where the agent will intelligently advise the customer what to buy—from an air ticket to VIP reservations at a hot new restaurant, from ski rentals to the after ski massage—the new travel brands will attempt to anticipate every need and deliver a service or product that satisfies the customer.

Prediction #3—Specialty Retailers Will Thrive

While the dominant trend may be consolidation around a handful of powerful travel brands, that does not mean that they will be the exclusive winners. Indeed, the irony of the Internet is that, while it has been the catalyst for the rise of big brands, it also serves as a democratizing force—helping consumers find alternatives that they might have never found.

However, to survive and thrive in a world of big brands with superior economics requires different strategies and capabilities than competing against another local travel agent. In the pre-Internet world, it was sufficient to advertise the lowest lead price and to hope that you won more than your fair share of clients. However, competing on price against a big brand with scale economics is a recipe for disaster, as most local merchants found out when Wal-Mart moved to town.

In order to effectively compete against a superstore, a differentiated consumer proposition will be needed—which, in the best case, will have natural barriers that make it difficult for the superstore to replicate. Examples of differentiation that have proved successful in other industries include focusing on product niches (e.g., pet foods, music, books, etc.) or on unique services (e.g., local hardware stores that assist with installation).

In travel we are beginning to see more and more specialty retailers—but most have arrived there out of necessity (selling cruise only because it pays higher commissions) rather than as a dedicated strategy. In order to truly build a defensible specialty, travel retailers will have to turn these default strategies into dedicated strategies and invest in building differentiation across every aspect of their business.

Some potential examples:

- Virtuoso—This retailer is attempting to build differentiation as a high-end service provider, offering substantially more personal attention than offered by traditional agencies or by the contemporary superstores. They have identified a market that is willing to pay for more attention; the challenge now is investing in technology and service capabilities that truly are more personal and satisfying than their superstore competitors (who are also setting up luxury and VIP product lines).

- Hotels.com—This mega retailer has built differentiation by dominating the category for hotel sales. While some debated whether a single category such as lodging could keep a customer coming back, particularly when they have to go to another travel provider to buy their air ticket, this retailer has proved that they will. Much like Petsmart outflanked Wal-Mart (at least for now) by dominating the category for pet food and supplies, Hotels.com has outflanked the superstores by being much deeper and relevant in the very important category of lodging.

- National Leisure Group—This retailer is looking to be the service provider of choice whenever a consumer is looking to go on a trip, vacation, or cruise. It is a technology leader in these areas and offers consumers a seamless experience, whether they are shopping online, in a store, or over the phone. It competes effectively with the superstores for customers by selling its vacations and cruises under some of the world's leading brands.

- At-home agents—Many travel agents are taking their expertise and joining loose affiliations of agents who sell out of their homes. Much as Avon succeeds in the face of stiff department store competition, this model will be successful if these decentralized networks can truly deliver on service and personalization. Selling in a different location will not be enough—but understanding the needs of a small community of consumers and then delivering against those needs has the potential to be a sustainable proposition.

While these examples are not an exhaustive list, they do give us a glimpse at specialty retailers who may thrive in the face of the online superstores. They each have something in common—they are building a differentiated value proposition for the consumer—and they are using technology to build efficiencies into their business. While the process of creative destruction will wreak havoc on the traditional players (as in the other industries that we have referenced), it will give rise to new rivals that will find opportunity in the consolidation. Their success over time will be determined by how well they can innovate to remain relevant and differentiated to the consumer.

Prediction #4—GDSs Wither / Suppliers Go Direct

Given the significant changes going on in distribution, how does this impact the traditional epicenters of power in travel—the global distribution systems (GDS) and the suppliers? Michael Porter offers a framework—known as the five forces—to better understand how these dynamics interact with one another.

According to Porter, every industry has five characteristics—supplier power, buyer power, substitutes, competition / rivalry, and barriers to entry—that help to explain how that industry is likely to evolve. In travel, the emergence of a few powerful intermediaries, replacing the vast network of local travel agents, is fundamentally altering this landscape—increasing buyer power, reducing rivalry, and increasing barriers to entry caused by brand and scale. This shift in the balance of power away from suppliers and toward the intermediaries will pose significant challenges for the GDSs and cause suppliers to focus more on their direct channel.

The GDSs (Sabre, Amadeus, Galileo, Worldspan) have been fixtures on the travel distribution landscape—extracting a toll from suppliers whenever their proprietary database of information was used to facilitate a sale of the supplier's product. Pre-Internet, they were the exclusive communication link between buyer and seller—giving travel agents access to rates and availability. As closed systems, they had significant pricing power, and for good reason–travel commerce would come to a halt without them.

However, the Internet, coupled with low-cost application protocols now allows suppliers and distributors to interact without a gatekeeper. This would not be practical in a world of 50,000 travel agents, but given the consolidation going on in the distribution channel, suppliers are increasingly able to access the vast majority of their demand by directly connecting via the Internet to a few key distributors. At the very minimum, this will destroy the pricing power of the GDSs. More importantly, it is shifting the power they once held in the channel to the distributors themselves—which is causing the GDSs to attempt to recast themselves as some sort of newfangled distributors.

But while the GDSs will gradually wither in the face of consolidation, suppliers are harnessing the power of technology and their brands to reassert control over their own distribution. While all suppliers (airlines, hotels, cruise lines) are not alike, they each view the consolidating distribution channel and potential for upward pressures on distribution costs to be reasons enough to invest serious money and energy in their direct sales efforts. How successful suppliers are at controlling their own distribution will depend on several factors, including their starting share, the specific category characteristics (e.g., high fragmentation drives consumers to aggregator brands), and how well they execute at the complicated migration to retail—particularly retail technology.

As the graphs show, notwithstanding the significant investments that hotel companies will make in supplier direct distribution, the supplier channel is likely to shrink in absolute terms—while for cruises, supplier direct will increase by over 500 percent by 2010. Why? One reason is simply that hotels are starting off with significantly higher share of the direct market today—nearly 75 percent. Alternatively, fewer than one in 10 cruises is distributed directly today. So while any moves by cruise companies will increase their share, they are still only likely to distribute approximately 33 percent of their product in 2010, while hotels, despite losing share to the major online brands, will still control more than half of their own sales. In the area of vacation packages, supplier share is likely to increase from approximately 30 percent direct in 2000 to nearly 40 percent in 2010. Not coincidentally, while the distribution make-up for the different product categories looked very different in 2000, by 2015 they will look very similar— with the majority of sales split roughly equally between suppliers and a few major travel brands.

The channel conflict issue (a huge deterrent to direct sales pre-Internet) is a lesser evil to suppliers today when compared to the cost and problems associated with overdependence on a few powerful intermediaries. So they are gearing up and investing in technology and content that will allow customers to transact with them both online and over the phone.

However, while supplier direct distribution will expand, the most successful suppliers will view their direct sales as complimentary to, rather than in competition with, the agency distribution channel. A consolidating distribution channel can have major benefits for suppliers. While more powerful distributors may extract deeper net rates or higher commissions, they also reduce the overall cost of distribution for suppliers by providing a huge single source of directly connected distribution. Working in cooperation, rather than competition, will allow them to use massive databases to predict and stimulate demand and better yield manage supply (e.g., similar to the working relationship between Wal-Mart and Procter and Gamble for products like Tide).

In addition, larger and more profitable distributors will continue to reinvest in innovations that will make it easier for consumers to plan travel. After all, unlike suppliers, intermediaries satisfy the consumer desire to shop across brands with unbiased displays and advice. And these distributors will also be much more able to leverage their marketing to educate consumers about all of the great travel opportunities available, growing the pie for everyone.

Prediction #5—Change Begets Change

Like most other industries, the pace of change in the travel industry has never been greater. From external shocks like the terrorism of September 11, 2001 to rapid waves of technical innovation, upheaval is everywhere. But creative destruction has a way of creating even more winners than losers. Undoubtedly, new entrepreneurs will prosper in this new environment and consumers are likely to reap the rewards of increases in productivity.

What's next on the horizon is anyone's guess. The changes that we have already predicted are seismic enough for now. But change will continue—there will be the next "big thing." Who would have ever guessed that a start-up travel agent like Expedia would be three times the size of Sabre in fewer than five years? Or that Southwest Airlines would be worth more than American, United, and Delta combined?

So, as we look ahead, think about what we can learn from looking at the other industries we have referenced. How will globalization impact the status quo? Will vertical integration continue—perhaps distributors buying suppliers (e.g., Expedia buying Disney) or suppliers buying distributors (e.g., Carnival buying Liberty). The possibilities are endless–making travel marketing in the 21st century ever more challenging and fun.

48

The Future of Internet Travel— Building Loyalty and Making Sites Relevant

Jeffrey G. Katz
Chairman, President and CEO
Orbitz

A 20-year veteran airline industry executive and expert in electronic reservations systems technology, Jeffrey Katz is chairman of the board and president of Orbitz, the travel Web site founded by American, Continental, Delta, Northwest and United airlines. As chief executive officer, Katz drives the company's management and strategic direction.

Prior to joining Orbitz, Katz was president and chief executive officer of Swissair Group's core airline unit, Swissair, an airline known worldwide for outstanding customer service. Katz joined Swissair in 1997 and led its efforts to adapt to the newly liberalized European market, including enlarging its Zurich hub, reaching agreement with Swissair pilots to improve productivity and overhaul its price and yield management systems, and negotiating Swissair's broad anti-trust approved code share agreement with American Airlines. Additionally, he instituted a number of customer care improvements using cutting-edge technology, such as *Fast Track*, the industry's first smart card-based, check-in system.

Before joining Swissair, Katz spent 17 years at American Airlines where he honed his industry expertise in positions including finance, pricing and sales, and Managing Director—In-flight Service. In 1993, the AMR Corp. board elected Katz vice president of American Airlines and president of the Computerized Reservation System Division (CRS) of SABRE, where he was responsible for its worldwide CRS business. During his tenure, SABRE expanded rapidly outside the United States in Europe, Mexico, South America and Asia, and formed joint ventures with the national airlines of Mexico, India and Japan. Under Katz's leadership, SABRE launched its first Web-enabled applications—Planet SABRE for Travel Agents and SABRE Business Travel Solutions—the industry's first comprehensive business-to-business travel arrangement tool for corporate travel.

Katz was named one of four "People to Watch 2001" (leisure travel) in *USA Today*, and is published in *The Heidrick & Struggles Leadership Opus: Access and Influence in the 21st Century*. He is a well-known speaker at such prominent venues as the 2001 World Economic Forum in Davos, Switzerland, the 2001 PC Forum, the Aero Club airline industry gathering and 2000 E-travel World. He is frequently interviewed on airline and online travel issues by national and local media such as *USA Today*, *The Washington Post*, the *New York Times*, the *Wall Street Journal*, CNN and CNBC.

Katz holds a bachelor of science degree in mechanical engineering from the University of California-Davis, and master's degrees from both Stanford University in California and the Massachusetts Institute of Technology, where he specialized in transportation management/ operations research. Katz is a licensed pilot.

In 1998, two years after the launch of the first travel Web site, only six million people purchased travel online in the United States. Since then, as the Internet became a part of our daily lives, a revolution has taken place in the travel industry, forever altering shopping habits, revamping marketing strategies and delivering unprecedented convenience, choice and savings to consumers and suppliers who use the Web.

In 2002, more than 42 million households—or seven in 10 online households that travel—will shop on the Web before booking their trips, according to Forrester Research, with an increasing (and increasingly sophisticated) array of third-party and supplier Web sites vying fiercely for their business.

In its first phase of development, travel e-commerce has empowered consumers with an almost mind-boggling amount of information—more than they could ever get from a reservations agent over the phone, by studying glossy brochures or by paging through a phone book. Today, using Orbitz, for example, a New York–Los Angeles flight search returns fares on 12 competing carriers and 224 different itinerary options. A rental car search delivers a Matrix display of rates from 13 vendors at Los Angeles International Airport, and on 13 vehicle types, from economy to SUV. And a Los Angeles hotel search shows the lowest rates at a glance within a wide range of quality levels, from budget hotels to luxury properties in neighborhoods across the metropolitan area. An online shopper can retrieve all this information and compare it in fewer than three minutes.

Travelers have responded to this transparency by flocking to the Internet. By 2007, Forrester predicts that nearly $50 billion will be spent purchasing leisure travel online. Even during the worst travel recession on record, the Internet travel business continued to grow at double-digit rates, emerging as a sweet spot while the overall industry was shrinking.

While transparency has been a boon to consumers, the industry is on the verge of entering a new and even more dynamic phase. Successful travel sites will counter the frenzy of online cross shopping by developing a deeper knowledge of their users and delivering information and benefits that are personalized and relevant to individual customers. Customers, after all, want to know more than "What's out there?" They want to know "What's right for me?" This next evolution is key—these travel sites will offer a distinct experience to their customers, thereby increasing the conversion of Web site "lookers" into bookers and earning those bookers' long-term loyalty.

In the early phase of e-commerce, the challenge was clear—lure customers to the online travel marketplace. Once they were there, you'd convince them to purchase their travel on the Web. Before the Internet, consumers' only choice was to buy from a traditional travel agent or directly from a supplier. Online agencies now sell air tickets, hotel rooms, rental cars, cruises, packages, and more. But to move from merely looking online (and then calling a supplier or offline agent to buy) to booking online, customers need to feel comfortable with this virtual marketplace. The evolution was and still is about getting customers to change their buying habits—to think about travel differently, to migrate to a new channel, and to transact in a new way. Since only 15 percent of customers book their travel online today, there is still the need to generate this broad base awareness.

Gaining Consumers while Managing Profitability

Early category marketing was directed to the broadest customer base to gain the attention of the early adopters and get them online. While traditional offline marketing has been used to support brand-building efforts, more than half of total marketing spending is typically focused on the Web. The most common tactics employed by travel sites to attract visitors include partnerships with Web portals and search engine sites, e-mails and a variety of online banner, button, and pop-under ads. Targeting users (for instance, those searching for "New York hotels") of major search engines such as Google has provided the highest conversion rates of any paid marketing. According to industry data, partnerships with portals such as AOL and MSN account for more than 40 percent of transactions on some leading travel sites. The goal is to drive traffic to the site and get users to search for a flight in hope they'll find an attractive fare and book a ticket.

Managing customer acquisition costs (total marketing spend in relation to number of new customers generated) was and is important to ensure profitability, given the lifetime value of a customer. The Web allows marketers to precisely track the return on investment down to an individual marketing element. For example, a specific pop-under ad can be evaluated as to its effectiveness, and modifications can be made to deliver desired traffic levels. Current category cost per customer acquisition is about $30 in 2003.

Leisure travelers, who in 2003 made up the majority of online agency customers, take only three trips per year. Therefore, customer retention has become essential, demanding an increased focus on profitability, or revenue per customer less customer acquisition costs. E-mail merchandising is one of the lowest-cost retention tools to produce repeat purchases. Consumers are more likely to interact with e-mails about travel deals compared to other retail offers. Effective e-mails communicate the best deals, and target customers' personal interests, favorite destinations and home airports.

In addition to managing costs, managing revenue (typically consisting of customer fees, supplier commissions and inducements and advertising) is a very important piece of the profitability equation. Shrinking supplier commissions have increased the importance of other revenue sources to online agencies. Traditionally, efforts to incentivize multiple purchases to gain incremental revenue consisted of cross-selling rental cars and hotel rooms to air bookers. Revenue opportunities have been expanding greatly to include targeted advertising, travel insurance, cruises, vacation packages, and even destination attractions such as prepaid theme park tickets. The key to increasing revenue per customer is relevancy—getting the right message in front of the right customer at the right time. For example, offering the opportunity to purchase Disney tickets (or concert or theatre tickets) to a customer who books tickets and a hotel room for a trip to Orlando will generate more sales than a generic offer.

Comprehensive travel sites will develop better functionality to help sell more expensive products such as cruises. The development of sophisticated ship maps and video content will offer consumers tools to experience a taste of the product before purchase. Online cruise shopping will offer consumers some of the same benefits as air purchases, such as being able to research the most options with the lowest prices. Real-time cabin availability with pricing will provide ease-of-use to improve the shopping experience. Customers will no longer be limited to the select few sailings that their travel agents want to sell.

Selling discounted inventory via the merchant or markup model has enabled online travel agencies to raise profit per customer, adding 10 to 30 margin points in many cases. This strategy has been especially successful in selling hotel rooms and vacation packages on the Web. Combining merchant inventory with discount fares to create dynamic packages "on the fly" offers another level of savings to customers, while raising profitability potential for the supplier and Internet company.

The Evolution of Marketing and the Marketplace

As the marketplace is evolving, marketing is becoming more sophisticated, particularly to those early adopters who have been online a while and are comfortable transacting online. Marketing is becoming more and more customer-focused, from mass marketing, to specialty group marketing, to individual marketing. This customer focus will bring about new forms of distribution, customer segmentation, differentiation and value-added services for customers.

Online business travel spending is quickly approaching that of leisure (estimated to be close to $17 billion in 2003). Online travel sites provide a new, more efficient distribution channel for business travelers. Corporations can reduce transaction fees by as much as 75 percent versus an offline agency, obtain greater selection, reduce the time it takes to book flights and take advantage of Web discounts to reduce their travel budget. Orbitz was the first online travel site to launch a program for business customers. This segment is growing remarkably fast as small and large companies move to capitalize on its economic benefits. Similarly, travel agents who use online travel sites have access to a wider selection of fares, allowing them to lower costs and increase service level to their clients. To illustrate, with just a click, Orbitz gives instant access to published prices, including suppliers' highly attractive Web-only rates, for 455 airlines, 50,000-plus hotels and 25 rental car companies. The use of Web-based search and booking engines among travel agents is expected to increase significantly in the next few years.

Finally, the use of wireless technology, including PDAs, cell phones, laptop computers, etc., on travel sites with international reach, will provide new channels that allow customers to make travel plans anytime, anywhere.

Customer segmentation allows online sites to reach micro-segments of the market with personalized messages. It's now possible to communicate with smaller groups, even with individuals, in a more relevant way. Online sites can reward frequent users by sending them a coupon with savings on their next purchases, or target affinity groups and special interest groups with customized travel offerings. For example, travel packages are targeted to skiers, golfers, and gay travelers. In the not too distant future, a customer will be able to indicate that she wants to fly from Chicago to Dallas for $200. Then, the instant this fare becomes available, they will receive a wireless notification that also includes suggestions on hot hotel deals, rental cars, and destination-specific discounts on activities related to their personal interests. With segmentation comes a trend away from traditional offline marketing channels to online channels, because online affords the opportunity to better target specific segments.

Another example of market segmentation is the ability to differentiate and offer customized tools for the business traveler versus the leisure traveler. For example, businesses want negotiated corporate rates and Web fares integrated with standard search results, along with tracking tools like individual employee accounts.

The Internet is the perfect medium for customized marketing. Technology allows us to recognize a customer who visits our site again, and reengage them by tailoring what we show on the screen based on previous online behavior or purchases. Customization combined with superior customer care will create loyal customers who keep coming back and spend a greater share of their travel dollar on our site.

There are now millions of Internet users visiting and shopping at travel sites—an estimated 40 million people visit a travel Web site each month. Travel sites have attempted to win their loyalty by being different in one way or another, whether the differentiator is ease-of-use, superior technology, discount packages, opaque pricing, comprehensive product offerings or supplier-friendly policies.

However, in the eyes of consumers, most travel sites appear more or less the same. Their online shopping behavior includes visiting several sites and booking on the one that has the best deal. In many cases, if the deals are similar, they will book on the last site they visited. This demonstrates there is little loyalty among consumers, as they do not perceive the sites to be significantly differentiated. The online travel sites must find ways to distinguish themselves and stand out from the pack. If they don't, they risk becoming a commodity, trapped in a low-margin, price-driven category.

At Orbitz, we believe our customer care program will be one of our differentiators in the longer term. We have pioneered a customer care program that delivers more than two million "Care Alerts" to travelers a month, more than any travel agent online or brick and mortar. We notify customers of weather and air traffic delays, gate changes and other changes to their itineraries, saving them time and aggravation when delays occur.

In addition to low cost and ease of use, to keep customers satisfied and build long-term loyalty, the industry needs to continue to innovate and provide value-added services to its customers. Great values, customized travel offerings, a high level of customer service, and promotional offers are ways to build consumer value. For example, concierge services that simplify and streamline trip planning will be valued by consumers.

Potential Threats on the Horizon

Though there is no debating the huge success of travel sites to date (both online agencies, such as Orbitz, Travelocity and Expedia, and supplier-owned sites, like hilton.com or swa.com) or the projected continued growth of this marketplace, a rosy future is not completely assured. Foremost among the looming threats are some of the marketing practices of the travel Web sites themselves.

For instance, pricing power has shifted from the travel suppliers to the consumer. Ten years ago, a consumer who purchased an airline ticket (or hotel room or rental car, for that matter) was largely unaware of the lowest fare in the market on any given day of travel. Consumers relied on information that either an airline ticket agent or travel agent provided, often over the phone. Fast-forward to the present where, in just a few clicks, a consumer can see hundreds of flights and fare options for any given day with an emphasis on the lowest available price at the moment.

Increased transparency created by the Web has pushed the cost of travel down so much that it risks becoming commoditized. Too deep of a cut into the margins will make the industry unsustainable. This could have multiple negative effects that could include the consolidation or the failure of some travel Web sites altogether, or lead travel suppliers to rethink their distribution strategies.

One solution to ensuring that travel Web sites' margins remain sustainable in the future is by charging fees for their services. After Orbitz initiated a $5 service fee per ticket in 2001, consumers' response confirmed that they are willing to pay a nominal transaction fee in return for greater price transparency and access to the best deals, and competitors have followed.

Travel Web sites are also taking advantage of cost-efficient new technology to provide what offline agents cannot—personalized levels of service to a massive customer base.

No offline travel agency has the ability to constantly update large numbers of passengers to itinerary changes and flight delays. But, by leveraging wireless technology and the Internet, a single air traffic controller in Orbitz' customer care center can monitor the impact of weather and air traffic on flights across the country and then, through automation, electronically message tens of thousands travelers before and during their trips with information tailored specifically to their itineraries.

Another factor that will determine the success or failure of the online travel distribution industry is credibility. The leading travel sites do a good job of disclosing user privacy policies in user-friendly language and are doing a better job of explaining fare rules and other industry jargon. The danger area is the "pay for performance" and override deals with travel suppliers that affect flight, hotel or rental car search results. These deals manifest themselves in many ways, and can result in the exclusion of certain airline, hotel or rental car competitors from search results pages, or the reordering of search results to favor one travel supplier over another, regardless of price or convenience. (Contractually bound to be unbiased, Orbitz' airline search results are always listed in the following order: lowest fare, number of stops and duration of time.)

As consumers become more educated toward purchasing travel online, this bias could ultimately alienate them and could drive them to utilize other distribution channels that are perceived to be more "honest."

The industry also faces the risk of overmerchandising their wares. It is important to differentiate between what consumers perceive as "clutter" and what is relevant information. Merchandising is viewed by some as a beneficial form of margin management—it creates additional revenue streams for the travel Web site), but its overuse can damage consumer confidence in the long run and ultimately harm the industry.

Finally, it almost goes without saying that the overall health of the global travel and tourism industry directly impacts the health of Internet travel sites.

Opportunities for growth

Consumers already benefit from technological innovations that allow them to control steps of the travel purchasing process that five years ago they could not, such as selecting and reserving an airplane seat at the time of booking the ticket. At the rate technology is moving, six months from now that same consumer will be able to purchase an airplane meal from a gourmet airport restaurant and have it waiting for them at the gate. One year from now, customers who purchase travel online may have a single reservation locator number for air, rental car or hotel reservations that will allow levels of interconnectivity between travel suppliers that have not been seen before, and create opportunities for even more personalized or proactive communications.

Technology is the key to leveraging other opportunities as well. The move to a direct connection with airlines, hoteliers, car rental companies and other travel suppliers represents an opportunity for travel Web sites. By eliminating the traditional GDS intermediary and connecting an airline or hotel's reservation inventory directly to a travel Web, the high transaction fees that suppliers currently bear will decrease significantly. These distribution cost savings will be passed on to consumers in the form of lower airfares or rates. While direct connect technology remains relatively new and underused by travel suppliers today, industry analysts universally acknowledge the huge potential impact of direct connect and predict a move in that direction. According to a 2002 study by Forrester Research, direct connect has the potential to save the industry more than $1.4 billion.

In 2002, Orbitz became the first third-party travel site to link its system directly to an airline reservation system. Consumers receive better real-time information and airlines enjoy distribution costs that are up to 77 percent lower than those associated with a traditional GDS.

By leveraging advances in technology, online travel sites can create new and powerful search tools that give consumers more information in fewer mouse clicks. One example is Orbitz' Flex Search feature, which is aimed at the millions of consumers who have flexibility in their travel dates and want to save money by flying when fares are lowest. The technology that enables this is truly amazing—what used to take up to 94 searches on another site, takes one Flex Search on Orbitz.

Another example of consumer-friendly technology used by Orbitz is a "Deal Detector" that will alert potential travelers when fares drop to their preferred destinations. These kinds of features are made possible by the choice of newer, server-based Internet technology over legacy mainframe technology that lacks the processing power to execute the necessary algorithms.

The universe of potential customers for these technologies is immense: almost 85 percent of travel is still being purchased offline. As the category continues its amazing growth, PhoCusWright projects that $65.5 billion will be sold online in 2005—representing three out of every 10 travel sales.

Regulators can play a role in ensuring that further growth in the online travel marketplace takes place. The U.S. Department of Transportation is currently reviewing its regulations that govern how computer reservation systems (CRSs) distribute airline tickets. Liberalizing or repealing these arcane regulations will increase competition in the distribution channel and improve offerings for consumers and travel suppliers alike.

Winners and Losers

The winners in the online travel space will have several things in common. First and foremost, they will be sharply focused on customer needs. Those sites that invest heavily in customer care will obtain loyalty, thereby allowing them to retain a strong customer base long-term. Successful online sites will emulate offline companies that have successfully differentiated themselves by building strong brands. Additionally, the ability to move quickly, at Internet speed, in this fast-moving, dynamic marketplace, is critical.

The best sites will continually seek ways to differentiate their product offerings to make their sites faster and easier to use. They will continue to provide a breadth of options, along with value-added products and services.

Travel sites will become even more attentive to balancing the needs of suppliers and consumers. Access to low prices has been one of the critical ingredients of the online travel success story. Remaining the low-cost provider is very important because the high-cost offline travel distribution model isn't sustainable in its current form, especially in an industry where airline seats and hotel beds are empty and GDS fees have risen steadily since 1990.

The losers in the online travel space will not innovate and instead rely on old technology or travel distribution intermediaries. They will lose focus on their core business model, and erode their low-cost position. They will not focus properly on the customer, and therefore lose their relevancy.

Consumers will be the ultimate beneficiary of this Web revolution, not only because of the convenience and savings, but because the travel industry will become better positioned to satisfy their individual needs. The Web will become their trusted travel advisor, open 24/7, tailoring information to reflect their preferences, and providing the best deals and most reliable information whether they're at home, at work or on the road.

49

The Rise of the
Home-Based Agent

Michael Gross
Cofounder and CEO
Global Travel International

Michael Gross is the cofounder and CEO of Global Travel International. Michael attended American University in Washington D.C., where he also interned for Senator Tom Daschle. After graduating with a political science degree, Michael earned his law degree at American University.

In 1994, Michael teamed with his college roommate Randy Warren and founded Global Travel International (GTI) to revolutionize the home-based travel business. Today, GTI is a multimillion-dollar state-of-the-art operation with over 200 specialists supporting GTI's 35,000 independent travel agents in all 50 states and 85 countries.

Gross lives in Boca Raton, Florida with his wife, Alison, and two daughters, Danielle and Jessica.

Introduction

Gone are the days of paper tickets. Gone are inconveniences like office hours, commutes and searching for a travel agent that "does it all." If it were possible to describe the state of the today's travel industry in a single word, that word would be "change." Across all sectors within the travel industry, change is a constant. However, in no sector is that change more potent and apparent than on the distribution side of the industry.

Armed with new and evolving technology, suppliers are changing how they go to market, with whom they partner, how they compensate their partners and even whether or not they require partners. Simultaneously, consumers, equipped with boundless information, are changing how they research travel, buy travel and ultimately from whom they buy their travel. The travel agent, essentially caught between the suppliers and consumers, has been forced to reexamine her value proposition.

The emergence of a growing legion of home-based travel agents is the result of this change, the result of a market driven by technology and consumers still searching for personal interaction and expertise.

Section One: Shifting Dynamics in the Travel Industry and Beyond

To understand the emergence of the home-based travel agent, it is important to examine some of the trends and developments in the travel industry, as well as other broader business and social advancements. It is these influences that are both dictating and facilitating the future of the home-based travel agent.

Home-based businesses will explode in the 21st century

Since the late 1980s, futurists have been predicting the growth of telecommuting. In the early 2000s, working from home has become a significant trend. In late 2003, approximately 20 million Americans were working at least a day-and-a-half to two days a week from home. Experts predict that 51 million Americans will do at least some of their work from home by 2010.

Driving this trend is an unusual convergence of technology, environmentalism and business. The rapid acceptance of personal computers as part of our lives, combined with the introduction of faster means of transmitting data has allowed individuals to work from a desk at home just as efficiently as if they were in an office.

In fact, working from home may be more efficient. People working from home avoid commuting on crowded highways or battling subway lines, which produce higher stress and anxiety levels. Working at home actually facilitates more productive and content workers. Add the sensitivities of today's work force, a cohort that has clearly indicated they want a better balance between work and home, and it appears working at home is becoming an increasingly attractive option for both businesses and individuals.

Backed by technology that allows workers to work effectively from home, businesses are gradually creating tools and support mechanisms for workers to create productive workspaces at home. Rather than fight the trend, businesses like AT&T and PricewaterhouseCoopers have established formal telecommuting programs as part of a broader, flexible work policy. We should anticipate seeing more telecommuting and work-at-home programs emerge as we head into the 2010s and 2020s.

Travel agents are being forced home

Put simply, the traditional travel agency model of the past 50 years is no longer an economically viable business model. Traditional travel agencies based on "bricks-and-mortar" models are increasingly expensive to operate. Rents and maintenance costs are high. Marketing costs are spiraling. Competition is fierce. Spurred by falling commissions, the travel agent has been forced to slash overhead, streamline their operations and create a more efficient business.

Additionally, the need for a physical location, which was once a necessity, has disappeared. While visiting your local travel agency was once as commonplace as visiting your local dry cleaner, today it seems almost archaic. People no longer have to visit a travel agency for a brochure, or wait a week until an airline ticket or thick package of information arrives. Consumers can now satisfy their curiosity about golfing in Nova Scotia or leisurely cruising the Caribbean on a Carnival Fun Ship with the click of the mouse.

Unfortunately, travel agencies, particularly those who have not quickly adapted to these changes, have suffered. Closures of travel agencies and the displacement of skilled travel agent professionals have sadly become commonplace.

The Internet impact

In less than a decade, online commerce has become an important part of our daily lives. As evidenced by declining newspaper circulation figures and plummeting network television news viewership, the Internet is becoming the primary source of news for consumers. For younger people, not bound to the traditions of the morning newspaper and six o'clock news, the Internet is the medium of choice. Even for Baby Boomers and Generation X, whose memories hearken to the past, the Internet has changed how they work and live.

While every industry has embraced the Internet, none has had more success in changing consumer's buying habits than the travel industry. That is because booking travel has become an online experience. People research destinations on the Internet. They read Web logs and reviews posted by travelers who share their experiences. They know how to look for deals or, if they have registered with an online marketer, the deals will find them.

In a few short years, people have become comfortable making purchases online. Travel suppliers have adapted their sales methodologies to accommodate increased customer familiarity with online purchasing.

One of the most visible impacts of online activity has occurred in the airline industry. Since the start of the 21st century, we have seen airline-ticketing shift, almost overnight, from paper tickets that required delivery or pickup, to e-tickets that consumers print out in the comfort of their own homes. Online purchase of airline tickets has skyrocketed as airlines promote online purchases as a means of reducing costs. Consumers have become smarter, not just about travel purchases, but about business in general.

Section Two: The Home-based Agent. A Natural Evolution

When one surveys the landscape of the modern travel industry, it would be easy to predict the continued success and eventual domination of the Internet travel companies. It may appear equally tempting to forecast the natural demise of the individual travel agent. But, upon closer examination, it becomes clear that the travel businesses that can blend tomorrow's technology with the personal needs of the customer will be the real victors over the next decade. With that in mind, no travel retailer will be better positioned to succeed than the home-based travel agent.

While the major online booking engines might presently dominate the market, one must ask about customer loyalty. The computer literate traveler will research and book at the best price, with little regard to brand loyalty. Now, what if that same tech-savvy traveler knows a close friend or family member who had a similar booking engine on their very own travel Web site? The field then becomes wide open, with customer loyalty being the new name of the game. Those travel businesses that can harness technology and also create customer loyalty will be the leaders in the distribution channel.

Even with the increasing pervasiveness of the Internet as a means of buying and selling products and services, one element will always remain constant: the customers are still people. Therefore, effective marketing must revolve around identifying and satisfying customer wants and needs. Even with the greatest technology in the world, the fastest Internet connections and the most sophisticated data collection programs ever devised, it still comes down to knowing and connecting with your customer.

People trust their friends when booking travel

Eighty percent of Americans cite "recommendations of a friend or family member," as their top choice when asked about their confidence in travel recommendation sources.

While people can now explore places they want to visit online, see where they might stay, and learn more about the experiences awaiting them, they still want to hear firsthand about travel experiences. Consumers still want the reassurance and confirmation that their investment in a week or two away from home, along with the expenditure of several thousand dollars, is worth their time and money. People want to buy from other people with whom they feel comfortable.

Confirmation and assurance is where home-based travel sales excel. Home-based travel sales agents deal with people they know and who know them. They offer what still remains the single most powerful marketing tool—word-of-mouth confirmation and referrals.

"Loyalty" is the watchword. Consider again: Friends and family are the number one choice to deliver travel recommendations according to the 2002 YPB&R/Yankelovich National Travel Monitor.

When you blend the social trends pointing toward home-based businesses, the rapid advance of technology and the changes in the travel agency, the result is a natural evolution toward the home-based travel agency. An army of home-based travel agents, each marketing to their circle of influence, produce an enormous amount of travel spending.

Attitudes Toward Traditional Information Sources

CONFIDENCE IN SELECTED INFORMATION SOURCES 2003

When Considering Travel Destinations, Extremely/Very Confident in:

Recommendations of a friend or family member	80 %
Information in travel guidebooks	52 %
Recommendations of a travel agent	46 %
Information on a Web site online	41 %
Information in travel brochures	34 %
Articles in newspapers/magazines or programs on TV/radio	34 %
Information in travel advertising	21 %

Source: 2002 Yesawich, Pepperdine, Brown and Russel/Yankelovich Partners National Travel Monitor
On the Horizon: An Army of Home-based Travel Agents

Is it possible? Home-based sales models have been successful in nearly every industry. If we look at the success experienced by Avon, Tupperware or Mary Kay, we immediately see how this circle of influence promotes loyalty, success, and a sense of trust. With this model as our foundation, it is easy to draw parallels to the travel industry.

What makes home-based travel considerably different than the old "home party" or direct sales models, however, is that the Internet allows consumers to look for what they want, on their own time and own terms. Once a consumer has become inclined toward what they want to do or where they want to go, our home-based travel sales professionals can confirm a travel decision and, better yet, make the booking.

Section Three: Case Study: Global Travel International

In the early 1990s, my good friend Randy Warren, who co-founded GTI with me, identified a means of bringing together the exploding technological changes of the Internet with the increasing desire to operate one's own business.

We created an opportunity for people to sell travel to their friends, relatives, neighbors and acquaintances, backed up by the knowledge and information of full-time travel professionals.

Our business model effectively blended:

- A grassroots sales force

- The power of the Internet

- Access to the sophisticated technology relied upon by airlines, cruise ships, hotels, resorts, tour operators and other travel suppliers

- The support of professional travel specialists

- Partnerships with the leading suppliers in the travel industry

- Access to proprietary sales, marketing and training support

Today our membership has reached more than 40,000 travel agents across the globe, backed by a team of more than 200 travel professionals whose experience and resources are equal to those of any professional travel organization anywhere in the world. This is all made possible by a combination of three factors: emerging technologies like better booking engines and faster means of transmitting information; shifting social norms and values such as the desire and ability to work from home; and fundamental changes in the economics of the travel industry.

But most of all, our business revolves around the notion that people are loyal to people they know when making purchases, especially when it comes to emotional purchasing decisions like travel.

The home-based agent's competitive advantage

A home-based travel agent's competitive advantage is the local knowledge and contacts that the agent enjoys in his or her community and hometown—a circle of influence. A successful home-based agent sells travel by leveraging the relationships the agent has with friends, family, business associates, local charities and religious organizations. Similar to the "Avon Lady," selling cosmetics via a grassroots effort and capitalizing on existing relationships and trust, home-based agents sell vacations, cruises, hotels and more.

As noted, friends and family are the number one choice to deliver travel recommendations according to the 2003 YPB&R/Yankelovich National Travel Monitor. GTI has capitalized on these trusted relationships to build the home-based travel channel. Our home-based agents are the first ones to volunteer to organize the annual trip to Bermuda. They are the trusted friend to call when planning an anniversary celebration or the Web site to trust when business travel is becoming too expensive. GTI agents are the "boots on the ground," building relationships *before* their clients make their travel decisions.

Who is the home-based agent?

The prototypical home-based agent enjoys traveling, talking about traveling and selling travel. The home-based agent is emboldened with the entrepreneurial spirit. Whether a home-based agent is sitting around Thanksgiving dinner telling the family about her latest vacation or giving her friends advice on which cruise to take during Christmas, home-based agents are travel people. Generally, home-based agents fall into one of the following four categories:

- The Traveler—An individual who travels extensively and is looking to offset some of the expense. Often this person owns a small-to medium-sized business and would like to control his travel budget.

- The Part-Time Agent—An individual who wants to build a part-time business to supplement her income. This may be a stay-at-home mother, civic or organization leader, senior citizen or a student looking to pay for a spring break vacation.

- The Entrepreneur—An individual who is looking to build a full-time business. Possibly a retired individual or a person looking for a second career.

- The Travel Professional—This individual has built a career in the travel industry. Typically this candidate is struggling in today's no commission, high-overhead environment. A home-based business offers a low-overhead alternative, allowing the professional to keep her existing client base.

How home-based agents are trained

Extensive training programs are essential for the success of the home-based agent. To be successful in the marketplace, a competitive travel agent must have product knowledge, sales skills, and marketing support.

GTI's extensive training program begins the moment a new GTI agent signs up. At that time, a training session is scheduled with one of our in-house Global

Tutors™, who begin to acquaint the agent on the different educational and sales opportunities that GTI offers. During that initial contact, a series of comprehensive surveys are initiated by GTI and delivered to our proprietary customer relationship management software.

To educate and motivate GTI agents, we've developed proprietary training programs including Cruise College™, the Certified Vacation Specialist Curriculum and the Global U™ programs. Weekly instructional teleconferences and online courses are offered for GTI's home-based agents to review on their own time and at their own pace. Familiarization trips and Destination Specialist programs are made available to further increase their travel industry knowledge.

How the home-based agent is supported

In Orlando, GTI has built the infrastructure with 200 professionals to provide the support, training, marketing tools and backend systems for its home-based channel. Using proprietary technology, GTI has created the "Life of the Customer" program enabling GTI to manage and guide our agents in their business. Advertising material is designed for our agents to use, which provides them with a quick and inexpensive solution to assist in their marketing efforts.

GTI's business model translates seamlessly to the Internet. In fact, the Internet represents an opportunity for GTI to expand its reach. Just as GTI agents market their own travel business to their circle of influence, the Internet allows GTI agents to move beyond their circle of influence and market their very own travel site all over the world. GTI uses the Web as a tool and has tailored that tool to its agents. To expand our agents' business on the Web, GTI developed technology enabling each agent to have a personalized travel Web site, giving them the ability to market air, car, hotels, vacations and cruises online. All of the content and back-end support of the Web site is maintained by GTI, allowing the home-based agent to again do what they do best—market their Web site to their circle of influence.

Section Four: Where Does Home-based Travel Go From Here?

When you clear away all the clutter and distractions in today's travel industry, the fundamental role of the travel agent remains unchanged. While today's travel agents may take many different forms, their principal mission is to sell, market and distribute travel. In fact, one could argue that today's travel agent is no longer an agent in the traditional sense, but rather a travel retailer, much like retailers in nearly every other industry. To remain relevant, the travel agent must provide value to the agent's two primary constituents—travel suppliers and travel consumers.

For all travel companies, the future will be about building loyalty and remaining on the edge of how technology and social attitudes change. The home-based agent relies on grassroots marketing to build the sales and loyalty while relying on the professional resources of the organization they represent for the support and technology.

Home-based travel will become tomorrow's standard

The future for home-based travel sales agents looks bright. As corporate business changes and looks for ways to reduce work forces, the concept of operating one's own business from home will become more attractive. In fact, people may operate more than one business from within their home. Travel will be one of many services, such as insurance, real estate and information, sold by home-operated entrepreneurs who will possess the business know-how to adroitly operate in a powerful technologically-based environment.

Home-based travel agents are not confined by four walls, restricted by geographical location or bound by the typical overhead that encumbers most traditional travel agencies. More than custodians of information on travel, home-based agents are a trusted friend, family member or business associate to their customers, helping the latter to make informed travel decisions.

No matter how the travel business changes and no matter what kinds of technological advancements occur, people will still prefer to buy from people whom they trust. The success of the home-based agent is a natural evolution. While the past decade was about building mass at any price, the next decade will hinge on building loyalty. Many thought the Internet would destroy the travel agency as we knew it, but it has, in fact, brought it full circle. We have arrived back at the original local travel agency, minus the bricks and mortar. It is a travel agency operated by someone you know and trust, selling travel to friends and family.

50

Travel Distribution Services: The New Intermediary

Samuel L. Katz
Chairman and CEO
Cendant's Travel
Distribution Services (TDS)

Samuel L. Katz is chairman and CEO of Cendant's Travel Distribution Services (TDS) division, a position he has served in since the division was established in October 2001, following the corporation's acquisitions of Galileo International and CheapTickets, Inc.

In this role, Katz is responsible for all ten travel distribution businesses, including Galileo International, Travelport, and CheapTickets.com, supported by more than 5,000 employees in 115 countries. Under Katz's leadership, the TDS division has integrated its complementary travel services businesses around five key customer channels—(1) leisure consumers, (2) corporate clients, (3) travel agencies, (4) air travel suppliers, and (5) hospitality and leisure travel suppliers—to better serve the needs of these diverse groups in a dynamic industry environment.

Mr. Katz is also chairman of Cendant's financial services division.

Much can be learned from the ancient Phoenicians about creating a sustainable, lucrative role as an intermediary in day-to-day commerce. They became legendary for their ability to seek out desirable or desperately needed goods and trade them for handsome profits. Their legacy continues today, with intermediaries capturing a portion of economic value from the transactions they broker. While the 21st century has had a precarious start, with traumatic events and economic jitters, the intermediary that has redefined its role and provided value is proving its resiliency.

But nothing is guaranteed in the world of the intermediary. Rapid technological change and entrepreneurial innovation lurk around every corner, making "business as usual" an outdated concept. Just as the broker who relied on fixed commissions is becoming obsolete, so too are huge swaths of giant industries. Wal-Mart influenced the paradigm shift in the retail industry, transforming the distribution model into a supplier transaction generator and growth engine. The impact proved a death knell to thousands of companies, large and small, which held on to the past, relying on the way things had always been done rather than anticipating where the market was headed and how the needs of key industry players were changing.

The world of travel is no different. People once entered the profession for the glamour and excitement of its jet-setting ways, along with attractive compensation, perks and growth opportunities. But that was yesterday's travel industry. The advancements of technology and the proliferation of electronic transactions have caused a revolution in travel, particularly in the distribution sector, which encompasses those businesses serving as intermediaries between travel suppliers and its customers, providing technology, infrastructure, and customer services. The distribution sector includes online and traditional travel agencies, full-service travel management companies, and electronic connectivity systems, all centered around the powerhouse Global Distribution Systems (GDS) computer reservation platform.

The GDS model was created by airlines to expand their distribution capabilities through traditional travel agencies, which still account for more than 70 percent of travel transactions, even with the explosion of online travel bookings. Today, this model is plagued by legacy economics that the airlines themselves created, yet today vocally criticize. At the time this was published, the GDS industry was undergoing significant regulatory and executive branch debate in both the United States and European Union, as rules that were constructed in the 1980s—to protect fair competition amid airline ownership and control of primary distribution channels—were proposed to be radically altered. In 2002, airline ticket sales comprised the majority of GDS bookings as the global GDS market size declined, demonstrating the effects of economic pressures as well as consumers' shift to online channel purchases and suppliers' continuing interest in disintermediating travel agencies and other distributors in the name of cost savings.

In 2002, approximately half of all online air bookings were transacted through carriers' own Web sites, and that rate is expected to increase to roughly 59 percent by 2005.

Times are changing, and the old guard intermediary must face this new reality. To succeed, distributors must leverage the latest technology and service offerings to transform themselves and use comparative advantages to compete in a synthesized world. The market leaders must blend yesterday's assets with today's electronic capabilities to better serve the travel distribution needs of diverse customers to help all participants increase transaction volume for a total lower cost.

Cendant has built a framework to accomplish this result—with its collection of traditional travel assets and its core GDS electronic platform. Cendant is leading the industry as it moves beyond the historical GDS model, redefining its capabilities as a comprehensive travel distribution services (TDS) model, which has rapidly become the *new* intermediary. Cendant employs a more cohesive and integrated TDS model that approaches the market as a single services- and solutions-based entity. Its vision is simple: *to be a leader*. Its method is easy: *leverage the entire asset portfolio* to provide a single, one-stop source for multiple distribution services that help customers increase sales volume while reducing total distribution costs. As a travel distribution service, Cendant wants all industry players to be successful and is defining its TDS model to enhance profits for all businesses as efficiently as possible while ensuring travel consumers get access to the best value.

The Synthesized World

Each airplane ticket sold, each car rented, and each hotel night booked results in a processed travel transaction, and the majority of these are processed through an intermediary of some sort, contributing to a $500 billion global travel market. Previously, these transactions were conducted via telephone or by sitting down with a brick-and-mortar travel agent. In today's digital world, travel has become the largest e-commerce industry, accounting for more than one-third of all online transactions. By 2005, it is expected that $65.5 billion, or nearly three out of 10 travel sales, will be booked online.

This has driven favorable returns for many companies participating in travel e-commerce. By 2003—and after the dot-com fallout of the late 1990s—nearly all of the positive equity value in the travel industry is represented by electronic intermediaries Expedia and Hotels.com, and these are companies spending but a fraction of the hundreds of billions of dollars of capital spent by suppliers to accumulate airplanes, hotel rooms and rental cars.

Online travel booking will continue to grow, especially as travel suppliers encourage its use with a broad range of offerings and special Internet rates, making pricing more competitive and transparent than ever before. On the consumer side, broadband connections are bringing high-speed Internet access into more homes, making online browsing more convenient, with faster page downloads. Further, the explosion of wireless devices with Internet capabilities will make it even easier to arrange and manage travel plans, no matter where the consumer may be.

The migration to online channels for purchasing travel services, by both cost-conscious and convenience-seeking consumers and corporate clients, signals a permanent and significant shift in buying behavior. The travel distribution industry has responded with Web-based tools and technologies that continue to improve self-directed online search capabilities and facilitate booking with fewer screens and commands. Consumers are now able to quickly browse through all available rates and options before making their selections, and new applications are making this process easier for traditional travel agencies to integrate and better serve their customer base.

In this instant environment, the electronic intermediary—whether online or offline—provides a cheaper, more efficient way for airlines to sell seats, and hotels to sell rooms, and for both to sell excess inventory. The downside is that electronic intermediaries are getting less compensation for their services, with lower fees and reduced, or zero, commissions. This puts pressure on the business to use its traditional assets in new, more effective ways.

This new formula is inherent in the strategy Cendant has followed for years: assemble assets, build volume, reduce costs. Like the Phoenicians, Cendant has a knack for recognizing market and profit opportunities. In the travel distribution business, Cendant is focused on providing its many customers with the services they want and need. Its goal is to help all industry players become more efficient and effective in distributing and accessing travel content for greater value.

Strategy Drives Structure

In moving to a streamlined and transformational TDS model, Cendant has assembled one of the industry's most comprehensive and geographically diverse portfolios in the business. In a changing paradigm, Cendant has elected to abandon the practice of managing these complementary businesses by brand, and has instead amassed its portfolio under five business units designed to serve the unique needs of its five core customer segments: travel agencies and management companies, corporations, travel suppliers (divided between the distinct (a) airline and (b) hospitality-leisure market segments), and the king of retail—the leisure consumers. These business units, in turn, are supported by a common shared-services platform, contributing to improved operating efficiency and lower costs. Consolidating common functions across multiple businesses enables Cendant to operate with a shared vision and common priorities. This allows human and financial resources to be shifted and allocated from consolidating markets to growing ones to more effectively seize market opportunities. One such example is Cendant's decision to direct information technology personnel and investment funds from the GDS business to help accelerate Cendant's online penetration in the corporate and leisure markets.

By approaching the business from a macro-level, Cendant's comprehensive capabilities and distribution network connects all players in the travel industry. Over the years, Cendant has proven itself flexible and resourceful in cross-marketing its many related services to appeal to different market segments and drive incremental transactions. Its assets span the entire distribution spectrum, and add greater advantage through its supplier operations in the form of lodging franchises, vacation rentals and car rentals.

Cendant's new TDS model and comparative advantage in owning travel inventory and other marketing services is a key differentiator as it is managing its business units to cross-utilize its technology, products and services to provide its customers the broadest range of inventory and solutions possible through one easy channel, for one low price. This ease of access and ability to gain attractive content and lower total costs are making Cendant a preferred provider of transaction processing services in the industry for key market segments highlighted below.

Traditional Travel Agencies and Management Companies

Galileo Client Services

The travel agency community was once embraced by the airlines as a preferred intermediary, with technology and financial incentives; now it is faced with disintermediation—being taken out of the distribution loop—as part of the legacy GDS model. The impact of the events of September 11, 2001, commission cuts and the emergence of e-commerce have all had a profound effect on distribution, particularly involving traditional travel agencies. The danger is that they will be completely bypassed by people using self-directed travel Web sites and by suppliers looking to move closer to customers and to reduce costs.

Yet travel agencies remain an important and trusted resource to consumers in helping them plan vacations and find package deals. Cendant is helping its travel agency customers with a "business builders" philosophy, working to adjust the legacy business model to make it more sustainable with better content, more automated technology to reduce labor and transaction costs, and additional revenue through increased sales and other commission opportunities.

Partnering with companies like Cendant enables travel agencies to benefit from its continuing investment in technology and infrastructure. These applications are being tailored to serve the travel agencies' need to improve automation and efficiency.

Galileo International is core to Cendant's distribution business. Since its formation in 1971, years before the emergence of e-commerce, Galileo pioneered travel automation products that enhance service and productivity, including electronic ticketing and booking products for airlines and travel agencies. Today, it is the most geographically diverse GDS system, with more than 26 percent global share of the market. Galileo connects 45,000 travel agencies and other subscribers worldwide to more than 500 airlines, 30 car rental companies, and 52,000 hotel properties.

The GDS technology platform is the most efficient means of aggregating and distributing travel inventory, and on a fully allocated basis, remains one of the lowest-cost, highest-yielding channels for airlines and other suppliers. Yet, the current independent GDS business model, constructed by the founding airline owners, involves suppliers paying fees to distribute inventory to the GDS, and a portion of that fee being provided to travel agencies in the form of financial booking incentive or other in-kind technology and software applications. This current model is unsustainable over the long term, as suppliers look to make deeper cuts in the cost of distribution across the supply chain. Cendant has been applying its assets to fundamentally reshape this legacy distribution model to focus on volume and removing costs from the equation, resulting in higher net revenues and a more efficient system. Its solution includes the introduction of innovative programs that can benefit travel agencies, travel suppliers and Cendant at the same time. The programs may vary, but the fundamental premise is the same: all players work together, giving a little to gain something greater.

A recent example is an innovative industry program created by Cendant with participation from United Airlines, Continental Airlines, US Airways and Rosenbluth International, called "Momentum." A first for the industry, Momentum provides benefits to all industry participants in exchange for a concession. Specifically, Momentum lowers GDS fees for airlines by about 20 percent in exchange for access to all the airlines' publicly available fares. Enrolled travel agencies gain the competitive benefit of Web fares and other attractive Cendant airline inventory, leading to incremental sales and revenue opportunities, in exchange for foregoing some financial incentives. Cendant reduces its fees to suppliers, and in turn reduces agency dependence on financial assistance, making the model more efficient and sustainable over the long term. All participants enjoy more transactions for a greater total return.

Suppliers continue to benefit from the travel agency channel, which helps quell disintermediation, while travel agencies gain enhanced infrastructure and access to more attractive content while actively participating in changing the legacy distribution model.

Managed Travel Customers— Corporate Travel Solutions

As corporations look to reduce operating expenses, focus has shifted to reducing business travel-related expenditures and more focus and attention is being placed on managing corporate travel policies and automating business travel planning with online booking tools. In the United States, the $100 billion corporate travel market is expected to more than double its use of online booking; corporate online bookings went from 9 percent in 2001 to 19 percent in 2003.

Corporate clients are searching for turnkey solutions that enable them to effectively manage policies, take advantage of supplier booking incentives and rebates, while reducing fees and expenses. Sophisticated online booking applications or Web tools allow corporations to bring the GDS interface right to the employee's desktop, helping employees plan and purchase travel, saving time and money.

Most corporations need more sophisticated electronic solutions than the readily available Web-booking sites like Cheap Tickets or Expedia. They need tools that integrate corporate travel policies, expense-reporting requirements, negotiated rates and employee profiles. In addition to receiving the best rates, integrated and automated systems can increase compliance with company policy through seamless integration. And, for multi-national companies, the ability to process multiple currencies in multiple languages is preferred. The ease of use has translated into higher adoption rates by employees and significant savings for corporations—up to 25 percent savings annually, on average, for corporate travel-related expenses, as corporations pay lower booking fees and receive volume discounts as employee usage increases. Employee adoption of Cendant's online booking solution averages more than 35 percent among its leading clients, which is twice the industry average, and is as high as 90 percent for some leading corporations.

Cendant's corporate travel solution is currently employed by a number of high-profile corporate customers in North America, and it is beginning to make inroads in European markets. Using its full asset portfolio, Cendant is providing corporations what no other competitor can claim to be—a single source for all corporate travel needs, ranging from a customized online booking tool to a full service, end-to-end services portfolio that provides access to one of the largest global distribution systems, and complete reservations and ticketing services. This solution allows corporations to easily store and access policy information, travel history, preferred provider discounts and personal profiles, while providing fully integrated data reporting and processing tools.

Cendant is anticipating the needs of global, multinational companies and expects to be a prominent player in managed corporate travel well into the future. When they accept it as a solution, companies gain the benefit of a single source in contracting for managed travel options, helping more companies closely manage business travel expense and increase employee adherence to policy and adoption, all of which lowers associated costs through increased managed transactions and more efficient processes—which means that suppliers can also enjoy lower distribution costs.

Airline, Hotel, Rental Car and Tour Suppliers

Travel suppliers are the primary customers of distribution services—i.e., technology and products specifically designed to connect travel inventory holders with the customers they serve. Recognizing the unique characteristics of airlines relative to other suppliers, Cendant has categorized its core supplier groups into two business units, one serving airlines and the other serving hospitality and leisure suppliers.

Although the two groups are distinct customers, the parallels among their wants and needs are nearly identical, for all travel content providers want to grow incremental revenues while reducing overall costs of distribution. Cendant is specifically addressing these needs by leveraging its asset portfolio to create customized and flexible distribution programs for these suppliers, making it easier, more cost-effective and thus more attractive, to do business with Cendant rather than with multiple distribution partners.

Supplier relationships are forged with small, medium and large customers, giving them one point of contact for end-to-end capability. Hoteliers and other suppliers gain greater exposure to a wide audience, providing an effective outlet to move both premium and discounted inventory.

Cendant provides several points in the distribution chain at which suppliers can interact with Cendant businesses: Galileo, Cendant Travel, Cheap Tickets, Lodging.com, Neat Group, and Traveler's Advantage, an affiliated membership-based travel club. These services and capabilities give the airlines exposure to a wider distribution network while also providing additional revenue opportunities by integrating Web-based technology, such as Neat's dynamic packaging product, into suppliers' own Web sites for greater sales. Cendant's ability to package airfares with hotels or other travel services allows suppliers to move excess or heavily discounted inventory with less price transparency at a total lower price—an average 30 percent lower—to consumers. This stimulates consumer demand, thereby increasing volume for the supplier.

With its multiple and complementary distribution channels, Cendant can help travel suppliers customize flexible and comprehensive distribution programs that reward increased business and transaction volume with lower costs.

Hospitality and Leisure Services

While airline tickets continue to comprise the majority of travel sales, there is increased emphasis on growing the percentage of non-air transactions through the new TDS model, which currently account for approximately 10 percent of Cendant's GDS bookings worldwide and present great opportunity.

Consumers who fly often need a place to stay at their destination, as well as ground transportation. Cruises are likely to require air travel to the city of departure. This simultaneously benefits more non-airline travel suppliers with increased sales, and travel agencies with higher-margin and commissionable products and services, supporting strategies to encompass a more packaged sales approach.

Dynamic packaging technology has made it easier for agencies to cross-sell air, hotel and car inventory, and even to upsell customers. Sales of online vacation packages are expected to reach nearly $2.4 billion by 2005, representing 12 percent of all vacation package gross bookings.

Cendant strengthened its packaging ability in May 2003 through the acquisition of Neat Group, Inc., which employs leading dynamic packaging technology. With Cendant's new packaging capability, there is less price transparency to the consumer—the focus is on the total price for the combined elements of the trip. This technology is attractive to suppliers and functionally appealing to Cendant's leisure consumers, corporate clients and travel agency partners, who will all benefit from its functionality and increased sales potential.

Cendant owns, or is affiliated with, a number of specialty services that allow it to carve out a unique position, specific to these hospitality and leisure suppliers, hoteliers, in particular. In addition to supplier relationship and distribution management offered to all suppliers, Cendant offers hotel customers unique services in the form of technology, connectivity, marketing and reservations services. Cendant is integrating these assets to provide consolidated products and services to the hotel market through an easy "one-stop shop" from which distribution and connectivity programs may be customized to meet each suppliers' needs, delivering superior value and providing lower costs in exchange for increased business and transaction volume through Cendant.

Airline Services

The airline industry is experiencing rough turbulence—the result of a slower world economy, fears of terrorism, global hostilities, and regional health epidemics. People have responded by cutting back on trips and planning vacations closer to home. The airlines, which have historically served as the backbone of the travel industry, are again in financial crisis, with major domestic carriers either in or heading toward bankruptcy. Cendant's TDS model, with additional opportunities to grow revenues and cut costs, was designed to help the airlines, and all travel suppliers, regain their strength.

In addition to programs such as Galileo's Momentum, Cendant can customize distribution programs by airline to meet specific needs, aggregating its capabilities to increase value and ease of doing business, while lowering the overall cost. Cendant gives airlines a broad outlet for both their high-margin routes and discounted fares through Galileo's expansive travel agency network and its online and membership-based agencies.

Cendant also serves airlines and maintains relationships through Shepherd Systems, which provides sales and marketing intelligence, including systems that integrate travel agent GDS bookings, flown revenue and airline reporting data. By using these intelligence tools, airlines gain the competitive information they need to guide their strategic and tactical plans for better business results.

Low-cost carriers have forever altered the competitive landscape as these carriers have entered the market with force, proving collaborative work rules, no-frills service, and employee-shared success provide for a sustainable and profitable model that benefits employees, airlines, shareholders and most of all, customers. If the current rate of growth is maintained in the United States, it is expected that low-cost, no-frills airlines will account for approximately 40 percent of U.S. air travel within the decade. While some low-cost carriers have managed success without the GDS, such as Southwest Airlines, which processes 100 percent of their online sales on Southwest.com, many others recognize the benefit of distributing through the GDS—Cendant's Galileo is becoming a leader with low-cost carriers around the globe. As the popularity of low-cost carriers increases, Cendant is keenly focused on delivering efficient and cost-effective distribution solutions to low-cost carriers. The solutions surpass the perceived benefit of managing independent hosting systems or multiple direct connections, where the absolute, fully allocated costs render these alternatives cost-inferior.

Cendant firmly believes the health of the travel industry rests on the vitality of the airline industry and responsibility in restoring airlines to financial stability is shared among all industry sectors.

At press time for this book, there are a number of factors at play that will affect the health and well being of the airline industry, including review of regulatory rules governing airline-owned distributors, bankruptcy filings, direct connection attempts and failures, and the general state of the economy.

As it refines the TDS model, Cendant will support the airline revitalization movement by combining its assets and services to deliver a compelling portfolio that helps airlines increase sales volume through multiple channels with the benefit of both price transparency and opacity for a total lower cost. Additionally, Cendant will continue to serve as an intermediary between airlines and the travel agency community to broker win-win tradeoffs that help preserve the overall effectiveness of the travel agency channel.

The question we should continue to ask is—Which carriers will emerge as winners and leaders in this marketplace? While opinions may vary, consensus is likely to lead to those carriers that have abandoned the legacy airline model and taken corrective steps to adopt a more sustainable and cooperative TDS model, such as the one created by Cendant, to cut costs and increase distribution. Like travel agencies, airlines must be active participants in changing the old paradigm. Those that fail to actively participate should be challenged as to whether they may be more interested in irrational market control rather than the long-term savings and viability provided through a TDS model delivering increased transaction opportunity and lower costs.

Consumer Markets

In a global market, where the consumer is king, and demand drives important economic trends, it is no surprise that Internet booking growth continues to outpace the rate of all travel bookings. Consumers have become quite comfortable using the Internet for a variety of e-commerce services, from paying bills and ordering merchandise to applying for mortgages and trading stocks. They have come to expect that, with a few clicks of a computer mouse, they can comparison shop for just about any product or service imaginable. So, when it comes to travel, be it for vacation or business, consumers increasingly rely on online sources to give them the choice, control and convenience to which they are rapidly becoming accustomed. They shop for travel services, particularly airfares, as they would a commodity, with price, convenience and preferred manufacturer—or supplier—being heavily weighted factors in their purchasing decision.

Cendant meets and exceeds these requirements through such online offerings as Cheap Tickets and Lodging.com. Spending for information technology and product development has been a priority in order to create and implement the best online tools, providing a full range of discounted products and services. This investment comes in the form of buying, building or renting, depending on economics. For example, Cendant contracted with a leading airline faring technology company to incorporate more inventory into its Cheap Tickets consumer site. The result has been measurable. According to comScore, which tracks online traffic, Cendant's affiliated collection of Web sites is the fourth largest, with an average of 10 million unique monthly visitors and 30 million registered users. Not only is the Cheap Tickets site attracting new visitors, but many more of them are making purchases and they are becoming customers, and repeat customers. By employing leading technology and software, coupled with a shift to its Galileo booking platform, Cendant increased Cheap Tickets' look-to-book conversion three-fold, providing price competitive inventory to consumers more efficiently than competitors. Cheap Tickets' increased popularity with consumers benefits Cendant through increased electronic transactions that keep fulfillment costs low and drive revenue growth. In turn, suppliers gain increased bookings through the Cheap Tickets online agency channel, which has prompted Cendant to introduce specific online booking fees for airlines, contributing to further distribution cost savings. With its success in North America, Cendant is making plans to leverage its online retail expertise in international markets as the passion for transacting on the Web continues to grow around the globe.

TDS—the New Intermediary

The ultimate fate of the travel industry lies in the ability of participants to drive and embrace a new distribution model for the 21st century. The current model is not sustainable as participants struggle for survival and suppliers demand increased control over distribution costs.

Cendant has created a competitive portfolio with complementary benefits and the TDS model as the new intermediary. Its value is the ability to drive costs out of the supply chain, while increasing transaction volume and providing travel suppliers with multiple efficient channels to diversify and broaden their distribution of inventory. TDS is a timely and appropriate response to current issues in today's travel industry; but it will not likely be the final answer. As the industry continues to change and evolve, so will the need for new solutions to address emerging issues and market developments. The period of arbitrage distributor profits, capitalized on by some leading online players through excessive hotel mark-ups, is fading away as hoteliers and other suppliers demand more pricing and inventory control over discounted inventory. Therefore, the successful intermediaries will be those with the flexibility, expertise and assets to continuously reinvent themselves. The model is undergoing transformation and one cannot wait for demand to shift before preparing for the new world. Leaders must prove their ability to anticipate developments and provide reliable market-based solutions to serve the multitude of customer needs, while providing greater scale more efficiently and helping to simplify distribution for customers. Above all, they must continue looking for innovative ways to drive revenues and profits for all players.

Like the Phoenicians in the Ancient World, Cendant recognizes the value inherent in the intermediary role. Like Wal-Mart, Cendant knows the value of transforming its distribution model to better serve its customer base in a manner unrivaled in the industry. As Cendant delivers its new TDS model, it is charting a new course as the new travel intermediary. The strategy is simple, but effective: build volume and reduce costs so that all participants in the distribution chain can be successful.

51

Staying Close to the Customer

Cynthia Valles
Senior VP and General Manager
Consumer Travel Network,
USA American Express

Cynthia Valles, senior vice president and general manager, Consumer Travel Network, USA, leads American Express' U.S. leisure travel business, which includes Centurion Travel Services, Platinum Travel Services, the owned retail network, the U.S. Representative Travel Network and two wholly-owned travel subsidiaries: Travel Impressions of Farmingdale, New York, and American Express Mariner Club/Golden Bear Travel of Novato, California Valles was appointed to her position in 2001 and reports to Al Kelly, president, consumer and small business services, American Express.

Since assuming her position two years ago, Cynthia has unified the Consumer Travel Network with her "one network" approach to marketing, supplier relations, product development and customer service. She has placed an unprecedented emphasis on customer excellence and making American Express the premium travel provider of choice. She has redefined the goals of the leisure travel network with plans for retaining and attracting the best and most successful agencies.

Valles has more than 20 years' experience in the travel industry. Prior to joining the Consumer Travel Network, she had demonstrated outstanding leadership in a variety of senior roles within American Express, forging a record of driving growth, profitability, and positive organizational change in complex businesses. She also has a well-earned reputation for leadership, having engineered dramatic improvements in employee satisfaction in organizations that she has headed.

Valles has held other key assignments in the company's travel businesses. She was vice president and general manager for the corporate services large market-Eastern region from 1999 to 2001, responsible for more than $8 billion in corporate card, and travel and purchasing card, volume. As vice president of business travel from 1996 to 1998, Valles led an organization of 1,700 employees and $2 billion in sales in the Eastern Region.

Valles came to American Express from Thomas Cook Travel. She played a key role in the successful integration of Thomas Cook's and American Express' group travel divisions. Prior to the acquisition, she was vice president, convention and incentive services, for Thomas Cook.

Active in the community, Valles has been an advisory board member of the Academy of Travel and Tourism since 1998. She has also been co-chair for the United Way of New York City's Volunteer Committee since 1998, and became a board member of the Council of Senior Centers and Services of New York City in 2000.

Intense change has come to define business conditions throughout industries and around the world. And certainly this trend has been evident in the travel industry. The increasing use, and capabilities of, technology, the "shrinking" of the globe (with a marked increase in concern for security and personal safety), and demographic trends have combined to cause major shifts in the structure of the travel industry. With the elimination of air commissions, increased price transparency and aggressive efforts by travel suppliers to sell directly to consumers, the travel service economics of the past have been changed forever.

At the same time, individual traveler needs and concerns have become more diverse and complex as people access a greater array of travel options. The advent and widespread use of interactive technology have given the traveler a tremendous increase in choices at all levels of the travel equation. Technology has empowered consumers by commoditizing basic travel and allowing individuals to access the best price for their needs quickly and easily. In many cases, this has resulted in lower prices for consumers and reduced income for travel agents and travel suppliers.

Clearly, the travel industry faces challenges in the years ahead. Travel suppliers must work to effectively define and serve the needs of the powerful consumer population, while meeting the traveler's concerns for safety and security. American Express, a global travel and payment services company, uses strengths the company has built over the years to remain a leader in all environments. Our

153-year history as a premium service provider, combined with our strong brand and extensive global network, provide a substantial platform from which to execute our consumer travel strategy. At the same time, our relationships with American Express Cardmembers and powerful partnerships with travel suppliers throughout the world give us the tools to understand and meet travelers' needs.

In this new world of travel services, American Express has developed and is pursuing a thoughtful strategy that, we believe, will ensure its success in consumer travel well into the 21st century. Although uniquely tailored to the strengths of American Express, our strategy, and the thinking behind it, can provide important insights for travel marketers today and in the future.

Consumers: The New U.S. Superpower

Consumers today are more powerful than ever before. The post–World War II Baby Boomers are already acknowledged to be the largest, most powerful generation of consumers the world has ever seen. Their sheer numbers—76 million people between 39 and 57 years old—make Boomers a force to be reckoned with. But it's their growing affluence that portends continuing influence in the years ahead. More than 15 million U.S. households have income of $100,000 or more; another 12 million have $75,000 or more in income. And the percentage of high-income households continues to grow.

But time marches on, even for the Baby Boomers, and the aging of this huge slice of America carries implications as well. Each year, for the next 11 years, three to four million Baby Boomers will turn 50. With overall U.S. population growth slowing, we are arguably at the leading edge of a "senior boom." The individuals in today's 50+ market are healthier, more active and more influential than ever. With intense buying power at their command—people over 50 control nearly $9 trillion of net worth—this population group is breaking free of traditional expectations, approaching aging in their own way.

The men and women in this demographic group own more than 70 percent of the nation's financial assets. They account for 80 percent of all luxury travel. And while they are big consumers of budget travel, people over 50 spend 74 percent more on a typical vacation than 18- to 49-year olds. The affluence of this group also brings an increasingly prevalent trend: the perception that "luxury" is a necessity. More people can afford the best, and more premium goods and services are available than ever before. Nowhere is this trend more evident than in travel.

What today' travel consumer wants

With their dominance in cultural trends and travel spending, aging Baby Boomers warrant attention from travel suppliers. By and large, American Express has found that mature consumers want to purchase experiences, not just things. Customized, unusual, educational, stimulating—these are the adjectives that describe the vacations and journeys most favored by older affluent consumers. Most are willing to pay to realize their vision, but they are conscious of how much value they receive for the price and are becoming more interested in getting rewarded for their business. This group may use frequent flyer or Membership Rewards points to purchase airline tickets and then splurge on ultra-luxury hotels and fine dining experiences. Self-service options are well utilized, but mature consumers value assistance from professionals who bring tangible, useful knowledge to any transaction or relationship.

More affluent travelers also place high value on quality and safeguarding their financial investment when making a travel purchase. Working with a well-known, trusted travel provider can be an important factor in travel planning, especially when addressing the traveler's personal safety and security. Here's where a strong, recognizable brand can play a leading role. For example, the knowledge that travelers can quickly receive support and help if the need arises when they are far from home, provides them an additional level of comfort. Generally, those travelers who have encountered difficulties when traveling and have utilized the services of American Express develop a powerful emotional connection to our brand.

Convenience and access to information also rank as major concerns for today's consumers—such concerns are often as important as the product or service itself. The Boomer group is better educated than any previous generation, and they realize the benefits of technology. Online use by older Americans far surpasses the predictions made during the Internet's early days. In a recent survey by retail consultancy Unity Marketing, luxury consumers said the Internet was the top media choice influencing their purchase decisions. This educated, computer-literate group will seek out information, but they also tend to be discerning, seeking out validation from an expert.

And, true to the Baby Boomer image, most mature Boomer consumers want to be treated as unique individuals. For travel suppliers who can put the pieces together, this is an attractive group.

Technology Changes
the Travel Equation

For today's tech-savvy consumer, extensive information on virtually any topic is available with a few clicks of a mouse. Research is faster, easier and more thorough, thanks to the Internet. Empowered by this access, consumers are more willing to try to find the product, service or travel experience that fits their unique needs.

Buying online, or conducting a travel-related transaction over the Internet, has become an integral part of the travel service equation, with online travel flourishing in recent years. According to Internet research firm PhoCusWright, Inc., online travel gross bookings for the consumer sector reached an estimated $28.4 billion in 2002, up 37 percent from the year earlier, even as the overall travel market declined 5 percent. Fifteen percent of all travel was booked online in 2002, with almost all the online gains being siphoned from traditional travel agency and travel supplier 800 numbers, rather than as a result of generating new business.

Unfortunately, there are downsides to online buying that may not be apparent to the consumer until something unexpected happens. Errors can happen on both ends, and customer service from online providers, while improving, is still inconsistent given today's current high standard. As in other aspects of travel, a strong brand and a strong, reliable customer service orientation can be a critical competitive advantage in the online world as well.

On the other end of the transaction, travel suppliers put technology to use to better serve their customers. In addition to faster and better booking systems, technology gives companies the tools and information to analyze and understand customer preferences and buying patterns in real time. As a result, travel suppliers can tailor services and offers that appeal to certain customer groups, or even to specific individuals. Privacy concerns are obviously paramount, but gathering, storing and analyzing customer data can provide tremendous insight into how best to service customers.

For travel agents, advances in technology have effectively leveled the playing field by bringing a wealth of information and expansive capabilities to the desk of every agent. Knowing the most shortcuts on an airline reservation system is no longer a competitive edge. Today's outstanding agents have extensive destination and product knowledge, a deep understanding of their customers' needs and preferences, and superior customer service skills. They differentiate themselves with consultation and advice that adds value or a specialization that can't easily be replicated.

Sophisticated consumers recognize this differentiation and, although ready to use the Internet themselves when it makes sense, they also know when it's better to call on the services of a trusted, knowledgeable expert. American Express travel counselors act as just such experts on a daily basis for their customers. A great example of creating a unique travel experience occurred when a counselor arranged a 50th birthday party for a client onboard a private yacht complete with customized t-shirts. The client was so delighted, the following year he asked his counselor to arrange a similar party for his wife.

Travel agents or service providers who are concerned that the Internet will eliminate their role should look to the banking and investment industries for reassurance. In the 1980s, when ATMs were proliferating, many predicted the end of the bank teller position. Rather than eliminating that role, ATMs actually helped take the burden of small transactions off the tellers, allowing them to become more valuable to the customer because of their knowledge of more complex or difficult transactions. Similarly, in the 1990s, online investing grew quickly, causing many to question the viability of brokers and investment advisors. The reality is that most individuals who trade online continue to maintain a relationship with a licensed broker.

In travel, the Internet cannot replace the expertise of a trusted, competent travel agent, particularly for complex itineraries or customized vacation experiences. Multi-city itineraries, destination weddings, exotic cruises—these are the types of vacations people are looking for and only a well-trained, accredited travel agent can make them happen.

Delivering desired travel services

Today's sophisticated, powerful consumers want convenience, choice and control. In travel, they want memorable experiences that often extend beyond the description of a typical vacation. The consumer is willing to pay for the knowledge and expertise of a travel counselor, as long as such assistance truly adds insight and enables the trip to meet specific expectations. At the same time, today's empowered consumers enjoy the convenience of booking quick trips or last minute flights themselves. How can the travel industry effectively meet these needs within a viable and profitable business model?

The continued dominance of technology necessitates a solid, robust online presence for travel suppliers. Continuous improvement will be the norm as the interactive capabilities and service standards of today become the bare minimum required for tomorrow. Service weaknesses must be addressed and corrected; success in the future will require ongoing enhancement of capabilities.

This technology imperative will make the travel agent more valuable, not obsolete. Change, already well underway in this profession, will continue as agents move away from the old model to become travelers' agents, not just a convenient booking agent for the airlines. Pricing services becomes a more difficult and complex question, answered, in part, by the expertise required to enable transactions. Yesterday's compensation systems are fading quickly—the vast majority of U.S. travel agencies now charge transaction fees for their services to make up for the loss of commissions.

In this new travel paradigm, being all things to all people will be a difficult task, at the very least requiring a significant infrastructure. Smart travel providers will target the bulk of their energy and resources to a specific consumer segment or area of travel expertise. American Express, while providing a full range of services for virtually any type of traveler, focuses on the luxury traveler. This is the consumer segment we think we can serve best. As a result, we gear our services to this segment and train our travel counselors to meet this group's unique needs. Whatever the determined focus, travel counselors and service representatives must have the training needed to serve the target groups and offer the level of customer care and expertise that matches that concentration.

Even with a specific focus, travel agents must face the reality that choice in contact and interaction is now the norm for consumers. In addition to phone and online capabilities, travel providers must maintain a physical presence as well. American Express believes that our customers at various times will want to walk in, call in or click in to access our services, depending on the customer's needs and desires.

In this evolving world of travel service, trust is critical, and again a strong, identifiable brand can be a valuable asset. Consolidation will continue throughout the industry as travel agents exit the business or combine with larger agencies, migrating to those companies that can provide the benefits of a well-respected brand name and negotiate the best preferred relationships with travel suppliers.

Our aim: Premium travel service provider

American Express Consumer Travel Network's goal is to be the premium travel service provider of choice for American Express Cardmembers. How will we do this? By demonstrating rational value, providing exceptional customer service, and creating emotional connections with our customers. These are the fundamentals of our premium value strategy.

American Express provides a breadth of service and choices to meet the needs of the upscale, "experiential" traveler. At the same time, we provide the tools they need to book a last minute air ticket themselves. Our ability to effectively integrate today's diverse delivery channels differentiates us from other travel companies. Many of our Platinum Card members, for example, take advantage of the opportunity to book their own airline tickets on our dedicated Web site, but call our Platinum Travel Services desk when they want to book a cruise or a more complex vacation.

Given today's challenging travel supply economics, travel agencies must increasingly align with a network to provide their customers with access to the best values and global assistance. Our network of independently owned travel agencies provides a local American Express presence in communities around the world. The representative agencies in our network—highly experienced travel providers and leaders in their communities—are carefully selected to meet the highest customer service standards.

Our travel counselors are held to a high standard as well and receive extensive and ongoing training to fulfill American Express' commitment to employing the best travel counselors in the business. Our internal travel counselor training programs have been accredited by the Institute of Certified Travel Agents (ICTA), enabling our counselors to work toward industry certification while attending our training classes. Counselor training and development includes educational tours to give our counselors firsthand experience of our most popular destinations and products.

This training helps us maintain our reputation for excellent customer service, the second component of our strategy and a trait we have been proud to reinforce throughout our company's history. The walk in/call in/click in model, which ensures 24/7/365 availability, is part of this commitment to service. Whenever and wherever our customer needs us— we'll be there, providing premium service at a rational cost.

Creating an emotional connection is the third component of our premium value strategy. Excellent service and comprehensive availability certainly helps create that connection. In addition, we offer important services such as medical emergency services, prompt card replacement and having a friendly face available almost anywhere in the world.

In consumer travel, our counselors are on the front line—ready, willing and able to satisfy our customers. We encourage our people to say, "We can do that!" in response to our customers. We expect our people to address the overlooked details and take immediate action to address complaints, and to seek out and act on continuous feedback. Our travel counselors have expanded their role to address special requests, such as acquiring theater tickets or hard-to-get dinner reservations at popular restaurants around the world.

A challenging, exciting future

The travel industry has confronted and continues to face numerous challenges. With change remaining a constant, cookie cutter approaches won't work. Personal care will be critical, supported by knowledgeable, smart advice, and customized products and services. Travel service companies must concentrate on offering experiences, not simply selling travel products. Giving customers access to best-in-class travel providers will enable competitive differentiation.

While world events and economic conditions will undoubtedly contribute to shifts in overall travel activity, growth in the worldwide travel marketplace will persist. Customers' knowledge, and correspondingly their demands, will continue to expand. For American Express, staying close to our customers and rewarding their loyalty, offering customized products and services enabled through partnerships with leading suppliers, delivering excellent service by hiring and training the best people in the industry and providing a local presence through our network of the country's leading travel agencies, ensures that we will remain a premium travel service provider and the most trusted travel brand in the world. We take our job of fulfilling peoples' vacation dreams very seriously.

52

GDS—Recasting the Business Model

Tony McKinnon
President and CEO
North American Operations
of Amadeus

Tony McKinnon, a tourism and hospitality industry veteran of 27 years, is the President and CEO for the North American operations of Amadeus, the leading global distribution system (GDS) and technology provider to the travel industry worldwide.

Mr. McKinnon's career includes senior executive positions with Vacation.com, the industry's largest travel agency consortium, as well as American Hawaii Cruises, the Delta Queen Steamboat Co., Wyndham Resort Hotels, American Airlines, Delta Air Lines, Pan American World Airways, US Airways and Certified Vacations. McKinnon is a graduate of the U.S. Military Academy at West Point and Emory University School of Law.

Today, the four global distributions systems (GDSs) provide the technology backbone for the fast and efficient distribution of services for air, sea and land travel. The primary role of a GDS is to electronically connect the buyers and sellers of travel.

Via these computerized electronic distribution systems, travel providers such as airlines, hotels and car rental companies can efficiently and effectively disseminate information about their schedules, availability, pricing and ticketing of their worldwide services to travel "customers" such as travel agencies, Web sites, airline sales and ticketing offices, and consumers.

The downturn in global economic conditions and fallout from the terrorism events of September 11, 2001, put the brakes on what had been a booming worldwide travel industry. The fear of terrorism among a security-obsessed traveling public and the emergence in early 2003 of SARS (severe acute respiratory syndrome) as a global health threat changed consumer travel patterns in ways that are only imperfectly understood today. The travel industry continues to search for clues as to what will be the new paradigm for the future. What we know is that the once-globetrotting U.S. business traveler is now more reluctant to venture overseas, and the U.S. leisure traveler is now opting to stay closer to home; in fact, driving vacations are expected to continue to spike upward as a result of these developments. To say that travel providers are facing steep challenges would be an understatement.

Airlines are perhaps the hardest hit of all. Forced to seek operating savings wherever they can find them, air carriers have identified distribution costs as a key place to significantly cut their expenses. Today, airlines are relying more than ever on automated systems that can integrate data and streamline transactions. They seek to significantly lower the costs of GDS distribution.

The changes in the industry have all of the GDSs seeking and implementing new business opportunities, new commercial models, new revenue streams and continued innovation in serving the needs of their customers.

Based in Madrid, Amadeus Global Travel Distribution [MAD:AMS] is the travel industry's leading GDS—and its leading information technology provider. Since 1992, Amadeus has served the marketing, sales, and distribution needs of travel enterprises the world over.

Amadeus' strategy for this new environment is centered around three main lines of business: airline information technology, travel agency distribution, and online travel transactions. Amadeus has long been at the leading edge in front-line technologies. The Amadeus data center is located near Munich, Germany, and its principal development offices are located near Nice, France. Today, the Amadeus technology base sets the standard of an industry that's trying to play catch-up.

Amadeus' data processing center serves approximately 64,000 travel agency locations and more than 10,000 airline sales offices, which together total more than 272,000 points of sale in more than 206 markets worldwide. Through Amadeus, travel agencies and airline offices are able to make bookings on more than 450 airlines, covering 95 percent of the world's scheduled airline seats. Amadeus also delivers access to more than 60,000 hotels and nearly 50 car rental companies serving some 25,000 locations. Other client groups include ferry, rail, cruise, insurance, and tour operators.

At the same time, Amadeus is a leading information technology provider to the airlines. The Amadeus System User concept, unique to Amadeus, provides a common technology platform for user airlines, enabling them to utilize the same reservation and distribution platform as Amadeus travel agencies use on a world-wide basis. This common platform allows airline users to substantially reduce operating and development costs while delivering comprehensive functionality, as well as providing increased transaction convenience to their passengers. Some 130 air carriers are Amadeus' System Users who use this platform to run their sales and reservations functionality in airport and city ticket offices on the Amadeus GDS.

Today, British Airways—the world's largest international airline—as well as Qantas and Finnair are adopting Amadeus' newest generation of passenger service systems, which comprise all IT systems associated with inventory management and departure control. This is the most sophisticated passenger management system available, putting Amadeus years ahead of the competition.

In fact, British Airways and Qantas continue to work with Amadeus to develop the next generation of world-class airline systems for departure control, inventory and related information systems. This is expected to be available in 2004.

Amadeus' "NewGen" IT platform is the industry's first single solution, which integrates revolutionary departure control and inventory applications with reservation, fares and ticketing solutions. The value of the Amadeus NewGen platform lies in its future-oriented, community approach, providing these airlines with an advanced system to raise levels of customer service, optimize revenue management, strengthen alliance affiliation and improve code-share benefits, all at reduced development and maintenance costs.

Yet the story behind the story of large airlines turning to Amadeus for outsourcing, is more than just one of a massive, unprecedented airline IT migration. It is that of the airlines opting for an enterprise-wide, top-to-bottom simplification of their business systems to focus on core competencies and delegating key functions to outside firms so as to expand cost savings.

When competing in the airline IT arena, Amadeus' competition isn't necessarily the other GDSs. It's actually other information technology outsourcing companies, like Electronic Data Systems (EDS), which itself is an excellent example of how the GDSs are changing to adapt to the post-September 11 world. Some of Amadeus' GDS competitors have actually outsourced their own IT development infrastructures. This leaves Amadeus in a unique position—it retains total control over its own technology infrastructure.

Still, online entities such as Orbitz, Expedia and Travelocity are keeping the pressure on. Founded in 2001 by a partnership of American Airlines, Delta Air Lines, United Airlines, Continental Airlines, and Northwest Airlines, Orbitz introduced technology that provides airlines with the potential to book reservations directly into an airline's reservation system—bypassing the GDSs. To date, only one airline has developed the direct connection. The efficiencies and cost savings that airlines would hope to gain through such a direct connection are yet to be proven. Other online travel sites, such as Expedia and Travelocity (which, interestingly, also view themselves as travel agencies), with the encouragement of the same companies that originally created the GDSs, are helping to give the GDSs a run for their money.

The GDSs were created expressly to instantaneously deliver the managed information about flights, prices, and seats upon which travel agencies, ticket counters, and airline call centers rely. But airlines especially have grown leery of the cost of the sophisticated legacy systems that they must maintain to continue to have this stream of travel data at their fingertips. Increasingly, airlines and other travel players are looking to Web-based, self-service travel sites as a way to minimize their reliance on the GDSs. But again, the efficiencies, cost savings and customer loyalty that these travel providers hope to achieve is still yet to be proven.

As a new generation of consumers becomes ever more comfortable with shopping on the Internet, they are migrating in greater numbers from traditional travel agencies to book-it-yourself Web sites. Little wonder, then, that accommodation suppliers like resorts and hotels are turning to online agencies to market their inventory.

Traditionally, travel agencies booked flights by going through GDSs. Under the global distribution system, airlines paid fees for each segment of a trip. For instance, a roundtrip itinerary connecting through a hub city could involve several segments. Contrary to GDS practice, Orbitz, for one, has initiated a policy of charging airlines a flat fee for each ticket, with no added fees for segments, cancellations, or rebooking.

Nevertheless, the airline industry continues to desperately look for ways to trim costs as consumer and corporate spending on travel trends downward. In response, most U.S. and many international airlines have eliminated the commissions they paid to travel agencies for booking flights.

Cost-cutting and revenue management are an intertwined science the airlines have been sharpening since the 1970s. The carriers have established complex forecasting models, developing strategies that seek to match customers with fares they're willing to pay. Yet the balance between trying to fill every seat while ensuring that some full-fare seats are available for last-minute travelers has been crumbling with the advent of the low-cost carriers. The budget airlines are leveraging a considerably different revenue model—one that is proving hard for many of the hub-and-spoke carriers to overcome.

The so-called "low-cost" newcomers continue to outperform their older rivals. The low-cost airlines are changing the way people think about travel, and the way travelers think about the airlines. Expectations are being raised about "value" that the incumbent airlines may have trouble satisfying. While some of the big carriers are experimenting with service cutbacks, others are abandoning long-standing premium pricing policies.

To what extent the big airlines jump into the price war trenches to do battle with the budget carriers, only time will tell. The intricate hub-and-spoke networks of the big carriers dictate that planes make many different connections at different times, leaving customers with continued service concerns about connecting flights. The big carriers also fly many different models of planes, which complicates cost-cutting. With the advent of the Internet, they have taken more control and options over how they market their product, with Web fares an appealing alternative they are pursuing with a fervor. Their audience? The Net-savvy passenger who refuses to pay full fare.

There is an added challenge for the GDS with respect to these low-cost carriers. With their simplified route schedules and fare structures, most of the new low-cost carriers are not distributed or sell tickets via the GDS. Low-cost carriers rely on their own direct reservation call centers or their own airline Web sites for all their bookings.

Despite the growth of Net travel, online booking isn't for everybody. Nor does it always reveal the best choices or cheapest fares—even for informed and experienced Web surfers.

Synergies generated by the GDS teaming with the professional travel agent still provide leisure and corporate travelers alike with the best range of service and faring options, functionality and reporting. Several market studies have confirmed that travel agents who know their craft and how best to use the GDS technology at their fingertips invariably identify better schedules and lower fares faster, and more frequently, than any online shopper can.

For corporations, there's the built-in benefit of enhanced productivity and higher cost savings when the job of travel shopping is taken out of the hands of the talented amateur and turned over to a skilled professional travel agent or corporate travel manager. Corporations equipped with systems, such as those offered by Amadeus' e-travel/e-commerce business unit, significantly maximize those efficiencies.

Still, unlike the cyclical downturn of the travel industry, Web fares are indicative of a larger reality that the GDSs must address with far-reaching structural changes. GDSs simply cannot continue to do business as usual and survive. Travel agents are changing the way they do business. The airlines are changing the way they do business. Just as the traditional travel agency and air carrier will look very different ten years from now, the GDSs will look much different a decade hence—not only from what they are today, but from each other. Success will be measured in how well each GDS manages change. For each GDS, however, that transition has already begun.

New strategic direction is the definition of change—witness Sabre's move to transform itself primarily into a travel marketing organization. They have done so by divesting themselves of their IT services division by contracting with other technology companies to deliver those services and by taking full ownership of the Travelocity online site, thereby putting themselves in direct competition with the retail travel agency network.

Differentiation in products and services is a key way the GDSs are managing change. Amadeus is in the forefront of GDS reinvention. Amadeus Workplace Solutions is Amadeus' answer to the one-size-fits-all GDS conventional wisdom that is becoming increasingly archaic in today's travel climate. The polar opposite of so many of the cookie-cutter products sold by the other global distribution systems, Workplace Solutions was designed as a suite of solutions, commercial offers, training programs, support tools and technology that meet the specific needs of an individual travel agency. Amadeus is changing the way it does business with its travel agency customers because agencies more than ever want their GDS to play the role of "change agent" and partner in helping them becoming more nimble and adaptable to a market in flux.

Amadeus Workplace Solutions is emblematic of the new consultative approach that will propel the GDSs in the future. Driven by that "change imperative," Workplace Solutions stands the traditional GDS service model on its head by addressing agencies' needs from the bottom up, not the top down. Today, Amadeus is the only GDS that lets an agency pick and choose from a suite of business products and automation tools personalized just for them. Its Workplace Solutions suite, calibrated to each agency's individual needs, gives agents the flexibility they require to prosper in a challenging and changing environment.

Within the Amadeus Workplace Solutions framework is a compelling new program that is changing the relationship between the GDS and travel agents: ProfitChoice. An unprecedented commercial offering designed to arm agents with more control, choice, and revenue for their businesses, ProfitChoice is revolutionary. It replaces productivity-based pricing for agencies (which formerly measured the numbers of transactions made in the GDS) striving to cope in an uncertain world and an unpredictable marketplace by pinpointing the appropriate commercial option to fit each agency's needs. Designed to enable agencies to calibrate and maximize revenue opportunities, ProfitChoice offers flexibility—the new coda of the travel industry—in products, services, GDS connectivity, and contract terms.

The players in this volatile travel marketplace are only too familiar with the pressure to keep pace. With their position on the frontlines of travel, agencies feel the pressure first. They have been a catalyst driving change, because their frontline experience has schooled them in how hard it can be to change and adapt, let alone survive and thrive, when they are limited by the square-peg-in-a-round-hole philosophy of their GDS.

In an industry that continues to reverberate with the echoes of September 11, 2001, a slow economy and unprecedented marketplace evolution, each GDS is blazing its own path to profitability as each one manages changes that no one anticipated even a few short years ago. Not only are the GDSs recasting their business models, they are aiding partners like the airlines and travel agencies to recast themselves, as well. Like the airlines, the travel agency will survive. Although under pressure, the traditional retail travel agency channel continues to be the way six of ten travelers book their trips. Both the agent and the consumer will benefit from that trend of distribution channel reinvention now reshaping the industry. While no one can predict what the travel picture will look like five years from now, what we can say with assurance is that both the impetus for change and the ever-increasing velocity of that change are inherent in any people business, much less the travel business.

53

The Travel Agent Distribution System as a Marketing Arm

Dick Knodt, CTC
President and CEO, Vacation.com

Dick Knodt, CTC, is the president and CEO of Vacation.com, North America's Largest Vacation Selling Network, with 8,000 agency locations.

Knodt entered the travel industry in 1971 when he founded Carefree Travel in San Diego, California., which grew into a five-office retail agency, and national marketing firm focusing on special interest groups. It has a management consulting division.

In 1982, he was recruited by ASTA for its top-paid executive position. He left ASTA in 1984 to start the California Travel Academy. In 1992, he returned to ASTA again to lead the organization as CEO.

In 1998, Knodt left ASTA to head up a new marketing organization, which became Vacation.com.

Knodt earned his CTC in 1978 and has served on the board of the Travel Industry Association (TIA), chaired the Tourism Works for America Council, and served on the advisory board for the Academy of Travel and Tourism.

Knodt is a graduate of the University of Wisconsin, Eau Claire, with a degree in business administration and management.

The often-maligned travel agent industry, with a history that dates back more than 100 years, is evolving into a more professional business as a result of the emergence of the Internet, a plethora of online travel sales and the elimination of third-party commissions (especially from the airlines) which previously provided the bulk of the revenue earned by many agents.

The travel agent of tomorrow will become more of a marketing partner than ever before. Changing avenues of distribution have forced retailers to take more control of their own fate and focus more of their efforts on marketing disciplines than at any time in their history.

What many saw as possibly the demise of the travel agent industry, the elimination of base commissions to retailers by the airlines, has turned into the leisure travel distribution industry's savior. Travel agents have been forced to return to their roots and again become true travel counselors, instead of just processors of airline tickets.

Despite the fact that many industry pundits have been predicting the demise of the travel agent industry for the past 20 years, organizations such as Vacation.com, with more than 8,000 agency locations across North America, are firmly committed to the independent travel agency industry and believe it will be the backbone of a new "click-and-mortar" strategy that is evolving today.

There is no doubt in our mind that the travel agent of today needs to be more proactive. We are beginning to see a return to the true travel counselor concept that first emerged a century ago.

We will also see a more proactive stance taken by the travel agency consortia with a role change that will require a more focused attention to having member agencies generate preferred supplier sales.

But the combined change in roles for both agencies and consortia will result in continued success for a cadre of travel agencies across North America as consumers find a need for qualified agents, especially in the leisure market.

As busy, stressed-out consumers plan family vacations, honeymoon getaways, annual vacation escapes and long weekends away from work, many of them are seeking assistance from the thousands of qualified travel agents across North America. They look for agents who provide three critical (consumer research supported) elements that will help to ensure customer satisfaction with their travel experience:

- Travel agents validate consumers' choices.

- Travel agents serve as the consumer's advocate if anything should go wrong.

- Travel agents save consumers valuable time, and actually become a human mouse for consumers who do not have the time to search the Internet for the perfect trip.

Consumers want to know, with assurance, that when they make a choice on a dream vacation, they will get both what they expect and deserve, based on what they paid. And consumers do not want to rely on a computer screen alone if something goes awry. They want a knowledgeable professional to address the problem and fix it immediately.

The value of using the services of a travel agent became even more pronounced following the terrorist attacks on the United States and the resulting havoc wreaked on the world's travel and transportation system. Travel agents served as the frontline in addressing the myriad of problems and concerns of travelers worldwide.

Web sites and Internet selling agencies are great for information purposes. However, the missing link will always be the human touch that is provided by a live travel agent. Most online travel services are now adding human-staffed reservation centers to support this previously unrecognized need.

Consumer research also indicates that most consumers want the freedom to search the World Wide Web for travel information, choices and price comparisons. Similar research has found that there are so many versions of airfares, hotel rates and vacation alternatives available that it is nearly impossible for the average consumer to know whether or not he or she has paid the lowest price for the best product. That's where the knowledgeable travel agent enters the picture.

The 21st century travel agent will be using the latest in technologically enhanced tools to find information, perform the reservations process and market to their customers in ways unimaginable only a few years ago.

Travel Marketing Organizations

These independent travel retailers, located in every community across North America, will be supported in these efforts by new "travel marketing organizations" (TMOs), which differ demonstrably from the travel agent consortia model of the past. The TMOs will provide technology, design marketing programs and negotiate preferred supplier agreements that few independent retailers could initiate themselves.

Additionally, the TMO's relationship with preferred suppliers is evolving into a much more substantial marketing and partner relationship. In this new relationship, they will work together to promote travel products to the consumer on behalf of the member travel agent in a much more efficient and effective manner. This creates the win-win scenario that agents and suppliers both seek.

More than at any time before, the successful travel agency of the future needs to be aligned with an organization that understands the current marketplace and also anticipates and provides for future needs.

Vacation.com was formed in 1998 with that concept in hand and has led the field with a "clicks-and-mortar" formula in which Web sites provide the information and real people provide the final counseling and bookings.

Using a travel agent in today's fast-paced Internet world is the only way consumers can ensure that they are really getting the best price, the best value and the protection from potential fraud in a growing, uncontrolled electronic environment. Surveys done by Forrester Research and PhoCusWright have concluded that no one Internet travel site provides a consistent hold on the lowest air fares, hotel rates or any other travel product. Using a travel agent to assist in the search and securing the lowest rates can often be an advantage, especially for the busy executives and even for the leisure vacationer who does not have the time to sit and recheck rates.

Travel agents armed with the most up-to-date technology, including automated fare search tools, can snare the best rate as soon as it becomes available. Whereas the average traveler might only come upon this rate by sheer luck if searching the Internet.

Independent researchers have found that there are so many versions of airfares, hotel rates and vacation packages available that it is nearly impossible for the average consumer to know whether or not he or she has paid the best price for the best product. That's where the travel agents enter the picture.

And while we know that not every travel agent is the most professional, we have seen a shakeout in the industry in the past year which has resulted in better odds on finding a good travel agent—many of the poor ones have gone out of business and disappeared.

The number of agency locations has dropped by almost 10,000 from a high of more than 36,000 U.S. locations two years ago to about 27,000 locations today. Those numbers will continue to drop over the next few years, until they reach a level that can be adequately supported by the traveling public and that will require and utilize their expertise and service.

Vacation.com believes that it serves as a model for both the agency organization of the future and the independent travel retailer operating successfully in this new era.

We are predicting that building on the growing concept of "click-and-mortar," travel agencies, like their Web sites, will continually evolve with a growing portfolio of technology-driven solutions, with which the agencies can manage and expand their client base.

As for the consortium of the future, any successful company must create an organization with a "critical mass" of experienced travel agents with millions of existing customers; negotiate the very best preferred supplier lineup; develop internal technology that would bind the organization together; and, ultimately, develop a brand and consumer travel Web site that would incorporate member agent and preferred supplier involvement.

We see these initiatives, combined with services provided by travel agents, as the keys to creating the best buying experience for the consumers over the next decade.

The consortium model of the 21st century will focus on every aspect of the sale. In order to profit from a TMO membership, agents must be offered support with marketing, technology, preferred supplier relationships, education and training opportunities and business-to-business benefits. Such support must be readily available, with information accessible around the clock.

A strong communications link between the consortium, the suppliers and the agency members will be the key for the consortium in the next decade. An online communications platform needs to be the center of this communications network.

Many consortia are now developing these platforms. It must be designed to become to travel agents what the Bloomberg Box is to financial planners. It should provide critical sales information for agencies by streamlining the flow of information among suppliers, agents and the consortium. This would allow members easy access to important supplier product information, so that they can access that information and sell more efficiently, rather than sift through piles of faxes and brochures.

As these communication networks evolve into the single desktop solution with which travel agents will transact their business, it will help create the uniform, disciplined sales and marketing force necessary to increase the sales of, and move market share to, preferred suppliers.

New Focus on Marketing

Marketing, in particular co-op marketing with strong partnerships, will be one of the keys to success in the next decade.

Marketing relationships with suppliers will be based on cooperative marketing, not just lip service provided by the traditional consortia or individual agencies. This will move marketing into a realm not previously accomplished by older agency groups. Many have been involved in the growth of the travel agency market and found that, over the years, we tried, but often failed, to move market share for our preferred suppliers. Loosely connected independent agencies will now have to focus on selling only preferred suppliers in order to make up for the commission base that was lost when the airlines cut commissions to zero.

The marketing of travel is now being remolded on the old basics of "know your customer and give them what will make them happy." Which is not necessarily what they came in asking for.

However, at the same time, many agencies are now working in earnest to survive in a new era of travel distribution. They turned their sights on the Internet agencies that were succeeding in drawing many of their customers with low fares, attractive packages and ease of booking.

Suddenly, the competition was the focal point and these small, independent agencies were mocking their large Internet cousins with their own Web sites filled with product that were often as attractive and sometimes better priced than that found on the big Web sites.

But the secret was not only in the Web site per se; it would be in getting the customer to log onto their Web site or make the call to the toll-free telephone number to book their trips. The question of the day was how would independent agencies compete with large Internet-based travel companies and chains?

The answer was simple: Agencies that truly became engaged with their consortium and committed to a greater level of participation in their membership, would be rewarded with exclusive promotional opportunities, bonus offers and incentives. This new focus on becoming engaged was evolving with the development of the new travel marketing organization (TMO) model of consortium that we expect will rule the future for independent agencies.

In addition, the co-op marketing program orchestrated by the TMO in conjunction with the suppliers would drive the consumer to the individual participating agencies, thus generating real business. Those agents who become "engaged" with their marketing organization, consortium or franchise will have the highest business success rate and reap the largest profits.

Relationship Marketing

Another key ingredient for the travel agent over the next decade will be the travel agency's greatest asset, its customer list. Consumer lists and real time sales data are key assets but both tend to be underutilized.

Travel industry marketing and sales and the travel agent industry, which has traditionally orchestrated those sales into both business and leisure trips for consumers, will be forever changed in the 21st century. The travel agent of tomorrow will be based on a combination of the travel agent of yesterday using the technology tools of today.

The travel agent industry in the next few years will come full circle. We are an evolving species that began in the early 20th century as true travel counselors helping and advising clients on how they could travel across the seas to foreign lands.

Deal marketing over the Internet was the new wave of marketing as the twentieth century turned into the 21st. A new mature century would see the maturation of travel marketing and a return to yesterday for some travel agents; especially those that realized their was still gold out there, but it was not being held by the suppliers—rather it was in the hands of the consumers who were still looking for advice.

Advice for consumers comes from many sources now. It seeps through every crevice of the new information highway. It finds venues in old formats on television, radio and in print in newspapers and magazines. Advice even finds itself back on the billboards that line the roadways and top the buildings in the cities. But the new key was how to tap this new medium and once again control the flow of marketing and subsequently the flow of sales.

It is expensive to plan, produce and deliver the high quality marketing materials that today's consumer is accustomed to. Even the most successful individual agencies have a hard time justifying the funding required to stay in front of a savvy customer. As TMOs aggregate the mailing lists of thousands of agents, the cost per piece, the quality and the frequency of messaging desired by agents falls within their reach.

The rules of engagement are simple. It is a marketing discipline in which the agent stays focused on the client. It uses available information about the client to help him select the best product from the collection of preferred suppliers' offerings negotiated exclusively for them.

By aggregating the names and demographics of thousands of member agent customers, marketing organizations will be able to use permission marketing to reach millions of proven travelers with preferred supplier product offerings focused on their individual needs and desires.

Smart marketing is sending the right message to the right customer! Consortia are able to provide tremendous economies of scale to member travel agents and preferred suppliers while targeting the "right" customer with the "right" promotion at the "right" time, whether by direct mail or via e-marketing.

The next level of marketing will use "variable marketing," in which the organizations will drill down and create specific marketing messages for individuals, at the optimum time for the customer and in the delivery mode they want, all designed to motivate sales for the individual agency members. Variables will include destinations, photographs, pricing levels, trip length and commentary and descriptors. These messages will go only to consumers who are most likely to purchase that specific product at that time. This is the 21st century version of target marketing taken to a new level. It will enable travel agents to better relate to their customers and keep their customers coming back to their agency.

A New Wide Wide World

The Internet has obviously changed the entire way travel and many other products and services are marketed and sold. No longer are customers confined to working with a local travel agent or to shopping at hours dictated by store hours.

But the consumer's need for "validation" of a travel offering, uncovered while she surfed the Net, and a "single throat to choke" when dealing with unanticipated problems, will continue to provide knowledgeable travel agents, who keep abreast of information, technology and consumer demand in both service and product, an important and meaningful role to play well into the future.

Today the travel agent must use all of the Internet and electronic tools that are available for marketing and selling travel. And despite the fact that there are Web sites out there that lure consumers with the ever-present lowest price deals, the real travel agents can still maintain dominance by providing the customer a service that is not available on a machine.

Personal service and the human factor behind the screen is a commodity that is now being marketed by real travel agents as a competitive advantage over the Internet-only sites that promote and sell travel.

In today's world, any professional forward-thinking travel agent can be an "Internet travel agent" and compete handily with the likes of Travelocity and Expedia. All the sales, marketing and booking tools are, in fact, readily accessible to agencies and are intended to help them build their own cutting edge Web sites through their various consortia.

In fact, they can out-compete the Internet travel giants because they already have a relationship with the customer. But, as these customers evolve their shopping and buying habits, the travel agent must adapt in order to compete. Providing 24/7 information and service will be standard practice, and technology will be a key communications channel supporting the travel agent's role as the expert.

Customer relationship marketing (CRM) has come back into vogue as the leading marketing discipline, especially for the travel agent industry. Knowing the customer has never been more important than it is today, and will grow in significance in the next decade.

Tools of the Trade

While many view CRM as the database of consumers, it is really a collection of tools that complete the communication channel. The role of the consortium or new TMO is now changing to allow actual preferred supplier sales records to rule the market—with the result being an increase in co-op marketing and training programs for agencies that have proven sales support for those suppliers.

Online tools from systems like VacationPORT provide an agency with a fast and efficient way to search through a comprehensive list of preferred supplier inventory. The agent can personalize and forward offers, which take the form of colorful emails containing links for more information such as prices and booking window, with an easy interface for contacting the travel agent.

A travel agent can "pull down" preferred supplier content, containing real time pricing and inventory availability on thousands of package vacations and cruises, ship deck plans and detailed trip descriptions and integrate it with product offerings on his own Web site. Agents can also personalize their site with information on their own particular expertise and staff specialization.

Other tools like TripValue, a Web site now being promoted to consumers, on which agencies can post their product offerings to a much wider Internet audience. These provide an alternative to more costly newspaper, radio and television advertising and agents can use hyperlinks to link customers from the TripValue site to their own site.

The Merchant Model

Once the marketing drives a lead to the agent, it is becoming increasingly important that the agent be able to transact the reservation function efficiently and productively. This can be accomplished with the booking engines that are now becoming readily available, especially through TMOs, but directly from suppliers, as well.

The good news for agents is that many travel suppliers participate in paying additional commissions for electronic bookings, enhancing the agent's productivity and earning ability.

Dynamic packaging, wherein an agent can piece together customized vacations at net prices for her clients and mark up the entire package seamlessly, can be accomplished with other online travel tools.

Taking on risk inventory with net priced products that suppliers promote to agents and TMOs will begin to grow over the next decade. Selling vacation product directly to agents through this prototype program allows the consortia to manage product selling prices and margins and become a merchant in the travel marketplace.

If this "merchant model" takes meaningful hold TMOs, with the distribution technology and financial resources, will become meaningful players in helping shape the future of travel distribution.

With all these innovations there are both increased costs as well as cost efficiencies that impact the operational side of the business of being a travel agent. As time goes on, more and more agents want to shed themselves of the costs associated with the administrative and fulfillment side of the business and focus more on the customer in sales, marketing and servicing activities.

This can be accomplished through new programs that have been created to deliver end-to-end administrative and fulfillment support to agencies of all sizes that are searching for a more profitable way to run their day-to-day operations.

Services of a typical program include document processing, financial settlement and fulfillment services, commission tracking and Web reporting, ARC number access, IATAN benefits, GDS access, destination guide and client database tools.

If agencies want to stay in business and do what they are best at, marketing and selling travel, then a modern day TMO may have a solution for them.

Today's TMO must continue to focus on doing for its constituencies, both member travel agent and travel supplier, what they cannot do for themselves. The key ingredients are leading edge technology, innovative marketing programs, education and training initiatives and strong communication links.

Vacation.com is a travel services marketing company serving a network of more than 8,000 travel agency locations across the United States and Canada. Its membership network is focused on leisure travel distribution, accounting for approximately 33 percent of all travel agencies in North America. With more than $25 billion in annual sales, Vacation.com—"Powered By Real Travel Agents"—is North America's largest vacation selling network.

Vacation.com is a subsidiary of Amadeus Global Travel Distribution and maintains its headquarters in Alexandria, Virginia, as well as a Toronto office that serves its Canadian members.

Section VIII

Luxury Marketing

We purposely put the focus on this slice of the travel and tourism industry because we believe it has unique marketing challenges and opportunities. Likewise, we purposely chose to classify the supplier contributors in this chapter rather than in other sections of this book. The reader is encouraged, however, to cast these marketers' points of view against their peers in the other chapters—a sort of reality check, if you will.

What makes this chapter so unique is that the consumer targeted here is not Everyman but a relatively small group of folks who travel a great deal more than the average and spend far more in the process. How big this market is depends on your definition. Ron Kurtz of the American Affluence Research Center estimates that the market for upscale travel is about two million households with a net worth of $3 million or more and incomes in excess of $200,000 per year. This is just 2 percent of the households in the United States, representing roughly 6 million people (including children, or course).

While there is naturally a range of behavior within this group, they have, from a travel standpoint, a lot in common: They have money, they travel frequently, they enjoy and expect great service. They appreciate value; they like to be with their own kind (exclusivity); and they enjoy the cachet of the most sought-after hotels, resorts, cruises and destinations.

The contributors to this chapter have a vision as to how they fashion their products to appeal today and tomorrow to the affluent traveler. Branding is vital here. The affluent traveler must immediately recognize the brand and understand that the brand's property caters uniquely to him or her in a consistent, satisfying manner. When a Four Seasons or Ritz-Carlton puts its name on a new property, it's critical that the quality is on par (or better) than the norm of that brand. In fact, that's the challenge and opportunity of these international brands. On the one hand, they have tremendous scale, which gives their brands more clout: bigger advertising and public relations budgets, more rooms, more trial, more satisfied customers, than smaller entities like Canyon Ranch and SeaDream Yacht Club cruises.

On the other hand, there is more to control from a quality standpoint: more staff to train and manage and more physical plant to maintain. In other words, with greater scale, more things can go wrong. And make no mistake, as with any human endeavor, things will go wrong. How a luxury property handles problems with the affluent traveler is critical to the brand's long-term success and staying power. Curiously, this fact of marketing life was not discussed by our contributors. Perhaps they just took it for granted.

Reaching out to the affluent is a daunting task. Everyone is after the affluent. There is a great deal of clutter. And when it comes to targeted magazines such as *Travel + Leisure* and *Condé Nast Traveler*, the advertising exposure is not insignificant.

Four Seasons puts an emphasis on targeted public relation campaigns, Canyon Ranch relies on referrals from past guests and direct mail. SeaDream uses their cruise staterooms as auction items for upscale charity fundraiser events, giving them practically a no-cost exposure to the affluent. Ritz-Carlton seeks out and wins awards to promote their quality, including the prestigious Malcom Baldridge National Quality Award—the only company in the hotel industry to earn it, and, they earned it twice! The awards speak of quality. The public relations and promotion of these achievements speaks volumes to the affluent listener.

Strategic alliances with other affluent brands is also a strategy at play here. Ritz-Carlton has partnerships with American Express, Mercedes-Benz, and Saks Fifth Avenue. Canyon Ranch has a partnership with Cunard's Queen Mary II, the largest ocean liner ever built, and is launching a line of skin care products to further stretch the brand.

Glenn Fusfiled of Steiner Leisure Group shares his vision of a burgeoning spa industry by 2013, where massage and spa treatments become more mainstream but at the same time even more elaborate and routine for the affluent. The hard-driving type-A affluent business executive of today may be "too busy" for spa pampering. In time, he'll come to realize how salubrious and necessary these treatments are and make them part of his daily routine, not just an activity for vacation. Importantly, all the truly luxury resorts, hotels and cruise ships offer elaborate and extensive spa and massage treatments. At least today, it's a necessity for the affluent, not a perquisite.

If Larry Pimentel of SeaDream is correct, there is a meaningful subset of the affluent (consumers of independent attitudes, as he calls them) who will not seek out a "formula-based experience" or "processed luxury." These folks will seek out the one-off, truly unique properties. While that may be true, when alternatives aren't available, we are pretty confident that they will be well satisfied with a Ritz-Carlton or a Four Seasons.

We believe a growing consumer travel phenomenon is the multigenerational trip frequently arranged by an affluent traveler. Main stream hotel, cruise and resort properties need to have suites and extra services to satisfy the affluent purchaser, as well as all the things his or her children and grandchildren are looking for in a vacation. Kurtz' research data suggests that the affluent population in this country will have grown by 24 percent from 2000 to 2010. Clearly this is a segment that offers vast rewards for the astute marketer.

Exhibit 2

High Income Households (2003)

| Net Worth (000s) | Households | |
	No. (000s)	%
uent	$6,000 plus	500	0.5%
t	$4,000 to $6,000	500	0.5
Affluent	$1,000 to $4,000	4,000	4.0
	5,000	**5.0%**

Source: Federal Reserve Board/AARC Analysis

ewhat simplistic and arbitrary definition of the affluent could be based
ith a net worth of $1 million or more. There are approximately five mil-
holds (5 percent of the total) that qualify as millionaires.

p 5 percent of all households, based on net worth, can be segmented
shown in Exhibit 2.

it 3 provides a financial profile of the top 1 percent and top 5 percent
seholds in the United States based on net worth. The approximately five

Exhibit 3

Financial Profile of the Most Affluent (Based on Net Worth)

	Top 1 percent	Top 5 percent
useholds	1 million	5 million
m	$4.0 million	$1.0 million
	$9.8 million	$2.9 million
t of U.S. Total	34 percent	50 percent
e	$657,000	$225,00
t of U.S. Total	12 percent	21 percent

Source: Federal Reserve Board Study/AARC Analysis

54

Marketing Travel to the Affluent

Ron Kurtz
Cofounder and Director
American Affluence Research Center

Ron Kurtz is a principal of The American Affluence Research Center (AARC) and The Management Resource Group, which provide marketing research and strategic planning services to prominent clients such as Philip Morris, Merrill Lynch, Celebrity Cruises, the Bahamas government, and Rio Suites and Casino.

Prior to founding MRG in 1989, Ron's experience included over 20 years in senior management positions in the airline, hotel, and tour business. As the founding president of Sea Goddess Cruises, he created the product category of small deluxe ships for the very affluent. He also served as the chief marketing officer of four cruise lines, including Norwegian Cruise Line and Windstar Cruises.

Ron has been a key contributor to six start-ups and 11 turnarounds of substantial businesses. He holds an MBA from Harvard Business School.

The affluent market is very important to the travel industry. Most of the vacation business for the larger hotels/resorts and for the cruise and tour industries is derived from relatively affluent consumers.

About 80 percent of all overnight travel away from home is in the family automobile. One of the reasons for this is that most people cannot afford to fly to a nice resort, take a cruise, or go on tour for a vacation. On average, regardless of income level, people spend 5 percent to 6 percent of their income for all of their travel. This means a family of three or four people with an income of $75,000 (the threshold for the top 25 percent of all households) would have about $4,000 to spread over 14 days or so of vacation time. That equals less than $300 per day, which will not go far if it has to cover airfare also.

Based on these realities regarding the nature of the travel market, it is clear that the marketers of vacation travel that includes flying to a resort/hotel, taking a cruise, or going on tour need to have a good definition of the affluent market and who represents their best prospects.

Defining the Affluent Market

As a starting point, it may be helpful to define who or what the affluent market is. During the past 20 years, the affluent market has been the target of increasing interest among marketing executives in various industries. More published data and research on this market segment have become increasingly available, particularly in the past 10 years, from the Federal Reserve Board, the Internal Revenue Service, various market research firms, and companies such as U.S. Trust.

Despite the increasing attention focused on the affluent market, it is very interesting to note that there is no generally accepted definition of affluence or the affluent market. Some define affluence in terms of income, some define it by net worth, and others define it on the basis of investable assets. For none of these possible criteria or methods of measurement is there agreement on the minimum value that defines affluence.

Income as the Criteria for Affluence

Many choose to define affluence in terms of annual income. In fact, some of the more prominent research studies have used an annual income of $75,000 as the criteria for defining affluence. This definition seems too broad, as it encompasses about 25 percent of all U.S. households. A family of three or four is not likely to consider themselves affluent at this level of income.

Exhibit 1

High Income Househ

Adjusted Gross Income (000s)	Number (000s)
$100 under $200	9,907
$200 under $500	2,394
$500 under $1,000	418
$1,000 or more	226
Total	**12,945**

Source: Urban-Brookings Tax

Exhibit 1 shows the estimated distribution percent of the 133,835,000 tax returns anticipa

In 2010, there will be an estimated 17,816, (12.1 percent of the total returns) and two of th lowest bracket ($100,000 to $200,000).

It is difficult to define affluence just by ann snapshot of one point in time. Some may be on (and discretionary income, which is an importan ers may be on a downward curve in their incor stage where they have considerable expenses fo hold/family formation (including expenses for ch empty nesters with no mortgage and a home tha

Net Worth as the Criteria for Affluence

Some choose to define the affluent market in terms bilities), as does the AARC, which does syndicated among the affluent. Net worth represents the co income and expenses of a household and is a financ funding its required and discretionary expenditures income.

Category

Wealthy A
Very Afflue
Comfortal

Total

A so
on those
lion hou
The
roughly
Exl
of the h

No. of
Net W
Mir
Ave
pe
Inco
Ave
pe

million households in the top 5 percent control about 50 percent of the total net worth of all U.S. households, and they have an average net worth of about $2.9 million. Their average income is about $225,000, and they account for approximately 21 percent of total U.S. household income. For the top 1 percent of the households, the average income is about $657,000 and the average net worth is $9.8 million.

Howard Waddell, co-founder and director of the AARC, notes the market for the more upscale travel is probably around two million households with a net worth of $3 million or more and incomes in excess of $200,000. This market segment consists of one million households with a net worth of at least $4.0 million and another one million households with an estimated net worth between $3 million and $4.0 million.

General Profile of the Affluent

Major changes in the demographics, interests, and motivations of the affluent do not normally occur in cycles or time periods of less than 10 years. Exceptions to this "rule" might be experienced if there were some major events that affected the economy, the stock market, or world tensions. The research presented in the following material is therefore believed to be relevant to and indicative of the affluent market for the next several years.

The majority of those with a net worth of $1million or more are self-made millionaires (about 80 percent) who spend and save conservatively. Profiled in the bestseller *The Millionaire Next Door* by Thomas Stanley and William Danko, the typical millionaire is not a conspicuous or pretentious consumer and has accumulated wealth through hard work and careful saving.

In a 2002 *Money Magazine* research report on the affluent, Dr. Gary Buffone of The Family Business Center says his clients prefer the term "comfortable" even when their assets approach $10 million. He describes these people as "primarily self-made and they can't identify with being rich. They retain the middle-class values and lifestyle they grew up with, and even though they've accumulated millions, most live well below their means." He believes that "If you've grown up in the middle class, that's who you are, even when you become wealthy."

The profile of millionaires at different levels of affluence can be partially defined by results from surveys conducted by the AARC. Exhibit 4 shows the median age and income increase with increases in net worth. The same is true for the number of homes owned and the number of nights spent in homes other than the primary residence. This latter attribute is competition for the cruise and resort industries, perhaps more than ever after the events of September 11, 2001.

Exhibit 4

Summary Profile of Millionaires

Net Worth

	$1.0 to $5.99 Million	$6.0 to $14.99 Million	$15 million or more
Median Age	53	55	58
Median HH Income (000s)	$400	$770	$1970
Avg. No. of Homes	1.5	1.9	2.3
Nights/Year in Other Homes	39	58	70

Source: AARC Surveys

Exhibit 5

Vacation Travel Profile of Millionaires

Net Worth

	$1.0 to $5.99 Million	$6.0 to $14.99 Million	$15 million or more
Vacation Nights/Spending			
Total Nights	30	45	54
International Nights	11	15	18
Avg.Total Spending (000s)	$16	$31	$46
Avg.HH Spend Per Night	$527	$687	$857
Cruises Prior 24 Months			
Yes	26 percent	35 percent	28 percent
Number	1.7	1.5	2.3
Nights Cruised	15	12	18

Source: AARC Surveys

Millionaires are very good prospects for travel marketers. Millionaires take a lot of vacation time and about one-third of it is spent at an international destination. As shown in Exhibit 5, total vacation time and dollar expenditures increase with increases in net worth. The same is true for the average expenditure per night of vacation.

Over 25 percent of all millionaires had cruised during the two years prior to the survey. Since they averaged almost one cruise per year, the equivalent of one quarter of all millionaires appears to cruise each year. This demand exceeds the capacity of the upscale cruise ships, thus reflecting the fact that half or more of the cruises taken by millionaires are on premium and contemporary category ships and not on the upscale, luxury brands.

This illustrates that millionaires will "trade down" in certain situations. For example, when traveling with children or grandchildren or when cruising in the Caribbean, the millionaires usually prefer a contemporary or premium category ship and will not pay the rates of the more deluxe ships.

Segments of the Affluent Market

The affluent market is not one homogeneous population. It can be viewed as consisting of several different segments. These segments can be defined in various ways, as evidenced by a review of the literature on marketing to the affluent and the promotion of luxury products.

Based on my personal experience tracking and researching the affluent market since 1982, it appears that the spending patterns of the affluent cannot be explained simply by their level of income or net worth. There is also a need to understand their attitude toward spending and enjoying life.

The segmentation of the market often is based on attitudes toward spending, which are typically a function of:

1. the level of affluence (as defined by net worth and/or income),

2. the life cycle stage (age, family status, etc.),

3. the source (self-made versus inheritance) and speed (accumulated savings versus quick gains) of achieving affluence,

4. their outlook for future earnings, and

5. their recognition, understanding, and appreciation of quality and style

For example, in the early years of the very deluxe Sea Goddess Cruises, it appeared that younger (mid-40s to mid-50s) high-income clients were better prospects and bigger spenders than more mature clients with much greater net worth were. The latter group, perhaps because their future earnings outlook was not as good and they were thus concerned about preserving their assets, seemed to be more conservative in their attitude toward spending.

Motivations of the Affluent Market

For guiding product design, the definition of promotional appeals, and other strategic marketing actions, it is important to understand the basic motivations of the affluent market and its various segments. Certain basic motives, as described below, are not likely to change anytime soon.

Marketing consultant Alan Rosenspan, in an essay on marketing to the affluent, expresses his belief that the primary motivations of the affluent include a desire:

1. to save money (find a good value),

2. to receive acknowledgement of their affluence,

3. to receive recognition as being something more than affluent (smart, sophisticated, worldly, gourmets, collectors, etc.),

4. to have exclusivity (being in good company with access to things beyond the average person's access), and

5. to acquire things money can't buy (a unique experience, access to people and things not normally accessible, etc).

Jane Coloccia in an article in *Marketing Review* (the magazine of the Hospitality Sales & Marketing Association International) makes a similar observation that "When it comes to travel, the affluent consumer wants to collect vivid and meaningful experiences to store as memories and to exchange as conversational currency."

While the population of the affluent is definitely aging with the maturing of war babies and Baby Boomers, there is also a growing number of younger affluent who have additional motivations to be satisfied.

Ms. Coloccia quotes Dr. Lalia Rach, dean of New York University's Hospitality and Tourism School, as noting that "the most dramatic change in the affluent traveler's profile is the decrease in the average age and their different mindset toward travel. They work hard and expect their relaxation to be as challenging. They want an atmosphere that reflects their earning status, provides a reward, and is fun and unusual. They want an unusual out-of-the-ordinary experience.

Exclusivity is but one aspect that interests them. They are looking for products and services that allow them to define themselves and to celebrate their success."

Pamela Fiori, editor-in-chief of *Town & Country Magazine*, also quoted in Coloccia's article, notes the emerging rich/emerging affluent are comprised of the top-level of Generation X who did not grow up surrounded by "the finer things." She feels it is important for luxury travel marketers to enlighten them because "once they experience the good life, they are not going to go backpacking again."

In her article, Coloccia also refers to research by Yesawich, Pepperdine & Brown in which they report the new younger affluent consumer "seeks life enriching experiences, wants to be assured of style and quality, wants to be recognized as knowledgeable and worldly, is not afraid of the unfamiliar or exotic, desires ways to simplify life, and is always pursuing obtaining more of life's most essential luxury, time."

To recap, the major motivations of the affluent, as they relate to the design and marketing of travel products and services, will be:

1. to acquire unique and exclusive experiences (access to people, places, and things that are not normally accessible),

2. to interact with similar (in terms of age and affluence) people,

3. to receive a personalized experience (with individual choice and freedom),

4. to receive recognition as an individual who is knowledgeable,

5. to be assured of quality, style, and good value

6. to participate in a life-enriching, educational and/or cultural activity, and

7. to enjoy the highest possible standards of comfort and convenience (including time-saving convenience).

These motivations have not been listed in any particular order of priority. In fact, travel marketers will do well to adhere to all of these motivations as guidelines for defining their product design, for determining what they will say in their promotional communications and how those communications will be delivered, and how they will develop their relationship with both prospects and current clients.

Marketing in the Future

The marketers of travel to the affluent will face, over the next several years, a potentially challenging and difficult marketplace. Forecasts of the future, like those in this chapter, are often strongly influenced by conditions and attitudes existing at the time the forecast is being made.

The United States has just forced a regime change in Iraq, the second major step (after the conflict in Afghanistan) in its campaign against those countries that are perceived to be threats to world peace and security and the sponsors of international terrorism. There are several other possible future targets after Iraq. At the same time, the stock market has been in a three-year bear market condition and the outlook for the economy is unclear.

International travel by Americans is negatively affected by world tension and acts of terrorism and, because it is typically more expensive than domestic travel, by weakness in the stock market and the economy. The latter are likely to be reversed in the next few years, although some people have a lot of ground to recover in their portfolio before they can begin to feel comfortable about returning to their former levels of spending.

AARC research indicates a number of the affluent will be deferring retirement and/or working part time to compensate for their losses in the stock market. This will depress the growth of the travel market more so than would have otherwise been anticipated due to the maturing of the relatively affluent and travel-oriented population of Baby Boomers.

The big unknown is how the U.S. campaign against the sponsors of terrorism will play out and how long it will last. If acts of terrorism against U.S citizens begin to occur with frequency and/or within the borders of the United States for an extended time period (perhaps lasting for several years), travel will be significantly affected. Everyone, including the affluent, is likely to want to vacation closer to home.

The affluent already have a high incidence of second home ownership (Exhibit 4) for weekend getaways, for vacations, and as primary residences on a seasonal basis. In addition, new concepts in vacation ownership for the affluent, such as fractional ownership and private residence clubs, are becoming popular as they create opportunities for the affluent to enjoy having a second home in several locations without a large upfront investment and continuing maintenance hassles. These new concepts represent an attractive and competitive alternative to the traditional travel options of hotels/resorts and cruises, especially in an environment where people do not want to travel too far from home.

On the positive side, the maturing of Baby Boomers and war babies is creating a vast population that places a high value on vacation travel, has relatively extensive prior international and cruise travel experience, and possesses the financial resources to travel frequently and in high style. At the same time, the travel market is being boosted by the younger segment of the affluent, who consider travel to be a top priority in the expenditure of their discretionary income, which is often considerable in households consisting of two well-educated professionals.

Both the Baby Boomers and this younger generation have, in many cases, the financial cushion of a substantial future inheritance from their parents.

As experienced travelers, the affluent market will increasingly consist of more sophisticated and demanding consumers. They will have considerable leverage over the suppliers of travel as a result of the "perfect information marketplace" created by the Web. The consumer can do extensive research on destinations and suppliers and shop for the best value/price with ever greater convenience and accuracy as the development of the Web evolves.

Travel services, such as hotel rooms/cruise cabins and airline seats, are perishable products with no residual value after their intended date of sale/usage. In addition, the economics of these businesses, comprising high fixed costs with relatively low variable costs, provide an incentive for suppliers to discount in order to achieve high occupancy. These two attributes make the travel industry vulnerable to pricing pressures that are facilitated by the Web.

While more and more travel will be sold over the Web, through the sites of intermediaries as well as suppliers, there will continue to be a role for travel agents, particularly for the affluent. Travel agents can provide valuable advisory services to the affluent in particular. First and foremost, they can help the affluent to save time in planning and making the more complex travel arrangements, and the saving of time is very important to the affluent.

A good travel agent can also be a source of endorsements and testimonials (from other clients as well as from themselves and other travel agents) that will have more credibility than the promotional information found on the Web. A travel agent should know the needs and expectations of their clients and be able to identify and recommend appropriate vacation options. An agent may be the first to learn about new options. Finally, an agent may have some extra influence with a supplier that can help in obtaining special service and/or deals and in securing attention if there is a problem.

The Yesawich study showed that about 80 percent of wealthy adults state they always look for the best prices when making a purchase. Similar findings have been reported by the American Affluence Research Center. This suggests a market segment of about 20 percent of the affluent for which price makes little or no difference. While that may be encouraging for some marketers of luxury travel, it means most affluent consumers will be exercising their power to obtain a good deal.

The affluent sometimes pose a challenge to those responsible for promoting customer loyalty. First, the affluent expect luxury brands to deliver a high standard of quality on a consistent basis. If there is a problem, they expect it to be resolved quickly, fairly, and in their favor, However, the affluent also want what is new and different. If a company does not keep their product(s) fresh and appealing, they are at risk of losing some of their repeat business. This can be more difficult for a specific hotel or resort, whereas cruise ships and tour operators can vary their itineraries and more easily take other actions to introduce diversity to their product line.

If one looks far enough into the future, it is possible to see a whole new collection of travel experiences becoming available to the affluent. Space travel has already been experienced by a privileged few at a cost of about $20 million. Eventually the costs can be reduced to make this option (at least short trips) affordable to a larger segment of the affluent market.

New technology in air travel will make it faster and easier to reach distant destinations (e.g. Asia and the South Pacific) and thus expand the demand for such options as short (one week or less) vacations. Cruise ships may be given speeds that will enable them to reach a larger number of (and more exotic) ports in a shorter time and to offer even more cruises from embarkation ports to which people can easily drive from their home. The design (and location) of resorts/hotels and cruise ships will continue to evolve to offer their guests a larger selection of more personalized experiences that cater to individual interests.

Marketing and promotional communications will increasingly utilize the Web. Companies will learn to use the Web more effectively to communicate with both their prospects and their past customers in a more personalized and individual manner. The process for obtaining information and making travel reservations will become much more user friendly.

Advertising and promotion, both the message and the medium (the types of publications, direct mail, special events, targeted Web sites, etc,) will need to be tailored even more effectively to the particular segment of the affluent market that is being addressed. This will be critical to break through the increasing clutter of promotional messages directed at the target audience, to show empathy for the customer or prospect, and to achieve credibility.

As part of the effort to tailor targeted messages that show customer empathy and have credibility, joint marketing programs that bring together two or more compatible companies that are serving similar segments of the affluent market will become even more important. These strategic partnerships facilitate the sharing of customers through cross selling that is reinforced by the implicit endorsement of one brand by another that already has the confidence of its customers.

The next several years will be an interesting period of time for marketers to the affluent because it will be characterized by both great challenges and opportunities.

55

New Consumers, New Attitudes, New Products

Larry Pimentel, CTC
Co-Owner, President and CEO
SeaDream Yacht Club

Larry Pimentel, CTC, is co-owner of Sea-Dream Yacht Club, founded in August 2001, and also serves as its President and CEO. The company operates the ultra-luxury, mega-yachts SeaDream I and II. Pimentel is a high-profile executive in international travel and tourism, widely known for his acumen in marketing luxury travel products to affluent consumers. His unique knowledge of the luxury marketplace complements exceptional skills as a compelling educator, lecturer and writer. Prior to the founding of SeaDream Yacht Club, Pimentel held posts as president and CEO of Cunard Line and Seabourn Cruise Line and earlier as president and CEO of Classic Hawaii.

Travel marketing requires the focus of a bullet in flight. Just when you think you've got it right and have zeroed in on your target audience, you discover that you really haven't. Your audience has shifted, morphed into something totally new, or moved out of range. The travel marketplace has always been like shifting sand in the desert—these days even more so.

Information technology rules the marketer. In the next decade, technological advances will outstrip anything we can imagine today. It will be like watching a one-hour television documentary on flight—the show opens in 1900 with the Wright Brothers at Kitty Hawk gliding only about 400 feet. The next scene, a hundred years or so later, the newest jet is streaking across the world's time zones—amazing and mind-boggling.

Technology is not only changing the way travel products are delivered to the marketplace, but is affecting their distribution as well. This will continue exponentially but perhaps the most important change over the next decade will be the change in the nature and mindset of consumers. This change will be caused by the inexorable advance of technology as well. I maintain that there is a new breed of consumers already just peeking over the horizon. I refer to them as consumers of independent attitudes (CIAs). In the future all marketers, not just travel marketers, will need to address these highly independent consumers. This will require new and revolutionary marketing strategies, new sales techniques and, most important for the travel industry, new and unusual travel products. That's why I say travel marketing requires the focus of a bullet in flight.

At my company, SeaDream Yacht Club, a leading edge provider of ultra-luxury travel products, we are already seeing these new consumers. As we move ahead we are learning to market to them diligently. We are finding them to be a highly intelligent, discriminating and eager audience. Here is what we are finding out about them.

First, they are fiercely independent; make no mistake about that. They are self-directed and self-reliant. The Internet has opened up their heads to new and infinite possibilities. They know what they want and they know how to get the information they need to make informed decisions about travel products and services. And they are perfectly capable of considering, interpreting and classifying this information themselves and then acting on it. The Internet, with its split-second availability, has also helped CIAs to learn about themselves—their minds, their bodies and their spirit. It has shaped their working and leisure lives.

As a result, the CIAs eagerly pursue a healthy lifestyle. What they put into their bodies is important to them. They want to dine well and in a healthful manner but they are hedonistic in that they want their food to be presented elegantly and to pass their rigorous taste test. Regardless of their age, these consumers are youthful. They are youthful in attitude and youthful in the casual and unstructured lifestyle they pursue. They have a fierce sense of self-image and pride. They seek active experiences, not passive ones. They want to do it all. Hence, they participate in sporting activities—especially ones that test themselves against themselves. They are highly conscious of the strength and suppleness of their bodies. They ski. They go ballooning. They enjoy whitewater river rafting. They are rock climbers, paragliders and sailboarders. Some of them can be found weekends gliding over our streets on inline skates. They play golf and tennis, but they also play squash, lacrosse, soccer and rugby.

They are adventurous, love to travel and have developed the habit of turning to new, sometimes extreme, travel products and services rather than traditional ones. While these consumers are frequently unpredictable and always opt for freedom of personal choice, when they do find a product or service that turns them on, they can be brand loyal.

Likewise, when a product or service disappoints or fails, that's it. It's time to move to something else. They are quick to reject what they believe to be "hype" and don't like to be pre-programmed and put into a preconceived box. The clutter and noise in the marketplace has made them skittish and hard to convince. They can be difficult to approach and extremely wary of the clumsy, overt sales pitch. They want to be pampered but in a casual, highly informal manner and they have no problem entertaining themselves and frequently even prefer to do so. However, they are by-and-large they are gregarious. They are mostly social animals with fine social skills. They lean toward the allocentric rather than the psychocentric. To call them "outgoing" is an understatement.

They are members of university alumni groups and go to home games. They attend new restaurant openings and wine tastings. They visit the wineries for personal, close-up experiences. They frequent museum openings, the opera, the ballet, the symphony, jazz and blues festivals and professional sporting events. During the holidays, they participate in singalongs of Handel's *Messiah*. Many of them belong to health clubs or have their own trainers. They work out. They have a lot of fun. The group also tends to be philanthropic.

Marketers desiring to appeal to these new consumers would do well to try to emulate them and live in their shoes, so to speak. Seek them out on their own turf. Study their interests. These consumers seek out the most unusual tour experiences they can find. For example, Buddy Bombard's Hot Air European Balloon Adventures, Tauck Tours Heli-Tour Ski programs, Intrav's private jet tour around the world, a SeaDream yacht charter on the Amalfi Coast, or a unique wine tour offered by some of the finest university alumni associations. Over-the-top experiences are at the heart of what they select.

From a hotel perspective, they are not interested in a formula-based experience. "Processed luxury" is simply not provocative enough for them. While this "processed luxury" may fit the requirements of many, these independents seek out the truly unique—perhaps the Hotel Hana Maui, Cap Jaluika in the Caribbean, the Hotel Cap Antibes or for a more rustic, but still extraordinary, experience the Gallatin River Lodge in Montana (devoted to flyfishing purists).

CIAs are not necessarily ultra wealthy. They are affluent and there is a difference. Affluence is a mindset; wealth is hard cash. Some are both wealthy and affluent. They don't mind spending money for what they deem to be good value.

Some of these new CIAs come from or have what we term "old money," a metaphor for those intellectually and socially cultivated Brahmins whose fortunes were established by brilliant but frugal antecedents who were known for spending "wisely and well." There is an old American proverb that seems to say it all: "Them that has—gits." "New money" is also a metaphor related to wealth. It is unfortunate that the phrase leans to a somewhat pejorative cast, but to the marketer of the luxury or ultra-luxury product or service, money is money. It is only the approach to it that differs. Geographically, "old money" is everywhere, just as is "new money." F. Scott Fitzgerald in his 1926 novel *All the Sad Young Men*, wrote: "Let me tell you about the very rich. They are different from you and me." Ten years later in *Esquire Magazine*, Ernest Hemingway replied to Fitzgerald's comment: "Yes, they have more money." He could have added that they have a different mind-set and much different imperatives in their lives.

There was a time when the very wealthy were known as the "leisure class." These days that is not necessarily true. Many affluent CIAs owe their upper-class position to the second income of a working spouse rather than to the buoyant cushion of inherited wealth. These new consumers frequently struggle to find a balance in their lives. But "old money" has its concerns as well. Those tagged by the term find that purchasing power frequently has shrunk and that they need to be careful custodians of their wealth. "New money" tends to be more open in spending patterns; one is tempted to refer to them not only as CIAs, but as the new "leisure class."

For example, I know a young affluent couple that travels to Europe almost every year. They shop around on the Internet until they find a bargain airfare and fly economy class. When they arrive in Paris, for example, they move into a modest Left Bank hotel they have carefully researched on the Internet. They arise early and go to an inexpensive sidewalk café for coffee and croissants. Then they walk around Paris, their backpacks bulging with guidebooks, bottles of water, a piece of hard cheese and a baguette. But it is more of the same for dinner? No! Prior to arriving in Paris, they have researched restaurants on the Internet. They send an e-mail to three or four of Paris' finest Michelin three-star restaurants. So, in the evening, she dons a Donna Karan pantsuit with an Escada silk blouse. He puts on a Brioni suit with an Ascot Chang custom-made shirt and a Hermes necktie and off they go into the world of affluence. And, if you were to ask them if they are being a bit extravagant, they would respond by saying that they felt they had their priorities straight, always shopped carefully and received good value for their money. Indeed, the perceived value of the three-star dinners and the up-market clothing are important to them. This couple has an affluent mindset. I comment on them here because I met them on one of our SeaDream sailings. I got to know and like them. They made good use of all of our watersports "toys." They snorkeled, used our waverunners, sailboats and swam like fish. They were up early every day jogging around on deck and swimming laps. They did yoga and tai chi and used our fitness center constantly. They frequented our Asian Spa every day and pampered themselves. When we put into a small port, they checked out a couple of the yacht's mountain bikes and off they went. They are gregarious and outgoing. They are curious, adventurous, open and friendly. In short, this young couple represents to me the archetype of what I have called the CIAs—a new leisure class, if you will.

This couple happened to be from the U.S. Midwest, but you will find their counterparts everywhere. They exist all over the map and in most advanced countries. Politicians, census takers, tax collectors, chambers of commerce, banks, credit and charge card companies, think tanks, research organizations, magazine publishers, broadcasting and telecasting gurus, sales "reps" and, of course, marketing executives—all look into their crystal balls and their computers to pinpoint the exact locations of these new consumers. While they are everywhere, geographically they tend to cluster in the larger cities and towns, not only of North America, but also in many other parts of the developed world. They are in the cities and the "burbs." Frequently they are living in satellite, or bedroom communities. Many of them have multiple dwellings—an apartment in the city, a condo elsewhere. They are in small towns and in no towns at all. The intelligent marketer needs to be aware that while many of these new consumers are living in, say, Central Park West in New York City or in nearby Westchester County or in the Hamptons, they are also in Ponca City, Oklahoma; Borger, Texas; Truth or Consequences, New Mexico and Yellow Knife, in Canada's Northern Territory. They not only live in London, Paris, Rome, Stockholm, Sydney and Hong Kong, for example, but also a short commuting distance from these international centers.

Specifically, marketers wishing to seek out new CIAs need to fish where the fish are. Not just blindly in the geographic areas mentioned, but with a narrow, highly focused searchlight that reaches into the complex social fabric of the area to be studied. These new consumers are strong supporters of cultural events and are involved with museums and performing arts institutions. They also belong to country clubs, golf club, yacht clubs, wine and food groups and university and other school organizations.

It is especially interesting and instructional to study how these new consumers give away their money by supporting favorite charities and not-for-profit institutions—private colleges and universities, private hospitals and a broad range of other philanthropic activities. At SeaDream Yacht Club, we have found it beneficial to ally ourselves with philanthropic events through auctions of sailings on our SeaDream yachts. We donate the sailing and charge only a minimal service fee. When the sailing is auctioned, it inevitably brings a fair market price or higher. The charitable organization gains and SeaDream not only benefits from the publicity but from a certain kind of favorable word-of-mouth. For example, frequently friends of the successful bidders join the sailing at full tariff. This has been highly successful for us and we gain long-term, happy clients. This is the ultimate win-win situation for all parties.

These new consumers are elusive and a moving target. However, there are some constants or "givens" in reaching them—and selling to them. They react to intelligent messages communicated to them in a straightforward (therefore, compelling) manner. Here are some guidelines to use when addressing them:

- Always tell the truth—Don't try to hide the truth behind thickets of endless bad prose or promises. Straightforward presentation of the facts and the benefits need to be communicated without smoke and mirrors or equivocation.

- Talk their language—Speak to the consumer's needs and desires and express the value of the product.

- Never talk down to them—They will know when you are doing this and will tune out.

- Don't work too hard to be clever or far out—It is easy to fall into the trap of thinking you are brilliant and that therefore your audience will agree. Usually it won't and, even if it does, it frequently becomes caught up in your cleverness and forgets just what it is you are selling.

- Deal with price head on—These new consumers are not afraid of price. They are looking for value and they yearn for quality.

- Let others do your talking—It is a good idea when you are addressing these new consumers to use third party endorsement. Real quotes from real folks.

- Don't bore them—This is a cardinal rule. Don't overexplain. Don't repeat the obvious. Don't try to force-feed them. Their eyes will glaze over and their interest will go elsewhere.

As I said earlier, SeaDream Yacht Club caters to these new consumers. But I question whether, at this point, the traditional cruise lines are doing so. I maintain that these new style consumers, with their new personal imperatives, are either not cruisers in the traditional sense or, if they are, the traditional cruise industry is in danger of losing them.

Let's take a look at the strengths and weaknesses of the cruise industry in general, as I see them, then measure them against these new consumers.

On the positive side, as I write this, all research points to the fact that mainstream cruising delivers unparalleled satisfaction. Generally, it is believed that with cruising consumers receive good value for their money.

On the negative side, as I see it, there are some weaknesses. Most of the newer ships are not able to personalize the service necessary to match the requirements of the emerging CIAs. They are simply not everyone's cup of tea. In some cases, cruising has become predictable—its own sea of sameness. It can be a highly structured, high profile, glitzy, pseudo-glamorous experience. It can be virtual reality, formula, force-fed fun. Generally the cruise industry fails to articulate the extraordinary value of the experience.

So where does the future lie for cruising? I believe we need new products for these new consumers. Herein lies the advantage of the small luxury cruise operators like SeaDream Yacht Club, which provide more casual and intimate luxury experiences that allow for active guest involvement. No lines, no tightly-timed and scheduled onboard programming where names and preferences are remembered; rather, there is a one-to-one ratio of staff to guests and the experience is basically all-inclusive—wine and spirits, for example, even gratuities. It is my belief that the smaller, more intimate seagoing experiences—yachting, if you will, in the case of Sea Dream—will be operated exclusively by entrepreneurs. In the future, the large operators won't be tempted by the more modest return on investment that those entrepreneurs will find highly acceptable. An apt analogy might be the small and exclusive restaurant versus the restaurant chain.

Certainly there is a sea of takers for the mass-market cruise experience. This has been demonstrated time and time again and is a successful formula. One has only to look at Carnival Corporation and its various brands to determine the great financial success that is possible in this product segment. As we all know, cruising is simply a good buy. But, as I am stating, we are in the early days of a major change in the style and desires of consumers—consumers whom I have described as having highly independent attitudes and lifestyles.

So I wonder if all passenger shipping companies—both mass market and those at the luxury end—can cater successfully to this new consumerism that embraces active, adventurous, more youthful, sports-minded, healthy lifestyles.

For these new consumers, at least in my SeaDream experience, luxury yacht cruising offers a great deal—including a favorable price-value equation. Without doubt, the up-end is good value. In fact, some will argue that high-end cruising is an even better value, based on its exclusivity.

So, small luxury cruising, as fine as it is today, needs to further separate itself from the mass market cruise companies. The luxury operators must also maintain costs in a more aggressive manner and focus on authentic luxury differences. The line between the mass-market cruise experience and the small luxury cruise experience cannot be allowed to become fuzzy and indistinct. If it does, the luxury operators lose and so does the new consumer.

The luxury cruise concept is a separate and distinct genre. It is not only about the hardware (the vessels themselves) but, when you look at the total package, it is really more about the software. And that software can indeed be distinguished by the most exacting standards. Service is as fine as can be found in some of the great land-based resorts and hotels or in elegant, private family dwellings. It can be quiet, understated and unobtrusive; it is usually superb. For example, staff members quickly not only address their guests by name, but they pick up on their likes and dislikes. If a diner requests that flowers be removed from a table because of allergies, the waiter remembers that and in the future the flowers are whisked away before the diner is seated. If a guest enjoys a particularly spicy Bloody Mary, it will be particularly spicy next time—without the guest's asking. Dining onboard these vessels is frequently as fine as land-based dining at some of the great restaurants of the world. Onboard amenities are lavish. Furniture, wall coverings, carpeting, silverware, crystal, china, linens, and towels—all are of the highest luxury quality. When you add to this software the operating standards of most luxury operators—such things as no-penalty cancellation policies and the all-inclusive nature of onboard offerings—you have an extraordinary leisure product of great value. This kind of ultra-luxury provides the ultimate travel experience. It is highly specialized—not a rigid, formula-driven luxury, but a loose, tailor-made cocoon of pleasure.

In my view, the future of the luxury segment of the cruise industry lies in two principal challenges—differentiation of the onboard product and reaching out to the new CIAs. It would appear that the luxury small ship experience may well offer the best advantages and return the highest satisfaction, when you consider the personalized service offered. Furthermore, the ships' mobility allows small, unique ports to be presented in alternative geographical locations, year after year. For instance, SeaDream can actually dock aft-in at the Monte Carlo Yacht Basin, which offers a fantastic vista and is within walking distance of the treasures and attractions of Monaco. These yachts' onboard and shoreside experiences are generally only approached or equaled by the world's best land-based resorts and hotels.

In a nutshell, small yacht cruising is personalized, intimate, casual, and an excellent value. It is hard to beat.

While I have drawn on my own field of expertise—upscale seagoing vacations—for many of these observations, the astute student of marketing will realize that the application of these views is valid throughout the entire field of leisure travel. In short, there are new consumers out there with new independent attitudes, and I believe they are searching for new and unusual travel products.

56

Growing a Legend

Simon Cooper
Co-Owner, President and COO
The Ritz-Carlton Hotel Company

Simon Cooper is president and chief operating officer of The Ritz-Carlton Hotel Company, LLC. In this position, he oversees the operations, development and strategic positioning of one of the world's most powerful brands encompassing 54 hotels in 19 countries.

Since joining the company in 2001, he has opened 19 hotels and grown The Ritz-Carlton Residences and Club. Under his leadership, the company continues to earn the highest accolades such as the 2003 J.D. Power and Associates Award for #1 Luxury Hotel Chain and being named as "The Top Employer in Asia" by *The Asia Wall Street Journal/Far Eastern Economic Review.*

Mr. Cooper joins Ritz-Carlton from Marriott International. Previously he was president and chief operating officer of Delta Hotels & Resorts. Before that he was with OMNI Hotels USA.

Mr. Cooper was educated in England and earned an MBA from the University of Toronto.

As The Ritz-Carlton Hotel Company, LLC, enters its third decade, the remarkable success of our luxury lodging business stands as a benchmark model for those seeking to establish a global brand. What makes our experience so unique compared to that of other start-up companies? We began by purchasing the rights to a brand that already enjoyed limited worldwide recognition for excellence in service, accommodations and luxurious settings. Recognizing that, our corporation's immediate task was to meet and exceed the century-old standards set by the famous European hotelier, César Ritz. His philosophy of service excellence and innovation has inspired all of our current practices at The Ritz-Carlton Hotel Company.

Having achieved those standards by our 20th year in the business, our company is now engaged in reshaping its marketing and management strategies. This is being done to meet the challenges of the new millennium in terms of addressing the rapidly changing global socioeconomic and political climate and the ever-changing tastes of our customers, while at the same time maximizing our profits. The central goal is surpassing all of our international competitors in the luxury-lodging niche. Capitalizing on our impressive performance during our first two decades, and adapting to the changing marketplace, should provide the momentum The Ritz-Carlton Hotels will need to fulfill this vision.

How Far We Have Come Since Our 1983 Startup

Currently, The Ritz-Carlton Hotel Company, LLC, is the largest luxury hotel management firm based in the United States, and is widely recognized by numerous industry organizations as the premier brand in high-end lodging. Hotels remain our largest business sector, and include 52 individual properties (as of April 2003), as well as an additional marketing contract for The Ritz London. In recent years, the brand has been extended to include exclusive residences and fractional ownership vacation homes. Our most dramatic growth has occurred since 1995 when Marriott International, Inc., acquired a 49 percent stake in our company—an interest that was increased to 99 percent in 1998. Since joining the Marriott family, Ritz-Carlton has continued to operate as an autonomous brand, while actually strengthening our marketing programs by being able to share some of the extensive resources that our owners possess. Worldwide, The Ritz-Carlton today has approximately 23,000 employees, annual revenues of nearly $2 billion, and a customer base of over one million—including the leisure, corporate, and group segments.

On September 1, 1983, exclusive rights to The Ritz-Carlton trademark, along with the venerable 56-year-old Ritz-Carlton, Boston, were acquired by Atlanta,

Georgia, developer W.B. Johnson. At the same time, The Ritz-Carlton Hotel Company, LLC, of Atlanta was founded (corporate headquarters relocated to Chevy Chase, Maryland, in mid-2003). Johnson became chairman of the new hotel management corporation, and Horst Schulze, formerly a Hyatt Hotel Corp. senior executive, was named president and chief operating officer. Thus began a new era in luxury lodging. During the late 1990s, we began extending our brand to include: The Ritz-Carlton Club (fractional ownership vacation homes), The Ritz-Carlton Residences (exclusive private homes and condominiums, serviced by the hotel), and The Ritz-Carlton Leadership Center (an educational division). Total Quality Management (TQM) practices have ensured the success of these divisions and the integrity of the brand.

In its quest to "measure up" to the high standards of César Ritz, the new company developed and pursued a comprehensive philosophy that still sets us apart from our competitors—a philosophy that stresses the delivery of quality customer service through specially trained employees.

This philosophy is reflected in the company's core values that are collectively expressed in our written "gold standards." These standards, as set forth on The Credo Card (carried by employees at all times) remain an industry first and are a blueprint for our success. Every employee has the business plan of The Ritz-Carlton in his or her pocket, which constantly reinforces in the employee's mind that guest satisfaction is our foremost mission.

Every new employee is expected to embrace these company standards, which include: The Credo, The Three Steps of Service, The Motto, The Twenty Basics, and The Employee Promise. The recurring theme of these guidelines is that personal attention to the needs of every guest is always a top priority. That's how to provide guests with their ultimate expectations: a memorable experience and exceptional value.

These are a few examples of The 20 Basics:

- "It is the responsibility of each employee to create a work environment of teamwork and lateral service so that the needs of our guests are met.

- "Each employee is empowered. For example, when a guest has a problem, or needs something special, you should break away from your regular duties to address and resolve the issue.

- "Be an ambassador of your hotel in and outside of the workplace. Always speak positively. Communicate any concerns to the appropriate person."

Hand in hand with our philosophy is our special approach to employee training. We are proud to maintain the lowest employee turnover rate in the hotel industry, year after year. Our training approach has often been cited as a textbook model for companies around the world—from Fortune 500 firms to smaller, family-run businesses.

Following a rigorous selection process, our new employees are introduced to the rich Ritz-Carlton culture with a two-day orientation at the property. All employees—from entry-level housekeepers, to sales and marketing professionals, to senior executives—learns to embrace and apply these founding principles on the job.

At morning "lineups," all staff and managers gather to reflect upon the company's "commitment to quality," recognize exceptional performance, and reinforce management objectives. Around the world, the daily message is the same: Exceeding guest expectations is our most important mission. Employees also learn about our self-empowerment policy, whereby they are each empowered to provide immediate corrective action should guest problems occur.

Every year, our employees receive more than 100 hours of customer service training. Many of them are on self-directed work teams that have originated many of our service innovations, subsequently increasing guest satisfaction and improving profitability.

This investment in training and service has yielded impressive results. Using the principles of total quality management (TQM), our company has received some of the highest ratings on guest satisfaction surveys; a near-perfect guest-return rate; and an employee retention rate of nearly 70 percent. This far-higher-than-the-industry-average rate of retention translates into significant savings and profitability.

Since its founding, our company has garnered every major honor that the hospitality industry and consumer surveys can bestow. In addition to frequently heading the annual "best" lists published by *Condé Nast Traveler*, *Travel & Leisure*, and *Gourmet*, the Ritz-Carlton hotels have placed exceptionally in rankings by *Business Travel News* and the *Zagat Survey*. A large number of our hotels, and their dining rooms, have also received the highest ratings from the American Automobile Association (AAA) and Mobil.

Of all our honors, the one of which we are proudest is the Malcolm Baldridge National Quality Award in the service category—the most prestigious recognition an American business can earn. The Ritz-Carlton is the only company in the hotel industry to earn this award, which recognizes exceptional achievement in the practice of TQM—and we did it twice (in 1992 and 1999)!

One of the award's key criteria was customer and market focus. Here the judges noted that: "The Ritz-Carlton has instituted an approach of customer customization that relies on extensive data gathering and capitalizes on the capabilities of advanced technology. Accessible to all Ritz-Carlton hotels worldwide, the database of customer preferences enables hotel staff to anticipate the needs of returning guests and to initiate steps that will help to ensure a high-quality experience."

Reemphasizing Brand Strength in the Future

No brand, no matter how respected or well known, can take it for granted that it will continue to grow and dominate the minds of consumers without the brand's marketing executives considering the changing demographics of its primary customer base. This has been a major factor in our plans for marketing the growing presence of Ritz-Carlton, and the brand extension of our "lion and crown" logo to include private residences, fractional ownership, and other luxury lifestyle products and services.

Not taking brand loyalty for granted is especially vital in the hotel industry, where evolving tastes and trends, like minimalist service and style, and the growth of boutique hotels, had impacted the definition of luxury by the end of the 1990s. Although the terms "ritzy" and "puttin' on The Ritz" have become almost generic, the challenge for Ritz-Carlton recently has been to reemphasize our brand strength through fresh marketing initiatives reflective of a changing world, a changing product, and a changing customer.

According to a 2002 study of its members, The Luxury Marketing Council said: "Luxury marketers fall into two groups: 1) those struggling to break through a 'legacy' approach; and 2) those who have seen the future and moved on to a 'leverageable' approach. Clearly, Ritz-Carlton has adapted the latter direction, which the Council defines as "new, more innovative, more disciplined visions, strategies, and tactics." Despite the company's very impressive number four ranking among world luxury brands (*Future Brands 2002*), senior management recognizes the need to develop brand loyalty among future generations of wealthy and affluent customers. The *Future Brands* ranking considered four areas of influence: the degree of control of distribution channels; effectiveness of marketing; media visibility; and impact of the brand in the buying decision. Four Seasons Hotels, our nearest hospitality competitor, *ranked 19th.*

Described in *Forbes Global* as the "best-driven brand," The Ritz-Carlton is using new approaches in advertising, and leveraging strategic partnerships with "like" brands to create a value proposition for customers. These brands include American Express (Amex), Mercedes Benz, and Saks Fifth Avenue. The relationship with Amex alone is expected to generate over $40 million in revenues in 2003.

In the early years, Ritz-Carlton directed its marketing and sales messages to the top five percent of the luxury market. Later, economic factors such as the "dot.com bust," and the declining stock market caused us to look beyond our traditional wealthy customer base towards the promising "affluent" and "aspirational" customer whose wealth was created in the 1990s. Although the wealthy continue to travel, even in a down economy, there simply are not enough of them on which to base a luxury strategy.

So who are today's Ritz-Carlton customers? It's the wealthy, plus the affluent and the aspirational customers as defined by these profiles published in *The Virtuoso Luxe Report* of 2002:

The wealthy customer. . .

- is 53+ years-old

- is conservative

- wants to be "taken care of"

- seeks status "badges"

- and wants recognition.

The affluent customer. . .

- is 35+ years-old

- is savvy, stylish

- has heightened expectations

- and wants memories and experience.

The aspirational customer (potentially our newest future guest). . .

- is a current traveler

- is a user of quality hotels

- is younger

- is slightly less affluent

- and is a proven user of lifestyle products.

An Evolving Product and Customer Message

One of the most frequent negative comments we heard in the early years was that our product had become "cookie cutter" and "stuffy." To address this, we broadened our design philosophy. Beginning with some of our new properties in Asia, where contemporary flair is a luxury hotel signature, we introduced a wider design concept. At The Ritz-Carlton Millenia Singapore, for example, everything about the hotel embraces modern influences, including a multimillion-dollar art collection. While we also lessened some of the formality, we did not compromise quality and service. Many of our competitors claim to follow these concepts, but none have been able to sustain their required commitment of resources and time that we have.

While our company continues to open hotels in the classic and traditional-European style in destinations such as Santiago, Chile, we have also added cutting-edge designs to our collection of hotels and resorts in locations such as South Beach, Florida, Miami, and Georgetown (Washington, D.C.). This eclectic grouping of traditional and trend setting properties has coincided with the addition of more image-enhancing amenities. For example, innovative services such as the Technology Butler, the Water Sommelier, and the Bath Butler have given Ritz-Carlton a strong public relations edge over our competitors. In 2002, we moved our advertising in a new tactical direction, with messages suggesting that "on occasion, the most memorable experiences can be within reach," in hopes of attracting those affluent and aspirational customers.

While the booming hotel occupancy days of 1998–2000 have been replaced by a vacillating economy and uncertain world conditions, Ritz-Carlton recognizes this is a cyclical business; we are prepared to change our strategies as necessary to be fully prepared for an eventual recovery. According to The Luxury Marketing Council, another trait of "leverageable" companies is that they have made certain that "all facets of the marketing mix are strategically integrated for maximum efficiencies and economies." This we are doing, as well.

As you can tell, The Ritz-Carlton has worked diligently over the past two decades to measure up to the ideals of our philosophical founder, Cesar Ritz. We have exceeded all expectations in providing elegant, award-winning accommodations and quality service for the most discriminating class of guests in the world. We have succeeded because we have created a flexible corporate culture that totally understands the product and the customer we serve.

In the 21st century, our management and marketing strategies cannot be allowed to stagnate. We intend to remain responsive to the changing world around us. If customers tell us they are dissatisfied with our hotel appointments, we will continue to listen and make the necessary corrections. If they seek specialized services to conform to their new lifestyle preferences, we will oblige. Being responsible to our customers' needs in a rapidly changing international environment will be our number one job, and this commitment will be prominently reflected in all our future marketing endeavors.

57

Looking Ahead: Marketing Luxury Hotels in the 21st Century

Barbara Talbott
Executive Vice President, Marketing
Four Seasons Hotels & Resorts

Barbara Talbott is executive vice president, marketing, for Four Seasons Hotels and Resorts, where her responsibilities include brand advertising and public relations, direct sales and e-commerce.

Four Seasons hotels aspire to provide exceptional guest experiences and superior business results. Named Top Hotel Chain in 2002 by the *Zagat Survey*, J.D. Power and Associates and *Gallivanters Guide* (UK), Four Seasons has also been recognized for the past six years as one of Fortune magazine's "100 Best Companies to Work for in America."

Barbara joined Four Seasons in 1989, when the company had 20 North American hotels and a plan to add both resorts and international locations. With that growth came the opportunity to help build a global marketing effort and organization; an opportunity that she continues to pursue today, as Four Seasons continues to grow.

Barbara began her career with the management consulting firm McKinsey & Company. Prior to joining Four Seasons, she served as vice president, marketing, Royal Viking Line. She earned a Ph.D. from the University of Wisconsin in 1978 and currently serves on the board of Cornell University's Center for Hospitality

Research. A native of Eastern Pennsylvania, she and her husband, John Riley, reside in Toronto.

Hotels of one kind or another have been welcoming the weary sojourner ever since travel began. Luxury hotels came later, first appearing in Europe during the 19th century. Palatial in style and service, they defined the top standard of luxury for many decades to come. In these elegantly formal environments, patrons were treated as royalty and expected to behave accordingly. Though there were famous names in hospitality even then, marketing or branding as we know it had yet to evolve. It was a world with relatively few of these establishments, and relatively few travelers to enjoy them.[1]

Today, luxury hotels are more numerous and more accessible than ever. They still capture our ideas about the good life, but those ideas are also much more diverse and dynamic. Once primarily an imitator, North America has become a source of important original trends in luxury hotel design and hotel keeping; an innovator, as well, in the marketing and branding of fine hotels. We owe this to the remarkable growth of affluence and technology during the second half of the 20th century, an opportunity that North Americans embraced wholeheartedly, and that has transformed the way we experience and purchase all kinds of travel.

As we begin a new century, there are more than 60,000 rooms and 150 hotels in the luxury category in the top 25 markets in the United States alone, and several hundred additional properties worldwide[2]. Virtually all have rooms available for reservation, 24 hours a day, in our increasingly electronic global marketplace. Along with fine service, effective marketing of top hotels has become a key factor in determining their success. The goal of effective marketing is to ensure that a luxury hotel or hotel group is consistently held in the highest regard and also delivers superior financial results.[3]

What will it take to do this in the future? Twenty-first century hotel marketing is likely to require a wide variety of things; some tried-and-true, some still emerging. What follows is a closer look at several of these factors, beginning with the consumer and the changing definition of luxury.

Focus on the Traveler

Tomorrow's luxury hotel guests will have much in common with the current generation of luxury travelers. Successful, often self-made individuals, these are people of exceptional accomplishments and resources. They have ambitious goals for all aspects of their lives, personal and professional. Most of all, they believe that time is precious; they are looking to use their limited time in the best way possible. In Maslow's terms, they are self-actualizers: people who want to become everything that one is capable of becoming.[4]

Travel is a key tool to accomplish that end. It allows them to connect with the most important people in their lives; to accomplish work that requires their presence; to rejuvenate their energies through rest and recreation; to enrich their perspective by discovering nature and culture firsthand. It even helps them to celebrate their most significant occasions, such as weddings and funerals.

Very frequent, affluent travelers, in their 30s, 40s and older, have been making a dozen or more significant trips a year throughout their adult lives. In the process, they have acquired a worldwide collection of family and friends, clients and colleagues, favorite places, tastes and memories. This is the fruit of globalization at a very personal level. To travel often is simply a part of who these people are; whom they need and want to be.

Their children and grandchildren, the generation born in the 1990s, began to travel even earlier, often as babes in arms do.

Looking ahead, it is hard to believe that this will change. E-mail and video conferencing are already in daily use; world events since September 11, 2001 have introduced challenging new issues to the travel equation. Most world economies have yet to regain the peak growth rates of 2000. And yet, the affluent, very frequent traveler has continued to travel and to choose fine hotels.[5] In a changing world, the real and perceived value of these experiences may in fact have risen.

New Definitions of Luxury

And it is not just the world itself that continues to change. Definitions of hotel luxury are evolving as well. Objectively, hotels are measured and compared by criteria such as price, features and service standards; there are established rating systems that do this on a national and international basis.[6] Travel magazines conduct annual reader polls. Travel guides and reviewers have their best lists and recommendations. The ways of judging quality continue to multiply, along with the growth of fine hotels.[7]

When guests give their own definition, however, it increasingly comes back to a few key things: comfort, style, service and pampering. More than ever, the sum of these equals luxury for the traveler who can choose to stay anywhere. For them, luxury means service that is worry-free, tailored to the guest and available 24 hours a day. It includes a great night's sleep; quiet, spacious surroundings; delicious and varied foods; and the tools required to accomplish the purpose of the trip, whether that is business or pleasure.

Beyond these basics, human moments are what this guest relishes most: a genuine and personal welcome; being greeted by name at the concierge desk; receiving immediate assistance with a sleepless child or a computer problem, whatever the hour; being asked at appropriate moments, How is everything? This guest wants his response carefully heard for any problems or suggestions he raises, which must be promptly addressed.

"For the large number of people who travel a lot, glitz and dazzle are not that impressive. It's a question of how simple things can be, how predictable, how comfortable. For most people, even an uneventful travel experience, one in which they don't get stuck in a traffic jam or one's flight isn't canceled, is somewhat tense. When they get back on the ground, they want to be somewhere that provides comfort in a style that reaffirms who they are. They want, in other words, to be greeted warmly, to be served promptly, to be pampered."[8]

This is luxury redefined by travelers who can be said not to seek luxury so much as a necessary support system for the life they want to lead when traveling.

The setting for this service, the size of the hotel, the style of its decor, the uniqueness of the destination near which it finds itself, can and do vary greatly. But luxury can be experienced in a sleek contemporary building in the heart of New York or London; in a historic prison or convent, reborn as a hotel; on an undiscovered beach or a well-loved mountain. The more the traveler has experienced, the more he or she tends to value authenticity and relevance: the degree to which a hotel reflects its surroundings and delivers an experience that evokes, in some sense, the surrounding community.

Many things combine to make the whole experience a pleasing one. What is essential is how the hotel functions to meet guests' individual needs. A modern luxury hotel, like a modern luxury automobile, is expected to deliver high performance in the form of efficiency, reliability and convenience. It is permitted to impress, but never to disappoint.

Unlike an automobile, however, hotel service is not something that can be engineered at a factory and periodically tuned up on the road. Memorable hotel service is created moment to moment, by people. In a typical luxury property of 200–300 rooms, thousands of encounters will occur between staff and guests every day.

Ironically, even as the world has become more dependent upon technology—or, perhaps, for that very reason—there has never been a greater appreciation of the value that service adds, not just to a hotel experience, but much more broadly as well. Adding concierge service to products ranging from homes to home electronics has become a recognized way to add value and differentiation. Multitasking consumers clearly agree that time is money. Service saves them time and greatly improves the quality of that time as well.

This increased demand for service has made great hotels attractive destinations in and of themselves, both for long-distance travelers and for those who live a short drive away. With the addition of spas and private residences, top hotels are also capitalizing on lifestyle trends that position expert service in one's midst as an integral part of the good life.

For all these reasons, the ability to attract and retain great service people is a true competitive advantage for hotels that serve the affluent traveler. Service quality is and will be the foundation on which these hotels build their clientele among satisfied guests who plan to return and are happy to share their good experiences with others.

Something Old, Something New

The sharing of these experiences is where luxury hotel marketing begins, since personal recommendations mean a great deal to discerning travelers when choosing a hotel. The process often starts when people potential guests know, including friends and family, as well as knowledgeable travel professionals, recommend a hotel. These are, after all, people with similar tastes and interests who have recent firsthand experience to share. Potential guests also extend their search for recommendations to a wide range of travel media, including books, magazines, newspapers and online sources.

Thus, reputation and image, two of the oldest methods by which luxury hotels have always established themselves, continue to have great impact today. Arguably, they are more important than ever—a variety of forces have combined to homogenize or commoditize many consumer choices, including the choice of hotels.

Now and in the future, effective public relations, image advertising and branding are some of the most powerful antidotes to that pressure to conform. Through their ability to convey meaningful differences, these modalities help make a hotel or hotel group a coveted experience and one which can command a premium price, as well.

The Role of Public Relations

After personal recommendations, editorial coverage in publications they trust is the biggest influencer of consumer decisions regarding staying in fine hotels. There is an ever-growing list of such publications, in hard copy and online. They feature travel and hotels on a regular basis. These include pure travel titles, as well as other men's, women's, food, fitness, business, wine and sport titles, that increasingly include some kind of travel content. Daily newspapers continue to dedicate sections to travel as well. Interestingly enough, for the most part, travel content has not been significantly reduced in the wake of September 11 and succeeding world events. What has happened is that travel *reporting* has become more thoughtful and much more closely attuned with what readers are feeling and experiencing. For example, North American publications have included more coverage on places closer to home, and the same has happened in Europe.

A successful public relations strategy reaches out to these publications, first of all with a constant stream of relevant news. What are the emerging trends? What's new in the way of facilities; awards and accolades? Updates are useful in and of themselves; they also help the sending hotel or hotel organization remain top of mind. The most lasting and strategic impact, however, comes from feature stories in top-tier publications. Accompanied by important visuals, these can go a long way toward successfully introducing or positioning a specific property or hotel group. When elicited and reused effectively, positive coverage results in benefits that multiply over time.

In addition to being an effective tool, public relations is also an exceptionally efficient one. It can be customized to specific markets and also coordinated at several levels for maximum impact. A few years ago, for example, Four Seasons learned from the American Automobile Association that our hotels had garnered 18 of the 58 AAA Five Diamond awards to be granted in that year. One of these, the Four Seasons Hotel Las Vegas, was the first to receive this honor only 12 months after opening; indeed, it was the first-ever Five Diamond winner in that city's history.

To honor the hotel's achievement, a satellite media tour from Las Vegas was conducted the day of the announcement. It enabled senior spokespeople to appear on network and local television stations around the country. Meanwhile, in New York, the company president conducted interviews with top national print publications. That same day, other Four Seasons hotels that had received Five Diamond honors issued local news releases and granted interviews to their local and regional media. Thus, for a modest investment, a large and lasting impression about service leadership was created—an impression that reflected on the award winners themselves and on every Four Seasons hotel.

The Role of Image Advertising

While editorial coverage is credible because it is independent, advertising messages can carry credibility of another kind. They do this when they evoke a satisfied current guest's most positive feelings and when they signal to others of like mind that something special awaits them in trying this experience.

While this kind of advertising has long been an effective tool for other luxury categories, for hotels it remains largely an area of opportunity. Historically, hotel advertising has been built around price, location or other specific features, a trend that tends to grow more pronounced during softer economic times. Looking ahead, marketers of fine hotels have the opportunity to do better by consistently positioning what they offer as a unique solution to important consumer needs. Even (or, perhaps, most especially) when advertising serves a tactical objective, this uniqueness or differentiation should be clear. Paid advertising messages are the one medium completely under the marketer's control. Using them only to communicate features or price means giving up a powerful tool for finding and keeping loyal customers.

This happens most often in cases where advertising is measured only by immediate results: for example, numbers of responses, inquiries and bookings. By contrast, the quantifiable impact of strategic advertising is achieved over time. It is best measured by positive results in awareness and reputation, as well as the sustained ability to generate premium pricing. As one of the long-term investments in a balanced marketing portfolio, it needs to be evaluated regularly and rigorously. But its best rewards come with patience and consistency.

The Role of Brands and Branding

Among top-quality hotels, the effective use of brands and branding is another area of opportunity in the future. Leading global brands have long been recognized in other categories prized by affluent consumers, including automobiles, jewelry, fashion and fragrance. Until rather recently, however, there were no luxury hotel brands with global reach. That is now changing and will continue to do so. Since 1990, for example, Four Seasons has grown from 20 hotels predominantly in North America, to 58 hotels and resorts in 27 countries. This growth has been of value to all Four Seasons properties, because it has created new customers and also extended the reputation for quality, which each individual hotel shares.

This trend will continue as new luxury hotel brands are launched and as regional brands are expanded. This is because exceptional brands have real value for high-end consumers. Where brand is a mark of substance and not merely a badge, it saves time and offers real peace of mind in the high-stakes process of choosing a hotel. And as Chanel, Mercedes, Hermes and Tiffany have shown, brands that enhance their quality and image as they grow can be both coveted and available everywhere.

Looking ahead, it is likely that brands will take on even more significance for affluent consumers. In their widely read book, *The Experience Economy*, Joseph Pine II and James H. Gilmore described a new value chain, along with a new and dynamic role for brands: an opportunity to create a brand image emphasizing the experience customers can have surrounding the purchase, use or ownership of a good. Experiences, as they point out, are the most valuable purchases consumers now make; brands that are invested with that level of value mean more and are thus worth more, as well.[9]

More recently, brand guru Scott Bedbury has made a similar point:

"Over time, products and services will come and go, but the brand that provides them will become a constant. And brands will be defined by the sum total of those experiences, rather than the products and services themselves . . . We must recognize that a great product by itself is just one more chit, one more token, one more piece of currency in the relationship between consumer and brand."[10]

For several reasons, fine hotels are ideally suited to succeed in this branded, experiential economy of the future. First, an exceptional hotel stay is an experience, one that is richly layered, memorable and tailor-made to the guest each time. The best hotel environments are beautiful, relaxing, and appealing to all the senses. The best hotel service is kind, intelligent and highly responsive to individual needs. It is there to prevent or to solve problems, to delight the guest whenever possible. As a result, the best hotels offer uncommon potential for bringing a brand to life and creating positive memories. These qualities are just what Pine and Gilmore prescribe as the way to avoid commoditization and to earn a different, more enduring place in consumers' lives.

Second, when they are away from their favorite hotels, affluent consumers voluntarily spend a lot of time thinking about, arranging and planning for future stays. This is reflected in their reading, and in other aspects of their decision process. Every point of contact in that process thus becomes a chance to evoke and reinforce positive values associated with the hotel, the experience and the brand. This might occur through a brochure or magazine; through a conversation with a reservationist on the toll-free line; through written or spoken contact with a member of hotel staff. When every interaction conveys a consistent tone and impression, then each offers the chance to build a growing, positive relationship with the brand.

For the 21st century hotel marketer, each of these channels hold potential. However, perhaps none has more power to build or to devalue a brand than the Internet.

The Role of the Internet

Bill Gates recently observed that "The Internet makes the world simpler." He went on to say: "Today's Internet is still roughly where the automobile was during the era of Henry Ford's Model T. . . . We're only at the dawn of the Internet Age."[11]

And the potential truly does seem almost limitless, for hotels and for many other travel categories. There are more than 140 million people now online in the United States alone, or about 67 percent of all adults. The affluent were among the earliest adopters and have also been quick to add broadband services. They are now using the Web extensively for travel research and travel purchases.[12]

Has the Web made these tasks simpler for them? The answer is both yes and no. Yes, because the Web unlocks so much information; because it is available to them 24 hours a day; because they alone can choose when and how to interact with it. And no, because the Web itself lacks some crucial elements.

It presents a wealth of facts, but not a perspective on which ones matter most. Further complicating the quality-minded consumer's relationship with the Web is the lack of price consistency it presents, even for well-established premium travel brands.

This is perhaps because many travel suppliers have looked upon the Web primarily as a discount channel, as a place to build incremental demand by offering different pockets of inventory at different prices on different sites. This has, in part, helped fuel the explosive growth and profitability of sites such as hotels.com, expedia.com and travelocity.com, which obtain discount inventory from hotels and hotel companies, then offer it to consumers at rates that undercut other retail channels. The result is meant to be incremental revenue, i.e., income derived from filling a room that would otherwise remain empty.

In practice, however, these marginal rates are likely to become the rates that most guests pay. This is because most Web shoppers investigate multiple sites, as well as multiple channels. Often, they will continue seeking until they have found the one place where price has fallen farthest. For premium products, the damage isn't limited to falling rates. Radical swings in price also undermine long-held consumer perceptions that the brand is truly worth more.

Does the discounting work? Conventional wisdom says yes, but there is growing evidence to the contrary, at least in the hotel industry.[13]

Is the discounting necessary? Affluent, quality-minded travelers remain willing to pay a premium for superior hospitality experiences. In one recent survey, for example, 63 per cent of respondents agreed that it is more important now to experience personalized service and to feel pampered when traveling.[14]

This is the same consumer who appreciates quality and seeks out trusted brands in other purchases; whose belief in the value of these brands has been reinforced over time, through consistent pricing. A classic Tiffany diamond solitaire never goes on sale. If it were priced at $20,000 one day and $10,000 the next, would the buyer not assume there was something different about Tiffany, the ring or both?

Whether in fine jewelry or travel, affluent consumers are seeking value. They define it as something that meets or exceeds their expectations, and for which they have paid a fair price. By understanding and aligning with this view, fine hotels can benefit from the dynamic global marketplace that is the Web, while continuing to assure consumers that their experience is worth every penny.

There appears to be growing awareness that taking back the Web by resisting commoditization and restoring confidence in their own pricing is the most important short-term challenge facing hotel marketers, if only they can also begin to contain transaction costs at an acceptable level.[15]

An even greater long-term opportunity, however, is to remember Scott Bedbury's advice about currency in the relationship between consumer and brand. Marketers with that goal in mind will strive as well to make the brand's own site a preferred destination, not only for booking but for browsing; for receiving helpful information; for spending enjoyable time.

They will understand that third-party sites are, in retail terms, a warehouse environment where both branded selections and generics are sold side by side, strictly on price. Their branded site, on the other hand, can be a travel boutique or showcase carefully crafted to offer value, service, and a wide range of other benefits. Depending upon the breadth of their product offering, hotel marketers may find themselves needing to be present in both environments. But, by ensuring price consistency in all channels, by offering unique merchandise and a uniquely appealing environment on their own sites, they can begin to unlock even more of the Web's potential.

The Role of Travel Industry Partnerships

The Internet was predicted to spell the demise of travel retailing, and it has, along with other factors, wrought dramatic change in the structure and economics of that business. In the United States, there are now 28,696 accredited travel agencies, in comparison with 40,937 only 10 years ago. As more travelers are required to serve themselves when it comes to air tickets, hotels and other travel purchases, the number of travel agencies is projected to decline further in the years ahead.[16]

For those who want service and are willing to pay for it, however, professional travel agents have become more important than ever. In supporting this relationship by, in effect, partnering with the agencies whose clients value their service and expertise, marketers of fine hotels have much to gain.

Today's leading travel professionals have taken the time to understand their clients' specific needs and expectations. They read and travel widely. Many of them specialize in particular destinations, or types of vacations. The Web is a tool they use every day to inform themselves as well as to share information with clients in real time. In many cases, the travel counselor is the one who provides the qualitative element which is otherwise missing from the Web. Once choices are made, their goal is also to ensure that the trip goes off as seamlessly and worry-free as possible.

Wendy Perrin, consumer news editor for *Condé Nast Traveler* magazine, has documented this evolving role in a series of annual articles on 21st century travel agents. In a recent story, "Travel Superheroes," she tells the tales of various travelers seeking to return home after September 11, 2001. Those who booked online found there was no one to assist them; they were on their own. Those who worked with top travel agents related very different experiences.

Perrin tells the story of a couple that was traveling in Turkey at that time. Their longtime travel counselor pulled strings with personal contacts in Istanbul to get them on the first flight out, in the same business class seats they had on the way there.

The value of these travel couturiers, as Perrin has dubbed them, goes far beyond crisis management, however. Their knowledge and background permit them to create one-of-a-kind experiences tailored to individual travelers: whether they are golfers, wine lovers, or proud grandparents. Often these special experiences can make the difference between a good trip and an unforgettable one.[17]

For premium travel brands targeting the affluent, these travel professionals are strong allies. Because client satisfaction is their focus, they will always consider quality as well as price, and they like to recommend the brands they trust.

That is why luxury hotel brands need a highly effective sales force to inform and to support the travel channel and to work with other distribution partners as well: in the meetings, incentive and wholesale segments of the travel industry.

Looking ahead, it would be shortsighted to count on the disappearance of these channel customers. As long as they continue to add value for service-minded travelers, they will continue to play an important role.

Conclusion

In the spring of 2001, Four Seasons celebrated its 40th anniversary with a publication entitled Four Seasons, Four Decades. Several articles reflected our experience growing from one Toronto motor inn to, at that time, more than 50 hotels in 25 countries. One, entitled "The Future of Travel," looked ahead. Exploring the factors that produced more than 700 million international travelers in the year 2000, it concluded by asking, What holds more promise than exploring the world?

Just a few short years later, everything has changed, or has it? It's clear that the demand for fine hospitality experiences has continued to grow during the turbulent early days of the 21st century, filling durable lifestyle priorities that will continue to motivate the affluent of all nations well into the future.

Looking ahead, there is every reason to believe that the future of luxury travel will be bright. For centuries, now, it has continued to gather momentum. Luxury travel has sometimes been slowed by world events or economic cycles, but it has nonetheless always grown with time and the pace of progress.

This is the opportunity for hotel marketers of the future to meet an enduring need with the best of tools both new and old. With service that comforts, welcomes and delights; with experiences that stay top of mind and create the desire for new ones; with a consistent stream of meaningful contact between stays—in print, online and in person; most of all, with a continuing focus upon the traveler and the traveler's needs, especially his need to stay in a place with all the comforts of home, only better.

Notes

[1] Among the first grand hotels in Europe was Hôtel Des Bergues in Geneva, Switzerland, built in 1834. Other luxury hotels which opened during the 19th century include The Ritz, Paris (1898), The Connaught, London, (1897, originally The Coburg Hotel), Il Palazzo, Venice (1880) and Grand Hotel Qvisisana, Capri Italy (1845).

[2] Branded luxury hotels include those of Four Seasons Hotels & Resorts, Starwood Luxury Collection, Mandarin Oriental, Pan Pacific, Park Hyatt, Peninsula Group, Regent International, St. Regis and Ritz-Carlton Hotels. Many fine hotels are also managed independently, and affiliate with organizations such as Leading Hotels of the World for reservations services.

[3] Two widely used measures of hotel performance are RevPAR and GOP. RevPAR, Revenue per Available Room, is the standard hotel industry method of measuring guest room sales performance. Based on the comparison of total room revenue and total number of available rooms, this measure determines whether a hotel is achieving optimal results from both measures. GOP,

Gross Operating Profit, is the measure of gross operating revenue, e.g. guest rooms, food and beverage, departmental revenues, less operating costs, not including fixed costs. When calculated as a percentage of gross operating revenues, the results determine overall profit margin of hotel goods and services. Successful hotels consistently out-perform their relevant competition on both these measures.

[4] Abraham Maslow, *Toward a Psychology of Being* (New York: John Wiley & Sons, 1962). Maslow's pyramid outlines a hierarchy of human needs, with self-actualization at its peak.

[5] John Tagliabue, "Tourists Think Twice about Travel to Europe During War," The New York Times, April 2, 2003, para.. 25. In this article, Francesco Frangialli, the secretary general of the World Tourism Organization in Madrid, notes, "In 2001, tourist arrivals fell globally by 0.5 percent . . . yet they rose 3 percent last year, to 715 million, despite a sour world economy."

ASTR Lodging *Review Special Analysis*. Smith Travel Research, (February 17, 2003). This full-year 2002 analysis discusses performance of North American hotels by region, price level, location, and chain scale. The results note that both demand and occupancy increased for luxury priced properties in 2002.

[6] The most widely recognized rating systems in the hospitality industry include Diamond Awards (*American Automobile Association*), Star Ratings (*Mobil Travel Guide*) and Hotel and Restaurant Ratings (*Zagat Survey*).

[7] Publications which produce widely cited lists of best hospitality-related products and services include *Condé Nast Traveler, Andrew Harper's Hideaway Report, Gallivanter's Guide, Fortune Magazine, Travel + Leisure, Business Travel News* and *Institutional Investor*.

[8] The Future of Travel. Four Seasons Four Decades, Jim Fitzgibbon, President of Four Seasons Asia-Pacific Operations, 2001.

[9] Joseph Pine II and James H. Gilmore, *The Experience Economy* (Boston: Harvard Business School Press, 1999), p. 3.

[10] Scott Bedbury, *A New Brand World* (New York: Viking Penguin, a member of Penguin Putnam Inc., 2002), p. 16.

[11] Bill Gates, (2003). "Shaping the Internet Age." Retrieved February 6, 2003, from http://www.microsoft.com/billgates/shapingtheinternet.asp.

[12] (February 12, 2003). "Affluence Online." Survey conducted by Harris Interactive. Retrieved February 13, 2003 from http://www.emarketer.com/news/article.php?1002051 &cnewsltr &n'brief-&t'ad.

[13] Cathy A. Enz, "Hotel Pricing in a Networked World." *Cornell Hotel and Restaurant Administration Quarterly*, (February 2003), pp. 4–5.

[14] "Adventure and Pampering Top Travel Priorities." *Travel and Leisure*, (December 2002/January 2003), Para. 3.

[15] Motoko Rich and Julia Angwin, (March 14, 2002). "Inn Fighting: Big Hotel Chains Are Striking Back Against Web Sites; Dot-Com Discounters Apply Fierce Pricing Pressure on Industry Hit by Slump; Rich Profits for Barry Diller." *The Wall Street Journal Online*. Retrieved April 14, 2003 from http://www.factiva.com.

[16] Motoko Rich and Julia Angwin, (May 3, 2002). "Ticket to Ride: Two Tycoons Make Same Unlikely Bet: On Travel Business; Messrs. Diller and Silverman Dive into Turbulent Market; The Internet vs. the Agents; 'For a Week, We Agonized.'" *The Wall Street Journal Online.* Retrieved April 14, 2003 from http://www.factiva.com.

[17] Wendy Perrin, "Travel Superheroes." *Condé Nast Traveler*, (August 2002), pp. 98–100.

58

Capitalizing on the Canyon Ranch Difference

Mel Zuckerman
Founder and Chairman of the Board
Canyon Ranch

Mel Zuckerman is the founder, developer and chairman of the board of Canyon Ranch, one of the most celebrated health resorts in the world.

A native of New Jersey, Zuckerman worked there as a CPA until 1958, when he and wife Enid moved to Tucson. There, he became a successful builder and real estate developer. Over-stressed, overweight and on medication for asthma and high blood pressure, Mel checked into a spa in 1977 and had an experience that changed his life—and his health profile—forever. Wanting to continue his healthy lifestyle—and offer it to others— the Zuckermans opened the original Canyon Ranch in Tucson in 1979. Ten years later, they opened Canyon Ranch in Lenox, Massachusetts, in the Berkshires.

The Zuckermans decided to expand the reach of Canyon Ranch with the development of new properties and projects: In 1999, Canyon Ranch opened its first SpaClub at The Venetian Resort in Las Vegas, Nevada, followed the next year by another at Gaylord Palms Resort in Kissimmee, Florida. In 2004, Canyon Ranch will debut its third SpaClub onboard the Queen Mary 2 luxury ocean liner. The nation's first healthy living community, Canyon Ranch Living, will open in 2005 in Miami.

It's hard to market something that's not easily described. *What is Canyon Ranch?* It's so perfect, yet so different, for everyone—and for such a wide variety of reasons.

We know we're not a "fat farm," though it's true we've helped thousands of people shed more than a few pounds since our inception in 1979. We know we're not a "pamper palace," though we do believe that giving yourself a break from your daily life stresses—and indulging in massage, meditation, facials, or just 30 minutes of peace and quiet—can do wonders for your emotional state. And though we possess a highly credentialed medical and wellness staff to offer guests leading-edge disciplines in integrative health services, we are not a clinic.

So, what *is* Canyon Ranch? Perhaps that can best be answered by explaining our intention as an enterprise with a vision that is bigger than our business. Our aim is to provide inspiration, guidance, education and support to further the achievement of healthier living. How we go about that has shifted over the years, but our core values remain the same. We have not wavered in our focus and determination to set the standard in the spa industry. Our great resort experience has been, is and always will be, the *seduction* that opens our guests to the possibilities of health and a better quality of life. We have been greatly successful in this endeavor.

Our mission is not merely selling vacations, but promoting a direct, emotional connection between what people know they should be doing and what they actually do on a daily basis. A Canyon Ranch resort experience is devoted entirely to what The Boston Consulting Group calls "taking care of me" and "questing"—an experience of physical, emotional, and spiritual attention and improvement. Today's new luxury consumers are seeking out this type of product—one that addresses their emotional drivers as well as offers tangible results.

Who Goes to Spas and Why?

The reasons people go to a spa are as varied as the day is long. Some come to heal after a loss or illness; those who have control over their business lives seek to better manage their personal health; still others wish to become stronger, thinner, more fit, less stressed, and so on. The beauty of a Canyon Ranch stay is that it *can* be all things to all people. The possibilities exist for a life-changing experience like no other. In fact, thousands—about 60 percent of our guest population—return to Canyon Ranch for yet a different focus, a new direction, reinforcement or a shot in the arm, along with more health information than they already have.

"Boomers" Are Booming

Lately, there has been an explosion of information and opportunity in the wellness arena. Baby Boomers, people ages 38 to 56, are among the largest demographic of spa-goers. They are the new generation of active participants in their health and well being, unafraid to ask questions and accustomed to taking action. They are, by definition, well traveled, well heeled, well healed and well versed in the importance and sanctity of feeling good. They know they want to enjoy life to the fullest and want to be able to spend quality time with their children and grandchildren. They use Canyon Ranch as a portal for that transformation. Retirement is just around the corner, and they will go into it kicking and screaming with a desire to be healthy, wealthy and wise.

These assertive consumers will not "settle." Unlike their parents, who were largely of the Depression era, they understand that prolonged stress can translate into serious illness and they are ready to take action. Perhaps most importantly, they are aware they have choices. I have always maintained that good health is a matter of choice, not chance. Don't wait for a "death sentence" to be visited upon you in the doctor's office one day, followed by a litany of *"if onlys . . ."*

In a wonderful book, *Successful Aging*, John Wallis Rowe, M.D., and Robert Louis Kahn, Ph.D., wrote about a 10-year study of several thousand people aged 60 to 95. They found that 70 to 75 percent of the likelihood that a person will have good health and functionality at age 65 is determined by lifestyle. And, by the time you reach age 80 to 85, how well you're doing will be based 100 percent on your current and previous lifestyle. As an awesome *lifestyle* vacation, Canyon Ranch offers the connection to your "intention toward health"—igniting your emotional energy for genuine and permanent life change.

So What's Really Important?

Recent studies in the spa industry mirror trends in the marketplace: What is really important to people these days? The spa paradigm has shifted—it was in the process of doing so even before the terrorist attacks of September 11, 2001. Now, more than ever, these Baby Boomers are seeking deeper connections in relationships, a sense of control and authentic experiences—everything a spa like Canyon Ranch has to offer. A comfort zone, a starting point, a community of well being.

People are looking to spas to provide sanctuary and camaraderie. The sense of community is an oft-overlooked benefit of a spa vacation. People with shared values and commonality of purpose come together and offer each other much in the way of support and information—an energizing part of the spa experience.

Case in point: The Canyon Ranch Life Enhancement Center. Built in 1989 on the premise of small-group healing, this beautiful facility on the Canyon Ranch campus combines collective wisdom and personal discovery as powerful keys to lasting change. Quitting smoking, living well with arthritis or diabetes, or optimizing the aging process is a much easier journey when shared.

Captain's Tables in our dining rooms—a simple, yet significant nicety—also speak to this sense, this *need*, for communal gathering and socialization.

Living, by Example

The future of Canyon Ranch is moving in a similar direction. Canyon Ranch Living—a residential community concept built on the same precepts as our highly successful destination spas—will allow people to live in an environment that nurtures the shared value of healthy living—it's anything but a retirement village with a golf course.

We are confident this new concept will be embraced by the Boomers who seek to feel better, look better and live longer. A national study conducted by American LIVES, Inc, concluded that 30 percent of the U.S. population seeks a lifestyle that embraces community, wellness, cultural diversity and environmental awareness—a design that creates an important "sense of place."

Staying active and educated are among the Boomers' main goals, supported in words and deeds by a Canyon Ranch Living community. Fitness facilities, healthy dining establishments, availability of spa services and treatments, lifestyle boutiques and the eventual offering of medical and behavioral components, closes the loop on living your desired lifestyle and achieving the ability to "feel this good forever" (the words that resounded after my own transformation almost three decades ago).

It also allows parents to teach their children, by example, how to live healthier and happier. Those are our up-and-coming spa guests—the offspring of the "Me Generation," who grew up knowing the value of vitality *and* a great massage. We have the ability to address their existing sensibilities, which will bring about an even bigger challenge in future marketing endeavors. They'll want—and expect—more, bigger, better spa facilities and opportunities, similar to Canyon Ranch.

In this day and age of the "quick fix"—*express* service, *hi-speed* Internet, *instant* breakfast and *direct* deposit—the $11 billion spa industry must market long-term benefits. We must sell the quality of our experience, the advantage of the investment and the intangible effects that come with understanding. "Getting it," or what I like to refer to as "the aha moment," is that undeniable, emotional connection between *knowing* and *doing*. And it is well worth the wait. Because after that, everything makes sense.

The Seduction of Good Health

Canyon Ranch's marketing efforts have always been based on an experiential sell, primarily successful due to word of mouth and personal expression. After all, how do you write a brochure explaining the feeling of satisfaction that comes from not being winded after a 30-minute exercise session? Or describe the sense of accomplishment after completing a 10-mile hike? If you write about those feelings, will people understand you?

Personal achievement is another seductive intention of the spa experience—what I like to call Special Personal Adventure (SPA). Each person is unique, each visit is unique and each accomplishment should be celebrated.

Nurturing word-of-mouth marketing is essential to our future. Canyon Ranch doesn't use a lot of discounts or specials to promote what we offer—good health. It is not a commodity, nor a given. It comes with commitment.

Our satisfied guests have always been our best marketing tools. More than 80 percent of our business comes from personal referral. Guests act as apostles of good health and vitality and preach the value of Canyon Ranch to those of their friends and loved ones whom they want to experience it. We will continue to nurture this phenomenon by always strengthening the staff/guest engagement from pre-arrival to well past departure.

The better you feel, the better you want to feel. We will always be able to teach you something new, catch you if you fall, provide a new experience. Sure, we expect you to have fun while you're at Canyon Ranch. But we measure our value by what you do when you leave the Ranch—what you take away in new awareness and a sense of control about issues in your life. A vacation with purpose.

Day Spa Alternative

Knowing that people can't always take a break from their lives when they need it most, Canyon Ranch now provides alternative boosts. In recent years, we've opened Canyon Ranch SpaClubs inside resort hotels in Las Vegas and Florida. Our next venture is onboard a new luxury cruise ship, Cunard's *Queen Mary 2*.

Canyon Ranch created SpaClub as a new kind of day spa, more complete and a true reflection of what Canyon Ranch stands for. It offers past guests—and those who have only heard of the Ranch—the ability to experience a "touch of Canyon Ranch." These venues offer the same professional expertise and quality of services offered at our successful resorts, including hands-on training to maintain healthy habits in "the real world"—whether you're in a hectic city or the middle of an ocean.

Doctor, Doctor

It is the desire of most people to age well—or, as I like to say, "live younger longer." By the year 2030, our country's older population (65+) will more than double to about 70 million, with the average life expectancy at about 82 years of age (according to information compiled from the U.S. Bureau of the Census, the National Center on Health Statistics, and the Bureau of Labor Statistics).

In the last 20 years, the medical community has discovered that every biomarker of aging (measurement of how old your body really is) is 70 to 80 percent reversible. While the hands on your chronological clock can't be turned back, your biological one can be reset. You, however, are the only one who can do it; with motivation and inspiration, you can take responsibility for your own aging process.

More and more people are recognizing this fact—and turning to spas with highly regarded medical components to show them the way. Canyon Ranch has always been a leader in this arena. With the most incredible array of top-notch physicians, nurses, nutritionists, psychologists, behaviorists and exercise physiologists assembled anywhere, Canyon Ranch has positioned itself differently than its competition—and we've charged ourselves with communicating that difference to the public. We've instituted a speaker's bureau, comprising about a dozen outstanding professionals, to take our philosophy and our name out into the world.

It doesn't hurt, too, that many of our health and healing staff are published authors, with books in the stores and on the Internet touting not only their message, but their place of employment. Indirectly this, too, builds the Ranch's credibility as a serious health vacation spot.

Integrated Approach to Medicine and Marketing

Performing high-level diagnostics and assessments outside of a hospital setting is a boon to our clientele. Features such as a sleep lab to diagnose and treat apnea and other sleep-related disorders, genomics testing (the study of genetic predispositions), functional medicine (managing chronic conditions by addressing nutritional, metabolic and psychological factors) and digital mammography (offered at a nearby clinic), give further credibility to our leading-edge claims.

Guests revel in our integrative approach to well being. The combined talents of our staff, who treat you as a whole entity, make Canyon Ranch a one-stop shop for your lifestyle prescription. Add to that the option of alternative therapies—acupuncture, healing touch, Chinese herbal medicine—and you have the best of Western and Eastern medical diagnostics and treatment at your fingertips.

The medical component is so much a part of what Canyon Ranch is that we are making the most of our reputation to initiate new services and programming. The corporate world, a previously untapped sector for the Ranch, has become a prime market for annual physicals and small-group retreats. Partnering with Fortune 500 companies will allow us to grow this market in a way that is naturally viable and mutually beneficial. We believe there is a market for simultaneous high-end leadership training and lifestyle training, which might as well take place in our nurturing environment.

Discussions are taking place with hospitals to have Canyon Ranch services integrated into their facilities. It makes perfect sense. Why not make the hospital also a place to discover and experience preventive medicine?

My good friend and best-selling author Andrew Weil, M.D., says, "Hospitals of the future might more resemble spas—where patients could learn and practice the principles of healthy living, where they could learn to eat and prepare healthy food, learn to use their minds in the service of healing, and become less, rather than more, dependent on health professionals." Amen to that.

A Rising Awareness

Canyon Ranch is in a wonderful position to reach more people through different markets and venues. We're considering a variety of innovative approaches to help people aim higher, live up to their potential and enjoy fuller lives.

We continue to spread the word about healthy living to the masses, not just those who visit us. It has always been our mission to benefit people of all ages, from all walks of life and at all levels of health. We are currently launching the Canyon Ranch Institute, a nonprofit arm of the Ranch, to help perpetuate this objective by gathering, synthesizing and distributing health information to underserved areas and populations.

Brand New

Canyon Ranch has become synonymous with quality—it's the gold standard, if you will, for spas. To that end, we are expanding the brand, not only via new facilities, programs and avenues of healthy living, but with retail pursuits. A Canyon Ranch line of skin care products and amenities will soon be produced to strengthen our name in the marketplace while providing scientifically proven means of keeping the skin, face and hair healthier. Also under consideration is the creation of Canyon Ranch-label vitamins and supplements, under the direction of our outstanding physicians.

The Canyon Ranch Way

Change is inevitable but healthy growth is optional. The marketplace can change, the environment can change, consumers' needs can change, and Canyon Ranch will be right in there, addressing those changes, growing new business, developing new programs and undertaking new projects.

One thing that won't change will be our dedication and strength of purpose in offering the best healthy vacations in the world. I've built my life around that, and staked my reputation on it. I'm still kicking around the real definition of what Canyon Ranch is . . . a spa? A health resort? A vacation destination? No, it's a way of life!

59

The Spa Industry in 2013

Glenn Fusfield, CEO
Steiner Leisure LTD

Glenn J. Fusfield is the chief operating officer of Steiner Leisure LTD. Steiner Leisure LTD is a worldwide provider of spa services. The company's operations include spas and salons on 108 cruise ships, 58 resort spas and two luxury day spas. Mr. Fusfield is a 20-year veteran in the Leisure Industry, including the hospitality, maritime and spa segments. In his current role, he orchestrates the daily operations of the various groups within the company with a primary focus on its largest segment, the maritime industry.

Fusfield joined Steiner in 2000 as senior vice president of group operations. He was appointed CEO in January 2001. Prior to joining Steiner, Mr. Fusfield was with Carnival Cruise Lines for 12 years as director, hotel operations until 1997 and as vice president, hotel operations through October 2000. Mr. Fusfield is a resident of Miami, Florida, where he resides with his wife, Susan, and children, Bryan and Jenna.

It's very easy to forecast a utopian future for the spa industry. It goes like this: You wake up in the morning and, after an hour of disciplined meditation; your massage therapist gives you a massage—because, by 2013, a massage a day is as common as a taking a shower a day. You go to work, or work from home, and every couple of hours, your computer automatically switches to relaxation music and demands that you take 15 minutes to go inward and restore your equanimity with a cup of herbal tea. The lunch snack machine and local restaurants only offer health-conscious foods—high in fiber, low in fat and artificial ingredients. Before you leave work you visit the office gymnasium, the office massage therapist (if you feel you need another massage) and a psychologist (just to release the day's frustrations). Then you return home for a great evening with your family or friends.

Even though we don't believe we will be living this Spatopian ideal in 10 years' time, what is described is a lifestyle that brings well being to the forefront of modern consciousness. And when we take a look at how far the spa industry and self awareness have come compared to 20 or even 10 years ago, maybe it's not that far-fetched.

In 1983, there was not a single cruise ship with a complete spa by today's standards and extremely limited facilities in hotels and resorts. Yes, massage and facials were offered in a couple of small treatment rooms—an afterthought addition to the oversized hair salon. The facilities, the majority of the time, were in the bowels of the ship. As technology was also embryonic at this time, there was no direct button on the telephone to call the spa from the guestroom, nor were there in-cabin promotional videos, or strategically located plasma screens highlighting the spa and treatments. The guest had to work much harder to find the salon—though, inevitably, most of the women did. The salon was a bustling place, especially as twice-weekly formal evenings—normally two per seven days—were considered black tie/gala affairs. The massage columns (industry vernacular for appointment schedule) however, were quite sparse and mostly accommodated men. American women, at this time, did not have massage treatments and would more than likely opt for a facial or beautifying treatment. Hence, spa and salon staffing was also weighted toward the hairstylists, who earned the most revenue for the facility. The salons either had separate barbering sections for the men, and if not, someone was always employed who specialized in barbering with cutthroat razors and shaving brushes.

What happened from 1983 until today is, of course, just a continuation of trends in the 1960s. A change in public consciousness. There were many "movements" that have directly affected the surge in "spa consciousness," with the most significant being the Women's Movement.

The Women's Movement started in the 1960s with the sexual revolution. The sexual revolution was a rebellion against the strict codes of social conduct. The gray area of the male/female threshold basically gave birth to a woman who not only embraced her independence and equality, but made huge efforts to ensure it. Concurrently, it was in the 1960s that the first health farms were born. These health farms were supposed to be soul searching places, that included the power of touch, combined with nature and spiritual practices in a program that would last from a couple of days to a few weeks. For the most part, the majority of society could not afford such indulgences and before the mass spa experience would actually come into being, there needed to be another, less self-indulgent pastime to lead us there. This came in the form of fitness. Fitness, for men, was always available as a lifestyle choice, but for women this was a new phenomenon. Not surprisingly, aerobics were largely created for the more flexible woman. Fitness took off first and, with this focus on physical health, a subsequent interest in other holistic, and health-reinforcing, activities emerged.

Of course, the Women's Movement was only one of the many developments in the 1960s that directly affected the spa development. Another was a renewed interest in Eastern philosophies, triggered by our newfound mobility in the skies. In India and China, massage, aromatherapy, meditation, acupuncture and other forms of ancient healing arts persist as bona fide medical therapies in those countries. Whereas the West had, for the most part, traded its natural healing arts for modern-day medical practices, in the East there was more of an integration between the ancient and modern health care practice. It was time to uncomplicate our lives and go back to the basics.

All the social movements have had a positive effect on the spa industry—racial equality, sexual equality, the technological revolution and the general leveling of the playing field—have all made the spa lifestyle both a fashion accessory and a necessity—for both men and women. While women are by far the largest spa consumer, men are becoming more and more spa-seasoned. After all, conventional white-collar jobs may seem less grueling than blue-collar jobs, but they can actually be more stressful, leaving the body physically "unused." Thus there's a real need among Boomer Men to help the body detoxify with exercise and spa treatments; to drain toxin buildup caused by stress with massage and to use the spa experience to think with the body instead of with the mind. The spa, for many, has become a place for reconnection—a temple of solitude, where the other aspects of our being can be remembered and acknowledged.

Of course, this quick synopsis of the past decade or two misses many other factors that have contributed to the spa enthusiasm. One of which is the media. Without the media, would the spa be so sought after as a destination? Probably not. Whereas friends used to be everyone's most common avenue for knowledge, the media has largely replaced this avenue. People are becoming more dependent, for better or worse, on their own judgments based on their new trusted friend—

the TV announcer, radio jock. Then again, many of spa clients visit the spa on their own, without prompting from a personal friend. Various forms of media, therefore, play an increasingly important role in revealing the benefits of the spa industry and informing the public of the newest trends in the spa lifestyle.

Before we move on to the future, there is one other important spa observation to note. There are many spa segments, some of which never cross market. First (and fundamentally), we have the holistic spa. It is the purest type of spa experience. From it, other aspects of the spa experience have sprung. The holistic spa offers hands-on, nonmedical, noninvasive therapies. This would include massage, yoga, facials, herbology, aromatherapy, tai chi, acupuncture, meditation, chanting, music therapy, walking, running and natural healing of any kind. The holistic spa has a goal of offering natural redemption. It is whole-istic—treating the body, mind and spirit as one phenomenon. It is metaphysical in nature and many spiritual treatments, like Reiki healing, also attempt to treat the body on all levels. A health spa offering purely holistic treatments could have a spiritual guru (normally nondenominational in practice) for guidance, astrology and other emotional/psychological activities to help provide complete balance to the client. These spas focus upon evoking the naturally joyful person within and aim at providing the client with a feeling of self-acceptance and love. The holistic spa is treating the beauty within with sensuous treatments. The other end of spa spectrum is the newly emerging medi-spa. It focuses on exterior or physical beauty. Today the medi-spa industry brings doctors into the spa mix with treatments like Botox, Collagen, Hyaluronic acid, Cellular Renewal, microdermabrasion and other, more invasive treatments. The medi-spa is not aimed at helping a guest find the "promised land," but prolonging for him or her the unpromised land of youth. Again, this, too, has emotional and psychological benefits. By looking better, we feel better. Therefore, as diverse as both ends of the spa spectrum are, they are both aimed at making the client feel better and may both appeal to the same client at different times of life. However, the medi-spa is brand new and has emerged from the medical industry and not the spa industry. "Marketeers" have tied this phenomenon to beautifying and hence the medi-spa was born. It will be very interesting to watch this new industry develop over the next 10 years.

The majority of spas mix the above extreme spa philosophies based on the demands of the client, and so what we have is the emergence of the integrated spa. This is a spa that will offer perhaps the Indian Ayurvedic system of healing side by side with Botox. For the most part, this integration of both health care systems is where we believe the future of the spa industry lies. The spa of the future must have an open mind to all "healing" treatments and therapies in all their forms.

In assessing the future trends of the spa industry, it is vital that we look at what the spa is to the generations that exist today. We have the veterans from World War II, the Baby Boomers who created the industry in the first place, Generation

Xers and now the new entry-level workers called Generation Y. And, then, of course, these groups must be classified into subcategories, depending on the nature of their individual wealth. The veterans for the most part are from a different financial climate and have a completely different worldview. The spa experience does not, generally speaking, appeal to them. The Baby Boomers have proved to be ardent spa fans because they are, after all, the creator, but largely this has been the wealthier Baby Boomer who has both the time and the money. The working class Baby Boomer may never have had a spa treatment. Generation Xer, professionals in their mid-30s, are very aware of the spa and its offerings and may or may not go weekly, but for the most part, urban Xers have a treatment every few months and on vacations. Because technology has made basic living easier, they have more time than their forebears and generally more excess cash to spend on health maintenance, which includes spa treatments. Spending habits have changed immensely, so it is not that the Xers have more money, they just spend it differently. The Generation Yers are as yet unfolding, but, judging by the number of teen spa programs available, for the Y group, the spa, won't be a "Why?" but instead a "What time is my appointment?" proposition.

When looking into the future of the spa industry, there is one target that we must focus on and this is the public habit. Habit is what defines the social consciousness. English pubs are successful because of a habit—a way of life—became a cultural phenomenon that has been passed down through the ages. The spa industry needs to wean itself away from this concept of a lifestyle for the rich and famous, and become part of the culture as a whole—a way of living—if it is to continue its growth pattern. There is every indication that this will happen, but it is each spa operator's responsibility to make this his/her goal and help the spa consciousness become part of everyone's psyche. The spa experience is not elitist. Of course, there are spas that cater to niche groups and higher income patrons, but, in the big picture, the basic spa treatments and principles can and should be offered to all walks of life.

Some insurance companies are beginning to see savings implied by preventative health care measures. Psychologists and occasionally acupuncture are now covered by insurance. However, unless there has been an injury, massage is not covered as preventative health care. This is quite absurd when over $100 billion every year is spent on stress-related illnesses. Anything that starts because of some form of stress can be soothed and helped, if not completely eliminated, through regular massage. So, in the next 10 years, we would expect that specific treatments could be partially, if not fully, covered by insurance.

Mirroring this, work environments need to become more well being oriented. Even today there are massage therapists that visit offices, but the truly *avant-garde* employer will look to the future and see how investing in his/her employee's well-being will actually save the company money in the long run.

Massage and relaxation techniques in general have been proven to improve productivity. Hence, even if you crack the whip and run a really tight ship, when your inventory manager's mind starts wandering, there is really nothing an employer can do about it. In every work day, there is down time, so why not pre-empt it and make it downtime that helps your employees produce? Being proactive as an employer can in the long run be more productive for shareholders and business at large. Whereas the small entrepreneur cannot necessarily afford to invest in these ideas, the larger corporation can and must do so if it is going to compete with other corporations for the highest-level employees.

The corporatization of the spa experience is another trend that we are going through now that is bound to continue. Therefore, the need to brand the spa and to become a household name will almost force the spa operator to invest in strong marketing practices. Although the familiarity of a local spa and its individuality is something highly valued, the standardization of hygiene practices, customer service, spa etiquette, and licensing laws (every state has different licensing laws for spa personnel) are desperately needed for spas to be able to offer discerning spa clientele another great experience at another great outlet. Because the spa industry is such a "human" industry, employees must be treated as family members and retained. Employee retention is client retention and the spa corporation must take this consideration very seriously. Clients love beautiful surroundings, certainly, but more than attaching themselves emotionally to any beautiful wall hanging, or comfy massage bed, they grow accustomed to their spa operator.

Another growing trend that we believe will unfold over the next 10 years is the integration of spa practices into the consumer's own household. To some extent we have seen this already—with the advent of in-home massage, the use of aromatic oils in the bath, cleansing, toning and moisturizing the face, morning and night—for many women, and some men, these are standard practices. However, we think we will see this trend even more with respect to a person's lifestyle in general: a morning walk, herbal tea, natural detoxification programs, meditation, reading, burning aromatherapy and self massage. Just as some people convert their garages into gymnasiums, some will convert a room into a mini spa, to include a massage bed and shower at the very least.

We think that what we have seen since the 1960s is a growing reaction to complex, highly technical lifestyles. The spa has in large part provided a pathway back to simplicity. Also, lives are more and more isolated. As we become less and less reliant on each other, what we gain in independence, we lose in togetherness. The spa experience is a modern day remedy and provides the simplicity of doing nothing and being touched. The Touch Institute has done hundreds of surveys that undoubtedly prove the inherent need we have of being touched, so the spa fills a real need in the modern world.

According to a study sponsored by ISPA (International Spa Association), spa industry revenues have increased by 114 percent since 1999. There are over 9,000 spa locations that combine the day spa, resort spa and cruise ship spa segments. Day spas account for 75 percent of spa venues with the balance spread over the hotel/resort spa segment. This study reveals a couple of very interesting facts. Firstly, that the growth in just four years is astounding and is continuing in this vein. The second is that for the resort spa to continue growing, the day spa segment must also continue to grow. SpaFinder, a travel company dedicated to the spa industry, estimates the total revenues generated in the spa industry to be $12 billion, including travel and lodging. It is the urban spa aficionado that demands to continue that part of their lifestyle while on vacation. The growth in resort spas will be seen in square footage allocated to the spa itself and in the number of qualified operators employed. In 2002, 282,000 people were employed by spas in the USA—a huge jump from the 151,000 employed in spas in 1999. We would assume that, in the next five years, the numbers will continue to grow exponentially.

The spa industry of the future knows no boundaries. It seeps into every facet of life because the spa lifestyle is as much about a way of thinking as it is an activity. At one time, a shower in the morning was a luxury. And so it is with the spa experience today. For some it is a luxury, but soon it will have a permanent thread in the social fabric of our lives.

Section IX

Niche Marketing

Bear with us for a moment. You may wonder what a true story about dog food has to do with travel marketing, but we think this one does. Once upon a time, a large packaged goods manufacturer decided that there was a huge market for dog food in the United States and wanted to capitalize on it. They asked their advertising agency for help. From a marketing point of view, they wanted to see if there were any niche markets that had been overlooked in dog foods. They wanted to know if they could create a new dog food that would appeal to a sizable number of dog owners—i.e., what ingredients should they put in it and, of course, how should they position it to capture that niche.

The agency took the problem to their research director. He said this would be a difficult and expensive question to answer. First of all he said, in traditional research that the agency was used to doing, they would go out and question consumers about what kind of food they liked to eat. In this case it was not possible to interview the consumers at all. Then he allowed that interviewing the consumers in this case might not be important because they didn't purchase the dog food anyway. The important thing to do would be to interview the people who purchased the product, the dog owners. But what do you question them about? What you really want to know is how they feel about their dogs. This determines how they decide what kind of dog food they like to use. Asking these questions directly would not produce useful data. Call up a dozen people and ask them how they feel about their dogs and they are likely to say, "He's nice" or "She's okay."

There was another problem as well. In traditional research, you often started out by assuming that people fall into certain categories and, in questioning them one purpose is to figure out how many people fall into each of your predetermined categories. For instance, if you are questioning travelers about their travel habits, you assume they travel for either business, pleasure, or to visit friends and relatives. In questioning them, all you have to do is ask. You use this information to determine the size of each submarket. But, in this case, you didn't know how many groups there were that comprised the total market. There could be three or 23. You would have to send interviewers into the home and administer a lengthy questionnaire and then use a process called "factor analysis." This process looks for patterns in how questions are answered and then sorts the questionnaires into groups, depending on which pattern they fall into. Since people could not easily answer questions about how they felt about their dogs, it would be necessary to ask questions like. Do you like (a) big dogs or (b) little dogs? Is your favorite dog name (a) Fido (b) Wolf or (c) Pumpkin? Do you appreciate your dog best when he is (a) sleeping in bed with you, (b) playing with your kids, or (c) barking at people who come to your door?

The questionnaire was duly administered to 500 dog owners in their homes. Each interview took roughly 30 minutes. The answers were then fed into the computer for factor analysis. When the answers came back, it was found that, based on the way they had answered the questions, there were three distinct groups of dog owners. In other words, all of the respondents had answered the questions in a way to clearly put them into one of three groups.

The first group was called the utilitarians. Utilitarians felt their dogs were useful members of their households. They were there to do a job. Maybe the dog was a watchdog. Maybe he was there to play with the children. Maybe he was a seeing-eye dog. Whatever the case, the dog had a job and the dog owners could quickly tell you what it was. These dogs tended to be larger animals like German Shepherds and often had names like "Dragon" and "Sampson."

The second group of people they named companions. This group kept a dog for an entirely different reason. To them, the dog was a companion. He was there to keep them company. The dog went with them everywhere—often on errands or to the office. They talked to the dog. He was their best friend. These dogs tended to be smaller and had names like "Tiffy," "Skippy," and "Snookums." A poodle was a typical companion dog breed.

The third group was a surprise. No one expected that this group even existed. They were substantial in number and they were called "dog haters." These were people who had a dog but hated him. Often they disliked, say, a puppy that Uncle Charlie had bought the kids for Christmas and they couldn't return, or an abandoned dog that had followed little Jenny home after school. Mother, who had to take care of the dog, hated him, but what could she do?

Immediately, you can see that there is not one dog food market, but rather three niche markets. It is not likely that the same dog food would satisfy all three of them. Take the utilitarians. What they want in a dog food is something that will keep the dog healthy so he can continue to do its work. This should be a dog food with lots of vitamins and minerals; one that helps keep the teeth clean (and sharp); one that has protein, and whatever else sounds like it will keep that dog in shape to do his work. The companion also wants a healthy dog. But he or she is more interested in feeding the dog good food—food that tastes like what they eat. Typically companions fed their dogs hamburger or chicken, or even steak. And they didn't want their dogs to get bored by having to eat the same tasting food every day. They wanted different flavors—Lamb Stew, Beef Bourgogne, Chicken-a-la King. The dog haters were easy to figure out. They wanted the cheapest, easiest-to-serve, product they could buy. Their ideal dog food was dry and came in a bag that they could tear open. They could simply put it in a bowl. The dog would lap it up quickly and go back to sleep.

Market segmentation is not a new concept. But it is an important one when it comes to niche marketing. Niche markets are simply segments of a larger market. Experienced marketers slice their markets demographically and/or psychographically. Then they develop different campaigns for each segment or one campaign for all of them. If they are only interested in one segment, that's a "niche." But to find a meaningful, viable, and profitable niches is extremely difficult. That's where the trap lies: Here are some of the things you need to remember if you aspire to be successful:

1. Niche markets are part of bigger markets.

2. The size of the niche market is critical. Suppose we told you that only three percent of dog owners are dog haters (the real figure is much higher). Would you spend a lot of money on R&D to formulate the product and then mount an extensive advertising campaign to sell it?

3. Niche markets are often unprofitable ones to communicate with. Granted, there are a lot of dog haters out there. How are you going to reach them? It's easy to find people who have dogs and like them. They read dog magazines, watch TV movies like "101 Dalmatians" and go to dog shows. But there are no magazines or other media for dog haters, at least that we can think of.

Landry and Kling found a niche market in the cruise business, the corporate charter, and figured out early in the game what that niche wanted and how to provide it to them. CIEE's niche market is students and others seeking educational experiences. That's a sizable market and one easy to reach. Every school has a newspaper! The RV market is self-explanatory. There are plenty of media covering that group as well. Renowned chef Todd English, who run's Olive's Restaurant in Charlestown, Massachusetts, has identified his niche as people who want restaurants with "deep roots in their community" which customize their offerings to suit a local customer base. They may well support local growers of fresh, organic produce and indigenous ingredients." English knows his community, supports it, and cooks great food for it. How can he lose?

60

Marketing the RV Industry

David J. Humphreys, President
Recreation Vehicle
Industry Association

David J. Humphreys has served as president
of the Recreation Vehicle Industry Association (RVIA), of Reston, Virginia, since 1979,
following 10 years of service as RVIA's outside legal counsel.

Humphreys is the leading spokesman
for the RV industry. A popular interview
guest, he has appeared on television and
radio shows from coast to coast explaining
the advantages associated with RV travel.

In recognition of his leadership and
numerous accomplishments, Humphreys
was given the RV industry's highest honor,
the Distinguished Service to the RV Industry Award, in 1977. In 1981, he was awarded

the industry's National Legislative Award and in 1997, he was inducted into the
RV Industry Hall of Fame.

Humphreys was the leading force in the creation of the American Recreation
Coalition (ARC) in 1979, a nonprofit, Washington-based federation of more than
100 recreation-related associations and companies active in government policy-
making on recreation issues, and has served since as chairman of its board of directors. In 2001, ARC's members honored Humphreys with the prestigious Sheldon
Coleman Great Outdoors Award in recognition of his more than two decades of

service as a central player in national policy matters affecting recreation, travel and tourism.

He has been active for many years in the Travel Industry Association of America (TIA), the umbrella organization for all segments of the travel and tourism industry. He has been a member of TIA's board of directors since 1985 and was its national chairman from 1990 to 1991. He is a former member of TIA's executive committee, and has chaired the compensation committee through two retiring and incoming TIA presidents. Humphreys received the travel industry's highest honor in 1994 when he was inducted into the Hall of Leaders. He is also a member of the board of directors of the American Highway Users Alliance (formerly Highway Users Federation), whose membership includes representatives of the oil, trucking, automobile and tire industries.

Humphreys is a member of the bar in the District of Columbia and Virginia, and is admitted to practice before all federal courts, including the U.S. Supreme Court. He was born in Scranton, PA, and attended high school and college in Baltimore, MD. He earned his law degree from Catholic University of America, Washington, D.C.

A commercial pilot and certified flight instructor, Humphreys and his wife, Peggy, have five children and reside in Shepherdstown, West Virginia.

RVIA is the national association representing nearly 500 manufacturers and component suppliers producing 95 percent of all RVs made in the United States. Its manufacturer members produce motorhomes, conventional and fifth-wheel travel trailers, folding camping trailers, truck campers and conversion vehicles. In addition to its headquarters in the Washington, D.C., suburb of Reston, Virginia, the association has a regional office in Riverside, California.

The recreation vehicle (RV) industry is a relatively small, but very remarkable, part of the travel and tourism industry in the United States. RVs refer to vehicles that have wheels and temporary living quarters. These include motorhomes, travel trailers, fifth-wheel trailers, folding-camping trailers, and truck campers.

While RVs have existed almost from the time the automobile was invented, RVs as we know them evolved after World War II, when the trailers that had been used for housing during the war changed. Some became larger and were known as mobile homes. These units were designed to be permanent housing and were seldom moved once they were placed on site and connected to city water, sewer, electricity and telephone services. Others became smaller vehicles that were designed as temporary living quarters. They were designed to be readily moved about and were self-contained. They did not need to be connected to anything to be fully functional and self-sufficient, and they were primarily used for recreational travel. They became known as recreation vehicles (RVs).

The RV industry did very well after World War II—that is, until the Arab oil embargo hit the United States in late 1973 and early 1974. This resulted in long lines at gas stations. The industry came to a virtual standstill. But, fortunately, the problem only lasted about four months.

In 1979, the United States encountered a severe energy crisis that again resulted in long lines at gas stations. The year 1980 brought interest rates that were over 20 percent. These two problems combined to cause the RV industry to lose 70 percent of its volume and 80 percent of its employees in a 24-month period. This second energy crisis also caused many RV owners to feel unpatriotic when they needed to fill their gas tanks. Yet full tanks were necessary in order to enjoy the RV lifestyle. There was also serious doubt about the future availability of vehicles that would be adequate for use as towing vehicles, since fuel economy became a top priority for the United States (more than half of all RVs are not motorized and require good towing vehicles).

In addition, the RV industry had another very serious problem. The typical RV purchaser was a retired person who had adequate discretionary time and income to enjoy the RV lifestyle. The age of the average RV owner was climbing steadily. It was obvious that if the industry did not find ways to appeal to the Baby Boomer group, the future of the RV industry would be bleak indeed.

As serious as the problems were in 1973–74 and in 1979–80, these crises did bring the various segments of the RV industry together. In the past, the industry was not very united, and was poorly equipped to deal with national problems. In 1974, the two major associations that represented RV manufacturers and suppliers merged, after spending many years feuding with one another. They became the Recreation Vehicle Industry Association (RVIA). This alliance was a very uneasy one at first, but it gradually strengthened between 1974 and 1979.

The story of what the RV industry accomplished after 1979 is truly amazing. In 1999, the RV industry had its best sales in 20 years. In 2000, it had the second-best sales year in 20 years. There was a downturn in 2001 when the economy took a dip and the terrorist acts of September 11 occurred. However, in 2002, when the travel and tourism industry was severely impacted, the RV industry posted a 20 percent increase over 2001. In 2003, the industry is not only sustaining these dramatic gains, it is enjoying about an additional 8 percent increase. The RV industry now sells in excess of 300,000 new RVs each year for over $12 billion.

In addition to success in sales, the RV industry has had a dramatic turnaround in its image and how the RV lifestyle is viewed in the United States. In fact, it is very common for RVs to be featured in national advertising campaigns for products that have nothing to do with RVs. The creators of these ads, in an attempt to relate their products to positive virtues such as family togetherness, outdoor fun and travel independence, physically present their products proximate to RVs. They spend millions of dollars on these campaigns. The creative people in advertising continue to do this year after year for a wide variety of products. Clearly they have been motivated to do this by the positive publicity that now surrounds RV use and ownership.

Two other indications that the image of RVs has become very positive are (1) that RVs are regularly featured, always in a very positive way, in sitcoms and movies. The RV industry has really encouraged this, but, for the most part, it has happened because the writers and producers of sitcoms and movies have decided on their own that RVing will be popular with their audiences.

Perhaps the best news of all for the future of the RV industry is that (2) the fastest-growing group of powerful purchasers—the Baby Boomers, those Americans between 35 and 55 years of age, are buying. This is the largest and most influential segment of our population. When this change is combined with research by the University of Michigan Consumer Research Center that indicates that RV owners have an incredibly high appreciation of, and loyalty toward, the RV industry, it bodes well for the RV industry's future.

The question is, how did the RV industry market itself so effectively to the American public after losing 70 percent of its volume and 80 percent of its employees between 1979 and 1980?

While individual manufacturers worked hard to meet the needs of the Boomers and to improve the overall image of the RV industry, the main tools that resulted in the industry's successful turnaround resulted from the combined effects of its PR campaign and the industry advertising campaign known as "Go RVing."

RVIA mounted a major public relations effort in the 1980s that gradually gained momentum and effectiveness. The campaign had many of the traditional elements of PR campaigns, such as programs aimed at obtaining positive print and TV coverage. In addition, RVIA sponsored a national weekly cable television series on RV travel on The Nashville Network, which introduced the joys and benefits of RVing to millions of prospects. The show had a successful nine-year run from 1986 to 1994.

Once the industry had attained substantial success in its public relations efforts, RVIA sought professional advice as to whether it had the best combination of programs. The advice was very positive as to what was being done, but concluded with the goal of increasing "top-of-mind awareness." It seemed that RVs were viewed more as a hobby than as a significant segment of travel and tourism. In fact, RVs were not even on the menu of many Americans, when they considered their vacation alternatives.

This advice resulted in a substantial increase in the PR efforts mounted by the RVIA on behalf of the industry. A wide variety of industry spokespersons were added to the program, and these have been very effective. RVIA's PR efforts have continued at about an annual $2 million level from 1990 to the present.

This program has been responsible in large part for the very positive improvement in the image and popularity of the RV lifestyle in America.

Once this success was obvious, the industry began considering the wisdom and practicality of an industry-wide national lifestyle advertising campaign. Go RVing was the result.

The Go RVing campaign is basically a partnership between the RV manufacturers and the RV dealers, but all industry segments (campgrounds, state associations, suppliers, etc.) participate in the funding and design of the program. The first part of this program was referred to as Phase I. It covered a three-year period from 1997 through 1999, and had a $20 million budget, including production and placement of five two-page print ads and four 30-second TV spots. The theme was "Wherever you go, you're always at home."

Phase II ran from 2000 through 2002 and had a $40 million budget for the same number of new print and TV executions, along with three Web banner ads for the first time, and a more aggressive media schedule. The theme was "Go RVing. Life's a Trip."

Phase III runs from 2003 through 2005 with a $55 million budget. The theme is "Pursue Your Passions." The Phase III budget was increased to allow for the addition of national network television and radio to the heavy direct response cable emphasis of the first two phases, along with production of the first 60-second TV spot of the campaign. This was designed to showcase the great diversity of experiences and product types available to potential RV buyers.

It was decided at the outset of the Go RVing advertising campaign that the results had to be carefully measured each year. However, using industry sales as the sole measure would not be valid—if the economy boomed, sales would increase whether the campaign had been run or not. Conversely, if there were a recession, sales would drop whether the campaign had been conducted or not. It was decided that the best way to measure the effectiveness of the program was to measure awareness of the campaign messages in the target audience. A firm that specialized in this type of research and was not affiliated with the advertising agency was chosen.

Extensive psychographic research into the attitudes, awareness and potential purchase barriers among potential RV buyers was also critical to planning the campaign launch and fine-tuning the approach in subsequent phases. In 1995, the renowned Harris research organization was tapped to determine the best qualified prospects and the best marketing communications messages to reach them, resulting in the selection of the Baby Boomers' parents as the primary target of the campaign. An updated study performed in 2001 identified aging, empty-nesting Boomers as a key secondary market, with their own set of psychographic attributes and messages. Focus groups within both the primary and secondary target audiences were conducted in each phase of the campaign to test the appeal of the messages and their creative executions.

The good news during Phase I was that awareness in the research-based primary target audience improved by about 20 percent each year. The bad news was that the ads were only run for about four months—awareness decreased sharply during the ensuing eight months. Those who viewed the ads were encouraged to call a toll-free number and order a free video that explained the types of RVs that were available and the advantages of the RV lifestyle. About 167,000 people called the 888 number. They also became leads that were forwarded to RV dealers in their area.

The budget for Phase II was doubled in order to have the ads on the air for 10 months in the hope of greatly reducing the sagging awareness numbers. This worked very nicely. The 888 number was also given more visibility in the commercials—both print and TV. A major Web site was also developed. It contained a great deal of information and had direct links to manufacturers and dealers, as well as complete information about the types of RVs, how to finance and insure them, where to use them, etc. Over 300,000 requests for information were received; all of the requestors became leads for RV dealers and manufacturers.

The budget for Phase III was increased in order to provide more primetime network TV coverage, as opposed to cable programming. Many improvements were made in how leads were sorted and forwarded to dealers. Also, a series of radio ads were produced and a celebrity voice (Tom Selleck) was used in the TV and radio commercials. Banner ads on popular Internet sites were also used for the first time, and these have been surprisingly effective.

There were several unanticipated but very positive results of the Go RVing program. One was that it was unique and successful in its own right, so that it became newsworthy, resulting in a great deal of free news coverage that was very positive and effective. Another surprise is that industry unity has benefited from the program, since all industry segments, were invested in it, and were consulted in the design of the ads.

In addition to the advertising component of this program, a RVIA committee on excellence was created. The purpose of this effort was to do research concerning how the consumers viewed the industry so that their concerns could be addressed by the industry. In other words, the industry was not content with merely attracting new customers. They wanted to find ways to please current and new customers even more than they had been pleased in the past. Every other year, the committee on excellence has surveyed 30,000 owners of RVs of about one year's standing. Each participating manufacturer receives a very detailed report on how consumers view their vehicles, as compared to the average ratings for their competition. Naturally, complete confidentiality is essential to the success of this. Fortunately, no problems have been reported. Consumers' views as to how dealers handled the sales process and how service was done as well as what their experiences were at both public and private campgrounds were sought. The result of this research has been a constant improvement in consumer satisfaction in almost all aspects of the RV industry.

The final test of the Go RVing program is how it was viewed by advertising professionals. The answer is that the program has won many awards and has gotten a great deal of positive publicity in the advertising trade press.

How was the Go RVing program funded? This seems to be the most common question RVIA has received. The main tool that was used was a mandatory assessment on all new recreation vehicles built by RVIA manufacturers, attached to what we refer to as the RVIA Standards Seal. For many years, RVIA has required member manufacturers to affix this seal to each RV they produce.

The seal contains a statement by the manufacturer that the vehicle complies with ANSI (American National Standards Institute) A119.2. This is a national standard that was independently developed covering the plumbing, heating, electrical and propane systems in RVs. RVIA employs its own inspectors, who inspect all members' factories every six to eight weeks to assure compliance. The cost of the program was divided by the number of RVs produced; that amount of money was added to the cost of the standards seal.

These new unit assessments, coupled with additional voluntary contributions made by many RVIA members through a supplemental fundraising program, represent roughly 96 percent of the overall Go RVing budget. Industry suppliers contribute another 3 percent through surcharges on booth space at RVIA trade shows and voluntary contributions.

RV park operators also contributed voluntary sums through the National Association of RV Parks and Campgrounds—ARVC). Many industry members contributed to the "Go The Extra Mile" program. This resulted in some $700,000 to $800,000 dollars in additional funds for each phase of the campaign, and showed how highly the program was valued by the industry.

In 2003, the RV industry has come a very long way from where it was in 1980. Sales are booming, the image of the industry is amazingly positive, the quality of the vehicles is improving, customer satisfaction has increased across the board and the average age of the RV consumer has dropped dramatically. According to the University of Michigan Survey Research Center, which compiles demographic information on the RV consumer, the number of RVs owned by 35- to 54-year-olds is growing faster than any other age group, and more RVs are now owned by 35- to 54-year-olds than any other age group. The rate of ownership among younger Baby Boomers, ages 35 to 44, has seen especially impressive growth, rising from 6.9 percent to 9.6 percent since the campaign began.

The RV industry has been very fortunate in a number of other ways as well. The popularity of SUVs and pickup trucks has provided the industry with a wide variety of excellent tow vehicles. This has helped the growth of our less expensive non-motorized vehicles, which still make up well over half of all RVs produced.

Sociological trends have even helped the industry. It is "in" to be physically active and fit. People are looking for ways to reduce the stress in their life and spend more quality time with their families. Americans love the outdoors. They want to enjoy the land and do not want to harm it. Most people are eager to find ways to put their children in positive environments away from numerous temptations and distractions that are not positive. Flexibility and safety in travel is more critical than ever after the events of September 11, 2001. We view all of these factors as helpful and long term.

We have successfully appealed to the Baby Boomers. We are now starting to find ways to reach the youngest groups of RV prospects identified by our research: Generation X, ages 21 to 39. This cohort exhibits an interest in outdoor activities that is highly compatible with RVing. Go RVing ads are now being crafted and placed in appropriate media to encourage younger buyers to "pursue their passions," from extreme sports to mountain biking, with an emphasis on Internet communications to this tech-savvy market.

As we go forward, we are confident that the RV industry will be able to continue to identify and appeal to various groups of consumers by continuing its research-based approach and constantly refining its public relations and advertising programs.

61

Where We Dine Is Who We Are

Todd English
Executive Chef and Restaurateur

One of the most decorated, respected, and charismatic chefs in the world, Todd English has enjoyed great accolades during his remarkable career. His accomplishments include recognition by several of the food industry's most prestigious publications, establishing one of the best-known restaurant brands in the nation, publishing three critically acclaimed cookbooks, and being recognized as one of *People Magazine*'s "50 Most Beautiful People."

In the Spring of 1991, English caught the culinary world's eye when the James Beard Foundation named him its National Rising Star Chef. The James Beard Foundation subsequently named him Best Chef in the Northeast in 1994. In 2001, English was awarded *Bon Appetit*'s Restaurateur of the Year award and was also named one of *People Magazine*'s 50 Most Beautiful People.

Todd is currently the chef and owner of Olives in Charlestown, Massachusetts. Olives opened in May of 1989 as a 50-seat, storefront restaurant. It has drawn national and international applause for English's interpretive rustic Mediterranean cuisine. Olives now occupies a larger space down the street from its original location in Charlestown. In recent years, English has established Olives as one of the most prestigious names in the nation by opening other locations across the country: Olives New York at the W Hotel on Union Square; Olives Las Vegas at the

Bellagio Hotel in Las Vegas; Olives DC in the heart of Washington, D.C., and Olives Aspen at the St. Regis Hotel in Aspen, Colorado. Olives Tokyo is opening in late spring of 2003.

English also has four Figs restaurants in the greater Boston area and two locations at LaGuardia Airport in New York City. Figs serves traditional and eclectic pizzas and handmade pastas. Among English's other restaurants are Tuscany at Mohegan Sun in Connecticut, which serves Italian inspired foods and pays homage to his Italian roots; Bonfire, a steakhouse that is a celebration of ranch cooking around the world, from the United States to Australia; and KingFish Hall, Todd's first seafood concept, in Boston's Historic Faneuil Hall. Todd's second seafood concept, Fish Club, is opening in Seattle in late spring of 2003. Two other ventures are scheduled to open in 2003 as well: the Cunard Line's Queen Mary 2 will be welcoming the restaurant Todd English, and Disney World will host Blue Zoo at the Swan and Dolphin.

Like English himself, his restaurants have received numerous accolades. The original Olives was voted Best New Restaurant by *Boston Magazine*. Since then, it has been honored for best food and top table by *Gourmet Magazine* and consistently named Boston's #1 favorite restaurant by *Zagat*. Figs was given the "Hot Concept" award from *Nation's Restaurant News*. KingFish Hall was named "Best of Boston" by *Travel + Leisure Magazine*.

Todd English began his cooking career at age 15, when he first entered the doors of a professional kitchen. At 20, he attended the Culinary Institute of America, graduating in 1982 with honors. He continued to hone his craft with Jean Jacques Rachou at New York's *La Côte Basque* and then relocated to Italy, where he apprenticed at the well-established *Dal Pescatore* in Canto Sull O'lio and *Paraccuchi* in Locando D'Angello. It was in Italy that English, drawing from his Italian heritage, developed his unique style and approach to cooking. English returned to the United States at 25 and was asked to be executive chef of the award-winning Northern Italian restaurant *Michela's* in Cambridge, Massachusetts. He served there as an executive chef for three years, garnering high praise from both the press and the public.

English's television credits include his public television series, "Cooking In with Todd English," produced by Connecticut Public Television. Other TV credits include: "Iron Chef USA" on UPN; Martha Stewart's *Living*; TVFN's "Chef du Jour," "The Main Ingredient," "In Food Today," Bobby Flay's "Food Nation," CBS "This Morning," "Live with Regis and Kelly," "The Today Show," Discovery Channel's *Great Chefs of the Northeast* series, WGBH's "Hot Off the Grill," and public television's "America's Rising Star Chefs." Todd has authored the critically acclaimed cookbooks, *The Olives Table*, *The Figs Table* and *The Olives Dessert Table*, published by Simon & Schuster.

Todd is very involved with several local and national charities including Big Brother, the Anthony Spinazzola Foundation, Community Servings, Share Our Strength, the Boys and Girls Clubs, and City Year.

After nearly 20 years of submersion in the restaurant business, cooking and managing in freestanding restaurants and those within hotels, I have certainly seen many ups and downs in this industry. When I started out in this business, professionals were still very much a utilitarian force working behind closed doors of kitchens that offered no recognition of their hard work and talent. The average diner had little interest in the actual process of his or her food's preparation; as long as the food came out beautifully presented and delicious, everyone was happy. In the past, closed door kitchens created almost a mystery. Today's open kitchens have transformed culinary "secrets" into a showplace offering a kind of stage where chefs are able to display their talents in an all-night performance (the industry owes the first major marketing of this concept, of course, to Rocky Aoki, founder of Beni-Hana). Flames dance and the energy among the crew on the line moves gracefully, similar to the perfect choreography of a ballet. It's very entertaining! Tomorrow's trends will continue to be influenced by those who have developed an interest, a rock star's or groupie's devotion, to the food and wine world. They will travel the world to see and be seen, to sample and experience the food and ambience of this stimulating and sometimes intoxicating industry.

Because food plays such an important role in our lives, I feel it is reasonable to believe that how we dine, where we dine and what we eat are significant indicators of where we are currently as a culture, as well as where we are headed. One example to consider is the impact of interstate travel on dining. As automobile usage increased after World War II, there was a greater need for highways traversing the country. When these roadways were established, it became apparent that roadside restaurants such as Howard Johnson's were needed to feed traveling families and businessmen.

Or, consider that as the country became more focused on speed and efficiency in the 1950s, the same principles were applied to the food industry. That's how a small, quick-serve hamburger restaurant in Southern California mushroomed into McDonald's. I believe there are some undercurrents of change afoot that will be just about as significant on the food and restaurant industry in the future—as significant as those that drove the beginnings of roadside dining and fast food.

Today, with the Baby Boomer population in middle age and approaching senior status, a huge segment of the population is entering its peak spending years. They have accumulated wealth, put their kids through college. Now it is time for them to focus on themselves and spend. This is the new "luxury" class. Unlike old money, they are willing to pay for what they perceive to be an excellent value. But they will not pay a premium for what they consider unimportant. They are smart and selective with their money. An example of this: Old money might go to Longchamps; the new luxury seeker goes to Burberry. However, the new luxury buyer will also not hesitate to shop at Target for simple, everyday items, such as cotton socks.

This group will have a huge effect on industries like healthcare and real estate. Hotel and restaurant industries will need to focus on elements that matter to this class. Expensive menu jackets and/or fancy matches may not be important anymore. Instead, a knowledgeable service staff, exceptionally high food quality and the offering of a "unique" and consistent product are more important than ever. Service is also something to earmark for the next decade. Faced with more choices, this consumer will not tolerate "attitude" any longer. Service in the future will be more unique and personalized than ever. This crowd demands comfort, consistency and personal attention.

I believe that we have lost the distinctiveness and identity of place, characteristics that distinguish one community from another, one region of the world from another. While it's clear that today's customer may demand the same product or service no matter where he is, as a result of the effectiveness of mass media, advertising and the Internet, it is apparent to me that we deliver that product at a substantial cost, the cost of local individuality and personal identity.

Contributing to the sense of identity loss is the "cookie cutter" quality found today in the retail and restaurant environments. The face of today's chain retail and service environments have permeated our communities to such an extent that independent retailers and restaurants in many markets struggle to stay in business. As a consumer, I find it impossible to know if I am standing in a mall in central Florida, upstate New York or Southern California. And as a diner, I struggle to separate one casual dining chain from another; the menus and interiors are practically identical.

Perhaps as a reaction to the growing economic uncertainties and global political upheaval, my sense is that over time, this loss of community identity will become more unsettling to the population. Ultimately, as a result of the desire for community, stability and sense of "home," these distinguishing differences will reignite our sympathies. My guess is that this need will manifest itself in a growing awareness and appreciation for those qualities that have historically characterized and helped to define a community. Today there is a growing interest in living a healthier lifestyle. This trend has clearly been hastened by the number of healthcare issues arising in our society, as well as by increased interest in the obtaining the healthiest lifestyles. Awareness of how our lifestyles affect our health is at an all-time high, particularly in the Baby Boomer age group.

Today's consumer is exceptionally educated and well informed. With issues of heart disease and cancer on the rise, we are taking better care of ourselves and making demands on industries for their support. More consumers are demanding natural and/or organic products, free of artificial additives and chemicals. This is true for restaurant, as well as food market, customers.

Another example of this trend may be a return to more regionalized styles and materials in architecture. Residential housing subdivisions that presently appear to vary little from one another, may begin to take on the characteristics for which the regions in which they are located were previously known. Families that have spread out throughout the country may reunite, finding comfort and support from one another. Or, we may see a resurgence of interest in local art forms, local forms of entertainment and local customs and traditions.

The implications for retailing, restaurants and menu products are significant. I would not be surprised to see an increasing interest in the local retailer who tailors his offerings to closely match the needs and interests of the community in which he is located—who personalizes his goods and services, ultimately giving the consumer the absolute most for his "smart" money. Familiar with his neighbors' tastes and preferences, he will offer the customer a product that is appropriate for the community. He may then be perceived to be giving a higher level of service. And while he may not match the lower-priced chain, the customer may feel that the local retailer is an overall better value as well as a "reinvestment" of sorts in one's community.

Local independent restaurateurs with roots that run deep in their communities may become the preferred choice, as they are also able to customize their offerings to suit a local customer base.

They may well support local growers of fresh, organic produce and indigenous ingredients. They will have more flexibility and be able to react more quickly to adapt their menus as necessary to meet local demand or to reflect a "local catch."

An owner/operator will have a much greater investment in the success of his enterprise than the salaried general manager of the local chain unit, who will probably be reassigned within a 12-month period anyhow.

Clearly there are benefits for both the consumer and the multiple unit "chain" operator who provided a variety of merchandise, services or food and drink at competitive prices. However, I feel we must begin to consider the alternative approach that may be required in the future; that recognizes the community as one that demands high quality, unique and individualized product; an approach that is customized for the community. It may become necessary to create food products that are uniquely suited to a particular location. An interior and exterior design that reflects local tastes and materials may also be called for, as well as a name for the business that is unique or, at least, very special.

It is my best guess that there will be some backlash to the domination of national brands that have managed to eliminate much of what was interesting and defining about our communities. It is possible that the reaction will be tempered, perhaps more so than I have anticipated, but I do not think it is one that will be ignored.

As the owner and operator of restaurants across the country, my team has internalized these issues and structured an organization that is highly responsive to emerging trends. Almost all of my restaurants feature open kitchens that invite the diner to become visually involved in the from-scratch preparation of his meal. We recognize the demand for fresh, high-quality ingredients that today's health conscious customer demands by providing daily specials that feature locally grown fruits and vegetables, fresh fish and bold, distinctive tastes. The menus at my three fish restaurants, located in very different parts of the country, are designed to take advantage of the daily local catch.

We change our printed menu offerings at least four times a year. At Olives, although we have locations in New York, Boston, Las Vegas, Aspen, Washington, D.C., and Tokyo, we have different menus tailored to the dining preferences of our local customer base. In Seattle, where there is a strong interest in Asian flavors, my restaurant provides many Asian-inspired alternatives.

My Figs restaurants are designed to fit into the local city, town or village landscape, integrating themselves into the community by utilizing storefronts of existing downtown facades. Each is retrofitted into the space and decorated to reflect the life of the community in which it resides.

62

Staying Ahead of the Curve to Avoid Getting Run Over

Joyce Landry
President and CEO,
Landry & Kling Inc.

Joyce Landry is president and CEO of Miami-based Landry & Kling Inc. She formed the company in 1982 with partner Josephine Kling, specializing in corporate events at sea. Landry's strong sales background and her years of experience in the cruise industry enabled her to identify a niche that had not yet been plumbed in the meetings and incentive market.

Prior to Landry & Kling's inception, Landry held the position of manager of Holland America Tours. She was responsible for the implementation of the first air/sea department of Holland America Line.

She also served as regional sales director of Delta Queen Steamboat Company, where she introduced travel agents and meeting planners within a 13-state territory to the concept of steamboat cruising.

Landry has held positions on several cruise line advisory boards, including those of Disney Cruise Line, Radisson Seven Seas, Royal Caribbean International and Cunard/Seabourn Cruises, as the point person for the meetings/incentive market. In the mid-1980s, Landry urged cruise line executives, via presentations made at the international shipping conference known as Seatrade, to incorporate purpose-built meeting facilities into new ship designs. Such designs were finally fulfilled when the vessels were completed in the early 1990s. It is now standard for ships to be equipped with meetings and conferences in mind.

Over the years, Landry has spoken to thousands of meeting planners about the viability of meetings and events on cruise ships. She has addressed audiences of the Insurance Conference Planners Association (ICPA), Meeting Professionals International (MPI) and the Society of Incentive Travel Executives (SITE). In addition, she is active in a number of associations and events relating to women in business and was formerly a keynote speaker treating Women's History Month at the annual meeting of the United States Coast Guard.

Landry has been nominated for several prestigious awards from organizations like the Athena Foundation, which recognizes women for their professional excellence and community service. She actively and generously assists women in their attainment of professional excellence. She was also named to the Women's Hall of Fame in recognition of Miami's Centennial, by the City of Miami Commission on the Status of Women, and was named one of the "Top 25 Most Influential People in the Meetings Industry" by *Meeting News* magazine in 2002.

Landry is also founder and president of the Miami Executive Women's Golf League, which introduces golfing to professional women. She has organized multiple golf tournaments on corporate cruise programs throughout the Caribbean. Her involvement in other organizations includes being president of the Youth Crime Watch of America, a troop leader for the Girl Scouts, and president of her local chapter of ToastMasters, USA.

Running a successful business in today's environment requires a variety of talents from its leaders, but most importantly, an ability to adapt to changing trends. Those who are sensitive to subtle changes in the business atmosphere, and those who are agile enough to adapt to change in their business model, will not only survive—they will become undisputed leaders in their industry.

In the 20-plus years of running one company, I've seen enough changes to make one's head spin. Clearly, we would have suffered great losses after the fact if we hadn't anticipated and adapted. Over this period, companies in our industry have been deregulated, have become technologically advanced, have merged, split, had great economic years, engaged in ship building booms, endured two recessions, several wars and numerous disasters (environmental, biological and manmade). Through it all, we reacted immediately and took the lead in shaping the outcome for the benefit of our clients, employees and stockholders.

In the beginning, as a fledgling company with few employees, we initiated twice yearly "partner meetings." Most small companies operated by the seat of their pants, but we knew that our growth was dependent on clear, cogent strategic thinking. Thankfully, we had the instinct to leave the office during these meetings and find a quiet place away from our daily responsibilities (usually an ocean-front property) for inspiration. Most of our visionary thinking came from these meetings. Over the years, we expanded the menu of partner meetings to include participation from our advisory board, senior management training sessions, and valuable input and guidance from a business coach. At the point that Landry & Kling was targeted for acquisition in 1998, we had grown to a $20 million business. We attribute much of our success to thinking ahead and being ahead of the curve—not sweeping up the remains.

As an example, shortly after the September 11 terrorist attack on the World Trade Center, we swung into action and issued a press release assuring clients that their safety was paramount. We evaluated each program that had been planned to take place during the following months—preempting client calls with our own, explaining the options that had been negotiated on their behalf. Our cruise line partners were receptive to the solutions that we suggested. In many cases, they were "outside-the-box" ideas that issued from our sales and operations teams' strategy sessions. Virtually every program was salvaged in some way—either by refund, transfer to a different ship, sailing date or even a different year of operation. Among our partners, we discovered who our true allies were—management reacted quite differently from cruise line to cruise line. Strategic decisions were made that—to this day—affect the volume of business transacted with certain lines. In fact, the cruise line that was most flexible during this period was rewarded with a three-fold increase in business one year later.

A trend that we identified immediately after September 11 was the desire for flexibility from our clients. No longer were they agreeable to the industry norm of locked-in charter contracts, committed by irrevocable letters of credit. They were looking for attrition clauses, contract verbiage that addressed State Department travel advisories and flexibility with payment options. These were all new concepts. Our company was on the leading edge of producing contract clauses that were acceptable to both our clients and cruise line management. Once we knew that a workable system was in place, we communicated this information through our marketing materials—inviting corporations who were still in the decision-making process to choose a cruise instead of land *because* of the flexibility and safety of such a choice—not *despite* it. And clients came back as a result. There is no question that this was a particularly difficult period in our industry; still, we maintained our profitability and actually completed the following fiscal year ahead of projections. We know that most other travel companies did not fare as well. The key was reacting immediately and anticipating the needs and newly formed sensitivities of our clients.

Personal Service in an Increasingly Impersonal World

If there is one thing that Landry & Kling has been known for over the years, it is personal service. That distinction continually separates our company from others, and keeps us ahead of the competition via recommendations and referrals. By personal service, we don't mean smiles and gestures of simple courtesy—although they're certainly part of it. We mean *genuinely liking* our clients; treating them as part of the L&K family; and getting a kick out of serving them.

In 1982, the year we were founded, this idea was actually quite conventional. As technology has grown, we have all gotten accustomed to less and less personal service. We have become more accepting of sterile interactions in our day-to-day life. It occurred to me several years ago that I was getting tired of being treated this way and began to assume that I was not the only one. Unconsciously, I gravitated toward smaller, personal establishments where I was treated more as a human being. And, the more I encountered impersonal interactions in my own life, the more fiercely I protected the personal touches we had initiated at Landry & Kling.

Recently, at an insurance industry conference, our management received a standing ovation when we announced that we still have live phone answering at our office. The response was astounding, and put to rest any thoughts about switching to voicemail prompts. Some other "old-fashioned" service concepts:

- sending a bottle of champagne with a signed contract

- initiating a welcome aboard phone call from the president of our firm—to thank our clients for their business

- awarding our client with a customized plaque on site; with a photo of the Landry & Kling team who serviced their program—as a remembrance to place in their office

We also strive to take note of our clients' personal preferences and deliver them whenever possible. For example, the wife of the founder and chairman of a major insurance company has a passion for popcorn. Whenever they travel with us, we place fresh popcorn in their suite, so she can enjoy it while getting dressed for dinner. In another example, the vice chairman of a major technology company has a penchant for powdered doughnuts. During our last program with this company, our staff bought a few boxes; took them aboard ship and placed them with the meeting break refreshments every morning. The vice chairman was able to enjoy his favorite doughnuts with coffee each morning, and he was noticeably pleased. The cost of these gestures is often negligible, but the impression they leave is invaluable. And while these kindnesses may not immediately translate into business, they certainly keeps us top of mind among our customers and insulate us, to some extent, from the competition.

A typical client remark is "someone recommended another company but I wouldn't think of it—Landry & Kling will always handle my cruise programs." Our repeat factor is over 60 percent—which is highly unusual in the corporate and incentive market. Most companies look for new destinations and venues every year, but our clients regularly come back to cruising because we demonstrate value; we provide successful programs, and they genuinely *like* working with our team.

Do You Really Know Who Your Competitors Are?

A major change in the cruise industry over the last 10 years is the shift in how travel is marketed and sold. When Landry & Kling was first formed, the travel agent network was golden; suppliers wouldn't think of circumventing the system. The change to direct bookings started with the automation of airline reservations systems in the 1980s. Gradually the cruise lines came aboard in the 1990s. In our sector (corporate and incentive travel), the lines have committed more resources to direct selling—for example, utilizing BDMs (business development managers) to make calls on major corporations. When someone asks us who our biggest competitor is, they are often startled to hear our response: the cruise lines themselves.

Fortunately, we anticipated this shift and tailored our processes to capture more business with net-rate pricing and cost-plus services. Many companies couldn't or wouldn't adapt and are either suffering business losses or did not survive. Worse, there were the companies that whined about the changes in the distribution system instead of using the information as an opportunity to take a hard look at their business practices.

We have the benefit (and challenge) of being a unique provider of services. Over the years, we've had few direct competitors—companies that only specialize in cruises, that also have experience with corporate groups and charters. We carved out a niche and enjoyed a free playing field for a good long run. Eventually others caught on to the business, but not until after we became well known and had operated many successful programs. At that point, it was hard for others to catch up and we found that we had an edge when competing in presentations and proposals to prospective clients. No one could match the number of ships we had chartered or the variety of programs we managed. We operated the first multi-ship dockside charter using ships as floating hotels; chartered ships for the Olympics and Super Bowl, managed all kinds of complex projects and events on cruise ships, all the while adding to our list of Fortune 500 clients. Our volume was growing, along with our profits. Had we suffered from hubris, it would have been a dangerous situation. Nevertheless, we were about to learn a good lesson.

Enter the broker/dealmaker. Our Achilles heel was the fact that we didn't offer minimal service programs. Landry & King's operational procedures were developed to handle full, personal service, with all of the costs associated with it. While a number of our current clients were still requesting full service—we were missing out on a growing number of new potential clients who were easily wooed by a new breed of brokers offering "direct" net pricing. In the age of stockholder value and bottom line consciousness, our clients were being forced to buy cheaper.

We spent some time marketing the Landry & King "difference" and, while it was effective for some clients, we discovered there were many new buyers who's singular mission was to secure the best price. So, after a strategic planning meeting, we decided to overhaul our services to include this new buyer—without compromising our high standards of service for the companies that required it. The result: a flexible buying program tailored to give clients what *they want*, instead of what we *think they need*. This is a menu driven program, giving clients the flexibility to choose the extent of services they want with corresponding cost. It provides us with a competitive tool that is quite effective in today's business environment.

Marketing with OPM

Future marketing executives would do well to fine-tune their negotiating skills. As the lines merge and grow, they are looking for partners to help build their business. Large funds are allocated to support this effort, and as long as the volume is being delivered, the funds will keep flowing. Typically, the money is used for print advertising, e-marketing, and mailings.

The support doesn't have to come only in the form of advertising dollars—the standard of the past. It can come in the form of partnership. Today, in our business, we work with our cruise line partners, for example, to co-produce seminars at sea, to sponsor events (industry trade shows, etc.), to produce corporate videos, DVDs or CD-ROMs. Sometimes our partners' support comes in the form of overrides or bonus commission. Higher volumes can command more lucrative partnership relationships with cruise lines and there is a tremendous financial opportunity here that will fall by the wayside unless it's picked up. So, sharpen that pencil and make a few calls.

I should note that when Landry & Kling was founded, we had little money and no clients. At that time, there was little that the cruise lines could do to support our efforts—especially when we had no track record. My business partner, Josephine Kling, started writing press releases and sending them to the New York Times and other papers. Within six months, we had had a half-page article written about our company that made appear to be a substantial company (the world was none the wiser). We booked over $300,000 in business that month and haven't looked back. Soon after, I wrote a letter to the producer of "The Today Show" (after we saw a cruise line executive interviewed on the air) and received the usual regret letter. Years later, when the show was scheduled to be broadcast on the S. S. Norway, we called again . . . remember us? They did and included us on the show—with Jane Pauley. Not long after that, we were requested to appear again as industry experts with Bryant Gumbel for the launching of the (then) largest ship in the world, the Sovereign of the Seas. None of this terrific public exposure cost us a penny—although it did require some intestinal fortitude.

Help Your Customer Solve Business Issues

How many times have you been approached by salespeople who never ask what your goals are? What are you trying to accomplish? You can either beat someone over the head with a product or service or offer a buyer the right fit after patiently and carefully finding out what that person wants. We train our sales team in the latter method. Our four-page client profile questionnaire prompts the answers that we need to determine the right fit; even after all these years, we simply don't offer a proposal until we have enough information to provide an effective recommendation.

Another trend that we've observed is that people don't have the time to read volumes of information. Thus, over the years, we've streamlined our proposal process to provide the necessary pieces of information (so a customer can make a decision), in an easy to read, visually stimulating format. As far as content delivery goes, I'm a firm believer in two things: bullet points and a friendly writing style. We take impersonal information and make it personal—tailoring the features and benefits to each customer's needs. For example; instead of listing 20 features of a vessel, we may pick out two or three that really stand out as pertinent to the client's needs:

- Meeting Rooms: Your general session can be accommodated in the main theatre, which seats 900 people and offers unobstructed sight lines. State-of-the-art technology is a strong feature on this ship, so it is not necessary for your production crew to ship or store equipment. There's no cost for meeting breaks; that should substantially help your budget.

- Golf: This cruise ship features a PGA pro, who will be available to offer clinics to your attendees. New Calloway clubs can be rented aboard ship. We can arrange tournament play on three different well-known courses in the Caribbean, considering the itinerary chosen for you. Your chairman will be delighted with the golf activities on this program.

As cruise experts, it is our goal to offer added value. When that makes the entire process of choosing the right ship easier, then we've accomplished our loftiest goal.

STAND-OUT . . . it's easier than you think

You'd be surprised at how many businesses function at the level of the ordinary. Customers have gotten so numbed by ordinary service, that it is refreshing and delightful, if sometimes shocking, to encounter the unexpected.

We have a good creative team of people at Landry & Kling. Here are some of the "memorable moments" that we have created for our clients:

- A longtime client from Texas visits our office in Miami. We announce in our office that, on the specified day, everyone is to wear the client's corporate colors (red and white). Before arriving, we hang an enormous banner outside our second floor balcony that can be seen from the street—with the client's logo emblazoned on it. And we have cold champagne ready in the conference room (her favorite). Smiles all around... you bet!

- After seven cruises and full ship charters, we anoint our frequent client with a new name: "Cruise Goddess." A customized plaque is ordered and presented at a ceremony in her honor. To this day, she calls and announces herself to our staff as the goddess.

- Picture a conference room filled with suits in a typical corporation. Enter the Landry & Kling sales team, equipped with a total knockout visual presentation. But, before the presentation starts, we introduce an activity to lighten up the room... by passing out serpentine streamers and giving instruction on the proper throwing technique. Within minutes, everyone is wrapped in colorful paper and laughing. Lights out, presentation begins and everyone is ready for cruising.

Somewhere along the line, we adopted the phrase "Friendships made at sea are said to last a lifetime." We've used this phrase on awards, plaques, and engraved on client gifts. The beauty of this phrase is that it really sums up the expression about what cruising means to all of us and allows us to share that with our clients.

63

Trends in Student Travel

Stevan Trooboff
President and Chief Executive Officer
Council on International Education Exchange

Stevan Trooboff is the president and chief executive officer of the Council on International Educational Exchange (CIEE) and its related subsidiaries. CIEE, founded in 1947, is a one of the oldest, largest and most respected educational and student exchange organizations in the world. Each year, through its various activities, the organization serves more than 100,000 students and education professionals. The company operates in more than 30 countries worldwide and has administrative offices in the United States, Europe, Asia and Australia. While mission driven, and organized as a nonprofit, CIEE is nonetheless a fee-for-service organization with virtually no government or endowment income. As the saying goes, "It earns its keep every day."

Prior to joing CIEE, Dr. Trooboff was involved in both business and academic life. In the business world, he was the founder and president of Corporate Services International (CSI). The company was one of the largest value-added services organizations in the business travel market. It was sold to Reed Travel Group in 1985. Prior to founding CSI, Dr. Trooboff spent almost 10 years in the management consulting business with the Forum Corporation, now a unit of Pearson Learning. His clients there included a host of organizations such as

Citibank, U.S. Navy, AT&T, TWA, CIGNA, and a wide variety of other Fortune 1000 organizations.

In academic life, Dr. Trooboff was involved in the Harvard Business School international teachers program in France and Switzerland, where he focused on pedagogy. Later, he served as professor of management and chair of the department of management at the Suffolk University School of Management. His area of specialization was organizational behavior and its impact upon business performance.

Dr. Trooboff is the author of a travel services textbook, numerous trade press and other articles, and has written extensive educational materials for general management and sales development. Is addition, he is a well-known speaker and seminar leader in travel and related industries. He is a graduate of Georgia State University, where he received his bachelor's degree with highest honors. He holds a master's and doctorate in business administration from Harvard Business School, where he was a Baker Scholar and George F. Baker Foundation scholarship award winner.

Those of a certain age will remember the famous scene in the movie *The Graduate*, in which the partly drunken businessman offers unsolicited career advice to the young Dustin Hoffman: "Just remember this one word—plastics!" As we think to the future of travel marketing, particularly in the 17- to 27-year-old student travel sector, my advice is to just remember these two words, "The Web."

The Internet has already changed student travel marketing and there is much more to come. While there are still product brochures and mailings, and some advertising (traditionally how marketers have reached students), the Web is already overpowering these media. Every student, with any level of education and disposable income, has and will continue to have lifetime access to the Web. As an offshoot of their education, former and current students will use the Web as their primary means of finding information.

Many schools are already 100 percent wired and even at the lower ends of the economic spectrum, the Web is becoming ubiquitous. Students who grow up on MTV, reality TV and IM (for you Luddites, instant messaging) are not interested in waiting for snail mail to arrive or in reading brochures. They want information, they want it now, and they want it at their fingertips—online. While there are many elements of pre-Web marketing still in place, over the coming years, advances in Web delivery systems, including expanded bandwidth, hardware portability, and improved user interfaces, will make the Web an even more integral part of the student market than it is today.

This is not brave new world stuff. It's easy to reject technology scenarios when applied to marketing. Good marketing will always be good marketing is always the argument for not embracing technological advances. And, while that's true, technology will mean fundamental changes in the shift of product sales and delivery in the travel business. Those of us who handled air reservations before any GDS really existed or controlled the market, and shopped and booked hotels before even WATS lines existed, have solid examples that remind us how markets and marketing will shift and change with technology. In all, the Web poses enormous opportunity but equally has pitfalls to be avoided.

Everyone who markets to students has already built a Web site or Web sites. But most of these are still really first generation. Marketers have discovered, sometimes painfully so, that the cost of developing and managing a quality Web site is far more expensive and difficult than originally thought. Bells and whistles on the site that seemed important are, in fact, counter-productive. As marketers pass through this first stage of Web development, the takeoff, we're seeing second-generation Web sites change in a variety of important ways.

First, the second generation (or the third, the fourth or more, for the most sophisticated) Web sites are far more user friendly than their historical antecedents. Ease of navigation, information retrieval and search engines and document retrieval via downloadable formatting are essential elements of a high quality, client-oriented, market-driven Web site.

Next, the best sites in terms of reaching customers and producing business are transactional. Various early stage enterprises such as www.travelocity.com; www.expedia.com; and www.hotels.com have proven beyond a doubt that buyers will buy via the Web. As the speed and availability of information improves, so will the desire of the buyer to buy while shopping. Many sites are still in the first generation of development in this regard. Over the next 10 years, there will be less and less need for human intervention in the sales process. To the extent humans intervene, it will be to provide substantive advice, not basic information and transaction assistance.

The net result of this is that the gap from producer to buyer will become increasingly narrow. And, when there is human intervention, it is likely to be more and more via Web mail, email, instant messaging and/or Internet phone. Traditional WATS lines will slowly diminish in influence as these alternative communications technologies take hold. Those of you who have used online assistance in this manner know the power and those of you footing the bills have seen the advantages in cost structure.

Finally, the best Web sites will capture a great deal of user information. For example, today, it is possible to capture every line of availability information on a destination request asked for by a potential, online client. So, a student shopping for a summer trip to England can be captured in the database via email address. Then, automatically, when a special in England becomes available, the student can receive an email blitz with special offer and buyer response mechanism.

For those who have tried this technology, they know its produces results. This type of very targeted and empirically based marketing will increase dramatically in the coming years as the information derived from systems for tracking, storing and responding to client preferences demonstrated by shopping patterns and information access is mined.

Point made: The Web is going to be at the core of product distribution. This decade's students are next decade's adults, the following decade's parents, and so forth into their adulthood. Those who have been insulated from these patterns up to now will find out in the coming years that students are the precursor of the future and the leaders in marketing trends. What's hip with the young today is mainstream in tomorrow's world. Those who ignore this evolution will do so to the detriment of their business.

Early stage Web marketing was mostly the province of "techies" and true believers. Mainstream marketing executives were often skeptics. Today, and surely tomorrow, the sophisticated marketing executive needs to be familiar with everything from Web mail to Web tracking and trends. To retain executives who profess that they don't understand the technology is simply not acceptable. Marketers, you don't need to bake "cookies," but you do need to understand what a cookie is, how it works, and when and how to use it as part of a Web marketing effort. Without this knowledge, marketers are unlikely to maximize the use of this high-potential medium. My experience indicates that many people in responsible marketing positions simply don't understand how to fit the Web into their distribution program. It is still seen as an add-on rather than a paradigm shift in marketing.

Wedded to the "old ways," these dinosaurs have missed a wide variety of opportunities. They know the virtues of bleeds on brochure covers and pricing specials or yield management, but they don't know nearly as much as they should about shopping cart systems and data mining. How many travel marketers missed the business built by www.hotels.com and now pay significant reservation fees to these distributors? Even now, it's hard to find specials on many hotel sites that are too busy showing pictures of their lobbies rather than the price information that buyers want. They are displaying electronic brochures, not transactional savvy. This is but one small example.

While some sites offer buying options, some of these are really cumbersome and make buying too difficult. How many fill-in forms can the seller expect someone to complete? How many times can the buyer be expected to have to call customer service for assistance? How many sites can anyone be expected to register for, remember a new password for, a new "secret question" for, etc.? These are all impediments to buying. This will change in time as the process is accelerated by a variety of methods. Those sites that lag in "zip" will pay in lost sales and customers. While this will be true in all markets, it will be even truer in student markets, the most responsive of all.

Three other trends related to students and student travel deserve attention; industry structure, mainstream participation and product packaging. For many years, student travel was a world unto itself. A large number of relatively small entities served these markets. For the most part, they were highly localized. It's what economists call a fragmented industry. During the last 15–20 years, there was some amalgamation within the industry, both on the product packaging and distribution side of the equation. Today, there are fewer and fewer student travel marketing companies but there's still plenty of product in the marketplace. The market is dominated by a smaller number of much larger players, many of them global in reach and service. The first billion-dollar companies have begun to emerge. This consolidation will continue. Whether we are thinking about tour programs, educational products or independent travel, service to students will be dominated by large, well-financed, highly sophisticated marketers. Mom-and-pop operators, the little guys, are history. This is as true for spring break in Cancun as it is for studying in Russia. Rising costs of entry and distribution require a far more significant business base to support overheads than they did 15 years ago.

Large marketers of travel in many sectors have stayed away from student markets. It was believed that student markets were relatively small, somewhat downscale (i.e., no student spends enough money to make marketing to them worthwhile), and hard to reach. This, too, is changing. There are now more than 15 million students in the United States alone, and many times more than that worldwide. While the demographics will shrink a bit in the richest countries, where birth rates are declining, there will be plenty of potential buyers for decades to come. These youth markets more and more have the same characteristics as other sectors of the travel industry. So, for example, youth cruises, while not a large business, could easily be developed and expanded. Educational travel that has largely been the province of universities and alumni clubs is a logical expansion for sophisticated tour operators. Service learning is another hot seller these days, as is language learning. In the decades ahead, we expect to see more of the big players in travel start to offer their existing product portfolio to students or develop product specifically for the student marketplace.

The final trend of importance in student travel marketing is product packaging. The days of the totally independent traveler constituting a viable market, at least in the context of student travel, are numbered. Disintermediation—the process of replacing middlemen in the distribution channel—is already well underway within student segments of the travel enterprise. Students going it alone will be able to buy air, hotel and lodging online, direct from suppliers. There is no place for middlemen, there is little added value they can provide. The gap between producer and buyer is going to completely disappear. We believe the future only belongs to those who produce experiences. Those that simply sell someone else's experiences (travel agents) or package them and then sell them (various levels of tour operators) will continue to vanish. In each of these categories, there might be room for one or two enormous operators who, through economies of scale and innovation, can survive. However, overall margins will continue to be squeezed and only the very top end of the food chain will avoid extinction.

CIEE has operated a variety of travel and educational programs including student travel for more than 55 years. We intend to be here when the century turns again. Towards that end, we have moved from being a company focused on transactions, the sale of products owned and controlled by others, to the operator of programs wherein we provide the lion's share of the goods delivered. These products all have extensive educational and experiential learning components and, in many cases, are formally integrated with students' study programs both within the United States and abroad. We believe that there are still many undeveloped opportunities to create new programming that explores untouched market niches and/or to grow by entering segments where our reach and distribution gives us a unique advantage in program operations.

Today, we do business in more than 54 countries. While our traditional markets were Western Europe and United States, today, we have high-growth activities in China, other parts of the Pacific Rim, Latin America and especially Eastern Europe. In these latter markets, newly found prosperity and freedoms are driving growing demand far faster than in mature markets. We believe this will continue over the next two decades and that these markets will constitute a growing share of our business.

To make this work requires a global strategy. We need to recognize that all markets are not like our present markets. Our staff of more than 450 people speak about 40 languages and have experience living and working in a wide variety of marketplaces. We are as happy to earn a crown as a dollar, a pound as penny. Managing a truly global organization is very different than managing a homogeneous one. Cultural sensitivity, management systems and a wide myriad of business practices that work in one market simply don't travel very well. Building truly global expertise takes time, money and a good deal of patience.

While we are a mission-driven organization, focused on service to our markets, not profits, we have found over a long period of time that's doing what's right, and good business, usually go hand in hand. Our foundation in 1947 was built on the premise that the world would be a safer place if young people had a chance to see the world beyond their own borders while they are still young. Over the years, we've honed this belief into a clear mission statement: "To help people gain understanding, acquire knowledge and develop skills for living in a globally interdependent and culturally diverse world." Our business plans are evaluated in light of this mission. We are truly one of those organizations that says "no," even at the expense of profits, when we believe a product doesn't serve our mission.

For many years, we have toyed with the idea of trying to follow our clients as they mature. Simply stated, the proposition is that, since we serve students while they are young, why not follow them through their lifecycle and sell them products for a lifetime? Without going into all the details, what we've discovered is that marketing to students, and serving their needs, is distinct from marketing to "former students." In the simplest sense, there are fundamental shifts in consumer needs that take place when a student leaves the student market and enters adult life. Our know-how, systems, product line, expertise, and brand advantage doesn't fly in the adult world the same way it does in the student world. And, the cost of entry into the adult markets, where there is significant competition, is very high. My granddaddy used to say that life was like poker: "It's not the bets you make, but the ones you don't make, that make the difference." After considerable evaluation, we've concluded that betting on the adult markets is not a good idea. The last 30 years in travel marketing, and in travel markets, as in many other kinds of markets, have been extremely good ones. We believe the next 30 years hold the same or greater potential. But, to seize this potential, will require greater resources in money and people, more technological know-how and a more global perspective than in the past. In the words of Rudyard Kipling: "This time like all times is a very good one if we but only know what to do with it."

64

The Fastest-Growing Market: Travelers with Disabilities

Roberta Schwartz, CTC, MCC
Professor
Johnson & Wales University

Roberta Schwartz, CTC, MCC started her career in the travel industry in 1981 as a travel agent and is currently a professor at The Hospitality College of Johnson & Wales University in North Miami, where she specializes in courses in the cruise industry. She also is the director of education for the Society for Accessible Travel & Hospitality (SATH), a nonprofit membership organization providing education for the industry on meeting the needs of travelers with disabilities and those that are mature. Roberta holds a bachelor's degree in Education from Brooklyn College as well as a master's degree in liberal studies from the State University of New York at Stony Brook.

The past few years have proved to be very challenging times in the travel industry. Thus, finding new ways to be profitable can really help a travel company's success. One market that is often overlooked but is actually the fastest-growing market segment comprises the approximately 54 to 60 million Americans with disabilities. And that's not including the "mature market," those people over 50 who don't consider themselves disabled but have "challenges" when they travel. It's estimated that this market represents over $250 billion in disposable income in the United States alone. Worldwide estimates put the market for people with disabilities at over $800 million! These people want to live the good life and travel is included in that lifestyle. So how can you capture your share of that pie?

For the most part, the market for travelers with disabilities is below everyone's radar. But most of us have only one or two degrees of separation between ourselves and someone with a disability. Unless you have a disability yourself, have a close friend or family member with a disability, or a friend with a family member or friend with a disability, you really don't pay much attention to this potent market. But you should!

Who Is the Market?

As with any market, you will want to recognize the characteristics of this market. A disability is defined as a limited ability in basic life activities. The disability travel market has several distinct segments. People using wheelchairs, walkers, service animals, or oxygen are the most visible. So it is assumed that this is the disability market. But disabilities come in two main varieties: visible and invisible! What many people don't grasp is that people with mobility impairments represent only about 15 percent of the total market. Most disabilities are the "invisible" type.

The largest segment of the disability market is people with hearing impairment (27 million, approximately 50 percent), followed by visual impairments (14 million, approximately 25 percent), with mobility impairments representing only about 8-10 million (about 15 percent). Hearing impairments can range from mild to total hearing loss. Baby Boomers who have spent years listening to loud rock music can easily expect to suffer substantial hearing loss in middle age. Another fact about people with hearing loss is that there are two different schools of communication; those who use sign language and those who lip read. Most people will use one form or the other, and not be familiar with the other form. Assistive listening devices are a great tool for many hearing impaired travelers, as are kits for hotel rooms with lights for the phone and doorbell. Visible flight information screens at airports are important to communicate with those flyers who cannot hear the announcements.

People with visual impairments range from those with some vision to those with total loss of sight. Much vision loss also comes with age. All too often people who lose their sight later in life never learn to read Braille, but they will often use a white cane and/or service animal. Using large print and audiotapes is a good way to reach this market.

Mobility impairments represent the most visible segment of the market. In fact, the universal symbol for disability is the wheelchair, although, in reality, this segment of the disabled in the United States constitutes only about 8 to 9 million people. This disability also becomes more common with age due to arthritis and stroke, but there is a large percentage of younger people with mobility impairments that may have occurred because of congenital causes, through accidents, or sports injuries. This market is often the hardest to meet the needs of because of the challenges in construction and existing infrastructure. But due to the ADA (Americans with Disabilities Act), almost all places are accessible today in the United States, though some are more accessible than others, and more people with disabilities are mainstreamed into everyday life, including travel.

Many people have "hidden" disabilities due to medical reasons and don't appear to need any extra attention. Diabetes, heart, lung and kidney disease, and cancer are leading causes of hidden disabilities. And then there are cognitive and learning disabilities such as autism, representing about four million souls, or 8 percent of the market. According to the U.S. Census Bureau, people with disabilities represent the largest minority segment in the country. The market represents over $1 trillion in total income, and, in 1995, spent over $82 billion total on travel! Is this a segment any savvy travel and tourism marketer should ignore?

What else do you need to know about the disability travel market? Forty-six percent of people with disabilities are married—they rarely travel alone, often traveling with companions and family members. Group travel is becoming a big part of the experience, with family reunions leading the charge. Family reunions frequently find older family members who have disabilities. Travel destinations range from the expected (Orlando, Las Vegas, cruises) to the unexpected (Macchu Picchu, Dubai). Cruises represent a popular travel decision for people with disabilities. About 12 to 15 percent of people with disabilities have taken a cruise (about the same as the general population). Many "mature" travelers don't consider themselves disabled—they just have "special needs" when they travel! Very important to those with disabilities who travel is a source of information who truly addresses their needs (a knowledgeable travel agent), and travel products and services that offer consistency and comfort. Travelers who find a travel agent, supplier or destination that can fulfill these requirements become loyal customers who can spread the word to others. The disabled travelers' market is *very* strong on word-of-mouth.

SATH

The Society for Accessible Travel & Hospitality (SATH— www.sath.org), founded in 1976, is a nonprofit educational membership association. Its mission is to educate the travel, tourism and hospitality industry worldwide on how to meet the needs of travelers with disabilities. In addition, SATH acts as a clearinghouse for consumers searching for information about accessibility when they travel. SATH refers them to those organizations (travel agencies, tour operators, attractions, lodgings, transportation companies, destinations, etc.) that have been proven to meet their needs.

Each year, SATH holds a world congress and trade show for travelers with disabilities. It's an ideal venue for travel agents, suppliers and destinations wanting to learn more about how to serve this market. One of the highlights of a recent congress was the release of the results of a survey conducted by Harris Interactive for Open Doors Organization, in conjunction with SATH and the TIA, examining the spending trends and market scope of U.S. resident travelers with disabilities. The major findings indicated that people with disabilities could spend at least $27 billion a year on airlines and hotels alone if certain of their needs were met. The top requests were a "meet and greet" welcome at airports and preferred seating on airlines, while lodging issues included being able to find rooms close to amenities and staff who go out of their way to accommodate guests with disabilities. People with disabilities spent $13.6 billion on 31.7 million air trips and hotel stays in the past year, and respondents indicated they would at a minimum double their travels if their needs were better met. These numbers indicate a major opportunity for travel firms and tour operators.

Another study, conducted by travel and tourism students at Johnson & Wales University's North Miami campus, looked at the number of disabled parking permits issued in the United States, as well as the criteria for acquiring one. The results indicated a large potential market—the state of Florida alone issued approximately two million permits!

SATH has also worked with The Travel Institute on an educational module on "Traveling with Disabilities" that focuses on understanding the needs of the market for disability travel, and how to position your business to serve that market. SATH also presents workshops at travel and tourism industry conventions and conferences to spread the word about reaching the market for travelers with disabilities, and also was instrumental in the writing of the Americans with Disabilities Act (ADA) and the Air Carriers Access Act. A code of conduct towards travelers with disabilities written by SATH was adopted by the World Tourism Organization in 1991. SATH has also lobbied for legislative changes in the European Community and assisted numerous governments to develop national access guidelines. SATH also sponsors Travelers with Disabilities Awareness Week, created in 1990 by SATH founder and ASTA Hall of Famer, the late Murray Vidockler, CTC, to commemorate the creation of the ADA.

SATH has an interactive Web site (www.sath.org), featuring an easily searchable resource guide. For example, if a traveler were looking for companies that work with travelers needing dialysis, a list would come up of those companies, as well as articles relating to traveling with kidney disease and dialysis. Sample articles from SATH's travel publication *Open World* are also online, and visitors can post questions to be answered by SATH staff and its members.

Etiquette

One of the biggest challenges facing our industry is getting people to feel comfortable working with people with disabilities. W.C. Duke Associates (www.wcduke.com), a Virginia-based firm providing disability sensitivity training to many travel and hospitality industry companies, asserts that over 50 percent of people claim to feel uncomfortable around people with disabilities, and about 40 percent express outright fear, mainly because they don't know what to do. This is primarily an issue that is easily addressed with training and awareness of the needs of people with disabilities. In my role as director of education for SATH and as a member of the faculty at The Hospitality College at Johnson & Wales University in North Miami, I see this challenge often. My students over the years have commonly emphasized the impact their heightened awareness of the disability market and their knowledge of basic etiquette has had on their career development. Creating a curriculum where sensitivity to people with disabilities is taught across the board in travel, tourism and hospitality programs is a major goal of SATH, so that the future workers and leaders of our industry will have the knowledge and comfort level to service these guests.

A simple thing to remember is that disability etiquette is most importantly a "people first" concept. Say "person with a disability" rather than "disabled person." Use "handicapped" to describe a situation, not a person. Speak directly to the person with the disability, not to their companion. Offer to help, but don't jump in unless your offer is accepted; some people are "a little bit independent." When talking to a person using a wheelchair for more than a few minutes, try to sit at their level so you're eye to eye, rather than have them strain their neck looking up at you. Don't lean or hang on to a person's wheelchair; that is their personal space. Say "uses a wheelchair" instead of "wheelchair bound;" most people using wheelchairs will tell you the chair frees them rather than confines them! Don't shout at someone who is hearing impaired; look directly at them and speak slowly and clearly if they lip read. Get their attention by tapping their arm or waving. Have paper and pen nearby—with which to communicate via the written word if necessary. If they use a sign language interpreter, speak to the person, not the interpreter. For people using service animals, don't pet or feed the dog without the owner's permission. These animals are working when on their harness and are trained accordingly. Service animals are used not only by people with visual impairments, but also those with hearing, mobility and medical impairments. People with severe vision impairments appreciate your identifying yourself and others when you join them, and letting them know when you are leaving, as well. Always offer your arm to someone with a vision impairment, rather than you taking their arm. When handling money, describe the bills so they can fold them in a special way or put the money in separate compartments according to denomination; coins they can tell by touch. If they use a sign language interpreter, again, speak to the person, not the interpreter.

Tapping the Market

So if you are intrigued by really tapping into this potential market, where do you begin? Any good marketer will ask three basic questions:

1. Where am I now?

2. Where do I want to go?

3. How do I get there?

This translates into the simplest form of creating a marketing plan.

"Where am I now?" is the basic of a SWOT (strengths, weaknesses, opportunities and threats) analysis. What do you currently know about the market, what has your experience been with people with disabilities, how comfortable do you feel around them, and what is your competition doing with respect to them—these are some initial questions to ask in order to analyze your position.

"Where do I want to go?" examines your goals. What do you want to achieve? The more specific, realistic and quantifiable your goals, the better. Do you need to provide access for all levels of disabilities, or can you focus on one particular disability? That will be answered by the nature of your business.

"How do I get there?" looks at the strategies and tactics necessary to reach your goals. What education is needed and how do you get it? How do you reach the market? SATH can be a good starting point for education. Getting involved with disability organizations, being visible at consumer shows, and reaching these consumers where they live, work and play are strategies and tactics that will get you noticed by the market. Remember, this is a very strong word-of-mouth market; a kind of "viral marketing" occurs when friends encounter an ostensibly good deal, competent operator, or stellar adventure . . .

Some Final Thoughts

The market for travelers with disabilities is the fastest-growing niche market today. At some point, everyone crosses the path of someone with a disability who wants to travel. Not only is marketing to those with disabilities enlightened and the "right" thing to do; it promises great financial rewards to those who do so properly. Of course, it is especially rewarding to help people who may have thought they could never travel because of their disability; but it can also be very profitable. Having the right attitude, getting the right education and being in the right place at the right time will truly make you and your organization a recognized disability specialist before you know it!